The Maritime Engineer

Careers in Naval Architecture and Marine, Ocean and Naval Engineering

CELESTE BAINE

Engineering Education Service Center

Eugene, OR

The Maritime Engineer

Careers in Naval Architecture and Marine, Ocean and Naval Engineering

by Celeste Baine

Published by:

Engineering Education Service Center (an imprint of Bonamy Publishing)
1004 5th St
Springfield, OR 97477 U.S.A.
(541) 988-1005
www.engineeringedu.com

Publishers Cataloging-in-Publication Data

Baine, Celeste

The maritime engineer: careers in naval architecture and marine, ocean and naval engineering / by Celeste Baine.

p. cm.

Includes bibliographical references and index.

ISBN 13: 978-0-9819300-2-2 (pbk.)

1. Engineering–Vocational guidance–United States 2. Naval Architecture–Vocational guidance–United States 3. Marine Engineering—Vocational guidance–United States 4. Ocean engineering—Vocational guidance–United States I. Title. II. Baine, Celeste.

TA157.B65 2011 620'.0023–dc20

How to Order:

Single copies may be ordered from the Engineering Education Service Center, 1004 5th Street, Springfield, OR 97477; telephone (541) 988-1005; Web site: www.engineeringedu.com. Quantity discounts are also available.

Dear Reader:

It is with great pride that we present *The Maritime Engineer* to you. This book was written to provide you with a better understanding of the exciting careers of naval architecture and marine, naval, and ocean engineering, along with other important maritime-focused technologies.

Did you even know these careers existed? Are you aware of the possibilities of a career within the maritime engineering world, but want more information? Are you a guidance counselor with a student who could perhaps find their calling within these pages? Are you a parent with a child who loves the water, science, math, engineering, or anything that floats (or dives?) Maybe you are a teacher with the need to spark an interest in a particular student.

Written with middle and high school students in mind, this book was designed to provide a brief glimpse into what we call "maritime engineering" careers, realizing that the field is much broader and deeper. Nevertheless, we hope it will spark discussions, questions, and for some students, the beginnings of a plan to join the ranks of professionals designing ships, boats, ROV's, submarines, or conducting important research that will further our nation's competitive edge and strengthen our country's security.

There are many who contributed to this book. First and foremost, this book was funded by the Office of Naval Research, the organization responsible for the coordination, education and promotion of science and technology programs for the United States Navy and Marine Corps. Without ONR's commitment to K-12 STEM Outreach, this book would not have been possible.

This book was the vision of The Society of Naval Architects and Marine Engineers and Celeste Baine, author and passionate engineering advocate, who painstakingly researched, patiently endured delays and revisions, and finally brought the vision to life.

Finally, thank you to those who participated in the interviews for this book. We are most grateful for the time you shared, providing insights into your careers. You have made a tremendous

contribution, and we appreciate your sharing your knowledge and experience with us.

Enjoy this book, and please take an opportunity to explore the other resources listed herein as you continue your journey to determine if "maritime engineering" is for you!

Susan Giver Nelson, CMP, CAE
Director of Outreach and Strategic Development,
The Society of Naval Architects and Marine Engineers
Executive Director, SeaPerch Program

Author Acknowledgments: This book wouldn't be possible without the vision of SNAME and in particular, my first mate, Susan Giver Nelson. Her direction of the SeaPerch program and commitment to inspiring future maritime engineers is a great thing to behold. I'd also like to thank my peer reviewers, Philip Kimball, Toby Ratcliff and David Helgerson. Without their encouragement and gentle persuasions, this book would not be all that it is today. Along the way, I also had some fantastic contributors: Jay Carson, Peter Noble, Charles Cushing, William Garzke, John Lehmen, Alan Rowen, Jose Fermenia and David Helgerson. Your quotes and insight into the maritime world are invaluable. I'd like to thank Ann Avary from Skagit Valley College for her interview, cheerleading and for setting up my Janicki tour. I'm also grateful to the many people I met and talked to along the way that encouraged me to keep digging, keep writing and reminded of the importance of this book.

Edited by: Marjorie Roueche

Cover design by: Amy Siddon

Revolutionary Research . . . Relevant Results

Contents

- What Now?
- Choosing the Right School
- The Successful Student
- Co-ops and Internships
- Professional Engineering and Licensure
- Summary

Appendix

"Not all who wander are lost."

-JRR Tolkien

About this Book

"The desire to build a house is the tired wish of man content thenceforward with a single anchorage. The desire to build a boat is the desire of youth, unwilling yet to accept the idea of a final anchorage".
- Arthur Ransome, English author

It's a sunny day at the International Hot Boat Association (IHBA) Drag Boat World Finals. The boats are pure engineering marvels—so powerful they can reach speeds of 250 miles per hour and fly over the surface of the water. The spectators have been waiting anxiously for this event. Two boats are lining up to drag race in this quarter-mile (1320 feet)

Retired Navy Cmdr. Paul Becker takes the lead in the UL-14 Go Navy hydroplane during the 2010 Lucas Oil Firebird Spring Nationals Drag Boat Races at Firebird Raceway.

race. Drag boat racing is just like drag racing with cars except that the race takes place on the water instead of on land. The

thunder of the engines is deafening as the racers gun their motors. All eyes are on the countdown clock—red, yellow, green! The roar of the engines explodes the air, and water shoots everywhere as the boats blast into the chop, and scream to the finish line. At high speeds, these boats force the water downwards and use the resultant upward force to create the lift that allows them to hydroplane on the water. Don't blink or tweet or text—this five-second race is extraordinarily fast with both boats trying desperately to outrace the other. In a fraction of a second, one hydroboat nudged out the competitor to claim the win. The crowd goes wild as the winner takes a victory lap, and two more boats approach the starting line.

This book is a gateway to the adventure, travel, and gratifying challenges of maritime engineering. Maritime engineers design the technologies that allow us to build underwater structures and explore the mysterious depths of the ocean. In these pages, you'll learn about the engineers that design boats for racing by motor or sail; boats for recreation such as rowboats, dinner boats and jet skis; working boats such as tugs, workboats, ferries, and barges; boats for the military; cargo and container ships and other vessels such as drill rigs, oil spill clean-up boats, floating power plants, and many other fascinating vessels. You will learn about different sectors such as large ocean-going vessels, small watercraft, offshore energy engineering, underwater robots such as Remotely Operated Vehicles (ROVs) and Autonomous Operated Vehicles (AUVs), and underwater habitats. Lastly, you'll get help on getting started in this one-of-a-kind amazing career path.

As we turn to the oceans for energy supplies and seek to transport vast resources around the world, the opportunities for maritime engineers grow. According to Peter Noble, Chief Naval Architect at ConocoPhillips

I believe that today we can see ever-expanding opportunities for naval architects, marine and ocean engineers. World trade is ever increasing, most cargoes are carried in ships of all sorts; development of the oceans is still in its early stages with many parts still not fully explored; we feed much of the world with protein harvested from the oceans or increasingly grown there in mariculture projects; and we are also developing systems to extract much needed minerals and precious metals, energy and power from the water-covered areas of our planet. We have tools to aid us in our engineering and construction that were denied to earlier generations, and we have enthusiastic and well-educated individuals entering our profession.

Maritime engineers that are interested in naval ship-building can be in the military or be a part of the Navy's civilian workforce. They can assist in the building and design of military ships such as aircraft carriers, submarines, cruisers, destroyers, frigates, corvettes, fast attack craft, ocean patrol cutters, amphibious landing ships and docks, oilers, supply ships, crane ships, and many more.

Peter Noble says, "25 percent of all the ships in the world will call at a U.S. port at least once in the next year. This gives opportunities for port development; tug, fireboat and other service craft design and construction; dredging and waterways engineering; ship-to-shore interface engineering and many other maritime engineering related activities. In addition, the disciplines of ocean and offshore engineering offer immense challenges for any who choose to enter."

With so much opportunity on the horizon, it's a great time to begin exploring careers in the maritime industries.

Part I – The Maritime World

What is Maritime Engineering?

In this book, maritime engineering refers to the engineers who work in the maritime and ocean industries. They design anything that can be used as transportation on water, such as commercial, cargo or Navy ships, yachts, submarines, seaplanes, and icebreakers. Maritime engineers also design underwater structures and ocean technology such as offshore drilling platforms, wind farms, diving gear, underwater robots (both remotely operated and autonomous) and underwater "cities" such as *Aquarius*, the

Boat building in a shipyard

underwater astronaut training center. Working in and near the ocean is unpredictable, corrosive, and sometimes hostile, so special training and systems are often required.

Engineers are life-long learners because there are many considerations in the design of each and every ship. For example, a Navy ship has to have systems that can detect airborne, surface, and subsurface threats, operate over long periods of time in any area of the world, and defend themselves and others against attacks. To do this, Navy ships must be able to withstand shock and blast effects, operate when damaged, prevent detection in hostile waters, have propulsion systems that are acoustically quiet, and much more. The demands are uncommon and therefore, the training to enter these fields is very specialized.

Marine structures, vehicles, and systems are unique and often expensive because they are large and complex, and only a few of each design are built. Anything that operates in or on the ocean has special design requirements for seakeeping, staying upright, capsizing, station-keeping, and enduring the random motions and loads of rogue waves and intense winds. Due to these unique requirements, manufacturing is often more challenging. David Helgerson, the technical director for CSC's Advanced Marine Center says, "Ships are large complex integrated systems; they require large teams to design, and it can take a long time. At the same time, the rewards are in proportion to the challenges." As with most things in life, the more heart and soul you put into a project, the more rewards you may get out.

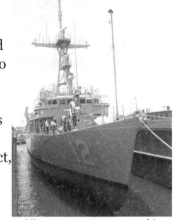

Mine countermeasures ship
USS Ardent

It's very important that you choose a career field that you are naturally interested in. If you love being by or in the water, going to the beach, sailing, swimming, scuba diving, paddleboarding, surfing, kayaking, canoeing, or fishing, then maritime engineering might be a great fit. If *The Deadliest Catch* is your favorite television show, or if you like to watch boats come in and out of the harbor, or dream of taking a cruise to an exotic destination, this may be the career for you.

Who are Maritime Engineers?

Maritime engineers are usually known as naval architects, marine engineers, ocean engineers, or naval engineers, and have a bachelor's or master's degree in these fields. Sometimes maritime engineers study civil, mechanical, or electrical

engineering with an emphasis or special training in marine or ocean engineering. All maritime engineers usually love to travel, and want to work near the water to enhance the world's transportation and energy systems and make the world a better place. These engineers may be married or single; they can have disabilities, and include men and women from every culture in the world. But they share a problem-solving orientation. Maritime engineering students can be right out of high school, just out of the military, returning to school after several years, or seeking a second degree.

An important part of understanding and thriving in this career is your worldview. The work is global in nature and has never been more important because these professions connect people and places in a way that is unmatched by other engineering careers. Think of the planet Earth as one big web of biodiversity that connects us to all living things. Many people may say that the United States and Japan are separated by the Pacific Ocean. However, in the maritime industry, we say that the oceans connect them.

Maritime engineers design

- Sailboats and yachts used in the America's Cup races;
- Hydroplane racing boats;
- Underwater cities or habitats used for astronaut training or research;
- Scuba-diving and other deep sea exploration equipment;
- Underwater robots;
- Boats such as small rowboats, Jet skis, tugs, workboats, barges, yachts, floating cranes, dredges, supply boats, dinner boats, ferries, tankers, container ships, car carriers, dry bulkers, gas carriers, drill rigs, jack-ups, semi-submersibles, trawlers, factory ships, floating power plants, and many others;

- Boats and ships for the military (Army, Navy, Marine Corps, and Coast Guard) such as aircraft carriers, submarines, cruisers, destroyers, frigates, corvettes, fast attack craft, ocean patrol cutters, littoral combat ships, hydrofoils, air cushion vehicles, amphibious landing ships and docks, oilers, supply ships, crane ships, sealift ships, and command-and-control ships;

- Ways to harvest energy from the ocean, such as offshore wind turbines, tidal and current converters, wave energy converters and many others;
- The gear that helps fishermen catch 800 lb fish or pull crab pots from the ocean floor;

Sailors man monkey lines in a landing craft as it is hoisted into its davit during small boat operations

- Boats and machinery needed to clean oil spills and protect the surrounding marine environment;
- And much, much more.

When you think about being near, in, or on the water, think about maritime engineering. Without these important people, we could not understand, research, or use the 73 percent of our planet that is covered in water.

The History of Maritime Engineering

The most famous ship of the last century was the "unsinkable" *Titanic*. The Hollywood movie about it was the largest grossing movie of all time until *Avatar* (Both movies were directed by James Cameron, a famous director and deep sea explorer.) The *Titanic* sank on its maiden voyage in 1912—an event that was catastrophic to the maritime industry and had a profound impact on ship design and construction.

CAD drawing of the Titanic

In those days, naval architects had to rely on having a sharp eye for detail and the skill to design a ship without the help of a computer and CAD software. At the time, not many scientific papers on ship design had been published. The tools that designers have today—the Internet, affordable air travel, long-distance communication, wireless computers, hand held devices capable of performing calculations and storing drawings and designs, and ship-tracking systems—have enabled naval architects and marine engineers to achieve much more than was possible when building the *Titanic*.

But the history of maritime engineering started long before 1912. It is not known exactly when the first person sat on a log to cross a river or other stretch of water, but from the 8th to the 11th Century, the Vikings were designing and building ships for raiding, trading with, and settling wide areas of Europe. And into the 15th Century, Europeans were bringing cargo by boat to trade with the Middle East. The Age of Exploration (the 15th Century to the early 17th Century) was a period when many nations explored the world, mostly by ship. Remember that before air travel, the only way to cross

the ocean was by boat. In the early 1800s, the steam engine
was invented, and many ships traded their sails for engines.
In the 1840s, ship designers were building hulls from iron and
moving them through the water with a propeller.

Little by little, naval architects, marine engineers, and ship
builders refined their skills and increased the performance and
safety of ships and other vessels. However, after the Civil War,
ship building waned and not many naval ships were built. At
the same time, people in the United States were headed West
by land, and the ocean frontiers were put on hold. It wasn't
until 1940 that boat building was back in full swing.

A timeline of important maritime dates

1891 – The first submerged oil wells were drilled from
platforms in the Mercer County Reservoir in Ohio.

1893 – The first diesel engine was patented by Rudolf Diesel.

1912 – The *Titanic* sank.

1915 – The United States Coast Guard was established.

1916 – The first ship-to-
shore radio telephone
conversation.

1922 – The Navy's first
aircraft carrier was
commissioned.

1922 – Navy Day was
established to focus
public attention on the
importance of the U.S.
Navy. This date was
also Theodore Roosevelt's birthday.

USS Enterprise Aircraft Carrier

1936 – Merchant Marine Act passed creating the U.S.
Maritime Commission.

1938 – A prototype of shipboard radar was invented by the Naval Research Laboratory.

1940 – The Navy awarded contracts for 210 ships, including 12 aircraft carriers and seven battle ships.

1945 – The first U.S. warship named after a woman, the USS Higbee, was launched.

1945 – As the U.S. prepared to enter WWII, the Maritime Commission began a shipbuilding program that used every available resource to quickly build as many ships as possible. These shipyards completed more than 2700 "Liberty" ships and hundreds of "Victory" ships, tankers, and transports.

1946 – A U.S. postal stamp honoring the ships and men of the Merchant Marine during WWII was issued.

Merchant Marine Stamp

1955 – The USS Nautilus, the first nuclear powered submarine, was launched.

1956 – The world's first container ship was built.

Container Ship

1960 – Submarine USS Triton went around the world (46,000 miles) in 84 days.

1960 – Bathyscaphe Trieste dove deeper (35,799 ft) than any manned submersible before it.

1977 – The first Liquid Natural Gas carrier was completed.

1985 – The *Titanic* wreck was discovered on the ocean floor.

1989 – The Exxon Valdez tanker runs aground in Alaska.

1989 – Recovery of an estimated billion
dollars worth of gold–one of the
greatest sunken treasures ever
found–from the 1857 wreck of the SS
Central American.

1992 – The USS Missouri, the last active
Battleship, was decommissioned.

2006 –BP pipeline corrosion leak in
Prudhoe Bay, Alaska, is the largest
oil spill on Alaska's northern slope.

USS Missouri

2010 – Deepwater Horizon drilling rig explosion causes the
largest marine oil spill in the history of the petroleum
industry.

Part II – Professional Opportunities

"Creating ships and boats is difficult and rewarding. It is not straightforward. Enormous percentages of what we need in life move across the oceans on ships. Our nation relies on ships to defend not only our own country, but other countries too. Ships and boats provide pleasure. While we have some rules that we must follow, there is enormous room for creativity in our profession. This creativity is not expressed so much in color choices or styling, as in fashion, but rather in crafting effective engineering solutions for challenging problems. When you stand on a ship that you helped design, or operate a boat that you designed, it is very satisfying."

- David Helgerson, Technical Director for the CSC's Advanced Marine Center

Go to any coastal town and look out across the ocean. You may see waves, birds, seals, fish jumping, sailboats, fishing boats, surfers, swimmers, or paddleboarders. However, the one thing that everyone will see no matter which coast they are on is water. Water covers 73 percent of the Earth's surface, and the size and power of the ocean demands our respect.

Coastal town

The ocean can be accompanied by hostile winds and large waves with unpredictable intensity. The intense nature of the marine environment is notorious, and movies such as *The*

Perfect Storm remind us to never underestimate the power of the ocean. This dynamic environment presents unique challenges for naval architects, marine engineers, ocean engineers, and naval engineers. The structures and vessels that these professionals design and build are often complicated and specialized to weather the elements.

Marine engineering is a smaller field than mechanical or civil engineering, but the impact is far-reaching and greatly enhances our quality of life. Consider these numbers.

- 74% of the world's trade is carried by ships,
- 95% of U.S. international trade is transported by ships,
- 55% of the U.S. population lives within 50 miles of a coastline, and
- 60% of U.S. energy is imported by ships.

Some naval architects and marine engineers also put their entrepreneurial skills to work designing boats. One entrepreneur, John Lehman, says

"I'm head of a naval architecture private practice in Philadelphia that I started in 1993. We're very small, one full time employee and some part time people, so I do everything from design, to analysis, research, sales, estimating, personnel and accounting/administration. Our work is design and engineering consulting for commercial shipping companies: ships, tugs and barges, and primarily oil/chemical transportation. It's perfect for me because I enjoy the endless variety, not because of the business 'hats' I wear, but more importantly, we handle technical challenges across all engineering disciplines. I also have the benefit of working and conversing with vessel operators, crews, shipyards and vendors on a regular and frequent basis. While most of our time is spent in the office, but we regularly visit vessels on projects to inspect them for

first-hand information about the situation, so we get some 'messing about in boats'."

If owning your own business is appealing, start by interning with small firms in which one person wears many hats or does many different jobs. Lehman goes on to say, *"My advice is that an inquisitive mind, coupled with a very strong background in math and physics, and very good communication skills is the foundation for a successful career; of course that's true in any endeavor, not only naval architecture and marine engineering. The difference is that an appreciation and knowledge of all the elements involved in (and packed into) ships/marine vehicles: arrangements; speed and power; seakeeping and maneuvering; structure; cargo handling; mooring, anchoring and towing; people systems; propulsion; machinery; fluid, heating, ventilating and air-conditioning (HVAC) and electrical systems marks the difference between the master naval architect, or marine engineer, and the ordinary one. Of course, a love of boats and the sea makes all of one's work more interesting and especially meaningful."*

Naval Architecture

Naval architects are engineers who design all kinds of watercraft, or anything that can be used as transportation on or under water. This may be a ship, boat, submarine, seaplane, icebreaker, or offshore drilling platform. The vessels may be used for commerce, recreation, or naval operations, and can be big or small. They may be

Submarine researcher

powered by sails, diesel, or gas turbine engines, electricity, or nuclear power.

Marine environments are tricky. One minute the seas are calm and the next can be a white-knuckle ride as the waves pound the side of your boat or seagoing vessel. To design for this unpredictability provides a challenge for the naval architect. Naval architects design boats with the following elements in mind:

- Hydrostatics—the study of the pressures exerted on the hull. For example, buoyancy is a hydrostatic force which enables an object to float.
- Stability—the boat's ability to remain afloat and right itself after a strong wind or wave.
- Hydrodynamics—the study of water in motion around the ship. It includes powering through the water, maneuvering and controlling the direction of the vessel, as well as the effects of water resistance around the hull.
- Strength, structure and construction—the selection of materials for the hull as well as the rudder, steering, and propeller design. Naval architects analyze the ocean forces that the boat may encounter during a storm at sea. This also includes the boat's strength in a collision or during accidental grounding.
- Interior Design—Ships are complicated, self-sufficient structures. They must carry all of the systems that enable the crew to live aboard for weeks or months at a time. Naval architects decide on the arrangement of the cabin, sleeping quarters, galley, head (bathroom), ventilation, fire protection, floor plan, capacity, water and sewage, weapons (on naval ships), propulsion, and cargo handling.

Naval architects often test the performance of newly designed boats and vessels in long towing tanks. These tanks are

typically housed in government laboratories and universities around the U.S. and the world.

As you can see, naval architects have many considerations for each design element. There are some stock designs available for mass production boats, but the future of ship design is wide open. Every time a materials engineer designs a lighter, stronger, or faster hull, rudder, or propeller, it has the potential to change the hydrostatics, hydrodynamics, construction techniques, strength, or interior design of future boats and ships. Every time a new paper is published or new research is completed, there are opportunities for advancement, changes in existing strategies, and new horizons to sail.

Marine Engineering

Naval architects may design the frame or structure of a boat, but marine engineers design all of the internal power and machinery systems in the boat. Without marine engineers, the boat would have no engine, electronics, hydraulics, lighting, refrigeration, or controls. According to Jose Femenia, a professor of Marine Engineering at the United States Merchant Marine Academy,

> "Marine Engineering is a very strong energy conversion discipline and very broad based. The subjects learned can be

The Ohio class fleet ballistic missile submarine USS Michigan (SSBN 727) enters into the Puget sound naval shipyard and intermediate maintenance facility.

*applied to shore side industries as well as the marine
industry. I strongly recommend it, especially if you
are interested in boats and/or ships." Because most
boats cannot be designed without regard to the control
systems, marine engineers often work closely with
naval architects.*

To be a good marine engineer, you must be versatile, creative,
and open to learning. Marine engineering is an exciting
career because every boat or ship is different, and you will
be responsible for every system on board. Almost every boat

*Person operating the fuel console in an aviation fuel pump
control room of an air-craft carrier.*

needs an engine, propeller, steering, transmission, pumps,
electrical systems, etc. Marine engineers make it all happen.
They understand the needs of the unique environment and
know many different kinds of boating systems and controls.

Marine engineers determine and design different types
of engines to propel a boat such as electric engines, diesel
engines, steam turbines, water jets, gas turbines, and nuclear
reactors. They also design hydraulic systems that can lift a
300 lb Marlin or crab nets out of the water for fishing boats,

and the automated refrigeration systems for cruise lines or other pleasure yachts. Marine engineers may find themselves designing the electrical or fluid systems on an aircraft carrier, or the mechanical control systems on a tugboat or other bay-, lake-, swamp- or ocean-going vessel. There are almost no systems on a maritime vessel that they don't have a hand in designing.

Marine engineers and naval architects may work on a ship at sea, in a shipyard, in factories where marine machinery is built, in design offices, in ship owners' offices, or for government agencies including military services.

Alan Rowen, technical director for The Society of Naval Architects and Marine Engineers (SNAME) and professor emeritus of marine engineering at the Webb Institute of Naval Architecture, explains that the sea-going engineers aboard ships tend to the operation and maintenance of the ship's machinery. They will also be responsible for the unlicensed crew working under their supervision. They may be in charge of an emergency team, damage-control team, or a life-boat. As the ship is traveling across the ocean, the sea-going, watch-standing engineer tends the machinery in the engine room of a ship for two, four-hour watches

Yellow Submarine

each day with eight hours off in between. They may use hand tools and machine tools, cutting and welding equipment, and machinery of all types—all while not getting seasick! In

addition, computer skills are absolutely necessary. They must possess:

- Good mechanical aptitude,
- An ability to visualize systems in three dimensions,
- An ability to think things through in a logical manner,
- Good common sense,
- Persistence,
- Willingness to learn,
- An open mind, and
- An ability to clearly express ideas verbally, graphically, and in writing.

Sea-going marine engineers and naval architects, as well as those stationed overseas managing new construction or major repairs, may miss their family life at home, and a ship at sea can be dangerous and uncomfortable in heavy weather. On the other hand, sea-going engineers typically have more days off. Typically, for every seven days at sea, they may get four days at home. Whether they are in a shipyard or at sea, marine engineers and naval architects must be physically fit to meet the demands of the job.

Licenses
There are a few types of licenses necessary to be a marine engineer.

1. Sea-going engineers start with a third assistant engineer's license, issued by the U.S. Coast Guard to those who meet the requirements of classroom instruction and practical experience aboard a ship. The exam may take several days to complete.
2. Many naval architects and marine engineers are licensed Professional Engineers, and some are certified marine surveyors.
3. Many marine engineers are sea-going marine engineers licensed by the U.S. Coast Guard or other national regulatory bodies.

When you think of marine engineers, think of them as the keymakers of the ship world. Without a key, you can't even get onboard and you certainly can't go anywhere. They give millions of people the ability to have fun on a Jet Ski, small sailboat, or vacation cruise, as well as enabling the military to race across the oceans, clean-up oil spills, and rescue boats in distress.

Ocean Engineering

Miles below the surface, a Remotely Operated Vehicle (ROV) or underwater robot is exploring the ocean floor. The ROV

ROV

may be taking pictures, collecting samples of the ocean floor, recovering treasures from a shipwreck, or performing repairs on an underwater structure such as an oil platform.

In the tragic BP oil spill of 2010, underwater robots were the first on-scene to try to fix the spewing oil pipe. Every instrument, device, and process in an ocean environment is the responsibility of ocean engineers. These engineers are at the top of their game because the ocean environment is so corrosive, volatile, and changeable. Waves are never-ending and the devices or gear that is used to explore the marine environment must be able to withstand the "typical" forces of Mother Nature, such as high winds, never-ending waves, and saltwater.

Ocean engineering is a fast growing and dynamic field with opportunities that are expanding as people turn to the oceans for food, transportation, and energy. Ocean engineers must be creative and visionary to use the oceans effectively.

Offshore Wind Turbine

Government, industry, and academia are hungry for ocean experts and researchers to develop new processes and systems to explore this natural resource without threatening its habitats.

One of the great things about ocean engineering is that many different types of engineers can work together to find solutions for ocean infrastructure, research, and utilization. Ocean engineering integrates disciplines such as oceanography, materials science, and mechanical, civil, computer, software, marine, chemical, electrical and electronics engineering. In addition to creating ROVs, ocean engineers develop underwater structures, oil rigs, wave buoys for data collection; and they are hard at work developing ways to capture the energy of waves and turn it into electricity. They develop transportation systems, plan new uses for waterways, design deep-water ports, and integrate land and water transportation systems and methods. They are concerned with discovering, producing, and transporting offshore petroleum, and developing new ways to protect marine wildlife and beaches against the unwanted consequences of offshore oil production and storm erosion.

Ocean engineers study all aspects of the ocean environment to determine people's influence on the oceans and the ocean's effects on ships and other marine vehicles and structures. *For more on ocean engineering, be sure to read the "Sectors" section of this book.*

Naval Engineering

The American Society of Naval Engineers (ASNE) defines naval engineering as follows.

Naval Engineering includes all arts and sciences as applied in the research, development, design, construction, operation, maintenance and logistic support of surface and subsurface ships and marine craft, naval maritime auxiliaries, ship related aviation and space systems, combat systems, command control, electronics and ordnance systems, ocean structures and fixed and mobile shore facilities which are used by the naval and other military forces and civilian maritime organizations for the defense and well-being of the Nation.

As a naval engineer, you can design, build, operate, and maintain ships as diverse as Navy aircraft carriers and submarines, U.S. Coast Guard cutters, or commercial passenger and cargo vessels. The profession is both traditional and cutting edge. Just like naval architects, naval engineers must consider hydrostatics, hydrodynamics, strength, weight distribution, stability, structure, and efficiency.

According to the ASNE Web site, combat systems and technologies related to command, control, communications, computers, intelligence, surveillance, and reconnaissance (C4ISR) are the most exciting, challenging, and rapidly changing fields in naval engineering. Weapons systems include guns, missiles, torpedoes, and the weapons carried by Navy aircraft. Weapon design includes its placement in the ship and integration with equipment such as radar, sonar, periscopes, launchers, and missile control systems (including lasers and satellites). Weapon design, installation, and operation require a variety of disciplines including aeronautical engineering for air frames; chemical engineering for propulsion; electronics

engineering for tracking, guiding, and controlling; physics for acoustics and electro-optics; and mechanical engineering for loading, rotating, and elevating weapon launchers.

Research, Development, Test and Evaluation (RDT&E) offers both naval engineers and architects a unique and creative opportunity to perform collaborative work with other scientists. The process of developing an engineering concept begins with fundamental theories and ideas, and proceeds through scientific analyses, feasibility studies,

Instructor showing a sailboat model.

collection and analysis of model and full-scale data, design, computer simulation and modeling, fabrication, model testing, evaluation at sea, and final adoption. RDT&E depends on the physical sciences such as physics, chemistry, and metallurgy. The fields of naval architecture and engineering span the entire spectrum of engineering and scientific disciplines, and applies to issues such as advanced hull forms, behavior of ships at sea, and development of new materials and technical processes.

Marine Engineering Technology

Marine Engineering Technology (MET) is a multidisciplinary associate degree that combines marine engineering, engine repair and maintenance, power systems, and the mechanical and electrical systems of ships. These technicians usually work aboard commercial and military vessels on:
- Power cycles,
- Principles and methods used to convert available energy into useful power,

- Selection and operation of major components of power-related machinery, and
- Support systems for the power cycle.

Marine technicians also know the basics of naval architecture, marine applications of electrical engineering, and

thermodynamics. MET is usually a two-year degree program, and students are often trained aboard a ship during school.

Choosing between engineering and engineering technology is a matter of preference for either hands-on

Engineering Officer on Watch monitors the ships propulsion plant.

or theoretical work, as well as consideration of working environment, opportunities for advancement, financial constraints, and time in school. An engineer goes to school for four or five years. A technician goes to school for two years to obtain an associate's degree or gets a certificate in one year or less.

Engineering technicians use the principles and theories of science, engineering, and mathematics to solve technical problems in research and development, manufacturing, sales, construction, inspection, and maintenance. Their work is more limited in scope and more application-oriented than the work of engineers. Many engineering technicians assist engineers, especially in research and development. Others work in quality control, inspecting products and processes, conducting tests, or collecting data. In manufacturing, they may assist in product design, development, or production.

Engineering technicians who work in research and
development build or set up equipment, prepare and conduct
experiments, collect data, calculate or record results, and help
engineers in other ways, such as making prototype versions
of newly designed equipment. They also assist in design
work, often using computer-aided design (CAD) and drafting
equipment.

Engineering technology is concerned with the applications of
technology. A technician is an expert at applying technology
to solve problems. An engineer may design a product to solve
a problem, but the technician will build, install, and maintain
it. There is some overlap in the two fields. Occasionally,
with additional coursework, the technician can also design a
product, but most of the time, that is the work of an engineer.
Conversely, some engineers are also involved in the build
process, but most of the time that is the work of a technician.

An advantage to studying engineering technology is that
students can quickly get a job after graduation from high
school or a community college. Employers are happy to
hire technicians because their training has given them the
knowledge, hands-on skills, and ability to succeed in the
workplace.

Other advantages of MET degrees include
- Less time in college (this option saves money, too),
- Less math and science coursework (depending on your perspective, this may not be an advantage),
- Great salary right out of school, and
- Abundant job opportunities worldwide.

Disadvantages of MET degrees include
- A difficult transition from a technician to an engineer because the science classes in a two-year technology program are not calculus based,
- Less flexibility in the career and less opportunity for advancement unless you seek advanced training, and
- Salary increases may get smaller over time.

Marine Maintenance Technology

Marine maintenance technicians are hands-on people. They usually work as
- Marine carpenters,
- Composite technicians,
- Marine welders,
- Painters,
- Diesel or gasoline engine mechanics,
- Electrical installers,
- Riggers, or
- Systems technicians.

Marine maintenance technicians have training in the repair and maintenance of vessel hulls, decks, and small parts along with the installation of on-board electrical and mechanical systems. They may also study structural development, hull repair, and marine coatings. In addition, they may also have training in engine and auxiliary equipment repair such as
- The repair and maintenance of inboard engines,
- Drive train systems,

- Inboard outdrive propulsion systems,
- Outboard engines,
- Auxiliary systems, and
- Vessel electrical systems.

Marine Maintenance Technology is a two-year degree that prepares you for entry-level employment in the marine trades. This type of training is focused on the repair and maintenance of recreational and small commercial craft that are located in boat repair yards, production boat shops, boat and motor dealerships, charter companies, and marinas. In addition, students with an entrepreneurial streak can become independently employed.

Technicians in this industry can show their expertise by becoming certified by the American Boat and Yacht Council (ABYC). Certification allows the technician to be listed on the ABYC Web site for employment by anyone looking for a specific skill. It's a prized addition to any resume. Currently, there are eight possible certifications through ABYC:
- Composite boat builder certification,
- Diesel engine and support systems certification,
- Gasoline engine and support systems certification,
- Electrical certification,
- Marine corrosion certification,
- Refrigeration and A/C certification,
- Marine systems certification, and
- ABYC standards certification.

Any one of these certifications can make you more competitive in the job market, more attractive to potential employers, and be the difference between getting the job or not.

There are many other degrees available in schools all over the U.S. There are too many other career possibilities to cover

in this book, but a few of the other degrees in the marine engineering and technology industries include

- Marine Transportation,
- Marine Engineering Operations,
- Maritime or Marine Systems Engineering,
- Maritime Administration,
- Marine Transportation Operations,
- Marine Safety and Environmental Protection,
- Small Vessel Operations,
- Small Craft Design,
- Small Craft Systems,
- Power Engineering Technology,
- Power Engineering Operations,
- Ocean and Coastal Resources (environmental marine sciences), and
- Marine Resources Management (MARM).

See the Appendix for a more detailed list of the ABET certified programs at specific schools.

The career opportunities for naval architects, marine, ocean, and naval engineers and technicians are diverse and plentiful. Anyone who enjoys working and living by the ocean may find these careers to be very satisfying and enriching. No matter your personality, if you are interested in being a part of this industry, there is something here for you.

PART THREE — SECTORS

Large Ocean-Going Ships

Grab a walking map of your city and study it for a few minutes. You'll see retail and grocery stores, streets, walking paths, houses, schools, movie theatres, and restaurants, just to name a few. Think back to all of the activities that you did in your hometown yesterday or last week or last month—maybe you rode your bike, went to school, saw a movie, surfed the Internet, or hung out with friends. Now imagine that your city or hometown is floating and today you are in the Atlantic Ocean, even though last week you were in the Mediterranean Sea. Every amenity in a regular city is also available in your floating home. How is this possible? It's only possible if your city is a ship.

Marine engineers, naval architects, and naval engineers are the professionals who are responsible for building these huge floating cities. Usually, these ships are engaged in military activity, such as carrying aircraft, but they can also be for entertainment and pleasure like cruise ships. Because people are on these vessels for seven days, two months, or even six months at a time, everything that is needed to sustain life for extended periods must be considered when the vessel is designed.

Cruise Ship

According to Jay Carson, a retired naval architect and marine engineer,

> *Concept designs are often performed for large complex ships with large bid teams, customers, and suppliers. $5–$10 million in pre-contract labor may be expended by a bidder to develop a large complex ship design into a contract design over a period of 18 months to two years. A large commercial ship may require one million to one and a half million hours of labor to design, develop material procurement documents and produce plans, schedules, working drawings and work instructions. In contrast, a large complex naval ship may require two or three times as much effort; submarines and aircraft carriers may require over 10 times this amount of effort. Remember, every piece of the ship is now built in electrons on a CAD system as electronic data descriptions, before anyone builds it in steel or physical materials.*

According to Charles Cushing, president of a naval architect and marine engineering consulting firm in New York, there are five phases of ship design:

1. Planning—The engineer works with ship owners and investors to develop a strategic plan and mission statement.
2. Concept design—This is the most innovative stage where brainstorming takes place. For small boats, the team size could be as low as a single person or a small group of engineers. For complex ships, teams could be much larger and this phase can take up to three weeks.
3. Preliminary design—This is where ideas start to take form. It may require a small team of 5 to 10 engineers to carry the design to a level where the technical operational and economic feasibility of the design can be validated. Also included in this step or during

the contract design are experimental model tests and Computer Fluid Dynamics (CFD) assessments.

4. Contract design—This phase takes the design to a high level of specificity, that is, sufficiently far so that an owner can negotiate and agree with a shipbuilder as to what will be built and exactly how much it will cost without any extra costs or hidden surprises—a total meeting-of-the-minds. It requires a team of 10 engineers and takes two to three months.

5. Detailed design—This phase is carried out by the engineering department of the shipyard. It results in hundreds (sometimes thousands) of drawings and a very large staff of engineers, designers, and draftsmen or CAD designers. The engineering may run many months.

After the design is approved and the contract is awarded, the building can begin. Depending on the size of the ship, this can take from six months to more than a decade.

The Engineers Who Design Large Ocean-Going Ships

Virtually every type of engineer is involved, including:

- **Naval Architects** who are responsible for the ship floating, including floating upright when damaged, being steerable and steering straight, holding together in hundred-year storms, having motions that are tolerable to people and onboard equipment, surviving ice storms that encrust the vessel with heavy topside weights, protecting cargo and people from fires and explosions; all while allowing efficient operations at sea and pier-side with required maintenance and repair.
- **Marine Engineers** who develop the propulsion plant, power plant, and all support services necessary for the safety and comfort of people onboard.

- **Electrical Engineers and Electronic Engineers** who design electrical power plants, automation systems, alarms, communication systems, radar, surveillance systems, navigation systems, and lighting.
- **Production Engineers** who work with planners and production personnel to develop best practices, process descriptions, facilities, and tooling to build the design in the most cost-effective fashion.
- **Materials Engineers** who identify appropriate metals, plastics, paint, lubricants, equipment, cable, furniture, and other goods necessary to meet performance requirements over the lifetime of the ship. They also work with manufacturers to ensure that the materials purchased perform as specified.
- **Welding Engineers** who define the best methods and joint designs to connect parts of the ship, its piping, and other metal parts.
- **Corrosion Control Engineers** who define how the ship and its parts will be protected from rusting and deterioration by salt water and corrosive cargoes.
- **Quality Engineers** who set up systems to monitor the performance of participants in the design and construction processes.
- **Environmental Engineers** who design ways to protect people and the environment by limiting toxic materials, and assess the processes used in the shipyard during construction of the ship.
- **Safety Engineers** who ensure that the ship and its equipment are ergonomically appropriate for men and women of all sizes, and can be operated without danger to the people aboard or to the cargo.
- **Rigging Engineers** who ensure that the parts of the ship that must be lifted during construction are safely picked up with wires and gear that has sufficient load capacity.

- **Test Engineers** who observe how equipment, systems, and the ship run in actual conditions of service, including noise and other signatures that may emanate from a vessel.

Naval Ships and Craft

Historically, the U.S. Navy has driven the development and delivery of advanced marine technologies. As the largest user of many different types of boats and ships, the Navy has also funded significant research in boat design and safety.

Carrier Ship

A naval ship is very complex, and one of the largest engineered systems. It's much more complicated to design a naval ship than almost any other form of transportation or structure. Engineers in this field must balance cost, new technology, hull design, materials, and all of the systems aboard (such as the weapons management, electronics, HVAC, propulsion, ventilation, sleep quarters, galley, head, etc.). The real trick for the naval engineer is to pull all the pieces of designing and building this enormous structure together.

According to the paper "Naval Engineering: A National Naval Obligation," by Chryssostomos Chryssostomidis, Michael Bernitsas, and David Burke, some unique aspects of naval engineering are that:

- Naval ships have specialized operational requirements such as:
 - ◊ The need to detect airborne, surface, and subsurface threats, which requires extensive and

extremely capable electronics packaged in a very small platform;

◇ The need to operate over long periods of time in any area of the world; and

◇ The ability to defend themselves and other forces against actions by opposing forces.

To provide these capabilities, the design of naval ship structures must:

- Be capable of resisting or sustaining damage while continuing to operate. These include requirements to withstand shock and blast effects;
- Be able to prevent detection by others without compromise to other demands. To do this, they must have non-magnetic and low radar cross section structures;
- Be acoustically quiet and have low non-acoustic signatures (leave no trace);
- Be able to dive very deep (submarines) and utilize nuclear propulsion and high strength, low-weight materials; and
- Have extra strong surface and subsurface platforms to fire weapons.

More important are the unique future requirements that are pushing the state-of the-art in technology for naval ships, which are:

- Future ships will be required to go at high speeds efficiently;
- These ships will require new structural materials to enable lighter weight, and increased stealth and survivability; and
- These attributes must be achieved at an affordable cost.

The size and complexity of ships incorporating advanced technology in war fighting systems for naval application makes these designs unique.

The Engineers Who Design Naval Ships and Craft

- **Naval Engineers** who are responsible for the ship floating, floating upright when damaged, being steerable and steering straight, holding together in hundred-year storms, having motions that are tolerable to human beings and onboard equipment, surviving ice storms that encrust the vessel with heavy topside weights, protecting cargo and people from fires and explosions; all while allowing efficient operations at sea and pier-side with required maintenance and repair.

- **Marine Engineers** who develop the propulsion plant, power plant, and all support services necessary for the safety and comfort of people onboard.

- **Materials Engineers** who identify appropriate metals, plastics, paint, lubricants, equipment, cable, furniture, and other goods necessary to meet performance requirements over the lifetime of the ship, and work with manufacturers to ensure that materials that are purchased perform as specified.

- **Mechanical Engineers** who design specific items of machinery like cranes, hoists, elevators, and equipment for anchoring, steering, controlling submarine depth, or moving weapons and other supplies within the ship, as well as between ships, at sea. A knowledge of fluid systems is required for designing fuel, lubrication, and water installations, as well as firefighting, compressed air, and heating, ventilation, and air conditioning systems.

- **Civil Engineers** who specify the actual structure of the ship including framing, shell, decks, bulkheads, and equipment foundations. They ensure that the ship can withstand the weight of cargo and the impact of waves. Combat ships must be able to withstand battle damage from weapons such as missiles, torpedoes, and underwater mines.

- **Electrical Engineers** who provide for the generation and distribution of electricity throughout the ship for lighting, power, system controls, and various other ship services. Modern ships also require a multitude of electronic navigation, communication, and combat systems.

- **Ocean Engineers** who concern themselves with work both on and below the surface of the sea, and study ocean movements and their affect on ships and craft both on the surface and below it. An ocean engineer may design small subsurface vehicles that perform ocean bottom scanning, salvage operations, object recovery, and submarine rescue. The work includes structural, propulsion, and hull-form design for resisting deep ocean pressure, and the selection of materials for this hostile environment.

Small Craft

The Navy and U.S. Coast Guard define small craft as a non-commissioned, waterborne unit of the Fleet, which is not designed as a service craft and is capable of limited independent operation. Small craft may be assigned to and carried on a ship as a ship's boat, or assigned to a shore station or fleet operating unit.

An airboat, also known as a fanboat or swampboat, has a flat-bottom and is propelled by a large propeller. Airboats are a very popular means of transportation in the Florida Everglades, and Louisiana Bayou, where they are used for fishing, bowfishing, hunting and eco-tourism

The term small craft also refers to boats that don't race across the oceans, clean oil

spills, or provide a living space for its passengers. Small craft can be inshore boats used for recreational purposes such as airboats, small fishing boats, sailboats and yachts, ski boats, party barges, power boats, ferries, riverboats, dinner cruise boats, floating casinos, and other boats designed to travel short distances.

One of the most innovative small crafts and an example of the changes in boat design materials is the 2010 'USA' Yacht for the 33rd America's Cup. The boat was a trimaran (first one ever in an America's Cup race). Many of the components were carbon fiber and rumor has it that the boat was so fast it scared the racing crew. For many months after it was built, nobody knew how fast it could go. The carbon fiber and Kevlar wingsail was 223 ft long (more than twice the span of a Boeing 747 wing) and made from a manufactured mold that provided

Sailboat Racing

increased maneuverability and speed. Wingsails have a built-up airfoil cross-section and act like an airplane wing. It can provide a better lift-to-drag ratio than conventional soft sails. In the past, all sailboats had soft sails that could be rolled up and stored on the boat. USA's sail, made of carbon fiber, is rigid and stays put once installed.

Advances in technology will continue to shape the future of boat design. Engineers in this industry must become life-long learners as new materials are discovered, tested, and implemented. Much of the technology designed for the America's Cup will eventually trickle down to consumer boats.

The Engineers Who Design Small Craft

- **Naval Architects** who are responsible for the small craft floating, floating upright when damaged, being steerable and steering straight, having motions that are tolerable to human beings and onboard equipment, protecting cargo and people from fires and explosions; all while allowing efficient operations at sea and pier-side with required maintenance and repair.
- **Marine Engineers** who develop the power systems and all support services necessary for the safety and comfort of people onboard.
- **Electrical Engineers and Electronic Engineers** who design electrical systems, automation systems, alarms, communication systems, radar, GPS systems, navigation systems, and lighting.
- **Materials Engineers** who identify appropriate metals, plastics, paint, lubricants, equipment, cable, furniture, and other goods necessary to meet performance requirements over the lifetime of the small craft, and work with manufacturers to ensure that materials that are purchased perform as specified.

Offshore Engineering

Offshore engineering refers to the design, installation, and construction of oil rigs, pipelines, wind turbines, and other ocean structures that produce oil, electricity, gas, or are used for underwater exploration, living, and research. The

construction of offshore structures is considered so dangerous
that often these enormous structures are built on land and
then installed in the ocean.

Once a structure is built on land, it has to be towed on a barge
or lifted with a crane vessel to the installation site. Crane
vessels can lift a structure that weighs up to 14,000 tons! If the
structure has to be anchored to the ocean floor, the structure
must be forced to the bottom. The engineering involved in
getting the structure to the installation site and installing it in
the proper location is a colossal challenge. Each step must be
carefully planned so equipment is not damaged, people are not
hurt, and the marine environment is minimally disturbed.

Because most structures cannot be installed in a day or two,
floating hotels are needed for the workers. In this case, the

Oil rig

naval architects and marine engineers have designed this boat-
hotel for the ocean, civil, structural, electrical, and mechanical
engineers that work in the offshore engineering industry.

Other common offshore engineering projects include designing
and developing wind farms or turbines, wave energy and data

collection buoys, tidal/current energy devices, and ocean thermal energy converters (OTEC). *For more on this, see Section IV.* In addition, NASA astronauts train in underwater habitats, and other marine researchers sometimes study the marine environment in these same structures. However, historically, the most common offshore engineering projects have been oil platforms.

Oil platforms are used to drill for oil. Many types of drilling rigs are utilized, although these rigs can also be used for the installation, maintenance, and repair of offshore wind turbines and other underwater structures. Oil platforms can also be used to dismantle ships that were wrecked at sea, or to install or repair any other structures found in and on the water. A few of the more popular drilling rigs include:

- Floating vessels—Used primarily for deeper water. They are a type of mobile offshore drilling unit that floats and is not secured to the seafloor (except for anchors). Floating units include inland barge rigs, drill ships, and semi-submersibles;
- Jack-up rig—A barge with liftable legs. According to the Jack-up Primer, "A Jack-up is an offshore structure composed of a hull, legs and a lifting system that allows it to be towed to a site, lower its legs into the seabed and elevate its hull to provide a stable work deck capable of withstanding the environmental loads. A typical modern drilling Jack-up is capable of working in harsh environments (wave heights up to 80 ft, wind speeds in excess of 100 knots) in water depths up to 500 feet."
- Drill Ship—Ship that provides a platform for a drill rig and is primarily used for drilling. Drill ships are capable of drilling exploratory wells in deep, remote waters.
- Semi-submersible—Floating offshore drilling units that have pontoons and columns that when flooded cause

the unit to submerge in the water to a predetermined depth. Semi-submersible rigs are either self-propelled or towed to a drilling site and either anchored or dynamically positioned over the site, or both. In shallow water, some semi-submersibles can be ballasted to rest on the seabed. Semi-submersibles are more stable than drill ships and are used extensively to drill wildcat wells in rough waters such as the North Sea.

A few examples of offshore rigs, drilling and production platforms. Left to right: onshore platform; fixed platform; jack-up rig; semi-submersible; drill ship; tension leg platform.

The Engineers Who Design Offshore Structures

- **Ocean Engineers** who concern themselves with work both on and below the surface of the sea and study ocean movements and their affect on the rig on the surface and submerged. The work includes structural design for resisting deep ocean pressure, and selecting materials for this environment.
- **Ocean Engineers with an Electrical Engineering Emphasis** who may develop the technology to generate, store, or distribute the renewable energy harvested from an offshore wind turbine. They may

be responsible for grid connections, designing the transmission lines, and the offshore logistics of bringing energy underwater and back to land.

- **Ocean Engineers with a Mechanical Engineering Emphasis** who may design turbines, generators, or control systems. They may build and test prototypes, make CAD models, or write and apply for patents.

- **Ocean Engineers with Civil Engineering Emphasis** who may design the OTEC structures that are embedded in the ocean floor and that can withstand hurricane winds; or they may be responsible for mooring systems and running electrical cable underwater. Every engineer works to make the systems more efficient and affordable.

- **Naval Architects** who are responsible for offshore structures staying upright when damaged, holding together in hurricanes and ice storms, determining how to fix, upgrade or maintain a structure that is old or damaged by corrosion, protecting cargo and people from fires and explosions, all while allowing efficient operations at sea.

- **Marine Engineers** who work with all other engineers to develop and support all machinery and the services necessary for the safety and comfort of people on the rig or offshore structure.

- **Electrical Engineers and Electronic Engineers** who design electrical power systems, automation systems, alarms, communication systems, radar, surveillance systems, navigation systems, and lighting.

- **Materials Engineers** who identify appropriate metals, plastics, paint, lubricants, equipment, cable, furniture, and other goods necessary to meet performance and environmental requirements over the lifetime of the structure,and work with manufacturers to ensure that materials that are purchased perform as specified.

- **Environmental Engineers** who participate in the design to protect people and the environment by limiting toxic materials, and assess the processes used during construction of the structure.
- **Safety Engineers** who ensure that the structure and its equipment are ergonomically appropriate for men and women of all sizes, and that they can be operated without danger to the people aboard or to the cargo.
- **Mechanical Engineers** who design specific machinery such as cranes, hoists, elevators, and equipment for anchoring, steering, or moving supplies within the rig, as well as between the structure and ships at sea.
- **Civil Engineers** who specify the actual structure of the rig or turbine including framing, shell, decks, bulkheads, and equipment foundations. They ensure that the structure can withstand the pressure of the water and the impact of waves.

Underwater Habitats

In 1962, Jacques Cousteau designed the first underwater habitat. It was called *Conshelf* and it enabled several researchers to work and live underwater for up to a month while they explored the ocean around them. Three of these habitats were built in the Red and Mediterranean Seas.

Scuba divers exploring the ocean.

The researches preferred to live underwater to escape the limitations of regular scuba diving. Usually, a scuba diver can only dive 130 feet down without changing the air mixture or getting sick. If a diver wants to go deeper, a technique referred to as 'technical diving,' they must decompress on the way to the surface.

Technical diving is a term used to describe all diving methods that exceed the limits of depth or immersion time for recreational scuba diving. Technical diving often involves the use of special gas mixtures (other than compressed air) for breathing. The gas mixture is determined either by the maximum depth planned for the dive, or the planned length of time that the diver intends to spend underwater. While the recommended maximum depth for conventional scuba diving is 130 feet, technical divers may dive 170 feet to 350 feet, or more.

Technical diving almost always requires one or more mandatory decompression "stops" upon ascent, during which the diver may change breathing gas mixtures. Decompression stops are necessary to allow the gases (primarily Nitrogen) that have accumulated in the diver's tissues to be released in a slow and controlled manner. If an individual exceeds the limits of time or depth, or ascends too quickly, large bubbles can form in the tissues, joints, and bloodstream. The formation of these bubbles leads to an extremely painful condition known as Decompression Sickness (DCS), more commonly known as the "bends," which can cause paralysis and even death.

When living underwater, researchers can return directly to the undersea laboratory after diving instead of coming to the surface. Because it doesn't matter if the dive was one day or 30, most researchers prefer to stay underwater to maximize their research time and minimize their need to decompress. As long as the researchers don't go back to the surface, they can

use special dive tables (which list the maximum time that a diver can safely stay underwater at a certain depth) to increase their dive time to nearly ten times greater than conventional surface-based diving.

Since *Conshelf,* other underwater habitats such as Sealab I, II, and III, and Hydrolab have been home to hundreds of scientists. Today, NASA astronauts train in underwater cities to experience living in near zero-gravity environments. The most famous of these is the *Aquarius* underwater laboratory which rests 60 feet below the surface. The astronauts typically live and work building the city for months at a time. These engineer/astronauts are often referred to as aquanauts.

The *Aquarius* is the only undersea laboratory in the world dedicated to marine science operating. Owned by the National

Aquarius undersea laboratory before its 1986 deployment.

Oceanic and Atmospheric Administration (NOAA) and managed by the University of North Carolina at Wilmington (UNCW), *Aquarius* operates 4.5 kilometers offshore of Key

Largo, Florida. The underwater laboratory is 20 meters
beneath the surface next to deep coral reefs. *Aquarius*
provides life-support systems that allow scientists to live and
work underwater in reasonably comfortable living quarters,
and offers sophisticated research capabilities. Scientists
have access to email, telephone, and video conferencing to
anywhere in the world.

Aquarius was originally conceived and funded by NOAA's
National Undersea Research Program (NURP) in the mid
1980s. The underwater laboratory was built by Victoria
Machine Works in 1986-87. Initial deployment was in the
U.S. Virgin Islands where 13 missions were conducted before
Hurricane Hugo struck in 1989, and devastated St. Croix.
Aquarius was retrieved from the seafloor in 1990, and moved
to North Carolina where it was refurbished. In 1993, the
laboratory was redeployed in the Florida Keys National Marine
Sanctuary, and supported 22 missions during the next three
years. In 1996, *Aquarius* was retrieved, and improvements
were made to the system. *Aquarius* was redeployed in 1997 and
operations resumed in 1998.

The fully equipped underwater laboratory includes several
components. The *Aquarius* "habitat" module is an 82-ton
double-lock pressure vessel that measures approximately 14
meters long by 3 meters in diameter. Scientists live and work
inside the habitat when they are not diving outside on the
reefs. Entry is through the wet porch, which contains an open
moon pool, dive equipment storage areas, hot water heater,
and shower.

There are two main compartments in the *Aquarius* module.
The 14 cubic meter "entry lock" contains bench space for
computers and experiments, power equipment, life support
controls, small viewports, and bathroom facilities. The largest
living space is the 40 cubic meter "main lock," which includes

berths for a six-person crew, computer work stations, two large viewports, and kitchen facilities. The kitchen has a microwave, instant hot water dispenser, refrigerator, sink, and dining and work areas. The main lock also contains life-support controls so that both the entry and main locks can be independently pressurized.

The *Aquarius* baseplate is a 116-ton structure that provides a stable and level support base for the habitat. Each of the four legs contains 25 tons of lead ballast. The legs have seven feet of adjustment for leveling it in variable seafloor terrain through the use of hydraulically-driven screw jacks. The habitat and baseplate were designed to survive severe storm conditions, and have successfully weathered hurricanes in both the Caribbean and Florida.

A shore-based Mission Control center is located in Key Largo, approximately 12 kilometers from *Aquarius*, and includes a specially designed "watch desk." The watch desk has computers and communication equipment linked to *Aquarius* by wireless telemetry. Also located on shore are docks for the program's boats, office space, storage and work rooms for dive gear and equipment, an electronics shop, a six-person dual-lock decompression chamber for emergency evacuation, two laboratories, and living accommodations for staff and visiting scientists.

The aquanauts who train in this underwater facility:
- Test lunar exploration concepts and long-duration spaceflight medical objectives;
- Conduct a variety of undersea "moon walks" to test concepts for future lunar exploration using advanced navigation and communication equipment;
- Receive training to make real-time decisions about daily operations similar to what may be necessary for lunar and Mars missions. The idea is to show

how procedures and training for future missions can be adapted, considering the reduced direct communication with Mission Control those crews will encounter;

- Learn about our oceans and coastal resources; and
- Work to understand our changing ocean and the condition of coral reefs.

Unfortunately, coral reefs are threatened worldwide by increasing pollution, overharvesting of fisheries, disease, and global climate change. Scientific achievements of *Aquarius* include discoveries related to the damaging effects of ultraviolet light on coral reefs, geological studies that use fossil reefs to better understand the significance of present-day changes in coral reefs, research that is rewriting the book on how corals feed, water-quality studies that evaluate sources of pollution, and long-term studies to help distinguish between reef changes caused by natural system variability and humans (due to pollution and overharvesting).

The next generation of underwater laboratories will build on the success of *Aquarius*, but challenges exist to provide even more cost-effective and flexible operations. A national debate is also underway regarding the use of remotely operated vehicles to replace human exploration and presence underwater based on cost and safety considerations. However, programs like *Aquarius* and manned submersibles satisfy an essential element of the human spirit that cannot be met by robots. Furthermore, human eyes still exceed the capabilities of cameras, and the creative potential of our brains to observe, explore, understand, and solve problems cannot be matched by computers. Human exploration in the extreme environments of the sea and outer space has captured the attention and imagination of our nation for almost half a century. *Aquarius* may be the only underwater laboratory operating in our oceans today, but based on its record of productivity and

accomplishment, and the human spirit of exploration, it won't be the last.

For more information on the *Aquarius* Underwater Laboratory, please visit the *Aquarius* Web site at www. oceanservice.noaa.gov.

The Engineers Who Design Underwater Structures

- **Ocean Engineers** who work both on and below the surface of the sea, and study ocean movements and their affect on the habitat both on the surface and submerged. Their work includes structural design for resisting deep ocean pressure, and selecting materials for this environment,
- **Ocean Engineers With an Electrical Engineering Emphasis** who may develop the technology to generate, store, or distribute the energy systems within the habitat. They may be responsible for backup electrical and oxygen systems.
- **Ocean Engineers With a Mechanical Engineering Emphasis** who may design the power and control systems to get the habitat to and from its location on the ocean floor. They may build and test prototypes, make CAD models, or write and apply for patents.
- **Ocean Engineers With Civil Engineering Emphasis** who may be responsible for mooring systems or running electrical cable underwater.
- **Marine Engineers** who develop all of the systems required to make the habitat functional, safe and comfortable for all of the people onboard.
- **Electrical Engineers and Electronic Engineers** who design electrical and computer systems, automation systems, alarms, communication systems, surveillance systems, navigation systems, and lighting.

- **Environmental Engineers** who participate in the design to protect people and the environment by limiting toxic materials, and they assess the processes used during construction of the vessel.
- **Materials Engineers** who design the helmets used by technical divers that are made from advanced materials that allow them to be both lightweight and extremely durable.
- **Mechanical Engineers** who design specific items of machinery like cranes, hoists, elevators, and equipment for anchoring, steering, or moving supplies.
- **Civil/Structural Engineers** who specify the actual structure of the habitat including framing, shell, decks, bulkheads, and equipment foundations. They ensure that the habitat can withstand the weight of cargo and the impact of waves.

Underwater Robots, Vehicles and Exploration

The oceans hold many mysteries, and people have always wanted to explore it. Finding new species of fish or other aquatic organisms, exploring the bottom of the ocean, and investigating new forms of life are just some. What's down there? Ships have sunk and treasure hunters line up to look for the loot. Historians marvel at the lives that can be recreated using artifacts that were brought back up to the surface after a ship such as the *Titanic* had sunk.

Humans, with our fragile bodies, cannot live in water without the aid of technology. Some of this technology has been invented, but more engineering is needed to explore the vast bodies of water on the planet. For more than 2000 years, people have been working underwater and exploring the seas. From Alexander the Great to the Japanese and Korean pearl divers to Jacques Cousteau and many others, finding ways to explore the oceans has interested some of the greatest minds in history.

Underwater Vehicles

To explore the ocean, engineers have invented many different types of vehicles. To better understand engineering, you need to think about it as a journey instead of a job. In this journey, you will always be working to make your inventions or designs better. This means that your designs will often be modified over time to meet the needs of society or to incorporate new technology. This continual refinement is what makes products and processes better.

Your cell phone is a great example of this "technology-in-motion" concept. Just five years ago, cell phones were large and only made phone calls. Today, because engineers continued to make the phones and networks better, we can send and receive text messages, take photos, get email, surf the net, and download apps to do almost anything or instantly get almost any information that we need. Without engineers working on every part of this infrastructure, this would not be possible.

The same is true for underwater vehicles. In the early 1700s, John Lethbridge made a diving chamber that was basically a waterproof wooden barrel with holes cut out for arms and for visibility. It was lowered from a boat with a rope to a maximum depth of 65 feet. In this rudimentary diving chamber, he successfully salvaged shipwreck treasures and artifacts from the ocean floor.

But humans wanted to explore deeper and we didn't want to be in wooden barrels. In the 1800s the first submarine was designed and constructed in France by Robert Fulton. It was 25 feet long, powered by hand, and had a mast and sail for when it was on the surface.

In the late 1800s, the U.S. Navy bought its first submarine, which was developed by John Holland and used in World Wars

I & II. It had an electric motor for underwater propulsion, and a gasoline motor to travel on the surface. Surface travel also recharged its batteries making it very beneficial on long trips.

Today, these designs and many others have improved because of engineering and technology. There are five main types of underwater vehicles.

1. **Remotely Operated Vehicle (ROV)**
 ROVs are robots that are operated with a cable or tether. They can be any shape or size, and are usually designed for the specific job they will perform. Underwater ROVs search for treasure or artifacts, research the lives of sea creatures, salvage materials on the ocean floor, and maintain oil rigs or other underwater structures. Usually, an ROV is unmanned— meaning that no man, woman, or child is riding in or on the robot.

 Usually, the ROV operator has a hand-held control device, similar to a video game controller, that is used to give the robot commands and power (electricity). The advantage of this system is that the ROV does not need an on-board battery, and if a video camera is attached, the footage can be seen in real time.

Deploying a ROV

The majority of devices in this category are considered to be "free swimming". With the help of the operator, they can swim in any direction as well as crawl along the bottom. Other ROVs are towed by boats or dragged along the ocean floor to dig trenches for underwater cables or fiber-optic Internet lines. Some are more like tractors that crawl on the bottom in very deep waters, and some conduct research on underwater structures such as oil rigs.

2. **Autonomous Underwater Vehicle (AUV)**
 Autonomous means that the underwater robot can be operated without a tether. If you have ever seen the LEGO® Mindstorms kit or watched a robotic competition, you know what I mean. These robots swap the tether for wireless or Bluetooth communication. Similar to the ROV, they can be operated by a person using a videogame-like controller directly or by a computer that has been programmed to give it specific commands.

 Like most autonomous vehicles, AUVs can be fully equipped with sonar and sensors to detect depth,

Autonomous Underwater Vehicle (AUV)

obstacles, currents, temperature, and time that help it navigate and perform specific tasks. Being untethered can help it explore underneath structures, shipwrecks, or ice patches in the Arctic regions.

It is expected that once underwater Wi-Fi or Bluetooth and battery technology improves, the AUV will become the most common robot for exploration. In addition, smaller computers with larger storage capacities will enable researches to acquire the vast amounts of data that each sensor captures.

3. **Manned Submersibles**
Don't let the name mislead you—a manned vehicle can be manned or operated by a woman! Just like the term implies, manned submersibles are underwater vehicles that have one to three people onboard. It can be tethered or untethered, and only differs from a submarine in that a submarine is usually larger, has a crew of people onboard, and is used for tourism or military operations. This smaller submersible is for one to three people to do research, fix oil rigs, or perform salvage operations.

Other types of manned submersibles include diving bells, observation chambers, and Newtsuits (atmospheric diving suits).

4. **Hybrid Vehicles**
This is a combination of a manned submersible and an underwater robot. It can be tethered or autonomous.

5. **Swimmer Recovery Vehicles (SRV)**
SRVs are great for going fast underwater. It's like

One Person Submarine or Manned Submersible

putting a motor on your bicycle. Suddenly, you don't have to do all the work to get from point A to point B, you just have to hold on.

Imagine that you only have one hour of air in your scuba tank and it would normally take you 30 minutes to swim to the work site. You wouldn't be able to get anything done. But with an SRV, you can get to the work site quickly, and even carry extra air and tools on its platform.

The Engineers Who Design Underwater Robots, Vehicles and Exploration Technology

- **Ocean Engineers** who work both on and below the surface of the sea, and study ocean movements and their affect on the habitat both above and below the waterline. Their work includes structural design for resisting deep ocean pressure, and selecting materials

for this environment. Ocean engineers may also be responsible for developing underwater tools and devices that aid underwater research.

- **Ocean Engineers With an Electrical Engineering Emphasis** who may develop the electrical systems and technology to generate, store, or distribute the energy to underwater vehicles. They may be responsible for battery systems, wired and wireless cameras, waterproof computers, sensors, underwater lighting and the logistics of collecting data.
- **Ocean Engineers With a Mechanical Engineering Emphasis** who may design turbines, generators, or control systems for underwater robots and vehicles. They may build and test prototypes, make CAD models, or write and apply for patents.
- **Ocean Engineers With Civil Engineering Emphasis** who may design the mooring systems for any structure that needs to be anchored to the ocean floor either temporarily or permanently. They make sure that the attachments can sustain hurricanes, corrosion and water pressure.
- **Marine Engineers** who develop the propulsion systems and work with other engineers to integrate all the systems together in any powered vehicle. They also provide all support services necessary for the safety and comfort of people onboard.
- **Electrical Engineers and Electronic Engineers** who may design or develop the electrical systems and technology to generate, store, or distribute the energy to underwater vehicles. They may be responsible for battery systems, wired and wireless cameras, waterproof computers, sensors, underwater lighting and the logistics collecting data.
- **Environmental Engineers** who participate in the design to protect people and the environment by limiting toxic

materials, and they assess the processes used during construction of the robot or vessel.

- **Materials Engineers** who design the helmets and wetsuits used by technical divers that are made from advanced materials that allow them to be both lightweight and extremely durable.
- **Mechanical Engineers** who design specific items of machinery like cranes, hoists, elevators, and equipment for anchoring, steering, or moving supplies. They may also may design turbines, generators, or control systems for underwater robots and vehicles. They may build and test prototypes, make CAD models, or write and apply for patents.
- **Civil/Structural Engineers** who specify the actual structure of the vehicle including framing, shell, decks, bulkheads, and equipment foundations. They may also may design the mooring systems for any structure that needs to be anchored to the ocean floor either temporarily or permanently. They make sure that the attachments can sustain hurricanes, corrosion and water pressure.
- **Chemical and Biomedical Engineers** who may design scuba diving equipment such as the air tanks, wet suits, and oxygen regulators. They may also determine the gas mixtures needed by divers at different depths.

PART FOUR—OUR WORLD

Global Climate Change

It's impossible to separate the future of careers in naval architecture, marine, ocean, or naval engineering from the future of the planet. Every career has pros and cons about what the future may hold, but these types of careers are even more sensitive to changes in the world. Fortunately, because the world is moving toward increased sustainability and conservation of resources, the future looks very bright for these types of engineers. One of the most rewarding aspects of being

Sailors and marsh restoration volunteers ride a fan boat to help replant grasses in Hitchcock, Texas.

this type of engineer is that you can meet the demand for sustainability and make a difference from the first day on the job through the rest of your career. The opportunities offer a challenging and satisfying chance to protect the health and safety of people and our environment.

According to The Department of Transportation, a ship carrying cargo uses only 10-20 percent of the energy that would be used by trucks. An inland barge can move one ton of freight about 514 miles on one gallon of fuel, a train can move one ton of freight about 202 miles on one gallon of fuel, and a

truck can move one ton of freight about 59 miles on a gallon of fuel.

Environmental Advantages of Inland Barge Transportation
Source: U.S. Department of Transportation

You would enjoy this career if you have an interest in renewable energy, reducing pollution, or assessing environmental impacts. If you want to work with people, make a more sustainable future, work to protect the planet, or develop renewable energy sources, you may be very happy in the naval, ocean, or marine industries. Sustainable engineering is a booming field with new jobs to find environmentally sustainable solutions to support population growth and preserve our limited natural resources. Sustainable engineers concentrate on preserving the environment for the public through knowledge, research, a caring attitude, and common sense.

We know that climate change is occurring. According to NASA, the evidence that suggests it includes:

- The levels of atmospheric carbon dioxide are higher today than at any time in past years. Scientists reconstructed past climate conditions through evidence in tree rings, coral reefs, and ice cores. For example, ice cores from two miles deep in the Antarctic contain samples of tiny atmospheric air bubbles that date back as far as 650,000 years. These samples have allowed scientists to construct a historical record of greenhouse gas concentrations stretching back thousands of years;

- The global sea level rose about 17 centimeters (6.7 inches) in the 20th century. The rate of rise in the last decade, however, is nearly double that of the last century;

- All three major global surface temperature measurements have increased since 1880. Most of this warming has occurred since 1981 with the 10 warmest years occurring in the last 12 years;

- The oceans have absorbed most of this heat with significant portions of ocean showing a warming of 0.302 degrees Fahrenheit since 1969. With a rise in the overall temperature of the ocean, tropical storms and hurricanes could increase in force.

Energy Concerns

We, society, use energy every day. Not only do we use energy to walk, talk, play sports, and function (in units called Calories), but we also use energy to power our cars, toast our bread, watch TV, etc. Energy is everywhere and there are multiple forms of it. Energy can be electrical, chemical, thermal, geothermal, nuclear, light, kinetic, sound, potential, or water. However, the only way we will solve our energy crisis is to learn how to convert any of these forms of energy into electricity.

Types of renewable energy include solar, wind, ocean, and geothermal. Types of non-renewable energy include coal, natural gas, oil, and other fossil fuels. When energy is renewable it means that it can be reused. For example, energy from the sun can provide power when it hits a solar panel. The sun's energy is renewable because the energy from the sun is still available even after you use it. Power provided by natural gas is non-renewable because, once you burn the gas, it is gone forever.

Developing sources of renewable energy is critical because someday, non-renewable energy sources, such as fossil fuels, will be depleted. Renewable energy technologies are also clean sources of energy and better for the environment. Continuing to rely heavily on fossil fuels will continually limit our access to clean water, clean air, and energy independence.

Engineers are hard at work designing new ways to use renewable energy to help slow global warming and protect our planet. Engineers in this industry are designing cleaner engines for improved efficiency as well as electric and hybrid vehicles. Other engineers are working to improve the efficiency of wind, water, and solar power. And still other engineers are exploring the potential of future technologies to help shape the world.

Energy from the Ocean (Wave, Tide, Geothermal, Current, and Wind)

As you read this, engineers are hard at work developing technologies that use the ocean and its resources to generate electricity. Energy from the ocean is usually renewable, can help reduce our dependence on foreign oil and may provide enough energy to light the world in the future. It's important to minimize the disturbance that these technologies cause to the ocean floor and the fish.

The element that's important to understand about engineering is that it's a constantly changing process, and more like a journey than a destination. Engineers constantly strive to make things better. They may develop ocean technology that can be used to power our homes today but they don't stop there. The next week, they may be working on improving a design, or they may have a new idea about how to harvest energy more efficiently.

For most engineers, the ideas don't stop once a product is designed. There are always improvements that can be made. Some improvements happen because there is new technology or systems available, and sometimes improvements happen because the needs of society or the funding organization have changed.

With further research, you will notice that there are many ways to harvest energy from the ocean and many different designs. The five ways you will read about below; wave energy converters, tidal energy devices, OTEC, ocean current converters, and offshore wind energy are general methods of energy extraction. This list of methods is not comprehensive and by the time this book is published, there may be other methods available. There are many forms of this technology and several that can also be used in rivers and lakes. Engineers are at the forefront of solving the energy crisis, and are desperately needed to solve the world's energy problems.

Wave Energy Converters

Just like the name implies, this technology converts wave energy into electricity. Wave power is used both in the ocean and in lakes that have enough waves to be useful. Although it is a relatively new technology, it may hold the most promise because wave energy can be caught anywhere on the ocean.

The technology can consist of:

- A buoy either on the water's surface or just below it that can capture the wave energy. The buoy system has a column that is filled with air. When a wave enters the buoy, the air in the column is forced upwards and the air turns a turbine. When the water recedes, the space left by the water creates a vacuum that also turns the turbine. In other words, the air movement caused by the water moving up and down in the column turns the turbine, which turns a motor to produce electricity. However, due to the relentless pounding of the waves and the corrosive nature of the ocean, these buoys often break or become nonfunctional, as seen off the Oregon coast where only 50 percent of all the buoys are in working order;

- A sea snake-looking device that is semi-submerged in the ocean. The "snake" generates power in the hinged joints that connect its sections. When a wave rolls by, the forward and back and side-to-side swells activate hydraulic rams located in the hinges (by resistance) that pump high-pressure oil into hydraulic motors that drive electrical

Pelamis Wave Energy Converter.
Photo courtesy: Pelamis Wave Power Ltd.

generators and produce electricity. The electricity is transported back to the shore in an underwater cable. Currently, this technology has been installed successfully as a 2.5 Mega Watt wave farm off the coast of Portugal. A wave farm that takes up less space than a half square mile of ocean can generate 30 Mega Watts of power, which is enough to power 20,000 homes.

Tidal Energy Devices

A tidal energy device is just like a wind turbine except that it is underwater and instead of wind, the current makes it turn. Just like the name implies, this type of system captures the energy of the tides or currents that run below the waves, and turns them into electricity. This is most often done by installing a turbine underwater that rotates in the current. The turbine may be bidirectional or may only be able to turn in one direction. In other words, some of these underwater turbines generate electricity only when the tide is going out, and some generate electricity when the tide is going out or coming into the shore.

OpenHydro's Open-Center Turbine is designed to be deployed, directly on the seabed. The first 6-m test unit produces enough energy to supply 150 average European homes and save the emission of over 450 tons of CO2 greenhouse gas per year.

These devices may be close to the shore or far out in the ocean. The ones deeply submerged in the ocean are often strategically placed where the cold fresh waters of the Polar Regions meet the warmer, tropical waters that have absorbed more solar radiation. These areas create intense water circulation that has the potential to generate large amounts of electricity.

With turbines, the amount of energy generated is directly proportional to the density of the fluid passing through it. Because water is much denser than air, a water turbine has several hundred times the power of an air turbine. On the flip side, the marine environment is so corrosive that repairs costs for underwater turbines can be substantial.

Ocean Thermal Energy Conversion (OTEC)

OTEC is like a big, slow heat pump. It only works if there is a 40 degree difference in the temperature of the surface water and the temperature of the water deep in the ocean. It generates electricity by pumping the colder water from deep in the ocean into a heat exchanger without using oil, coal, natural gas, or any other fuel. As you might have guessed, this is installed in island nations such as Hawaii and Puerto Rico. Forty floating OTEC power stations can generate enough electricity to power all of Puerto Rico forever.

To harvest this solar energy stored in the oceans, engineers have built an all-weather, hurricane-proof floating power station that uses the temperature difference to turn a turbine that generates electricity. The hot tropical water is used to boil a liquid such as propane that has a very low boiling temperature. The propane is turned into a gas that turns the turbine, which generates the electricity that is carried to land in an underwater cable. The cold water of the deep ocean is then pumped into the exchanger where it cools and condenses the propane so that it can be turned back into a liquid and used again.

OTEC System

Think of it like this, 70 percent of the earth's surface is covered by water and 97 percent of that water is ocean water. In the tropical waters near the equator, the oceans can store 1000 times more heat than the atmosphere. That means that all of this heat (solar power) that is stored in the upper layers of the tropical oceans has the potential to supply more than 300 times the earth's electrical needs.

The additional benefit of this kind of energy generation is that it produces the useful by-product of fresh drinking water and a supply of cool, nutrient-rich seawater that can be used to enhance such activities as mariculture (growing food in the ocean).

Ocean Current Energy

Ocean currents created by tides are generated from the gravitational attraction between the earth and the Moon. High tide and low tide both occur twice a day and at regular intervals, so the direction of the current changes four times a day. Because of the regularity of the tides, the amount of energy that the current can generate can be estimated with accuracy. For example, current can travel at speeds of 10 knots or 11.5 miles per hour. Water traveling at 10 knots over an area of one square meter can generate up to 6 Kilowatts of power, or a little more than what is needed to power two houses.

Ocean current energy is at an early stage of development. There are no commercial grid-connected turbines currently operating; Only a small number of prototypes and demonstration units have been tested.

There are also non-tidal ocean currents such as the Gulf Stream that are created by the solar heating of the tropical waters near the equator. Because the hot

water wants to cool down (Newton's law of thermodynamics), the hot tropical water makes its way North to the cold fresh waters of the Arctic. The rotation of the Earth, the salinity of the water, and the temperature differences that make the currents race are known as the "Coriolis Force."

Offshore Wind Energy

Wind turbines are different from windmills. Windmills are used to pump water up from an underground well or to grind grain, whereas wind turbines are used to produce electricity. Wind is a renewable resource and engineers design wind turbines to change the kinetic energy of the wind into mechanical and electrical energy.

Wind farms are usually found in regions that have strong and steady winds (most often in open fields, on top of mountains, or in the ocean). For most wind turbines to turn fast enough to generate electricity, the wind must roar at a minimum of 12-14 miles per hour. When the wind blows, the angled blades of the turbine turn gears in a transmission box that is connected to a generator that generates electricity. To avoid damage to

the blades, the turbine includes a brake just in case the wind gets too strong.

A turbine usually produces 50–300 Kilowatts of electricity. 300 Kilowatts of electricity can light up 3000 100-Watt light bulbs. Most jobs in the field of wind energy research require an electrical, computer, or mechanical engineering background. The challenges for engineers in this industry

are how to make wind turbines or farms more efficient, and finding better ways to store or transport the electricity that is generated.

According to "Careers in Wind Energy" by Robin Arnette, the five major areas of wind energy research are:

- Turbine research—involves research to improve turbine design (aerodynamics), understanding the nature of wind (inflow and turbulence), and using computer models to design efficient and low-cost turbines (modeling structures and dynamics).
- Wind resource assessment—provides maps of a country or state/province that includes specific wind data such as average wind speed and its variability.
- Forecasting—uses weather models (i.e., Doppler radar) to predict wind speeds and patterns at various altitudes. It also uses old data to predict how the wind will behave at a certain time.
- Utility grid integration—integrates the energy produced by wind into a utility grid. New techniques and models will ensure that grid operators can manage variable-output technologies like wind and solar with maximum efficiency.
- Energy storage—uses technology to store wind energy as electricity. Some methods include converting it to chemical energy (like hydrogen), and flywheels.

Fortunately, the ocean technology resources named in this section can meet a considerable proportion of our energy needs, and they can help alleviate many problems while providing other important benefits. Researching and harvesting renewable energy from the ocean can:

- Protect our environment and public health by avoiding or reducing emissions that contribute to smog, acid rain, and global warming;

- Increase economic development and create new green-collar jobs;
- Create more competition to help restrain fossil fuel price increases;
- Diversify our fuel sources and enhance the reliability of fuel supplies;
- Insulate our economy from fossil fuel price spikes and supply shortages or disruptions;
- Reduce a growing reliance on imported fuel and electricity;
- Reduce the cost of complying with present and future environmental regulations; and
- Conserve our natural resources for future generations.

The Engineers Who Help Harvest Ocean Energy

- **Ocean Engineers with an Electrical Engineering Emphasis** who may develop the technology to generate, store, or distribute the renewable energy harvested. They may be responsible for grid connections, designing the transmission lines and the offshore logistics of transporting energy underwater and back to land.
- **Ocean Engineers with a Mechanical Engineering Emphasis** who may design energy and control systems that can withstand corrosion, wave impacts, storms and the constant motion of the ocean. They may build and test prototypes, make CAD models, or write and apply for patents.
- **Ocean Engineers with a Civil Engineering Emphasis** who may design the OTEC and offshore wind turbine structures that are embedded in the ocean floor that can withstand hurricane winds. They may be responsible for mooring systems and running electrical cable underwater.

- **Marine Engineers** who develop all of the support services necessary for the safety and comfort of installers, operators and/or maintenance technicians.
- **Electrical Engineers and Electronic Engineers** who design electrical, computer and automation systems, alarms, and communication systems. They may also develop the technology to generate, store, or distribute the renewable energy harvested. They may be responsible for grid connections, designing the transmission lines and the offshore logistics of transporting energy underwater and back to land.
- **Environmental Engineers** who participate in the design to protect people and the environment by limiting toxic materials, they assess the processes used during construction and study the potential impact on sealife, birds and the water.
- **Materials Engineers** who research advanced materials that may be able to withstand corrosion, wave impacts, storms and the constant motion of the ocean while also lowering cost and improving the stability of the integrated systems.
- **Mechanical Engineers** who design specific items of machinery like cranes, hoists, elevators, and equipment for installing, anchoring, or moving structures and supplies. They may also manage the manufacturing processes for the turbines, gearboxes, towers, and blades and other technology. They may also research ways to improve turbine aerodynamics while lowering the cost.
- **Civil/Structural Engineers** who specify the actual structure and mooring of the ocean energy technologies including framing, shell, foundations and anchoring. They ensure that the structures can withstand the weight of ice and the impact of waves.
- **Aerospace Engineers** who may research ways to improve turbine aerodynamics while lowering the cost,

study the nature of wind (inflow and turbulence), build and test prototypes, make CAD models, or write and apply for patents.

Part Five — Getting Started

When you work with other people, good communication is very important. Communication skills include the ability to listen, write clearly, and speak well. In addition to being good communicators, engineers need to be passionate, energetic, creative, and excited about their work. The maritime industry is always evolving and changing. Being a good engineer is so much more than being a brain. Take extra classes in technical

writing, develop excellent presentation skills, choose an industry that makes you excited about your career, and commit yourself to being the best you can be. Four years in engineering school may not be enough. To succeed, focus your energy, meet your goals, pay attention to details, and push yourself to be creative.

Remember that this book is only one source of information to help you decide whether you want to become a maritime

engineer. Right now, you should begin reading everything you can find about engineering, and talk to every engineer or engineering student you know about the challenges ahead and how to prepare for them. Attend a summer camp or program pertaining to engineering at your school. Obtaining this information now may save you lots of heartache if you decide later that you are on the wrong path.

If you want to work in the maritime industry, the most valuable thing you can do is to get practical hands-on experience. Get out and do the actual work. Take classes in hull design or marine electronics in college, and learn the basics from a technical standpoint. Try to get down to the nuts and bolts of what you are learning, and then get out and do it. If you go to work for a manufacturer that experience will be invaluable because you'll be able to relate to the customer for the products you design, and will be able to talk on their level. And your experience will also be invaluable to the company, because you can bring hands-on, practical information back to the company from actually knowing how to use the products that the company makes.

David Helgerson, the technical director for CSC's Advanced Marine Center says,

> *"I would advise students to gain as much practical experience as possible before and during school; this helps them understand the opportunities that will present themselves, will make more opportunities available, will provide money and will differentiate the student from other students with less experience. In*

> *high school, I would look for internships. In college I would look for intern opportunities in other geographic areas because moving when young is easier than later and I would go to Europe or the Far East to experience shipbuilding in those cultures. For some with a highly design-oriented interest, I would recommend working for an independent naval*

*architect, essentially as an apprentice; that is difficult
and not as financially rewarding, but the training can
be more intense. If you are dreaming of yacht design,
find the best yacht designer that will take you and
then make that work experience the primary thing
in your life for a few years. Read everything. Collect
reference information. Develop your own designs. I
am a Professional Engineer and recommend becoming
licensed. I strongly recommend active participation in
professional societies by joining SNAME: www.sname.
org.*

*Naval architecture, marine engineering, and
associated disciplines are challenging and interesting.
I recommend the field without question. My advice
to individuals depends on their personal interest and
skills. Employment in the community that serves the
Navy and U.S. Coast Guard is much different than the
community that serves the purely commercial industry,
or the yacht design community. You do not need to
'love the water' to be good at naval engineering. I
believe that it helps and makes it more enjoyable. For
yacht design, it probably does help much more to love
the water and to have hands-on operating experience.
Important skills include: good mathematics skills,
excellent communication skills, patience, creativity
balanced with practicality, ability to work with others,
AutoCAD, Rhino, MS Office, and proficiency with other
specialty software (e.g. CFD, FEA) can be important for
some careers. It helps to be responsive to direction and
willing to work long hours when necessary."*

Academic preparation is also essential to exploring
engineering as a career. In addition to coursework, getting

involved in extracurricular activities pertaining to engineering can give you invaluable exposure. In high school, classes in algebra I and II, trigonometry, biology, physics, calculus, chemistry, computer programming, or computer applications can tell you if you have the aptitude and determination to study engineering. These courses are not all required to get into every engineering school, but early preparation can mean the difference between spending four years in college or six. Some universities also require two to three classes in a foreign language for admission. Check into the programs that interest you and begin to fulfill their requirements. Advance Placement (AP) or Honors courses are recommended, as well as an ACT score of 20 or a SAT score of at least 1000.

SeaPerch

One of the best ways to get involved in this field is to build an underwater robot, or SeaPerch, that will help you figure out if you enjoy these types of adventures. It's the beginning of it all and your future career can ride right on top of your SeaPerch experiences. By building a remotely operated vehicle or ROV out of PVC pipe and other materials, you'll learn about waterproofing motors, ballast, underwater mobility, soldering, propulsion, balance, teamwork, communication, and much more.

After the SeaPerch is constructed, you are encouraged to test your vehicles, deploy them on "missions," and compete in a culminating event, the SeaPerch Challenge. The SeaPerch

Challenge is a district-wide one-day design competition, to take it to the next level.

Events at the challenge can include:
- Vehicle Performance;
- Innovative Design;
- Team Presentations;
- Design Planning, Construction, Testing, and Learning;
- Team Spirit and Sportsmanship.

The SeaPerch Program is funded by the Office of Naval Research as part of the National Naval Responsibility for Naval Engineering (NNRNE) to find the next generation of naval architects, marine engineers, naval engineers, and ocean engineers.

Become Well-Rounded

Engineering is much more than just being a brain. Companies want to hire engineers who are well-rounded, work well in teams, and communicate effectively. When it comes to inspiration, conceptualization, and rock-solid prototypes that really work, every engineering discipline is important. Every engineering student today must study multiple disciplines so they can be well-rounded and very creative in their thinking. You may find yourself working with other engineers, scientists, private entrepreneurs, inventors, investors, technicians, urban planners, accountants, politicians, and policy makers. The collective knowledge of the entire group may be needed to deal with a serious problem.

It's like playing in a band—the guitarist sets the bass line or melody, the drummer sets the rhythm, and the singer adds words and meaning. Beautiful music is made by each person doing what they do best, and working together. Each player

brings different strengths to the band, and the band can't function as efficiently or achieve the sound it wants without each part. Teamwork is integral to the success of the band. Engineering design works in the same way. Each member of the team contributes according to his or her individual strengths, and as a result, society gets new boats, benefits from improved renewable energy sources, and an increased quality of life.

Communication Skills

Are communication skills necessary? Absolutely! Rarely do people work alone. Any engineer must be able to tell other people what is happening, what to expect, and what is needed, verbally or in writing. Specifications, proposals, briefings, and reports are all part of the job.

Most ships trade internationally, and many are built in foreign countries or outfitted with a mixture of domestic and foreign equipment. Crews of many nationalities are common. Repairs in foreign shipyards are frequent. There is a lot of contact with professional people, shipyard workers, and merchant mariners from other countries and cultures, and an understanding of their languages and cultures is certainly helpful and probably essential. Many ships are government owned, but even privately owned ships are built and operated under regulations of a multitude of domestic, foreign, and international agencies.

Learn to communicate effectively—you won't regret it.

Summer Camps

Summer camps provide another innovative approach to preparing for a career in engineering or evaluating if that career is right for you. Find out what it is like to study engineering; learn about the different types of engineers and what engineers do on a daily basis. Almost every college of engineering offers a summer engineering camp for high-school students. These camps offer a week or two of fun while developing leadership, professional, and personal organizational skills, and they provide opportunities to meet and talk with engineers during visits to local engineering companies. Check with the college of engineering at a university near you to see if any summer programs are offered, or visit the Engineering Education Service Center's Web site at www.engineeringedu.com to find a camp in your area.

Student Competitions

A great way to get a feel for engineering is to look at the student design competitions that are sponsored or co-sponsored by various engineering societies and organizations. These competitions are developed to encourage and motivate students. The competitions focus on teamwork and allow you to get a "real-world" feeling for the design process, including working with the cost of materials and team dynamics.

BEST student getting ready for the competition.

A few of the more popular competitions include

- Boosting Engineering, Science, and Technology (BEST). A robotic competition that provides students

with an intense, hands-on, real engineering and problem-solving experience that is also fun. (www. bestinc.org)

- FIRST Robotics Competition. Corporations and universities team up with high schools in a high-tech robot sporting event. (www.usfirst.org)
- Mathcounts. A national math coaching and competition program for 7th and 8th grade students. (www. mathcounts.org)
- Future City. Students learn about math and science in a challenging and interesting way through reality-based education using SimCity 2000 software. (www. futurecity.org)
- TEAMS. A national academic competition hosted by the Junior Engineering Technical Society (JETS) that enables groups of high school students to learn team development and problem-solving skills. Students learn how math and science concepts are applied to real-world problems. Teamwork is promoted in an open-book, open-discussion environment, and students often work with an engineering mentor. The wide range of real-world problems shows students the diversity of specialties within the engineering field. (www.jets.org)
- International Bridge Building Contest. The construction and testing of model bridges promotes the study and application of fundamental principles of physics and also helps high-school students develop "hands-on" skills through bridge construction. By participating in the Bridge Building Competition students get a flavor of what it is to be an engineer by designing structures to a set of specifications, and then seeing how they perform. (www.iit.edu/~hsbridge)

- Odyssey of the Mind. A worldwide program that promotes creative team-based problem solving for kids from kindergarten through college. (www.odysseyofthemind.com)
- National Science Bowl. A U.S. Department of Energy academic competition where teams of high-school students answer questions on scientific topics in astronomy, biology, chemistry, mathematics, physics, earth, computer and general science. (www.scied.science.doe.gov/nsb)
- BattleBotsIQ. A comprehensive educational program where students learn about the science of engineering through robot building. This unique curriculum fuses mathematics, physics, and engineering into tangible and relevant lessons for high-school students. (www.battlebotsiq.com)

For a current and more comprehensive list of competitions, visit the Engineering Education Service Center's website: www.engineeringedu.com.

What Now?

Now that you have decided to pursue an engineering education, you should prepare for it as soon as possible. Search the Internet, and contact any societies that interest you. Be sure to visit SNAME.org. Browse their Web pages. Ask about their programs to

The commanding officer of Afloat Training Group Western Pacific (ATGWP), explains the purpose of the navigation simulator during a tour of the facilities.

help you prepare for college. Ask to talk to students currently participating in programs that interest you. Contact local engineering firms and ask for a tour. Most firms would be happy to show you around and explain what they do. Several companies encourage continuous improvement in engineering education. For example, a company may have a summer intern program that allows college-level science students to work at their facility each year. They may sponsor a job-shadow program to bring junior high and high school kids into the facilities or labs to see what their researchers are doing.

If you like the companies you've contacted, ask if they offer summer internships or job shadowing programs. Through this simple effort, you will make a contact, and more importantly, a potential job opportunity may await you when you finish your degree.

Choosing the Right School

Choosing the engineering school that is right for you is as important as wheels are to automobiles. Your choice should incorporate your preferences. The advantages and disadvantages of each school will depend on your personal needs and wants. Important considerations for most college-bound students include location, cost, faculty, school size, and academics.

1. Location: In addition to distance from home, location refers to the climate and the types of industry in the surrounding area. If there is an industry specific to your degree, then opportunities

for summer internships, co-op programs, and part-time work experience increase dramatically. These work experiences often lead to jobs after graduation.

2. Cost: Cost of attendance may be a critical factor in determining which school to select, although your decision should not be based on cost alone. Generally, public institutions are less expensive than private schools, but there are many ways to fund your education at any institution. Most engineering societies offer scholarships, and the government offers grants and loans. Part-time work, co-op programs, and campus jobs also help reduce the cost of attendance. Check with the financial aid department of the schools you are interested in to see what grants and loans you qualify for. Call the engineering department to find out about scholarships offered to incoming students through the college. The military may also offer opportunities for financing your education. The National Guard is a popular program among college students. The Air Force, U.S. Coast Guard, Marines, Merchant Marine, Army, and Navy offer education at reduced cost in exchange for a commitment to serve in the Armed Forces for a certain period of time.

3. Faculty: A fine faculty makes it easier to get a good education. A faculty that includes women and minorities will broaden your experience and better prepare you to work with people from diverse backgrounds. Faculty members can bring numerous experiences and expertise to their lectures. Check to make sure that faculty rather than graduate students teach the classes. As you proceed to your junior-level and senior-level classes, the research of the faculty becomes more important. Try to select a school that has at least one faculty member performing active

research in your area of interest. That person can be
a role model. You can talk and learn directly from
someone whose interests you share.

4. School Size: School size matters for some students.
 Large schools offer a greater diversity of people and
 more things to do, but often lack the professor-student
 interaction found at smaller schools. In a small school,
 you may get to know a larger percentage of classmates,
 but in a large school you can meet more people. You
 can receive an excellent education at a large school or
 a small one; which one you choose is purely a matter of
 preference.

5. Academics: Academics is probably the most important
 factor in choosing the school that's best for you. The
 program should be accredited by the Accreditation
 Board for Engineering and Technology (ABET).
 ABET accreditation ensures that the program
 follows national standards for faculty, curricula,
 students, administration, facilities, and institutional
 commitment. By choosing an ABET program, you
 can be sure that the faculty has met certain national
 standards and that the program is highly regarded
 by the profession. *See the appendix for a list of ABET
 accredited schools.*

Some students like the competitive atmosphere that
accompanies attending a very prestigious school, and some
students find they work better in a more relaxed environment.
Both will require a great deal of studying, although some
programs will be more challenging than others. Pick the
atmosphere that best fits your personality and aspirations.
Questions you might ask yourself at this point include: Do I
want to be on the cutting edge of technology? Do I want to find

better solutions to existing identifiable problems (even if a current solution already exists)? Or do I want a combination of the two?

Some schools require their students to have computers, and other schools provide computer laboratories. Find out if free tutoring is offered and if the professors have posted office hours. Can you e-mail questions to professors? Will your questions be answered in a timely fashion? Another consideration is the campus library. Is it easy to find the information you are looking for? Does the school have a special engineering library or carry engineering journals?

Student working in the electronics lab

Students frequently enjoy joining student chapters of professional organizations. These organizations can be an excellent resource during your college experience and in your career search. Many offer competitions against other colleges. Check to see if the society for the branch of engineering you want to study has student chapters at the schools you are considering.

Other school selection criteria to consider include sports facilities, leisure activities, community events, cultural events, and campus activities.

The Successful Student

Engineering is a rigorous and demanding major. To be successful in engineering school, you will need certain tools. You must be self-disciplined, organized, and manage your time effectively. In college, the "real" learning often takes place outside the classroom, and less time is spent in the classroom. A general rule of thumb is that for every hour spent in the classroom, engineering students can expect to spend three hours outside the classroom, compared with two hours for non-technical majors. A good time-management system can also allow you to participate in extracurricular activities, which broaden experience and are of interest to potential employers.

Engineering curricula vary from school to school; however, most schools don't require you to declare a specific field of interest until the end of your second year. The first two years of engineering school are focused on learning the fundamentals such as chemistry, calculus, physics, and mechanics such as statics and dynamics. Courses in English, the humanities, and biology are usually also required.

The third and fourth years of engineering school are most often spent studying your chosen specialty. Most universities require their students to complete a design project in their senior year. The project may be completed in teams or individually and solves a real-world problem. Students may be able to select a problem of personal interest, or local industry may present a problem they are currently exploring. Typically, the project requires a research report, the presentation of the design process, and an analysis of the results.

Co-ops and Internships

A cooperative, or co-op, educational experience is one where an engineering student alternates academics with work experience in government, industry, or business. For example, a student may do a parallel co-op where they work part-time and go to school part-time, or complete a traditional co-op where they work for six months and go to school for six months. A good co-op program may be the perfect answer for the non-traditional student who has financial responsibilities.

Because a co-op program usually takes longer to complete, your experience can be more meaningful. Additionally, a co-op experience can show employers that you have the experience and a solid desire to work in your chosen field. In today's competitive market, you need to do everything possible to stand out.

Engineering internships are another way to get your foot in the door. They generally consist of a summer job related to your major at an engineering company. David Tanaka of Industrial Light and Magic began his successful career by interning every summer. By the time he graduated, he was the first choice when a position became available. If you are interested in obtaining an internship position at an engineering firm, find a company you like and apply (send a resume) as early in the school year as possible.

Professional Engineering and Licensure

A professional engineer (PE) has been licensed by the state. Just as attorneys need to pass the bar exam, and doctors need to pass the state medical board exam, engineers need to pass an eight-hour written exam called the Principles and Practices of Engineering.

Generally, to become a PE, you must have graduated from an accredited college or university, worked for four years under the guidance of a professional engineer, and then passed the exam. Most states, however, offer a pre-registration certificate called the Engineer Intern to those who do not yet have four years of experience. You can obtain the Engineer Intern certificate by passing an eight-hour Fundamentals of Engineering (FE) exam. The first half of the FE exam challenges your general engineering skills. The last half pertains to a specific concentration in engineering such as chemical, civil, electrical, environmental, industrial, or mechanical. Although the certificate does not authorize the practice of engineering, it is the first step to full registration. Then, after you gain four years of experience, you can take the PE examination. This test relates specifically to a major branch of engineering.

Although registration is not mandatory, there is a strong trend in the engineering community toward licensure. For example, licensure is a legal requirement to be in private practice as a consulting engineer. Many high-level government positions can be filled only by professional engineers, and many states now require university instructors to be registered PEs. Most employers expect that students fresh out of college will be well versed in the basics or fundamentals of engineering. Engineer Intern certification proves them right.

Summary:

- Take as many math and science classes in high school as possible.
- Get involved in extracurricular activities such as robotics clubs.
- Practice your communication skills.
- Become well-rounded.
- Enter engineering and technology competitions. When you win, it's very rewarding.

- Read everything you can about engineering to make sure it's the right career for you. This book is only one source of information and only mentions a few of the hundreds of things that you can do with an engineering career.

- Tour colleges of engineering. See what kinds of projects their students are doing, and try to figure out if you would enjoy going to school there. While on campus, talk to engineering students about their experiences and how they decided to become an engineer.

- Tour ship yards, and ocean research centers such as aquariums, fish hatcheries, and marine science centers.

- Learn to scuba dive. Investigate the equipment.

- Take night and summer classes at your local community college. College-level classes are sometimes free for high school students. Take classes that are not offered at your high school, and focus on subjects that might be fun to learn about.

- Visit SNAME online, and the Web sites of other engineering organizations that have sections for students.

- Go to engineering camp, or seek opportunities for summer employment or internships with engineering firms or government research laboratories.

- Visit the U.S. Dept. of Labor Web site for information on career opportunities, growth trends, and salary ranges.

- Talk to your principal about bringing SeaPerch into your school.

You are writing the script for your future and you should make it as interesting and engaging as possible.

APPENDIX

ABET Certification of Programs

Marine Engineering
State University of New York Maritime College
U.S. Naval Academy

Marine Engineering and Shipyard Management
U.S. Merchant Marine Academy

Marine Engineering Systems
U.S. Merchant Marine Academy

Marine Engineering Technology
California Maritime Academy
Maine Maritime Academy
Texas A&M Galveston

Marine Systems Engineering
Maine Maritime Academy

Maritime Systems Engineering (Ocean Engineering)
Texas A&M Galveston

Mechanical and Ocean Engineering
MIT

Naval Architecture
State University of New York Maritime College
U.S. Naval Academy

Naval Architecture and Marine Engineering
University of Michigan
University of New Orleans
U.S. Coast Guard Academy
Webb Institute

Ocean Engineering
Florida Atlantic University
Florida Institute of Technology
University of Rhode Island
Texas A&M University
U.S. Naval Academy
Virginia Polytechnic Institute and State University

Ocean and Resources Engineering
University of Hawaii at Manoa

Glossary of Maritime Terms

Aft — the back or stern of a boat

ASNE — American Society of Naval Engineers

Barge — an unpowered boat pushed by a tow boat

Beam — width of the hull

Body plan — end view of a hull as if it were cut crosswise at regular intervals

Bow — front of a boat

Bow wave — wave that forms in front of a hull as it moves through the water

Cargo hold — location designated for the cargo

Chine — the intersection of the bottom and sides of a flat- or V-bottomed boat

Container Ship — vessel designed to carry cargo in large metal boxes for rapid loading and unloading.

Deck — any horizontal floor in a hull (Some ships have many decks; on smaller ships, the deck is the covering over the top of the hull.)

Displacement — amount of water that is pushed out of the way when a hull is floating on its waterline (usually measured in pounds)

Displacement hull — a hull designed to push the water out of the way as it moves

Draft — distance from the water line to the bottom of the hull

Drag — the force that acts between a moving object and the fluid medium, slowing the motion of the object.

Drill Ship - a self-propelled floating offshore drilling unit that is a ship constructed to permit a well to be drilled from it. Used in deep, remote waters.

Floating Offshore Drilling Rig — a type of mobile offshore drilling unit that floats and is not secured to the seafloor (except for anchors).

Freeboard — distance from the waterline to the top edge of the hull

Freighter — a cargo carrier.

Fore — toward the front, or bow, part of the boat.

Half-breadth plan — top view of the hull (Usually, only half is drawn because the hull is symmetrical.)

Hydrodynamics — Hydrodynamics is the science of fluid behavior and movement.

Hydrofoils — underwater wings to lift entire hull out of the water for increased speed

Hull — the frame or body of a vessel (boat, ship), without masts, yards, sails, or rigging

Inboard — a boat in which the engine is located inside the hull and drives a propeller mounted under the hull

Jack-up Drilling Rig — a mobile bottom-supported offshore drilling structure whose legs rest on the sea floor.

LOA (Length overall) — the entire length of the boat

LWL (Length waterline) — the length of the waterline of the hull.

Pitch — the falling and rising of the hull in the fore and aft direction.

Planing hull — a hull designed to rise up over the bow wave and move across the surface of the water.

Port — left side.

Profile Plan — side view of the hull.

Propulsion — providing force to move an object in a desired direction.

Prototype — a first full-scale and functional form of a new design.

Roll — the motion of a hull tipping from side to side

Rudder — vertical plate that can angle left or right; used to control yaw.

Semi-submersible Drilling Rig — a floating offshore drilling unit that has pontoons and columns that when flooded cause the unit to submerge in the water to a predetermined depth.

SNAME — The Society of Naval and Marine Engineers

Starboard — right side.

Stem — structural piece that forms the front of the hull

Stern — back of a boat.

Three-view plan – a drawing of a boat's profile, body and breath views.

Thrust — The force that pushes a vehicle forward.

Waterline — a line on the hull to correspond with the surface of the water.

Wetted surface — the surface area of the hull below the waterline.

Wildcat — a well drilled in an area where no oil or gas production exists.

Yaw — The motion of a hull turning to the left or right.

Further Reading

Books on Design

Bohm, Harry and Jensen, Vicki (1997). Build Your Own Underwater Robot: and Other Wet Projects. Vancouver, B.C. Canada: Westcoast Words. Spiral Bound. ISBN: 978-0-9681610-0-5. (A great book that introduces readers to the excitement and the technology of underwater exploration.)

Bohm, Harry and Jensen, Vicki (2001). Build Your Own Programmable LEGO Submersible. Vancouver, B.C. Canada: Westcoast Words. Spiral Bound. (Project: Sea Angel AUV.)

Brewer, Edward S. (1994). Understanding Boat Design. Camden, ME: International Marine. Paperback, Fourth Edition. ISBN: 0070076944. (A classic primer for the boat buyer, builder, or designer. Gives simple answers to basic questions: Round or V-bottom? Full or fin keel? What size engine and propeller?)

Devlin, Samual. (1995). Devlin's Boatbuilding: How to Build Any Boat the Stitch and Glue Way. Camden, ME: International Marine. Paperback, Reprint Edition. ISBN: 00721579907. (The author has designed and built wooden boats for a living for more than 20 years. The book is a complete guide to boatbuilding with sheet plywood, wire stitches, and epoxy glue, and is described as "covering everything from sharpening the tools to launching the finished boat.")

Dear, Ian and Kemp, Peter. (1997). An A-Z of Sailing Terms. New York: Oxford Paperbacks, Oxford University Press. Paperback, Second Edition. ISBN: 019280068X. (many definitions, plus detailed entries on topics such as navigation, hydrodynamics, rudder, mercator projection; excellent reference book.)

Gerr, Dave. (1992). The Nature of Boats: Insights and
 Esoterica for the Nautically Obsessed. Camden, ME:
 International Marine/Ragged Mountain Press, The
 McGraw Hill Companies. Paperback. ISBN: 007024233X.
 (Author is a naval architect who designs yachts and
 commercial craft. He weaves stories of boats, boat building,
 and boat voyages through a highly useful compendium of
 information on the physics, technology, and common sense
 of boatbuilding.)

McLaren, TA and Jensen, Vicki (2000). Ships of Steel: A
 British Columbia Shipbuilder's Story. Vancouver, B.C.
 Canada: Westcoast Words. Spiral Bound. ISBN: 978-
 1550172423. (Chronicles the industry from the early
 development of steel construction facilities, equipment
 and qualified personnel; to the World War II boom when
 BC yards delivered two 10,000-ton freighters every week;
 to the postwar production of tugs, barges, fish boats and
 sophisticated supply vessels; to the present day.)

Monk, Edwin. (1992). How to Build Wooden Boats, with
 16 Small-Boat Designs. New York: Dover Publications,
 Inc. Paperback. ISBN: 048627313X. (for the amateur
 boatbuilder; clear, concise directions and designs, with
 plenty of diagrams.)

Nicolson, Ian. (1999). Boat Data Book, Fourth Edition. Dobbs
 Ferry, NY: Sheridan House. Hardback. ISBN: 1574090445.
 (complete specifications, mostly in graph and table form,
 for all things boat-related: anchors, masts, propellers,
 rigging wire, ropes, and much more; invaluable for boat
 owners and builders.)

Payson, Harold H. (1989). Boat Modeling with Dynamite
 Payson: A Step-by-Step Guide to Building Models of Small
 Craft. Camden, ME: International Marine. Paperback.
 ISBN: 0071573712. (instant approach to building tabletop
 replicas of small rowing and sailing craft, by a real Maine
 boatbuilder.)

Payson, Harold H. (1997). Building New Instant Boats. New York: McGraw-Hill. Paperback. ISBN: 0071559663. (a book on building a ready-for-water boat, containing necessary fundamentals, step-by-step instructions, and several plans, ranging from a six-foot rowboat/sailboat to a fast 25-foot schooner.)

Teale, John. (1998). How to Design a Boat. Dobbs Ferry, NY: Sheridan House. Paperback, Second Edition. ISBN: 157409050X. (Step-by-step instructions from the first sketch to the completed design, including the reasons behind the process and simple, well-explained mathematical calculations.)

Trower, Gordon. (1992). Yacht and Small Craft Design: From Principles to Practice. Wiltshire, U.K.: The Crowood Press, Ltd. Hardback. ISBN: 1852237090. (explains the physics of boat design.)

Trower, Gordon. (1999). Yacht and Small Craft Construction: Design Decisions. Wiltshire, U.K.: The Crowood Press, Ltd. Hardback. ISBN 1861261187. (a companion volume to the previous book, with emphasis on boat construction.)

Books on Cruising

Coote, Jack (Editor). (1992). Total Loss. Dobbs Ferry, NY: Sheridan House. Paperback. ISBN: 092486333. (This book relates true stories of actual emergency situations experienced by sailors, what they did, and what worked and didn't work.)

Gleckler, Walt. (1998). All About Cruising. Seal Beach, CA: Passagemaker Publications. Paperback. ISBN: 0966141636. (covers all aspects of planning an extended cruise, from finding the right boat, to finding provisions and cooking at sea, to dealing with bad weather.)

Hood, Jeremy R. (1997). Safety Preparations for Cruising. Dobbs Ferry, NY: Sheridan House. Hardcover. ISBN: 1574090224. (Excellent reference for "Cruising the World". It covers safety throughout the boat, plus how to prepare for emergencies on the water, such as fire, weather, and man overboard.)

Leonard, Beth A. (1998). The Voyager's Handbook: The Essential Guide to Bluewater Cruising. Camden, ME: International Marine. Hardback. ISBN: 0070381437. (Called "the new bible of long-distance cruising," this book includes detailed information.)

Schult, Joachim, and Jens, Detlev (translator). (1997). Mayday! Yachts in Distress. Dobbs Ferry, NY: Sheridan House. Paperback. ISBN: 1574090399. (It summarizes stories of actual sinkings, fires, shipwrecks, and other disasters befalling yachts.)

Books on Traveling the Seas—Adventure and History

Callahan, Steven. (1996). Adrift: Seventy-Six Days Lost at Sea. New York: Ballantine Books. Paperback. (Callahan's sloop capsized six days out, and he survived 76 days and 1,800 miles of ocean in a small, inflatable life raft.)

Farrington, Tony. (1995). Rescue in the Pacific: A True Story of Disaster and Survival in a Force 12 Storm. New York: McGraw-Hill. Hardcover, Third Edition. ISBN: 0070213674. (This is the true story of a freak storm in the South Pacific that overwhelms a fleet of nine small yachts.)

Jensen, Vickie (1995). Salt Water Women at Work. Vancouver, B.C. Canada: Douglas and McIntyre. Paperback. ISBN: 1-55054-436-5. (A compilation of stories about women that work on boats.)

Johnson, Donald S. and Turner, Philip (Editor). (1995). Charting the Sea of Darkness: The Four Voyages of Henry

Hudson. New York: Kodansha International, 247 pp. Paperback. ISBN: 156838105X. (Johnson uses Henry Hudson's original logs to piece together a picture of Hudson's little-known voyages in the early 1600s.)

Kinder, Gary. (1998). Ship of Gold: in the Deep Blue Sea. New York: Grove Press. Paperback, ISBN: 978-0-8021-4425-6. (The full horror as the mighty Central American, a ship carrying almost 600 people and a wealth of gold, sank in a "perfect hurricane" in 1857 is brilliantly re-created.)

Rediker, Marcus. (1993). Between the Devil and the Deep Blue Sea: Merchant Seamen, Pirates, and the Anglo-American Maritime World, 1700-1750. New York: Cambridge University Press. Paperback, Reissue Edition. ISBN: 0521457203. (This entertaining account of the world of pirates includes descriptions of the dangerous and backbreaking lives of both pirates and "legal" sailors, who lived in equally brutal circumstances.)

Rudeen, Louisa (Preface) and the Editors of Motor Boating & Sailing. (1998). Against the Sea: Great Adventure Stories from the Pages of Motor Boating & Sailing. New York: Avon Books. 258 pp. Paperback. ISBN: 0380798611. (This anthology of 24 exciting true-life adventures on the high seas is drawn from the pages of Motor Boating & Sailing Magazine. It is short, easy reading; good for younger students.)

Testa, Serge. (1988). 500 Days. Naples, FL: Trident Press. Paperback, Second Edition. ISBN: 0731648498. (A travel journal by a sailor who sailed around the world in a 12-foot boat, this book describes many of the ports he visited.)

Boating Magazines

Blue Water Sailing
 Monthly magazine of cruising and offshore sailing.

Boating Magazine
Regular articles on boat buying and financing, powerboat accessories, seamanship, maintenance, sport fishing, racing, and sport cruising.

Boating World
Boating lifestyle magazine for active boaters who enjoy family boating, fishing, cruising, and waterskiing.

Boating Life
Magazine dedicated to recreational boating. Includes information on boating activities & destinations, family boating, fishing, navigation, buying and maintaining boats.

BoatTest.com
Boat reviews and tests on over 750 major powerboats, comparisons, criticisms, features and benefits for new and used boats for sale.

Catamaran Sailor
Magazine covering any and all news concerning beach cats of all brands and breeds.

Go Boating
Features boat tests, the latest boating gear, tips and tricks.

Great Lakes Boating
Recreational interest magazine written specifically for Great Lakes power and sail boaters.

Hot Ribs
Magazine for enthusiasts of rigid hull inflatable boats (RIBs) and inflatables.

Houseboat Magazine
Offers a directory of suppliers, travel guides, classified ads, archived articles and information on houseboat manufacturers.

Lakeland Boating
Travel and boating magazine for the Great Lakes. Boat tests, features on weekend getaways, product roundups, more.

Nautica
> Provides information on yachting and leisure boating in Italy, Europe and Mediterranean with documents, articles, technique, regulations and news.

Pontoon and Deck Boat
> Features topics of concern and interest to the pontoon and deck boating community including how-to articles and maintenance tips.

Powerboat Magazine
> Performance boating magazine offering product reports, classified ads, photos, news, notes and links.

Powerboat Reports
> Independent evaluations of today's boating equipment and gear.

Practical Sailor
> Famed for its rigorous and demanding tests, magazine separates the good gear from the bad. Discover which equipment is best for your boat, your budget and your sailing.

Sail
> Features include articles on boat and equipment design, racing news, piloting, boat handling, navigation and new product news.

Sailing Anarchy
> Ezine about the world of sailboat racing. Includes articles, interviews, editorials, rumors, and message board.

Sailing World
> Magazine featuring the latest performance sailing equipment, tactics, racing, and sailing techniques.

Sportsboat and Rib
> UK power boat magazine with articles, news, tests, features & reviews.

Trailer Boats
: Magazine dedicated to the hard-core boating enthusiast, with articles on trailerable boats, maintenance, repair, tow vehicles, boat trailering, etc.

Waterfront News
: Southeast Florida's nautical newspaper covering the yachting and boating communities.

Yachting and Boating World
: Boating portal presenting Motor Boat and Yachting, Motor Boats Monthly, Practical Boat Owner, Classic Boat, Yachting Monthly and Yachting World magazines.

Yachting World
: Features the latest yacht racing and super-yachting news from events across the world.

Yachts and Yachting
: Provides reports, results, fixtures & photographs from racing sailing.

References

1. Shipbuilding Technology and Education, Committee on National Needs in Maritime Technology, Marine Board, Commission on Engineering and Technical Systems, National Research Council; National Academy Press 1996.

2. Ferreiro, L. D., "A Definition of Naval Architecture", Marine Technology, Vol. 36, No. 4, Fall 1999, pp.xiv-xv.

3. American Society of Naval Engineers (ASNE) web site: http://www.navalengineers.org/

4. Society of Naval and Marine Engineers (SNAME) web site: http://www.sname.org/

5. Marine Log website: http://www.marinelog.com/

6. M. M. Bernitsas, "Engineering for the Marine Environment at a USA Research University," Proceedings of MEET'99, Maritime Engineering: Education and Training, Saint Petersburg, Russia, June 21-24, 1999.

7. National Aeronautics and Space Administration, Global Climate Change website: http://climate.nasa.gov/

8. National Security Assessment of the Maritime Industry, Industry Survey: Building and Repairing of Ships, Boats, and Other Marine Platforms, A Joint Project Between the U.S. Department of Commerce, Bureau of Export Administration and the U. S. Department of the Navy, Naval Surface Warfare Center, Carderock Division. September 1999

9. U.S. Department of Education. National Center for Education Statistics. Chartbook of Degrees Conferred, 1969-70 to 1993-94, NCES 98-071, Thomas D. Snyder, Project Officer. Washington DC: 1997. URL: http://www.nces.ed.gov/pubsearch/pubsinfo.asp?pubid=98071

10. U.S. Department of Education, National Center for Education Statistics, [E.D. Tabs] Degrees and Other Awards Conferred by Degree-granting Institutions: 1995-96, NCES 98-256, by Frank B. Morgan, Washington, DC: 1998. URL: http://www.nces.ed.gov/pubsearch/pubsinfo.

asp?pubid=98256

11. University of Michigan website: http://www.engin.umich. edu/dept/name/overview/overview.htm

12. Office of Strategic Industries and Economic Security, U.S. Department of Commerce, Maritime Summary website: http://www.bis.doc.gov/news/2001/ annualreport/01annualchap4sies.pdf

13. ConocoPhillips website: http://www.conocophillips.com/ EN/about/energy/energy101/Pages/index.aspx

14. U.S. Census Bureau Census Data - http://www.census.gov/ Press-Release/www/emergencies/coast_areas.html

15. Barth, B. 2000. Sea Dwellers: The humor, drama and tragedy of the U.S. Navy SeaLab programs. Doyle Publishing Company, Inc. Houston, TX. 184 pages.

16. Bond, G.F and H.A. Siteri (Editor). 1993. Papa Topside: The Sealab Chronicles of Capt. George F. Bond, U.S. Navy. United States Naval Institute. Book News Incorporated. Portland, OR 270 pages.

17. Heidelberg, K.B. 1999. The effects of water flow and zooplankton prey behavior on scleractinian coral and heterotrophy. University of Maryland (USA). 207 pp.

18. Koblick, I.G. and J.W. Miller. 1995. Living and Working in the Sea. Flagstaff, AZ. Best Publishing Company. 438 pages.

19. Leichter, J.J. and S.L. Miller. 1999. Predicting high frequency upwelling: Spatial and temporal patterns of temperature anomalies on a Florida coral reef. Cont. Shelf Res. 19:911-928.

20. Accreditation Board for Engineering and Technology (ABET) website: http://www.abet.org

Index

Author building a SeaPerch

ABOUT THE AUTHOR

Celeste Baine is a biomedical engineer, the director of the Engineering Education Service Center and the award-winning author of over 20 engineering career and education books and publications. She won the Norm Augustine Award for Engineering Communications which is given to an engineer who has demonstrated the capacity for communicating the excitement and wonder of engineering; the American Society for Engineering Education's Engineering Dean Council's Award for the Promotion of Engineering Education and Careers; and, she is also listed on the National Engineers Week Web site as one of 50 engineers you should meet!

Other Engineering Career Publications by Celeste Baine

Engineers Make a Difference: Motivating Students to Pursue an Engineering Education. $21.95

The Musical Engineer: A Music Enthusiast's Guide to Engineering and Technology Careers. $17.95

The Fantastical Engineer: A Thrillseeker's Guide to Careers in Theme Park Engineering. $17.95

High Tech Hot Shots: Careers in Sports Engineering. $19.95

Is There an Engineer Inside You? A Comprehensive Guide to Career Decisions in Engineering. $29.95

Ideas in Action: A Girl's Guide to Careers in Engineering $7.95

Is There a Civil Engineer Inside You? A Student's Guide to Exploring Careers in Civil Engineering & Civil Engineering Technology. $7.95

Is There a Computer Engineer Inside You? A Student's Guide to Exploring Careers in Computer Engineering & Computer Engineering Technology. $7.95

Is There a Mechanical Engineer Inside You? A Student's Guide to Exploring Careers in Mechanical Engineering & Mechanical Engineering Technology. $7.95

Is There a Chemical Engineer Inside You? A Student's Guide to Exploring Careers in Chemical Engineering. $7.95

Is There a Biomedical Engineer Inside You? A Student's Guide to Exploring Careers in Biomedical Engineering & Biomedical Engineering Technology. $7.95

Is There an Electrical Engineer Inside You? A Student's Guide to Exploring Careers in Electrical Engineering & Electrical Engineering Technology. $7.95

Is There a Manufacturing Engineer Inside You? A Student's Guide to Exploring Careers in Manufacturing Engineering & Manufacturing Engineering Technology. $7.95

To Order:
call toll free 1-877-NGINEER or 1-541-988-1005
Fax orders to 1-541-988-1008
Online orders www.engineeringedu.com

SHARK TANK
SECRETS TO SUCCESS

HOW TO PROPEL YOUR BUSINESS FROM THE TANK TO THE BANK

MICHAEL PARRISH DuDELL

SHARK TANK
SECRETS TO SUCCESS

KINGSWELL

LOS ANGELES · NEW YORK

Copyright © 2016 Sony Pictures Television Inc.

All photography © American Broadcasting Companies, Inc.

All rights reserved. Published by Kingswell, an imprint of Disney Book Group. No part of this book may be reproduced or transmitted in any form or by any means, electronic or mechanical, including photocopying, recording, or by any information storage and retrieval system, without written permission from the publisher. For information address Kingswell, 1101 Flower Street, Glendale, California 91201.

Editorial Director: Wendy Lefkon
Executive Editor: Laura Hopper
Cover designed by Shannon Koss

Printed in the United States of America

First Edition, May 2016

10 9 8 7 6 5 4 3 2 1

FAC-026988-16078

Library of Congress Cataloging-in-Publication Data on file

ISBN 978-1-4847-2325-8

CONTENTS

This book is dedicated to those who embrace the hard things—the difficult choices, the uncharted paths, the relentless quests. To those who bravely abandon comfort in pursuit of meaning. Keep going. You're closer than you think.

INTRODUCTION

t's 4:45 A.M. and a twenty-something CEO in New York City is wearily climbing out of bed. The sun has yet to peek over the horizon, but his day has already begun. Two thousand miles and three time zones away, a mother of two is putting the finishing touches on a pitch deck she's been obsessing over for months. Her family is fast asleep as she vigilantly toils away. Neither founder has ever met, nor do they have much in common, yet in many ways they share a parallel reality, underscored by an insatiable ambition that few will ever understand. A light goes on. A light goes off. This day is no exception; it is the rule.

Success is a complicated thing. What appears idyllic to one person could very well be viewed as unappealing by another. Like beauty, its meaning lies in the eye of the beholder and must first be defined before it can ever be fully realized. What does real, measurable accomplishment look like? What are the various steps required to claim it? How do you turn ambiguous ambition into tangible results? The answers to these simple yet powerful questions make up the bedrock of

an entrepreneur's experience and serve as the starting point for this book.

Each week, millions of Americans tune in to *Shark Tank* and watch as bold and savvy entrepreneurs face off against some of the world's most celebrated investors. Whether pragmatic executive or quirky inventor, each founder enters the tank in hopes of raising the capital required to turn his or her budding enterprise into a booming empire. Seven seasons and hundreds of episodes later, many have gone on to do just that—some of whom you'll meet in these very pages.

In *Shark Tank Jump Start Your Business*, the first *Shark Tank* book, readers get an inside glimpse of what it takes to start, run, and grow a prosperous organization. Each chapter contains valuable insights from the Sharks and select entrepreneurial alumni on steps from assessing an idea to launching and even selling a business. Combining tactical advice with actionable tips, it serves as a comprehensive resource for anyone looking to turn his or her concept into a company. And the response has been outstanding.

Shark Tank Secrets to Success picks up where its predecessor leaves off by sharing the real-life stories behind a selection of the show's most successful ventures. Featuring nine different companies from memorable episodes, this book will give you an up-close-and-personal look into each entrepreneur's rise to the top, complete with firsthand accounts of some of the most meaningful triumphs and gut-wrenching failures.

You'll discover how the husband-and-wife cofounders of Grace and Lace turned overwhelming despair into boundless opportunity, what it took for TITIN CEO Patrick Whaley to close $2.5 million in sales in just six weeks, and why the mother-and-daughter team behind Wicked Good Cupcakes

will always have a special place in their hearts for the Transportation Security Administration (TSA).

Each chapter fuses inspiring anecdotes with actionable advice and concludes with a personalized "Playbook for Success"—a detailed breakdown of the respective company's most impactful principles and time-honored practices. And, back by popular demand, scattered throughout the book are "Shark Bites"—tidbits of professional wisdom from the Sharks themselves.

More than just concepts and theories, *Shark Tank Secrets to Success* provides an in-depth look at what it means to be an entrepreneur and details the incredible journeys of a handful of founders who took their ideas from the tank to the bank.

CHAPTER ONE

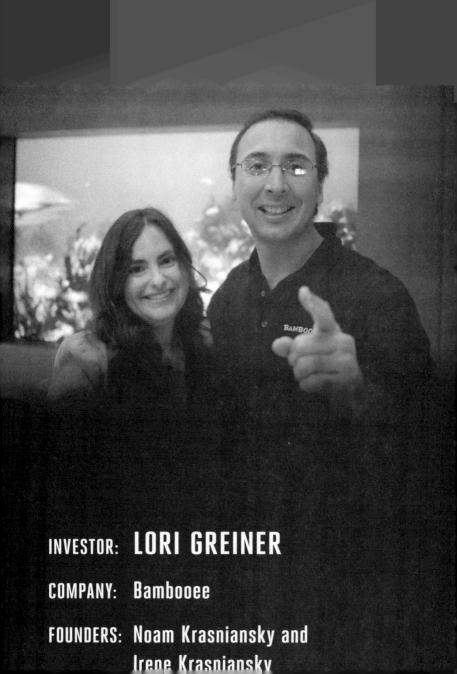

INVESTOR: **LORI GREINER**

COMPANY: **Bambooee**

FOUNDERS: **Noam Krasniansky and Irene Krasniansky**

A CLEAN VICTORY

S tarting a business is like scaling a cliff—a slow and steady ascent to a destination unknown. As the wanderer proceeds up the vertical slope, each step presents yet another uncertainty, supporting or impeding the ultimate goal. At times, this expedition can feel liberating, like a great unshackling from the outside world. As with any steep climb, however, there are also moments of fatigue—when the indignity of surrender feels easier than the strain of pushing onward. It's in these moments when having a cofounder can make the difference between total victory and absolute defeat.

The cofounders of Bambooee are more than just business partners, of course; they're husband and wife. The couple appeared on season five of *Shark Tank* and walked away with a $200,000 investment from Lori Greiner for their line of reusable paper towels made from 100 percent organic and sustainable bamboo.

While their experience in the tank was undoubtedly thrilling, the real adventure lay in what came before, co-creating what is today a wildly successful company and life.

THE BIRTH OF A SALESMAN

Noam Krasniansky stood perched on the edge of the noisy street corner with a handful of freshly gutted orange peels.

Through the chaos of whooshing cars and busy passersby, he climbed atop the rickety old milk carton and began his pitch. It was time to get to work.

It didn't matter that Noam was only five years old or that he had yet to begin elementary school; the young business-man had already developed one of the fundamental skills required of any entrepreneur: the ability to sell. And boy, could he ever.

Earlier that day, a neighborhood friend had gifted him a small bag of oranges. Unlike other children, who may have hastily eaten the fruit, Noam decided to erect a roadside juice stand. He rushed home and asked his nanny for a knife, jar, and as many cups as she could find. The young boy couldn't explain this sudden urge—it surely wasn't out of necessity. All he knew was that it had to be done.

Within minutes of opening for business, Noam's inven-tory had disappeared and his pockets were full of *colones*— the local currency of Costa Rica, his childhood home. It was his first taste of success and one he would not soon forget.

As the years progressed, Noam continued cultivating his entrepreneurial tendencies. While some cultures may have celebrated such relentless ambition, in Costa Rica it was per-ceived as peculiar and at times even uncouth. Noam's family was well-off, and it was uncommon for somebody of means to solicit in such flagrant ways. But he remained unaffected and continued honing his skills throughout adolescence.

"In America it's common for a kid to get a summer job," says Noam. "But South America is very classist. People look down on that if your family is of a high social or economic class."

During his teenage years, Noam was sent to a boarding school in England. Although he didn't much care for the

courses, he was grateful to be in an environment where he could pursue his professional goals without disdain or judgment. It wasn't until he left the hallowed halls of the institution's dormitory, however, and moved into a small flat on the other side of town that his fate began to come into focus.

Noam's roommate was a foul-mouthed young sailor who had recently taken a sabbatical from his post at sea to sell Didi Seven—a once-popular cleaning solution. Each morning the London native would wake up early, head to the town square, and spend the afternoon pitching his product to curious housewives and amused tourists. On a good day, he would return home with as much as £3,400—the equivalent of $5,300.

"He had money everywhere," says Noam. "Instead of washing his socks, he would just buy a new pair. The guy was nuts."

Noam was awestruck by what he saw and pleaded with his roommate to show him the ropes. The following day, almost fifteen years after selling that very first cup of orange juice, Noam found himself back on a bustling street, hooting and hollering atop a flimsy milk crate.

"I sold four bottles right away," says Noam. "I was hooked to pitching from that day onwards."

After high school, Noam set out on the road, selling Didi Seven and other cleaning products in small towns across Europe. Eventually, however, he grew tired of the cold and dreary winters native to the continent. So in early 1994, after a particularly long and frigid season, the traveling salesman packed his bags and headed west to Los Angeles, where he planned to "spend the next six years wearing shorts."

With a new California address and a refreshed outlook on life, Noam decided it was time to stop selling other people's

products and finally create one of his own—a world-class carpet cleaner that could rival the competition. He asked his godfather for a small loan and began crafting the concoction.

"I moved into an apartment in Hollywood that was full of cockroaches," says Noam. "It didn't even have a bed. I would make the product in the kitchen sink and sleep underneath my desk."

It was around that time that Noam first met Irene—a bright-eyed nineteen-year-old designer who had recently returned from studying abroad in Italy. Like Noam, she had also demonstrated an entrepreneurial streak from an early age and had even started her own venture in high school. Irene still recalls one of their first encounters.

"He was trying to hit on my friend with a business card," says Irene. "I saw that the name of his company was 'Useful Products USA' and said he should hire me to design products."

Noam was taken by her confidence and moxie—a fondness Irene reciprocated. It didn't hurt, of course, that he'd just emigrated from Europe and, like her, was of the Jewish faith.

"I liked what I had experienced in Italy and knew I wanted to be with a foreign guy," says Irene. "But I also knew my parents wanted me to marry someone Jewish. Noam was a perfect combination."

The connection was palpable, and the two immediately started going out. Noam couldn't resist expressing his affection, and on only their second date, he made a bold confession.

"I told her I wanted to marry her," says Noam. "We had only known each other for a week, but I was positive she was the woman for me."

Although it would be almost three years before the couple

walked down the aisle, Noam and Irene moved in together just a few months later. There would be no more sleeping under desks.

The relationship moved fast, and so did Noam's business. This newfound love inspired him to push harder and put everything he had into building the company. The stakes were higher; he was now creating something for two people.

Meanwhile, Irene attended the Art Center in Pasadena and spent weekends tagging along to flea markets, trade shows, and other venues where he might be pitching. After graduation she began working for Noam's organization, which at that point had become a formidable operation.

As the venture grew, however, so did tensions between Noam and his business partner. Deep down, the young entrepreneur knew the relationship had deteriorated, but the rapid expansion made it difficult to sever ties.

Noam wasn't the only one beginning to resent the arrangement. Irene had taken a job in the accounts department—a far cry from her passion for design. She felt uninspired in her role and hungry for something more.

"I was really upset because I felt like I hadn't gotten anywhere," says Irene. "You reach a point in your life where you want to achieve certain goals. I hadn't done that yet."

After the terrorist attacks that occurred on September 11, 2001, many small companies went out of business. Like many of his competitors, Noam's margins had evaporated overnight, and the enterprise was hemorrhaging money. With no salvation in sight, he was forced to close up shop.

"When you've never had any real failures, you can get very cocky," says Noam. "All of a sudden the business went kaput. I was in a state of shock."

*It is not possible to overemphasize how incredibly impor-
tant your pitch will be to the success of your product. In
many cases, it will make or break your invention.*[1]
 —Lori

OUT WITH THE OLD, IN WITH THE NEW

Noam was devastated over the demise of the company but
grateful to be out of the toxic relationship with his cofounder.
Although neither husband nor wife knew what lay ahead,
they were committed to rebuilding something meaningful.
And this time they would do it as a couple.

When a venture goes under, it's not only the employees
and shareholders who suffer. Suppliers, landlords, and other
vendors also feel the effects in the form of broken contracts
and outstanding invoices. While it's common in such circum-
stances for an organization to declare bankruptcy, Noam
and Irene were dedicated to settling their debts.

"We were committed to paying everyone back," says
Irene. "We had been working with those suppliers for years.
We knew their families."

To secure the necessary funds, the husband-and-wife team
gathered all that remained of their carpet-cleaning product
and formed a new enterprise. Together, they hit the road, sell-
ing at fairs, festivals, and trade shows across America. Once
again, Noam's salesmanship proved invaluable.

It took over two years to repay their debts, during which
time Noam and Irene built key relationships with VIPs at
some of the country's most profitable consumer shows. What

was supposed to be a short-term method of raising money accidentally became the start of a whole new chapter.

"As you gain more experience, you get better positions at the shows," says Noam. "With the right spot at the right show, it's possible to sell $120,000 of product in twenty days."

Free of debt and quickly gaining momentum, Noam and Irene began producing additional products, until soon they had amassed a small arsenal of inventory. Meanwhile, they expanded their outreach to include industry trade shows—events attended by buyers looking to acquire new products for their retail stores.

Still the couple faced a steep learning curve. Neither founder knew anything about the retail industry or how to secure corporate accounts. In fact, most of their products didn't even come with standard packaging. While the industry trade shows proved profitable, the husband-and-wife team recognized they could be selling more. They just didn't know how.

Then, during one of the busiest shows, a curious onlooker approached their booth with a snarl. The man, a trade show veteran, had watched as buyer after buyer admired their product but walked away empty-handed. He offered them an unsolicited piece of advice that would revolutionize their entire business.

"You guys are idiots," he said. "Why are you selling like you're at a swap meet? Go get some packaging and these retailers will start to buy from you."

Noam and Irene were skeptical at first but decided to test the feedback by concluding each pitch with an offer to provide custom packaging to any retailer who made a bulk purchase. This, the couple figured, would allow them to assess demand before making such a sizable investment.

The new approach worked and soon earned them the attention of a high-power buyer who was enthralled with their best-selling product—an innovative household cleaning cloth. There was just one catch: the retailer he represented needed a supplier who could provide a massive quantity of units. Ever the consummate salesman, Noam insisted that he and his wife could meet the challenge.

When the buyer followed up later that week, however, Noam's confidence began to fade. The retailer needed specific information about logistics such as case size and shipping quantities. Unsure how to reply, Irene and Noam both froze.

"We didn't e-mail back," says Irene. "The buyer eventually said that if we didn't turn in the paperwork, he wouldn't be able to work with us for another six months."

Realizing they risked losing what could potentially be their biggest sale to date, Noam and Irene filled out the forms with "imaginary, guesstimated numbers" and got to work creating homemade packaging for the small test sample the store had requested. Within days, the samples sold out, and the couple received word that an official purchase order (P.O.) was on its way. Neither husband nor wife had any idea what to expect.

"I remember coming into the office on Friday morning, seeing the P.O. in the fax machine, and just sort of staring at it," says Noam. "It was for a quarter of a million dollars."

Noam and Irene had never closed a deal that large and knew they faced a major problem. Fulfilling the order would require significant capital—capital the business did not have. With limited options, they approached Irene's mother for a loan. Fortunately, she was willing and able to lend a hand.

The couple returned to the office on Monday morning

feeling calm and composed. They had dodged a near-fatal bullet and were proud of the cleverness and dexterity they had so keenly demonstrated.

"When we walked into the office, Noam noticed the fax machine was out of paper," says Irene. "So he filled it up, and right away three more purchase orders started printing out, each bigger than the next."

When the last page had finally emerged, the order totaled over five million units—an unfathomably massive number.

"We began jumping up and down," says Noam. "I was just laughing hysterically. It was like winning the lottery."

But it didn't take long for the merriment to give way to reality. Once again, they faced the daunting task of financing a massive order.

After researching various funding options, Noam and Irene chose to bankroll the order by factoring—a type of debt financing where an enterprise sells its accounts receivable to a third-party company at a reduced price. They figured it was the only way they stood any reasonable chance of meeting the fast-approaching deadline.

As the organization grew, the husband-and-wife team focused their attention on obtaining more retail accounts and designing new products. Within only a few years, they had a comprehensive catalog of cutting-edge inventions and were earning substantial profits. But the end goal had never been exclusively to make money; they yearned to do something that made a positive impact in the world.

"We didn't want to wait to become philanthropists until we were old," says Noam. "We wanted to make a difference when we were young and still working."

After reading an article in 2009 about the destruction of the Brazilian rain forests, Noam and Irene decided to use

their extensive industry knowledge to create a product that could serve as an alternative to traditional paper towels, which in the United States contribute nearly three thousand tons of waste each day.

"We wanted to make something on a roll that could actually fit on a dispenser," says Irene. "That way it would be easy for people to make a conscious choice."

To ensure they manufactured the highest-quality product, the couple spent nearly two years developing the idea. With practices such as sourcing 100 percent of the material from sustainable bamboo and planting a tree for every roll sold, they modeled Bambooee after their own set of personal values. It was more than just a clever product idea; it was a passion project.

As retailers began to carry their bamboo towels, Noam got to work pitching. On weekends, he would bring his daughter, Bella, to various stores around town and together they would demo Bambooee for local shoppers. As usual, the professional salesman received a flood of customer feedback, but there was one response he hadn't anticipated.

"People started saying we should be on *Shark Tank*," says Noam. "I had no idea what they were talking about."

The family didn't own a TV and had never seen an episode of the hit ABC show. But the recommendations kept pouring in, until finally they decided to find out what everyone was raving about.

"In business you have to see the opportunities," says Noam. "And you see the opportunities by observing what is already successful."

After just one episode, Noam and Irene were hooked. There was no doubt about it: they knew they had to be part of the show.

> When you're an entrepreneur, you just can't let anything or anyone get in your way, no matter how dire the situation. You can almost always find a solution if you try hard enough.[2]
> —Lori

HOLD YOUR MONEY, HOLD YOUR MONEY

While attending their next trade show, Irene spotted a neighboring booth with a large sign that read AS SEEN ON SHARK TANK. She wasn't sure if it was coincidence or fate but figured it was a perfect opportunity to get the inside scoop.

"I really only had two questions," says Irene. "Did the founder like her experience and would she recommend it to other business owners?"

The *Shark Tank* alum spoke highly of the show and suggested that the couple attend an open casting call. That was all it took to convince the husband-and-wife team to proceed.

The live auditions had already passed, however, which meant their only option was to submit an online application. Three entries and one very animated video later, they received a call from the production team and were eventually given a time slot to tape.

Noam had spent his entire life as a salesman but knew pitching on *Shark Tank* would be a completely different experience. So he and Irene practiced for weeks, drilling their presentation and carefully studying previous episodes.

"We watched every single show from the beginning," says Noam. "And by doing that we were able to figure out which questions were the common denominators."

When the big day finally arrived, the pair was confident in their pitch and preparation. While they were eager to make a deal with any of the Sharks, their first choice was Lori Greiner—a QVC veteran with an outstanding track record of turning inventive consumer products into overnight successes.

The couple asked for $200,000 for 10 percent of the business, which may have seemed high considering Bambooee had sold only $122,000 worth of towels during the previous year. But Noam and Irene were giving away more than just the one product; they were offering 10 percent of their entire company, which had annual sales of $1.6 million.

The pitch started out strong, and Noam's charisma electrified the room. But it didn't take long for Kevin O'Leary to chime in with some very serious apprehensions. The feeding frenzy had begun!

Since bamboo cloth isn't proprietary, Kevin felt the product could be easily replicable. What would stop a competitor from coming in and dominating the market?

Irene quickly addressed his concern, explaining that they had developed a "proprietary manufacturing process" and had even applied for a design patent. But Kevin continued to push back.

Each roll of Bambooee contains twenty-two sheets that can be laundered and reused numerous times. Although one roll of the bamboo-based product can replace up to 286 rolls of its paper counterpart, the per-unit price is significantly higher. Kevin wondered whether consumers would pay a premium for such a product. And if so, was the value proposition strong enough to convince the average American to wash their paper towels instead of throwing them away?

"You've made an assumption that people are going to

treat this as a replacement for paper towels," said Kevin. "I don't buy it."

But Robert Herjavec disagreed, explaining that in Europe many people already use reusable paper towels. He didn't see why the same practice couldn't be adopted in the United States.

Although Kevin remained skeptical, he *was* impressed by Noam's salesmanship and complimented the entrepreneur on being "a kindred spirit." And for that reason he decided to make the founders an offer: he would loan them $200,000 with an 8 percent interest rate but would also require the full 10 percentage points of equity.

"I didn't understand the deal when he said it," says Noam. "When you're in the tank, everyone is talking to you at the same time. I was just trying to keep my cool."

But Irene understood the deal perfectly and knew it was a poor one. With all the Sharks still in, she thanked Kevin for the bid and waited patiently to hear what others had to say.

"I think it's a great demonstrable product," said Lori. "I think you two are heroes, and I think the product is a hero."

Lori was both impressed by the invention and inspired by their mission, so she offered them precisely what they had asked for: $200,000 for 10 percent of the business.

Thrilled by Lori's generous bid, Irene began to accept the offer. But before she could finish, Noam cut her off.

"I know that the rest of you have not had the opportunity to give an offer," said Noam. "Would you like to pitch in?"

It's rare that an entrepreneur leaves the tank with exactly what he or she has requested, so naturally the Sharks were taken aback. Many at-home viewers were also surprised by this unorthodox move, taking to social media to call it rude and arrogant. But a closer examination of Noam's story

reveals that the unusual reaction was not an act of greed but of habit.

When Noam was first learning to pitch, during those early years in London, his roommate shared one critical piece of advice that he never forgot.

"Don't ever let someone pay you before you finish your pitch or you'll lose everyone else," he said. "Instead, shout 'hold your money, hold your money.' This will make the rest of the crowd want your product even more."

Without consciously realizing it, Noam had just told Lori to hold her money and risked jeopardizing the entire deal. Lucky for him, Irene was not going to let that happen.

"We decided in advance that we only wanted to give away ten percent of the company and that we wanted to work with Lori," says Irene. "So when she made the offer, the answer was yes."

Before Noam could say another word, Irene interjected and accepted Lori's offer. She had saved the deal and proved yet again the value of their extraordinary partnership.

TRADE SHOW STOPPERS

Bambooee's episode aired on Friday, February 28, 2014—more than five months after it taped. For the easily excitable Noam, this waiting period proved to be an exercise in patience.

"We were not allowed to talk about it with anybody," says Noam. "That was the hardest part of all. We literally couldn't say anything."

Companies that appear on *Shark Tank* are generally notified two weeks before their episode airs, during which time they're advised to make any last-minute accommodations. Most important, Lori suggested, was that the husband-and-wife team take the necessary steps to ensure their website would not crash. Otherwise, they'd risk losing potential sales.

On the night their episode aired, the couple loaded their kids in the car and headed to Noam's brother's house to watch the big premier. Although confident in their performance, they were anxious to see how they would come across on TV.

"You don't know how your episode will be edited," says Noam. "One of my biggest fears was that I would look like a schmuck."

The segment went off without a hitch, and just minutes later the orders came pouring in.

"People started calling us immediately," says Irene. "We were actually answering customer service calls that night."

Within only a couple of days, Bambooee had sold over $150,000 in product—more than they had during the entire previous year.

When Noam and Irene attended a popular consumer show the following week, they were mobbed by fans. They had been prepared for what they hoped might be a sudden boost in sales but not for such a surge in popularity.

"We had CEOs of huge companies coming up to us with business cards," says Noam. "People were taking pictures and asking for our autograph. Now I know how celebrities feel."

Thanks to Lori's help, Bambooee was able to get on QVC and has since made over half a dozen appearances. But it's more than just promotional help that the savvy Shark has

been able to provide. The cofounders rely on Lori's finely tuned business acumen when making important strategic and executional moves.

"She's always available to us, which is incredible," says Irene. "We can text her at 8 P.M., and she'll text us right back."

Today, Bambooee's line has expanded to include a variety of new innovations, including a bamboo-based pillow that's already setting record-breaking sales. But the couple is not stopping there. They have big plans to continue growing the company and creating new products that both delight customers and help make the world a better place.

> **SHARK BITE**
>
> Once you create a product that succeeds, the possibilities are endless. As time goes on, you can learn more about your market and consumer demand, you can enhance your technology, and you can use that knowledge to make improvements and to fuel an endless stream of creation and innovation.[4]
> —Lori

THE BAMBOOEE PLAYBOOK FOR SUCCESS

Noam and Irene believe that the only way to attain success is to recognize it from the outset. That means it's crucial to appreciate each individual triumph, from daily accomplishments to larger, more impactful victories.

"It's very important that you sit down and acknowledge what you've achieved, because nobody is going to do that for you," says Noam. "We entrepreneurs are a very small group of people and not everybody understands what it's like."

While celebrating a milestone is important, Noam and Irene are careful never to get too comfortable or content in their accomplishments. For a founder to remain successful, he or she must always possess a modicum of hunger.

"When you're an entrepreneur it's like you're right on the crest of the wave," says Noam. "And as long as you catch all the waves, you can jump from crest to crest and never end up on the beach."

Noam and Irene have ridden out the best of them, from minor whitecaps to mile-high tidal waves, and emerged with their very own Playbook for Success.

PRACTICE UNWAVERING PERSISTENCE

The path to success is winding and littered with an array of complicated challenges that test the very core of an entrepreneur's spirit. While each experience is unique, there are certain inevitable roadblocks that every small-business owner will face—rejection being one of the most common.

Throughout their nearly two decades as cofounders, Noam and Irene have experienced countless rejections in various arenas, from peddling at flea markets to negotiating multimillion-dollar corporate accounts. But no matter how large the setback or crushing the blow, they always persist.

"Sure, it can be upsetting when somebody says no," says Irene. "But to us, 'no' always translates to 'maybe.'"

An example of this is when a large retail chain announced it would stop carrying the Bambooee line, despite a previous agreement to stock the item through the end of the year. A new buyer had joined the company and delivered the news via e-mail, refusing to discuss the matter in person. Worse still, the buyer wouldn't provide a reason for the decision, which the cofounders were told would go into effect immediately.

While many might have quietly accepted that outcome, Noam and Irene pushed back. They had already purchased the inventory required to fulfill the order and, at the very least, insisted the new buyer meet with them face to face to explain the decision.

"We sent this person an e-mail or two every day for a week and a half," says Irene. "And all of the e-mails were quite lengthy."

Eventually, the buyer replied with a short response, claiming that the product's low sales were to blame for the ruling.

In that moment, the couple knew they had leverage. Working swiftly, they e-mailed back a detailed spreadsheet of all past and current sales, which were five times higher than the minimum required by the organization to remain compliant. Furthermore, they added, the retailer was not treating them in

a way that aligned with the company's core values, which were proudly plastered on the walls of each of their stores.

Shortly thereafter, both husband and wife were granted an in-person meeting and convinced the large chain to continue stocking their product. Crisis averted.

"Most people have been told no all of their life and reach a point where there's only so much they're willing to risk," says Noam. "But if you want to be successful you have to learn to overcome rejection."

Fail Fast, Recover Faster

Although Noam and Irene have used sheer grit and determination to overcome many calamitous situations, even tenacity has its limits. Every entrepreneur will experience a situation in which failure is imminent, and only then will his or her true determination be tested.

"There will be times where you're going to get down," says Noam. "But when you hit a bump, you can't allow it to last longer than a day."

This sentiment is echoed by many of the Sharks, including Barbara Corcoran, who believes that learning to recover quickly is an essential component to one's overall ability to succeed.

"You can't lick your wounds if you want to be an entrepreneur," says Barbara. "You have to be able to continuously jump back up and say, 'Hit me again! Hit me again!'"

There's a reason why the Krasnianskys don't own a television. Noam is a self-professed TV addict and will happily stay up until 4 A.M. binge-watching "just about anything." Knowing this about himself, he avoids the medium at all costs, except under one condition: when he's recovering from a disappointment.

In moments of turmoil, Noam allows himself to partake in as much television as he'd like . . . for twenty-four hours. After that, he picks himself up, bandages his wounds, and begins searching for creative solutions.

"Failure is the most important moment for an entrepreneur," says Noam. "Because that's when you really start working. That's where you find the solutions that can take your business to the next level."

Beware of Analysis Paralysis

A founder will make thousands of complicated decisions throughout the life cycle of his or her company—some carrying more weight than others. And as Noam and Irene have learned, the line between careful consideration and self-defeating contemplation is thinner than most realize.

"The most important thing an entrepreneur can do is to take action," says Noam. "You can't overthink a problem so much that you do nothing. A lot of people get stuck there."

Like all good partners, Noam and Irene each bring their own set of unique skills to the organization. Combined, these talents help ensure a well-rounded approach to challenges big and small. Such is the case when it comes to this principle.

While Noam has a tendency to overthink situations, Irene is naturally action-oriented and vigilant about ensuring they never get too bogged down by deliberation.

"She's such an amazing person, because she can take a task, create a plan of action, and complete it," says Noam.

If their own experience has taught them anything, it's that analysis paralysis is often spawned by a past failure or fear of the unknown. Take, for instance, their interaction with the meddling stranger who suggested packaging their product for retail buyers.

Neither knew anything about selling to corporate clients. Surely, it would have been easy for them to overthink the situation or get caught up in their own lack of knowledge. But instead of letting fear stand in their way, they chose to take action and landed a $1.5 million account.

"When you run a small business, you have to be the CEO and the factory worker at the same time," says Noam. "That

means you need to have vision while doing the work required to make things happen."

Let Creative Solutions Trump Financial Resolutions

Although Noam came from a wealthy family, he had very little money when first starting out, especially after the failure of his initial company. But it was during those lean years that Noam first learned what has become one of his most valuable guiding principles: a million-dollar idea doesn't always come with a price tag equivalent in size.

"When you have resources you try to solve problems by throwing money at them," says Noam. "When you don't, you come up with creative solutions that often cost nothing."

Although today Bambooee is tremendously successful, the couple still spends money as though it's sparse. By doing this, they found they're able to grow the enterprise in more nimble and imaginative ways.

Most recently, they asked some of their employees to shoot and edit a series of funny videos for the website. After speccing out the project, the team came back with a whopping $10,000 price tag. Noam knew it could be done for less—way less.

"I gave them $1,000 and told them to figure it out," says Noam. "Well, not only did they figure it out, they kept it under budget."

Approach the Masses

Each month, about 543,000 small businesses are started in America,[5] adding to the nearly 28 million that already exist. But the sobering reality is that more than half of those companies will close within the first five years.

While there are many reasons an organization ceases to succeed, Noam believes much of this failure can be attributed to one primary issue: obscurity.

"Most entrepreneurs don't get their product in front of enough customers," says Noam. "You need to find a place that

allows you to present to thousands and thousands of people."

The founder recently rediscovered this principle when his ten-year-old daughter, Bella, expressed interest in starting her own business. She had heard tales of her father's orange juice operation and wanted to try her luck at a lemonade stand. Noam was thrilled by his daughter's enthusiasm and spent the week helping her develop a plan.

He explained to the young child that since the "company" had yet to bring in revenue, she would have to pay close attention to her start-up costs. Fortunately, her main ingredient is native to California and readily available. In fact, many of their neighbors have lemon trees in their front yards. So together, Noam and his daughter went door-to-door asking for any fruit that could be spared.

Instead of buying ice, yet another expense, Bella spent the next week making ice and storing it in large freezer bags. She also managed to convince her mom to donate some leftover paper cups and a spare bag of organic sugar. Start-up costs: zero.

When Sunday morning finally arrived, Noam and Bella awoke early and set up shop on a nearby street. But to their amazement, they found not a single paying customer. So they packed up the car and tried another location. Once again, their prospects were less than impressive.

"When you're not getting any sales you start to put yourself down," says Noam. "But most of the time it's not about you. It's that you're not getting in front of enough people."

Finally, on the third try, they found a street with traffic snaking around the block. It was just what they had been looking for: hundreds of potential customers with nothing but time (and hopefully a spare dollar or two) on their hands. By their third Sunday on the busy street corner, Bella was averaging sales of $200 per day.

"The most important part was that she figured out how to present her product to a large group of the right people," says Noam. "It wasn't just one person at a time."

CHAPTER TWO

INVESTOR: **ROBERT HERJAVEC**

COMPANY: Tipsy Elves

FOUNDERS: Evan Mendelsohn and Nick Morton

THE VERY MERRY APPAREL COMPANY

Since the dawn of the industrial revolution, the suburban garage has served as an important symbol of American entrepreneurship. From Walt Disney to Steve Jobs, some of the world's most celebrated founders, makers, and creators began their journeys in drafty, homemade workshops just a few small steps away from the kitchen table.

It should come as no surprise, then, that this fabled room played an integral role in the formation of Tipsy Elves—a whimsically festive apparel company started by Evan Mendelsohn and Nick Morton.

But unlike the early days of Hewlett Packard or Mattel, the garage in this story serves not as a physical laboratory but as the backdrop for a conversation that would lead to a multimillion-dollar apparel venture.

Years before the two aspiring cofounders appeared on *Shark Tank* and made a deal with famed investor Robert Herjavec, Nick Morton sat parked in his garage, transfixed as his former fraternity brother pitched an idea that would forever change the course of both their lives: ugly Christmas sweaters.

AN UNLIKELY ENTREPRENEUR

Evan Mendelsohn never planned on being an entrepreneur. The youngest son of two medical professionals, the California

native grew up in a highly educated family and knew from an early age that he was destined to pursue an academic career.

"There was always some inherent thought that I would go to graduate school for something," says Evan. "That was the expectation."

But deep down, the budding founder was wary of a traditional 9–5 job and wanted nothing more than to experience the freedom that comes with running his own business.

"To me, the idea of building something, being independent, was what everyone wanted," says Evan. "If I could do that, I knew I'd be one of the lucky ones."

At only eighteen years old, however, the Tipsy Elves cofounder had no actual concept of what it would take to start and grow an organization and was keenly aware of his academic obligations. So, after graduating from high school, Evan enrolled at the University of California with the goal of eventually attending law school and becoming a lawyer. Sure, it wasn't his dream job, but he believed it was the best way to achieve financial independence. And at that point in his life, wealth was his single greatest measure of success.

During Evan's second year of graduate school, he became friends with an enterprising classmate who had already launched a few small yet profitable Internet businesses. Fascinated by the e-commerce model, Evan began daydreaming about building his own online company and even experimented with starting a small textbook lending venture, which at the time was a relatively new concept.

After graduating from law school with a minor in business and passing the bar exam, Evan embarked on a month-long voyage to China. With a flight time of nearly thirteen hours, he brought with him an array of reading material,

including one particularly compelling book on search engine marketing (SEO).

"Basically it explained how SEO works and gave some pretty simple ways to rank for key terms on Google," says Evan. "It's funny looking back, because none of the information in that book would be relevant today."

As he learned the basics of SEO and discovered how to use keyword research to assess consumer demand, Evan began to see opportunity everywhere. By the time he returned home to San Diego just a few weeks later, he had already concocted a plan to build his first online project.

Using lessons from the book, the newly minted lawyer spotted an interesting trend. Each day, thousands of people were browsing the Internet for dates of upcoming holidays. Evan concluded that if he could purchase just a few of the keywords associated with the popular search terms, he could capture enough traffic to earn significant advertising revenue. So, just weeks before starting his first full-time job at a law firm, Evan launched a side project called Day Finder.

Day Finder began to generate traffic almost immediately, and with it a steady flow of passive income. The first-time entrepreneur was ecstatic. Not only was he utilizing his new-found SEO knowledge, he had achieved his goal of creating a profitable online venture.

The site continued to perform well, but it wasn't bringing in enough money for Evan to walk away from his $170,000-a-year corporate law career, which he was quickly growing to resent.

"I remember expressly thinking that if I could find a way to just make $70,000 for three years I could quit my job," says Evan. "I would have even been okay with earning that

much for the rest of my life, if it meant I could do something I enjoyed."

As the months ticked by, however, Evan became less confident that Day Finder would ever bring in enough revenue to make it a sustainable enterprise, so he dove back into keyword research in hopes of finding another profitable idea. It didn't take long to uncover a potentially lucrative, if not highly unusual opportunity: ugly Christmas sweaters.

Each year countless people attend holiday gatherings themed around tacky Christmas fashion: Evan and Nick had even gone to a few of these parties themselves as college students. But where does one go if one lacks the necessary attire required for such a festive dress code? The Internet, of course. And as he soon learned, this overly zealous audience was highly underserved.

Evan saw an opportunity to own the ugly Christmas sweater market. But was the idea big enough to be a business? Could this really be his ticket out of a passionless career? He wasn't sure, but he knew he needed to find out. And this time he didn't want to do it alone.

Meanwhile, some 500 miles away in San Francisco, Nick Morton hovered over the gaping mouth of an anesthetized patient, toiling away at a mischievous tooth. An up-and-coming dentist with an emergent practice, Nick had chosen the field in college as a way to combine medicine with his lifelong entrepreneurial aspirations.

"Most of my family thought I should have a professional, stable job," says Nick. "But I always wanted to work for myself."

Dentistry seemed to be the perfect combination. He could satisfy his family's expectations while at the same time

running his own firm. There was just one minor issue: he wasn't particularly interested in the trade.

"I don't think I was ever passionate about dentistry," says Nick. "Everyone around me thought I should go into medicine, so I found something in the field that worked."

Then in the spring of 2011, less than a year after launching his practice, he received a phone call that would change the trajectory of his entire life. Evan Mendelsohn, an old friend and former fraternity brother, was starting a new venture and was on the hunt for a cofounder—someone who might share his energy and passion. The moment Nick heard the concept, he was certain he wanted in.

"I remember sitting in the garage thinking that this was really a good idea," says Nick. "It may have sounded crazy to a lot of people, but to me it made perfect sense."

Just days later, the two twenty-somethings decided to move forward with the partnership and began making plans for the future. Although neither Evan nor Nick had ever worked for, let alone run, an apparel company, they were confident in their ability to succeed and hungry for a challenge. And a challenge they did find.

SHARK BITE

Don't ask your mom, your wife, your friends, your barber what they think—those are opinions (and often biased one's at that!). Test the idea with the only people who really matter: the ones who are going to cut you a check for it. Call on some potential clients and see if they will buy whatever it is you're selling.[6]
—Robert

SANTA SELLS OUT

Although Evan and Nick had hoped Tipsy Elves would one day grow into a legitimate business, during the initial stages of development they treated it more as a "fun project."

"It wasn't like we quit our day jobs right away," says Evan. "Our initial plan was to order 1,000 sweaters and see if we could sell them."

The game plan, however, would soon change. Shortly after partnering, the friends attended a trade show in Las Vegas and immediately attracted crowds of amused passersby. They were even approached by a few buyers who expressed interest in carrying the product at their retail stores. It didn't take long for the cofounders to recognize that it would require more than 1,000 sweaters to meet the demand. So they scraped together whatever money they could find and purchased another 4,000 pieces of inventory. Now the proud owners of 5,000 ugly Christmas sweaters, the pressure was on.

Over the next few months, Evan and Nick worked tirelessly to build the organization from the ground up. Still holding down full-time jobs and living in separate cities, they spent nights and weekends eagerly preparing for the holiday season. It was a grueling schedule, but they were relentless in their pursuit.

"Most people think you just design a product and then sell it," says Nick. "But there is so much more to it than that. You have to secure a manufacturer, develop samples, find a fulfillment house, and build a website. There are so many steps we didn't think about."

The Tipsy Elves site went live in October of 2012, and by December 1—less than three months after launching—all 5,000 sweaters had been sold. With $380,000 in sales, and

not a single piece of inventory left in stock, Evan and Nick were convinced they were on to something groundbreaking.

"We got some good press that first year, but the majority of our business came from SEO," says Evan. "It was a great validation of our strategy."

Although growth is generally a positive thing, it also brings an onslaught of unanticipated challenges. Evan and Nick knew that by selling out so early in the season they were leaving an undetermined amount of money on the table—an agonizing prospect for any new venture. But without additional capital they couldn't afford to buy more inventory, so Nick decided to approach his family for an investment. And what better time for a holiday pitch than at the annual Christmas get-together?

"I put together a PowerPoint presentation and pitched the company during the party," says Nick. "All we were trying to do is raise enough money to buy more inventory."

While his aunts and uncles weren't entirely sold on the company, his grandfather—a former entrepreneur—saw the potential and agreed to invest in the young company.

Tipsy Elves had officially raised their first round of capital. It wasn't a huge sum of money, but it allowed them to purchase the much-needed inventory and continue growing the business.

With the new year just around the corner, Evan and Nick put together a strategic plan for the next 365 days. They needed to fine-tune designs, hire a better fulfillment company, and make crucial updates to the website. And that was just the beginning. Each day seemed to present an endless array of new tasks.

By June of 2012, Evan had quit his job at the law firm

and was working full-time on Tipsy Elves. His entrepreneurial dream had now become a reality, whether he was ready for it or not.

"I think Evan downplayed how much risk was involved in quitting his job," says Nick. "We had no money to pay him and in his field you can't really go back. He would never be able to practice corporate law again."

At this point, however, Evan was thoroughly invested and had no time to consider the consequences; the holiday season was fast approaching and there were ugly Christmas sweaters to be sold. Determined to exceed the demand, they placed an order for 12,500 units.

"We bought every sweater we could afford," says Evan. "I even sold all my stock and liquidated my Roth account."

Yet even with the additional 7,500 units, Tipsy Elves once again sold out all of their merchandise by the beginning of December—generating almost a million dollars in sales but leaving precious money on the table.

Desperate for capital, the two founders began approaching banks to secure additional financing. But no matter how many doors they tried, nobody would give them a loan.

"We had trouble raising capital from a traditional bank," says Nick. "We were a seasonal business with only two years of sales. Plus, we had yet to establish enough of an upward trend. As a investment, we had all the issues a conservative bank tries to avoid."

If they were serious about growing Tipsy Elves, Evan and Nick realized they would need to raise enough money to guarantee they didn't sell out of product during the following year. Only then could they accurately assess the company's true earning potential. But they needed more than

just financial assistance. The enterprise had reached a critical turning point and could greatly benefit from a strategic partner who possessed industry experience and a proven track record of business excellence. What they needed was a Shark.

> *There are so many people that will say, "No—bad idea, it's never going to work." You have to have a senseless belief in your idea and yourself—almost to the point of being delusional.[7]*
> *—Robert*

SHARK BITE

A DIP IN THE TANK

Each year, *Shark Tank* receives over 30,000 submissions from eager business owners who are looking for an investment. Evan and Nick were convinced they had a great product but realized it would take more than that to stand out from the crowd. They wanted to do something different, something unique, something . . . tipsy.

The duo came up with a plan to turn Nick's new, unfurnished condo into a homemade television studio and shoot a high-energy audition video. Wearing their ugliest of Christmas sweaters, the team filmed an off-the-wall pitch—complete with festive song and dance. They hoped the colorful presentation would win over the casting team. If not, at the very least they'd have a good story to tell at their next holiday party.

Luckily, the lively performance was well received, and a couple of weeks later they were on the phone with a producer.

"It all happened really fast," says Nick. "There was only about a one-month turnaround from the time the show contacted us to when we actually taped."

With only a brief window of time to prepare, Evan and Nick meticulously constructed their pitch. Worried that such a quirky product might subtract from their credibility and general business expertise, they made it a top priority to highlight their proficiency and professionalism.

"I remember watching past seasons of the show and making a list of all the questions that were asked," says Nick. "We even made flashcards so we could drill our numbers."

The preparation paid off. Less than a month later, they were headed to Los Angeles to tape an episode. Little did they know just how important that trip would become.

On the morning of the big day, Evan and Nick woke up

early to practice their pitch and review their plan of attack. They were asking for $100,000 for 5 percent of the company, valuing the venture at $2 million—not an outrageous calculation but certainly an optimistic projection. Although they were open to working with any of the Sharks, they were especially interested in making a deal with Daymond John, Mark Cuban, or Robert Herjavec.

"There was something about Robert that we both really liked," says Nick. "He seemed like a nice guy, and we really related to his story."

When the big day finally arrived, the founders made their way to the studio and waited patiently in the dressing room until they were called to set. With a passionate customer base and over a million dollars in sales, they felt optimistic about their chance of securing a deal but unsure of whether or not the Sharks would relate to their nontraditional product.

"If we were given an opportunity to tell our story, we knew we could land a deal," says Evan. "We just needed to show them that we were thoughtful guys and had a decent idea of what we were doing."

After only a few minutes in the tank, the bidding war began. Offended by the $2 million valuation, Kevin O'Leary countered with a royalty deal. Tipsy Elves would pay him $2 for each unit sold until he recouped his initial capital. From there, the royalty would drop to $1 per unit in perpetuity (i.e., for the lifetime of the organization).

"The average royalty for a licensing deal in the clothing world is around eleven percent," says Nick. "So asking for one dollar of a sixty dollar sweater really wasn't such a bad deal."

But money wasn't the only reason the business partners

had come on the show. Yes, they needed to raise capital, but they were also looking for a trusted advisor—a partner who was just as excited about investing in the company as he or she was about investing in them. They didn't believe Kevin O'Leary would be interested in building that type of relationship.

As Mark and Lori went out, things began to look bleak. That is, until Robert Herjavec stepped in and made an offer that instantly caught the young cofounders' attention. Robert was willing to invest $100,000 but only if he could get 10 percent of the business, instantly cutting their value in half.

"I'm really investing in you guys," said Robert. "I want to participate in the company. Kevin just wants to suck money right off the top."

Robert's desire to become a fully engaged partner was all it took to convince both founders that he was the right investor. And although his offer was lower than their original ask, they felt it was the right opportunity to pursue.

"Honestly, his valuation made sense," says Nick. "We didn't think we were going to leave with exactly what we wanted, and it would have been petty to argue over a couple points of equity."

Overjoyed to have scored a deal, Evan and Nick immediately began brainstorming new ways to scale operations and source additional inventory. They weren't going to let anything stand in their way of taking Tipsy Elves to the next level.

"It was a totally surreal experience," says Nick. "Neither of us had ever really been on TV before. I think we both sort of blacked out."

> On Shark Tank, I watch the entrepreneurs very closely. I will attack the business idea, not the person, but I have a keen eye for the type of entrepreneur that I like to work with. If they've got drive, I never worry about getting a return on my investment.[8]
> —Robert

GROWING PAINS (AND GAINS)

Tipsy Elves' episode aired on December 13, 2013, and overnight, sales began to soar. By the end of the fourth quarter, the company had grossed over $8.5 million—a 700 percent increase from the prior year. Evan and Nick couldn't have been more exhilarated. But with great expansion comes great responsibility.

"When an entrepreneur sees an immediate spike in growth, it's common to feel as though the organization is bigger than it actually is," says Evan. "It was important for us to stay grounded and remain focused on building the company in the right way."

If Tipsy Elves was going to continue to evolve, Evan and Nick needed to make some critical adjustments, which would affect everything from the model to the growth plan.

First they had to assess their core strategy. Should they double down on e-commerce or create a wholesale division and expand to retailers? They agreed that establishing a retail presence was a crucial part of elevating the brand and attracting new consumers. They even acquired a small company in the UK with a strong wholesale business and began looking for a dedicated manager to pitch new corporate accounts.

"We started wondering how much we could actually drive sales through our website," says Evan. "We thought wholesale was an option worth pursuing."

Over time, however, they began to second-guess the approach. As more retailers carried the product, Tipsy Elves' SEO stronghold started to diminish. It became increasingly clear that having too many retail partners could damage the business.

Still convinced that brick-and-mortar was integral to growth, Evan and Nick considered opening a flagship retail store in San Francisco. They even went as far as to put an offer on a space. But after re-examining the numbers, they concluded it wouldn't be worth the time and energy required.

"We have a tendency to bite off more than we can chew," says Evan. "Especially if we have a couple slow weeks. It's important to keep things in perspective."

Ultimately, the company chose to adopt a hybrid approach, investing heavily in the e-commerce business while also partnering with select retailers who could amplify the brand offline. Today, they view brick-and-mortar more as a marketing channel than as a direct driver of sales.

"There's a lot of advantage in being the only place online to buy our products," says Nick. "We've made sure our retail partners can't compete with us there."

The challenges continued to mount, however, and the next hurdle had the potential to threaten the very core of their enterprise. In order to achieve significant expansion, Tipsy Elves needed to evolve beyond a seasonal business, which meant developing new products and retooling the brand.

"We still thought there was a lot of room for growth

within the Christmas market," says Evan. "But we knew we'd hit a cap at some point."

Going back to his SEO roots, Evan began researching popular keywords in hope of discovering new commercially viable categories. Using data from the research, the team developed two additional product lines: USA- and university-themed collections. This, they believed, would put them on track to achieving their goal of becoming a company that sold fun apparel for *all* occasions—not just the holidays.

But there was still one unanswered question: would consumers buy non-holiday products from a business called Tipsy Elves? Would the brand name hinder their ability to grow? Evan and Nick were about to find out.

"As founders the branding is in your control," says Nick. "The example I always give is Banana Republic. They started out as a safari-themed clothing company. Nobody thinks of them that way now."

To help facilitate the reimagined identity, they removed the elf from their website and changed the tagline. They also developed a range of color schemes for their logo, so they wouldn't be limited to strictly a red and green Christmas palette. The rebrand proved successful, and today the company has more than quadrupled its collection, offering a wide array of products for all types of holidays and occasions.

As an investor and partner, Robert Herjavec has patiently guided the business through each critical phase. But his mentoring doesn't end there. He actively promotes the company through a multitude of channels and plays a key role in their annual planning.

"Robert has helped us maintain focus," says Nick. "When we were trying to develop a secondary line of products, for example, he stepped in and convinced us it was a bad

decision. That one piece of advice saved us a lot of time and money."

Perhaps Robert's most instrumental contribution was convincing Nick to leave his dentistry practice and dedicate himself full-time to the company. It was a difficult decision to make, but the cofounder knew it was the right move.

"To be successful in business you have to take big risks or you won't get there," says Nick. "It was time for me to come on board full-time."

At the start of 2015, Tipsy Elves had sold over 125,000 units, grossing more than $11 million. Evan and Nick remain passionate about the business and feel confident they can grow the enterprise to more than $50 million in revenue. Robert, however, believes they're capable of soaring to even greater heights.

"Mark my words," says Robert. "These guys are going to build a one-hundred-million-dollar clothing company. We're going big time."

SHARK BITE

Your business is a living, breathing thing, and it has to be fed and grow to survive. There is no balance in your life when your business is in trouble. If you are under the illusion that you can start a business and run it at your life's schedule, you are mistaken.[9]
—*Robert*

THE TIPSY ELVES PLAYBOOK FOR SUCCESS

The definition of success is rarely static and must constantly evolve with the company and founder(s). As first-time

entrepreneurs, Evan and Nick have experienced this principle throughout the life of their business.

"When I was younger, I thought success meant getting a stable job and earning a good income," says Evan. "That's changed a lot. Today I define it as just being happy and doing what I enjoy."

Evan first noticed this shift shortly after becoming a lawyer. Although he assumed the money and prominence of a high-status job would bring satisfaction, instead it left him feeling deflated and trapped. It was then he realized that if he was ever to be truly happy, he would need to reevaluate how he measured achievement.

Although Nick pursued a different career path, he, too, faced a similar challenge. After graduating at the top of his class and building a thriving practice, the young dentist felt as though something was missing. It was only when he gave himself permission to redefine expectations that he was able to find genuine fulfillment.

"Evan and I have similar ideas about success," says Nick.

"That's part of why we work so well together. We just want to be happy and have the freedom to do something we both love."

But identifying success is only the first part of achieving it. As cofounders, Evan and Nick have developed an unspoken set of guiding principles that help them maintain perspective and stay on track. Combined, these core beliefs create a customized Playbook for Success.

UPGRADE YOUR ATTITUDE

For Evan and Nick, success can be boiled down to one essential factor: attitude. Maintaining a positive perspective, they believe, is the most effective way to transcend the daily challenges of running an organization and ensure permanent, lasting progress.

Like any start-up, Tipsy Elves has faced a slew of obstacles along the way. Early in the development of the business, for example, their manufacturer unknowingly used a graphic that was protected under a copyright. They received the shipment just days before the holiday season and were forced to sacrifice 20 percent of their product—a damaging blow to the bottom line.

While some might have panicked, Evan and Nick chose to remain calm and channel their frustration into motivation.

"We weren't happy," says Evan. "But we knew we couldn't do anything about it. At least we had eighty percent of the product to sell."

This productive approach to adversity has become a hallmark of their leadership style and stems from an uncompromising belief that no matter how steep the challenge, they will ultimately prevail.

"There are as many reasons to believe something will work as there are that it won't," says Evan. "Success is about deciding to believe the reasons that prove you can instead of those that prove you can't."

Still, Evan will also be the first to admit that this philosophy is often easier said than done.

"I used to think that entrepreneurship was reserved for people who had a certain set of skills or who knew something that I didn't," says Evan. "But I had to change my thinking. To be successful at something, you first have to believe you can be successful at it."

Risk Smarter, Not Harder

While it's true that business owners must learn to cultivate a certain propensity for risk, the cofounders believe you can greatly reduce the chance of failure by approaching unpredictability in smarter, more calculative ways.

"We were never in a situation where we were living off ramen and down to our last dollar," says Evan. "Those stories are popular and get a lot of press, but it's not a smart way of building a business."

From its original inception, Tipsy Elves has relied on customer feedback to launch more targeted products. You could even say the organization was founded on this practice.

Instead of dreaming up an idea he *thought* consumers would buy, Evan came up with Tipsy Elves after scouring through mounds of keyword data. By doing this, he was able to tap into an existing market and produce a product with a previously established audience.

"To me it was the safest way to create a business," says Evan. "So many people try to start a cool T-shirt company or apparel brand, but they have no idea who their audience is. We wanted to find something with built-in demand."

While this approach didn't guarantee the enterprise would succeed, of course, it greatly reduced Evan's fear of failure, empowering him to take bigger risks that might otherwise have felt unsafe. The company still uses this technique today, especially when introducing new products to market.

"We start by looking closely at what worked well in the past," says Nick. "From colors to sizes, we try to explore all the numbers and trends."

In recent months they've even gone so far as to break down products into specific subcategories based on humor and tone. From risqué to more family-friendly designs, they've spent countless hours mapping and measuring their entire collection.

"We then take this data and compare it to things like size ratio," says Evan. "It helps us make the right product for the right person."

Using this method, they've been able to quantify how much of each product to manufacture and who specifically they should target, thus reducing waste and streamlining costs.

"We take a lot of risks," says Nick. "But we're always careful in our approach."

Lean Hard on Others

Nobody will ever care as much about a business as its founder. That doesn't mean, however, that he or she will always have the right answers or be the ideal candidate for every task. As Evan and Nick have discovered, doing what's best for the organization often means learning to lean on others.

"You have to accept that you don't know what you don't know," says Evan. "We're constantly asking questions and trying to seek out the best information."

In Tipsy Elves' early days, Evan created all the products and Nick provided feedback and edits. While this scrappy approach worked on a temporary basis, neither founder had any legitimate design experience, and they eventually sought outside help.

"We didn't know what it meant to hire a designer," says Nick. "Once we brought someone on, we quickly realized just how important that role was."

Today, Evan and Nick put great emphasis on ensuring their employees feel valued and appreciated. This, they believe, is paramount in developing a passionate and engaged team and maintaining a productive workplace culture.

"We try to always be kind," says Nick. "We pay our employees well and treat them fairly because we know how much they bring to the business."

Outwork the Competition

It's no secret that building a profitable enterprise requires hard work and dedication. But more than that, Evan and Nick believe success is earned by using every opportunity to go above and beyond the competition.

"At the end of the day, can you honestly and confidently say that nobody could have worked harder or smarter than you? That's a question I ask myself every day," says Nick.

For the first three years, Tipsy Elves was primarily a seasonal business. Although there was plenty of work to be done year-round, the third and fourth quarters were always the most time-intensive.

"During the busy season Evan would often sleep at the office," says Nick. "And I would put in a full day at my practice and then rush home to work on our business."

The cofounders have discovered that stamina is crucial for an entrepreneur and that the best way to maintain the hectic pace is to "become obsessed" with the business. In other words, one must develop a deep appreciation for each part of the process.

"If you want to succeed you can't just love the product," says Evan. "You have to also love running the company and everything it encompasses."

Stay True to Your Mission

As founders of a rapidly growing organization, it's easy to get distracted by new and potentially profitable opportunities. But as Evan and Nick have learned, staying true to their mission and core competencies is a crucial part of achieving sustainable success.

"When you start a business you have to know deep down who you are as a company and what you do best," says Nick. "Otherwise you can risk losing focus."

This principle hasn't always been easy to practice, especially when faced with the many hurdles of expansion. From pursuing a wholesale strategy to creating a less expensive sub-brand, the founders have experienced turbulence each time they've strayed from their primary areas of expertise. Fortunately, Robert Herjavec has been there to ensure they stay on track.

During a recent annual retreat, Robert shared a story about Under Armour—the multibillion-dollar sports clothing brand—that left a strong impression on both founders.

"He told us that at Under Armour they still end each meeting the same way," says Nick. "By saying, 'remember to sell T-shirts.'"

Under Armour is a global brand with thousands of products, but the enterprise started by selling high-performance athletic T-shirts made from moisture-wicking synthetic fabric. Although they've experienced incredible growth over the past twenty years, at the heart of the business they're still a T-shirt company.

From Tipsy Elves' early days as a fledgling start-up to its current status as a million-dollar brand, Evan and Nick have learned that knowing who they are—and perhaps, most importantly, who they aren't—is a critical part of building a powerful and profitable organization.

"You have to identify your strengths and recognize where the growth model has proven itself," says Evan. "Otherwise you'll chase after any opportunity."

CHAPTER THREE

INVESTOR: MARK CUBAN

COMPANY: ZooBean

FOUNDERS: Felix Lloyd and Jordan Lloyd Bookey

AN EDUCATION IN EDUCATION

Winston Churchill once said, "To improve is to change; to be perfect is to change often." While perfection in and of itself is a futile pursuit, progress—growth—is what most entrepreneurs spend a lifetime chasing. And if Felix Lloyd and Jordan Lloyd Bookey's experience proves anything, it's that Churchill got it right: the ability to evolve is a prerequisite for achievement.

The husband-and-wife team appeared on season five of *Shark Tank* and secured a deal with Mark Cuban for $250,000 in exchange for 25 percent of their company, Zoo-Bean, which at the time was an online platform that "delights kids with books curated just for them."

Today, however, ZooBean has expanded beyond the concept Felix and Jordan first pitched in the tank. And, not unlike the couple who founded the technology venture, its trajectory has been anything but ordinary.

THE BUSINESS OF LEARNING

When Jordan arrived at Hartsfield-Jackson Atlanta Airport on that humid afternoon in the spring of 2000, she had no idea what lay just around the corner. At only twenty-four years old, the recent college graduate had but two years of professional experience and was on her way to the nation's

capital with little more than a carry-on bag and a hunch. But Jordan knew better than to ignore a good premonition. If two decades of life experience had taught her anything, however, it was that a good premonition should never be ignored. And this was more than a premonition; it felt like a calling.

Waiting at the other end of that auspicious flight was Felix Loyd—a rising star in the education sector and a fellow serial risk-taker. As a film major at Syracuse University, he had graduated at the top of his class and been chosen to deliver the commencement speech at the year-end ceremony. But unlike many of his peers who had dashed off to the illustrious hills of Hollywood or the bustling streets of New York City, Felix returned to his hometown and took a job as a history teacher at The SEED School of Washington, D.C.—the first public boarding school in the United States. Was it an unconventional move? Perhaps. But convention, as Felix had learned, is often overrated and rarely to be trusted.

As Jordan's flight began its initial descent into Reagan National Airport, she tried to imagine what her future might be like if she obtained the coveted teaching job at the charter school where she was scheduled to interview. Never did she guess that, mere hours later, she would be offered the position and meet the man who would become her future husband and eventual business partner.

"When I got hired, Felix was assigned as my mentor teacher," says Jordan. "We were dating before the school year even started."

The couple spent the next two years advancing quickly in their respective roles at the institution. Felix was voted teacher of the year in 2001 and became vice principal and dean of students shortly thereafter. Still, the twenty-something educator yearned for something more.

Since graduating from college, Felix had been itching to write his first novel. But a busy life and budding career had served as a much-welcomed distraction. Recognizing that the book project would require his undivided attention, he submitted his resignation in 2003 and headed west to an artist colony in Indiana that was run by a group of Franciscan monks.

For two years, Felix lived and breathed his novel. As the monastery's artist in residence, he received free room and board but collected no salary. So each summer, he returned to Washington D.C. to spend quality time with his then-girlfriend and replenish his savings.

"I ran the summer program at The Seed School and lived with Jordan," says Felix. "I think everyone was very patient with me."

By 2005, Felix had finished his novel and applied to Washington University in St. Louis, where he was accepted into the graduate writing program. Similarly, Jordan had also decided to seek an advanced degree.

With a passion for arts, culture, and social progress, her plan was to major in a subject like theater or education and eventually work for a nonprofit. Her mentor, however, suggested she take a different approach and consider a degree in business. An MBA, he claimed, could be a tremendous asset in whatever career she chose to practice. Jordan wasn't as convinced.

"I thought that was the dark side," Jordan says. "There was no way I was going to do that. I wanted to work *for* the people."

Eventually, she conceded and agreed to visit a few business schools before making a decision. If nothing else, she thought, it would verify that pursuing an MBA was the

wrong choice. But, in fact, just the opposite happened.

As Jordan toured each campus, she was surprised to find so many students who shared a similar worldview and who also had an interest in social entrepreneurship—a type of for-profit entity that seeks to use business practices to solve major social problems. After much consideration, she applied to the University of Pennsylvania's Wharton School of Business and was accepted for the following academic year. Although separated yet again by distance, the couple was united by a shared desire to succeed.

Jordan thrived at the university and was soon elected president of the Wharton Social Impact Initiative—a program designed to help students, faculty, and alumni use "business knowledge and practices to enhance the greater good of the local community, the nation, and the world." And Jordan wasn't the only one who found the program intriguing.

Felix was fascinated by what his now fiancée was learning, even if it did trigger a somewhat frightening realization that a bachelor's degree in film and a master's in writing might not be the most marketable combination of credentials for a future job-seeker. For the first time in his life, he began to see entrepreneurship as a meaningful path—a belief that, in the past, he had rather vehemently rejected.

Felix's father was a self-described entrepreneur, which, according to Felix, "basically meant he was unemployed and irresponsible." Felix had watched as his dad bounced from one botched idea to the next, from selling pickled eggs and school lunches to attempting to launch a gypsy cab company. As a result, Felix associated small business with instability and failure—both of which he had spent a lifetime actively trying to avoid.

"I think watching his experience showed me it wasn't a real or viable way to live," says Felix.

The reality, however, was that Felix had always been somewhat enterprising and unquestionably imaginative; part of what inspired him to pursue a career in the arts was the freedom such a career provided. The way he saw it, it was either that or spend the rest of his life stuck in a cubicle.

"The big thing was that I never wanted to have a traditional 'job,'" says Felix. "So I decided to be a writer and filmmaker because I knew that would allow me to be independent."

As graduate school came to a close, Jordan found herself in a slight panic. At the eleventh hour, she had decided to deviate from her original plan of working in education or government to find a job in the corporate sector. This last-minute shift meant that when it came time to secure an internship, she was uncharacteristically behind schedule. It's possible that Jordan's anxiety would have continued to rage if not for a random e-mail she received from a recruiter at Google shortly before the spring semester concluded.

"I checked my inbox one evening and there was this one-line message from a recruiter," says Jordan. "He asked if I had any interest in interning at Google for the summer."

At first she thought the note was a prank, but Jordan soon discovered the opportunity was legitimate. Google was looking for an MBA student to work in the People Operations department—a division of human resources. After a series of interviews, she received an offer and the couple headed off for a three-month stint in Mountain View, California.

Jordan excelled during her summer at the technology company and, upon graduation, was offered a full-time job managing the diversity programs at numerous sites around

the country. It was the last job she would have before start-
ing her own organization.

Meanwhile, Felix was hard at work preparing to launch
his first business—a financial education video game called
Cents City (which has since been rebranded as *Money
Island*). The concept behind the game was to build a virtual
world where kids could learn critical financial skills. Hav-
ing lacked such information as a child, Felix felt the game
could help countless children while also becoming a profit-
able operation.

To raise the necessary start-up funds, the first-time founder
applied for a fellowship grant through Echoing Green—a
global nonprofit that provides seed funding and technical
assistance to emerging social entrepreneurs. After months of
back and forth, Felix was awarded the endowment, which
consisted of a $30,000 annual salary and a health insurance
plan for two years.

"For the first six months, I had no idea how to run the
business," says Felix. "I was just sort of bumbling around
until I got accepted into a business accelerator program in
Pittsburgh, PA called AlphaLab."

Similar to many of the popular tech accelerators that
exist today, AlphaLab is a concentrated six-month incubator
program that provides entrepreneurs with capital, resources,
and support in exchange for a small percentage of equity.
From incorporation procedures to financial projecting, it was
there that Felix learned many of the essential skills required
to start and run a venture.

In the final week of the program, each founder was asked
to pitch his or her idea to an audience of investors during
a competition called Demo Day. Having spent much of
his career as a teacher, Felix was confident in his ability to

communicate his strategy and articulate his vision. It was an experience he would not soon forget.

"I gave my fifteen-minute pitch, after which one investor came up to say hello," says Felix. "He saw something in me as an entrepreneur and salesman, and eventually made a fifty-thousand-dollar investment to help me continue building the product."

Felix used the money to hire a developer and complete the first consumer-facing iteration of *Cents City*. With a working beta version and a growing list of users, the newly minted founder pitched the game at Finovate—a big-stage seven-minute pitch competition for financial innovation products.

Once again, Felix's presentation skills impressed the crowd and captured the attention of yet another VIP—the CEO of an Austin-based company called BancVue. Just four months later, the financial services firm acquired *Cents City*. Felix had successfully sold his first venture.

SHARK BITE

> If you really want to know where your destiny lies, look at where you apply your time. Time is the most valuable asset you don't own. You may or may not realize it yet, but how you use or don't use your time is going to be the best indication of where your future is going to take you.[10]
> —Mark

TAG, YOU'RE IT

When a business is acquired, it's common for the buyer to retain the founder (or founding team) of the purchased company for a designated period of time. Such was the case in the *Cents City* deal. As part of the transaction, Felix was

required to relocate to Austin, Texas, and work directly for BancVue. With both husband and wife now working traditional 9–5 jobs, they began to get restless.

"Felix and I knew we wanted to start another company together," says Jordan. "We were always coming up with different ideas and buying new domain names. That was sort of our nightly activity."

The couple did more than just daydream, however. Using SurveyMonkey—a popular platform where users can create and publish online polls—they conducted market research to uncover which of their many ideas might have the most potential.

"We had ourselves in the right mindset," says Jordan. "That's a really important part of starting a business."

While none of their initial concepts made it past the ideation phase, Felix and Jordan kept their eyes open for potential challenges that needed tackling. Finally, at the end of 2011, they came across a problem they felt uniquely positioned to solve.

With their second child on the way, the couple was searching for a "big brother" book for their son, Cassius. As they browsed the shelves at their favorite local bookstore, they were surprised by how few books showcased a multiracial family such as their own.

Frustrated by the lack of options, Felix and Jordan reached out to a librarian friend who suggested they check out a copy of *All the World*. Featuring a white mother and black father, it was the first children's book they had found that mirrored their own family dynamic.

"It was a perfect book for us," says Jordan. "Our son would look at the pictures and say, 'That's me, that's me.'"

Although they were happy to have finally found a book with identifiable characters, the experience of locating it had been daunting. Surely, they thought, there must be other parents who were struggling to uncover similar reading material for their children. They began to wonder if there was a way to create a hyper-curated service that could provide a customizable solution for families of all backgrounds.

To assess the scope and complexity of the problem, Felix and Jordan cataloged countless children's books, tagging each with a multitude of relevant keywords. From general topics like baseball to larger themes such as "strong girls" and "big brother," they tracked each category in a master spreadsheet.

"We would tag something that we thought a family might want, which is very different than what an adult may be looking for," says Jordan.

As the database grew to include more than 1,600 keywords, their confidence grew, too. They knew, however, that if their product was to offer a truly personalized experience, they would need substantially more data. So, using their network of fellow educators, they recruited a team of librarians to dig through material and uncover new categories.

The couple felt certain they had stumbled upon a great concept, but was the market big enough? To help gauge demand, they once again launched a series of online surveys that were targeted to their specific audience. This allowed them to zero in on the most critical features, which they then used to build a minimum viable product (MVP)—a popular phrase in the tech industry that is used to describe a product with the highest return on investment versus risk.

"At the time, it was very basic," says Felix. "We just

needed something that would allow us to capture credit card information and start providing services."

By May of 2013, ZooBean was ready to go live; they just needed to find users. In an effort to generate buzz around the product launch, the couple participated in a two-day pop-up pitch event sponsored by NewME—a technology start-up accelerator for "businesses founded by underrepresented groups."

"I think we did it a little reluctantly," says Jordan. "We were both working full-time jobs and had just moved to Washington, D.C. But we decided to hire a babysitter for a couple nights and just go for it."

By that point, Felix had participated in a slew of similar events and had become somewhat of a pitching expert. Not surprisingly, their presentation was a success, and ZooBean won the entire competition. It was a victory that would set the pace for the future of both their business and their lives.

> **SHARK BITE**
>
> I personally think that the only way you can connect to your customers is to put yourself in their shoes. For me personally, if I can't be a customer of my own product, then I probably am not going to do a good job running the company.[11]
> —Mark

FROM PRODUCT TO PLATFORM

It's estimated that each day more than 2.5 million blog posts are published on the Internet—a number that continues to climb. With such a huge surplus of digital content, the odds

are slim that the right post will end up in front of the right person at exactly the right time. But Felix and Jordan are proof that rarities like that can and do occur.

The morning after the pitch event, NewME published a blog post announcing the winner of the competition, which just so happened to appear in the newsfeed of someone on the *Shark Tank* casting team. With the fifth season scheduled to begin taping later that summer, the associate reached out to Felix and Jordan with an offer to audition for the show.

At first, the couple was wary of the unsolicited e-mail—especially Felix, who has been an enormous *Shark Tank* fan since it first premiered on August 9, 2009. But after Googling the name of the sender, he realized the offer was genuine.

"Felix always thought he was going to be on *Shark Tank*," says Jordan. "And I would always tell him he was crazy."

Crazy or not, it was clear the opportunity was legitimate, and the duo had an important decision to make. They knew that getting the opportunity to pitch in front of the Sharks was an incredible honor and could potentially provide the business with vital capital. However, they weren't entirely sure the company was mature enough to endure such scrutiny.

"It was incredibly exciting, but I had a sense that we may not be ready for it," says Felix. "We had only been around for eight weeks and, at that point, neither one of us were working on it full-time."

Jordan was also nervous about the idea of going head-to-head with five of America's most infamous investors. She was confident in the couple's work ethic and track record, but she'd seen how the Sharks could pulverize entrepreneurs who appeared unprepared. So together, Felix and Jordan came up with a plan to ensure they were as equipped as possible.

First they combed through the previous four seasons of the show, carefully studying each pitch and tracking a wide set of data, ranging from topics like popularity of question to frequency in which a particular Shark made an offer. Using this robust database of information, they built custom profiles for each investor and identified who would be most likely to make a deal.

Next they began crafting their pitch, making sure to maximize their strengths while also trying to minimize any potential weaknesses or liabilities. Once it was complete, Jordan reached out to a consultant she had met at Google who specializes in helping founders improve their presentation skills. Working in tandem with the coach, the couple spent weeks drilling each sentence line by line.

"We must have practiced that thing a thousand times," says Jordan. "It got to the point where our son was walking around the house reciting it."

By late June of 2013, only one month after they had initially been contacted, Felix and Jordan were on their way to Los Angeles. Ready or not, it was time to face the Sharks.

As the duo waited backstage, they could feel the intensity building. In high-pressure situations, Felix enters what he calls his "zen place," while Jordan tends to be more outward in her emotions. With only minutes to go, she started to panic.

"I freaked out," says Jordan. "We wanted to say the pitch one last time before going out there, but all of a sudden I couldn't remember any of my lines."

Jordan recovered quickly, however, and soon the husband-and-wife team made their way down the narrow corridor and began their presentation.

The ZooBean founders asked for $250,000 for 15 percent equity in their company. Earlier in the year, they had closed an initial round of funding with another investment firm—the valuation of which they used to determine their funding request in the tank. Still, they were familiar enough with the show to recognize their numbers would likely be contested.

Kevin O'Leary was the first Shark to respond. As the cofounder of Softkey Software Products, which eventually changed its name to The Learning Company and was acquired by Mattel, Inc. in 1999, he had "lived in the space" for nearly twelve years and understood the market well.

"I'm going to guess that eighty percent of your sales are [to children] between the ages of three and eight years old," said Kevin. "Acquiring the customer at that age . . . is a huge challenge . . . because you have about twenty million people moving through that zone every twelve months."

Because of this inherent challenge, the Shark wanted to know how much it cost to acquire each new customer—a

question the husband and wife had, of course, anticipated. Jordan revealed that, on average, it cost ZooBean roughly $6.03 to gain a new user.

Recognizing that acquisition cost is directly related to the size of one's clientele, Barbara Corcoran and Mark Cuban probed deeper into the scope of ZooBean's user base.

That was another pain point the founders would have to swiftly overcome. The product had been live for less than two months and had only obtained a small group of just eighty-five subscribers. This concerned Lori Greiner, who questioned whether or not there was sufficient demand to make ZooBean a big enough opportunity.

"It seems to me there's a need for what you're doing," said Lori. "I don't know, though. Is this something that people are actually needing that you're fulfilling in the marketplace?"

Hoping that an in-depth description would help demonstrate the value of the service and the viability of their model, Felix offered a more technical explanation of how the product functioned. He clarified that, by matching user data with specific keyword tags, each person was assigned a relevancy score, which the platform uses to curate hyper-customized product recommendations.

Unfortunately, the explanation only further dissuaded Lori and Barbara, and they both quickly went out. With three Sharks remaining, the husband-and-wife team knew they needed to regain control of the conversation.

Hoping to emphasize their areas of strength, Felix and Jordan shared their impressive professional backgrounds, highlighting their technical training and work experience.

"Jordan left her job as head of K–twelve education at Google a week ago," said Felix. "I'm a former Washington,

D.C. teacher of the year and then after that I started a technology venture that I had an exit from three years ago."

Their attempt to impress the remaining Sharks worked, but it wasn't enough to keep all of them interested. Unable to see a clear path to success, Kevin and Robert eliminated themselves from the bidding process.

"My children are voracious readers, but I got to tell you, they can go online and search for almost book that they want," said Robert. "I just currently don't see it."

Lucky for them, Mark Cuban had a different opinion. Believing that trusted curation is "the future," he was curious to know if the business could grow outside of just books. For example, could the software be extended to include other forms of media, such as kid-appropriate television shows and movies?

"The value in this has nothing to do with books," said Mark. "It has everything to do with helping grandma find something when she doesn't know what to get."

For the first time, Felix saw a real opportunity to land a deal. The couple explained that, yes, ZooBean could be extended to catalog and curate an assortment of different items—an answer that satisfied Mark.

"One thing I've learned as an entrepreneur is that you should never interrupt agreement," says Felix. "My goal in that moment was to help him see this as a platform, not a product."

Felix's attempt to persuade Mark worked, and after a short negotiation they accepted his offer of $250,000 for 25 percent of the company. Less than three months after launching the business, they had secured one of world's most prominent tech investors.

STACKED TO WIN

Felix and Jordan taped their segment in July of 2013, but the episode didn't actually air until April of the following year. For an established business, nine months can feel like no time at all, but ZooBean was still in its infancy and experiencing a litany of growing pains. In fact, in the three quarters that had elapsed between the time they taped and aired, the company had undergone a dramatic transformation.

While in the tank, they had pitched ZooBean as a book-of-the-month service that provided families with personalized reading material based on specific profile criteria. Soon thereafter, however, Felix and Jordan began to see some inherit flaws in their approach.

"The original idea was to send users a book per month," says Felix. "But over the course of that year we saw just how small the margins were and how complicated each order was to fulfill."

So, like any savvy founder might do, the couple decided to pivot—a common practice wherein an organization shifts their business model or overarching strategy in response to market feedback or to test a new hypothesis.

Instead of curating and shipping a physical book, Felix and Jordan repositioned ZooBean to become a software-based

subscription service that provided customers with high-quality, personalized content delivered via e-mail. In other words, for twenty-five dollars a year, parents would receive a series of content and product recommendations tailored to fit their family's specific needs. It was a risky move, but one the couple felt compelled to make.

To prepare for their television debut, the ZooBean team launched a redesigned home page, which featured a special offer wherein *Shark Tank* viewers could gain access to a free sixty-day trial of the new service. The sign-up form was purposefully brief and required no credit card or payment information. In doing this, their goal was to create a low-barrier lead generation tool and capture as many e-mails as possible. This, they assumed, would allow them to eventually convert the free users into paying ones.

"I'll be honest; I was nervous about that decision," says Felix. "I knew we shouldn't pursue a direction as an inventory business, but I wasn't sure if the opt-in strategy was right."

On the night their episode aired, Felix and Jordan hosted a small viewing party at their home and waited to see how the reimagined product would be perceived. They watched anxiously as their web traffic ebbed and flowed. By the end of the evening, ZooBean had signed up roughly ten thousand free accounts. Immediately, Felix realized they had made the wrong decision.

"What I regret is that we didn't collect credit card information," says Felix. "The challenge of trying to convert people at a later date was just too great. We had their attention and we should have capitalized off of it."

It wasn't long before these feelings of temporary disappointment gave way to another more profound revelation:

the subscription-based content service simply would not work. The pivot had failed.

"I woke Jordan up that night at four in the morning and told her I needed to go to the hospital," says Felix. "I was literally having a panic attack."

If ZooBean was going to change direction for a second time, they would need to move fast. Working in tandem with their three employees, Felix and Jordan spent the following week in a conference room, brainstorming as many ideas as they could. By the end of the seven days, they emerged with two potential strategies.

The first was to give the consumer-facing business one last push by removing the free offer and investing in a digital marketing campaign. For $5,000, they would engage with a network of relevant bloggers to promote ZooBean through native content and blog posts. Meanwhile, their internal team would aggressively work on turning the *Shark Tank* leads into paying customers.

The second strategy was to develop a business-to-business (B2B) service that could be sold directly to library systems. They still believed their concept of building a curation tool for parents was sound; they just weren't sure if consumers would pay for it. By licensing the software to libraries, Zoo-Bean could provide the service to families for free.

To test the idea, the couple purchased a booth at the American Library Association trade show—a globally recognized and highly trafficked industry event in Las Vegas. With no time to develop an actual product, they devoted all their effort to crafting a pitch and creating marketing materials that could be distributed to attendees.

"We just needed to find one good customer," says Jordan.

"That way we could use them as a pilot partner to validate the idea and test the product."

As first-time exhibitors, Felix and Jordan were given a booth in the very back of the convention center. It certainly wasn't the ideal location, but they had come too far to let something so trivial stand in the way. Knowing they needed to capitalize on their experience on *Shark Tank*, they draped a large poster over the booth that featured an image of them in the tank. The tactic worked, and soon they were bombarded with conference-goers, including one particularly important attendee from the Sacramento Public Library.

For the next month, the couple aggressively courted the contact, digging deep into the library system's specific challenges and offering an interactive webinar that explained exactly how their product could provide a solution. By the end of the summer, the library confirmed it was on board.

Today, the company has rebranded the B2B platform as Beanstack and works with more than forty different library systems throughout the United States and Canada. Similar

to the original concept, parents fill out a profile and receive a personalized list of book recommendations. From there, Beanstack allows the user to place each title on hold at his or her local library branch. With just a minor tweak, Felix and Jordan have transformed the platform into a powerful tool for both content discovery and lead generation.

"Forty-three percent of consumers who are signing up for Beanstack do not yet have a library card," says Jordan. "That's great because it means we're helping libraries get more traffic."

Through all of the ups and down, Mark Cuban has remained a loyal partner. From offering support and guidance to providing the enterprise with additional capital, he's been instrumental in helping the business grow to where it is today.

"When we decided to move forward with Beanstack, we were able to hire two employees and build the product in-house," says Jordan. "Mark's investment has allowed us to do so much."

SHARK BITE

It doesn't matter how many times you almost get it right. No one is going to know or care about your failures, and neither should you. All you have to do is learn from them and those around you because all that matters in business is that you get it right once.[13]
—Mark

THE ZOOBEAN PLAYBOOK FOR SUCCESS

Part of being a successful entrepreneur is understanding when and how to reinvent. This has been a constant theme

throughout Felix and Jordan's journey and one that continues to play an important role.

"You're going to make mistakes whether you accept it or not," says Felix. "Part of being successful is knowing how to move beyond those mistakes and turn them into new opportunities."

Reinvention, however, does not only occur in moments of failure. Jordan's decision to leave Google after more than seven years is a perfect example of how mastering the personal and professional pivot can lead to enduring career growth.

This ability to recognize potential and take real-time action is one of the many principles that guides the ZooBean founders and has become a central part of their Playbook for Success.

MAKE IT PERSONAL

Felix and Jordan first got the idea to start ZooBean after struggling to find a children's book that showcased a family similar to their own. And since launching, the couple has made a conscious effort to ensure the organization remains intensely personal.

"It's a long road and not every moment is going to feel like being on *Shark Tank*," says Jordan. "Most days are a grind, so you need to find something that you can get behind."

For the husband-and-wife team, this means accepting that sometimes the line between personal and professional can blur. They've learned to use that ambiguity as an asset instead of a liability.

"There've been times when we've even had to take our son to sales meetings," says Felix. "Whether it's the right approach or not, people seem to appreciate that it's personal to us."

This personalized approach, however, shouldn't be strictly limited to the entrepreneur's individual experience. Being a savvy business owner means finding unique ways to make the company feel personal to clients, as well. Before pitching to a new library, for example, the ZooBean founders do hours of research in an attempt to identify, specifically, what matters most to each person in the room.

"There's so much information out there and everybody's so busy," says Felix. "The more personal you can make it to the individual customer, the better off you'll be."

Focus on What's Next

When Felix and Jordan glance down at their to-do lists, the sheer volume of tasks can feel stifling. From big-ticket items to smaller, more mundane, chores, even the most productive person can become unraveled by such boundless responsibility.

"Having a lot of tasks to complete can feel overwhelming in any job," says Jordan. "But there's ten times more pressure

when it's your company and when you've taken other people's money."

To ensure they remain grounded, the couple abides by a simple yet powerful mantra: focus on what's next.

"As an entrepreneur, time is your greatest asset," says Felix. "With so much on your plate, you have to be dead set on accomplishing whichever task is the most pressing at that specific moment."

To uncover which chore is the most vital, he looks for the one item that's standing in the way of the completion of others—or the one that, if neglected any longer, could jeopardize a vital part of the business.

As important as this practice is, however, it should not detract from the larger strategic plan. No matter the size or scope of each daily task, Felix and Jordan believe a founder must never lose sight of his or her ultimate vision.

"You have to always keep your eye on the finish line," says Felix. "Even if that finish line changes."

Talk Less; Listen More

To survive in the competitive world of business, an entrepreneur must be brave enough to boldly share his or her idea with the world. Whether pitching an investor or closing a sale, effective communication is an important skill to learn. But conversation is a two-way street and, according to Felix and Jordan, should include less talking and more listening.

"It's shocking how many people just don't ask questions," says Jordan. "You'd be surprised at how much you can learn about your company just by becoming a better listener."

Not only has this approach made them better communicators, but it's become one of their most effective sales techniques. Instead of blindly pitching a new customer, the couple begins each meeting by asking a series of tactical questions designed to shed light on the exact needs and concerns of the client.

"Certain library systems care more about certain issues," says Jordan. "By asking questions and really listening to the answers, we can highlight specific solutions that speak directly to their challenges."

The husband-and-wife team credits this commitment to curiosity for many of their greatest victories and believe it to be one of their most pivotal practices.

"In most cases there are just one or two things that can make or break a deal," says Felix. "The fact is you have a better chance of closing the sale when you become a better listener."

Let Cash Be King

During his time at AlphaLab, Felix was introduced to a slew of local business leaders, including one well-known entrepreneur and financier named Frank Denver. Considered "the godfather of investment in Pittsburgh," Frank shared a lesson that left a lasting impression.

"He came in to give a presentation on the very first Wednesday night of the program," says Felix. "I remember he walked in the room and wrote on the board, 'Cash is king. No really, cash is king. Cash is more important than your mother.'"

While Felix is quick to point out that he doesn't entirely agree with the statement—his mother happens to be quite important to him—he does concur with the overall sentiment. Without stabilized cash flow, an enterprise is destined for failure.

This philosophy is part of why the couple was so willing to negotiate in the tank. Although they had hoped to give up no more than 20 percentage points of equity, eventually they agreed to the extra 5 percent that Mark Cuban requested.

"When you're in the tank, it's really easy to get caught up in the equity," says Felix. "But the lifetime of this business is going to be cash. That's important."

Discover Applicable Experiences

You'd be hard-pressed to find anyone who'd disagree with the notion that knowledge is power. But in Felix and Jordan's experience, acquiring information is one part of a two-part process. To transform understanding into capability, one must constantly seek out diverse experiences that allow for each teaching to be applied.

The couple first adopted this principle while Jordan was finishing her master's program at Wharton.

"I learned a lot in the classroom," says Jordan. "But so much of what I gained from that experience was outside the university."

At the time, Felix had begun working on his own start-up and was relying heavily on his wife's newfound knowledge. In fact, there were many times when he was required to produce the very same model or financial framework that Jordan was learning in school.

"In some ways I felt like I was paying for Felix's education," says Jordan. "I think if I was getting an MBA while running this, if I could ever possibly do that at the same time, it would be so valuable because I would immediately be able to apply what I was learning."

Today, the couple makes a conscious effort to engage in new applicable experiences, which was part of what motivated them to audition for *Shark Tank*.

"Our business had only been around for about six weeks when we did the show," says Felix. "But had we not put ourselves out there, we may never have learned what we did or made the changes that we needed to."

CHAPTER FOUR

INVESTOR: **DAYMOND JOHN**

COMPANY: **TITIN**

FOUNDER: Patrick Whaley

SEASON: Six

GEARING UP FOR VICTORY

Are entrepreneurs born or are they made? It's an age-old question and the cause of much debate among the Sharks.

Barbara Corcoran, for example, believes that successful founders are gifted with a special set of talents that allow them to prosper as business owners. Robert Herjavec, on the other hand, thinks that starting a company requires a unique combination of learned skills and natural abilities. While neither opinion is necessarily right or wrong, for Patrick Whaley, the answer is clear: this guy was born to be an entrepreneur.

Patrick appeared on season six of *Shark Tank* and closed a deal with Daymond John for $500,000 in exchange for 20 percent equity in TITIN—a patented line of weighted compression gear designed to boost training endurance and performance.

Although the Millennial CEO has yet to celebrate his thirtieth birthday, one must not be fooled by his youthful glow. Beneath the boundless optimism and fresh-faced veneer lies an inspired leader and determined go-getter who's well versed in the art of invention.

BEYOND THE LEMONADE STAND

Patrick can't remember the exact date and time when the idea first popped into his head. Maybe it came to him while

sitting in class, anxiously awaiting the chime of the final school bell. Or perhaps it was later in the evening, over dinner with his family. Although it's unlikely he'll ever recall the precise moment the epiphany transpired, what he does know is that it ignited something deep within—an unquenchable desire that has since become his guiding force.

True, Patrick was only in kindergarten when this breakthrough incident occurred. And yes, in hindsight the concept itself was undoubtedly silly. But like so many of life's milestones, the act of revelation is often more meaningful than the revelation itself. And in this case, the verb most definitely outweighed the noun.

"That's when I had the idea for my first business," says Patrick. "My plan was to make and construct what I called 'artistic ladders.'"

The concept came about after Patrick noticed that many of his neighbors spent large amounts of money on "decorative art pieces" for their homes. After a closer examination of these trinkets, the perceptive youngster realized he could make his own collection that rivaled the competition. So that's exactly what he did. Armed with a handful of borrowed tools, he retired to the backyard and chopped down as many small trees as he could find.

"Basically, I would cut each tree into three- or five-foot sections, decorate them, and sell them to my neighbors," says Patrick. "Sometimes I would even 'hire' their children to help me build them."

It wasn't long before the "business" was gaining momentum, but the artistic ladder market appeared to have a cap. As it turns out, there's a limit to how many ornamented logs one household needs. What's more, Patrick recognized that

his primary competitive advantage (i.e., the adorableness of youth) also came with a built-in expiration date. To succeed as an entrepreneur, he would need to find a new idea and fast.

Patrick's parents were entertained by their son's creativity and encouraging of his ambitions. His mother, a "tough-minded Irish woman" with a high-ranking marketing position at a technology company, related to her son's unyielding persistence and tenacity.

"My mom is the kind of woman who knows what she wants and is very motivated to get it," says Patrick. "I think that's trickled down into my personality. I don't stop until I've given one hundred and ten percent."

His father, conversely, has a more mild temperament and a gentle approach to life. Soft-spoken and measured, he, too, possessed an "entrepreneurial mindset" and had once dreamed of building his own company. But after starting a family at a young age, Patrick's father found it difficult to devote the time and attention required to launch an enterprise and raise a small child at the same time. With a profusion of new responsibilities, he took a job as an airline pilot and devoted himself to fatherhood.

"The hardest part of starting a business is identifying the obstacles and knowing in which direction to go," says Patrick. "My dad has always been really great at helping me focus my ideas."

With "artistic ladder" sales on the decline, the young inventor began searching for a new opportunity. Where he was raised, in the suburbs of Atlanta, Georgia, there were plenty of odd jobs to be found. But Patrick craved more than just a j-o-b; he wanted to build a company—something

that could eventually grow into a legitimate operation. And it wasn't long before he was struck by yet another bolt of inspiration.

When Patrick was in the fourth grade, a classmate of his revealed that he'd been earning extra money by cutting his next-door neighbor's grass. Patrick couldn't believe it; he'd been mowing his parents' lawn for years and never considered that somebody might pay for the service. The two friends formed a landscaping business and, together, hit the pavement, pitching the service to friends and neighbors.

"Anyone can mow a lawn, but we took it further," says Patrick. "We offered a full landscaping experience for a very reasonable price."

The basic lawn care package started at twenty dollars. But for just ten dollars more, customers would receive the full bundle of services, which included weeding, trimming, and other premium accruements. Within only a few months, the boys had signed up over twenty customers and were bringing in significant profits, especially considering their age (ten) and lack of overhead costs (zero). Eventually, however, they reached a crossroads and were forced to reorganize.

With only a limited number of hours in a day, the boys began to realize that there was a limit to how much they could earn. If the organization was going to expand, Patrick and his friend would have to shift their roles from workers to managers. This, of course, meant hiring other neighborhood children to do the actual yard work. For the aspiring tycoon, it was a game-changing moment.

"That business taught me a pivotal lesson about scaling a company," says Patrick. "Growth wasn't about how many lawns we could mow. It was about how many deals we could close."

Shortly before his thirteenth birthday, Patrick's family relocated to Duluth, Georgia, and he was forced to leave the business and part ways with his cofounder. While he was disappointed about abandoning the enterprise, he was confident that the next opportunity was just around the corner.

Throughout the remainder of his teenage years, Patrick focused his efforts on athletics, schoolwork, and developing new concepts. Partnering with another friend, he started a company that provided computer services to small businesses. Unlike his other initiatives, however, getting this one off the ground proved harder than anticipated. For the first time in Patrick's life, he found that his age worked against him—a burden that would foreshadow the next decade of his journey.

"Landing a client was the biggest obstacle," says Patrick. "When it comes to mowing grass, it's easy to take anyone seriously. But once you start dealing with businesses and technology, it becomes a much harder sell."

Still, Patrick pushed onward, and soon secured three significant clients, including American Sportsplex—the athletic facility where he trained.

It was the late nineties and digital technology had yet to become a pervasive force in American culture. Patrick recognized that a computer that allowed members to check themselves in could save the organization money by reducing the number of front desk staff they had to employ. The owner accepted Patrick's proposal and a deal was struck.

"Each facet of a business has a cost," says Patrick. "And it was at that point where I realized if I could save someone that money, I would become invaluable."

Like many of the previous challenges he'd faced, this, too, offered an important lesson: optimism plus persistence equals success.

Let your imagination go crazy, because that's where your budget is truly unlimited. It doesn't cost a cent to come up with a great marketing idea; it's the execution of that marketing idea that might be hard to afford.[14]
—Daymond

FROM IDEATION TO REVELATION

Patrick's parents were insistent that, no matter what career path he chose to pursue, earning a degree was an important milestone. While he understood their point of view, he also felt somewhat torn on the issue. Knowing that his interests lay in entrepreneurship, Patrick wasn't sure that a diploma would have much of a direct impact on his goals. On the other hand, he realized that college could potentially be an empowering experience. Since being diagnosed with dyslexia as a child, he has constantly felt a desire to prove himself.

"I'd been told from a very young age that I was never going to be accepted to a four-year university," says Patrick. "People said I'd never be successful at academics and that I should just find a trade craft."

While some may have been discouraged by that negative feedback, comments like those only encouraged Patrick to push harder. So when it came time for college, he didn't pursue just any school; he applied to the one place where he'd always dreamed of attending: Georgia Institute of Technology.

A revered university that's recognized for its engineering program, the celebrated institution is often ranked among the world's best colleges. Patrick knew getting accepted

would be no simple task, but he was committed to pursuing the quest with unrelenting fervor.

Insistent that Georgia Tech was the only "acceptable choice," he spent the latter portion of high school studying for his standardized tests, even signing up for practice classes and hiring a tutor to help him prepare. Moreover, he secured a copy of Georgia Tech's submission packet from the previous year, so that he might have a full twelve months to perfect his own application. He hoped that, with any luck, the questions would remain relatively static from year to year.

Patrick's labor paid off, and the high school senior was admitted for the following academic year. It was a triumph unlike any he'd ever known, but the battle had only just begun. The real test would be enduring the rigorous workload and graduating with passing grades.

"When the school year started I put all my other ambitions aside," says Patrick. "I wanted to be one hundred percent dedicated to succeeding in college, so all I did was study."

After successfully passing each of his freshman classes, Patrick's confidence increased, and soon he felt comfortable entertaining other interests. By the beginning of his sophomore year, his entrepreneurial tendencies were beginning to reemerge.

"I wanted to start a business that could grow into a multimillion dollar company by the time I graduated," says Patrick. "I had this vision of being the first undergraduate student to start a scholarship fund while still enrolled in school."

Hoping to boost the creative process, Patrick sat down with a large yellow legal pad and separated each page into

three distinct columns: high-level ideas, needs and requirements, and prospective rewards.

For days, he poured over the notepad, jotting down decades' worth of nascent business concepts. After reviewing the list and examining the full scope of each item, he chose the idea with what he perceived to be the most potential: an Alka-Seltzer-powered engine.

In high school, Patrick had crafted an initial prototype of the invention and, with just a bit of tweaking, thought it could "get people off their dependency on oil." Upon further investigation into the costs of research and development, however, he decided that building a sodium bicarbonate–based engine might be too ambitious a task for his first mission.

Sticking with the automotive theme, his next idea was to design a scented, antimicrobial air filter for cars and trucks— another concept he had first dreamed up during his adolescent years.

While riding to middle school in his dad's old Chevrolet Stingray one afternoon, Patrick noticed a musty smell coming from the air conditioner. He was curious as to the origin of such a noxious odor, and his father explained that it was caused by a bacterial growth on the filter. That got Patrick thinking. If he could design a filter that contained an antimicrobial property, it would prevent the formation of bacteria and "cut the smell at the source," which he had decided would be the product's slogan. But once again the invention proved too complicated to execute.

Frustrated by his general lack of progress, Patrick put down the legal pad and took a much-needed break from the ideation session. It was then that the revelation finally occurred. After happening upon a Band-Aid that contained a mysterious solidified gel, he was reminded of an idea that

he'd first contemplated while in grade school: weighted compression gear.

As a child, Patrick was always one of the skinniest boys in his class, which made him feel deeply insecure. With dreams of one day looking like Rocky Balboa, he would stuff his backpack full of extra books and do shoulder shrugs on the way to class.

"Rocky Balboa was a guy who could overcome any obstacle in his path," says Patrick. "And that really resonated with me, because that's what I wanted to be able to do."

Soon, however, he noticed that an overstuffed backpack did nothing more than deteriorate his posture and hurt his back. If he wanted to be "Rocky strong," he would need to come up with a better solution.

Throughout middle and high school, Patrick experimented with different techniques for designing the perfect training apparel. From lead-based threads to rubbers and silica, he underwent an exhaustive search to find the perfect material but found no such solution. But the tacky substance on the Band-Aid contained a material he had yet to explore: hydro-gel.

A solid yet gelatinous material with properties ranging from soft to firm, the hydro-gel could be used to create weighted inserts that, when strategically placed in each shirt, provided maximum stabilization without limiting one's range of motion. It appeared to be the perfect solution.

"There was just one problem," says Patrick. "Because it's a liquid gelatin, it takes on the properties of its container. This meant it would need a corrugated pouch or the material would just sag at the bottom."

For the next two years, Patrick devoted himself to researching various fabrics and methods of manufacturing.

Using YouTube, he taught himself to sew, and by the end of his junior year, he had successfully built an initial prototype.

"I made that first one on my grandmother's sewing machine," says Patrick. "It was incredibly ragged, but it proved to all the naysayers that the idea was sound. Sometimes people have to see something to believe in it."

In theory, he was confident the invention was sound, but could it actually enhance the training experience and help athletes achieve better results? Unbeknownst to Patrick, he was about to become his very own case study.

> The key to any successful new product launch is to start small. Aim too high right out of the gate and you're bound to come up short. Keep it simple and within reach, and at least you'll have some kind of shot.[15]
> —Daymond

AN UNFORTUNATE PROOF OF CONCEPT

During the summer before his final year at Georgia Tech, Patrick decided to wave good-bye to the dingy college dormitory and rent a place of his own off campus.

"I was going to be a senior," says Patrick. "And I wanted to finally feel like a real adult."

After a bit of researching, the soon-to-be college graduate found a one-bedroom apartment in the popular Midtown district of Atlanta—less than a mile from the university. It seemed like an ideal building.

Late in the evening on May 4, 2009, while Patrick was finishing up his move, a suspicious van pulled up next to

his car. At first he thought nothing of it, but that quickly changed when three armed teenagers jumped out of the vehicle. Before he had a moment to think, one of the gunmen pulled out a weapon, ordered him to the ground, and instructed that he surrender his wallet and cell phone.

"To be honest, at first I thought it was a joke," says Patrick. "But when he put the gun on my neck, I could feel the weight of the barrel and knew it was real. That's when I realized it was a situation where I could possibly lose my life."

It's likely the conflict would have ended there, but just as Patrick was forfeiting his belongings, two students, a male and a female, appeared from the elevator bank located adjacent to the van. The heist had been compromised.

In a moment of panic, the man with the gun rushed over to the couple while his partner directed Patrick to the van. Soon the assailants began harassing the young woman, rummaging through her purse and threatening her with the gun.

At the time, Patrick was a semipro bodybuilder and had just finished an intense workout. Standing six-foot-four and weighing 215 pounds, his body was coursing with adrenaline. As he watched the assault commence, he grew increasingly infuriated until, finally, he couldn't help but take charge.

"I started to make a commotion," says Patrick. "I was getting so frustrated that they were treating this girl with such disrespect. It got me so riled up."

As the TITIN founder approached the couple, one of the teenagers aimed a gun in Patrick's direction and barked at him to stand back. But it was it too late; the situation had escalated beyond control.

"He went to go pull the trigger, but the safety was on," says Patrick. "I didn't want to let him shoot at me twice, so

I reached out and grabbed on to his wrist, but the gun went off in my chest."

When Patrick arrived at the hospital, he learned that the bullet had gone through two lobes of his lungs, pierced his liver, and rushed through his inferior vena cava—the large vein that carries blood from the lower body to the heart. He had survived the attack but was critically injured.

Over the next few months, Patrick regularly attended physical therapy sessions but found the rehabilitation process to be painstakingly slow. After six weeks of recuperation, he was finally limber enough to wiggle his way into the prototype of his weighted compression shirt. If nothing else, he thought, this could be a good opportunity to test the effectiveness of the product.

"I would wear it for an hour every day," says Patrick. "And I saw more improvement in fourteen days with the shirt than I had during the previous six weeks of physical therapy. That's when I realized it wasn't just for athletes; it was for anyone who wanted to live a better life."

As his body began to heal, the young entrepreneur worked diligently to enhance the product, making improvements to the design and rebranding it to reflect the new direction. After going through a list of more than five hundred potential ideas, he changed the name from Omega Wear to TITIN—the word for the longest protein in the human body.

"My mom and I would play this game as a kid," says Patrick. "Whenever we'd pass a billboard or watch a commercial, she'd ask me whom I thought the ad was being targeted to and why. So when I was coming up with business ideas, I would always try to imagine how I could market them."

With a revitalized brand and elevated mission, he applied

for the Georgia Tech InVenture Prize—an interdisciplinary innovation competition hosted by the university—and won both first place and people's choice. Nicknamed "the American Idol for Nerds," the contest provided him with a cash prize of $20,000 and a slew of media attention, including one very influential feature on CNN.

Anticipating the broadcast would bring traffic to the site, Patrick designed a simple landing page that could collect the names and e-mail addresses of potential customers. In addition to the standard questions one might find on an opt-in form, however, users were also polled as to how much they might pay for such an invention. Still early in the development phase, Patrick hoped this type of market research would help him uncover the perceived value of the product and determine a realistic price point.

Motivated by his recent win and flurry of good press, the young founder began competing in pitch events at universities across the country. There was no doubt that TITIN had crossed a threshold, but Patrick still lacked the necessary funds required to bankroll the first round of production. So in the winter of 2011, he launched a presale campaign to raise money for an initial order. This, he thought, would be the most effective way to turn prospective interest into actual sales.

Using data he'd collected from the CNN newscast, Patrick sent a mass e-mail to his entire database with an exclusive preorder offer. Thirty-six hours later, TITIN had sold over one hundred units, grossing nearly $20,000. Organic traffic continued to trickle in throughout the year, and by the end of the summer, he had closed his first significant deal: 120 units to the University of Georgia's football team.

"I was ecstatic," says Patrick. "I negotiated that we could

use the brand to promote the product on our website. I knew that's what we needed to get other schools."

Money was starting to flow into the business, but it wasn't enough to stay afloat. Although his father had provided an initial investment, Patrick realized substantially more capital would be required to grow the organization.

"I had the same problem that almost every start-up has," says Patrick. "All my capital reserve was going to inventory. I never seemed to have any money left over."

Patrick began searching for an investor. And, after a series of tumultuous incidents and one particularly catastrophic fundraising round, he soon found himself swimming straight toward the Sharks.

> **SHARK BITE**
>
> *You start out as one thing and end up another. It happens all the time in every business. You have to be willing to adapt—and this needs to be part of a company's branding strategy.*[16]
> —Daymond

SCIENCE? FICTION?

Patrick's time in the tank wasn't his first experience negotiating with investors. During the previous year, TITIN had raised nearly $1 million from a UK-based investment group—a partnership that proved to be disastrous in just about every way imaginable.

As part of the deal, the outside firm brought in their own management and sales force which, according to Patrick, misappropriated funds and ran the organization straight into

the ground. In the end, he offered them a leveraged buyout—a transaction wherein a management team purchases a controlling share in a company using outside capital.

The conflict with the venture firm lasted for more than a year, during which time TITIN experienced relative growth. Still, Patrick was unimpressed with the external sales team's numbers and knew revenue could be higher.

"The sales force they brought in couldn't sell the product the way it needed to be sold," says Patrick. "It's an educated product that needs to be sold with an educated mind-set. They were trying to hawk it like it was just your everyday weight vest."

By the time his relationship with the investors had concluded, TITIN was in desperate need of new business. So Patrick hit the road, dedicating 100 percent of his time to acquiring wholesale accounts.

In only six weeks, the ambitious entrepreneur sold $2.5 million worth of product, increased organic web revenue tenfold, and locked a product placement deal in *The Expendables 3*. Patrick was on a roll, but it wasn't enough to stabilize cash flow. Buying out his previous partners had cost him a pretty penny, and he needed more capital to keep TITIN solvent.

A fan of *Shark Tank*, he applied for season six in early 2013. Just a few months later, he was on his way to Los Angeles for the pitch of a lifetime.

Patrick asked for $500,000 for 5 percent of the organization—valuating the business at a cool $10 million. Although TITIN only had $1.4 million in pending purchase orders, he was confident that year-end sales would reach between $10 and $16 million. It was a bold estimation, and one the Sharks didn't take lightly.

From the moment the pitch concluded, Mark Cuban began his attack, questioning the validity of the company's assertions and demanding that Patrick explain the science behind the elaborate claims.

"You're saying it's just like the old ankle weights that we used to wear when we were kids that make you feel lighter?" asked Mark. "You want to give me a valuation of ten million dollars for ankle weights?"

Surprised by Mark's aggressive tone, the nervous entrepreneur tried to maintain his cool while going more in-depth into

the research behind the data. His attempt proved futile, however, and it wasn't long before the pitch began spiraling downward. It was only when Kevin O'Leary brought up the issue of sales that the TITIN founder was able to regain his footing.

Patrick revealed that in the previous month, he had brought in $1 million in revenue and closed a deal with the largest medical distribution company in the United States. Impressed by the sales numbers, Daymond John wanted to know more about TITIN's history.

"In 2012, I actually closed a deal with a venture capitalist," said Patrick. "They decided it was in the best interest for us to bring in an executive chair. We burnt through the investment within six months."

Operating at 30 percent net profit and no longer carrying debt, Patrick shared that just two days prior, he had bought out his previous investors and was now completely independent. But losing nearly $1 million in just six months was a hard pill for the Sharks to swallow, and one by one, they began to lose interest.

"I'm struggling with your ten-million-dollar valuation," said Kevin O'Leary. "It's all based on you hitting a stratospheric growth rate. I have to pay for next year's sales as if they've already occurred today."

Patrick, however, would not have a chance to respond to the comment. Before he could reply, Mark abruptly went out, claiming his "BS meter" was going through the roof. Soon Lori Greiner and Robert Herjavec followed suit.

"You're straddling the line," said Robert. "Mark has real athletes, professional athletes, professional doctors. Either you're in that market with a tremendous amount of credibility . . . or this is purposely geared to the weekend athlete, like me."

With sales in the millions, Kevin saw things differently. TITIN, he explained, didn't belong in the sports category; it was a clothing company and carried "the same merits and risk of the apparel industry." Intrigued by the venture's growth, he offered Patrick $500,000 for 15 percent equity, decreasing the valuation by nearly $7 million.

"Your style sort of fits within the arrogant ass factor," said Kevin. "I'm okay with that. I'm not trying to make friends. You want a friend? Buy a dog. I'm trying to make money."

Kevin may have been able to spot TITIN's potential, but what he didn't see was that his comment had cost him the deal.

"Character is a driving force for me," says Patrick. "I had just gotten out of a relationship with an investor who'd always attack my character. The second Kevin said that, it was over."

Luckily, Mr. Wonderful wasn't the only Shark interested in making a deal. Daymond believed in the product and felt he could add particular value to the manufacturing and distribution processes. So he made the Millennial CEO an offer: $500,000 for 20 percent of the business.

Although Daymond requested a higher percentage of equity than Kevin had, Patrick felt he would make a better partner, especially since he offered to handle many of the inventory and production challenges that plagued the organization. The TITIN founder accepted the deal and left the tank with the capital he needed.

"I wanted a deal more than anything," says Patrick. "And I felt like Daymond really got what the company was all about."

> *Even when they're asleep, sharks are slipping through the ocean, swimming, scheming, getting ready to attack-- which is pretty much the approach you have to take when you're starting out in business. You have to be relentless, nimble, moving ever forward. No matter what.*[17]
> —Daymond

THE TITIN PLAYBOOK FOR SUCCESS

From achieving financial prosperity to scaling the operation on a global level, Patrick's personal definition of victory is multilayered and includes a plethora of internal and external milestones. Ultimately, however, he believes true success boils down to one thing: the ability to have an impact on the world.

"Success for me is making a difference in people's lives," says Patrick. "And that's what we're doing on a daily basis."

In the aftermath of *Shark Tank*, TITIN experienced a 100 percent increase in sales and continues to sell out of many of its most popular SKUs. Thanks to the help of Daymond John, the apparel company has been given numerous opportunities to amplify the brand and connect to a loyal community of advocates.

Today, TITIN is focused on expanding its product line and developing new ways to serve its growing base of avid consumers. Through it all, Patrick remains dedicated to leading the organization from a place of passion and integrity—two of the fundamental principles in his Playbook for Success.

TRUST YOUR GUT

In the eight years since the product was invented, TITIN has gone through various iterations—some more successful than others. While the business has experienced considerable change, Patrick has always tried to remain constant in his vision and loyal to his intuition.

"You have to make sure you're happy with yourself and the decisions you make," says Patrick. "As long as you're satisfied with your choices, you can always find a way to salvage a situation."

The TITIN founder first experienced this principle while negotiating with his original investors. Deep down, Patrick knew the transaction was flawed but chose to pursue the opportunity anyway, hoping the funds would soothe any lingering uncertainties. The result, of course, was just the opposite: a turbulent relationship that cost the organization copious amounts of time, energy, and money.

More than anything, the lesson he derived from that experience was how dangerous it can be to make decisions solely based on the desire to satisfy others.

"My grandma used to say that if you try to please everybody, you're not going to please anybody," says Patrick. "And you know what? She was absolutely right."

Get Passionate or Get Out

Talk about entrepreneurialism for long enough and the topic of stamina will inevitably arise. How do you "live and breathe the business" without burning out? Where do you find the energy and endurance to push onward when the going gets tough? While Patrick admits these can be challenging questions, for him, the answer is fairly straightforward.

"You have got to be passionate about your business," says Patrick. "Because if you're not, you won't ever be able to put in the full effort it requires."

To get TITIN off the ground, the young founder has made

tremendous sacrifices both in his personal and professional life. Although at times this can be a difficult way to live, Patrick remains motivated thanks to a deep desire to improve the lives of others.

"I'm passionate that there's a better way to train," says Patrick. "That's what inspired me to design and develop this product, and that's what keeps me going."

Build a Reliable Team

Delegation is a challenge for many entrepreneurs, especially those who are used to being actively engaged in all parts of the business. Running a company requires unparalleled focus and dedication, and it's natural to feel as though others may lack the same level of intensity or dedication that a founder brings to the venture. But Patrick has learned that, while taking on an abundance of roles may be an effective temporary solution, in the long run it only leads to regret and fatigue.

"Doing a little bit of everything can work when you're still in the early stages," says Patrick. "But as the company grows you're going to find yourself strapped for time."

When building a team, Patrick looks for people he can believe in—those who understand the business and subscribe to the company's mission. What's more, he tries to find employees with a broad range of talents and abilities that round out his skill set.

"You have to sit down and ask yourself: what is it that you do better than anyone else?" says Patrick. "For all other tasks, you should hire A-players who can do it for you. That's the only way a business ever reaches its full potential."

Understand the Role of Timing

Coming up with new and original concepts has never been much of a challenge for Patrick; the young inventor has been dreaming up ideas for most of his life. But it takes more than innovation to make a product successful. As any accomplished

founder will reveal, timing plays a critical role in one's ability to prevail.

When Patrick began working on TITIN, he saw that production would be his greatest challenge.

"I spent all the time and energy trying to manufacture something that couldn't be done at scale," says Patrick. "Eventually I realized that I would need to create a whole new manufacturing process."

Exasperated by this development, he placed TITIN on a temporarily hold and began brainstorming more practical solutions.

"I hoped that maybe at some point there would be a machine or piece of fabric that could solve it," says Patrick. "Much like I had to wait for the solidified hydro-gel, I had to wait for the technology to catch up to my idea."

As he's gained more experience, Patrick has found this to be a frequent challenge for inventors and one that is often difficult to accept.

"Even if you have a great idea, sometimes the technology just isn't there," says Patrick. "It can be incredibly frustrating when you're trying to build a new product."

Keep Your Eye on the Prize

While the TITIN founder considers himself to be a highly optimistic person, he's experienced plenty of hardships along the way. And it's in those moments—the turbulent ones—where Patrick relies heavily on his fifth and final principle.

"You always have to focus on the end goal," says Patrick. "Otherwise you're going to lose your way and get off target."

From regaining his health after a near-fatal act of violence to overcoming the daily trials and tribulations of running a business, Patrick's spirit remains strong thanks to an unyielding determination to carry out his long-term vision for the organization—one that has progressed with each new year.

"Your goal doesn't have to be unwavering," says Patrick.

"It can change from year to year or quarter to quarter. What's important is that you have a goal and always keep it in mind."

In addition to establishing quarterly goals, the TITIN founder often considers where the company will be five or even ten years down the line. Sure, the course will likely shift, but focusing on a perceived destination allows him to remain motivated and inspired, especially in moments of chaos.

"This is probably the most useful principle any entrepreneur can practice," says Patrick. "You always have to be able to see the forest through the trees."

CHAPTER FIVE

INVESTOR: **KEVIN O'LEARY**

COMPANY: Wicked Good Cupcakes

FOUNDERS: Tracey Noonan and Danielle Vilagie

THE FAMILY THAT BAKES TOGETHER MAKES TOGETHER

When picturing the typical family business, one might envision a tiny operation on some out-of-the-way street in a humble, quiet town—maybe a restaurant or nail salon. The reality, however, is very different. In fact, there are roughly 5.5 million family-run companies in the United States, which contribute 57 percent of the GDP (i.e., $8.3 trillion) and employ over 60 percent of the workforce.[18] In other words, family business is big business. And nobody knows this better than the mother-and-daughter team behind Boston-based bakery Wicked Good Cupcakes.

Tracey Noonan and her daughter Danielle Vilagie appeared on season four of *Shark Tank* and made a deal with Kevin O'Leary for $75,000. Less than a year later, their venture had experienced unprecedented growth, and today boasts sales in the millions.

To many onlookers, this could be seen as one of those fabled tales of overnight success—an instantaneous triumph. But the true story behind Wicked Good Cupcakes' fascinating ascent to greatness is deeply complex and far less conventional than most people realize.

FROM BALLET TO BAKING

Growing up in Milton, Massachusetts—a well-to-do suburb just outside the city limits of Boston—Tracey Noonan

always felt a little different. The eldest of three siblings, she resisted the priggish "country club life" relished by her parents and brothers. Instead, she gravitated more toward artistic endeavors like music, theater, and dance. By age thirteen, those interests had developed into passions. But passion, as she soon learned, is not always met with enthusiasm.

As the sole daughter of two "very traditional parents," Tracey's creative aspirations clashed with family expectations. If she were going to achieve her goals, it would be up to her and her alone to make them happen.

In an effort to earn money, the young entrepreneur went door-to-door, pitching babysitting services to neighbors and friends of the family. It wasn't long before she had saved up enough to enroll in the Boston School of Ballet. It was through this experience that Tracey first learned the intrinsic value of independence and the true cost self-reliance—a lesson that would stay with her for years to come.

"That's where I would go every day after school," says Tracey. "Milton is the first town outside of Boston, so I would get on the train and head straight to the city."

When it came time to attend college, Tracey had but one goal: to attend a performing arts college and pursue a degree in dance. Once again, however, a lack of family support stood in the way.

"My dad told me that I didn't need to go to college because I was a girl," says Tracey. "And that was really devastating because I was at an all-girls high school and everyone else was going."

But the ambitious teenager persisted, and eventually her father relented—with one condition: he would help pay for college only if she pursued a nursing or secretarial career.

Not surprisingly, Tracey refused, and once again decided to take matters into her own hands.

"I auditioned for performing arts schools without telling anyone," says Tracey. "Luckily, I got into the Boston Conservatory of Music with a scholarship. My parents weren't happy about me going, but they knew they couldn't stop me."

Tracey excelled at the conservatory and was on track to become a professional dancer; she even got the opportunity to perform with the renowned Boston Lyric Opera. But shortly before graduation, Tracey became pregnant and was forced to reevaluate her future.

"I didn't have to look very far to see that there weren't many pregnant ballerinas on tour," says Tracey.

Certain her career as a dancer was over, she dropped out of school and married her high school sweetheart. It wasn't the future she had expected, but the new mother was committed to making it work.

Without dance in her life, Tracey felt an artistic void and started to search for a creative outlet that could be both personally fulfilling and professionally rewarding. It was then that she discovered photography and began making plans to launch her first real business.

With little training or means, Tracey faced an array of immediate challenges, many of which would have deterred a less motivated person. But instead of backing down she doubled down, doing anything it took to achieve her goal.

"I had no training, and I couldn't pay for school," says Tracey. "But I knew that if I worked for someone I could learn on the job and from there start my own thing. So that's exactly what I did."

After just a couple of years working for other photographers, Tracey set out on her own and quickly became one of Boston's most sought-after commercial photographers. But the revelry didn't last for long.

The mid-nineties were fast approaching and digital photography was beginning to dominate the trade. Technology had disrupted the industry, and Tracey found herself on the wrong side of history. Within only a few short years of starting the business, her fast-growing enterprise had become all but irrelevant.

"I became a dinosaur overnight," says Tracey. "I knew nothing about technology, and even if I did, I wouldn't have been able to afford to make the switch. Back then, entry-level digital photography equipment started at fifty thousand dollars. I lost all my clients."

Tracey felt overwhelmed but had no time to let grief stand in the way. She had just gone through a challenging divorce and was raising two small children on her own. Once again, she faced a crossroads and had no choice but to reinvent.

Over the next ten years, Tracey started a series of small businesses—some more successful than others. She sold real estate, got her massage license, and wrote screenplays. At one point she even owned and operated an animal talent agency. (Author's note: should you ever run into Tracey, be sure to ask about the piano-playing pig.)

While her career might have been in flux, her personal life was flourishing. In 1996, she met and eventually married her current husband Scott Noonan and focused on raising her family. Tracey cherished the time she spent time with her children and was particularly close to her younger daughter, Danielle.

Like her mother, Danielle often felt different from the

other kids her age. Artistic and highly creative, she had gone to college for graphic design but dropped out after losing interest in the career.

"I just really wasn't getting a feel for it," says Danielle. "So I just kind of bowed out and started to think about other things I could do."

In late 2009, Danielle got engaged and left the family home to live with her fiancé. Nervous the move might jeopardize the close relationship she had developed with her daughter, Tracey suggested they sign up for a weekly cake-decorating class at a bakery near their home.

"It was honestly just an excuse to see her once a week," says Tracey. "At the time we were watching the show *Ace of Cakes*, and I thought it looked like a lot of fun."

Neither mother nor daughter could ever have guessed just how transformative that humble cake-decorating course would become.

SHARK BITE

Here's the cold, hard truth: no matter how much money you make, the world is designed to take it away. Right from the day you're born, your money is under siege.[19]
—Kevin

A WICKED GOOD IDEA

By the end of the first class, it was clear that Tracey and Danielle had found an enjoyable new hobby. But even more than that, they seemed to possess a natural talent for the craft. Sure,

they had casually baked together before, but this was the first time they'd attempted anything so elaborate. Both women were surprised at just how well their desserts turned out.

"I can still remember that first day of class," says Scott. "I came home late from work and there was a white fondant cake sitting on the island in the kitchen. I couldn't believe how professional it looked."

Scott wasn't the only one to recognize their abilities. Tracey began posting pictures on social media and the positive feedback came pouring in. Soon friends and family were commissioning the mother-and-daughter team to cater parties and small events.

"When I first started posting pictures on Facebook, it was never to solicit business," says Tracey. "But right away people started ordering."

Although Tracey was delighted by the attention, what she found most inspiring was how this new hobby seemed to impact her daughter. For the first time in recent history, Danielle seemed to be truly passionate about something. Like most parents, it was exactly what Tracey had always hoped her daughter might one day discover.

Over the next few months, the duo spent nights and weekends fulfilling orders and perfecting new recipes. They called the enterprise Cranberry Coast Cupcakes and continued marketing on social media. But it wasn't until May of 2010 that they got their first real taste of what was to come.

In a few short days, the company received two of their largest orders ever for back-to-back events—one for 500 cupcakes and the other for 250 cupcakes. While they normally would have been excited by such a large sale, instead they were petrified. Tracey was scheduled to be out of the country during the week of both events, which meant Danielle would

be responsible for overseeing the production and delivery of all 750 cupcakes.

"It was a disaster," says Danielle. "Our small convection oven could only bake two dozen cupcakes at a time, so I had to work around the clock. I called two friends and we just baked all weekend."

Although the experience was exhausting, Danielle pulled it off and the cupcakes were a huge hit. It wasn't long before they were partnering with local organizations and receiving larger, more intricate orders.

But as the business grew, Tracey started to have second thoughts about the name. She didn't feel Cranberry Coast Cupcakes captured the essence of the brand. It needed to have more personality—something memorable and fun that could be uniquely their own. So one afternoon, between batches of baked goods, she sat down at the kitchen table with a notepad and began to brainstorm.

"The first name I loved was Pink Monkey," says Tracey. "But that name was already taken by a chain of strip clubs, so that was out."

Eventually, she came up with Wicked Good Cupcakes—a play on the popular Boston colloquialism "wicked." The next day, she and Scott trademarked the name and filed the necessary incorporation paperwork. Wicked Good Cupcakes was now a legitimate enterprise.

With a catchy name, a new brand image, and a steady flow of customers, Tracey and Danielle felt it was time to take the company to the next level. So in the winter of 2010, after being chosen to appear on the cover of a local New Hampshire magazine, they organized their next move: the opening of a flagship retail location.

Tracey's husband Scott was thrilled by the idea. He loved

that his wife and stepdaughter had found something they could build together and saw tremendous potential in the concept.

"I spent about a month doing market research and putting together a business plan to test viability," says Scott. "And when I was finished I saw that this could be a legitimate business."

Scott recognized it would require a considerable investment to get the retail operation off the ground, so he offered them a $50,000 loan—$30,000 of which could be allocated for the build-out and the remaining $20,000 to be used for working capital, once the store was up and running. With a fleshed-out business plan and money in the bank, the trio began searching for their first storefront.

Instead of launching in Boston proper, they felt it wiser to open on the South Shore. The cupcake industry was booming, and the city was already saturated with bakeries. By setting up shop just outside of town, they could bypass much of the competition and slowly build their fan base while gaining crucial experience.

Ten painstaking months and one 800-page lease later, Wicked Good Cupcakes officially opened its doors in Cohasset, Massachusetts on October 1, 2011. Thanks to some local press, a well-placed grand opening sign, and a lack of viable competition in the area, the business was an immediate hit. But the mother-and-daughter team were in way over their heads.

"It was absolutely crazy," says Tracey. "On that first day there was a line out the door before we even opened. By two P.M. I wanted to quit."

The plan had always been for Tracey and Danielle to run the shop together and, when the time was right, to hire an

additional employee, maybe two. But after putting in over one hundred hours of backbreaking work during the first week, it was clear they needed to reevaluate their strategy. Within weeks, they had hired five part-time employees.

"I look back at those early days and realize how stupid we were in thinking that running a bakery would be easy," says Tracey. "But if we had known then just how hard it was going to be, I'm not sure we would have done it. It really was a case of ignorance is bliss."

Although Scott had yet to come on board as CEO, he was deeply committed to the company's success and was already thinking about how to grow the operation. As the cofounder and CTO of a highly successful digital agency, he was a technology expert and believed investing in e-commerce would be the most efficient way to achieve scalability.

"I'd always thought the long-term play would be online because you can cast a wide net and reach a national audience," says Scott. "So I began researching packaging solutions. I even tried to engineer one of my own."

Shipping a cupcake, however, proved more difficult than it seemed. Then, late one evening, while mindlessly flipping through channels on the TV, Scott turned to a special on canning and had an epiphany. Wicked Good Cupcakes could use glass jars to ship its product. Not only would it preserve the ingredients, but it would offer a new take on a classic dessert. He was sure it would be a huge hit.

Tracey, on the other hand, was less convinced. At that point, Wicked Good Cupcakes was known for its elaborate designs and custom-made creations. Would stuffing their high-quality confections into jars hurt their reputation? Tracey wasn't confident it was the right move, but she was willing to giving it a try.

"My goal from the beginning was just for the online sales to cover the cost of rent," says Scott. "To do that we needed to sell thirty jars each day."

They launched the e-commerce operation on December 1, 2011. Two days later, they had sold a measly three jars. Five days after that, they were still in the single digits. But then, on December 10, less than two weeks after going live, they sold thirty-six jars—six more than their daily goal. It was then that Scott realized the idea had real promise and could potentially become a viable part of the enterprise.

As the holidays approached, customers began buying cupcake jars as gifts for friends and family, including one student from Salem State who purchased two for his professor. It was a sale that would alter the entire course of the business.

"I'll never forget that order," says Tracey. "We used to handwrite each note, and I still remember writing that card."

On December 27, 2011, while returning home from holiday travel, the Salem State professor was stopped by the TSA at McCarran International Airport and forced to surrender the jar. But before giving up her coveted dessert, the instructor snapped a picture of the TSA agent holding the cupcake and posted it on her blog.

Within only a few days, the popular site Boing Boing had picked up the piece, and it soon spread. Tickled by the incident and recognizing it as a potential marketing opportunity, Tracey called the local news channel and suggested they feature the story. They loved the idea, and overnight their coverage went viral, appearing on national late night talk shows and daytime news programs.

"We were deemed a national security threat by the TSA,"

says Tracey. "The Department of Homeland Security was on our website two hundred times in the next month."

It was the kind of press every entrepreneur dreams of getting, and just like that the small business went from selling an average of thirty jars a day to one hundred and twenty-five. Without a fulfillment center or dedicated online team, Tracey and Danielle had to shift into overdrive.

A few weeks later, the TSA released an official statement on the incident, saying the product "wasn't your everyday, run-of-the-mill cupcake." With Valentine's Day just around the corner—one of Wicked Good Cupcakes' busiest times of the year—they'd hit the PR jackpot. Business had never been better.

> **SHARK BITE**
>
> *I've discovered that money is the most forgiving energy on the planet. The second you begin to make even the most minor positive adjustments to your spending, saving, or investment habits, money begins to flow back to you.*[20]
>
> —Kevin

IN THE PRESENCE OF ROYALTY

With booming sales and a steady dose of national press, Tracey and Danielle were more motivated than ever to grow the operation. But they faced one major challenge: material costs.

Although sales were on the incline, they were still a new enterprise with a relatively conservative budget. This

prevented them from taking full advantage of bulk purchasing prices, which in turn meant steep variable costs—those that fluctuate relative to a company's output. In other words, they faced what is an all-too-common catch-22 for many small businesses: they were not large enough to gain access to better pricing—but without that preferred pricing they would never expand to the size where they could afford it.

Having watched *Shark Tank* since its premiere, Tracey and Danielle knew that an investment from one of the Sharks could help solve this dilemma. So in April of 2012, Tracey logged on to the show's website and applied.

"The TSA incident really gave me the confidence I needed," says Tracey. "It made me feel like our product was unique enough to stand out and that we could do well on the show."

Getting on *Shark Tank* is an elaborate process and doesn't always follow one specific formula. Some entrepreneurs attend an open call while others are scouted at trade shows or local events. Tracey chose to fill out an online application and submit a video. Just five days later, the casting manager got in touch.

Over the next few months, the duo had weekly phone meetings with the casting team to brainstorm and develop their pitch. Like every founder who appears on the show, a strong presentation is crucial to landing a deal.

"We practiced our pitch ad nauseam," says Tracey. "I still remember drilling it over and over again as we baked cupcakes and put together jars."

After much preparation, they were invited to fly out to Los Angeles and tape an episode. Tracey and Danielle had just two weeks to get ready.

"I was so pumped," says Danielle. "I had never been to

Los Angeles before, and now I was getting the chance to visit *and* be on a television show."

When it came time to present, the mother-and-daughter team made its way into the tank and confidently began their pitch. They asked for $75,000 for 20 percent of the company, valuing the business at $375,000. Although they had only sold $150,000 worth of cupcakes, their projected annual sales was $360,000.

The presentation went off without a hitch, and the product seemed to resonate with the Sharks. But it wasn't entirely smooth sailing; each investor had his or her own list of potential concerns.

Since it's impossible to patent the process of putting cake into a jar, Kevin O'Leary was curious how they planned to protect themselves against copycats, especially now that they were appearing in front of millions of people on national television.

Lori Greiner, on the other hand, was worried about the limited shelf life. Because Wicked Good Cupcakes never uses preservatives, the product remains fresh for only seven to ten days. Lori was worried this would prevent the enterprise from ever being truly scalable.

What the Sharks found most troublesome, however, were the narrow margins. At the time of air, it cost $2.15 to make just one small jar and even more for the larger sizes. This, the investors believed, posed a substantial threat to their long-term profitability. Tracey had anticipated this might be a concern and revealed how, with a capital infusion, she could bring the cost down to $1.45 per cupcake jar.

"We need more money to buy in bulk," said Tracey. "That's why we're here."

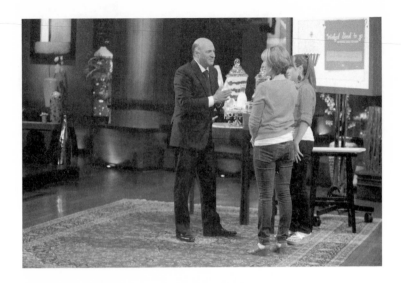

With a taste for the product and a clear understanding of the company's trajectory, it was time for the Sharks to get down to business.

Before the negotiations even began, Robert Herjavec went out, claiming his healthy lifestyle and disinterest in sweets would make him a bad partner. Daymond John, conversely, felt he would have the opposite problem. With a voracious sweet tooth, he liked the product too much and was concerned that becoming an investor would wreak havoc on his waistline. For that reason, he also decided to remove himself from the bidding process.

Lori Greiner and Mark Cuban went out next, citing concerns with shelf life and a lack of expertise in the space, respectively. With only one Shark remaining, Tracey and Danielle began to feel the pressure mount.

"At that point we were starting to panic," says Tracey. "Kevin was the only Shark remaining and never in a million years did we think he would invest in us."

Their assumption, however, was incorrect. Kevin had taken a liking to the product and was interested in making a deal. But there was one catch. He offered to give them $75,000, but he didn't want any equity. Instead, he proposed a royalty deal. Wicked Good Cupcakes would pay him one dollar per cupcake until he recouped his initial investment and then fifty cents per cupcake in perpetuity. It wasn't the deal Tracey and Danielle had anticipated, but they liked the idea of maintaining full control.

After a brief negotiation, Kevin agreed to reduce the long-term royalty to forty-five cents and Tracey and Danielle accepted the offer. The rest, as they say, is history.

"At the time, everyone said the deal was a disaster, but it has actually been one of the most successful in *Shark Tank* history," says Kevin. "This is a family business. There's no room for a non-blood relative to have equity. Today, the family still owns one hundred percent of the company."

SHARK BITE

> Negotiations may take time, but the most important moments are always at the beginning. Everything matters here, from your body language to the way you dress to the way you start out the discussion. Establish your credibility by showing the other party that you're not a bad use of their time.[21]
> —Kevin

A CUPCAKE EMPIRE IS BORN

Wicked Good Cupcakes' episode aired on April 26, 2013, and immediately sales began to soar.

"We really had no idea what to expect," says Scott. "All

of a sudden, orders just started coming in like a tsunami. It was incredible to watch."

While nobody could have anticipated the massive influx of traffic, Tracey, Danielle, and Scott had spent the previous eight months putting systems in place to prepare for a potential surge. From technology to infrastructure, the team was ready for anything. They even hired an outside firm to serve as co-baker for orders that couldn't be fulfilled in-house.

"That process was actually a bit of a nightmare," says Tracey. "A lot of the bakeries we met with refused to follow our recipes and insisted we use generic mixes. That was a deal-breaker."

But quality wasn't the only issue they had to consider. Wicked Good Cupcakes are always prepared fresh, which meant they needed a facility that could bake, pack, and ship the product all in a centralized location. Typically, most vendors only manage one or two parts of the process.

After hours of research, they managed to find a co-baker who was capable of handling the nontraditional request. Today, they still rely heavily on their vendors.

"We absolutely love the company we work with now," says Tracey. "The owner is a classically trained pastry chef from Paris and he really cares about our product. I can't begin to explain how good of a job he does."

Thanks to their careful preparation, Wicked Good Cupcakes was able to take full advantage of the astonishing buzz their episode generated. Not only did they manage to fulfill each new order, they remained on schedule and within budget—no easy feat considering the speed and intensity of their growth.

Within twenty-four hours of appearing on *Shark Tank*, the company sold 7,500 cupcakes jars—7,454 more units

than the forty-six they had sold the day before. A week later, that number had climbed to eighteen thousand units.

"After the spike we saw a pretty good tail for about six weeks before it leveled off," says Scott. "But where it eventually leveled was far beyond anything we had before. To this day we're still experiencing month-over-month growth."

As the enterprise continued to expand, it faced a bevy of unique challenges. *Shark Tank* had provided the growth needed to stabilize the business, but it was time to scale the operation. To help facilitate this new direction, Scott left his job at the agency he had cofounded and joined Wicked Good Cupcakes as CEO.

One of his first tasks was to close the Cohasset bakery that had first put the company on the map. They had recently opened a kiosk location at Faneuil Hall—the seventh largest tourist attraction in the world—that exclusively sold cupcake jars. Maintaining a small local bakery no longer aligned with the larger strategy.

"The business model had obviously changed. We were now an e-commerce company," says Scott. "It just didn't make sense to allocate so many resources to bake for a daily case."

Clearly the new strategy is working. Wicked Good Cupcakes boasts sales in the millions and is a shining example of a prosperous family business. Not only is the organization massively successful, but each team member has found a role that fits their skills and interests.

Danielle handles the daily operations, manages the employees, and runs logistics. Tracey is responsible for marketing, branding, and developing the overarching creative vision. And Scott oversees the "general infrastructure" of the business, including financials, supply chain management, and vendor relationships.

Kevin O'Leary also remains an active partner, advising on key moves and providing Wicked Good Cupcakes with priceless PR opportunities. It's thanks to him, the team says, that they are on track to become a household name.

"At O'Leary Ventures, my team and I are always thinking about what we can do to elevate Wicked," says Kevin. "I'll do anything in my power to increase sales because our interests are totally aligned."

> It's hard to be self-critical. This is especially true for entrepreneurs, since you need confidence to take risks. But it's because you take such risks, often with your family's money, that you owe it to yourself to face up to your strengths and weaknesses.[22]
> —Kevin

THE WICKED GOOD CUPCAKES PLAYBOOK FOR SUCCESS

There's no doubt that appearing on *Shark Tank* greatly helped Wicked Good Cupcakes grow its brand and business. But it takes more than appearing on national television to be successful.

"A lot of people think that just because you get on the show you'll be successful," says Scott. "What they don't understand is that it's an opportunity. And like any opportunity, you can either make the most of it or screw it up."

In order to achieve sustainable success, Wicked Good Cupcakes has developed and cultivated a series of basic philosophies that, combined, keep the organization on track and have become a critical part of their Playbook for Success.

KNOW THE DIFFERENCE BETWEEN WILL AND WANT

In the early stages of starting or growing a company, it's common to feel a slightly euphoric sense of invincibility. With a seemingly endless reserve of inspiration, the newly minted entrepreneur may feel as though he or she can muscle through any challenge. But the team behind Wicked Good Cupcakes believes there's a difference between determination and perseverance.

"Having the will to succeed isn't enough," says Scott. "That eventually wears off. But if you have the 'want,' you'll always be able to break through those sixteen-hour days."

For Tracey, the "want" is about producing the very best cupcake she can. For Scott, it's the day-to-day process that feels the most meaningful.

"I'm not super passionate about a cupcake itself," says Scott. "But I *am* super passionate about growing a company that people love. My 'want' is to make every single customer happy."

This principle impacted Danielle both personally and professionally as a first-time entrepreneur, especially during the initial stages of building the business.

"Those early days were super hard," says Danielle. "My friends didn't understand why I couldn't hang out as much. I really had to give the company all of my attention."

The Wicked Good Cupcakes team believes in this concept so much, they've even coined their own spin on a popular adage: "if there's a *want*, there's a way."

Assess Whether You Can Be the Best in the World

No matter what kind of enterprise you choose to build, there's bound to be a steady dose of cutthroat competition, which in reality can actually end up being a positive thing. A competitive market proves there's a built-in need for your product or

service. Without it, you'd be creating an entirely new category, and that means it's your job to educate the consumer—a costly and time-intensive task.

In order to stand out from the crowd, the Wicked Good Cupcakes team believes you must first determine whether you're capable of being the best in the world. And, like many small-business owners, they often had to learn that the hard way.

"When we first had success with the cupcake jar, I foolishly thought we could expand into brownies," says Scott. "It seemed like a no-brainer."

But the brownies were a flop, and Scott immediately recognized he had broken his own rule. Being the best in the world isn't just about making a great product; it's about being the best at all aspects of selling a product.

"There are eight billion people trying to do brownies," says Scott. "Of course we couldn't be the very best at selling them."

So how do you decipher whether your concept is capable of achieving that coveted world-class status? The first step is to develop a keen knowledge of the marketplace and to honestly assess whether your idea has the potential to stand out. Next you must identify what Tracey, Danielle, and Scott refer to as "the acquisition differentiator."

"What is it that you do that nobody else does?" says Scott. "Your customers should be able to figure this out on their own. You shouldn't have to tell them."

For Wicked Good Cupcakes, the glass jar has become their primary acquisition differentiator. This, along with their inventive flavors and clever branding, has helped them attract attention and become one of the best in the business.

Control Your Costs (or They'll Control You)

Most successful companies are started in order to solve a problem in the market. But coming up with a creative solution

to a common challenge is only the first part of developing a company. Next you must determine if your idea has the potential to make a profit.

"It sounds so simple," says Scott. "But ninety-five percent of small businesses fail because they don't spend enough time looking at the numbers."

From material costs and payroll fees to run rates and employee salaries, Wicked Good Cupcakes keeps a constant watch on where and how they spend money. While it may sound obvious, it was a practice that took considerable time to adopt.

Shortly after opening the Cohasset bakery, their accountant called with some very disturbing news. They only had $1,100 left in the bank and were on track to run out of money in two weeks.

Tracey and Danielle were stunned by the news. They were actively bringing in revenue, and by all accounts the organization was doing well. But they hadn't been keeping a close eye on their costs and were unaware of their daily, weekly, and monthly spend.

At the time, Scott was the sole investor, not the CEO, and he was forced to sit down with the cofounders for a tough conversation. He told them that he wouldn't be providing the company with any additional capital. They would either have to find a way to control their costs or close up shop.

"That was a really bad day," says Tracey. "We had to lay off some of our staff for a short period of time and run everything ourselves until we could get it all figured out."

After three months of closely monitoring each dollar that went in and out of the business, they uncovered their problem areas and took immediate action to rectify the situation.

"It was a defining moment for the company," says Scott. "Like many start-ups, they had been so focused on gaining revenue that they had forgotten to control their costs."

Make the Most of Each Failure

Like death and taxes, there's no escaping the occasional failure. Whether you're a first time founder or a seasoned veteran, you're bound to make mistakes—and it's up to you to determine how to fix them.

Since Wicked Good Cupcakes' inception, Tracey has made "many, many mistakes," but she's learned to lessen the blow by following a simple three-step process.

First she makes a conscious effort to face the incident head-on and experience the full gravity of the incident. No matter how big or small, she never denies or diminishes the situation.

"It has to really hurt," says Tracey. "Maybe you've let somebody down or you've hurt your business. Either way, you have to really feel that hurt."

Next she takes immediate action to right the wrong, or at the very least minimize the blunder.

"There's no time to lay blame or point fingers," says Tracey. "You just have to focus on immediately getting the problem solved."

The final and perhaps most important step is the hardest to master and one that many never learn: self-forgiveness.

"You have to give yourself permission to move past it," says Tracey. "Don't forget the lesson you learned, but don't dwell on the failure, either."

Remain Flexible with Your Vision

When Tracey and Danielle first considered turning their newfound hobby into a business, the vision was simple: sell enough product to one day open a small bakery on the South Shore. Today, Wicked Good Cupcakes is far from small and anything but local.

This highlights an important principle that can be challenging for even the most experienced small-business owner to adopt. In order to stay relevant, a company must constantly evolve—and that means maintaining a flexible vision. When

coaching young entrepreneurs, Scott often analogizes this concept to organizing a road trip.

"Let's say I get a bus and ask a small group of people to come on board," says Scott. "I can't tell them where we're going, what their role will be, or even how long it will take. But what I can tell them is that every single one of us will benefit by the time we reach our destination."

Having owned and operated a wide range of ventures, Tracey knows that staying flexible isn't easy, especially when passion gets in the way of logic.

"You have to be smart enough to know when to change course," says Tracey. "A lot of people get stuck on one idea and can't admit that the business might be better if they go in another direction. You can't hang on to something that isn't working."

CHAPTER SIX

INVESTOR: **BARBARA CORCORAN**

COMPANY: Grace and Lace

FOUNDERS: Rick Hinnant and Melissa Hinnant

SEASON: Five

THESE BOOTS ARE MADE FOR SOCKING

Behind every flourishing business is a story—one of passion, prosperity, and success. For Rick and Melissa Hinnant, however, the tale is a bit more complicated and begins not with triumph but tragedy.

In 2010, the couple experienced one of the greatest traumas of their life: the loss of their unborn daughter. Married for only two years, they found themselves facing a challenge the likes of which they had never known. But through hope, faith, and a little good fortune, the resilient husband and wife transformed excruciating heartbreak into vibrant opportunity and, in the process, changed the lives of countless people around the world.

Rick and Melissa appeared on season five of *Shark Tank* and made a deal with Barbara for $175,000 in exchange for 25 percent equity of Grace and Lace—an Austin, Texas–based apparel company that sells high-quality, on-trend knits and clothing.

How did they overcome such grief and sadness? Where did they find the courage to choose optimism over despair? The answers, of course, are woven deep within their narrative and have become a central part of their life and business.

ONCE LOST, NOW FOUND

Rick Hinnant was one of those kids you could never forget. Strong-willed and wildly ambitious, he was on a constant quest to find the next big adventure. From selling coffee cups and "other knickknacks" as a small child to launching a landscape business in middle school, the Texas native was drawn to entrepreneurialism from an early age.

"I've been starting businesses since the fourth or fifth grade," says Rick. "I was never afraid to knock on a door or pick up a phone. It was always fun for me."

His passions, however, were not strictly limited to commerce. A natural-born athlete, he was a top-ranked tennis player and was even sponsored by Wilson Tennis Racquets— a leading industry brand. Whether scoring a point on the court or landing a sale in the neighborhood, Rick, it seemed, was destined for success.

Melissa, on the other hand, had a different vision in mind for her future. The daughter of two enterprising parents, she saw firsthand what it took to run a company.

"I grew up in a very successful family," says Melissa. "From as far back as I can remember, everyone has been entrepreneurial in some way or another."

While inspired by her family's accomplishments, she had no interest in pursuing the same goals. For Melissa, the dream was to grow up, get married, and raise a family. Until that day arrived, she devoted her time and energy to her second passion: philanthropy.

"I've always been called to charity and mission work," says Melissa. "From the age of thirteen, I spent every summer in a foreign country working with the poorest of poor."

Throughout high school and college, Rick and Melissa led divergent lives. Melissa continued to focus on philanthropy

and eventually relocated from Michigan to East Texas to work for the missionary group she had volunteered with as a teenager.

Melissa was passionate about the work and inspired by the group's mission of providing volunteer opportunities in impoverished communities around the world. When the organization offered to pay for her college tuition after just a year of employment, she knew she'd found the perfect job.

Just a few cities away, Rick attended the University of Texas at Austin, where he majored in kinesiology with plans of becoming a doctor. But things were not as sublime as they might have looked on paper. The reality was that he was not the slightest bit interested in medicine. In fact, he abhorred seeing people in pain and would often pass out at the mere site of blood. Rick had chosen the major only after a high school guidance counselor suggested it would be the best way to make a living while maintaining his independence. Needless to say, he never did make it to medical school.

In the years following college, Rick's feelings of purposelessness began to take a toll on his mental health. He had lost the fire and determination that had defined his youth, and he desperately wanted it back. With no real prospects in site, he took a series of odd jobs and even tried his luck at an acting career, but nothing seemed to fit.

"It was a scary point in my life," says Rick. "I didn't know how to do what I wanted to do, and I was absolutely miserable."

There was more to this restlessness, however, than a mere lack of direction. Years of bad habits and too much partying had left him feeling empty and out of control. If he didn't make a dramatic change, Rick felt as though he may never build the career and life he'd always wanted.

Then, in October of 1996, shortly after returning home from a raucous night of drinking and carousing at a local bar, Rick got down on his knees and started to pray—something he hadn't done in years.

"God, I think I'm blowing it," he said. "I don't know what it means to be a man. Can you help me? Will you forgive me?"

The next morning Rick awoke a changed person. It was as though the destructive habits and negative behaviors he had developed over the years had evaporated into thin air. He was back on track and determined not to let anything slow him down.

Over the next five years, Rick found a supportive group of friends who provided necessary guidance and mentorship. He started a handful of successful companies, which netted him a large amount of money by the time he'd reached his late twenties. But after one of his most ambitious ventures failed to succeed, he fell into a downward financial spiral and soon found himself more than $80,000 in debt. The timing couldn't have been worse; he and Melissa had just met.

"I don't think I was all that shocked when he told me about the debt," says Melissa. "I believed in him and knew he was going to be successful in whatever he did."

Motivated to regain his financial independence, Rick decided to go back to the basics, reviving the landscape business he had started as a middle school student. With the clock working against him, he took to the streets and began searching for new customers.

"I just started knocking on doors," says Rick. "I literally went door-to-door talking to each customer personally. It was a humbling experience, but I knew it's what had to be done."

Eighteen months (and many doors) later, Rick's new company Four Seasons Landscape was booming. As profits increased, Rick was able to pay off his debt and eventually hire a team.

Meanwhile, Melissa had gone into real estate and was one of the highest performing agents at her firm. But no matter how much she accomplished, she remained uninspired by the work and concerned that she was moving further away from her ultimate goal of having a family.

"Growing up, I always wanted to be a wife and mother," says Melissa. "I never wanted to be some professional career woman. That just wasn't me, and I felt like somehow I had turned into that."

Shortly after getting married, with both husband and wife confident that Rick's landscape company was stable enough to support the family, Melissa left her job and the couple began trying to get pregnant.

In 2010, after numerous attempts and one miscarriage, Melissa became pregnant with a baby girl. The first-time mother was overwhelmed with joy; her dream of parenthood was finally coming true—or at least she thought it was.

Halfway through the pregnancy, while at a routine doctor visit, Melissa received alarming news that she was about to give birth and that the child would likely not survive. Immediately, she was rushed into emergency surgery.

"I couldn't believe what was happening," says Melissa. "It felt like everything came crashing down all at once. It was a massive whirlwind."

The procedure was successful and they were able to prevent the baby from being delivered. But the doctor insisted

she stay in the hospital for the remaining five months of the pregnancy, tipped backwards in bed to avoid further complications.

It was a scary time for both soon-to-be parents, but their confidence never wavered. They were committed to doing whatever it took to ensure a safe and successful delivery.

"The thought of having to stay in the hospital that long was completely overwhelming," says Melissa. "But honestly, at that point I would have done anything to keep her until full-term."

By the third day of bed rest, Melissa was growing increasingly bored. Longing to do something creative, she began knitting a baby blanket for her daughter and was surprised by the comfort it provided. Such comfort, however, would only be temporary.

Just two weeks into her five-month hospital stay, the doctors could no longer prevent Melissa from going into labor, and she was forced to deliver the severely premature baby. Tragically, their daughter was unable to survive. In a flash, Rick and Melissa's world came shattering down.

"We had so much faith," says Rick. "We never thought it was going to turn out like that. We never thought we were actually going to lose her."

SHARK BITE

My favorite entrepreneurs on Shark Tank *have had the same spirit, the same gumption, to keep going after what they believed in, even in the face of tremendous personal and professional obstacles. So when I'm watching pitches . . . I know what to look for: the people who know how to pick themselves back up.*[23]
—*Barbara*

A NEW BEGINNING

The couple returned home from the hospital, overcome with grief. Determined to finish the blanket she had started for her daughter, Melissa spent hours at the sewing machine fervently stitching away.

"I found so much healing through sewing," she says. "It was the only thing that brought me peace."

Soon Melissa began making baby blankets for her friends and relatives who, impressed by the craftsmanship, suggested she sell her pieces on Etsy—an online marketplace for handmade or vintage items, art, and supplies. Melissa had never considered turning the new hobby into a business, but she found the idea exciting.

"I'd sell a few here and there," says Melissa. "It was nothing significant, but it was the first time I had been passionate about anything in years."

Then, in the fall of 2011, Melissa created a product that would forever change the course of her and Rick's life. After exhaustively searching for a pair of lacey socks that could ascend above her boots, Melissa decided to take a stab at making them herself. Ever the DIY aficionado, she was confident she'd be able to whip them up in no time at all. Nine long hours later, the exhausted seamstress descended down the staircase with socks in hand.

"They turned out great," says Melissa. "But they took so much work. I swore I'd never make another pair again."

Proud of her accomplishment, Melissa wore her homemade socks everywhere she went and was bombarded with compliments and queries. It wasn't uncommon for her to return home from a trip to the store with a pocketful of phone numbers and e-mail addresses from strangers who'd expressed interest in purchasing a pair.

Shocked by all the attention, Melissa snapped a quick picture of the socks and uploaded them to her Etsy page. This, she thought, would be a perfect way to assess demand and see if there really was a need in the market for her product. The experiment worked.

"Those socks sold instantly. I mean instantly," says Melissa. "I couldn't believe it."

Orders continued to pour in, and just two days later she had sold over four hundred pairs. Melissa was ecstatic at the response but unsure how she was going to fulfill so many orders.

"I was in big trouble," says Melissa. "I knew I wouldn't be able to make all of them myself. But I'm a business-minded person, so I wasn't about to turn down all that interest."

With limited time and resources, she set up a makeshift workshop in her house and began hurriedly recruiting any friends, family members, or neighbors who could sew. After only two weeks on Etsy, Melissa received a call from Nordstrom department store with a request for fifty thousand pairs.

Although she couldn't supply the massive order, it provided the validation she needed to continue pursuing the idea—even if she wasn't entirely sure what she was doing.

"My high school volleyball coach used to tell me that if you can't do it, just fake it," says Melissa. "Because if you fake it for long enough, eventually it will become a reality. So that's what I did: I faked it."

After two months of "faking it," Melissa looked up from her sewing machine to find that she had done over $40,000 in sales. The couple recognized that if they wanted the growth to continue, it was time to seek outside counsel.

Through one of Rick's longtime mentors, they were connected to an industry veteran with over thirty-five years of manufacturing experience. The executive-turned-investor shared crucial guidance and support, and even offered to come on board as a partner.

"She was passionate about the product and fell in love with our story," says Rick. "During our fourth month of business, she made an offer to buy a large percentage of the company."

Rick and Melissa were grateful for the offer, but felt it was too early to raise capital. The organization was only twelve weeks old, and they had yet to embark on any long-term strategic planning. Plus, they had other investment plans in store.

"We've been avid *Shark Tank* fans since day one," says Rick. "I really felt like we were supposed to be on the show. I thought it was the route God had in store for us."

Although Melissa appreciated Rick's enthusiasm, she was less than convinced. Battling with the Sharks in front of millions of viewers didn't seem like her idea of a wonderful time.

"I thought he was nuts," she says. "I had absolutely no interest in going on TV and being eaten alive by Mr. Wonderful."

Melissa relented, however, and finally agreed to let Rick submit an application. With so many entrepreneurs vying for a spot, she didn't actually think they'd be chosen. And she was right, at first.

Rick filled out the lengthy form and eagerly awaited a reply, but no response ever came. So he submitted another one, and then another one. After a third attempt, he decided

Shark Tank just wasn't in the cards and moved on to other things.

Then, just days after he'd given up hope, Rick was on a call with his former business partner and mentioned he'd applied for the show. As luck would have it, his friend knew a producer at ABC and offered to put them in touch. By the end of the afternoon, Rick was on the phone with *Shark Tank* casting. Shortly thereafter, they were chosen to tape an episode.

"It was a mad rush to get everything together," says Rick. "Melissa was pregnant with our son, and because it was a high-risk pregnancy we had to get permission from our specialist to fly to Los Angeles."

Although the couple did eventually manage to secure the necessary consent, the *Shark Tank* production team felt the risk was too large. So the husband-and-wife team were asked to resubmit for the following year.

"I was crushed," says Melissa. "I felt responsible for us losing this big opportunity."

Rick was also disappointed but felt confident everything would work out in due time. Less than one year later, he was back on the phone with *Shark Tank*.

"When we first started talking to them, we only had a few months of sales," says Rick. "But at this point we had been in business for over a year and had sold more than eight hundred and fifty thousand dollars."

Blown away by their progress, the producer felt that Grace and Lace would be a perfect fit for the show. After a few months of back and forth, Rick and Melissa landed a spot and headed off to sunny California. Rick's vision had become a reality.

SHARK BITE

The Corcoran Group became the innovator in my industry because I was always willing to fail. Most of my innovations were built on a leap and a prayer, using money I should never have spent in the first place.[24]
—Barbara

BARBARA OR BUST

As tried-and-true *Shark Tank* fans, the couple had been watching the series for years and were acutely familiar with each investor. Still, they put in hours of additional research before boarding the flight to California.

"That was a really big deal for us," says Melissa. "If you're going to give up a portion of your company, you owe it to yourself to have as much information as possible."

Rick and Melissa started the preparation process by re-watching each of the previous seasons, carefully studying the most and least effective pitch techniques. Next they read each of the Sharks' books and scoured the Internet for interviews and articles that could provide additional insight into their personal and professional stories. They'd only have one shot to land a deal, so they wanted to be as prepared as possible.

It didn't take long for the duo to reach a unanimous decision. There was but one Shark who could help elevate the organization to new and uncharted heights: Barbara Corcoran.

"Of course any smart person would love to do business with all of the Sharks," says Rick. "But for this particular business we knew we had to get Barbara."

Convinced that Barbara was the right partner, they made

a pact to only accept an offer if Barbara was somehow involved. She didn't need to be the only Shark in the deal, but her participation was required. Armed with a concrete plan of attack, Rick and Melissa entered the tank.

With almost $1.5 million in sales, they asked for $175,000 for a 10 percent equity share in the enterprise, valuating the business at almost $1.75 million—an indisputably fair sum.

Although nervous at first, they felt confident in their pitch and that their sales would speak for themselves. But right away they experienced an unexpected curveball: Lori Greiner went out.

"That totally threw me off," says Melissa. "She kept saying that she felt like we were hiding something—that the business was too good to be true. It really surprised me."

Luckily, the other Sharks had different outlooks, including their top choice, Barbara Corcoran. In fact, it was she who made the initial offer, but it came with a catch. Barbara

was willing to put up half the money but only if they could convince another Shark to go in for the remaining half. It wasn't exactly what they were hoping for, but Rick had faith he could make it work.

"At that point I knew we were gold," says Rick. "We had it in the bag. We were in."

Kevin O'Leary was the next Shark to make a bid, offering $175,000 for 20 percent equity, which would drop to 10 percent once he had recouped his initial investment. While they were grateful for the interest, it didn't align with their strategy.

"He gave us a good offer," says Rick. "But we knew it wasn't the right deal for us."

Impressed by their numbers and entrepreneurial spirit, Robert Herjavec was the next investor to step up to the plate, offering the husband-and-wife team exactly what they had asked for: $175,000 for a 10 percent equity stake.

This threw Rick and Melissa for a loop. They didn't expect to get so many offers and certainly not one that echoed their initial valuation. Still fixated on working with Barbara, Rick asked if she could come in on the deal.

"All I was trying to do was buy time," says Rick. "I was just stalling to get Barbara to reconsider her offer."

But stalling isn't always the best tactic, especially when a Shark is willing to honor a full valuation. Frustrated with the back and forth, Robert rescinded his offer, accusing the founder of "mistaking his kindness for weakness." They were back to square one.

"At this point I'm just thinking I got to get Barbara in somehow," says Rick. "I just kept looking back at her and making it pretty obvious that she was the one we wanted."

Mark Cuban was the final Shark to chime in and he

made the same proposal as Robert: $175,000 for 10 percent of the business—once again, the exact deal Rick and Melissa had proposed. But without Barbara they wouldn't accept.

And then, just when they thought they'd be leaving the tank empty-handed, Barbara revised her offer: $175,000 for 10 percent of the company—half in cash and half in a line of credit.

"At the last second Barbara decided to revise her offer and gave us the deal we wanted," says Rick. "I had been holding on to faith the whole time."

Rick and Melissa immediately accepted the offer and left the tank feeling triumphant. They came. They pitched. They conquered.

> **SHARK BITE**
>
> I have never met a really smart person who didn't over-prepare, and after flunking my audition for the high school cheerleading squad because I hadn't bothered to learn the cheers, I swore to myself that I would never be caught unprepared. I find that over-preparation and the insecurity that drives it have always guaranteed my success.[25]
> —Barbara

GROWING, GROWING, GONE

Grace and Lace's episode aired on November 22, 2013, and, as the couple recounts, what happened next can only be described as "absolute and utter insanity."

Rick and Melissa were aware that it's common for companies that appear on *Shark Tank* to experience a sudden burst of rapid growth and wanted to ensure they were adequately

prepared. Uncertain of how many orders to expect, they met with Barbara to review potential outcomes.

"Barbara couldn't give us an exact number," says Rick. "But she estimated that we might sell an additional seven thousand to ten thousand units."

With fifty-four thousand pieces of inventory in stock, the husband-and-wife team were certain they could weather the busy holiday season. Even taking into account the most optimistic of projections, fulfilling ten thousand extra orders would be more than manageable. Little did they know just how enthusiastically America would respond to their product.

"The night our episode aired we were at our viewing party and my phone wouldn't stop buzzing," says Melissa. "We sold ten thousand units almost instantly. I couldn't believe it."

Nervous they might run low on merchandise if orders continued to come in at such a steady pace, she excused herself from the celebration and called their manufacturer. Her instinct was correct.

Over the next five days, Grace and Lace sold one hundred and fifty-thousand units—bringing in over a million dollars in revenue. To say the company was unprepared for the flood of business would be a gross understatement.

"We went from getting one hundred and fifty orders a day before *Shark Tank* to getting ten thousand orders a day after," says Melissa. "We actually thought about taking the site offline, but I just couldn't do it."

Instead of closing up shop, Rick and Melissa changed the shipping notifications to allow for additional time and alerted customers that orders wouldn't arrive for the holidays. But it would take more than extra time to fulfill the influx of orders. If they were going to survive the year, they needed additional inventory and staff.

"We grew from six employees to thirty-six in about two or three days," says Rick. "We asked everyone to bring in their friends, their neighbors, anyone they knew."

But even with thirty new employees, they still faced an array of complex challenges. Prior to going on *Shark Tank*, Grace and Lace had fulfilled each order in-house. With one hundred and fifty thousand additional orders, continuing such a laborious process became impossible. Time was running out, and they weren't sure where to turn.

"I remember getting a call from Barbara one day while I was shopping at Target," says Melissa. "I hadn't slept or showered in days and just sat down in the middle of the aisle and started crying."

Barbara knew the small company didn't have the infrastructure capable of processing such a high volume of orders, so she recommended they hire a fulfillment center—an outside firm that specializes in receiving, packing, and shipping goods on a company's behalf.

Melissa agreed and quickly began searching for vendors, eventually hiring two local companies to offload some of the labor. Even with the additional help, however, it took almost two months to fulfill all the orders. The business was booming, but Rick and Melissa were fading fast.

"It was two months of hell," says Rick. "Literally, hell. "We were not prepared for that."

Most disturbing was the barrage of angry e-mails and phone calls they received from customers who had grown frustrated with the wait. In the few years since launching, Grace and Lace had never received a single piece of negative feedback from a customer—not one. And now all of a sudden they were bombarded with complaints.

"We had to play Santa Claus to thousands upon thousands of people," says Melissa. "And we just couldn't keep up. I took it really personally."

Fortunately, Rick was able to take a step back and help Melissa put the situation in perspective.

"I didn't take it as hard as she did," says Rick. "It wasn't the end of the world, nobody was dying. We were just two weeks late on getting a few people their socks."

Eventually, the storm subsided and daily operations stabilized. Although the initial spike has mellowed, today business continues to flourish, with a growth rate of 1,000 to 1,500 percent over the prior year.

While Rick and Melissa recognize the enterprise's massive

expansion would never have been possible without *Shark Tank*, they attribute much of their continued success to their committed team of loyal employees.

"Our staff is just absolutely incredible," says Rick. "I've never seen anything like it in all my years. It's just mind-boggling how dedicated they are."

Melissa seconds Rick's praise and insists that it's the people working behind the scenes who've turned Grace and Lace into such a flourishing venture.

"It really is all about them," says Melissa. "Everyone we've hired has been directly connected to the company— either through friends, family, or neighbors. There's a whole cul-de-sac that works here. That's something you don't see a lot in business, and that's a huge reason why we've been successful."

SHARK BITE

The fact is, it's a huge personal challenge to navigate the uncharted waters of a big second act, especially without a map to guide you. I soon learned that the trusted old blueprints that had worked for me in life so far were pretty much obsolete the moment I decided to move on, shift gears, and start fresh.[26]
—Barbara

THE GRACE AND LACE PLAYBOOK FOR SUCCESS

As both business and life partners, Rick and Melissa believe it's crucial for their definitions of success to remain consistently aligned. While they're passionate about growing the brand, they're equally dedicated to their roles as parents.

"I think of success in a larger context than just business," says Rick. "Am I a good husband and father? Do I have an

identity outside of just what I do? Of course I'm prosperity-minded, but it's by no means the barometer to which I measure success."

Melissa shares Rick's sentiment and believes it's crucial to view achievement through a wider lens that promotes both personal and professional satisfaction.

"I think of success as contentment," says Melissa. "It's not about the fulfillment of what you want, but the realization of the things you already have."

As a first-time business owner, Melissa has found that "constantly striving" for the next best thing only breeds emptiness and doubt—not joy or meaning. This ideology is contrary to how many of Melissa's entrepreneurial counterparts view achievement and is paramount to who she is as a founder, mother, and wife.

"I feel peaceful and content," says Melissa. "I get to exercise my God-given abilities in business, and also have the freedom to spend time with my family."

Balance, gratitude, appreciation, respect: these are just a few of the values that Rick and Melissa practice on a daily basis and have infused into their Playbook for Success.

FOSTER A STRONG COMMUNITY

Spend an afternoon with the Grace and Lace team and you'll quickly observe just how much emphasis they put on community. One of their first hires, a neighbor, now runs the warehouse. Chris Cowden, a longtime family friend, is the director of operations and Rick's "number two." For Rick and Melissa, community is what their company is and always will be about.

"There is no way we would be successful if we didn't have such a strong community," says Melissa. "Every aspect of this business was built around it."

But their circle isn't limited to just staff and colleagues. Rick has maintained an influential circle of mentors who've advised and guided him along the way. Likewise, Melissa relies on the support of a close group of like-minded entrepreneurs.

"There are very few people who understand what it's like to run a small business," says Melissa. "It's priceless to be able to learn from and lean on those who've had a similar experience."

Barbara Corcoran has also become an important part of Rick and Melissa's community, connecting them with a large pool of thought leaders and media influencers.

"Those connections have been huge," says Rick. "Barbara adds instant credibility to us and to our business."

Devise a Give-Back Strategy

From as early as she can remember, Melissa has been driven by a single motivator: to make the world a better place. Rick also champions this philosophy and believes altruism to be a critical piece of long-term prosperity.

"Our mission is really simple," says Rick. "We're going to change the world. Period."

To help them achieve this important goal, Grace and Lace has developed a partnership with Angel House—a nonprofit organization that brings abandoned children from the slums of India to safety and empowers them to become "future leaders of their generation."

Melissa first visited India during the summer of her senior year of high school. Having previously done mission work in other indigent communities, the destitution she witnessed there was unlike any she'd ever experienced, and it left a lasting impression.

"I had never seen poverty like this before," says Melissa. "I left there with a note in my journal that said, 'I've been so broken for this place. They need help so badly. I have to do something more.'"

Never would Melissa have guessed that one day she'd own a profitable company and be able to contribute in such a meaningful way.

Today, Grace and Lace donates a portion of each sale to Angel House and has thus far funded two orphanages, which, combined, house fifty children.

"There's poverty here in the U.S., but there's deep utter depravity there," says Rick. "We're trying to give these kids hope and show them they have a chance in this world."

In addition to building orphanages, they've also begun funding the organization's first Freedom House, which provides a safe haven for victims of human trafficking. Already home to more than thirty girls and young women, Freedom House offers shelter, counseling, and job training.

"We're equipping them with the healing they need while also giving them a trade skill so they can enter back into society," says Melissa.

To its customers, Grace and Lace may be a hub for quality fashion-forward clothing and apparel. But for Rick and Melissa, the company has always been about so much more than the product they make.

"This is the motivation," says Melissa. "This is why I do what I do—to see that we're giving these lives a chance. It's why I wake up every morning."

Pay Strict Attention to Detail

Although Grace and Lace has already achieved incredible success, Rick and Melissa have a larger vision for the enterprise.

And they believe that to accomplish the big tasks, one must first learn to master the small ones.

"Everything we do as an organization can impact the larger vision," says Rick. "And if we execute each detail with absolute excellence, we'll ultimately build a better business."

Rick first developed an appreciation for strict attention to detail after reading a navy seal book and applying the principals to his own life. Immediately surprised by the overlapping viewpoints, he made a commitment to become a more detail-oriented person and approach even the most mundane tasks with precision and finesse.

"We're not in a war here," says Rick. "But if we don't pay attention to the little stuff, we may not be able to build the next orphanage. So in some way, Grace and Lace is about saving lives."

While Melissa shares this approach, she's better at tackling more big-picture creative projects and relies on Rick for many of the day-to-day tasks.

"The operations side is not my strong suit," says Melissa. "When Rick came on full-time I was able to focus on what I'm naturally good at and let him handle a lot of the details."

Prepare for Adversity

There are many who view success as a finish line—a threshold that, once traversed, can never be uncrossed. But as any seasoned entrepreneur will reveal, achievement is leased, not owned, and rent is due every day in the form of hard work, sacrifice, and dedication.

"It's like the classic iceberg visual," says Melissa. "The public only sees a small part of the business: the product. But underneath is this huge, complicated operation."

For Rick and Melissa, part of running an effective company means anticipating adversity before it occurs and making a mindful effort to manage hardship in a direct and productive way.

After appearing on *Shark Tank* and experiencing such intense demand, they were bombarded with an endless stream

of complicated challenges that pushed both founders far beyond their comfort zones.

"Honestly, we thought about shutting the business down," says Melissa. "I didn't know if we would be able to survive."

But even though they were left feeling disoriented and overwhelmed, the husband-and-wife team chose to recommit to their mission and power through the storm.

"As a business owner you have to decide from the beginning how you'll deal with adversity," says Rick. "Do you face it head-on? Do you find solutions? Or do you let the challenges conquer you?"

Practice Absolute Honesty

At Grace and Lace, honesty isn't just the *best* policy; it's the most important policy. And it's one the company expects each employee to faithfully respect and observe.

"I'm a huge proponent of being totally truthful with everyone involved," says Rick. "Whether it's with those you're working for or those you're working with, there's got to be a base level of trust."

But as Rick and Melissa have experienced, practicing absolute honesty isn't always easy or comfortable, especially in times of turmoil.

"Some of our employees get really upset when they make a mistake, even when it's just a minor one," says Rick. "When that happens we try to remind them that we're all figuring this out together and that it's a process. As long as it doesn't jeopardize our core values or break the law, we're okay with mistakes and want everyone to be open about them."

This commitment to honesty doesn't only apply to their employees. As cofounders, Rick and Melissa uphold the same commitment and always try to be both communicative and forgiving of their mistakes.

"We're not perfect," says Rick. "But we always try to extend grace to ourselves and to each other. That's such an important part of running a business."

CHAPTER SEVEN

INVESTORS: DAYMOND JOHN AND **LORI GREINER**

COMPANY: Scholly

FOUNDER: Christopher Gray

SEASON: Six

NO FREE RIDES IN A SCHOOL OF SHARKS

Starting a small business is no easy feat and requires a finely calibrated combination of brass, brawns, and brains. Intelligence, however, is multifaceted and can be assessed in many different ways. While some entrepreneurs are more traditionally "book smart," others have strong intuition or demonstrate an elevated emotional IQ, more commonly thought of as "street smarts." Scholly's Christopher Gray is one of those rare founders whose versatile business acumen includes valuable traits from both categories.

Christopher appeared on season six of *Shark Tank* and underwent one of the most highly charged, controversial negotiations in the show's history. But controversy isn't always a bad thing. The young entrepreneur left the tank with a $40,000 investment from Daymond John and Lori Greiner for 15 percent of his company, Scholly—a mobile app that makes finding scholarships quick and easy.

Many viewers were shocked when Christopher revealed that as a student he earned over $1.3 million in financial aid. More inspiring than the lucrative sum, however, is the story behind the triumph—the true-life tale of how a kid from the inner city pulled himself up by his bootstraps to become the head of a powerful and profitable technology enterprise.

PREPARATION MEETS OPPORTUNITY

From an early age, Christopher had been driven by a deep motivation to succeed. Growing up in a low-income household in Birmingham, Alabama, the twenty-four-year-old entrepreneur knew the path to success would be fraught with challenge and saw education as his ticket to a more prosperous future.

"I always did very well in school," says Christopher. "I think some people just have a fundamental desire to rise up and do better for themselves."

A sharp thinker and creative problem solver, Christopher was a lively kid and constantly scheming up new projects and ideas. He had barely reached adolescence before his penchant for entrepreneurship began to surface.

As a thirteen-year-old, the Scholly founder was fascinated by technology and enamored with video games. But his mother's demanding work schedule meant trips to the video game store were few and far between. Recognizing that other kids might be grappling with this same dilemma, Christopher began planning his first business: Games to Go—a delivery service that brought the latest titles straight to the customer's door.

"I developed a model where I could partner with GameStop and other retailers," says Christopher. "Think of it like Instacart but for video games."

Although Games to Go never did take off, developing the concept was an eye-opening experience and one that served as an important prelude to Christopher's eventual career goals. Surely, he thought, there were other, more pressing challenges that needed to be solved.

By the time Christopher entered high school, he had

already begun researching potential colleges. He noticed that the top institutions favored well-rounded candidates over those who only had good grades—students who were active members of society and had a solid track record of participating in service-related activities. This insight only magnified his desire to get more involved in the community.

Christopher began searching for an organization that paired young people with local volunteer opportunities. When he discovered no such group existed, the eager youth did what any budding entrepreneur might: he took matters into his own hands.

"I wanted to find a way to bring volunteer opportunities to my community," Christopher says. "We didn't really have that in the inner city."

It was around this time that he got involved in a neighborhood program designed to teach young people the fundamentals of running an enterprise. This, along with the advanced business classes offered at his magnet high school, provided the necessary framework to successfully transform his concept into a company.

By his junior year of high school, Christopher had launched a nonprofit organization dedicated to bringing volunteer opportunities to urban communities. It was his first legitimate operation and a critical landmark in his narrative.

"I remember getting six of my friends together to meet at the library," says Christopher. "We put together a board of directors and started working on a business plan."

How, you might wonder, did a teenager with no traditional business experience undertake the complicated process of starting such a venture? The same way he had navigated many of life's other major challenges: through inventiveness,

resourcefulness, and support. Specifically, he made sure to surround himself with a team of knowledgeable mentors who helped nurture his curiosity and focus his passion.

"Growing up in a neighborhood with such a different culture and mindset created a lot of friction for me," says Christopher. "Having mentors outside my immediate community was helpful because it provided real-world guidance."

To do this, Christopher made a constant effort to broaden his reach and expand his influence. Approaching such luminaries often felt scary and uncomfortable, but he knew his future depended on it.

"Sometimes our school would invite local business owners to come in and talk," says Christopher. "I would always stay after the event and introduce myself. I was usually the only student who would do stuff like that."

By the time his first company launched, Christopher had amassed a vast network of strategic advisers. It was through this network that he connected to a local venture organization and law firm that, together, sponsored the expensive incorporation process and provided critical guidance along the way.

It wasn't long before Christopher's company was partnering with world-renowned organizations. As the operation grew, it became a valuable pipeline for national nonprofits that were looking to find local volunteers. You didn't need half of Christopher's smarts to see the obvious: this kid was going places.

With high school graduation only two years away, Christopher began to give more thought as to where he might attend college. There was never any doubt as to whether or not he would continue his education; Christopher was determined to be the first in his family to graduate from a

university. But it would take more than drive to achieve such a prodigious goal. With limited resources available, Christopher realized his academic future hinged on his ability to secure financial aid.

"I started aggressively looking for scholarships," says Christopher. "And it took me about seven months of searching to find the right ones."

On paper, it may have appeared as though he would have been the perfect candidate for financial assistance; he was a minority student from a low-income background with outstanding grades and unparalleled ambition. But the pursuit proved more difficult than he had imagined—and at times it even felt like an impossible pursuit.

"That hardest part about getting money for college is actually finding it," says Christopher. "There are so many scams, and a lot of the websites make it impossible to filter results."

Tuition, however, wasn't the only expense he had to consider. Most colleges require candidates to pay an application fee that can range from $50 to $90—a substantial figure for a family with limited means. And the timing couldn't have been worse.

The year was 2009 and the country had just gone through a damaging economic recession. For Alabama residents, this collapse was particularly grisly, driving up the state unemployment rate from 3.4 percent to 9.7 percent. Christopher's mother was one of many who found themselves out of work.

With money tight, the ambitious student approached his high school guidance counselor and asked about securing a fee waiver, which is often made available to low-income college applicants. Regrettably, however, his query was met with little more than a shrug of the shoulders and an uncertain remark.

"She didn't really know how to do it," says Christopher. "But in her defense, there were several hundred students per counselor, and most kids went to local colleges."

Without access to fee waivers, Christopher was forced to narrow his search from a long list of universities to a handful of schools that he felt were within reach. It was through this process that he first discovered Drexel University.

Based in Philadelphia, Drexel had many distinct characteristics that Christopher found appealing, including a co-op program that allowed students to get real-world experience while earning their degrees. He also liked that the campus was in close proximity to other major cities like New York, Boston, and Washington, D.C. With a full scholarship in place, he applied and was accepted for the fall semester of 2010.

SHARK BITE

You will get nowhere if you carry around the idea that you are less important or less deserving of success than anyone else. The inventor's arena is no place for self-doubt. You need to believe in yourself as passionately as you believe in your product.[27]
—Lori

THE COLLEGE YEARS

Christopher was excited to expand his wings outside the narrow city limits of Birmingham. His hometown had given him much, and he was grateful for the friends, family, and mentors who had supported him over the years. But he was ready to finally be surrounded by a group of like-minded people, even if the relocation was a bit nerve-wracking.

The transition from high school to college is difficult for students from any background. Add an out-of-state move and a substantial cultural shift to the mix and you have what could be a recipe for disaster. There were no two ways about it: Christopher knew he would either sink or swim.

"I was aware that the adjustment might be difficult or that I may not fit in," says Christopher. "But the exact opposite happened: the moment I hit the ground at Drexel, I began to grow exponentially."

Not only did the Scholly founder excel academically, he immersed himself in the university's vibrant community. Soon Christopher became president of the finance club and a founding partner of the Dorm Room Fund—one of the first venture capital funds run by students, for students. For the first time in his life, Christopher felt he was in his element. It was the college experience he had always dreamed of, and he wanted to empower others to achieve the same.

Having logged countless hours researching scholarship opportunities, Christopher offered his services to friends and classmates. He was surprised to find such an obvious disconnection between the young people who needed scholarships and the organizations that provided financial aid. By the fall of his sophomore year, students were lining up for help. Demand had quickly outgrown supply.

"That was really the beginning of Scholly," says Christopher. "It was bred out of a frustration. I wanted to figure out how to scale my efforts to help the most people."

A lifelong digital enthusiast, Christopher understood the best way to achieve his goal was through technology. More specifically, he needed to build something mobile—an app that could succinctly bridge the gap between student and scholarship. This, of course, would require technical skills he

did not have, like coding and design. So he began searching for a team—a talented crew that could transform his vision into a product.

Eventually, Christopher brought on Rick Pirollo and Bryson Alef—two talented developers and user-experience designers with whom he'd worked on previous projects. Upon coming on board as official cofounders, Rick focused on building the web and Android platforms, while Bryson worked on iOS—Apple's operating system. But it was more than just their individual skill sets that made them a diverse team. Each founder came from a different socioeconomic background and brought with him a unique point of view.

Bryson had earned a variety of scholarships to pay for college, even though his family was well off. Meanwhile, Rick, who was raised in a typical middle-class home, had racked up over $100,000 in student loan debt. And then, of course, there was Christopher, whose humble beginnings inspired him to raise over $1 million in financial aid. This broad amalgamation of experiences allowed them to build a product that was hyper-relevant and authentically addressed the needs of a broad scope of students.

"We each added our own cultural perspective to the product," says Christopher. "That's one of the reasons that it's so important for teams to be diverse."

With Rick and Bryson focused on development, it was up to Christopher to create the business model and piece together an executable plan of attack. Each task, from building the brand and marketing strategy to coordinating launch details, brought with it a barrage of important decisions.

The first major issue Christopher faced involved Scholly's price point. He could either charge for the app or find other ways to monetize the platform, like encouraging in-app

purchases or relying on third-party advertisers. Another alternative, of course, was to ignore monetization entirely and focus solely on acquiring a user base.

While the latter approach may seem counterintuitive when attempting to create a profitable company, it's a popular strategy among many tech start-ups that wish to achieve critical mass—the crucial stage at which a company earns significant market share and is able to grow and compete. If Christopher were to follow this path, he would need to raise enough capital to float the venture until it became profitable.

"So many tech companies build their entire business model around raising investor money, and it ends up taking them years to make a profit," says Christopher. "We wanted to build a business that was sustainable from the start."

Logistics aside, Christopher recognized another, more strategic reason to charge for the app: market differentiation. At the time, most of their competitors were offering a free product. With a price point just slightly above market rate, Scholly would stand out from the crowd and send a message to users that their platform was superior.

"We wanted to be the luxury, high-end scholarship product," says Christopher. "For only $1 we could position ourselves as a premium product."

Another early decision Christopher made was to make the app and its vast database accessible when a user is offline as well as online. Once again, this decision served two purposes. The first was to enhance the platform with yet another notable feature; the second was to ensure that students of all economic classes could access the information.

Growing up in a low-income household, Christopher understood that not all families have access to regular Internet use. Making Wi-Fi connectivity a requirement could

potentially restrict those students with the greatest need. Even if it made the app more difficult to build, the team believed it was critical.

By the spring of 2013, less than a year after Christopher had come up with the idea, Scholly was ready to go live. He had spent months planning a comprehensive public relations (PR) strategy and knew just who to call when it came time to launch.

Earlier that year, the first-time founder had been interviewed by Philadelphia's local Fox TV affiliate about a story on financial aid. Although the app was still being developed, he couldn't ignore such a valuable opportunity.

"After the interview I told them about what we were working on" says Christopher. "I showed them a quick demo and they offered to cover it when we launched."

True to their word, Fox 29 News featured the start-up on May 28, 2013. Within twenty-four hours, Scholly had received several thousand downloads and attracted the attention of a brigade of local media outlets.

"PR is the best kind of marketing because it's free," says Christopher. "We just kept getting request after request, which led to tons of organic growth."

SHARK BITE

Get the word-of-mouth machine cranking, so that your product is talked about and seen as widely as possible. Create a perfect storm. Hit every marketing platform as hard and as fast as possible.[28]
 —Lori

A TANK DIVIDED

After saturating the local media market, Scholly began gaining national attention. From *Inc.* magazine and *Forbes* to *TechCrunch* and *Bloomberg*, each story helped grow the user base and expand the overall brand presence. But it was a feature in *USA Today* that ultimately caught the attention of the *Shark Tank* casting team.

"I remember getting an e-mail from one of the producers asking if I'd be interested in auditioning," says Christopher. "I watched the show religiously, so I was really excited when they reached out."

With the help of his cofounders, Christopher filled out an application and submitted a video pitch. Just a couple weeks later, he received word that the Scholly app was being considered.

Over the next few months, the young entrepreneur spent countless hours on his presentation, mapping out potential questions and coming up with various answers for each one. He knew he needed to be prepared for any scenario.

By the summer of 2014, Christopher was notified that he'd been chosen to tape the show and headed off to California. Though just twenty-three years old, he was about to embark on one of the most pivotal experiences of his life.

As the large wooden doors swung open, Christopher entered the tank and began his pitch. Having received 92,000 paid downloads in less than a year, he felt confident with his offering: $40,000 for 15 percent of the company.

Robert Herjavec and Kevin O'Leary commented first, asking questions about the product's design, functionality, and development. Robert was curious to learn how the young entrepreneur had come up with the idea. This, the

Scholly founder felt, was a vital question and one that had the potential to influence the rest of the negotiation.

Christopher recounted his story of growing up poor and raising over $1.3 million in financial aid. He shared the difficulties of applying for scholarships and revealed that each year millions of dollars slated for college go unclaimed. As he explained how Scholly provided a fast and effective solution to this problem, the Sharks became visibly enthralled.

"I think we can all relate to that story," said Robert. "I'm the first person in my entire family to go to college. I get the value."

The investors continued examining the app and probed deeper into the technical details. But before Christopher could respond, Lori Greiner made an unprecedented move.

"I'm going to do something that I've never done before," said Lori. "I haven't heard a whole lot, but I'm going to make you an offer right now."

Lori explained that she would provide the $40,000 for 15 percent of the company—the exact deal he requested—but only if Christopher agreed to the bid immediately.

"I believe in you, I believe that what you're doing is good, and I believe that we will make it together," said Lori. "So I hope you just say yes."

Christopher was taken aback to have received an offer so quickly. He had been in the tank for only a few minutes and had barely even explained the product. Mark Cuban and Robert were also surprised that Lori made such a hasty proposal and insisted they be allowed to ask "some real questions" before the bidding process officially commenced.

Like Lori, however, Daymond John was also convinced

and required no further information. Having been raised in a single-parent household by a mother who often worked three jobs to support the family, Daymond expressed the feeling that getting involved was a "personal matter" for him. Not only was Scholly a good investment, Daymond believed it was good for the world.

"I resonate with this," said Daymond. "So I'll offer you the same deal: forty thousand dollars for fifteen percent."

By this point, the mood in the tank had dramatically shifted. Two offers had been made, but Mark, Robert, and Kevin refused to back down, firing off more questions about the product, team, and business model.

Once again, Lori interjected.

"I don't care how we're going to monetize it," said Lori. "I just want you to take my hand and say deal . . . but I'd like you to do it right now."

Frustrated that Christopher was being forced into a deal

so quickly, the conversation between the Sharks quickly escalated from spirited banter to full-fledged yelling.

"I was in shock," says Christopher. "I just really didn't want to lose both investors and leave the tank without a deal."

With a shared passion for the product and founder, Lori suggested partnering with Daymond. With two Sharks on his side, the Scholly founder felt he'd hit the jackpot. Daymond agreed and the deal was accepted.

But the drama didn't end there. When Christopher left the tank, Robert accused Lori of having offered a "charity case" deal.

"When I had nothing and couldn't rub two pennies together, you know what I really hated?" asked Robert. "I hated when people gave me a break because they felt bad for me."

His comments hit a nerve, and the room erupted in chaos. In a fit of passion, Robert stormed off the set, followed by Kevin and eventually Mark. It was the first time in the show's history that three Sharks had abandoned the tank.

"I wasn't even aware of the fighting until it aired," says Christopher. "I heard there was a debate, but I had no idea it was anything like that."

SHARK BITE

I know firsthand what it's like to lack access and resources, and to be told no by lenders. That's why I'm excited to be able to work directly with emerging digital influencers in helping them build customer bases and brands.[29]
 —Daymond

FROM THE SHARK TANK TO THE WHITE HOUSE

When the Scholly episode premiered on February 20, 2015, Christopher, his two cofounders, and one hundred of their closest friends and family members gathered together to watch it live.

It's common for entrepreneurs who appear on the show to find the viewing experience somewhat nerve-wracking. Many are committed *Shark Tank* fans and describe the process of seeing themselves on television as "surreal" or "bizarre." But the Scholly team watched the segment with delight, excited to showcase their product and CEO—that is, until Christopher left the tank and the infamous battle ensued.

At first Christopher was worried it might have a negative impact on the business. He certainly didn't feel as though his deal had been a "charity case" of any kind and hoped the viewing public didn't either. Curious to see how America was responding, he logged onto Twitter and began monitoring comments.

"Right away I saw that the audience was on my side," says Christopher. "We ended up being the number three trending topic in the U.S. that night."

Not only did the dispute spawn a flood of Tweets, it also brought a steady flow of traffic to the Scholly platform. With over 8,000 hits per second, many sites would have crashed under such strain. But the team had taken extra precautions to ensure it remained strong.

Prior to airing, Christopher reached out to Amazon Web Services (AWS)—their hosting provider—and alerted them of the pending surge. AWS used the opportunity as a real-time experiment to test their capacity. Needless to say, the site remained live.

There was, however, one rather large glitch the founders had not anticipated. Upon downloading Scholly, a user gains access to thousands of scholarships from various third-party vendors across the web, which he or she is then automatically redirected to via the app. Although the Scholly platform was prepared for the massive influx of traffic, their partner sites had not taken such precautions.

"We were sending them so much traffic that we actually started shutting them down," says Christopher. "So our users thought the app had a bunch of dead links."

Although this initially earned them a smattering of bad reviews, they recovered quickly and soon climbed to number one in the app store, where they remained for three prolific weeks.

In the days following the episode, traffic continued to spike. A week later, Scholly had received over 300,000 downloads—more than triple their total sales from the previous year. In less than two years since launching, they have helped students raise over $15 million in scholarships and still receive a minimum of 1,500–2000 new downloads per day.

"It's so cool to see how excited people are about Scholly," says Christopher. "We've had MIT and Harvard promoting it on Twitter. Some schools have even made it a requirement."

Since Christopher appeared on *Shark Tank*, Scholly has hired nine employees and created a series of new initiatives, including Scholly Awards—a program that allows universities and scholarship providers to connect with students directly. It also gives users access to fee waivers, subscription services, and real-time financial aid opportunities.

"Imagine flash deals but for scholarship opportunities," says Christopher.

Additionally, Scholly has secured partnerships with a

wide array of organizations and municipalities, including the city of Memphis, Tennessee, where all junior and senior high school students receive the app. Scholly has even attracted the attention of the White House.

In the spring of 2015, Scholly teamed up with the Obama Administration on My Brother's Keeper Alliance—a nonprofit organization that helps young men of color gain access to educational and work-related opportunities. As part of this program, roughly 275,000 students will be given free access to the platform.

Through it all, Lori and Daymond have continued advocating for Christopher and the venture, helping him secure important deals and take the product to new heights.

"A lot of tech companies might get a spike in traffic, but they can't sustain it," says Christopher. "We've maintained our relevancy by creating a ubiquitous brand and partnering with other credible organizations."

> *Successful companies go through external and internal progressions, and both sides need to come together in a seamless way if you want your business to survive and thrive in a competitive marketplace.*[30]
> —Daymond

SHARK BITE

THE SCHOLLY PLAYBOOK FOR SUCCESS

It's been said that success is in the eye of the beholder. But as the beholder evolves, does his or her definition of success do the same? The answer, if based entirely off experiences shared by entrepreneurs in this book, is unequivocally yes.

Almost all of the small business owners interviewed for *Shark Tank Secrets to Success* expressed the belief that accomplishment is not a static milestone marked by a clearly defined borders. Instead, they suggest, it's an ever-changing entity that closely mirrors their own personal growth and development. So what does that mean for Christopher Gray—the youngest founder featured here? No matter his level of sophistication, has he gathered enough life experience or real-world perspective to define achievement in any meaningful or comprehensive way? Once again, the answer is affirmative.

As it turns out, Christopher has spent the majority of his life thinking about what it means to prosper. From his early years dreaming up new ideas in his hometown of Birmingham, Alabama, to his current role as CEO of Scholly, Christopher has spent countless hours meticulously crafting his own personal Playbook for Success.

FIND GREAT MENTORS

Christopher believes that it's crucial for entrepreneurs of all ages, backgrounds, and cultures to seek out talented and gracious mentors. It's a principle he's practiced for years and one that has undoubtedly shaped his personal and professional trajectory.

"One of my core mantras is that you are the average of the five people you spend the most time with," says Christopher. "So I try to surround myself with people who raise me up."

The Scholly founder first learned this lesson in high school when his AP Literature teacher took a special interest in his development. Having grown up in a similar economic environment, she had a deep understanding of the particular challenges Christopher faced and went above and beyond to ensure he was on the right path.

"She helped me with all the scholarship essays," says Christopher. "She's the one who stayed after school, missed lunches, took the time to make sure I was successful."

Although Tara was Christopher's first mentor, she wouldn't be his last. Their relationship cemented the notion that having a robust community is vital to achievement and helped jump-start a practice that has remained strong ever since.

"As a young entrepreneur, I realize there are a lot of things I don't know," says Christopher. "I try to avoid mistakes by surrounding myself with people who have more experience than I do."

It's important, however, that this type of relationship never be passive or submissive. While a mentee must be humble enough to accept the guidance being offered, Christopher believes that he or she must also possess enough self-assurance to take full responsibility for any and all actions.

"At the end of the day you have to make your own decisions," says Christopher. "A mentor can provide perspective, but ultimately it's you who makes the call."

Obey Your Strengths and Weaknesses

When launching a new venture, a business owner typically wants to be involved in all aspects of the operation. And sometimes, especially at the beginning, that may be the only option; this was definitely true in Christopher's case. At a certain point, however, he discovered that for the organization to move forward he had to learn to take a few steps backward.

"When you're starting a company, it's very common to become overextended," says Christopher. "But you can't allow yourself to get distracted by a million different things."

How do you know which tasks to spearhead and which to abandon? The Scholly founder believes this answer lies in one's ability to fully recognize and accept his or her strengths and weaknesses.

"I'm much better at big-picture stuff," says Christopher. "When I get inundated by a lot of little tasks, I tend to get flustered."

Armed with this knowledge, Christopher has built a dynamic team made up of high-performing employees who round out his skill set. Now that he's no longer distracted by having to address several issues at once, he's free to focus on tasks that are more aligned with his natural talents.

One of Christopher's greatest strengths is the ability to infuse his life story into all of Scholly's efforts. Anyone can build a scholarship app, but few have personally raised over $1 million in financial aid. This narrative adds credibility to the brand, and over time has become one of the product's most powerful differentiators.

"I've built a strategy where I could leverage my story to get press and PR," says Christopher. "It's been a good way to market and brand the business."

Read More Books

In *Shark Tank Jump Start Your Business*, the Sharks shared their thoughts on MBA programs and discussed whether they were a wise path for entrepreneurs to pursue. This conversation

led to a broader dialogue about learning and development, specifically the difference between hard and soft skills.

Soft skills relate to a person's emotional intelligence and directly influence how they manage, lead, and communicate. Hard skills, on the other hand, are more quantitative abilities that can be measured and defined. While hard skills are teachable (i.e., writing, math, etc.), soft skills are harder to impart through academic practice and usually require some degree of life experience or real-world contextualization.

Although Christopher learned much in school, he's found that one of the best ways to improve both his hard and soft skills is through a regular and dedicated reading practice.

"When I needed to figure out how to write my first business plan, I went to the library," says Christopher. "Even today I read at least two books a month."

When choosing a new title, the Scholly founder likes to float freely between topics and genres. Specifically, he enjoys books that offer a glimpse into the lives of noteworthy trailblazers.

"I like to read biographies and autobiographies that profile great leaders," says Christopher. "I think it's important to learn how to approach life from people who did it well."

Develop a Personal Brand

When most people hear the word "brand," they think of an assortment of tangible assets—a name, logo, or design. But brand is much bigger than a mere icon or element of typography; it's the emotional response to a person, product, or service—the concentrated essence of who you are, what you do, and why you do it.

As the world becomes increasingly globalized and consumers gain access to a wider pool of choices, building a pervasive brand is more important than ever before—for both businesses and individuals.

Each of the Sharks, for example, has a distinct and identifiable personal brand, not unlike a product you might find in the

store. Expressed through various channels, his or her brand plays a significant role in what makes you a fan or foe.

Christopher believes that it's every entrepreneur's responsibility to develop a well-defined personal brand. As he's witnessed firsthand, it's one of the most potent ways to earn short-term attention and long-term credibility.

"Everyone needs to be his or her own personal PR machine," says Christopher. "If you want to control what people think, control what they know."

This, of course, isn't to say that such a process requires dishonesty or manipulation. In fact, just the opposite is true: a lasting brand demands absolute authenticity. Rather, when you're purposeful in your words and actions, you're able to subtly alter perception and play a larger role in how you're viewed.

"Think about how you want to be seen and then approach the world with that point of view," says Christopher. "You can't control how someone perceives you, but you can control the information you choose to provide."

Maintain a Positive Reputation

Unlike the archetypical tech CEO you may see portrayed in the media, Christopher isn't obsessed with getting rich. Yes, money matters, but it's not his greatest motivator nor is it his solitary measure of success. Instead, Christopher strives to make an impact on the world and achieve professional longevity.

"Money's just a way of keeping score," says Christopher. "I think influence is worth more than almost anything."

The Scholly founder knows that in order to earn the authority he desires, he must make an active effort to maintain a positive reputation and never let ego stand in the way. Not only is this important for his personal legacy, it's crucial to the livelihood of his enterprise.

"A lot of our growth has been through referrals," says

Christopher. "If people like and trust you, they'll want to work for your company."

Part of how Christopher earns trust is through generosity. He recognizes that his success as an entrepreneur is, in part, thanks to the kindness bestowed upon him by others. So today, Christopher tries to pay that goodwill forward whenever he can.

"I make a lot of effort to help people," says Christopher. "And it's not always about making introductions; sometimes it just means making yourself available."

No matter how much he achieves, the Scholly founder believes that a solid reputation is the cornerstone of a successful life and works hard to build a positive one.

CHAPTER EIGHT

INVESTORS: MARK CUBAN AND **ROBERT HERJAVEC**

COMPANY: Lollaland (formally Lollacup)

FOUNDERS: Hanna Lim and Mark Lim

SEASON: Four

A CUP ABOVE THE REST

Nineteen ninety-two was an eventful year in America: Bill Clinton became the forty-second president; Hurricane Andrew decimated the South Florida coastline; Johnny Carson retired from *The Tonight Show*. And at a small Christian summer camp, just outside Glendale, California, two unassuming middle schoolers were paired together for a group project. It was the beginning of a partnership that would carry the young couple all the way from the chapel to the *tank*.

Hanna and Mark Lim appeared on season four of *Shark Tank* and landed a deal with Robert Herjavec and Mark Cuban for $100,000 in exchange for 40 percent of their company Lollaland—a modern line of infant and toddler goods that are designed to be functional and fun.

Although the couple has spent a lifetime traveling on parallel paths, the ground has not always been steady. From personal to professional disasters, this husband-and-wife team has experienced a plentitude of trials and tribulations—the culmination of which has led to an unwavering marriage and a business that's poised for epic success.

TWO WORLDS COLLIDE

Hanna Lim never wanted to be an entrepreneur. Born into a traditional Korean family, her parents immigrated to America

by way of Brazil and worked tirelessly to create a stable and comfortable life for their daughter. Her father ran his own company in the Garment District and, although successful, discouraged Hanna from going the same route.

"My father saw entrepreneurship as something you did when you had no other options," says Hanna. "He didn't have a college degree and barely spoke the language. Starting a business was the only thing he thought he *could* do."

Determined to provide their daughter with a top-notch education, Hanna's parents enrolled her in the best schools they could afford and nurtured her innate academic abilities. It could be a strict household at times, but the discipline and order helped the bright young student blossom.

From an early age, Hanna dreamed of becoming a pediatrician. She excelled in math and science and loved working with children. Becoming a physician seemed like the most effective way to combine her talents and passions into a career that was both stimulating and lucrative. Once again, however, her father had reservations.

"He never wanted me to be a doctor," says Hanna. "He said that all his friends who were doctors were miserable and that it would be a difficult career to have while also being a mother."

Less than ten miles away, Mark was being raised in a family with a resoundingly parallel dynamic. Similarly, his father had also moved to America barely speaking the language and started a company in the garment industry. While he was equally disparagingly of entrepreneurship, unlike Hanna's father, he encouraged his son to pursue a career in the medical field.

"He thought being a doctor meant guaranteed success,"

says Mark. "I went through life saying that's what I wanted, but secretly I loved business."

Hanna and Mark first met when they were twelve and thirteen, respectively, while attending a small, local church camp. Mark was smitten from the moment he laid eyes on her, but it wasn't until he learned they'd be attending the same middle school that his affection grew into an all-out crush.

During the following year, Mark looked for any excuse to pass Hanna in the hallway. The one-year age difference prevented them from being enrolled in any of the same academic courses, but as fate would have it, they happened to be assigned to the same PE class. Ever the hopeless romantic, Mark took it as a good omen.

After months of flirting, the lovesick teen decided it was time to ask Hanna out on a date. She had attracted the attention of other boys, and he didn't want to risk losing her to a fellow classmate. With a quivering voice and a sweaty brow, Mark nervously made his move.

"It was December 17, 1992," says Mark. "I walked right up to her after school and asked if she would be my girlfriend."

Hanna was flattered that an older boy had taken an interest in her. It didn't hurt, of course, that the feelings were mutual. Hanna agreed to the courtship and the pair officially started "dating," which primarily consisted of passing notes and exchanging flirtatious grins. Still, Mark believed their relationship was more than just a middle school crush.

"From the very beginning I knew she was going to be my wife," he says. "I just had a gut feeling that she was the person I would spend the rest of my life with."

The pair continued to date throughout high school, but decided to separate shortly before Mark headed east to attend Bucknell University in Pennsylvania. The pause, however, would only be temporary. During the following year, Mark transferred to a school in Boston just as Hanna had begun her freshman year at Wellesley College—a private women's liberal-arts college just thirty minutes outside the city. Reunited in a new town, the couple resumed their relationship.

While at Wellesley, Hanna started to realize her dream of becoming a pediatrician was motivated more by a love of children than it was by a desire to practice medicine. So with help from her college adviser, she switched her focus to education and, upon graduation, accepted a teaching position at a nearby school for children with autism.

By that point, Mark had moved to New York City and was working for a globally recognized international bank. Although he'd majored in finance, he'd given little thought to his long-term career path. Working at a well-regarded financial institution seemed like the obvious next step—even if the work itself wasn't always enjoyable.

"To be honest, I had no idea what I wanted to do," says Mark. "I wasn't one of those guys that woke up and read the *Wall Street Journal*. I was good at math, and banking sounded sexy."

Then in early 2002, Mark received a surprise. The acquaintance was the CEO of a $100 million denim company who happened to be passing through town on business. Assuming that Mark might be lonely in a new city, he invited the recent graduate to attend a high-profile work dinner later in the week.

One dinner became two and then three and eventually

four. At the end of the week, the fashion mogul asked the young man to return to California and work for his firm. The organization was about to launch what they believed would be a promising new brand and was in need of a junior-level operations expert. It was an opportunity Mark couldn't resist.

Meanwhile, Hanna had transitioned to a job teaching science at an urban school on the outskirts of Los Angeles. She found the work itself rewarding, but the administrative politics and enormous class sizes made it nearly impossible to keep up.

"I had sixty-five students per period—for five periods a day," says Hanna. "That meant if I gave an assignment, I would have to grade three hundred papers."

Hanna wasn't the only one dealing with shattered expectations. Mark's new employer was nothing like he had imagined. Similar to Hanna, he loved his role, but the rigid workplace culture left him longing for something more.

"It was a very Korean-run company," says Mark. "There was a hierarchy to how every decision was made. You had to shut your mouth and listen to seniority, even if you had a good idea."

To succeed at the organization, Mark knew he'd need to devote years, decades even, to climbing the corporate ladder. It was a sacrifice he was unwilling to make. So less than two years after accepting the position, he resigned and went to work for his father—a move he never could have anticipated.

Mark and his dad had a strained relationship, especially after Mark had decided to forgo a career in medicine. But unlike the denim company, which had evolved with the times, his father's business was quickly becoming commoditized and was in need of a serious overhaul. Mark believed

that with just a little tweaking he could stimulate growth and help the enterprise regain profitability.

"I tried to apply the model that I had learned at the other company," says Mark. "I knew that by creating a brand we could turn a sixty-cent T-shirt into a sixty-two-dollar product."

His father was hesitant to embrace the new direction, but Mark proceeded anyway, designing a custom T-shirt line that could appeal to the masses. When the collection was complete, he flew to New York City and pitched the new brand to buyers from some of the country's biggest retail stores.

"I decided I wasn't going to come home until I had a sale," says Mark. "At my first meeting, the buyer at Barneys [New York] committed to a twelve-thousand-dollar order. My dad was in shock."

Shortly after that first meeting, his collection was bringing in upwards of $60,000–$70,000 per month. With Mark making (and spending) heaps of money, Hanna left her teaching job shortly after the two got married in 2006. Six months later, she was pregnant with their first child.

Mark's flourishing venture, however, would soon take a dramatic nosedive. Technology had disrupted the apparel industry, lowering the barrier to entry and allowing new players to enter the space. Within a year, their direct competitors increased from seven companies to ninety.

"Things began to fall apart very quickly," says Mark. "Reality set in and I realized we wouldn't be able to survive at the rate we were going."

Sensing a potential collapse, Mark sold his BMW and enrolled in UCLA's part-time MBA program. Executive by day and student by night, it was a grueling schedule for the new husband and dad, but he was determined to make it work.

"I wanted to be in business in some capacity, but I didn't know how," says Mark. "I thought graduate school would be a great place to get more skills and find new opportunities."

SHARK BITE

You are going to screw up. We all do. I can't tell you how many times I did and [still] do. No matter what happens, every morning, the minute after you wipe away the crust from your eyes, remind yourself that you are going to enjoy every minute of the day.[31]
—Mark

FROM BABY BRAIN TO BABY EMPIRE

Hanna enjoyed the initial few months of domestic life, but motherhood brought challenges she didn't expect and with them a flood of confusing emotions. As Mark juggled a full-time job and heavy class load, the first-time mom was often alone with the baby and felt isolated from the world.

"It was like my brain was literally rotting away," says Hanna. "There were moments when I actually thought I was losing my mind. Looking back, I can see now I had post-partum depression."

After six months of barely leaving the house, Hanna decided to "take charge" of her situation and signed up for a few of the Mommy and Me classes offered near their home.

Engaging with a community of mothers provided Hanna with an important emotional outlet and proved she wasn't alone in her struggles. What's more, the outings helped stimulate the healing process and served as a key source of inspiration for the soon-to-be company's very first product: the

Lollacup—a valve-free sippy cup that allows infants to easily and effectively drink from a straw.

Hanna and Mark's daughter had been born three weeks prematurely and, as a result, was developing slower than other children her age. Certain tasks, like drinking from a traditional kids' cup, proved difficult for the toddler to master. As Hanna connected with more parents, she realized it was a challenge that many families shared.

"Most sippy cups have spill-proof valves, which is great for parents but can be incredibly difficult for kids," says Hanna. "I couldn't understand why there weren't more open-straw cups."

The new mother searched high and low for a functional solution, but couldn't find anything she liked. The only cup that seemed to work was one that her parents had found while vacationing in Korea.

"It was really easy for my daughter to use," says Hanna. "But it wasn't very cute and didn't have much of an aesthetic. I thought I could make something that was more tastefully done."

At the time, one of the most popular baby items on the market was a teething product called Sophie the Giraffe. Free of PVC and Phthalates, the French toy had a $25 price tag and was a favorite among celebrity and other noteworthy parents. Hanna believed she could do for sippy cups what Sophie the Giraffe had done for teethers.

When she approached Mark about the idea, he was instantaneously supportive. Recognizing that Hanna had never started a venture, however, he gave her a large stack of books and advised that she spend the following months examining the market and writing a business plan. If, after

his graduation, she was still interested in building the company, Mark agreed to come on board full-time. That was all it took to send Hanna off to the races.

"I immediately got to work doing research," says Hanna. "I would put my daughter down for a nap and spend hours on Google searching for how to manufacture plastic products. At first I didn't know any of the terminology, but soon it all started to make sense."

Within only a few months, Hanna had put together a thirty-five-page business plan and drafted a long list of local manufacturers. Ever the ambitious student, the more information she gathered, the more determined she grew.

"Mark's mom would babysit, and I would go out and meet with factories," says Hanna. "Most of the manufacturers thought I was clueless, but finally one offered to help."

Although Hanna had a clear vision of what the product should look like, she wasn't a professional graphic artist and required a physical rendering to get it produced. So she hired a small team of design students whom she'd met while attending a letterpress class at the local art college. Her instructions were simple: the cup had to resemble an animal and include both handles and a retractable straw. From frogs to bears, a flood of design concepts soon came pouring in.

It was clear that Hanna was more passionate than ever about building the business, and Mark could tell she was getting restless. So in mid-2009, shortly after his graduation, the pair sat down for a final discussion.

"I wanted to make sure she was one hundred percent certain that this was the right decision," says Mark. "I knew this was going to be the hardest thing we'd ever done and that it would test us both individually and as a couple."

Hanna confirmed that she was up for the challenge, and the two began mapping out their respective roles and responsibilities.

"We decided that she would handle everything related to sales, design, and product development," says Mark. "And I was responsible for anything that had to do with finances, operations, and production."

Unlike some businesses that require minimal start-up costs, manufacturing a physical product is generally an expensive undertaking. So, using their house as collateral, Hanna and Mark borrowed $100,000 from the bank and got to work creating the first prototype.

As Mark dove into production tasks, Hanna went from boutique to boutique, pitching buyers and attempting to secure their first set of clients. With no real sales experience, this was the first time she'd ever pitched anything—let alone something she'd created herself.

"It was definitely hard at first," she says. "But I believed so much in the cup that I felt confident walking into a store and pitching."

Selling door-to-door was a good initial step, but it proved time intensive and not particularly effective. So in the fall of 2010, the couple purchased a booth at the ABC Kids Expo—one of the world's largest trade shows for baby products. This, they hoped, would broaden their reach and allow them to connect with a targeted audience of prospective customers. It was a significant expense for the fledgling company, but one that ultimately proved invaluable to the business.

From the moment the expo began, it was clear that Lolla-cup was a hit with attendees. By the end of the show, Hanna and Mark had signed their first ten accounts and attracted a barrage of outstanding press. They were even selected to be

in *People* magazine's Holiday Gift Guide. There was just one problem: they had no actual merchandise.

It takes months to get a new product off the ground, and Lollacup was still in the development phase. At that point, all they had were a few prototypes and some very basic packaging samples.

"We signed up our first accounts before we even had product to sell," says Hanna. "We actually didn't even start fulfilling orders until April of 2011."

Although they weren't able to directly capitalize off the positive press, Hanna used the articles as leverage to attract more clients. Soon, boutiques from around the country were taking her calls.

"That's when I could really sell," says Hanna. "I finally had some real ammunition to present to buyers."

Less than three months later, Hanna had signed up thirty more retail locations and attracted the attention of countless more. Now all they were missing was just one tiny thing: inventory.

ALTERNATE, REALITY

Hanna and Mark were optimistic about their progress but worried they weren't expanding fast enough. Their savings were dwindling and they needed to secure additional sources of capital to meet the growing demand.

At the time, *Shark Tank* was still a relatively new series, with fewer than forty episodes in the can. Although the husband-and-wife team had watched the show before, they had never seriously considered auditioning. That is, until one of their close friends suggested they give it a try.

"We needed an investment to get more inventory," says Hanna. "So, one evening around midnight we decided to log on to the website and see how to apply."

What happened next can only be described as pure serendipity. As it turned out, the show was holding an open casting call the very next morning in Studio City, California—a mere twenty-minute drive from the couple's home. While these days, *Shark Tank* hosts numerous auditions in cities across America, in 2011 there was only one live casting event each year. Hanna and Mark couldn't believe their luck.

With only six hours to prepare, they stayed up for most of

the night filling out the thirty-page application and preparing their pitch. Was it a crazy idea? Maybe. But they knew it might also be the chance of a lifetime.

The next morning, Hanna and Mark woke up early, dropped their daughter off at day care, and headed straight to the audition. After seven hours of waiting in line, they were assigned a room and given one minute to present.

"We had a great elevator pitch," says Mark. "I knew there was a lot of competition, but I really thought they liked us."

Mark's intuition was correct. Just a few weeks later, the Lollaland founders received a call from the casting director with an invitation to advance to the next round. From that moment on, Hanna and Mark treated the opportunity as though it was life or death.

"We made a rule that we would get the producers anything they needed within two hours or less," says Mark. "It didn't matter what it was. If they wanted something, we would put our lives on hold."

For the next month, the husband-and-wife team participated in regular calls with the casting team, where they practiced their pitch and perfected their approach. Eventually, they were given a time slot to tape and asked to attend a live orientation. Their good fortune, however, would soon run out.

The night before the meeting was scheduled to occur, Hanna and Mark received some disappointing news. Due to a show scheduling conflict, they had been demoted to an alternate role. In other words, they could still attend the training session but would only get a time slot if another entrepreneur failed to show up or was disqualified for any reason. It was a devastating blow, but they refused to give up hope.

At orientation, each company was provided with detailed information about the taping process and asked to perform their pitch to one or two dozen members of the production team. Mark spotted the executive producer in the crowd and, determined to stand out, delivered the pitch directly to him.

"All I wanted was for him to lose sleep that night," says Mark. "I wanted him to see that they had made a massive mistake."

While neither founders will ever know for sure if the strategy worked, just a month later they were standing backstage, getting ready to present to a room full of Sharks.

"Before we entered the tank, I gave Hanna a little pep talk," says Mark. "I reminded her that we were there looking for business partners, not a charity handout. We were equals, and no matter what, we shouldn't beg."

With their confidence high, Hanna and Mark entered the tank and started their pitch, asking for $100,000 for 15 percent of the company—a daring valuation considering they'd only sold $30,000 worth of product.

Once the presentation was complete, the Sharks began a series of rapid-fire questions, delving deep into their sales figures and performance history.

Lollaland manufactures all of its inventory in the United States, which at the time meant each cup cost $4.50 to produce—a significantly higher number than the industry average. Kevin O'Leary was taken aback by the inflated expense and insisted they move production offshore to a country like China, where it's considerably cheaper.

"If we have to sell it at $9.99, which is a very popular retail price point, you have to make it for $1.07," said Kevin.

But Hanna and Mark had no interest in taking the

recommendation. Their research showed that parents prefer baby products that are made in the United States and Europe. Not only was an American-made product perceived to be safer, local manufacturing was an important part of their value proposition.

As the negotiation continued, the couple revealed that they had recently entered into an exclusive agreement with a third-party sales agency. This meant that all deals needed to be run through the vendor—a service that came with a steep 15 percent fee. Without any legally binding metrics to ensure performance quality, the Sharks felt as though Hanna and Mark had made a disastrous decision and would have to "learn the hard way."

"We're not dumb," says Mark. "We did our homework. The less established you are, the more you have to give away. We were a brand-new company and they were taking a chance on us."

Even with the controversial sales contract, Kevin believed in the cup and made the couple an initial offer: $100,000 for 50 percent of the company. Not only did the deal dramatically reduce their valuation, it came with an unsavory contingency—Lollaland would have to move all manufacturing offshore and get costs below two dollars per cup.

Daymond John was the next Shark to chime in, matching O'Leary's offer of $100,000 for 50 percent of the organization but providing his own contingency—Hannah and Mark would have to break their agreement with the sales agency.

"There was no way that was going to happen," says Mark. "I've been burned by partners before, and I wasn't going to do that to somebody else. When I make a deal, I give my word. That's not something I take lightly."

Knowing that both contingencies posed a threat to their core values, they were relieved when Robert expressed interest in getting involved. He had invested in this industry before and knew the product category well. Robert, however, felt as though their valuation was too high and asked the entrepreneurs to make a counteroffer. Unsure of how to proceed, Mark revised his ask: 40 percent of the company for $100,000.

Before Robert could respond, Mark Cuban shot up from his chair and announced he would do the deal for the same terms. Robert, of course, was offended that a fellow Shark was meddling in his negotiation, but the Lollaland founders had no time to smooth over hurt feelings. Mark's deal was time-sensitive; they had just twenty-four seconds to respond.

As the clock ticked down, Daymond made a counteroffer, lowering his proposed share of equity to 30 percent. But the couple was too slow to respond, and the FUBU founder quickly went out.

Recognizing they might lose both Kevin's and Mark Cuban's offers, Hanna tried to disarm the situation by asking if they would consider partnering on the deal. After a brief moment of tension, both investors agreed, and Lolla-land received its first investment. It was a dream come true.

"Aside from my marriage and the birth of our children, that was the happiest moment of my life," says Mark. "We were almost to the point where we didn't think we could drive home. We were *that* happy."

> SHARK BITE
>
> *A perfect pitch is when people know their numbers, capture my fleeting attention quickly, feed me when I'm hungry (which is most of the time), and allow me to interact and play. But most importantly, you need to be passionate.*[33]
> —Robert

BREAKING THE MOLD

Hanna and Mark's experience on *Shark Tank* did more than just provide their company with a much-needed infusion of capital; it substantiated their product and confirmed that they had reached a certain level of legitimacy.

"Sure, we'd achieved some success before going on the show," says Hanna. "But for these moguls to actually believe in what we were doing and put their money into the business felt like real validation."

The feelings of excitement, however, would soon wane. On January 30, 2012, Hanna and Mark received yet another

discouraging call from the production team. Their segment had been cut.

There are myriad factors that go into producing a television show, and it's rare that every piece of footage makes it to broadcast. Knowing that this can be distressing, the casting department regularly reminds participating entrepreneurs that, even if they make it to the tank and land a deal with a Shark, it's possible their episode may not air.

Hanna and Mark were aware this might occur, but couldn't help but feel disappointed. Their ascent from alternate to contender had been an emotionally exhausting process and, while grateful to have secured an investment, they were saddened that the segment would now go unseen.

"We were so bummed," says Mark. "From the early days of talking about starting the company to landing a deal with Mark Cuban and Robert Herjavec, it just felt like we had come so far."

Once again, however, timing would work in their favor. When a television network green-lights a show, they place an "order" for a certain number of episodes. This can range from a single "pilot" to a full twenty-two-episode season. *Shark Tank* hit its stride in the fourth season and, at the very last minute, ABC ordered three additional episodes, one of which included Lollaland's pitch.

"We got the call two or three weeks before we were scheduled to air," says Hanna. "We were shocked. At that point we didn't think it was going to happen."

With less than a month to prepare, Hanna and Mark had no time to doddle. It takes eight weeks from start to finish to manufacture a cup, which meant they were already behind schedule. Unsure of how many orders to expect, the couple

increased their production run from 1,000 units to 10,000 units and braced themselves for a potential surge.

When their segment finally aired on April 27, 2012—almost a full year after they had taped it—the Lollaland founders hosted a private party at the school where they had first begun dating. Surrounded by friends and family, they prepared for what would quickly become a record-breaking night.

"It was insane. Our phone was ringing nonstop from the moment the episode aired on the East Coast," says Mark. "That night we did $100,000 from our website alone, so basically we doubled our business in one evening."

The couple awoke the next morning to over 3,000 e-mails and more sales than they could have ever imagined. To help handle the flood of new orders, Hanna and Mark recruited their parents, as well as two of their unemployed friends. For nine days straight, the scrappy team worked around the clock to fulfill each and every order.

The joyride, however, would soon come to a screeching halt. Just eleven days after the Lollaland episode aired, their factory called with horrifying news: the mold that was being used to manufacture their cups had broken. This meant all production would be frozen until a new one could be made—a process that would take eight weeks to complete and cost $60,000.

"I've never in my life felt more defeated," says Mark. "Pretty much all the money we made that night went into the mold."

But the expense was just one of many concerns. By this point, Lollaland had secured 150 corporate accounts—all of which had pending orders. With manufacturing halted, it would take months for the inventory to be delivered.

"Our retailers were not happy," says Mark. "Everyone kept saying we were through, that we were going to go out of business."

Fortunately, each customer maintained their order, and by the fall of 2012 the company was back in business. It had been a trying time, but in the end, the husband-and-wife team emerged victorious.

Today, Lollacup offers a range of merchandise and has been rebranded as Lollaland. Their products can be found in over 1,000 stores across the globe, including such well-known retailers as Whole Foods and Nordstrom, and both Hanna and Mark continue to develop new ways to grow the enterprise.

"This next year is really going to be pivotal," says Mark. "I always say that, but I really think the next twelve months are do-or-die. We've achieved a lot, but we still have a long way to go."

Everyone gets down; the key is how soon you get back up. The people who will be truly successful are those who fight through the quickest and come back stronger and smarter.[34]
—*Mark*

THE LOLLALAND PLAYBOOK FOR SUCCESS

Maintaining success is easy when everything's running smoothly. It's only when faced with an extreme challenge that one's passion and dedication is truly put to the test.

The couple faced such a challenge during their third year of business.

Since childhood, Hanna has suffered from a variety of skin ailments that have resulted in the prescription of countless steroid creams, which are generally provided on a strictly temporary basis.

After visiting a new dermatologist in 2012, she was told that the high dosages of steroids had compromised her vascular system and essentially shut down her adrenal glands. The doctor suggested she go off all medications immediately but warned her the withdrawal process could be "intense"—a word that doesn't begin to describe the hardship she encountered.

For fifteen months, Hanna lived in a constant state of agonizing pain. Losing much of her hair and eyebrows, the symptoms got so bad she was forced to leave the family home and move in with her parents. At one point, her skin even appeared to take on a mummified state.

"I couldn't wear clothes for four months because my skin was so raw it would stick to the fabric and peel off," says Hanna. "I literally was forced to live in a bathtub."

With no choice but to step down from her role in the business, it was up to Mark to ensure the family and organization stayed afloat. It was a trying year and a half, but one that made both their business and marriage stronger in the end—thanks, partly, to their Playbook for Success.

HUSTLE HARDER AND FASTER

In a world that grows more rapid with each passing year, Hanna and Mark believe it's crucial for entrepreneurs to hustle harder and faster than what feels comfortable. On numerous occasions, for example, the couple has dragged their feet on a new idea or innovation only to find that a competitor has swooped in and dominated the market.

"It starts from the moment you first get the idea," says Hanna. "If you don't move fast enough, someone else will beat you to it."

It takes more than speed, however, to be a good hustler. One must also learn to develop a keen eye for opportunity and be willing to take chances that others may resist—a habit Mark first established as a teenager.

The high school he and Hanna attended allowed seniors to travel off-campus during their lunch periods. While most students used the free time as a chance to socialize with friends or relax, Mark saw it as a business opportunity.

"I would buy McDonald's for all the ninth graders and charge them a dollar premium on each item," says Mark. "Sure, that meant I didn't get to eat lunch, but I didn't care. I just wanted to make a few bucks so I could buy a gift for Hanna."

Build Your Network

For the fifteen months that Hanna was ill, Mark worked around the clock to close new sales. Trade shows had become one of their most effective lead generation tools, so each month he would travel to a different expo, totaling thirteen in just one year.

Being away from his family, especially during such an emotional time, was taxing. But instead of feeling sorry for himself, Mark decided to use each trip as an opportunity to build new relationships.

"I knew I couldn't sit around in my hotel room and sulk,"

says Mark. "So I always made an effort to take someone out for a drink or just start a conversation. I met so many great people that either I've been able to help or who have helped me."

From fellow vendors to new clients, Mark amassed a vast network of associates and colleagues. Most importantly, it was while traveling that he met Lollaland's current sales manager. What started as a simple discussion over drinks eventually blossomed into a meaningful friendship and a prosperous business relationship.

"We're a small company, and that's a very important role for us," says Mark. "We never would have met if I hadn't made a conscious effort to connect."

Remain a Constant Learner

In the seven years since Lollaland first began, Hanna and Mark have gone through a litany of ups and downs—from the joy of securing their first accounts to the pain of dealing with Hanna's illness. Through it all, however, the husband-and-wife team has remained dedicated to using each experience as an opportunity to learn valuable new lessons about themselves and their organization.

"The desire to learn was a big part of why I wanted to start the company in the first place," says Hanna. "I was at home with a baby all day and didn't feel like I was using my brain. I needed intellectual stimulation."

Cultivating a deep thirst for knowledge isn't a principle reserved strictly for first-time entrepreneurs. In fact, the couple has found that the most successful business tycoons tend to also be the most avid learners, including the Sharks.

"We were one of Mark Cuban's first deals on the show," says Mark. "He wasn't much of a product guy at the time, so it was up to us to teach him about our category."

Nervous the famous investor might be resistant to new ideas, both founders were pleasantly surprised at how eager Mark was to take their advice.

"Sometimes he'll send out a mass e-mail to all his

entrepreneurs asking for our thoughts on a certain issue," says Mark. "I mean this guy's a billionaire, and he's still trying to learn new things."

Master Prioritization

Just because a particular item may be listed in one's playbook, it doesn't mean he or she has necessarily perfected it. Such is the case with Lollaland's fourth principle: master prioritization.

From the moment they rise, Hanna and Mark begin to arrange their day, organizing their to-do list from most to least important item. Even if it's a simple five-minute conversation, they have found that prioritizing their daily goals is crucial to their success as business and life partners.

"As an entrepreneur, you're pulled in ten different directions," says Hanna. "You need to make sure you're focusing on the big things."

This, they admit, is often easier said than done, especially for new organizations with limited resources. While every CEO would love to focus strictly on high-level tasks, most small-business owners must wear a variety of hats. This is part of why the couple believes that learning effective and efficient task management is a skill worth investing in.

"Being responsible for making sure things get done isn't easy," says Mark. "Believe me, there are plenty of times when I wish a Shark would walk in here and tell me what to do."

Find the Balance

Like many founders, Hanna and Mark must be careful not to become too consumed by their company. While it's crucial they remain on the top of their game at work, they must also set aside enough time to be caring and devoted parents. To ensure they don't get swept up in the minutia of a busy day at the office, each partner has developed his or her own way of finding balance.

Mark does this by trying to give 100 percent to each task while it's being performed. When he's at work, for example,

he's fully invested in the operation. At home, he puts down the smartphone and spends focused, quality time with his family.

"I would give us a good grade when it comes to that," says Mark. "There's no greater motivating factor for us than our girls, and we make sure they know we're invested in them."

For Hanna, balance is about letting go of some of the unnecessary rules and expectations she placed on herself over the years.

"I used to think that every time I got on the phone I needed to appear like we were some big corporation," says Hanna. "But after being on *Shark Tank*, I felt like people had a glimpse into our reality. It helped me to relax a little bit."

Today, Hanna has no qualms about jumping on a conference call while changing a diaper or letting clients know she's working from home. By embracing this authentic approach, she's become a better mom and a more empowered business owner.

"I think that one change has really helped with balancing my own life," says Hanna. "It was a real revelation."

CHAPTER NINE

INVESTOR: **BARBARA CORCORAN**

COMPANY: Pipsnacks

FOUNDERS: Jeff Martin and Jen Martin

SEASON: Six

POP GOES THE BUSINESS

You might say that popcorn is somewhat of a tradition in the Martin family. Growing up in the suburbs of New Jersey, the brother-and-sister team sold their first batch over twenty years ago—at the ripe old ages of eight and five, respectively. Little did they know that, just two decades later, they would ascend to snack food stardom as the proud owners of a multimillion-dollar consumer packaged goods enterprise.

Jeff and Jen Martin appeared on season six of *Shark Tank* and landed a $200,000 deal with Barbara Corcoran for 10 percent of their company, Pipsnacks—an all-natural line of mini popcorn that's prepared in small batches and seasoned by hand. Today, the popular item is carried in thousands of stores and boasts a loyal tribe of fans, followers, and foodies.

Although the Brooklyn-based siblings have been peddling products since grade school, the birth of this now booming venture was relatively accidental and unlike anything either sibling could have predicted.

JEFF'S DINER WILL NO LONGER ACCEPT RESERVATIONS

Like so many entrepreneurs, both Jeff and Jen displayed a passion for business from an early age. As a child, Jeff was hyper-inquisitive and continuously tinkering with new ideas.

It didn't take long for the enthusiastic youngster to spot a challenge he knew he could solve: snack time.

With a family that consisted of four rowdy kids and two working parents, after-school meals were often left up to the children to manage. But after an exhausting day of sitting in a classroom, Jeff's siblings were too rambunctious to prepare anything from scratch. So, naturally, the enterprising elementary schooler opened Jeff's Diner—a casual eatery with a five-star location: just north of the living room and south of the kitchen.

Too young then to handle sharp knives or cook on the stove unsupervised, his specialty dish was "the Pickle Delight," which consisted of a small mound of deli meat atop a plain bagel with a handful of pickles and a smear of yellow mustard. It wasn't gourmet, but neither was his clientele.

"It was the best business plan ever," says Jen. "He would give my mom a grocery list, she would buy everything, and then he would charge us for it."

But the budding entrepreneur would soon feel the firm smack of parental oversight. After his "customers" ran out of money and began complaining of hunger pangs, Jeff's Diner was promptly shut down and forced to return all profits. His mother had no idea he'd been charging for his services.

Still, Jeff's parents were impressed by his drive and encouraged him to explore other ideas. They wouldn't let him starve his siblings, of course, but they also didn't want to starve him of his creativity and ambition. As an alternative, they handed over the family popcorn machine and encouraged him to work *with* his brothers and sister, instead of profiting from them.

Soon, he and Jen were peddling small bags of homemade popcorn on the street, and they would regularly sell out. Before long, they had broken the popcorn machine and

graduated to peddling more profitable items, namely, their toys.

"When we were kids, we never played house," says Jen. "Instead we would take all of my parents' old checkbooks and play business."

As Jeff and Jen grew older, they began to drift apart. With a three-year age difference separating them, they spent most of their time with the other siblings who were closer to their age. It wasn't until high school that the pair became close.

"I started driving Jen to school when she was a freshman," says Jeff. "At a certain point I realized she was really funny, and we just started hanging out nonstop."

But they shared more than just a sense of humor. Jeff and Jen took great pride in their after-school jobs—a relatively uncommon occurrence for most kids their age. Never could they have guessed that this mutual passion would one day lead to a million-dollar enterprise.

After graduating from high school, Jeff moved out of the family home and headed north to Bentley University, where he majored in business. Unlike his high school classes, which he felt lacked much real-world relevancy, the courses at Bentley offered a wide range of experiences. The work could be difficult, of course, but Jeff had never been one to back down from a challenge.

Jen, on the other hand, was less certain of her future. She knew she was expected to attend college but had little idea as to what she actually wanted to study. After dragging her heels for much of her senior year of high school, she eventually applied and was accepted into a small college in Connecticut. It was only upon arrival that Jen realized it was a commuter school and that "ninety-nine percent of the students lived off-campus."

While many of her peers may have found this distressing, Jen used the alone time as an opportunity for growth and development. Interested in health and healing, she would often retire to the local co-op where she'd spend hours perusing the shelves. Even though Jen had found a way to make the most of her time at college, deep down she felt it wasn't a good fit. So the following summer, she sat her parents down for a difficult conversation.

"I told them I wasn't going back," says Jen. "I didn't know what I wanted to learn, and it just didn't make sense for me to stay."

To her great surprise, her parents approved of the decision, but only if she agreed to actively explore other alternatives. They didn't want her sitting around the house all day—and quite frankly, neither did she.

With a passion for community service, Jen volunteered for a nonprofit in Costa Rica that gave her the opportunity to work with disabled adults. From there, she traveled to Australia and Thailand, where she participated in similar programs. Eventually, Jen decided to pursue a career in social work and moved back to the United States to attend Loyola University in Chicago.

Meanwhile, Jeff had relocated to New York City and begun a career in investment banking. The hours could be long, but for the most part, he found the work enjoyable. Still, something was missing.

"I learned a ton, which I'm really grateful for," says Jeff. "I just didn't love the culture of banking. I knew it wasn't for me."

Then in 2009, at the height of the recession, the bank where Jeff was employed began company-wide layoffs. After

just barely surviving the first three cuts, he was let go on the fourth and final round.

"I felt unbelievably anxious, but I refused to give into it," says Jeff. "So I left the office, went to the gym, and started the next phase of my life."

At that point, Jen was still in school and working part-time at a local health food store. It was there that she met a successful entrepreneur who shared her passion for juicing. One afternoon, while preparing a juice for her favorite customer—a successful entrepreneur who shared her passion for health—the businessman suggested they start a juicing company together.

As the organization began to flourish, the first-time business owner found herself inundated with work. Between school, a day job at the health food store, and the start-up, Jen was quickly falling behind. Aware that her brother was out of work and eager for a challenge, she asked Jeff to fly out for a week and help her catch up. It was an experience that would become a turning point in both their lives.

"I think I always knew we'd work well together," says Jen. "But that trip really proved it to me."

SNACKS ON SNACKS ON SNACKS

If the week comanaging the juicing company had taught them anything, it was that their skill sets were highly complementary. While Jen had a flair for the creative, she lacked much of the organizational abilities that her more analytically minded sibling seemed to naturally possess. It's no surprise then that when she decided to move to a new apartment in late 2010, she once again reached out to her big brother.

"I called Jeff and asked if he would come help me," says Jen. "I'm good at a lot of things, but organization is truly not one of them."

Happy to lend a hand, Jeff arrived in Chicago on the morning of the scheduled move and headed straight to her apartment. Jen had spent weeks preparing for the relocation, she assured him, and simply needed some last-minute help coordinating details and packing a few remaining items. When Jeff arrived on the scene, however, he found a very different situation.

"All she had packed were two shoe boxes," says Jeff. "Literally, there were two shoe boxes and a bag full of dirty yoga clothes."

Both brother and sister still debate the exact details of this story. What they can agree on, however, is that by the time the move was complete, they were both exhausted and starving. Lacking the energy to head back outside and forage for dinner, they began scouring through Jen's belongings in search of something, anything, to eat.

With the new apartment in disarray, all they found was a small bag of miniature popcorn kernels—a gift from a farmer whom Jen had met at a local outdoor market. Jeff

was surprised to find the kernels; since childhood his sister had suffered from an array of food-related allergies, including a sensitivity to corn. She'd accepted the present only after the farmer explained that the miniature kernels were lighter on the digestive system and could even be tolerated by people with corn allergies.

Although Jen wasn't entirely trusting of the mysterious seeds, she knew their options were limited. So, using a small dab of olive oil and a sprinkle of pink Himalayan sea salt, she got to work preparing a batch.

"We were really grumpy and just needed to eat," says Jen. "I decided to just try some and see what would happen."

By the second bite, both siblings were hooked. It was unlike any popcorn they had ever tasted, yet similar enough to evoke the same satisfaction. "The first thing I said was that we should try to sell this," says Jeff. "We'd been joking around about starting a business together and this seemed like the perfect product."

Like many who experience a momentary flash of inspiration, however, the feeling soon gave way to the realities of everyday life, and the idea was put on hold. Jeff continued to work at the small tech start-up where he'd recently been hired, and Jen went back to the health food store.

It took almost a full year, and a cross-country drive, for the brother-and-sister team to rekindle their concept and begin building the organization that would one day become their legacy.

During the summer of 2011, their older brother, Pete, was asked by his employer to relocate from Los Angeles to New York City. There was just one problem: Pete's car had recently been rear-ended and wouldn't be out of the shop

until after he had moved. With Jen on summer break and Jeff in need of a vacation, they approached their brother with a solution.

"We offered to fly to LA and drive the car back to New York," says Jeff. "It would cost him less than hiring a company, and it would be a fun experience for us."

Pete agreed to the plan, and Jeff and Jen traveled west to retrieve the vehicle. But this would be no ordinary road trip.

As they snaked their way across the southwest and up through the Rocky Mountains, the duo began putting together a business plan. From packaging and design, to development and start-up costs, they made a detailed list of everything that would be required to build a popcorn company. By the time they reached the East Coast, they were committed to making it happen.

Before they could begin selling the product, however, they needed to come up with a name—something bold and recognizable that would not only describe their brand but the mini popcorn category as a whole. Motivated to find something clever and industry-defining, they reached out to their friends for help.

It wasn't long until they were connected to Nina Beckhardt, a friend of a friend who had started The Naming Group—a New York City-based agency dedicated to changing the way brands name their products. Although engagements with the firm usually started in the six-figures, The Naming Group was looking to launch a pilot program for start-ups and small businesses. For only $500 they agreed to take on the fledgling organization.

"We were grateful for the opportunity, but that was still a lot of money for us," says Jeff. "At the time, we only had $1,300 in the bank."

After going back and forth about whether or not it would be worth the expense, they decided to take the leap—a smart move considering that only one week later they received a long list of potential names.

"We read through the document they sent over and immediately stopped at Pipcorn," says Jen. "That was it. There was no second choice."

With a refined recipe and a catchy name, Jeff and Jen incorporated their business under the name Pipsnacks and began searching for a venue to debut their product. On a whim, they applied to Smorgasburg—one of New York City's most well-known open-air markets, featuring packaged and prepared food that's handcrafted by some of the city's top purveyors.

Getting into the mega-popular bazaar is no easy feat. Because of its outdoor location, the market is open exclusively on weekends between April and November and draws crowds of upwards to 16,000 per day. It was a long shot at best, but at that point they figured they had nothing to lose.

As luck would have it, the Smorgasburg team was in search of a popcorn vendor for their upcoming season. After a formal pitch and brief product sampling, Pipsnacks was accepted to the market in January of 2012.

With a dwindling bank account and a hard deadline fast approaching, Jeff and Jen knew they'd have to get creative. Instead of hiring a design company to create their packaging, they used The Dieline—a comprehensive online platform that connects designers with those in need of creative services. In just a few days, they found an up-and-coming design student who had just what they wanted: exquisite taste and a reasonable price tag.

Next they began searching for a commercial kitchen and

soon found a Harlem neighborhood-based business incubator that offered both affordable kitchen space and valuable mentorship. But the affection proved unrequited.

After a brief interview process, the director of the incubator felt Pipsnacks wasn't ready for such an intensive program and turned down their application. It was a crushing blow, but one that both founders took in stride.

"From the first day, we decided this business was going to work," says Jeff. "We had no backup plan. There was no way we were going to fail."

Over the next three months, Jeff and Jen filed incorporation paperwork, secured the necessary insurance, and continued searching for a commercial kitchen. But no matter where they looked, they couldn't find anything that fit their budget and timeline. With the Smorgasburg premiere only a few weeks away, they returned to the incubator that had initially turned them down.

"We told them about our situation and asked if we could, at the very least, rent space by the hour," says Jeff. "We just needed to get it done."

The founder of the incubator agreed, and Jeff and Jen immediately got to popping. Less than a month later, on April 28, 2012, they debuted at the outdoor market and sold their very first bag of Pipcorn.

"I still remember the woman who bought that one," says Jen. "She had no idea how much she was blowing our minds. I wish I had gotten a picture with her."

But their mini popcorn attracted more than just the everyday shopper. Legendary designer Kate Spade was at the market that weekend and, unbeknownst to them, had purchased a bag. She was so impressed by the product, she

Tweeted it out to the world. They couldn't have asked for a better unveiling.

The summer of 2012 was a sweltering one, especially in the Northeast, where temperatures reached record highs. One afternoon in late May, only four weeks after Pipcorn's debut, Jeff and Jen noticed a young woman with a clipboard standing outside by their booth.

"It was clear she was doing some kind of work," says Jeff. "She was sweating her face off, so we invited her in to cool off in the shade."

Little did they know, the perspiring woman was a scout from the Oprah Winfrey Network on the hunt for items to be featured in the holiday edition of *Oprah's Favorite Things*. Once again, it appeared as though luck was on their side.

The scout loved their product and soon they were meeting with Oprah's creative team. After months of back and forth, and the development of four special holiday flavors, they were chosen to be showcased in the legendary feature.

To prepare for the increase in exposure, Jeff and Jen raised $100,000 from friends and family, which they used to hire employees and relocate to a larger space in New Jersey. Things were moving faster than they had anticipated, but the team knew they couldn't turn down such a remarkable opportunity.

When *Oprah's Favorite Things* aired in November of 2012, Pipcorn's sales went through the roof. It was a whirlwind experience, and at times Jeff and Jen felt unsure that they'd be able to keep up. Still an early-stage company, they had yet to build processes around much of their operations and were sprinting to fulfill the massive influx of orders.

"We didn't even have a solid cost structure yet," says

Jeff. "We knew it wasn't going to put us out of business, but we didn't know if we were going to make or lose money."

Although demanding, ultimately the experience proved to be a positive one. Not only did it create a deluge of publicity, it provided them with the credibility they needed to attract larger retailers and, eventually, the Sharks.

> *I find that all of us—rich, poor, or in between—are afraid of the same damn thing: running out of money. Along with that comes the fear of losing control of our lives, of not being able to pay our bills or remain self-sufficient. It's enough to make you lose sleep at night when you think about it, and so most of us don't.[36]*
> *—Mark*

SHARK TANK AUDITION, TAKE TWO

For most people, getting the opportunity to audition for *Shark Tank* is an once-in-a-lifetime opportunity. For Jeff and Jen, however, the auspicious chance came along twice.

Like millions of viewers who had seen Pipcorn on *Oprah's Favorite Things*, the *Shark Tank* casting team was impressed by their product and loved their relatable story. As avid fans of the show, Jeff and Jen were ecstatic when, out of the blue, they received an offer to audition for the fifth season.

"We were so excited to get the call," says Jen. "We immediately started filling out the paperwork."

But if their experience on the Oprah Winfrey Network had taught them anything, it was the crucial role that timing plays when undertaking any type of ambitious growth

opportunity. The organization had reached a critical juncture and demanded their utmost attention. Although an investment from a Shark would have been a dream come true, they felt it wasn't the right time.

"We weren't at the point in our business where we could have capitalized off of it," says Jeff. "We were still in a small kitchen, still hand-stamping each bag. We just weren't ready."

Recognizing that they wouldn't be able to devote the care and attention such an experience required, they reached back out to their contact and formally declined.

"It was a horrible call to make," says Jen. "We knew we had just turned down a chance that most people would have begged for."

But to their surprise, the casting team was understanding of their situation and promised to contact them again should another opportunity arise. While they were thankful for the generous offer, neither expected to ever hear from the *Shark Tank* crew again.

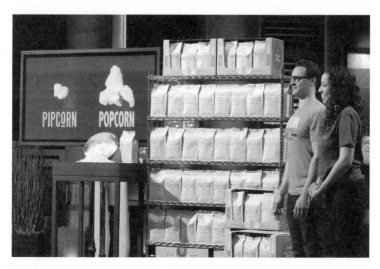

Over the next year, Jeff and Jen worked seven days a week to grow the company. They continued earning positive press and secured distribution with a handful of popular retailers. Slowly but surely, the enterprise was taking off.

But revenue isn't profit, and Jeff and Jen were struggling to make ends meet. Neither had yet to take a salary, and it was beginning to affect their livelihood. What's more, a lack of funds limited their ability to expand the operation.

Like many small-business owners, they faced a complex dilemma. In order to reduce costs, they would need to scale the manufacturing process, which would require additional capital. In other words, to make money in the long-term they would need to spend money in the short-term—money they did not have.

Then, in February of 2014, Jeff and Jen received an unexpected e-mail from the *Shark Tank* casting manager with yet another offer to audition for the show—this time for the sixth season. The timing couldn't have been better.

As winter turned to spring, the sibling cofounders alternated between running the day-to-day operations and furiously practicing their pitch. No matter what, they couldn't allow the time-intensive audition process to negatively impact the business or divert their focus, as the Oprah experience had done.

"We couldn't afford to walk away from the company for any period of time," says Jen. "Every penny counted. Every new store had to happen."

After months of preparation, the Pipsnacks founders were invited to fly to Los Angeles to tape an episode. They had but one simple goal: land a deal with Barbara Corcoran.

As Jeff and Jen entered the tank, they felt a rush of adrenaline course through their veins. They were asking for

$200,000 for 10 percent of the organization—a lofty valuation considering they hadn't yet turned a profit. Still, they were confident in their request. Pipsnacks had grown 125 percent in the six months prior and was on track to end the year with nearly half a million dollars in revenue.

When the pitch concluded, Kevin O'Leary weighed in first, questioning the steep valuation and lack of proprietary goods. What, he wondered, would stop a prospective competitor from purchasing the same kernels and replicating the idea. Jeff shot back quickly, revealing they were on the verge of closing a deal with their supplier for exclusive popping rights—a deal that did in fact close in the summer of 2015.

Mark Cuban and Robert Herjavec chimed in next, asking them to explain their cost structure, price point, and distribution model. At the time, one bag sold for $4.99—a premium compared to many of their competitors—and cost $1.80 to produce. Jeff explained that they had recently begun working with a co-packer and could eventually cut their manufacturing costs in half.

With a passion for healthy food and an insatiable appetite for a thriving business, Robert Herjavec was the first Shark to make an offer.

"Here's the deal: I love the belief, I love the popcorn, I really love the name," said Robert. "200K for twenty percent."

The bid threw Jeff and Jen for a loop. Robert liked their product, but he had cut the valuation in half. Although they desperately needed an investment, they were unwilling to give away such a large piece of the company.

"We knew the valuation was aggressive, but we were confident in it," says Jeff. "We were already doing $200,000 in just forty stores."

Jeff expressed his gratitude for the offer but explained they would be unwilling to sacrifice such a significant percentage of equity. Curious to see if they could meet in the middle, Robert asked him to counter. Jeff, however, refused to budge.

"Robert offered us a deal really early," says Jeff. "I turned it down partly to kill time and partly to show them that we were serious. Plus, we knew we wanted Barbara."

Passing on Robert's offer was a risky move, but their strategy worked. Barbara Corcoran appreciated their gumption and, even though she, too, felt the appraisal was exaggerated, decided to make them an offer.

"I happen to agree with his valuation," said Barbara. "I think you're overreaching. But you guys are winners. I can smell it a mile away. I'm giving you your full price."

Jeff and Jen were elated. Not only did they survive the tank, but they walked away with the exact deal and Shark they had wanted from the start.

"We were just so excited," says Jen. "We couldn't believe it. Even now I don't even think I could put that experience into words."

> *I was once young, broke, and ambitious, too, and I see a piece of myself in every entrepreneur I meet. I don't really think of myself as a "shark." It's a label I would have never given myself. I like to think I built my success on hard work, common sense, and playing nice.*[37]
> —Barbara

DOLLARS AND SENSE

Jeff and Jen's episode aired on November 14, 2014—five months after it had originally been taped. This meant there was plenty of time to prepare the business for what would hopefully be a massive growth spurt.

Their first step was to move the manufacturing facility from a small commercial kitchen in Englewood, New Jersey, to a much larger space back in Manhattan's Harlem neighborhood. They also upgraded their equipment, fine-tuned their package design, and made sure their website could handle a surge in traffic. Still, they were careful not to overspend or make any grand assumptions.

The Oprah experience had opened their eyes to the realities of modern-day media. Yes, they had successfully landed a deal, but there was no guarantee their episode would actually air. And if it did, who could say for sure how much it would affect their sales? It would be best, they decided, to remain cautiously optimistic.

"We've learned not to count on anything," says Jen. "So, while of course we were ready for our segment to air, we focused on growing the business as if *Shark Tank* wasn't going to happen."

In addition to expanding the wholesale operation and preparing for their *Shark Tank* premiere, they were also undergoing the due diligence process with Barbara and her team.

When a financier chooses to invest in a company, he or she commences an extensive appraisal process called due diligence. During this evaluation period, the investor reviews all relevant documents and confirms whether or not the organization and its owners are legitimate. From evaluating assets and liabilities to appraising the organization's overall viability, this procedure can take months to complete and requires an abundance of time and energy from all parties involved.

Although Jeff and Jen had made the initial deal with Barbara in June, it didn't officially close until the very week their episode debuted—a week that will go down in history as one their most memorable and emotionally charged.

"Every now and then we have one of these periods where all our wholesale orders come in at the same time," says Jeff. "This happened during the week our episode was scheduled to air."

To help ensure the Pipsnacks could meet the demand, their small team of dedicated employees put in countless hours of overtime. Jeff and Jen knew their team was extraordinary, but that experience proved just how committed and dedicated their staff was to the business. So you can imagine how horrified they were by what happened next.

Only hours before their episode was scheduled to air, the

cofounders received a phone call from one of their star employees. The paycheck, which she received earlier that afternoon, had bounced. It was the first time they were unable to make payroll. Both brother and sister went into panic mode.

"I was horrified. I mean that's just not okay," says Jen. "Luckily, a couple checks had come in that day, so I ran right over to the bank and got her the money."

The company's financial woes, however, would soon come to an end. Later that evening, their episode went live, and within twenty-four hours they had sold $296,000 worth of product—more than their total sales from the previous year.

"I had just bought a new phone and would get an e-mail every time an order came in," says Jeff. "By the next morning the phone no longer worked. It had vibrated over thirteen thousand times in one night."

In the three months following their episode, the enterprise catapulted to a whole new level of growth, bringing in roughly $1.1 million in revenue. And by September of 2015, they had expanded from forty stores to over two thousand.

"To me the coolest part is that all our clients keep reordering," says Jen. "In fact, every week Whole Foods places two orders: one for the shelf and one for customers who have preordered."

Meanwhile, their e-commerce business, which had previously brought in just $500–$700 a week, has also expanded, averaging sales of $2,000 per day—a number that has yet to taper off.

"A big part of the reason our e-commerce sales have stayed strong is Barbara," says Jeff. "She has a brilliant marketing mind and is constantly getting our product in front of the right people."

It's more than just marketing expertise Barbara brings to the table, however; she's become instrumental in keeping the brother-and-sister team motivated and empowered. "We're inspired to do better just by being around her," says Jen. "She's the best kind of investor you could ask for."

THE PIPSNACKS PLAYBOOK FOR SUCCESS

From a steadfast work ethic to an unquenchable commitment to quality, Jeff and Jen attribute much of their success to the values bestowed upon them by their parents—wisdom that continues to serve as inspiration.

During a recent trip to their childhood home, Jeff noticed the freezer had broken and would no longer produce ice. He tinkered with it for a bit, as he's prone to do, but eventually gave up and moved on to other tasks. When he and Jen returned home the following weekend, their mother announced that she had successfully fixed the appliance. Jeff was flabbergasted. How had she done it?

"In life," she explained. "I have found that if you can't make something work, you just need to find a button, any button, and I push it."

This simple philosophy has become more than just a credo for the siblings; it has served as the framework for their Playbook for Success.

"At some point everything will go wrong," says Jeff. "As an entrepreneur, it's your job to find a button, any button, and push it."

CULTIVATE A STRICT FOCUS

Like many entrepreneurs, the Pipsnacks founders have often been distracted by "shiny objects." It's easy, especially in the early stages of running a business, to pursue every potential opportunity. Over time, however, Jeff and Jen have learned that in order to achieve long-term, sustainable success, they must develop and cultivate a strict focus—even if it means sacrificing a short-term win.

They first learned this principle after being chosen as one of *Oprah's Favorite Things*. While the experience proved to be a game-changing one, it distracted them from their larger goal of building out their wholesale business and, ultimately, ended up putting them months behind schedule.

"Getting chosen was incredible, but it definitely was a distraction," says Jen, "It took us a long time to dig ourselves out of that."

This, they believe, is one of the most important lessons a first-time entrepreneur can learn. In other words, a great opportunity isn't always the *right* opportunity.

"You can't change your business for anybody or anything," says Jeff. "Otherwise, you're bound to get off track."

Respect the Phases of Growth

It's often said that it takes money to make money, and in no situation is this more accurate than when starting or running an enterprise.

"It takes a lot of capital to grow a business," says Jeff. "And if you don't respect and manage the phases of growth, you'll end up in a world of hurt."

For the Pipsnacks team, this means tempering enthusiasm with realism and sometimes even passing up potentially lucrative deals with powerful players.

"We've turned down huge accounts because we know we don't have the time or money to do it well," says Jen.

"We'd rather wait until the timing is right and do a good job."

This philosophy was the motivation behind withdrawing their first application from *Shark Tank*. Sure it was a risky move, but they recognized their current phase of growth couldn't support such an opportunity, so they did what they felt had to be done.

"We were a tiny company," says Jeff. "The valuation would have been garbage, and even if we had landed a deal we wouldn't have been able to keep up. It all ended up working out."

Embrace the Dirty Work

During high school, Jeff held a part-time job at a small, local chocolate factory near his home. The owner had inherited the organization from his family and was relatively hands-off when it came to the day-to-day operations. This meant it was up to Jeff, along with his fellow coworker and best friend, Evan, to make sure everything ran smoothly.

Of all the responsibilities he had, one of the most demanding was making the chocolate-covered pretzels. It was a backbreaking process that involved numerous steps and would often take a full day to complete.

"The kitchen would be like 300 degrees and we were just running for hours at a time," says Jeff. "But that experience taught me that in order to be successful, you have to be willing to do whatever it takes to get the job done."

Jen also learned this lesson from a young age and believes it's crucial for entrepreneurs to embrace even the most grimy or mundane tasks.

"I think that's a big part of what has made the company successful," says Jen. "We've made the popcorn, cleaned the dishes, and stamped the bags. A lot of people want others to do the work for them, but it doesn't work that way when you run your own business."

Practice 360-Degree Loyalty

From the first day of business, Pipsnacks has operated under its own unique code of conduct, which over time has become a larger part of their core brand promise. From the quality of their product to the ways in which they build workplace culture, Jeff and Jen are committed to staying true to their vision.

"We are very loyal to what we want this company to be," says Jen. "Sometimes that can make things difficult or more expensive, but it's worth it to us."

Innovating on flavor, for example, can often be a difficult task. With a commitment to only use all-natural, non-GMO ingredients, their options are sometimes limited. This means that competitors who don't abide by the same rigorous standards can manufacture a cheaper product with a wider variety of flavor profiles. Still, Jeff and Jen remain unwavering in their beliefs and unwilling to compromise the integrity of their brand.

"Loyalty is wildly important," says Jeff. "Not just to your customers and your retailers but also to yourself."

Find Your Own *Shark Tank*

From a distance, it's easy to chalk up Pipsnacks' success to a series of happy accidents. Whether it was getting into Smorgasburg, being featured as one of *Oprah's Favorite Things*, or landing a deal on *Shark Tank*, there's no doubt that good fortune has played a role in their accomplishments. But Jeff and Jen believe it's up to the entrepreneur to make his or her own luck.

"People always ask us how to meet Oprah or get on *Shark Tank*," says Jeff. "But you don't need either of those to be successful. You just have to find your own way."

The brother-and-sister team believe that uncovering the right opportunities comes down to three important steps: setting clear goals, developing an actionable strategy, and using real-time feedback to swiftly and succinctly pivot an idea.

If Pipsnacks hadn't been accepted to Smorgasburg, for example, it's likely they would have gone a completely different route, which would have led to a series of alternative experiences and taken the company in a different direction.

"As an entrepreneur you have to find your own *Shark Tank*," says Jen. "And you can't stop until you do."

CHAPTER TEN

A BLUEPRINT FOR SUCCESS

By now, of course, you've realized there is no actual template for success—no definitive process or guaranteed method—especially when it comes to building a profitable business. Some entrepreneurs appear to be genetically wired for innovation, while others seem to have simply stumbled upon a great idea at *around* the right time in *vaguely* the right place. This, of course, can feel as maddening as it does liberating.

In many ways, it would be more comforting to believe there is one proven recipe—a step-by-step formula that, if followed precisely, will lead to infallible triumph. If the stories recounted here have demonstrated anything, however, it's that just the opposite is true: accomplishment is more of a tailored pursuit. But that doesn't mean there isn't a basic through line.

From two siblings creating a popcorn company on the East Coast, to a group of college buddies launching an apparel venture out west, the entrepreneurs featured in these pages share a common set of core capabilities—a universal framework for achievement. While each individual playbook may be unique, the general outline remains the same and encompasses three fundamental practices.

THE AUDACITY TO INITIATE

Every business starts with an idea—a notion that maybe, just maybe, you have the solution to a common problem in the market. Perhaps it's ubiquitous, like the one Christopher Gray encountered after he learned that millions of dollars in scholarship money goes unclaimed every year. Or maybe the issue is specific to a smaller subset of consumers, such as the one Noam and Irene Krasniansky discovered when they were unable to find an eco-friendly alternative to the everyday household paper towel. No matter the size or scope of the problem, each founder in this book faced the same preliminary roadblock: fear.

In order to build anything, an entrepreneur must first make the conscious and often agonizing decision to advance beyond analysis and embrace bold and valiant action. This act of courage serves as more than just an obligatory prerequisite; it's a crucial proof point that victory can in fact be attained.

Take, for example, the story of Wicked Good Cupcakes. The mother-and-daughter team who started the company had no reason to believe they could own and operate a bakery. Neither possessed any sort of traditional training in the craft or experience in the trade. What's more, they were entering an industry rife with competition and littered with rules and regulations. Every stitch of hard evidence pointed to the notion that their organization would likely not survive. And yet today the company is thriving and boasts sales in the millions.

They were lucky, of course, to score some early press and get the opportunity to appear on *Shark Tank*, but that was only a very small part of their journey and occurred much later down the line. Before Tracey and Danielle could sell

that first cupcake, they had to conquer their own fear of failure and traverse the terrifying threshold of apprehension. Only then could they begin to take small, assertive strides toward their desired future.

"If we had done everything at once, it would have been too daunting," says Tracey. "From the beginning we've just taken everything one step at a time."

Across the country, Tipsy Elves' Evan Mendelsohn underwent a similar challenge. After having invested an abundance of time, energy, and money to pursue a law career, he made the risky decision to defy expectations and build a fun and quirky business he was proud to call his own. Was he certain the idea was going to catch on? Of course not. Without taking that initial leap, however, he would never know the answer.

Getting started isn't easy, but it *is* simple. You just start. That's it. And as each of the entrepreneurs highlighted here has proven, being audacious enough to initiate means you just might be audacious enough to succeed.

THE INGENUITY TO PROSPER

Benjamin Franklin once said, "In this world nothing can be said to be certain except death and taxes." With a slight alteration, a similar assertion can be applied to the plight of the small business owner: nothing can be said to be certain except *challenge* . . . and taxes.

From the launch of a new venture, an entrepreneur will face a bevy of uphill battles—some more demanding than others. The question, therefore, is not, will you experience struggle? The question is, how, in the face of such tumult, will you react? If the founders profiled here have demonstrated anything, it's that the best way to defeat a challenge is by discovering its hidden opportunity.

After watching his segment on *Shark Tank,* ZooBean's Felix Lloyd came to the startling realization that his enterprise's recent pivot had backfired.

"It was terrifying," says Felix. "I sat there watching our episode knowing that our idea wasn't going to work—that what we had built was never going to be our business."

Faced with the reality that his model was inherently flawed, the founder was forced to make a difficult decision. While his family slept, Felix paced the house, weighing each of his options. Three months later, ZooBean had successfully repositioned its model, and today the operation is flourishing.

In Georgia, TITIN founder Patrick Whaley experienced the same feelings of dread after clashing with his original investment firm. With his organization in dire straits, the young CEO had no choice but to find creative ways to weather the storm. Free of his partners and back in control of the company, Patrick packed his car full of inventory and headed north. Six weeks later, he returned home with over $2 million in purchase orders.

What Felix and Patrick experienced is *the* critical turning point in an entrepreneur's journey—the make-or-break moment that separates the amateurs from the professionals. Working swiftly and assertively, they each came up with their own method for turning potential hardship into vibrant opportunity.

THE RESILIENCE TO ENDURE

Inventiveness is an important skill for a small-business owner to possess, but sometimes sheer resourcefulness isn't enough. Failures are bound to occur, and when they do, it's up to the entrepreneur—and entrepreneur alone—to react in an appropriate manner. And, as confirmed by the stories shared in these preceding chapters, there's really only one suitable response: unremitting resilience.

Nobody understands the power of this concept better than Hanna and Mark Lim. The husband-and-wife team has experienced numerous setbacks throughout the life cycle of their organization. From their experience getting chosen, then rejected (then selected again), to appear on *Shark Tank*, to dealing with Hanna's incapacitating illness and surviving a mandatory cease in production, the Lollaland cofounders have encountered one conflict after another. Through it all, however, they've remained dedicated to maintaining their professionalism and coming out on top.

"We refuse to make excuses," says Mark. "And I truly believe that is what separates us from the people who fizzle out."

Hanna and Mark are not the only couple to embody such resilience. The husband-and-wife team behind Grace and Lace are also well versed in this practice. After the tragedy

of losing their first child, Rick and Melissa Hinnant were tested in ways they never thought imaginable.

"We had to make a decision," says Rick. "We could either be bitter and angry at God or accept that we don't know why that happened and have faith that something good will come out of it."

Although each couple's experience was distinct, the moral is the same: resilience is a choice and one that every entrepreneur must make on his or her own. Adversity will occur; that is certain. And only when it does will you gain true insight into the magnitude of your spirit and depth of your drive.

THE ULTIMATE PLAYBOOK FOR SUCCESS

In *Shark Tank Jump Start Your Business*, the first *Shark Tank* book, we explored the various phases of building and growing a company. While no two ventures are ever the same, most will experience four distinct phases: Prepare, Launch, Run, and Grow.

Below is a comprehensive *Playbook for Success* that combines practical tips and tricks from each of the entrepreneurs featured in this book. Organized to reflect the four aforementioned stages, it's designed to help you and your team effectively and efficiently navigate each phase.

PREPARE

"Just because you have a great idea doesn't mean you're on easy street. From finding the right packaging to going through the whole trademark process, there is so much that goes into starting a business. And we did all of it ourselves."

—TRACEY NOONAN, WICKED GOOD CUPCAKES

1. Make It Personal—*ZooBean*
2. Trust Your Gut—*TITIN*
3. Assess Whether You Can Be the Best in the World—*Wicked Good Cupcakes*

4. Obey Your Strengths and Weaknesses—*Scholly*
5. Get Passionate or Get Out—*TITIN*
6. Beware of Analysis Paralysis—*Bambooee*
7. Find Great Mentors—*Scholly*
8. Know the Difference Between Will and Want—*Wicked Good Cupcakes*
9. Understand the Role of Timing—*TITIN*
10. Remain Flexible with Your Vision—*Wicked Good Cupcakes*

LAUNCH

"At the beginning, we were masters at making it look like we had more than we did. For example, our business cards were letter-pressed. Nobody knew that we were the ones who rented the machine and pressed each one ourselves. Little things like that make a big difference."

—MARK LIM, LOLLALAND

1. Approach the Masses—*Bambooee*
2. Risk Smarter, Not Harder?—*Tipsy Elves*
3. Pay Strict Attention to Detail—*Grace and Lace*
4. Control Your Costs (or They'll Control You)—*Wicked Good Cupcakes*
5. Embrace the Dirty Work—*Pipsnacks*
6 Build Your Network—*Lollaland*
7. Make the Most of Each Failure—*Wicked Good Cupcakes*
8. Cultivate a Strict Focus—*Pipsnacks*
9. Keep Your Eye on the Prize—*TITIN*
10. Focus on What's Next—*ZooBean*

RUN

"Don't be swayed by shiny objects. Good things are going to happen and bad things are going to happen, but you can't allow yourself to be swayed. You have to keep working towards your goal."

—JEFF MARTIN, PIPSNACKS

1. Find Your Own Shark Tank—*Pipsnacks*
2. Build a Reliable Team—*TITIN*
3. Practice Unwavering Persistence—*Bambooee*
4. Upgrade Your Attitude—*Tipsy Elves*
5. Master Prioritization—*Lollaland*
6. Practice Absolute Honesty—*Grace and Lace*
7. Let Cash Be King—*ZooBean*
8. Outwork the Competition—*Tipsy Elves*
9. Fail Fast. Recover Faster—*Bambooee*
10. Find the Balance—*Lollaland*

GROW

"Try to find a way to test your concept before you bet the farm on it. Don't take out a second mortgage on your home before you know if the idea can really work."

—EVAN MENDELSOHN, TIPSY ELVES

1. Respect the Phases of Growth—*Pipsnacks*
2. Talk Less; Listen More—*ZooBean*
3. Prepare for Adversity—*Grace and Lace*
4. Stay True to Your Mission—*Tipsy Elves*
5. Let Creative Solutions Trump Financial Resolutions—*Bambooee*
6. Devise a Give-Back Strategy—*Grace and Lace*

7. Hustle Harder and Faster—*Lollaland*
8. Maintain a Positive Reputation—*Scholly*
9. Practice 360-Degree Loyalty—*Pipsnacks*
10. Remain a Constant Learner—*Lollaland*

BIOGRAPHY

Michael Parrish DuDell is an entrepreneur, keynote speaker, and the best-selling author of *Shark Tank Jump Start Your Business*—the official book from ABC's hit show *Shark Tank* on how to successfully launch and grow a company from concept to cash.

Ranked as one of the top three most popular business authors by Amazon.com, Michael is a recognized industry expert and television pundit who is regularly featured across numerous media outlets, including *CNBC, Fox News, CNN, Fox Business, Bloomberg TV, NBC News, Nightly Business Report, The New York Times, Fast Company, Inc. Magazine, Business Insider*, and many more.

Named as "one of nation's leading Millennial voices in the business sector" by IBM, Michael has collaborated with some of the world's most innovative and influential brands.

Previously, Michael served as the editor of ecomagination .com—GE's cleantech and sustainable innovation site—as well as the host of ecomagination.com's web series *Green Room Live*. Prior to that, he was the managing editor of The Domino Project—a publishing company started by marketing guru Seth Godin and powered by Amazon.com.

Learn more at www.MPDHQ.com.

NOTES

Chapter One

1 Lori Greiner, *Invent It, Sell It, Bank It! Make Your Million-Dollar Idea into a Reality* (Ballantine Books, 2014).

2 Lori Greiner, *Invent It, Sell It, Bank It! Make Your Million-Dollar Idea into a Reality* (Ballantine Books, 2014).

3 Lori Greiner, *Invent It, Sell It, Bank It! Make Your Million-Dollar Idea into a Reality* (Ballantine Books, 2014).

4 Lori Greiner, *Invent It, Sell It, Bank It! Make Your Million-Dollar Idea into a Reality* (Ballantine Books, 2014).

5 Jason Nazar, "16 Surprising Statistics About Small Business," *Forbes*, September 9, 2013, http://www.forbes.com/sites/jasonnazar/2013/09/09/16-surprising-statistics-about-small-businesses/.

Chapter Two

6 Robert Herjavec, "My Top Ten Tips for Entrepreneurs," LinkedIn, November 29, 2014, https://www.linkedin.com/pulse/20141129135810-3945137-my-top-ten-tips-for-entrepreneurs?trk=mp-reader-card.

7 Robert Herjavec, "My Top Ten Tips for Entrepreneurs," LinkedIn, November 29, 2014, https://www.linkedin.com/pulse/20141129135810-3945137-my-top-ten-tips-for-entrepreneurs?trk=mp-reader-card.

8 Robert Herjavec, "What's in a Perfect *Shark Tank* Pitch?" LinkedIn, May 16, 2014, https://www.linkedin.com/pulse

/20140516122440-3945137-what-s-in-a-perfect-shark-tank-pitch
?trk=mp-reader-card.

9 Robert Herjavec, "My Top Ten Tips for Entrepreneurs,"
LinkedIn, November 29, 2014, https://www.linkedin.com/pulse
/20141129135810-3945137-my-top-ten-tips-for-entrepreneurs?trk
=mp-reader-card.

Chapter Three

10 Mark Cuban, "Don't Follow Your Passion, Follow Your Effort,"
Blog Maverick, March 18, 2012, http://blogmaverick.com/2012/03
/18/dont-follow-your-passion-follow-your-effort/.

11 Mark Cuban, *How to Win at the Sport of Business: If I Can Do
It, You Can Do It* (Diversion Books, 2013).

12 Mark Cuban, *How to Win at the Sport of Business: If I Can Do
It, You Can Do It* (Diversion Books, 2013).

13 Mark Cuban, "Success and Motivation," Blog Maverick, May 13,
2009, http://blogmaverick.com/2009/05/13/success-motivation/.

Chapter Four

14 Daymond John, *The Brand Within* (Display of Power Publishing,
2011).

15 Daymond John, *The Brand Within* (Display of Power Publishing,
2011).

16 Daymond John, *The Brand Within* (Display of Power Publishing,
2011).

17 Daymond John. Crown Business. *The Power of Broke: How Empty
Pockets, a Tight Budget, and a Hunger for Success Can Become
Your Greatest Competitive Advantage.* 2016. Page 23.

Chapter Five

18 https://www.uvm.edu/business/vfbi/?Page=facts.html.

19 Kevin O'Leary, *Cold Hard Truth On Men, Women, and Money: 50
Common Money Mistakes and How to Fix Them* (Gallery Books,
2014).

20 Kevin O'Leary, *Cold Hard Truth On Men, Women, and Money: 50
Common Money Mistakes and How to Fix Them* (Gallery Books,
2014).

21 Kevin O'Leary, "How to Win in Business Negotiations: Never
Forget, It's All About the Money!" O'Leary Financial Group Blog,

December 6, 2011, http://kevinoleary.com/how-to-win-in-business
-negotiations-never-forget-its-all-about-the-money/.

22 Kevin O'Leary, *Cold Hard Truth On Men, Women, and Money: 50 Common Money Mistakes and How to Fix Them* (Gallery Books, 2014).

Chapter Six

23 Barbara Corcoran, "The Best Entrepreneurs Don't Know When to Quit, LinkedIn, September 6, 2014, https://www.linkedin.com/pulse /20140906172705-264544111-the-best-entrepreneurs-don-t-know -when-to-quit?trk=mp-reader-card.

24 Barbara Corcoran, *Shark Tales: How I Turned $1,000 into a Billion Dollar Business* (Portfolio, 2011).

25 Barbara Corcoran, *Shark Tales: How I Turned $1,000 into a Billion Dollar Business* (Portfolio, 2011).

26 Barbara Corcoran, *Nextville: Amazing Places to Live the Rest of Your Life* (Grand Central Publishing, 2008).

Chapter Seven

27 Lori Greiner, *Invent It, Sell It, Bank It! Make Your Million-Dollar Idea into a Reality* (Ballantine Books, 2014).

28 Lori Greiner, *Invent It, Sell It, Bank It! Make Your Million-Dollar Idea into a Reality* (Ballantine Books, 2014).

29 Daymond John, "Here's What I Plan to Do with My Presidential Appointment," LinkedIn, June 25, 2015, https://www.linkedin.com/ pulse/presidential-ambassador-global-entrepreneurship-daymond -john.

30 Daymond John, *The Brand Within* (Display of Power Publishing, 2011).

Chapter Eight

31 Mark Cuban, "Success & Motivation," Blog Maverick, June 9, 2009, http://blogmaverick.com/2009/06/09/success-motivation -2009/.

32 Robert Herjavec, "If You Aren't Taking Risks, You're Missing Out," LinkedIn, March 15, 2015, https://www.linkedin.com/pulse /5-tips-doing-something-first-time-robert-herjavec?trk=mp-reader -card.

33 Robert Herjavec, "What's in a Perfect *Shark Tank* Pitch?"

LinkedIn, May 16, 2014, https://www.linkedin.com/pulse
/20140516122440-3945137-what-s-in-a-perfect-shark-tank-pitch
?trk=mp-reader-card.

34 Mark Cuban, *How to Win at the Sport of Business: If I Can Do
It, You Can Do It* (Diversion Books, 2013).

Chapter Nine

35 Barbara Corcoran, *If You Don't Have Big Breasts, Put Ribbons
on Your Pigtails: And Other Lessons I Learned from My Mom*
(Portfolio Trade, 2003).

36 Barbara Corcoran, *Nextville: Amazing Places to Live the Rest of
Your Life* (Grand Central Publishing, 2008).

37 Barbara Corcoran, *Shark Tales: How I Turned $1,000 into a
Billion Dollar Business* (Portfolio, 2011).

37 Barbara Corcoran, *Shark Tales: How I Turned $1,000 into a
Billion Dollar Business* (Portfolio; Revised edition, February 9,
2011).

The Jungle Book

The Jungle Book

RUDYARD KIPLING

Word Cloud Classics

San Diego

Canterbury Classics
An imprint of Printers Row Publishing Group
10350 Barnes Canyon Road, Suite 100, San Diego, CA 92121
www.canterburyclassicsbooks.com

Printers Row Publishing Group is a division of Readerlink Distribution Services, LLC. The Canterbury Classics and Word Cloud Classics names and logos are registered trademarks of Readerlink Distribution Services, LLC.

All correspondence concerning the content of this book should be addressed to Canterbury Classics, Editorial Department, at the above address.

Publisher: Peter Norton
Associate Publisher: Ana Parker
Publishing/Editorial Team: April Farr, Kathryn C. Dalby
Editorial Team: JoAnn Padgett, Melinda Allman
Production Team: Jonathan Lopes, Rusty von Dyl, Lidija Tomas

Library of Congress Cataloging-in-Publication Data

Kipling, Rudyard, 1865-1936.
 The jungle book / Rudyard Kipling.
 pages cm
 Summary: Presents the adventures of Mowgli, a boy reared by a pack
of wolves, and the wild animals of the jungle.
 ISBN 978-1-62686-258-6 (paperback)
[1. Feral children--Fiction. 2. Jungle animals--Fiction. 3. Jungles--
Fiction. 4. India--History--19th century--Fiction.] I. Kipling, Rudyard,
1865-1936. Second jungle book. II. Title.
 PZ7.K632Ju 2014
 [Fic]--dc23
 2014006238

PRINTED IN CHINA
23 22 21 20 19 7 8 9 10 11

Editor's Note: This work has been published in its original form to preserve the author's intent and style.

CONTENTS

The Jungle Book

1. MOWGLI'S BROTHERS

Now Rann the Kite brings home the night
That Mang the Bat sets free—
The herds are shut in byre and hut
For loosed till dawn are we.
This is the hour of pride and power,
Talon and tush and claw.
Oh, hear the call!—Good hunting all
That keep the Jungle Law!

—Night-Song in the Jungle

It was seven o'clock of a very warm evening in the Seeonee hills when Father Wolf woke up from his day's rest, scratched himself, yawned, and spread out his paws one after the other to get rid of the sleepy feeling in the tips. Mother Wolf lay with her big gray nose dropped across her four tumbling, squealing cubs, and the moon shone into the mouth of the cave where they all lived. "Augrh!" said Father Wolf. "It is time to hunt again." He was going to spring down hill when a little shadow with a bushy tail crossed the threshold and whined: "Good luck go with you, O Chief of the Wolves. And good luck and strong white teeth go with noble children that they may never forget the hungry in this world."

It was the jackal—Tabaqui, the Dish-licker—and the wolves of India despise Tabaqui because he runs about making mischief, and telling tales, and eating rags and pieces of leather from the village rubbish-heaps. But they are afraid of him too, because Tabaqui, more than anyone else in the jungle, is apt to go mad, and then he forgets that he was ever afraid of anyone, and runs through the forest biting everything in his way. Even the tiger runs and hides when little Tabaqui goes mad, for madness is the most disgraceful thing that can overtake a wild creature. We call it hydrophobia, but they call it *dewanee*—the madness—and run.

"Enter, then, and look," said Father Wolf stiffly, "but there is no food here."

"For a wolf, no," said Tabaqui, "but for so mean a person as myself a dry bone is a good feast. Who are we, the *Gidur-log* [the Jackal-people], to pick and choose?" He scuttled to the back of the cave, where he found the bone of a buck with some meat on it, and sat cracking the end merrily.

"All thanks for this good meal," he said, licking his lips. "How beautiful are the noble children! How large are their eyes! And so young too! Indeed, indeed, I might have remembered that the children of kings are men from the beginning."

Now, Tabaqui knew as well as anyone else that there is nothing so unlucky as to compliment children to their faces. It pleased him to see Mother and Father Wolf look uncomfortable.

Tabaqui sat still, rejoicing in the mischief that he had made, and then he said spitefully:

"Shere Khan, the Big One, has shifted his hunting grounds. He will hunt among these hills for the next moon, so he has told me."

Shere Khan was the tiger who lived near the Waingunga River, twenty miles away.

"He has no right!" Father Wolf began angrily—"By the Law of the Jungle he has no right to change his quarters without due warning. He will frighten every head of game within ten miles, and I—I have to kill for two, these days."

"His mother did not call him Lungri [the Lame One] for nothing," said Mother Wolf quietly. "He has been lame in one foot from his birth. That is why he has only killed cattle. Now the villagers of the Waingunga are angry with him, and he has come here to make *our* villagers angry. They will scour the jungle for him when he is far away, and we and our children must run when the grass is set alight. Indeed, we are very grateful to Shere Khan!"

"Shall I tell him of your gratitude?" said Tabaqui.

"Out!" snapped Father Wolf. "Out and hunt with thy master. Thou hast done harm enough for one night."

"I go," said Tabaqui quietly. "Ye can hear Shere Khan below in the thickets. I might have saved myself the message."

Father Wolf listened, and below in the valley that ran down to a little river he heard the dry, angry, snarly, singsong whine of a tiger who has caught nothing and does not care if all the jungle knows it.

"The fool!" said Father Wolf. "To begin a night's work with that noise! Does he think that our buck are like his fat Waingunga bullocks?"

"H'sh. It is neither bullock no'r buck he hunts to-night," said Mother Wolf. "It is Man."

The whine had changed to a sort of humming purr that seemed to come from every quarter of the compass. It was the noise that bewilders woodcutters and gypsies sleeping in the open, and makes them run sometimes into the very mouth of the tiger.

"Man!" said Father Wolf, showing all his white teeth. "Faugh! Are there not enough beetles and frogs in the tanks that he must eat Man, and on our ground too!"

The Law of the Jungle, which never orders anything without a reason, forbids every beast to eat Man except when he is killing to show his children how to kill, and then he must hunt outside the hunting grounds of his pack or tribe. The real reason for this is that man-killing means, sooner or later, the arrival of white men on elephants, with guns, and hundreds of brown men with gongs and rockets and torches. Then everybody in the jungle suffers. The reason the beasts give among themselves is that Man is the weakest and most defenseless of all living things, and it is unsportsmanlike to touch him. They say too—and it is true—that man-eaters become mangy, and lose their teeth.

The purr grew louder, and ended in the full-throated "Aaarh!" of the tiger's charge.

Then there was a howl—an untigerish howl—from Shere Khan. "He has missed," said Mother Wolf. "What is it?"

Father Wolf ran out a few paces and heard Shere Khan muttering and mumbling savagely as he tumbled about in the scrub.

"The fool has had no more sense than to jump at a woodcutter's campfire, and has burned his feet," said Father Wolf with a grunt. "Tabaqui is with him."

"Something is coming uphill," said Mother Wolf, twitching one ear. "Get ready."

The bushes rustled a little in the thicket, and Father Wolf dropped with his haunches under him, ready for his leap. Then, if you had been watching, you would have seen the most wonderful thing in the world—the wolf checked in mid-spring. He made his bound before he saw what it was he was jumping at, and then he tried to stop himself. The result was that he shot up straight into the air for four or five feet, landing almost where he left ground.

"Man!" he snapped. "A man's cub. Look!"

Directly in front of him, holding on by a low branch, stood a naked brown baby who could just walk—as soft and as dimpled a little atom as ever came to a wolf's cave at night. He looked up into Father Wolf's face, and laughed.

"Is that a man's cub?" said Mother Wolf. "I have never seen one. Bring it here."

A Wolf accustomed to moving his own cubs can, if necessary, mouth an egg without breaking it, and though Father Wolf's jaws closed right on the child's back not a tooth even scratched the skin as he laid it down among the cubs.

"How little! How naked, and—how bold!" said Mother Wolf softly. The baby was pushing his way between the cubs to get close to the warm hide. "Ahai! He is taking his meal with the others. And so this is a man's cub. Now, was there ever a wolf that could boast of a man's cub among her children?"

"I have heard now and again of such a thing, but never in our Pack or in my time," said Father Wolf. "He is altogether without hair, and I could kill him with a touch of my foot. But see, he looks up and is not afraid."

The moonlight was blocked out of the mouth of the cave, for Shere Khan's great square head and shoulders were thrust into the entrance. Tabaqui, behind him, was squeaking: "My lord, my lord, it went in here!"

"Shere Khan does us great honour," said Father Wolf, but his eyes were very angry. "What does Shere Khan need?"

"My quarry. A man's cub went this way," said Shere Khan. "Its parents have run off. Give it to me."

Shere Khan had jumped at a woodcutter's campfire, as Father Wolf had said, and was furious from the pain of his burned feet. But Father Wolf knew that the mouth of the cave was too narrow for a tiger to come in by. Even where he was, Shere Khan's shoulders and forepaws were cramped for want of room, as a man's would be if he tried to fight in a barrel.

"The Wolves are a free people," said Father Wolf. "They take orders from the Head of the Pack, and not from any striped cattle-killer. The man's cub is ours—to kill if we choose."

"Ye choose and ye do not choose! What talk is this of choosing? By the bull that I killed, am I to stand nosing into your dog's den for my fair dues? It is I, Shere Khan, who speak!"

The tiger's roar filled the cave with thunder. Mother Wolf shook herself clear of the cubs and sprang forward, her eyes, like two green moons in the darkness, facing the blazing eyes of Shere Khan.

"And it is I, Raksha [the Demon], who answers. The man's cub is mine, Lungri—mine to me! He shall not be killed. He shall live to run with the Pack and to hunt with the Pack; and in the end, look you, hunter of little naked cubs—frog-eater—fish-killer—he shall hunt *thee*! Now get hence, or by the Sambhur that I killed (*I* eat no starved cattle), back thou goest to thy mother, burned beast of the jungle, lamer than ever thou camest into the world! Go!"

Father Wolf looked on amazed. He had almost forgotten the days when he won Mother Wolf in fair fight from five other wolves, when she ran in the Pack and was not called the Demon for compliment's sake. Shere Khan might have faced Father Wolf, but he could not stand up against Mother Wolf, for he knew that where he was she had all the advantage of the ground, and would fight to the death. So he backed out of the cave mouth growling, and when he was clear he shouted:

"Each dog barks in his own yard! We will see what the Pack will say to this fostering of man-cubs. The cub is mine, and to my teeth he will come in the end, O bush-tailed thieves!"

Mother Wolf threw herself down panting among the cubs, and Father Wolf said to her gravely:

"Shere Khan speaks this much truth. The cub must be shown to the Pack. Wilt thou still keep him, Mother?"

"Keep him!" she gasped. "He came naked, by night, alone and very hungry; yet he was not afraid! Look, he has pushed one of my babes to one side already. And that lame butcher would have killed him and would have run off to the Waingunga while the villagers here hunted through all our lairs in revenge! Keep him? Assuredly I will keep him. Lie still, little frog. O thou Mowgli—for Mowgli the Frog I will call thee—the time will come when thou wilt hunt Shere Khan as he has hunted thee."

"But what will our Pack say?" said Father Wolf.

The Law of the Jungle lays down very clearly that any wolf may, when he marries, withdraw from the Pack he belongs to. But as soon as his cubs are old enough to stand on their feet he must bring them to the Pack Council, which is generally held once a month at full moon, in order that the other wolves may identify them. After that inspection the cubs are free to run where they please, and until they have killed their first buck no excuse is accepted if a grown wolf of the Pack kills one of them. The punishment is death where the murderer can be found; and if you think for a minute you will see that this must be so.

Father Wolf waited till his cubs could run a little, and then on the night of the Pack Meeting took them and Mowgli and Mother Wolf to the Council Rock—a hilltop covered with stones and boulders where a hundred wolves could hide. Akela, the great gray Lone Wolf, who led all the Pack by strength and cunning, lay out at full length on his rock, and below him sat forty or more wolves of every size and colour, from badger-coloured veterans who could handle a buck alone to young black three-year-olds who thought they could. The Lone Wolf had led them for a year now. He had fallen twice into a wolf trap in his youth, and once he had been beaten and left for dead; so he knew the manners and customs of men.

There was very little talking at the Rock. The cubs tumbled over each other in the centre of the circle where their mothers and fathers sat, and now and again a senior wolf would go quietly up to a cub, look at him carefully, and return to his place on noiseless feet. Sometimes a

mother would push her cub far out into the moonlight to be sure that he had not been overlooked. Akela from his rock would cry: "Ye know the Law—ye know the Law. Look well, O Wolves!" And the anxious mothers would take up the call: "Look—look well, O Wolves!"

At last—and Mother Wolf's neck bristles lifted as the time came—Father Wolf pushed "Mowgli the Frog," as they called him, into the centre, where he sat laughing and playing with some pebbles that glistened in the moonlight.

Akela never raised his head from his paws, but went on with the monotonous cry: "Look well!" A muffled roar came up from behind the rocks—the voice of Shere Khan crying: "The cub is mine. Give him to me. What have the Free People to do with a man's cub?" Akela never even twitched his ears. All he said was: "Look well, O Wolves! What have the Free People to do with the orders of any save the Free People? Look well!"

There was a chorus of deep growls, and a young wolf in his fourth year flung back Shere Khan's question to Akela: "What have the Free People to do with a man's cub?" Now, the Law of the Jungle lays down that if there is any dispute as to the right of a cub to be accepted by the Pack, he must be spoken for by at least two members of the Pack who are not his father and mother.

"Who speaks for this cub?" said Akela. "Among the Free People who speaks?" There was no answer and Mother Wolf got ready for what she knew would be her last fight, if things came to fighting.

Then the only other creature who is allowed at the Pack Council—Baloo, the sleepy brown bear who teaches the wolf cubs the Law of the Jungle: old Baloo, who can come and go where he pleases because he eats only nuts and roots and honey—rose upon his hind quarters and grunted.

"The man's cub—the man's cub?" he said. "*I* speak for the man's cub. There is no harm in a man's cub. I have no gift of words, but I speak the truth. Let him run with the Pack, and be entered with the others. I myself will teach him."

"We need yet another," said Akela. "Baloo has spoken, and he is our teacher for the young cubs. Who speaks besides Baloo?"

A black shadow dropped down into the circle. It was Bagheera the Black Panther, inky black all over, but with the panther markings showing up in certain lights like the pattern of watered silk. Everybody knew Bagheera, and nobody cared to cross his path; for he was as cunning as Tabaqui, as bold as the wild buffalo, and as reckless as the wounded elephant. But he had a voice as soft as wild honey dripping from a tree, and a skin softer than down.

"O Akela, and ye the Free People," he purred, "I have no right in your assembly, but the Law of the Jungle says that if there is a doubt which is not a killing matter in regard to a new cub, the life of that cub may be bought at a price. And the Law does not say who may or may not pay that price. Am I right?"

"Good! Good!" said the young wolves, who are always hungry. "Listen to Bagheera. The cub can be bought for a price. It is the Law."

"Knowing that I have no right to speak here, I ask your leave."

"Speak then," cried twenty voices.

"To kill a naked cub is shame. Besides, he may make better sport for you when he is grown. Baloo has spoken in his behalf. Now to Baloo's word I will add one bull, and a fat one, newly killed, not half a mile from here, if ye will accept the man's cub according to the Law. Is it difficult?"

There was a clamor of scores of voices, saying: "What matter? He will die in the winter rains. He will scorch in the sun. What harm can a naked frog do us? Let him run with the Pack. Where is the bull, Bagheera? Let him be accepted." And then came Akela's deep bay, crying: "Look well—look well, O Wolves!"

Mowgli was still deeply interested in the pebbles, and he did not notice when the wolves came and looked at him one by one. At last they all went down the hill for the dead bull, and only Akela, Bagheera, Baloo, and Mowgli's own wolves were left. Shere Khan roared still in the night, for he was very angry that Mowgli had not been handed over to him.

"Ay, roar well," said Bagheera, under his whiskers, "for the time will come when this naked thing will make thee roar to another tune, or I know nothing of man."

"It was well done," said Akela. "Men and their cubs are very wise. He may be a help in time."

"Truly, a help in time of need; for none can hope to lead the Pack forever," said Bagheera.

Akela said nothing. He was thinking of the time that comes to every leader of every pack when his strength goes from him and he gets feebler and feebler, till at last he is killed by the wolves and a new leader comes up—to be killed in his turn.

"Take him away," he said to Father Wolf, "and train him as befits one of the Free People."

And that is how Mowgli was entered into the Seeonee Wolf-Pack for the price of a bull and on Baloo's good word.

Now you must be content to skip ten or eleven whole years, and only guess at all the wonderful life that Mowgli led among the wolves, because if it were written out it would fill ever so many books. He grew up with the cubs, though they, of course, were grown wolves almost before he was a child. And Father Wolf taught him his business, and the meaning of things in the jungle, till every rustle in the grass, every breath of the warm night air, every note of the owls above his head, every scratch of a bat's claws as it roosted for a while in a tree, and every splash of every little fish jumping in a pool meant just as much to him as the work of his office means to a business man. When he was not learning he sat out in the sun and slept, and ate and went to sleep again. When he felt dirty or hot he swam in the forest pools; and when he wanted honey (Baloo told him that honey and nuts were just as pleasant to eat as raw meat) he climbed up for it, and that Bagheera showed him how to do. Bagheera would lie out on a branch and call, "Come along, Little Brother," and at first Mowgli would cling like the sloth, but afterward he would fling himself through the branches almost as boldly as the gray ape. He took his place at the Council Rock, too, when the Pack met, and there he discovered that if he stared hard at any wolf, the wolf would be forced to drop his eyes, and so he used to stare for fun. At other times he would pick the long thorns out of the pads of his friends, for wolves suffer terribly from thorns and burs in

their coats. He would go down the hillside into the cultivated lands by night, and look very curiously at the villagers in their huts, but he had a mistrust of men because Bagheera showed him a square box with a drop gate so cunningly hidden in the jungle that he nearly walked into it, and told him that it was a trap. He loved better than anything else to go with Bagheera into the dark warm heart of the forest, to sleep all through the drowsy day, and at night see how Bagheera did his killing. Bagheera killed right and left as he felt hungry, and so did Mowgli—with one exception. As soon as he was old enough to understand things, Bagheera told him that he must never touch cattle because he had been bought into the Pack at the price of a bull's life. "All the jungle is thine," said Bagheera, "and thou canst kill everything that thou art strong enough to kill; but for the sake of the bull that bought thee thou must never kill or eat any cattle young or old. That is the Law of the Jungle." Mowgli obeyed faithfully.

And he grew and grew strong as a boy must grow who does not know that he is learning any lessons, and who has nothing in the world to think of except things to eat.

Mother Wolf told him once or twice that Shere Khan was not a creature to be trusted, and that some day he must kill Shere Khan. But though a young wolf would have remembered that advice every hour, Mowgli forgot it because he was only a boy—though he would have called himself a wolf if he had been able to speak in any human tongue.

Shere Khan was always crossing his path in the jungle, for as Akela grew older and feebler the lame tiger had come to be great friends with the younger wolves of the Pack, who followed him for scraps, a thing Akela would never have allowed if he had dared to push his authority to the proper bounds. Then Shere Khan would flatter them and wonder that such fine young hunters were content to be led by a dying wolf and a man's cub. "They tell me," Shere Khan would say, "that at Council ye dare not look him between the eyes." And the young wolves would growl and bristle.

Bagheera, who had eyes and ears everywhere, knew something of this, and once or twice he told Mowgli in so many words that Shere Khan would kill him some day. Mowgli would laugh and answer: "I

have the Pack and I have thee; and Baloo, though he is so lazy, might strike a blow or two for my sake. Why should I be afraid?"

It was one very warm day that a new notion came to Bagheera—born of something that he had heard. Perhaps Ikki the Porcupine had told him; but he said to Mowgli when they were deep in the jungle, as the boy lay with his head on Bagheera's beautiful black skin, "Little Brother, how often have I told thee that Shere Khan is thy enemy?"

"As many times as there are nuts on that palm," said Mowgli, who, naturally, could not count. "What of it? I am sleepy, Bagheera, and Shere Khan is all long tail and loud talk—like Mao, the Peacock."

"But this is no time for sleeping. Baloo knows it; I know it; the Pack know it; and even the foolish, foolish deer know. Tabaqui has told thee too."

"Ho! ho!" said Mowgli. "Tabaqui came to me not long ago with some rude talk that I was a naked man's cub and not fit to dig pig-nuts. But I caught Tabaqui by the tail and swung him twice against a palm-tree to teach him better manners."

"That was foolishness, for though Tabaqui is a mischief-maker, he would have told thee of something that concerned thee closely. Open those eyes, Little Brother. Shere Khan dare not kill thee in the jungle. But remember, Akela is very old, and soon the day comes when he cannot kill his buck, and then he will be leader no more. Many of the wolves that looked thee over when thou wast brought to the Council first are old too, and the young wolves believe, as Shere Khan has taught them, that a man-cub has no place with the Pack. In a little time thou wilt be a man."

"And what is a man that he should not run with his brothers?" said Mowgli. "I was born in the jungle. I have obeyed the Law of the Jungle, and there is no wolf of ours from whose paws I have not pulled a thorn. Surely they are my brothers!"

Bagheera stretched himself at full length and half shut his eyes. "Little Brother," said he, "feel under my jaw."

Mowgli put up his strong brown hand, and just under Bagheera's silky chin, where the giant rolling muscles were all hid by the glossy hair, he came upon a little bald spot.

"There is no one in the jungle that knows that *I*, Bagheera, carry that mark—the mark of the collar; and yet, Little Brother, I was born among men, and it was among men that my mother died—in the cages of the king's palace at Oodeypore. It was because of this that I paid the price for thee at the Council when thou wast a little naked cub. Yes, I too was born among men. I had never seen the jungle. They fed me behind bars from an iron pan till one night I felt that I was Bagheera—the Panther—and no man's plaything, and I broke the silly lock with one blow of my paw and came away. And because I had learned the ways of men, I became more terrible in the jungle than Shere Khan. Is it not so?"

"Yes," said Mowgli, "all the jungle fear Bagheera—all except Mowgli."

"Oh, *thou* art a man's cub," said the Black Panther very tenderly. "And even as I returned to my jungle, so thou must go back to men at last—to the men who are thy brothers—if thou art not killed in the Council."

"But why—but why should any wish to kill me?" said Mowgli.

"Look at me," said Bagheera. And Mowgli looked at him steadily between the eyes. The big panther turned his head away in half a minute.

"*That* is why," he said, shifting his paw on the leaves. "Not even I can look thee between the eyes, and I was born among men, and I love thee, Little Brother. The others they hate thee because their eyes cannot meet thine; because thou art wise; because thou hast pulled out thorns from their feet—because thou art a man."

"I did not know these things," said Mowgli sullenly, and he frowned under his heavy black eyebrows.

"What is the Law of the Jungle? Strike first and then give tongue. By thy very carelessness they know that thou art a man. But be wise. It is in my heart that when Akela misses his next kill—and at each hunt it costs him more to pin the buck—the Pack will turn against him and against thee. They will hold a jungle Council at the Rock, and then—and then—I have it!" said Bagheera, leaping up. "Go thou down quickly to the men's huts in the valley, and take some of the Red Flower which

they grow there, so that when the time comes thou mayest have even a stronger friend than I or Baloo or those of the Pack that love thee. Get the Red Flower."

By Red Flower Bagheera meant fire, only no creature in the jungle will call fire by its proper name. Every beast lives in deadly fear of it, and invents a hundred ways of describing it.

"The Red Flower?" said Mowgli. "That grows outside their huts in the twilight. I will get some."

"There speaks the man's cub," said Bagheera proudly. "Remember that it grows in little pots. Get one swiftly, and keep it by thee for time of need."

"Good!" said Mowgli. "I go. But art thou sure, O my Bagheera"— he slipped his arm around the splendid neck and looked deep into the big eyes—"art thou sure that all this is Shere Khan's doing?"

"By the Broken Lock that freed me, I am sure, Little Brother."

"Then, by the Bull that bought me, I will pay Shere Khan full tale for this, and it may be a little over," said Mowgli, and he bounded away.

"That is a man. That is all a man," said Bagheera to himself, lying down again. "Oh, Shere Khan, never was a blacker hunting than that frog-hunt of thine ten years ago!"

Mowgli was far and far through the forest, running hard, and his heart was hot in him. He came to the cave as the evening mist rose, and drew breath, and looked down the valley. The cubs were out, but Mother Wolf, at the back of the cave, knew by his breathing that something was troubling her frog.

"What is it, Son?" she said.

"Some bat's chatter of Shere Khan," he called back. "I hunt among the plowed fields tonight," and he plunged downward through the bushes, to the stream at the bottom of the valley. There he checked, for he heard the yell of the Pack hunting, heard the bellow of a hunted *Sambhur*, and the snort as the buck turned at bay. Then there were wicked, bitter howls from the young wolves: "Akela! Akela! Let the Lone Wolf show his strength. Room for the leader of the Pack! Spring, Akela!"

The Lone Wolf must have sprung and missed his hold, for Mowgli

heard the snap of his teeth and then a yelp as the *Sambhur* knocked him over with his forefoot.

He did not wait for anything more, but dashed on; and the yells grew fainter behind him as he ran into the croplands where the villagers lived.

"Bagheera spoke truth," he panted, as he nestled down in some cattle fodder by the window of a hut. "To-morrow is one day both for Akela and for me."

Then he pressed his face close to the window and watched the fire on the hearth. He saw the husbandman's wife get up and feed it in the night with black lumps. And when the morning came and the mists were all white and cold, he saw the man's child pick up a wicker pot plastered inside with earth, fill it with lumps of red-hot charcoal, put it under his blanket, and go out to tend the cows in the byre.

"Is that all?" said Mowgli. "If a cub can do it, there is nothing to fear." So he strode round the corner and met the boy, took the pot from his hand, and disappeared into the mist while the boy howled with fear.

"They are very like me," said Mowgli, blowing into the pot as he had seen the woman do. "This thing will die if I do not give it things to eat"; and he dropped twigs and dried bark on the red stuff. Half-way up the hill he met Bagheera with the morning dew shining like moonstones on his coat.

"Akela has missed," said the Panther. "They would have killed him last night, but they needed thee also. They were looking for thee on the hill."

"I was among the plowed lands. I am ready. See!" Mowgli held up the fire-pot.

"Good! Now, I have seen men thrust a dry branch into that stuff, and presently the Red Flower blossomed at the end of it. Art thou not afraid?"

"No. Why should I fear? I remember now—if it is not a dream— how, before I was a Wolf, I lay beside the Red Flower, and it was warm and pleasant."

All that day Mowgli sat in the cave tending his fire pot and dipping dry branches into it to see how they looked. He found a branch that

satisfied him, and in the evening when Tabaqui came to the cave and told him rudely enough that he was wanted at the Council Rock, he laughed till Tabaqui ran away. Then Mowgli went to the Council, still laughing.

Akela the Lone Wolf lay by the side of his rock as a sign that the leadership of the Pack was open, and Shere Khan with his following of scrap-fed wolves walked to and fro openly being flattered. Bagheera lay close to Mowgli, and the fire pot was between Mowgli's knees. When they were all gathered together, Shere Khan began to speak—a thing he would never have dared to do when Akela was in his prime.

"He has no right," whispered Bagheera. "Say so. He is a dog's son. He will be frightened."

Mowgli sprang to his feet. "Free People," he cried, "does Shere Khan lead the Pack? What has a tiger to do with our leadership?"

"Seeing that the leadership is yet open, and being asked to speak—" Shere Khan began.

"By whom?" said Mowgli. "Are we *all* jackals, to fawn on this cattle butcher? The leadership of the Pack is with the Pack alone."

There were yells of "Silence, thou man's cub!" "Let him speak. He has kept our Law"; and at last the seniors of the Pack thundered: "Let the Dead Wolf speak." When a leader of the Pack has missed his kill, he is called the Dead Wolf as long as he lives, which is not long.

Akela raised his old head wearily:—

"Free People, and ye too, jackals of Shere Khan, for twelve seasons I have led ye to and from the kill, and in all that time not one has been trapped or maimed. Now I have missed my kill. Ye know how that plot was made. Ye know how ye brought me up to an untried buck to make my weakness known. It was cleverly done. Your right is to kill me here on the Council Rock, now. Therefore, I ask, who comes to make an end of the Lone Wolf? For it is my right, by the Law of the Jungle, that ye come one by one."

There was a long hush, for no single wolf cared to fight Akela to the death. Then Shere Khan roared: "Bah! What have we to do with this toothless fool? He is doomed to die! It is the man-cub who has lived too long. Free People, he was my meat from the first. Give him to me.

I am weary of this man-wolf folly. He has troubled the jungle for ten seasons. Give me the man-cub, or I will hunt here always, and not give you one bone. He is a man, a man's child, and from the marrow of my bones I hate him!"

Then more than half the Pack yelled: "A man! A man! What has a man to do with us? Let him go to his own place."

"And turn all the people of the villages against us?" clamored Shere Khan. "No, give him to me. He is a man, and none of us can look him between the eyes."

Akela lifted his head again and said, "He has eaten our food. He has slept with us. He has driven game for us. He has broken no word of the Law of the Jungle."

"Also, I paid for him with a bull when he was accepted. The worth of a bull is little, but Bagheera's honour is something that he will perhaps fight for," said Bagheera in his gentlest voice.

"A bull paid ten years ago!" the Pack snarled. "What do we care for bones ten years old?"

"Or for a pledge?" said Bagheera, his white teeth bared under his lip. "Well are ye called the Free People!"

"No man's cub can run with the people of the jungle," howled Shere Khan. "Give him to me!"

"He is our brother in all but blood," Akela went on, "and ye would kill him here! In truth, I have lived too long. Some of ye are eaters of cattle, and of others I have heard that, under Shere Khan's teaching, ye go by dark night and snatch children from the villager's doorstep. Therefore I know ye to be cowards, and it is to cowards I speak. It is certain that I must die, and my life is of no worth, or I would offer that in the man-cub's place. But for the sake of the Honour of the Pack,—a little matter that by being without a leader ye have forgotten,—I promise that if ye let the man-cub go to his own place, I will not, when my time comes to die, bare one tooth against ye. I will die without fighting. That will at least save the Pack three lives. More I cannot do; but if ye will, I can save ye the shame that comes of killing a brother against whom there is no fault—a brother spoken for and bought into the Pack according to the Law of the Jungle."

"He is a man—a man—a man!" snarled the Pack. And most of the wolves began to gather round Shere Khan, whose tail was beginning to switch.

"Now the business is in thy hands," said Bagheera to Mowgli. "*We* can do no more except fight."

Mowgli stood upright—the fire pot in his hands. Then he stretched out his arms, and yawned in the face of the Council; but he was furious with rage and sorrow, for, wolflike, the wolves had never told him how they hated him. "Listen you!" he cried. "There is no need for this dog's jabber. Ye have told me so often tonight that I am a man (and indeed I would have been a wolf with you to my life's end) that I feel your words are true. So I do not call ye my brothers any more, but *sag* [dogs], as a man should. What ye will do, and what ye will not do, is not yours to say. That matter is with *me*; and that we may see the matter more plainly, I, the man, have brought here a little of the Red Flower which ye, dogs, fear."

He flung the fire pot on the ground, and some of the red coals lit a tuft of dried moss that flared up, as all the Council drew back in terror before the leaping flames.

Mowgli thrust his dead branch into the fire till the twigs lit and crackled, and whirled it above his head among the cowering wolves.

"Thou art the master," said Bagheera in an undertone. "Save Akela from the death. He was ever thy friend."

Akela, the grim old wolf who had never asked for mercy in his life, gave one piteous look at Mowgli as the boy stood all naked, his long black hair tossing over his shoulders in the light of the blazing branch that made the shadows jump and quiver.

"Good!" said Mowgli, staring round slowly. "I see that ye are dogs. I go from you to my own people—if they be my own people. The jungle is shut to me, and I must forget your talk and your companionship. But I will be more merciful than ye are. Because I was all but your brother in blood, I promise that when I am a man among men I will not betray ye to men as ye have betrayed me." He kicked the fire with his foot, and the sparks flew up. "There shall be no war between any of us in the Pack. But here is a debt to pay before I go." He strode forward to

where Shere Khan sat blinking stupidly at the flames, and caught him by the tuft on his chin. Bagheera followed in case of accidents. "Up, dog!" Mowgli cried. "Up, when a man speaks, or I will set that coat ablaze!"

Shere Khan's ears lay flat back on his head, and he shut his eyes, for the blazing branch was very near.

"This cattle-killer said he would kill me in the Council because he had not killed me when I was a cub. Thus and thus, then, do we beat dogs when we are men. Stir a whisker, Lungri, and I ram the Red Flower down thy gullet!" He beat Shere Khan over the head with the branch, and the tiger whimpered and whined in an agony of fear.

"Pah! Singed jungle cat—go now! But remember when next I come to the Council Rock, as a man should come, it will be with Shere Khan's hide on my head. For the rest, Akela goes free to live as he pleases. Ye will *not* kill him, because that is not my will. Nor do I think that ye will sit here any longer, lolling out your tongues as though ye were somebodies, instead of dogs whom I drive out—thus! Go!" The fire was burning furiously at the end of the branch, and Mowgli struck right and left round the circle, and the wolves ran howling with the sparks burning their fur. At last there were only Akela, Bagheera, and perhaps ten wolves that had taken Mowgli's part. Then something began to hurt Mowgli inside him, as he had never been hurt in his life before, and he caught his breath and sobbed, and the tears ran down his face.

"What is it? What is it?" he said. "I do not wish to leave the jungle, and I do not know what this is. Am I dying, Bagheera?"

"No, Little Brother. That is only tears such as men use," said Bagheera. "Now I know thou art a man, and a man's cub no longer. The jungle is shut indeed to thee henceforward. Let them fall, Mowgli. They are only tears." So Mowgli sat and cried as though his heart would break; and he had never cried in all his life before.

"Now," he said, "I will go to men. But first I must say farewell to my mother." And he went to the cave where she lived with Father Wolf, and he cried on her coat, while the four cubs howled miserably.

"Ye will not forget me?" said Mowgli.

"Never while we can follow a trail," said the cubs. "Come to the foot

of the hill when thou art a man, and we will talk to thee; and we will come into the croplands to play with thee by night."

"Come soon!" said Father Wolf. "Oh, wise little frog, come again soon; for we be old, thy mother and I."

"Come soon," said Mother Wolf, "little naked son of mine. For, listen, child of man, I loved thee more than ever I loved my cubs."

"I will surely come," said Mowgli. "And when I come it will be to lay out Shere Khan's hide upon the Council Rock. Do not forget me! Tell them in the jungle never to forget me!"

The dawn was beginning to break when Mowgli went down the hillside alone, to meet those mysterious things that are called men.

2. HUNTING-SONG OF THE SEEONEE PACK

As the dawn was breaking the *Sambhur* belled
 Once, twice and again!
And a doe leaped up, and a doe leaped up
From the pond in the wood where the wild deer sup.
This I, scouting alone, beheld,
 Once, twice and again!

As the dawn was breaking the *Sambhur* belled
 Once, twice and again!
And a wolf stole back, and a wolf stole back
To carry the word to the waiting pack,
And we sought and we found and we bayed on his track
 Once, twice and again!

As the dawn was breaking the Wolf-Pack yelled
 Once, twice and again!
Feet in the jungle that leave no mark!
Eyes that can see in the dark—the dark!
Tongue—give tongue to it! Hark! O hark!
 Once, twice and again!

3. KAA'S HUNTING

His spots are the joy of the Leopard: his horns are
 the Buffalo's pride.
Be clean, for the strength of the hunter is known by the
 gloss of his hide.
If ye find that the Bullock can toss you, or the heavy-
 browed *Sambhur* can gore;
Ye need not stop work to inform us: we knew it ten
 seasons before.
Oppress not the cubs of the stranger, but hail them as
 Sister and Brother,
For though they are little and fubsy, it may be the Bear
 is their mother.
"There is none like to me!" says the Cub in the pride of
 his earliest kill;
But the jungle is large and the Cub he is small. Let him
 think and be still.

— Maxims of Baloo

All that is told here happened some time before Mowgli was turned out of the Seeonee Wolf-Pack, or revenged himself on Shere Khan the tiger. It was in the days when Baloo was teaching him the Law of the Jungle. The big, serious, old brown bear was delighted to have so quick a pupil, for the young wolves will only learn as much of the Law of the Jungle as applies to their own pack and tribe, and run away as soon as they can repeat the Hunting Verse—"Feet that make no noise; eyes that can see in the dark; ears that can hear the winds in their lairs, and sharp white teeth, all these things are the marks of our brothers except Tabaqui the Jackal and the Hyaena whom we hate." But Mowgli, as a man-cub, had to learn a great deal more than this. Sometimes Bagheera the Black Panther would come lounging through the jungle to see how his pet was getting on, and would purr with his

head against a tree while Mowgli recited the day's lesson to Baloo. The boy could climb almost as well as he could swim, and swim almost as well as he could run. So Baloo, the Teacher of the Law, taught him the Wood and Water Laws: how to tell a rotten branch from a sound one; how to speak politely to the wild bees when he came upon a hive of them fifty feet above ground; what to say to Mang the Bat when he disturbed him in the branches at mid-day; and how to warn the water-snakes in the pools before he splashed down among them. None of the Jungle People like being disturbed, and all are very ready to fly at an intruder. Then, too, Mowgli was taught the Strangers' Hunting Call, which must be repeated aloud till it is answered, whenever one of the Jungle People hunts outside his own grounds. It means, translated, "Give me leave to hunt here because I am hungry." And the answer is, "Hunt then for food, but not for pleasure."

All this will show you how much Mowgli had to learn by heart, and he grew very tired of saying the same thing over a hundred times. But, as Baloo said to Bagheera, one day when Mowgli had been cuffed and run off in a temper, "A man's cub is a man's cub, and he must learn *all* the Law of the Jungle."

"But think how small he is," said the Black Panther, who would have spoiled Mowgli if he had had his own way. "How can his little head carry all thy long talk?"

"Is there anything in the jungle too little to be killed? No. That is why I teach him these things, and that is why I hit him, very softly, when he forgets."

"Softly! What dost thou know of softness, old Iron-feet?" Bagheera grunted. "His face is all bruised to-day by thy—softness. Ugh."

"Better he should be bruised from head to foot by me who love him than that he should come to harm through ignorance," Baloo answered very earnestly. "I am now teaching him the Master Words of the Jungle that shall protect him with the birds and the Snake-People, and all that hunt on four feet, except his own pack. He can now claim protection, if he will only remember the words, from all in the jungle. Is not that worth a little beating?"

"Well, look to it then that thou dost not kill the man-cub. He is no

tree trunk to sharpen thy blunt claws upon. But what are those Master Words? I am more likely to give help than to ask it"—Bagheera stretched out one paw and admired the steel-blue, ripping-chisel talons at the end of it—"still I should like to know."

"I will call Mowgli and he shall say them—if he will. Come, Little Brother!"

"My head is ringing like a bee tree," said a sullen little voice over their heads, and Mowgli slid down a tree trunk very angry and indignant, adding as he reached the ground: "I come for Bagheera and not for *thee*, fat old Baloo!"

"That is all one to me," said Baloo, though he was hurt and grieved. "Tell Bagheera, then, the Master Words of the Jungle that I have taught thee this day."

"Master Words for which people?" said Mowgli, delighted to show off. "The jungle has many tongues. *I* know them all."

"A little thou knowest, but not much. See, O Bagheera, they never thank their teacher. Not one small wolfling has ever come back to thank old Baloo for his teachings. Say the word for the Hunting-People, then—great scholar."

"We be of one blood, ye and I," said Mowgli, giving the words the Bear accent which all the Hunting People use.

"Good. Now for the birds."

Mowgli repeated, with the Kite's whistle at the end of the sentence.

"Now for the Snake-People," said Bagheera.

The answer was a perfectly indescribable hiss, and Mowgli kicked up his feet behind, clapped his hands together to applaud himself, and jumped on to Bagheera's back, where he sat sideways, drumming with his heels on the glossy skin and making the worst faces he could think of at Baloo.

"There—there! That was worth a little bruise," said the brown bear tenderly. "Some day thou wilt remember me." Then he turned aside to tell Bagheera how he had begged the Master Words from Hathi the Wild Elephant, who knows all about these things, and how Hathi had taken Mowgli down to a pool to get the Snake Word from a water-snake, because Baloo could not pronounce it, and how Mowgli was

now reasonably safe against all accidents in the jungle, because neither snake, bird, nor beast would hurt him.

"No one then is to be feared," Baloo wound up, patting his big furry stomach with pride.

"Except his own tribe," said Bagheera, under his breath; and then aloud to Mowgli, "Have a care for my ribs, Little Brother! What is all this dancing up and down?"

Mowgli had been trying to make himself heard by pulling at Bagheera's shoulder fur and kicking hard. When the two listened to him he was shouting at the top of his voice, "And *so* I shall have a tribe of my own, and lead them through the branches all day long."

"What is this new folly, little dreamer of dreams?" said Bagheera.

"Yes, and throw branches and dirt at old Baloo," Mowgli went on. "They have promised me this. Ah!"

"*Whoof!*" Baloo's big paw scooped Mowgli off Bagheera's back, and as the boy lay between the big fore-paws he could see the Bear was angry.

"Mowgli," said Baloo, "thou hast been talking with the *Bandar-log*—the Monkey-People."

Mowgli looked at Bagheera to see if the Panther was angry too, and Bagheera's eyes were as hard as jade stones.

"Thou hast been with the Monkey-People—the gray apes—the people without a law—the eaters of everything. That is great shame."

"When Baloo hurt my head," said Mowgli (he was still on his back), "I went away, and the gray apes came down from the trees and had pity on me. No one else cared." He snuffled a little.

"The pity of the Monkey-People!" Baloo snorted. "The stillness of the mountain stream! The cool of the summer sun! And then, man-cub?"

"And then, and then, they gave me nuts and pleasant things to eat, and they—they carried me in their arms up to the top of the trees and said I was their blood-brother except that I had no tail, and should be their leader some day."

"They have *no* leader," said Bagheera. "They lie. They have always lied."

"They were very kind and bade me come again. Why have I never been taken among the Monkey-People? They stand on their feet as I do. They do not hit me with their hard paws. They play all day. Let me get up! Bad Baloo, let me up! I will play with them again."

"Listen, man-cub," said the Bear, and his voice rumbled like thunder on a hot night. "I have taught thee all the Law of the Jungle for all the peoples of the jungle—except the Monkey-Folk who live in the trees. They have no law. They are outcasts. They have no speech of their own, but use the stolen words which they overhear when they listen, and peep, and wait up above in the branches. Their way is not our way. They are without leaders. They have no remembrance. They boast and chatter and pretend that they are a great people about to do great affairs in the jungle, but the falling of a nut turns their minds to laughter and all is forgotten. We of the jungle have no dealings with them. We do not drink where the monkeys drink; we do not go where the monkeys go; we do not hunt where they hunt; we do not die where they die. Hast thou ever heard me speak of the *Bandar-log* till to-day?"

"No," said Mowgli in a whisper, for the forest was very still now Baloo had finished.

"The Jungle People put them out of their mouths and out of their minds. They are very many, evil, dirty, shameless, and they desire, if they have any fixed desire, to be noticed by the Jungle People. But we do *not* notice them even when they throw nuts and filth on our heads."

He had hardly spoken when a shower of nuts and twigs spattered down through the branches; and they could hear coughings and howlings and angry jumpings high up in the air among the thin branches.

"The Monkey-People are forbidden," said Baloo, "forbidden to the Jungle People. Remember."

"Forbidden," said Bagheera, "but I still think Baloo should have warned thee against them."

"I—I? How was I to guess he would play with such dirt. The Monkey-People! Faugh!"

A fresh shower came down on their heads and the two trotted away, taking Mowgli with them. What Baloo had said about the monkeys

was perfectly true. They belonged to the tree-tops, and as beasts very seldom look up, there was no occasion for the monkeys and the Jungle People to cross each other's path. But whenever they found a sick wolf, or a wounded tiger, or bear, the monkeys would torment him, and would throw sticks and nuts at any beast for fun and in the hope of being noticed. Then they would howl and shriek senseless songs, and invite the Jungle People to climb up their trees and fight them, or would start furious battles over nothing among themselves, and leave the dead monkeys where the Jungle People could see them. They were always just going to have a leader, and laws and customs of their own, but they never did, because their memories would not hold over from day to day, and so they compromised things by making up a saying, "What the *Bandar-log* think now the jungle will think later," and that comforted them a great deal. None of the beasts could reach them, but on the other hand none of the beasts would notice them, and that was why they were so pleased when Mowgli came to play with them, and they heard how angry Baloo was.

They never meant to do any more—the *Bandar-log* never mean anything at all; but one of them invented what seemed to him a brilliant idea, and he told all the others that Mowgli would be a useful person to keep in the tribe, because he could weave sticks together for protection from the wind; so, if they caught him, they could make him teach them. Of course Mowgli, as a woodcutter's child, inherited all sorts of instincts, and used to make little huts of fallen branches without thinking how he came to do it. The Monkey-People, watching in the trees, considered his play most wonderful. This time, they said, they were really going to have a leader and become the wisest people in the jungle—so wise that everyone else would notice and envy them. Therefore they followed Baloo and Bagheera and Mowgli through the jungle very quietly till it was time for the mid-day nap, and Mowgli, who was very much ashamed of himself, slept between the Panther and the Bear, resolving to have no more to do with the Monkey-People.

The next thing he remembered was feeling hands on his legs and arms—hard, strong, little hands—and then a swash of branches in his face, and then he was staring down through the swaying boughs as

Baloo woke the jungle with his deep cries and Bagheera bounded up the trunk with every tooth bared. The *Bandar-log* howled with triumph and scuffled away to the upper branches where Bagheera dared not follow, shouting: "He has noticed us! Bagheera has noticed us. All the Jungle People admire us for our skill and our cunning." Then they began their flight; and the flight of the Monkey-People through tree-land is one of the things nobody can describe. They have their regular roads and crossroads, up hills and down hills, all laid out from fifty to seventy or a hundred feet above ground, and by these they can travel even at night if necessary. Two of the strongest monkeys caught Mowgli under the arms and swung off with him through the treetops, twenty feet at a bound. Had they been alone they could have gone twice as fast, but the boy's weight held them back. Sick and giddy as Mowgli was he could not help enjoying the wild rush, though the glimpses of earth far down below frightened him, and the terrible check and jerk at the end of the swing over nothing but empty air brought his heart between his teeth. His escort would rush him up a tree till he felt the thinnest topmost branches crackle and bend under them, and then with a cough and a whoop would fling themselves into the air outward and downward, and bring up, hanging by their hands or their feet to the lower limbs of the next tree. Sometimes he could see for miles and miles across the still green jungle, as a man on the top of a mast can see for miles across the sea, and then the branches and leaves would lash him across the face, and he and his two guards would be almost down to earth again. So, bounding and crashing and whooping and yelling, the whole tribe of *Bandar-log* swept along the tree-roads with Mowgli their prisoner.

For a time he was afraid of being dropped. Then he grew angry but knew better than to struggle, and then he began to think. The first thing was to send back word to Baloo and Bagheera, for, at the pace the monkeys were going, he knew his friends would be left far behind. It was useless to look down, for he could only see the topsides of the branches, so he stared upward and saw, far away in the blue, Rann the Kite balancing and wheeling as he kept watch over the jungle waiting for things to die. Rann saw that the monkeys were carrying something, and dropped a few hundred yards to find out whether their load was

good to eat. He whistled with surprise when he saw Mowgli being dragged up to a treetop and heard him give the Kite call for—"We be of one blood, thou and I." The waves of the branches closed over the boy, but Rann balanced away to the next tree in time to see the little brown face come up again. "Mark my trail!" Mowgli shouted. "Tell Baloo of the Seeonee Pack and Bagheera of the Council Rock."

"In whose name, Brother?" Rann had never seen Mowgli before, though of course he had heard of him.

"Mowgli, the Frog. Man-cub they call me! Mark my trail!"

The last words were shrieked as he was being swung through the air, but Rann nodded and rose up till he looked no bigger than a speck of dust, and there he hung, watching with his telescope eyes the swaying of the treetops as Mowgli's escort whirled along.

"They never go far," he said with a chuckle. "They never do what they set out to do. Always pecking at new things are the *Bandar-log*. This time, if I have any eye-sight, they have pecked down trouble for themselves, for Baloo is no fledgling and Bagheera can, as I know, kill more than goats."

So he rocked on his wings, his feet gathered up under him, and waited.

Meantime, Baloo and Bagheera were furious with rage and grief. Bagheera climbed as he had never climbed before, but the thin branches broke beneath his weight, and he slipped down, his claws full of bark.

"Why didst thou not warn the man-cub?" he roared to poor Baloo, who had set off at a clumsy trot in the hope of overtaking the monkeys. "What was the use of half slaying him with blows if thou didst not warn him?"

"Haste! O haste! We—we may catch them yet!" Baloo panted.

"At that speed! It would not tire a wounded cow. Teacher of the Law—cub-beater—a mile of that rolling to and fro would burst thee open. Sit still and think! Make a plan. This is no time for chasing. They may drop him if we follow too close."

"*Arrula! Whoo!* They may have dropped him already, being tired of carrying him. Who can trust the *Bandar-log*? Put dead bats on my head! Give me black bones to eat! Roll me into the hives of the wild bees that

I may be stung to death, and bury me with the Hyaena, for I am most miserable of bears! *Arrulala! Wahooa!* O Mowgli, Mowgli! Why did I not warn thee against the Monkey-Folk instead of breaking thy head? Now perhaps I may have knocked the day's lesson out of his mind, and he will be alone in the jungle without the Master Words."

Baloo clasped his paws over his ears and rolled to and fro moaning.

"At least he gave me all the Words correctly a little time ago," said Bagheera impatiently. "Baloo, thou hast neither memory nor respect. What would the jungle think if I, the Black Panther, curled myself up like Ikki the Porcupine, and howled?"

"What do I care what the jungle thinks? He may be dead by now."

"Unless and until they drop him from the branches in sport, or kill him out of idleness, I have no fear for the man-cub. He is wise and well taught, and above all he has the eyes that make the Jungle People afraid. But (and it is a great evil) he is in the power of the *Bandar-log*, and they, because they live in trees, have no fear of any of our people." Bagheera licked one forepaw thoughtfully.

"Fool that I am! Oh, fat, brown, root-digging fool that I am," said Baloo, uncoiling himself with a jerk, "it is true what Hathi the Wild Elephant says: '*To each his own fear*'; and they, the *Bandar-log*, fear Kaa the Rock Snake. He can climb as well as they can. He steals the young monkeys in the night. The whisper of his name makes their wicked tails cold. Let us go to Kaa."

"What will he do for us? He is not of our tribe, being footless—and with most evil eyes," said Bagheera.

"He is very old and very cunning. Above all, he is always hungry," said Baloo hopefully. "Promise him many goats."

"He sleeps for a full month after he has once eaten. He may be asleep now, and even were he awake what if he would rather kill his own goats?" Bagheera, who did not know much about Kaa, was naturally suspicious.

"Then in that case, thou and I together, old hunter, might make him see reason." Here Baloo rubbed his faded brown shoulder against the Panther, and they went off to look for Kaa the Rock-python.

They found him stretched out on a warm ledge in the afternoon sun,

admiring his beautiful new coat, for he had been in retirement for the last ten days changing his skin, and now he was very splendid—darting his big blunt-nosed head along the ground, and twisting the thirty feet of his body into fantastic knots and curves, and licking his lips as he thought of his dinner to come.

"He has not eaten," said Baloo, with a grunt of relief, as soon as he saw the beautifully mottled brown and yellow jacket. "Be careful, Bagheera! He is always a little blind after he has changed his skin, and very quick to strike."

Kaa was not a poison snake—in fact he rather despised the poison snakes as cowards—but his strength lay in his hug, and when he had once lapped his huge coils round anybody there was no more to be said. "Good hunting!" cried Baloo, sitting up on his haunches. Like all snakes of his breed Kaa was rather deaf, and did not hear the call at first. Then he curled up ready for any accident, his head lowered.

"Good hunting for us all," he answered. "Oho, Baloo, what dost thou do here? Good hunting, Bagheera. One of us at least needs food. Is there any news of game afoot? A doe now, or even a young buck? I am as empty as a dried well."

"We are hunting," said Baloo carelessly. He knew that you must not hurry Kaa. He is too big.

"Give me permission to come with you," said Kaa. "A blow more or less is nothing to thee, Bagheera or Baloo, but I—I have to wait and wait for days in a wood-path and climb half a night on the mere chance of a young ape. Psshaw! The branches are not what they were when I was young. Rotten twigs and dry boughs are they all."

"Maybe thy great weight has something to do with the matter," said Baloo.

"I am a fair length—a fair length," said Kaa with a little pride. "But for all that, it is the fault of this new-grown timber. I came very near to falling on my last hunt—very near indeed—and the noise of my slipping, for my tail was not tight wrapped around the tree, waked the *Bandar-log*, and they called me most evil names."

"Footless, yellow earth-worm," said Bagheera under his whiskers, as though he were trying to remember something.

"*Sssss!* Have they ever called me *that?*" said Kaa.

"Something of that kind it was that they shouted to us last moon, but we never noticed them. They will say anything—even that thou hast lost all thy teeth, and wilt not face anything bigger than a kid, because (they are indeed shameless, these *Bandar-log*)—because thou art afraid of the he-goat's horns," Bagheera went on sweetly.

Now a snake, especially a wary old python like Kaa, very seldom shows that he is angry, but Baloo and Bagheera could see the big swallowing muscles on either side of Kaa's throat ripple and bulge.

"The *Bandar-log* have shifted their grounds," he said quietly. "When I came up into the sun to-day I heard them whooping among the tree-tops."

"It—it is the *Bandar-log* that we follow now," said Baloo, but the words stuck in his throat, for that was the first time in his memory that one of the Jungle People had owned to being interested in the doings of the monkeys.

"Beyond doubt then it is no small thing that takes two such hunters—leaders in their own jungle I am certain—on the trail of the *Bandar-log*," Kaa replied courteously, as he swelled with curiosity.

"Indeed," Baloo began, "I am no more than the old and sometimes very foolish Teacher of the Law to the Seeonee wolf-cubs, and Bagheera here—"

"Is Bagheera," said the Black Panther, and his jaws shut with a snap, for he did not believe in being humble. "The trouble is this, Kaa. Those nut-stealers and pickers of palm leaves have stolen away our man-cub of whom thou hast perhaps heard."

"I heard some news from Ikki (his quills make him presumptuous) of a man-thing that was entered into a wolf-pack, but I did not believe. Ikki is full of stories half heard and very badly told."

"But it is true. He is such a man-cub as never was," said Baloo. "The best and wisest and boldest of man-cubs—my own pupil, who shall make the name of Baloo famous through all the jungles; and besides, I—we—love him, Kaa."

"*Ts! Ts!*" said Kaa, weaving his head to and fro. "I also have known what love is. There are tales I could tell that—"

"That need a clear night when we are all well fed to praise properly," said Bagheera quickly. "Our man-cub is in the hands of the *Bandar-log* now, and we know that of all the Jungle People they fear Kaa alone."

"They fear me alone. They have good reason," said Kaa. "Chattering, foolish, vain—vain, foolish, and chattering, are the monkeys. But a man-thing in their hands is in no good luck. They grow tired of the nuts they pick, and throw them down. They carry a branch half a day, meaning to do great things with it, and then they snap it in two. That man-thing is not to be envied. They called me also—'yellow fish' was it not?"

"Worm—worm—earth-worm," said Bagheera, "as well as other things which I cannot now say for shame."

"We must remind them to speak well of their master. *Aaa-sssh!* We must help their wandering memories. Now, whither went they with the cub?"

"The jungle alone knows. Toward the sunset, I believe," said Baloo. "We had thought that thou wouldst know, Kaa."

"I? How? I take them when they come in my way, but I do not hunt the *Bandar-log*, or frogs—or green scum on a water-hole, for that matter."

"Up, Up! Up, Up! *Hillo! Illo! Illo!* Look up, Baloo of the Seeonee Wolf-Pack!"

Baloo looked up to see where the voice came from, and there was Rann the Kite, sweeping down with the sun shining on the upturned flanges of his wings. It was near Rann's bedtime, but he had ranged all over the jungle looking for the Bear and had missed him in the thick foliage.

"What is it?" said Baloo.

"I have seen Mowgli among the *Bandar-log*. He bade me tell you. I watched. The *Bandar-log* have taken him beyond the river to the monkey city—to the Cold Lairs. They may stay there for a night, or ten nights, or an hour. I have told the bats to watch through the dark time. That is my message. Good hunting, all you below!"

"Full gorge and a deep sleep to you, Rann," cried Bagheera. "I will remember thee in my next kill, and put aside the head for thee alone, O best of kites!"

"It is nothing. It is nothing. The boy held the Master Word. I could have done no less," and Rann circled up again to his roost.

"He has not forgotten to use his tongue," said Baloo with a chuckle of pride. "To think of one so young remembering the Master Word for the birds too while he was being pulled across trees!"

"It was most firmly driven into him," said Bagheera. "But I am proud of him, and now we must go to the Cold Lairs."

They all knew where that place was, but few of the Jungle People ever went there, because what they called the Cold Lairs was an old deserted city, lost and buried in the jungle, and beasts seldom use a place that men have once used. The wild boar will, but the hunting tribes do not. Besides, the monkeys lived there as much as they could be said to live anywhere, and no self-respecting animal would come within eyeshot of it except in times of drought, when the half-ruined tanks and reservoirs held a little water.

"It is half a night's journey—at full speed," said Bagheera, and Baloo looked very serious. "I will go as fast as I can," he said anxiously.

"We dare not wait for thee. Follow, Baloo. We must go on the quick-foot—Kaa and I."

"Feet or no feet, I can keep abreast of all thy four," said Kaa shortly. Baloo made one effort to hurry, but had to sit down panting, and so they left him to come on later, while Bagheera hurried forward, at the quick panther-canter. Kaa said nothing, but, strive as Bagheera might, the huge Rock-python held level with him. When they came to a hill stream, Bagheera gained, because he bounded across while Kaa swam, his head and two feet of his neck clearing the water, but on level ground Kaa made up the distance.

"By the Broken Lock that freed me," said Bagheera, when twilight had fallen, "thou art no slow goer!"

"I am hungry," said Kaa. "Besides, they called me speckled frog."

"Worm—earth-worm, and yellow to boot."

"All one. Let us go on," and Kaa seemed to pour himself along the ground, finding the shortest road with his steady eyes, and keeping to it.

In the Cold Lairs the Monkey-People were not thinking of Mowgli's friends at all. They had brought the boy to the Lost City, and were very

much pleased with themselves for the time. Mowgli had never seen an Indian city before, and though this was almost a heap of ruins it seemed very wonderful and splendid. Some king had built it long ago on a little hill. You could still trace the stone causeways that led up to the ruined gates where the last splinters of wood hung to the worn, rusted hinges. Trees had grown into and out of the walls; the battlements were tumbled down and decayed, and wild creepers hung out of the windows of the towers on the walls in bushy hanging clumps.

A great roofless palace crowned the hill, and the marble of the courtyards and the fountains was split, and stained with red and green, and the very cobblestones in the courtyard where the king's elephants used to live had been thrust up and apart by grasses and young trees. From the palace you could see the rows and rows of roofless houses that made up the city looking like empty honeycombs filled with blackness; the shapeless block of stone that had been an idol in the square where four roads met; the pits and dimples at street corners where the public wells once stood, and the shattered domes of temples with wild figs sprouting on their sides. The monkeys called the place their city, and pretended to despise the Jungle People because they lived in the forest. And yet they never knew what the buildings were made for nor how to use them. They would sit in circles on the hall of the king's council chamber, and scratch for fleas and pretend to be men; or they would run in and out of the roofless houses and collect pieces of plaster and old bricks in a corner, and forget where they had hidden them, and fight and cry in scuffling crowds, and then break off to play up and down the terraces of the king's garden, where they would shake the rose trees and the oranges in sport to see the fruit and flowers fall. They explored all the passages and dark tunnels in the palace and the hundreds of little dark rooms, but they never remembered what they had seen and what they had not; and so drifted about in ones and twos or crowds telling each other that they were doing as men did. They drank at the tanks and made the water all muddy, and then they fought over it, and then they would all rush together in mobs and shout: "There is no one in the jungle so wise and good and clever and strong and gentle as the *Bandar-log*." Then all would begin again till they grew tired of the city

and went back to the tree-tops, hoping the Jungle People would notice them.

Mowgli, who had been trained under the Law of the Jungle, did not like or understand this kind of life. The monkeys dragged him into the Cold Lairs late in the afternoon, and instead of going to sleep, as Mowgli would have done after a long journey, they joined hands and danced about and sang their foolish songs. One of the monkeys made a speech and told his companions that Mowgli's capture marked a new thing in the history of the *Bandar-log*, for Mowgli was going to show them how to weave sticks and canes together as a protection against rain and cold. Mowgli picked up some creepers and began to work them in and out, and the monkeys tried to imitate; but in a very few minutes they lost interest and began to pull their friends' tails or jump up and down on all fours, coughing.

"I wish to eat," said Mowgli. "I am a stranger in this part of the jungle. Bring me food, or give me leave to hunt here."

Twenty or thirty monkeys bounded away to bring him nuts and wild pawpaws. But they fell to fighting on the road, and it was too much trouble to go back with what was left of the fruit. Mowgli was sore and angry as well as hungry, and he roamed through the empty city giving the Strangers' Hunting Call from time to time, but no one answered him, and Mowgli felt that he had reached a very bad place indeed. "All that Baloo has said about the *Bandar-log* is true," he thought to himself. "They have no Law, no Hunting Call, and no leaders—nothing but foolish words and little picking thievish hands. So if I am starved or killed here, it will be all my own fault. But I must try to return to my own jungle. Baloo will surely beat me, but that is better than chasing silly rose leaves with the *Bandar-log*."

No sooner had he walked to the city wall than the monkeys pulled him back, telling him that he did not know how happy he was, and pinching him to make him grateful. He set his teeth and said nothing, but went with the shouting monkeys to a terrace above the red sandstone reservoirs that were half-full of rain water. There was a ruined summer-house of white marble in the centre of the terrace, built for queens dead a hundred years ago. The domed roof had half fallen

in and blocked up the underground passage from the palace by which the queens used to enter. But the walls were made of screens of marble tracery—beautiful milk-white fretwork, set with agates and cornelians and jasper and lapis lazuli, and as the moon came up behind the hill it shone through the open work, casting shadows on the ground like black velvet embroidery. Sore, sleepy, and hungry as he was, Mowgli could not help laughing when the *Bandar-log* began, twenty at a time, to tell him how great and wise and strong and gentle they were, and how foolish he was to wish to leave them. "We are great. We are free. We are wonderful. We are the most wonderful people in all the jungle! We all say so, and so it must be true," they shouted. "Now as you are a new listener and can carry our words back to the Jungle People so that they may notice us in future, we will tell you all about our most excellent selves." Mowgli made no objection, and the monkeys gathered by hundreds and hundreds on the terrace to listen to their own speakers singing the praises of the *Bandar-log*, and whenever a speaker stopped for want of breath they would all shout together: "This is true; we all say so." Mowgli nodded and blinked, and said "Yes" when they asked him a question, and his head spun with the noise. "Tabaqui the Jackal must have bitten all these people," he said to himself, "and now they have madness. Certainly this is *dewanee*, the madness. Do they never go to sleep? Now there is a cloud coming to cover that moon. If it were only a big enough cloud I might try to run away in the darkness. But I am tired."

That same cloud was being watched by two good friends in the ruined ditch below the city wall, for Bagheera and Kaa, knowing well how dangerous the Monkey-People were in large numbers, did not wish to run any risks. The monkeys never fight unless they are a hundred to one, and few in the jungle care for those odds.

"I will go to the west wall," Kaa whispered, "and come down swiftly with the slope of the ground in my favour. They will not throw themselves upon *my* back in their hundreds, but—"

"I know it," said Bagheera. "Would that Baloo were here, but we must do what we can. When that cloud covers the moon I shall go to the terrace. They hold some sort of council there over the boy."

"Good hunting," said Kaa grimly, and glided away to the west wall. That happened to be the least ruined of any, and the big snake was delayed awhile before he could find a way up the stones. The cloud hid the moon, and as Mowgli wondered what would come next he heard Bagheera's light feet on the terrace. The Black Panther had raced up the slope almost without a sound and was striking—he knew better than to waste time in biting—right and left among the monkeys, who were seated round Mowgli in circles fifty and sixty deep. There was a howl of fright and rage, and then as Bagheera tripped on the rolling kicking bodies beneath him, a monkey shouted: "There is only one here! Kill him! Kill." A scuffling mass of monkeys, biting, scratching, tearing, and pulling, closed over Bagheera, while five or six laid hold of Mowgli, dragged him up the wall of the summerhouse and pushed him through the hole of the broken dome. A man-trained boy would have been badly bruised, for the fall was a good fifteen feet, but Mowgli fell as Baloo had taught him to fall, and landed on his feet.

"Stay there," shouted the monkeys, "till we have killed thy friends, and later we will play with thee—if the Poison-People leave thee alive."

"We be of one blood, ye and I," said Mowgli, quickly giving the Snake's Call. He could hear rustling and hissing in the rubbish all round him and gave the Call a second time, to make sure.

"Even ssso! Down hoods all!" said half a dozen low voices (every ruin in India becomes sooner or later a dwelling place of snakes, and the old summerhouse was alive with cobras). "Stand still, Little Brother, for thy feet may do us harm."

Mowgli stood as quietly as he could, peering through the open work and listening to the furious din of the fight round the Black Panther— the yells and chatterings and scufflings, and Bagheera's deep, hoarse cough as he backed and bucked and twisted and plunged under the heaps of his enemies. For the first time since he was born, Bagheera was fighting for his life.

"Baloo must be at hand; Bagheera would not have come alone," Mowgli thought. And then he called aloud: "To the tank, Bagheera. Roll to the water tanks. Roll and plunge! Get to the water!"

Bagheera heard, and the cry that told him Mowgli was safe gave him

new courage. He worked his way desperately, inch by inch, straight for the reservoirs, halting in silence. Then from the ruined wall nearest the jungle rose up the rumbling war-shout of Baloo. The old Bear had done his best, but he could not come before. "Bagheera," he shouted, "I am here. I climb! I haste! *Ahuwora!* The stones slip under my feet! Wait my coming, O most infamous *Bandar-log*!" He panted up the terrace only to disappear to the head in a wave of monkeys, but he threw himself squarely on his haunches, and, spreading out his forepaws, hugged as many as he could hold, and then began to hit with a regular *bat-bat-bat*, like the flipping strokes of a paddle wheel. A crash and a splash told Mowgli that Bagheera had fought his way to the tank where the monkeys could not follow. The Panther lay gasping for breath, his head just out of the water, while the monkeys stood three deep on the red steps, dancing up and down with rage, ready to spring upon him from all sides if he came out to help Baloo. It was then that Bagheera lifted up his dripping chin, and in despair gave the Snake's Call for protection— "We be of one blood, ye and I"—for he believed that Kaa had turned tail at the last minute. Even Baloo, half smothered under the monkeys on the edge of the terrace, could not help chuckling as he heard the Black Panther asking for help.

Kaa had only just worked his way over the west wall, landing with a wrench that dislodged a coping stone into the ditch. He had no intention of losing any advantage of the ground, and coiled and uncoiled himself once or twice, to be sure that every foot of his long body was in working order. All that while the fight with Baloo went on, and the monkeys yelled in the tank round Bagheera, and Mang the Bat, flying to and fro, carried the news of the great battle over the jungle, till even Hathi the Wild Elephant trumpeted, and, far away, scattered bands of the Monkey-Folk woke and came leaping along the tree-roads to help their comrades in the Cold Lairs, and the noise of the fight roused all the day birds for miles round. Then Kaa came straight, quickly, and anxious to kill. The fighting strength of a python is in the driving blow of his head backed by all the strength and weight of his body. If you can imagine a lance, or a battering ram, or a hammer weighing nearly half a ton driven by a cool, quiet mind living in the handle of it, you can roughly

imagine what Kaa was like when he fought. A python four or five feet long can knock a man down if he hits him fairly in the chest, and Kaa was thirty feet long, as you know. His first stroke was delivered into the heart of the crowd round Baloo. It was sent home with shut mouth in silence, and there was no need of a second. The monkeys scattered with cries of—"Kaa! It is Kaa! Run! Run!"

Generations of monkeys had been scared into good behaviour by the stories their elders told them of Kaa, the night thief, who could slip along the branches as quietly as moss grows, and steal away the strongest monkey that ever lived; of old Kaa, who could make himself look so like a dead branch or a rotten stump that the wisest were deceived, till the branch caught them. Kaa was everything that the monkeys feared in the jungle, for none of them knew the limits of his power, none of them could look him in the face, and none had ever come alive out of his hug. And so they ran, stammering with terror, to the walls and the roofs of the houses, and Baloo drew a deep breath of relief. His fur was much thicker than Bagheera's, but he had suffered sorely in the fight. Then Kaa opened his mouth for the first time and spoke one long hissing word, and the far-away monkeys, hurrying to the defense of the Cold Lairs, stayed where they were, cowering, till the loaded branches bent and crackled under them. The monkeys on the walls and the empty houses stopped their cries, and in the stillness that fell upon the city Mowgli heard Bagheera shaking his wet sides as he came up from the tank. Then the clamor broke out again. The monkeys leaped higher up the walls. They clung around the necks of the big stone idols and shrieked as they skipped along the battlements, while Mowgli, dancing in the summerhouse, put his eye to the screenwork and hooted owl-fashion between his front teeth, to show his derision and contempt.

"Get the man-cub out of that trap; I can do no more," Bagheera gasped. "Let us take the man-cub and go. They may attack again."

"They will not move till I order them. Stay you sssso!" Kaa hissed, and the city was silent once more. "I could not come before, Brother, but I *think* I heard thee call"—this was to Bagheera.

"I—I may have cried out in the battle," Bagheera answered. "Baloo, art thou hurt?"

"I am not sure that they did not pull me into a hundred little bearlings," said Baloo, gravely shaking one leg after the other. "Wow! I am sore. Kaa, we owe thee, I think, our lives—Bagheera and I."

"No matter. Where is the manling?"

"Here, in a trap. I cannot climb out," cried Mowgli. The curve of the broken dome was above his head.

"Take him away. He dances like Mao the Peacock. He will crush our young," said the cobras inside.

"Hah!" said Kaa with a chuckle, "he has friends everywhere, this manling. Stand back, manling. And hide you, O Poison People. I break down the wall."

Kaa looked carefully till he found a discoloured crack in the marble tracery showing a weak spot, made two or three light taps with his head to get the distance, and then lifting up six feet of his body clear of the ground, sent home half a dozen full-power smashing blows, nose-first. The screen-work broke and fell away in a cloud of dust and rubbish, and Mowgli leaped through the opening and flung himself between Baloo and Bagheera—an arm around each big neck.

"Art thou hurt?" said Baloo, hugging him softly.

"I am sore, hungry, and not a little bruised. But, oh, they have handled ye grievously, my Brothers! Ye bleed."

"Others also," said Bagheera, licking his lips and looking at the monkey-dead on the terrace and round the tank.

"It is nothing, it is nothing, if thou art safe, oh, my pride of all little frogs!" whimpered Baloo.

"Of that we shall judge later," said Bagheera, in a dry voice that Mowgli did not at all like. "But here is Kaa to whom we owe the battle and thou owest thy life. Thank him according to our customs, Mowgli."

Mowgli turned and saw the great Python's head swaying a foot above his own.

"So this is the manling," said Kaa. "Very soft is his skin, and he is not unlike the *Bandar-log*. Have a care, manling, that I do not mistake thee for a monkey some twilight when I have newly changed my coat."

"We be one blood, thou and I," Mowgli answered. "I take my life from thee tonight. My kill shall be thy kill if ever thou art hungry, O Kaa."

"All thanks, Little Brother," said Kaa, though his eyes twinkled. "And what may so bold a hunter kill? I ask that I may follow when next he goes abroad."

"I kill nothing,—I am too little,—but I drive goats toward such as can use them. When thou art empty come to me and see if I speak the truth. I have some skill in these [he held out his hands], and if ever thou art in a trap, I may pay the debt which I owe to thee, to Bagheera, and to Baloo, here. Good hunting to ye all, my masters."

"Well said," growled Baloo, for Mowgli had returned thanks very prettily. The Python dropped his head lightly for a minute on Mowgli's shoulder. "A brave heart and a courteous tongue," said he. "They shall carry thee far through the jungle, manling. But now go hence quickly with thy friends. Go and sleep, for the moon sets, and what follows it is not well that thou shouldst see."

The moon was sinking behind the hills and the lines of trembling monkeys huddled together on the walls and battlements looked like ragged shaky fringes of things. Baloo went down to the tank for a drink and Bagheera began to put his fur in order, as Kaa glided out into the centre of the terrace and brought his jaws together with a ringing snap that drew all the monkeys' eyes upon him.

"The moon sets," he said. "Is there yet light enough to see?"

From the walls came a moan like the wind in the tree-tops—"We see, O Kaa."

"Good. Begins now the dance—the Dance of the Hunger of Kaa. Sit still and watch."

He turned twice or thrice in a big circle, weaving his head from right to left. Then he began making loops and figures of eight with his body, and soft, oozy triangles that melted into squares and five-sided figures, and coiled mounds, never resting, never hurrying, and never stopping his low humming song. It grew darker and darker, till at last the dragging, shifting coils disappeared, but they could hear the rustle of the scales.

Baloo and Bagheera stood still as stone, growling in their throats, their neck hair bristling, and Mowgli watched and wondered.

"*Bandar-log,*" said the voice of Kaa at last, "can ye stir foot or hand without my order? Speak!"

"Without thy order we cannot stir foot or hand, O Kaa!"

"Good! Come all one pace nearer to me."

The lines of the monkeys swayed forward helplessly, and Baloo and Bagheera took one stiff step forward with them.

"Nearer!" hissed Kaa, and they all moved again.

Mowgli laid his hands on Baloo and Bagheera to get them away, and the two great beasts started as though they had been waked from a dream.

"Keep thy hand on my shoulder," Bagheera whispered. "Keep it there, or I must go back—must go back to Kaa. *Aah!*"

"It is only old Kaa making circles on the dust," said Mowgli. "Let us go." And the three slipped off through a gap in the walls to the jungle.

"*Whoof!*" said Baloo, when he stood under the still trees again. "Never more will I make an ally of Kaa," and he shook himself all over.

"He knows more than we," said Bagheera, trembling. "In a little time, had I stayed, I should have walked down his throat."

"Many will walk by that road before the moon rises again," said Baloo. "He will have good hunting—after his own fashion."

"But what was the meaning of it all?" said Mowgli, who did not know anything of a python's powers of fascination. "I saw no more than a big snake making foolish circles till the dark came. And his nose was all sore. Ho! Ho!"

"Mowgli," said Bagheera angrily, "his nose was sore on *thy* account, as my ears and sides and paws, and Baloo's neck and shoulders are bitten on *thy* account. Neither Baloo nor Bagheera will be able to hunt with pleasure for many days."

"It is nothing," said Baloo; "we have the man-cub again."

"True, but he has cost us heavily in time which might have been spent in good hunting, in wounds, in hair—I am half plucked along my back—and last of all, in honour. For, remember, Mowgli, I, who am the Black Panther, was forced to call upon Kaa for protection, and Baloo and I were both made stupid as little birds by the Hunger Dance. All this, man-cub, came of thy playing with the *Bandar-log*."

"True, it is true," said Mowgli sorrowfully. "I am an evil man-cub, and my stomach is sad in me."

"*Mf!* What says the Law of the Jungle, Baloo?"

Baloo did not wish to bring Mowgli into any more trouble, but he could not tamper with the Law, so he mumbled: "Sorrow never stays punishment. But remember, Bagheera, he is very little."

"I will remember. But he has done mischief, and blows must be dealt now. Mowgli, hast thou anything to say?"

"Nothing. I did wrong. Baloo and thou are wounded. It is just."

Bagheera gave him half a dozen love-taps from a panther's point of view (they would hardly have waked one of his own cubs), but for a seven-year-old boy they amounted to as severe a beating as you could wish to avoid. When it was all over Mowgli sneezed, and picked himself up without a word.

"Now," said Bagheera, "jump on my back, Little Brother, and we will go home."

One of the beauties of Jungle Law is that punishment settles all scores. There is no nagging afterward.

Mowgli laid his head down on Bagheera's back and slept so deeply that he never waked when he was put down in the home-cave.

4. ROAD-SONG OF THE BANDAR-LOG

Here we go in a flung festoon,
Half-way up to the jealous moon!
Don't you envy our pranceful bands?
Don't you wish you had extra hands?
Wouldn't you like if your tails were—so—
Curved in the shape of a Cupid's bow?
 Now you're angry, but—never mind,
 Brother, thy tail hangs down behind!

Here we sit in a branchy row,
Thinking of beautiful things we know;
Dreaming of deeds that we mean to do,
All complete, in a minute or two—
Something noble and wise and good,
Done by merely wishing we could.
 We've forgotten, but—never mind,
 Brother, thy tail hangs down behind!

All the talk we ever have heard
Uttered by bat or beast or bird—
Hide or fin or scale or feather—
Jabber it quickly and all together!
Excellent! Wonderful! Once again!
Now we are talking just like men!
 Let's pretend we are…never mind,
 Brother, thy tail hangs down behind!
 This is the way of the Monkey-kind.

Then join our leaping lines that scumfish through the pines,
That rocket by where, light and high, the wild grape swings.
By the rubbish in our wake, and the noble noise we make,
Be sure, be sure, we're going to do some splendid things!

5. "TIGER! TIGER!"

What of the hunting, hunter bold?
Brother, the watch was long and cold.
What of the quarry ye went to kill?
Brother, he crops in the jungle still.
Where is the power that made your pride?
Brother, it ebbs from my flank and side.
Where is the haste that ye hurry by?
Brother, I go to my lair—to die.

Now we must go back to the first tale. When Mowgli left the wolf's cave after the fight with the Pack at the Council Rock, he went down to the plowed lands where the villagers lived, but he would not stop there because it was too near to the jungle, and he knew that he had made at least one bad enemy at the Council. So he hurried on, keeping to the rough road that ran down the valley, and followed it at a steady jog-trot for nearly twenty miles, till he came to a country that he did not know. The valley opened out into a great plain dotted over with rocks and cut up by ravines. At one end stood a little village, and at the other the thick jungle came down in a sweep to the grazing-grounds, and stopped there as though it had been cut off with a hoe. All over the plain, cattle and buffaloes were grazing, and when the little boys in charge of the herds saw Mowgli they shouted and ran away, and the yellow pariah dogs that hang about every Indian village barked. Mowgli walked on, for he was feeling hungry, and when he came to the village gate he saw the big thorn-bush that was drawn up before the gate at twilight, pushed to one side.

"Umph!" he said, for he had come across more than one such barricade in his night rambles after things to eat. "So men are afraid of the People of the Jungle here also." He sat down by the gate, and when a man came out he stood up, opened his mouth, and pointed down it to show that he wanted food. The man stared, and ran back up the one street of the village shouting for the priest, who was a big, fat

man dressed in white, with a red and yellow mark on his forehead. The priest came to the gate, and with him at least a hundred people, who stared and talked and shouted and pointed at Mowgli.

"They have no manners, these Men Folk," said Mowgli to himself. "Only the gray ape would behave as they do." So he threw back his long hair and frowned at the crowd.

"What is there to be afraid of?" said the priest. "Look at the marks on his arms and legs. They are the bites of wolves. He is but a wolf-child run away from the jungle."

Of course, in playing together, the cubs had often nipped Mowgli harder than they intended, and there were white scars all over his arms and legs. But he would have been the last person in the world to call these bites, for he knew what real biting meant.

"*Arré! Arré!*" said two or three women together. "To be bitten by wolves, poor child! He is a handsome boy. He has eyes like red fire. By my honour, Messua, he is not unlike thy boy that was taken by the tiger."

"Let me look," said a woman with heavy copper rings on her wrists and ankles, and she peered at Mowgli under the palm of her hand. "Indeed he is not. He is thinner, but he has the very look of my boy."

The priest was a clever man, and he knew that Messua was wife to the richest villager in the place. So he looked up at the sky for a minute and said solemnly: "What the jungle has taken the jungle has restored. Take the boy into thy house, my sister, and forget not to honour the priest who sees so far into the lives of men."

"By the Bull that bought me," said Mowgli to himself, "but all this talking is like another looking-over by the Pack! Well, if I am a man, a man I must become."

The crowd parted as the woman beckoned Mowgli to her hut, where there was a red lacquered bedstead, a great earthen grain chest with funny raised patterns on it, half a dozen copper cooking pots, an image of a Hindu god in a little alcove, and on the wall a real looking glass, such as they sell at the country fairs.

She gave him a long drink of milk and some bread, and then she laid her hand on his head and looked into his eyes; for she thought perhaps that he might be her real son come back from the jungle where the tiger

had taken him. So she said, "Nathoo, O Nathoo!" Mowgli did not show that he knew the name. "Dost thou not remember the day when I gave thee thy new shoes?" She touched his foot, and it was almost as hard as horn. "No," she said sorrowfully, "those feet have never worn shoes, but thou art very like my Nathoo, and thou shalt be my son."

Mowgli was uneasy, because he had never been under a roof before. But as he looked at the thatch, he saw that he could tear it out any time if he wanted to get away, and that the window had no fastenings. "What is the good of a man," he said to himself at last, "if he does not understand man's talk? Now I am as silly and dumb as a man would be with us in the jungle. I must speak their talk."

It was not for fun that he had learned while he was with the wolves to imitate the challenge of bucks in the jungle and the grunt of the little wild pig. So, as soon as Messua pronounced a word Mowgli would imitate it almost perfectly, and before dark he had learned the names of many things in the hut.

There was a difficulty at bedtime, because Mowgli would not sleep under anything that looked so like a panther trap as that hut, and when they shut the door he went through the window. "Give him his will," said Messua's husband. "Remember he can never till now have slept on a bed. If he is indeed sent in the place of our son he will not run away."

So Mowgli stretched himself in some long, clean grass at the edge of the field, but before he had closed his eyes a soft gray nose poked him under the chin.

"Phew!" said Gray Brother (he was the eldest of Mother Wolf's cubs). "This is a poor reward for following thee twenty miles. Thou smellest of wood smoke and cattle—altogether like a man already. Wake, Little Brother; I bring news."

"Are all well in the jungle?" said Mowgli, hugging him.

"All except the wolves that were burned with the Red Flower. Now, listen. Shere Khan has gone away to hunt far off till his coat grows again, for he is badly singed. When he returns he swears that he will lay thy bones in the Waingunga."

"There are two words to that. I also have made a little promise. But

news is always good. I am tired to-night,—very tired with new things, Gray Brother,—but bring me the news always."

"Thou wilt not forget that thou art a wolf? Men will not make thee forget?" said Gray Brother anxiously.

"Never. I will always remember that I love thee and all in our cave. But also I will always remember that I have been cast out of the Pack."

"And that thou mayest be cast out of another pack. Men are only men, Little Brother, and their talk is like the talk of frogs in a pond. When I come down here again, I will wait for thee in the bamboos at the edge of the grazing-ground."

For three months after that night Mowgli hardly ever left the village gate, he was so busy learning the ways and customs of men. First he had to wear a cloth round him, which annoyed him horribly; and then he had to learn about money, which he did not in the least understand, and about plowing, of which he did not see the use. Then the little children in the village made him very angry. Luckily, the Law of the Jungle had taught him to keep his temper, for in the jungle life and food depend on keeping your temper; but when they made fun of him because he would not play games or fly kites, or because he mispronounced some word, only the knowledge that it was unsportsmanlike to kill little naked cubs kept him from picking them up and breaking them in two.

He did not know his own strength in the least. In the jungle he knew he was weak compared with the beasts, but in the village people said that he was as strong as a bull.

And Mowgli had not the faintest idea of the difference that caste makes between man and man. When the potter's donkey slipped in the clay pit, Mowgli hauled it out by the tail, and helped to stack the pots for their journey to the market at Khanhiwara. That was very shocking, too, for the potter is a low-caste man, and his donkey is worse. When the priest scolded him, Mowgli threatened to put him on the donkey too, and the priest told Messua's husband that Mowgli had better be set to work as soon as possible; and the village head-man told Mowgli that he would have to go out with the buffaloes next day, and herd them while they grazed. No one was more pleased than Mowgli; and that night, because he had been appointed a servant of the village, as it were,

he went off to a circle that met every evening on a masonry platform under a great fig-tree. It was the village club, and the head-man and the watchman and the barber, who knew all the gossip of the village, and old Buldeo, the village hunter, who had a Tower musket, met and smoked. The monkeys sat and talked in the upper branches, and there was a hole under the platform where a cobra lived, and he had his little platter of milk every night because he was sacred; and the old men sat around the tree and talked, and pulled at the big huqas (the water-pipes) till far into the night. They told wonderful tales of gods and men and ghosts; and Buldeo told even more wonderful ones of the ways of beasts in the jungle, till the eyes of the children sitting outside the circle bulged out of their heads. Most of the tales were about animals, for the jungle was always at their door. The deer and the wild pig grubbed up their crops, and now and again the tiger carried off a man at twilight, within sight of the village gates.

Mowgli, who naturally knew something about what they were talking of, had to cover his face not to show that he was laughing, while Buldeo, the Tower musket across his knees, climbed on from one wonderful story to another, and Mowgli's shoulders shook.

Buldeo was explaining how the tiger that had carried away Messua's son was a ghost-tiger, and his body was inhabited by the ghost of a wicked, old money-lender, who had died some years ago. "And I know that this is true," he said, "because Purun Dass always limped from the blow that he got in a riot when his account books were burned, and the tiger that I speak of, *he* limps, too, for the tracks of his pads are unequal."

"True, true, that must be the truth," said the gray-beards, nodding together.

"Are all these tales such cobwebs and moon talk?" said Mowgli. "That tiger limps because he was born lame, as everyone knows. To talk of the soul of a money-lender in a beast that never had the courage of a jackal is child's talk."

Buldeo was speechless with surprise for a moment, and the head-man stared.

"Oho! It is the jungle brat, is it?" said Buldeo. "If thou art so wise,

better bring his hide to Khanhiwara, for the Government has set a hundred rupees on his life. Better still, talk not when thy elders speak."

Mowgli rose to go. "All the evening I have lain here listening," he called back over his shoulder, "and, except once or twice, Buldeo has not said one word of truth concerning the jungle, which is at his very doors. How, then, shall I believe the tales of ghosts and gods and goblins which he says he has seen?"

"It is full time that boy went to herding," said the head-man, while Buldeo puffed and snorted at Mowgli's impertinence.

The custom of most Indian villages is for a few boys to take the cattle and buffaloes out to graze in the early morning, and bring them back at night. The very cattle that would trample a white man to death allow themselves to be banged and bullied and shouted at by children that hardly come up to their noses. So long as the boys keep with the herds they are safe, for not even the tiger will charge a mob of cattle. But if they straggle to pick flowers or hunt lizards, they are sometimes carried off. Mowgli went through the village street in the dawn, sitting on the back of Rama, the great herd bull. The slaty-blue buffaloes, with their long, backward-sweeping horns and savage eyes, rose out of their byres, one by one, and followed him, and Mowgli made it very clear to the children with him that he was the master. He beat the buffaloes with a long, polished bamboo, and told Kamya, one of the boys, to graze the cattle by themselves, while he went on with the buffaloes, and to be very careful not to stray away from the herd.

An Indian grazing ground is all rocks and scrub and tussocks and little ravines, among which the herds scatter and disappear. The buffaloes generally keep to the pools and muddy places, where they lie wallowing or basking in the warm mud for hours. Mowgli drove them on to the edge of the plain where the Waingunga came out of the jungle; then he dropped from Rama's neck, trotted off to a bamboo clump, and found Gray Brother. "Ah," said Gray Brother, "I have waited here very many days. What is the meaning of this cattle-herding work?"

"It is an order," said Mowgli. "I am a village herd for a while. What news of Shere Khan?"

"He has come back to this country, and has waited here a long time

for thee. Now he has gone off again, for the game is scarce. But he means to kill thee."

"Very good," said Mowgli. "So long as he is away do thou or one of the four brothers sit on that rock, so that I can see thee as I come out of the village. When he comes back wait for me in the ravine by the *dhak* tree in the centre of the plain. We need not walk into Shere Khan's mouth."

Then Mowgli picked out a shady place, and lay down and slept while the buffaloes grazed round him. Herding in India is one of the laziest things in the world. The cattle move and crunch, and lie down, and move on again, and they do not even low. They only grunt, and the buffaloes very seldom say anything, but get down into the muddy pools one after another, and work their way into the mud till only their noses and staring china-blue eyes show above the surface, and then they lie like logs. The sun makes the rocks dance in the heat, and the herd children hear one kite (never any more) whistling almost out of sight overhead, and they know that if they died, or a cow died, that kite would sweep down, and the next kite miles away would see him drop and follow, and the next, and the next, and almost before they were dead there would be a score of hungry kites come out of nowhere. Then they sleep and wake and sleep again, and weave little baskets of dried grass and put grasshoppers in them; or catch two praying mantises and make them fight; or string a necklace of red and black jungle nuts; or watch a lizard basking on a rock, or a snake hunting a frog near the wallows. Then they sing long, long songs with odd native quavers at the end of them, and the day seems longer than most people's whole lives, and perhaps they make a mud castle with mud figures of men and horses and buffaloes, and put reeds into the men's hands, and pretend that they are kings and the figures are their armies, or that they are gods to be worshiped. Then evening comes and the children call, and the buffaloes lumber up out of the sticky mud with noises like gunshots going off one after the other, and they all string across the gray plain back to the twinkling village lights.

Day after day Mowgli would lead the buffaloes out to their wallows, and day after day he would see Gray Brother's back a mile and a half

away across the plain (so he knew that Shere Khan had not come back), and day after day he would lie on the grass listening to the noises round him, and dreaming of old days in the jungle. If Shere Khan had made a false step with his lame paw up in the jungles by the Waingunga, Mowgli would have heard him in those long, still mornings.

At last a day came when he did not see Gray Brother at the signal place, and he laughed and headed the buffaloes for the ravine by the *dhak* tree, which was all covered with golden-red flowers. There sat Gray Brother, every bristle on his back lifted.

"He has hidden for a month to throw thee off thy guard. He crossed the ranges last night with Tabaqui, hot-foot on thy trail," said the Wolf, panting.

Mowgli frowned. "I am not afraid of Shere Khan, but Tabaqui is very cunning."

"Have no fear," said Gray Brother, licking his lips a little. "I met Tabaqui in the dawn. Now he is telling all his wisdom to the kites, but he told *me* everything before I broke his back. Shere Khan's plan is to wait for thee at the village gate this evening—for thee and for no one else. He is lying up now, in the big dry ravine of the Waingunga."

"Has he eaten to-day, or does he hunt empty?" said Mowgli, for the answer meant life and death to him.

"He killed at dawn,—a pig,—and he has drunk too. Remember, Shere Khan could never fast, even for the sake of revenge."

"Oh! Fool, fool! What a cub's cub it is! Eaten and drunk too, and he thinks that I shall wait till he has slept! Now, where does he lie up? If there were but ten of us we might pull him down as he lies. These buffaloes will not charge unless they wind him, and I cannot speak their language. Can we get behind his track so that they may smell it?"

"He swam far down the Waingunga to cut that off," said Gray Brother.

"Tabaqui told him that, I know. He would never have thought of it alone." Mowgli stood with his finger in his mouth, thinking. "The big ravine of the Waingunga. That opens out on the plain not half a mile from here. I can take the herd round through the jungle to the head of

the ravine and then sweep down—but he would slink out at the foot. We must block that end. Gray Brother, canst thou cut the herd in two for me?"

"Not I, perhaps—but I have brought a wise helper." Gray Brother trotted off and dropped into a hole. Then there lifted up a huge gray head that Mowgli knew well, and the hot air was filled with the most desolate cry of all the jungle—the hunting howl of a wolf at mid-day.

"Akela! Akela!" said Mowgli, clapping his hands. "I might have known that thou wouldst not forget me. We have a big work in hand. Cut the herd in two, Akela. Keep the cows and calves together, and the bulls and the plow buffaloes by themselves."

The two wolves ran, ladies'-chain fashion, in and out of the herd, which snorted and threw up its head, and separated into two clumps. In one, the cow-buffaloes stood with their calves in the centre, and glared and pawed, ready, if a wolf would only stay still, to charge down and trample the life out of him. In the other, the bulls and the young bulls snorted and stamped, but though they looked more imposing they were much less dangerous, for they had no calves to protect. No six men could have divided the herd so neatly.

"What orders!" panted Akela. "They are trying to join again."

Mowgli slipped on to Rama's back. "Drive the bulls away to the left, Akela. Gray Brother, when we are gone, hold the cows together, and drive them into the foot of the ravine."

"How far?" said Gray Brother, panting and snapping.

"Till the sides are higher than Shere Khan can jump," shouted Mowgli. "Keep them there till we come down." The bulls swept off as Akela bayed, and Gray Brother stopped in front of the cows. They charged down on him, and he ran just before them to the foot of the ravine, as Akela drove the bulls far to the left.

"Well done! Another charge and they are fairly started. Careful, now—careful, Akela. A snap too much and the bulls will charge. *Huyah!* This is wilder work than driving black-buck. Didst thou think these creatures could move so swiftly?" Mowgli called.

"I have—have hunted these too in my time," gasped Akela in the dust. "Shall I turn them into the jungle?"

"Ay! Turn. Swiftly turn them! Rama is mad with rage. Oh, if I could only tell him what I need of him to-day."

The bulls were turned, to the right this time, and crashed into the standing thicket. The other herd children, watching with the cattle half a mile away, hurried to the village as fast as their legs could carry them, crying that the buffaloes had gone mad and run away.

But Mowgli's plan was simple enough. All he wanted to do was to make a big circle uphill and get at the head of the ravine, and then take the bulls down it and catch Shere Khan between the bulls and the cows; for he knew that after a meal and a full drink Shere Khan would not be in any condition to fight or to clamber up the sides of the ravine. He was soothing the buffaloes now by voice, and Akela had dropped far to the rear, only whimpering once or twice to hurry the rear-guard. It was a long, long circle, for they did not wish to get too near the ravine and give Shere Khan warning. At last Mowgli rounded up the bewildered herd at the head of the ravine on a grassy patch that sloped steeply down to the ravine itself. From that height you could see across the tops of the trees down to the plain below; but what Mowgli looked at was the sides of the ravine, and he saw with a great deal of satisfaction that they ran nearly straight up and down, while the vines and creepers that hung over them would give no foothold to a tiger who wanted to get out.

"Let them breathe, Akela," he said, holding up his hand. "They have not winded him yet. Let them breathe. I must tell Shere Khan who comes. We have him in the trap."

He put his hands to his mouth and shouted down the ravine—it was almost like shouting down a tunnel—and the echoes jumped from rock to rock.

After a long time there came back the drawling, sleepy snarl of a full-fed tiger just wakened.

"Who calls?" said Shere Khan, and a splendid peacock fluttered up out of the ravine screeching.

"I, Mowgli. Cattle thief, it is time to come to the Council Rock! Down—hurry them down, Akela! Down, Rama, down!"

The herd paused for an instant at the edge of the slope, but Akela gave tongue in the full hunting-yell, and they pitched over one after

the other, just as steamers shoot rapids, the sand and stones spurting up round them. Once started, there was no chance of stopping, and before they were fairly in the bed of the ravine Rama winded Shere Khan and bellowed.

"Ha! Ha!" said Mowgli, on his back. "Now thou knowest!" and the torrent of black horns, foaming muzzles, and staring eyes whirled down the ravine just as boulders go down in floodtime; the weaker buffaloes being shouldered out to the sides of the ravine where they tore through the creepers. They knew what the business was before them—the terrible charge of the buffalo herd against which no tiger can hope to stand. Shere Khan heard the thunder of their hoofs, picked himself up, and lumbered down the ravine, looking from side to side for some way of escape, but the walls of the ravine were straight and he had to hold on, heavy with his dinner and his drink, willing to do anything rather than fight. The herd splashed through the pool he had just left, bellowing till the narrow cut rang. Mowgli heard an answering bellow from the foot of the ravine, saw Shere Khan turn (the tiger knew if the worst came to the worst it was better to meet the bulls than the cows with their calves), and then Rama tripped, stumbled, and went on again over something soft, and, with the bulls at his heels, crashed full into the other herd, while the weaker buffaloes were lifted clean off their feet by the shock of the meeting. That charge carried both herds out into the plain, goring and stamping and snorting. Mowgli watched his time, and slipped off Rama's neck, laying about him right and left with his stick.

"Quick, Akela! Break them up. Scatter them, or they will be fighting one another. Drive them away, Akela. *Hai*, Rama! *Hai, hai, hai!* my children. Softly now, softly! It is all over."

Akela and Gray Brother ran to and fro nipping the buffaloes' legs, and though the herd wheeled once to charge up the ravine again, Mowgli managed to turn Rama, and the others followed him to the wallows.

Shere Khan needed no more trampling. He was dead, and the kites were coming for him already.

"Brothers, that was a dog's death," said Mowgli, feeling for the knife he always carried in a sheath round his neck now that he lived

with men. "But he would never have shown fight. His hide will look well on the Council Rock. We must get to work swiftly."

A boy trained among men would never have dreamed of skinning a ten-foot tiger alone, but Mowgli knew better than anyone else how an animal's skin is fitted on, and how it can be taken off. But it was hard work, and Mowgli slashed and tore and grunted for an hour, while the wolves lolled out their tongues, or came forward and tugged as he ordered them. Presently a hand fell on his shoulder, and looking up he saw Buldeo with the Tower musket. The children had told the village about the buffalo stampede, and Buldeo went out angrily, only too anxious to correct Mowgli for not taking better care of the herd. The wolves dropped out of sight as soon as they saw the man coming.

"What is this folly?" said Buldeo angrily. "To think that thou canst skin a tiger! Where did the buffaloes kill him? It is the Lame Tiger too, and there is a hundred rupees on his head. Well, well, we will overlook thy letting the herd run off, and perhaps I will give thee one of the rupees of the reward when I have taken the skin to Khanhiwara." He fumbled in his waist cloth for flint and steel, and stooped down to singe Shere Khan's whiskers. Most native hunters always singe a tiger's whiskers to prevent his ghost from haunting them.

"Hum!" said Mowgli, half to himself as he ripped back the skin of a forepaw. "So thou wilt take the hide to Khanhiwara for the reward, and perhaps give me one rupee? Now it is in my mind that I need the skin for my own use. Heh! Old man, take away that fire!"

"What talk is this to the chief hunter of the village? Thy luck and the stupidity of thy buffaloes have helped thee to this kill. The tiger has just fed, or he would have gone twenty miles by this time. Thou canst not even skin him properly, little beggar brat, and forsooth I, Buldeo, must be told not to singe his whiskers. Mowgli, I will not give thee one anna of the reward, but only a very big beating. Leave the carcass!"

"By the Bull that bought me," said Mowgli, who was trying to get at the shoulder, "must I stay babbling to an old ape all noon? Here, Akela, this man plagues me."

Buldeo, who was still stooping over Shere Khan's head, found

himself sprawling on the grass, with a gray wolf standing over him, while Mowgli went on skinning as though he were alone in all India.

"Ye-es," he said, between his teeth. "Thou art altogether right, Buldeo. Thou wilt never give me one anna of the reward. There is an old war between this lame tiger and myself—a very old war, and—I have won."

To do Buldeo justice, if he had been ten years younger he would have taken his chance with Akela had he met the wolf in the woods, but a wolf who obeyed the orders of this boy who had private wars with man-eating tigers was not a common animal. It was sorcery, magic of the worst kind, thought Buldeo, and he wondered whether the amulet round his neck would protect him. He lay as still as still, expecting every minute to see Mowgli turn into a tiger too.

"Maharaj! Great King," he said at last in a husky whisper.

"Yes," said Mowgli, without turning his head, chuckling a little.

"I am an old man. I did not know that thou wast anything more than a herdsboy. May I rise up and go away, or will thy servant tear me to pieces?"

"Go, and peace go with thee. Only, another time do not meddle with my game. Let him go, Akela."

Buldeo hobbled away to the village as fast as he could, looking back over his shoulder in case Mowgli should change into something terrible. When he got to the village he told a tale of magic and enchantment and sorcery that made the priest look very grave.

Mowgli went on with his work, but it was nearly twilight before he and the wolves had drawn the great gay skin clear of the body.

"Now we must hide this and take the buffaloes home! Help me to herd them, Akela."

The herd rounded up in the misty twilight, and when they got near the village Mowgli saw lights, and heard the conches and bells in the temple blowing and banging. Half the village seemed to be waiting for him by the gate. "That is because I have killed Shere Khan," he said to himself. But a shower of stones whistled about his ears, and the villagers shouted: "Sorcerer! Wolf's brat! Jungle demon! Go away! Get hence quickly or the priest will turn thee into a wolf again. Shoot, Buldeo, shoot!"

The old Tower musket went off with a bang, and a young buffalo bellowed in pain.

"More sorcery!" shouted the villagers. "He can turn bullets. Buldeo, that was *thy* buffalo."

"Now what is this?" said Mowgli, bewildered, as the stones flew thicker.

"They are not unlike the Pack, these brothers of thine," said Akela, sitting down composedly. "It is in my head that, if bullets mean anything, they would cast thee out."

"Wolf! Wolf's cub! Go away!" shouted the priest, waving a sprig of the sacred *tulsi* plant.

"Again? Last time it was because I was a man. This time it is because I am a wolf. Let us go, Akela."

A woman—it was Messua—ran across to the herd, and cried: "Oh, my son, my son! They say thou art a sorcerer who can turn himself into a beast at will. I do not believe, but go away or they will kill thee. Buldeo says thou art a wizard, but I know thou hast avenged Nathoo's death."

"Come back, Messua!" shouted the crowd. "Come back, or we will stone thee."

Mowgli laughed a little short ugly laugh, for a stone had hit him in the mouth. "Run back, Messua. This is one of the foolish tales they tell under the big tree at dusk. I have at least paid for thy son's life. Farewell; and run quickly, for I shall send the herd in more swiftly than their brickbats. I am no wizard, Messua. Farewell!"

"Now, once more, Akela," he cried. "Bring the herd in."

The buffaloes were anxious enough to get to the village. They hardly needed Akela's yell, but charged through the gate like a whirlwind, scattering the crowd right and left.

"Keep count!" shouted Mowgli scornfully. "It may be that I have stolen one of them. Keep count, for I will do your herding no more. Fare you well, children of men, and thank Messua that I do not come in with my wolves and hunt you up and down your street."

He turned on his heel and walked away with the Lone Wolf, and as he looked up at the stars he felt happy. "No more sleeping in traps for

me, Akela. Let us get Shere Khan's skin and go away. No, we will not hurt the village, for Messua was kind to me."

When the moon rose over the plain, making it look all milky, the horrified villagers saw Mowgli, with two wolves at his heels and a bundle on his head, trotting across at the steady wolf's trot that eats up the long miles like fire. Then they banged the temple bells and blew the conches louder than ever. And Messua cried, and Buldeo embroidered the story of his adventures in the jungle, till he ended by saying that Akela stood up on his hind legs and talked like a man.

The moon was just going down when Mowgli and the two wolves came to the hill of the Council Rock, and they stopped at Mother Wolf's cave.

"They have cast me out from the Man-Pack, Mother," shouted Mowgli, "but I come with the hide of Shere Khan to keep my word."

Mother Wolf walked stiffly from the cave with the cubs behind her, and her eyes glowed as she saw the skin.

"I told him on that day, when he crammed his head and shoulders into this cave, hunting for thy life, Little Frog—I told him that the hunter would be the hunted. It is well done."

"Little Brother, it is well done," said a deep voice in the thicket. "We were lonely in the jungle without thee," and Bagheera came running to Mowgli's bare feet. They clambered up the Council Rock together, and Mowgli spread the skin out on the flat stone where Akela used to sit, and pegged it down with four slivers of bamboo, and Akela lay down upon it, and called the old call to the Council, "Look—look well, O Wolves," exactly as he had called when Mowgli was first brought there.

Ever since Akela had been deposed, the Pack had been without a leader, hunting and fighting at their own pleasure. But they answered the call from habit; and some of them were lame from the traps they had fallen into, and some limped from shot wounds, and some were mangy from eating bad food, and many were missing. But they came to the Council Rock, all that were left of them, and saw Shere Khan's striped hide on the rock, and the huge claws dangling at the end of the empty dangling feet. It was then that Mowgli made up a song that came up into his throat all by itself, and he shouted it aloud, leaping up and down on

the rattling skin, and beating time with his heels till he had no more breath left, while Gray Brother and Akela howled between the verses.

"Look well, O Wolves. Have I kept my word?" said Mowgli. And the wolves bayed "Yes," and one tattered wolf howled:

"Lead us again, O Akela. Lead us again, O Man-cub, for we be sick of this lawlessness, and we would be the Free People once more."

"Nay," purred Bagheera, "that may not be. When ye are full-fed, the madness may come upon you again. Not for nothing are ye called the Free People. Ye fought for freedom, and it is yours. Eat it, O Wolves."

"Man-Pack and Wolf-Pack have cast me out," said Mowgli. "Now I will hunt alone in the jungle."

"And we will hunt with thee," said the four cubs.

So Mowgli went away and hunted with the four cubs in the jungle from that day on. But he was not always alone, because, years afterward, he became a man and married.

But that is a story for grown-ups.

6. MOWGLI'S SONG

(That he sang at the Council Rock when he danced on Shere Khan's Hide)

The Song of Mowgli—I, Mowgli, am singing. Let the jungle listen to the things I have done.

Shere Khan said he would kill—would kill! At the gates in the twilight he would kill Mowgli, the Frog!

He ate and he drank. Drink deep, Shere Khan, for when wilt thou drink again? Sleep and dream of the kill.

I am alone on the grazing-grounds. Gray Brother, come to me! Come to me, Lone Wolf, for there is big game afoot!

Bring up the great bull buffaloes, the blue-skinned herd bulls with the angry eyes. Drive them to and fro as I order.

Sleepest thou still, Shere Khan? Wake, oh, wake! Here come I, and the bulls are behind.

Rama, the King of the Buffaloes, stamped with his foot. Waters of the Waingunga, whither went Shere Khan?

He is not Ikki to dig holes, nor Mao, the Peacock, that he should fly. He is not Mang the Bat, to hang in the branches. Little bamboos that creak together, tell me where he ran?

Ow! He is there. *Ahoo!* He is there. Under the feet of Rama lies the Lame One! Up, Shere Khan! Up and kill! Here is meat; break the necks of the bulls!

Hsh! He is asleep. We will not wake him, for his strength is very great. The kites have come down to see it. The black ants have come up to know it. There is a great assembly in his honour.

Alala! I have no cloth to wrap me. The kites will see that I am naked. I am ashamed to meet all these people.

Lend me thy coat, Shere Khan. Lend me thy gay striped coat that I may go to the Council Rock.

By the Bull that bought me I made a promise—a little promise. Only thy coat is lacking before I keep my word.

With the knife, with the knife that men use, with the knife of the hunter, I will stoop down for my gift.

Waters of the Waingunga, Shere Khan gives me his coat for the love that he bears me. Pull, Gray Brother! Pull, Akela! Heavy is the hide of Shere Khan.

The Man-Pack are angry. They throw stones and talk child's talk. My mouth is bleeding. Let me run away.

Through the night, through the hot night, run swiftly with me, my brothers. We will leave the lights of the village and go to the low moon.

Waters of the Waingunga, the Man-Pack have cast me out. I did them no harm, but they were afraid of me. Why?

Wolf-Pack, ye have cast me out too. The jungle is shut to me and the village gates are shut. Why?

As Mang flies between the beasts and birds, so fly I between the village and the jungle. Why?

I dance on the hide of Shere Khan, but my heart is very heavy. My mouth is cut and wounded with the stones from the village, but my heart is very light, because I have come back to the jungle. Why?

These two things fight together in me as the snakes fight in the spring.

The water comes out of my eyes; yet I laugh while it falls. Why?

I am two Mowglis, but the hide of Shere Khan is under my feet.

All the jungle knows that I have killed Shere Khan. Look— look well, O Wolves!

Ahae! My heart is heavy with the things that I do not understand.

7. THE WHITE SEAL

Oh! hush thee, my baby, the night is behind us,
And black are the waters that sparkled so green.
The moon, o'er the combers, looks downward to find us
At rest in the hollows that rustle between.
Where billow meets billow, then soft be thy pillow,
Ah, weary wee flipperling, curl at thy ease!
The storm shall not wake thee, nor shark overtake thee,
Asleep in the arms of the slow-swinging seas!

— *Seal Lullaby*

All these things happened several years ago at a place called Novastoshnah, or North East Point, on the Island of St. Paul, away and away in the Bering Sea. Limmershin, the Winter Wren, told me the tale when he was blown on to the rigging of a steamer going to Japan, and I took him down into my cabin and warmed and fed him for a couple of days till he was fit to fly back to St. Paul's again. Limmershin is a very quaint little bird, but he knows how to tell the truth.

Nobody comes to Novastoshnah except on business, and the only people who have regular business there are the seals. They come in the summer months by hundreds and hundreds of thousands out of the cold gray sea. For Novastoshnah Beach has the finest accommodation for seals of any place in all the world.

Sea Catch knew that, and every spring would swim from whatever place he happened to be in—would swim like a torpedo-boat straight for Novastoshnah and spend a month fighting with his companions for a good place on the rocks, as close to the sea as possible. Sea Catch was fifteen years old, a huge gray fur seal with almost a mane on his shoulders, and long, wicked dog teeth. When he heaved himself up on his front flippers he stood more than four feet clear of the ground, and his weight, if anyone had been bold enough to weigh him, was nearly seven hundred pounds. He was scarred all over with the marks

of savage fights, but he was always ready for just one fight more. He would put his head on one side, as though he were afraid to look his enemy in the face; then he would shoot it out like lightning, and when the big teeth were firmly fixed on the other seal's neck, the other seal might get away if he could, but Sea Catch would not help him.

Yet Sea Catch never chased a beaten seal, for that was against the Rules of the Beach. He only wanted room by the sea for his nursery. But as there were forty or fifty thousand other seals hunting for the same thing each spring, the whistling, bellowing, roaring, and blowing on the beach was something frightful.

From a little hill called Hutchinson's Hill, you could look over three and a half miles of ground covered with fighting seals; and the surf was dotted all over with the heads of seals hurrying to land and begin their share of the fighting. They fought in the breakers, they fought in the sand, and they fought on the smooth-worn basalt rocks of the nurseries, for they were just as stupid and unaccommodating as men. Their wives never came to the island until late in May or early in June, for they did not care to be torn to pieces; and the young two-, three-, and four-year-old seals who had not begun housekeeping went inland about half a mile through the ranks of the fighters and played about on the sand dunes in droves and legions, and rubbed off every single green thing that grew. They were called the holluschickie—the bachelors—and there were perhaps two or three hundred thousand of them at Novastoshnah alone.

Sea Catch had just finished his forty-fifth fight one spring when Matkah, his soft, sleek, gentle-eyed wife, came up out of the sea, and he caught her by the scruff of the neck and dumped her down on his reservation, saying gruffly: "Late as usual. Where *have* you been?"

It was not the fashion for Sea Catch to eat anything during the four months he stayed on the beaches, and so his temper was generally bad. Matkah knew better than to answer back. She looked round and cooed: "How thoughtful of you. You've taken the old place again."

"I should think I had," said Sea Catch. "Look at me!"

He was scratched and bleeding in twenty places; one eye was almost out, and his sides were torn to ribbons.

"Oh, you men, you men!" Matkah said, fanning herself with her hind flipper. "Why can't you be sensible and settle your places quietly? You look as though you had been fighting with the Killer Whale."

"I haven't been doing anything *but* fight since the middle of May. The beach is disgracefully crowded this season. I've met at least a hundred seals from Lukannon Beach, house hunting. Why can't people stay where they belong?"

"I've often thought we should be much happier if we hauled out at Otter Island instead of this crowded place," said Matkah.

"Bah! Only the holluschickie go to Otter Island. If we went there they would say we were afraid. We must preserve appearances, my dear."

Sea Catch sunk his head proudly between his fat shoulders and pretended to go to sleep for a few minutes, but all the time he was keeping a sharp lookout for a fight. Now that all the seals and their wives were on the land, you could hear their clamor miles out to sea above the loudest gales. At the lowest counting there were over a million seals on the beach—old seals, mother seals, tiny babies, and holluschickie, fighting, scuffling, bleating, crawling, and playing together—going down to the sea and coming up from it in gangs and regiments, lying over every foot of ground as far as the eye could reach, and skirmishing about in brigades through the fog. It is nearly always foggy at Novastoshnah, except when the sun comes out and makes everything look all pearly and rainbow-coloured for a little while.

Kotick, Matkah's baby, was born in the middle of that confusion, and he was all head and shoulders, with pale, watery blue eyes, as tiny seals must be, but there was something about his coat that made his mother look at him very closely.

"Sea Catch," she said, at last, "our baby's going to be white!"

"Empty clam-shells and dry seaweed!" snorted Sea Catch. "There never has been such a thing in the world as a white seal."

"I can't help that," said Matkah; "there's going to be now." And she sang the low, crooning seal song that all the mother seals sing to their babies:

You mustn't swim till you're six weeks old,
 Or your head will be sunk by your heels;
And summer gales and Killer Whales
 Are bad for baby seals.

Are bad for baby seals, dear rat,
 As bad as bad can be;
But splash and grow strong,
And you can't be wrong.
 Child of the Open Sea!

Of course the little fellow did not understand the words at first. He paddled and scrambled about by his mother's side, and learned to scuffle out of the way when his father was fighting with another seal, and the two rolled and roared up and down the slippery rocks. Matkah used to go to sea to get things to eat, and the baby was fed only once in two days, but then he ate all he could and throve upon it.

The first thing he did was to crawl inland, and there he met tens of thousands of babies of his own age, and they played together like puppies, went to sleep on the clean sand, and played again. The old people in the nurseries took no notice of them, and the holluschickie kept to their own grounds, and the babies had a beautiful playtime.

When Matkah came back from her deep-sea fishing she would go straight to their playground and call as a sheep calls for a lamb, and wait until she heard Kotick bleat. Then she would take the straightest of straight lines in his direction, striking out with her fore flippers and knocking the youngsters head over heels right and left. There were always a few hundred mothers hunting for their children through the playgrounds, and the babies were kept lively. But, as Matkah told Kotick, "So long as you don't lie in muddy water and get mange, or rub the hard sand into a cut or scratch, and so long as you never go swimming when there is a heavy sea, nothing will hurt you here."

Little seals can no more swim than little children, but they are unhappy till they learn. The first time that Kotick went down to the sea a wave carried him out beyond his depth, and his big head sank and his little hind flippers flew up exactly as his mother had told him in the

song, and if the next wave had not thrown him back again he would have drowned.

After that, he learned to lie in a beach pool and let the wash of the waves just cover him and lift him up while he paddled, but he always kept his eye open for big waves that might hurt. He was two weeks learning to use his flippers; and all that while he floundered in and out of the water, and coughed and grunted and crawled up the beach and took catnaps on the sand, and went back again, until at last he found that he truly belonged to the water.

Then you can imagine the times that he had with his companions, ducking under the rollers; or coming in on top of a comber and landing with a swash and a splutter as the big wave went whirling far up the beach; or standing up on his tail and scratching his head as the old people did; or playing "I'm the King of the Castle" on slippery, weedy rocks that just stuck out of the wash. Now and then he would see a thin fin, like a big shark's fin, drifting along close to shore, and he knew that that was the Killer Whale, the Grampus, who eats young seals when he can get them; and Kotick would head for the beach like an arrow, and the fin would jig off slowly, as if it were looking for nothing at all.

Late in October the seals began to leave St. Paul's for the deep sea, by families and tribes, and there was no more fighting over the nurseries, and the holluschickie played anywhere they liked. "Next year," said Matkah to Kotick, "you will be a holluschickie; but this year you must learn how to catch fish."

They set out together across the Pacific, and Matkah showed Kotick how to sleep on his back with his flippers tucked down by his side and his little nose just out of the water. No cradle is so comfortable as the long, rocking swell of the Pacific. When Kotick felt his skin tingle all over, Matkah told him he was learning the "feel of the water," and that tingly, prickly feelings meant bad weather coming, and he must swim hard and get away.

"In a little time," she said, "you'll know where to swim to, but just now we'll follow Sea Pig, the Porpoise, for he is very wise." A school of porpoises were ducking and tearing through the water, and little

Kotick followed them as fast as he could. "How do you know where to go to?" he panted. The leader of the school rolled his white eye and ducked under. "My tail tingles, youngster," he said. "That means there's a gale behind me. Come along! When you're south of the Sticky Water [he meant the Equator] and your tail tingles, that means there's a gale in front of you and you must head north. Come along! The water feels bad here."

This was one of very many things that Kotick learned, and he was always learning. Matkah taught him to follow the cod and the halibut along the under-sea banks and wrench the rockling out of his hole among the weeds; how to skirt the wrecks lying a hundred fathoms below water and dart like a rifle bullet in at one porthole and out at another as the fishes ran; how to dance on the top of the waves when the lightning was racing all over the sky, and wave his flipper politely to the stumpy-tailed Albatross and the Man-of-war Hawk as they went down the wind; how to jump three or four feet clear of the water like a dolphin, flippers close to the side and tail curved; to leave the flying fish alone because they are all bony; to take the shoulder-piece out of a cod at full speed ten fathoms deep, and never to stop and look at a boat or a ship, but particularly a row-boat. At the end of six months what Kotick did not know about deep-sea fishing was not worth the knowing. And all that time he never set flipper on dry ground.

One day, however, as he was lying half asleep in the warm water somewhere off the Island of Juan Fernandez, he felt faint and lazy all over, just as human people do when the spring is in their legs, and he remembered the good firm beaches of Novastoshnah seven thousand miles away, the games his companions played, the smell of the seaweed, the seal roar, and the fighting. That very minute he turned north, swimming steadily, and as he went on he met scores of his mates, all bound for the same place, and they said: "Greeting, Kotick! This year we are all holluschickie, and we can dance the Fire-dance in the breakers off Lukannon and play on the new grass. But where did you get that coat?"

Kotick's fur was almost pure white now, and though he felt very proud of it, he only said, "Swim quickly! My bones are aching for the

land." And so they all came to the beaches where they had been born, and heard the old seals, their fathers, fighting in the rolling mist.

That night Kotick danced the Fire-dance with the yearling seals. The sea is full of fire on summer nights all the way down from Novastoshnah to Lukannon, and each seal leaves a wake like burning oil behind him and a flaming flash when he jumps, and the waves break in great phosphorescent streaks and swirls. Then they went inland to the holluschickie grounds and rolled up and down in the new wild wheat and told stories of what they had done while they had been at sea. They talked about the Pacific as boys would talk about a wood that they had been nutting in, and if anyone had understood them he could have gone away and made such a chart of that ocean as never was. The three- and four-year-old holluschickie romped down from Hutchinson's Hill crying: "Out of the way, youngsters! The sea is deep and you don't know all that's in it yet. Wait till you've rounded the Horn. Hi, you yearling, where did you get that white coat?"

"I didn't get it," said Kotick. "It grew." And just as he was going to roll the speaker over, a couple of black-haired men with flat red faces came from behind a sand dune, and Kotick, who had never seen a man before, coughed and lowered his head. The holluschickie just bundled off a few yards and sat staring stupidly. The men were no less than Kerick Booterin, the chief of the seal-hunters on the island, and Patalamon, his son. They came from the little village not half a mile from the sea nurseries, and they were deciding what seals they would drive up to the killing pens—for the seals were driven just like sheep— to be turned into seal-skin jackets later on.

"Ho!" said Patalamon. "Look! There's a white seal!"

Kerick Booterin turned nearly white under his oil and smoke, for he was an Aleut, and Aleuts are not clean people. Then he began to mutter a prayer. "Don't touch him, Patalamon. There has never been a white seal since—since I was born. Perhaps it is old Zaharrof's ghost. He was lost last year in the big gale."

"I'm not going near him," said Patalamon. "He's unlucky. Do you really think he is old Zaharrof come back? I owe him for some gulls' eggs."

"Don't look at him," said Kerick. "Head off that drove of four-year-olds. The men ought to skin two hundred to-day, but it's the beginning of the season and they are new to the work. A hundred will do. Quick!"

Patalamon rattled a pair of seal's shoulder bones in front of a herd of holluschickie and they stopped dead, puffing and blowing. Then he stepped near and the seals began to move, and Kerick headed them inland, and they never tried to get back to their companions. Hundreds and hundreds of thousands of seals watched them being driven, but they went on playing just the same. Kotick was the only one who asked questions, and none of his companions could tell him anything, except that the men always drove seals in that way for six weeks or two months of every year.

"I am going to follow," he said, and his eyes nearly popped out of his head as he shuffled along in the wake of the herd.

"The white seal is coming after us," cried Patalamon. "That's the first time a seal has ever come to the killing-grounds alone."

"Hsh! Don't look behind you," said Kerick. "It *is* Zaharrof's ghost! I must speak to the priest about this."

The distance to the killing-grounds was only half a mile, but it took an hour to cover, because if the seals went too fast Kerick knew that they would get heated and then their fur would come off in patches when they were skinned. So they went on very slowly, past Sea Lion's Neck, past Webster House, till they came to the Salt House just beyond the sight of the seals on the beach. Kotick followed, panting and wondering. He thought that he was at the world's end, but the roar of the seal nurseries behind him sounded as loud as the roar of a train in a tunnel. Then Kerick sat down on the moss and pulled out a heavy pewter watch and let the drove cool off for thirty minutes, and Kotick could hear the fog-dew dripping off the brim of his cap. Then ten or twelve men, each with an iron-bound club three or four feet long, came up, and Kerick pointed out one or two of the drove that were bitten by their companions or too hot, and the men kicked those aside with their heavy boots made of the skin of a walrus's throat, and then Kerick said, "Let go!" and then the men clubbed the seals on the head as fast as they could.

Ten minutes later little Kotick did not recognize his friends any more, for their skins were ripped off from the nose to the hind flippers, whipped off and thrown down on the ground in a pile. That was enough for Kotick. He turned and galloped (a seal can gallop very swiftly for a short time) back to the sea; his little new mustache bristling with horror. At Sea Lion's Neck, where the great sea lions sit on the edge of the surf, he flung himself flipper-overhead into the cool water and rocked there, gasping miserably. "What's here?" said a sea lion gruffly, for as a rule the sea lions keep themselves to themselves.

"*Scoochnie! Ochen scoochnie!*" ("I'm lonesome, very lonesome!") said Kotick. "They're killing *all* the holluschickie on *all* the beaches!"

The Sea Lion turned his head inshore. "Nonsense!" he said. "Your friends are making as much noise as ever. You must have seen old Kerick polishing off a drove. He's done that for thirty years."

"It's horrible," said Kotick, backing water as a wave went over him, and steadying himself with a screw stroke of his flippers that brought him all standing within three inches of a jagged edge of rock.

"Well done for a yearling!" said the Sea Lion, who could appreciate good swimming. "I suppose it *is* rather awful from your way of looking at it, but if you seals will come here year after year, of course the men get to know of it, and unless you can find an island where no men ever come you will always be driven."

"Isn't there any such island?" began Kotick.

"I've followed the *poltoos* [the halibut] for twenty years, and I can't say I've found it yet. But look here—you seem to have a fondness for talking to your betters—suppose you go to Walrus Islet and talk to Sea Vitch. He may know something. Don't flounce off like that. It's a six-mile swim, and if I were you I should haul out and take a nap first, little one."

Kotick thought that that was good advice, so he swam round to his own beach, hauled out, and slept for half an hour, twitching all over, as seals will. Then he headed straight for Walrus Islet, a little low sheet of rocky island almost due northeast from Novastoshnah, all ledges and rock and gulls' nests, where the walrus herded by themselves.

He landed close to old Sea Vitch—the big, ugly, bloated, pimpled,

fat-necked, long-tusked walrus of the North Pacific, who has no manners except when he is asleep—as he was then, with his hind flippers half in and half out of the surf.

"Wake up!" barked Kotick, for the gulls were making a great noise.

"Hah! Ho! Hmph! What's that?" said Sea Vitch, and he struck the next walrus a blow with his tusks and waked him up, and the next struck the next, and so on till they were all awake and staring in every direction but the right one.

"Hi! It's me," said Kotick, bobbing in the surf and looking like a little white slug.

"Well! May I be—skinned!" said Sea Vitch, and they all looked at Kotick as you can fancy a club full of drowsy old gentlemen would look at a little boy. Kotick did not care to hear any more about skinning just then; he had seen enough of it. So he called out: "Isn't there any place for seals to go where men don't ever come?"

"Go and find out," said Sea Vitch, shutting his eyes. "Run away. We're busy here."

Kotick made his dolphin-jump in the air and shouted as loud as he could: "Clam-eater! Clam-eater!" He knew that Sea Vitch never caught a fish in his life but always rooted for clams and seaweed; though he pretended to be a very terrible person. Naturally the Chickies and the Gooverooskies and the Epatkas—the Burgomaster Gulls and the Kittiwakes and the Puffins, who are always looking for a chance to be rude, took up the cry, and—so Limmershin told me—for nearly five minutes you could not have heard a gun fired on Walrus Islet. All the population was yelling and screaming "Clam-eater! *Stareek* [old man]!" while Sea Vitch rolled from side to side grunting and coughing.

"*Now* will you tell?" said Kotick, all out of breath.

"Go and ask Sea Cow," said Sea Vitch. "If he is living still, he'll be able to tell you."

"How shall I know Sea Cow when I meet him?" said Kotick, sheering off.

"He's the only thing in the sea uglier than Sea Vitch," screamed a Burgomaster gull, wheeling under Sea Vitch's nose. "Uglier, and with worse manners! *Stareek*!"

Kotick swam back to Novastoshnah, leaving the gulls to scream. There he found that no one sympathized with him in his little attempt to discover a quiet place for the seals. They told him that men had always driven the holluschickie—it was part of the day's work—and that if he did not like to see ugly things he should not have gone to the killing grounds. But none of the other seals had seen the killing, and that made the difference between him and his friends. Besides, Kotick was a white seal.

"What you must do," said old Sea Catch, after he had heard his son's adventures, "is to grow up and be a big seal like your father, and have a nursery on the beach, and then they will leave you alone. In another five years you ought to be able to fight for yourself." Even gentle Matkah, his mother, said: "You will never be able to stop the killing. Go and play in the sea, Kotick." And Kotick went off and danced the Fire-dance with a very heavy little heart.

That autumn he left the beach as soon as he could, and set off alone because of a notion in his bullet-head. He was going to find Sea Cow, if there was such a person in the sea, and he was going to find a quiet island with good firm beaches for seals to live on, where men could not get at them. So he explored and explored by himself from the North to the South Pacific, swimming as much as three hundred miles in a day and a night. He met with more adventures than can be told, and narrowly escaped being caught by the Basking Shark, and the Spotted Shark, and the Hammerhead, and he met all the untrustworthy ruffians that loaf up and down the seas, and the heavy polite fish, and the scarlet spotted scallops that are moored in one place for hundreds of years, and grow very proud of it; but he never met Sea Cow, and he never found an island that he could fancy.

If the beach was good and hard, with a slope behind it for seals to play on, there was always the smoke of a whaler on the horizon, boiling down blubber, and Kotick knew what *that* meant. Or else he could see that seals had once visited the island and been killed off, and Kotick knew that where men had come once they would come again.

He picked up with an old stumpy-tailed albatross, who told him that Kerguelen Island was the very place for peace and quiet, and when

Kotick went down there he was all but smashed to pieces against some wicked black cliffs in a heavy sleet-storm with lightning and thunder. Yet as he pulled out against the gale he could see that even there had once been a seal nursery. And it was so in all the other islands that he visited.

Limmershin gave a long list of them, for he said that Kotick spent five seasons exploring, with a four months' rest each year at Novastoshnah, when the holluschickie used to make fun of him and his imaginary islands. He went to the Gallapagos, a horrid dry place on the Equator, where he was nearly baked to death; he went to the Georgia Islands, the Orkneys, Emerald Island, Little Nightingale Island, Gough's Island, Bouvet's Island, the Crossets, and even to a little speck of an island south of the Cape of Good Hope. But everywhere the People of the Sea told him the same things. Seals had come to those islands once upon a time, but men had killed them all off. Even when he swam thousands of miles out of the Pacific and got to a place called Cape Corrientes (that was when he was coming back from Gough's Island), he found a few hundred mangy seals on a rock and they told him that men came there too.

That nearly broke his heart, and he headed round the Horn back to his own beaches; and on his way north he hauled out on an island full of green trees, where he found an old, old seal who was dying, and Kotick caught fish for him and told him all his sorrows. "Now," said Kotick, "I am going back to Novastoshnah, and if I am driven to the killing-pens with the holluschickie I shall not care."

The old seal said, "Try once more. I am the last of the Lost Rookery of Masafuera, and in the days when men killed us by the hundred thousand there was a story on the beaches that some day a white seal would come out of the North and lead the seal people to a quiet place. I am old, and I shall never live to see that day, but others will. Try once more."

And Kotick curled up his mustache (it was a beauty) and said, "I am the only white seal that has ever been born on the beaches, and I am the only seal, black or white, who ever thought of looking for new islands."

This cheered him immensely; and when he came back to

Novastoshnah that summer, Matkah, his mother, begged him to marry and settle down, for he was no longer a holluschick but a full-grown sea-catch, with a curly white mane on his shoulders, as heavy, as big, and as fierce as his father. "Give me another season," he said. "Remember, Mother, it is always the seventh wave that goes farthest up the beach."

Curiously enough, there was another seal who thought that she would put off marrying till the next year, and Kotick danced the Fire-dance with her all down Lukannon Beach the night before he set off on his last exploration. This time he went westward, because he had fallen on the trail of a great shoal of halibut, and he needed at least one hundred pounds of fish a day to keep him in good condition. He chased them till he was tired, and then he curled himself up and went to sleep on the hollows of the ground swell that sets in to Copper Island. He knew the coast perfectly well, so about midnight, when he felt himself gently bumped on a weed-bed, he said, "Hm, tide's running strong tonight," and turning over under water opened his eyes slowly and stretched. Then he jumped like a cat, for he saw huge things nosing about in the shoal water and browsing on the heavy fringes of the weeds.

"By the Great Combers of Magellan!" he said, beneath his mustache. "Who in the Deep Sea are these people?"

They were like no walrus, sea lion, seal, bear, whale, shark, fish, squid, or scallop that Kotick had ever seen before. They were between twenty and thirty feet long, and they had no hind flippers, but a shovel-like tail that looked as if it had been whittled out of wet leather. Their heads were the most foolish-looking things you ever saw, and they balanced on the ends of their tails in deep water when they weren't grazing, bowing solemnly to each other and waving their front flippers as a fat man waves his arm.

"Ahem!" said Kotick. "Good sport, gentlemen?" The big things answered by bowing and waving their flippers like the Frog Footman. When they began feeding again Kotick saw that their upper lip was split into two pieces that they could twitch apart about a foot and bring together again with a whole bushel of seaweed between the splits. They tucked the stuff into their mouths and chumped solemnly.

"Messy style of feeding, that," said Kotick. They bowed again,

and Kotick began to lose his temper. "Very good," he said. "If you do happen to have an extra joint in your front flipper you needn't show off so. I see you bow gracefully, but I should like to know your names." The split lips moved and twitched; and the glassy green eyes stared, but they did not speak.

"Well!" said Kotick. "You're the only people I've ever met uglier than Sea Vitch—and with worse manners."

Then he remembered in a flash what the Burgomaster gull had screamed to him when he was a little yearling at Walrus Islet, and he tumbled backward in the water, for he knew that he had found Sea Cow at last.

The sea cows went on schlooping and grazing and chumping in the weed, and Kotick asked them questions in every language that he had picked up in his travels; and the Sea People talk nearly as many languages as human beings. But the sea cows did not answer because Sea Cow cannot talk. He has only six bones in his neck where he ought to have seven, and they say under the sea that that prevents him from speaking even to his companions. But, as you know, he has an extra joint in his foreflipper, and by waving it up and down and about he makes what answers to a sort of clumsy telegraphic code.

By daylight Kotick's mane was standing on end and his temper was gone where the dead crabs go. Then the Sea Cow began to travel northward very slowly, stopping to hold absurd bowing councils from time to time, and Kotick followed them, saying to himself, "People who are such idiots as these are would have been killed long ago if they hadn't found out some safe island. And what is good enough for the Sea Cow is good enough for the Sea Catch. All the same, I wish they'd hurry."

It was weary work for Kotick. The herd never went more than forty or fifty miles a day, and stopped to feed at night, and kept close to the shore all the time; while Kotick swam round them, and over them, and under them, but he could not hurry them up one-half mile. As they went farther north they held a bowing council every few hours, and Kotick nearly bit off his mustache with impatience till he saw that they were following up a warm current of water, and then he respected them more.

One night they sank through the shiny water—sank like stones—and for the first time since he had known them began to swim quickly. Kotick followed, and the pace astonished him, for he never dreamed that Sea Cow was anything of a swimmer. They headed for a cliff by the shore—a cliff that ran down into deep water, and plunged into a dark hole at the foot of it, twenty fathoms under the sea. It was a long, long swim, and Kotick badly wanted fresh air before he was out of the dark tunnel they led him through.

"My wig!" he said, when he rose, gasping and puffing, into open water at the farther end. "It was a long dive, but it was worth it."

The sea cows had separated and were browsing lazily along the edges of the finest beaches that Kotick had ever seen. There were long stretches of smooth-worn rock running for miles, exactly fitted to make seal-nurseries, and there were play-grounds of hard sand sloping inland behind them, and there were rollers for seals to dance in, and long grass to roll in, and sand dunes to climb up and down, and, best of all, Kotick knew by the feel of the water, which never deceives a true sea catch, that no men had ever come there.

The first thing he did was to assure himself that the fishing was good, and then he swam along the beaches and counted up the delightful low sandy islands half hidden in the beautiful rolling fog. Away to the northward, out to sea, ran a line of bars and shoals and rocks that would never let a ship come within six miles of the beach, and between the islands and the mainland was a stretch of deep water that ran up to the perpendicular cliffs, and somewhere below the cliffs was the mouth of the tunnel.

"It's Novastoshnah over again, but ten times better," said Kotick. "Sea Cow must be wiser than I thought. Men can't come down the cliffs, even if there were any men; and the shoals to seaward would knock a ship to splinters. If any place in the sea is safe, this is it."

He began to think of the seal he had left behind him, but though he was in a hurry to go back to Novastoshnah, he thoroughly explored the new country, so that he would be able to answer all questions.

Then he dived and made sure of the mouth of the tunnel, and raced through to the southward. No one but a sea cow or a seal would have

dreamed of there being such a place, and when he looked back at the cliffs even Kotick could hardly believe that he had been under them.

He was six days going home, though he was not swimming slowly; and when he hauled out just above Sea Lion's Neck the first person he met was the seal who had been waiting for him, and she saw by the look in his eyes that he had found his island at last.

But the holluschickie and Sea Catch, his father, and all the other seals laughed at him when he told them what he had discovered, and a young seal about his own age said, "This is all very well, Kotick, but you can't come from no one knows where and order us off like this. Remember we've been fighting for our nurseries, and that's a thing you never did. You preferred prowling about in the sea."

The other seals laughed at this, and the young seal began twisting his head from side to side. He had just married that year, and was making a great fuss about it.

"I've no nursery to fight for," said Kotick. "I only want to show you all a place where you will be safe. What's the use of fighting?"

"Oh, if you're trying to back out, of course I've no more to say," said the young seal with an ugly chuckle.

"Will you come with me if I win?" said Kotick. And a green light came into his eye, for he was very angry at having to fight at all.

"Very good," said the young seal carelessly. "*If* you win, I'll come."

He had no time to change his mind, for Kotick's head was out and his teeth sunk in the blubber of the young seal's neck. Then he threw himself back on his haunches and hauled his enemy down the beach, shook him, and knocked him over. Then Kotick roared to the seals: "I've done my best for you these five seasons past. I've found you the island where you'll be safe, but unless your heads are dragged off your silly necks you won't believe. I'm going to teach you now. Look out for yourselves!"

Limmershin told me that never in his life—and Limmershin sees ten thousand big seals fighting every year—never in all his little life did he see anything like Kotick's charge into the nurseries. He flung himself at the biggest sea catch he could find, caught him by the throat, choked him and bumped him and banged him till he grunted for mercy, and

then threw him aside and attacked the next. You see, Kotick had never fasted for four months as the big seals did every year, and his deep-sea swimming trips kept him in perfect condition, and, best of all, he had never fought before. His curly white mane stood up with rage, and his eyes flamed, and his big dog teeth glistened, and he was splendid to look at. Old Sea Catch, his father, saw him tearing past, hauling the grizzled old seals about as though they had been halibut, and upsetting the young bachelors in all directions; and Sea Catch gave a roar and shouted: "He may be a fool, but he is the best fighter on the beaches! Don't tackle your father, my son! He's with you!"

Kotick roared in answer, and old Sea Catch waddled in with his mustache on end, blowing like a locomotive, while Matkah and the seal that was going to marry Kotick cowered down and admired their menfolk. It was a gorgeous fight, for the two fought as long as there was a seal that dared lift up his head, and when there were none they paraded grandly up and down the beach side by side, bellowing.

At night, just as the Northern Lights were winking and flashing through the fog, Kotick climbed a bare rock and looked down on the scattered nurseries and the torn and bleeding seals. "Now," he said, "I've taught you your lesson."

"My wig!" said old Sea Catch, boosting himself up stiffly, for he was fearfully mauled. "The Killer Whale himself could not have cut them up worse. Son, I'm proud of you, and what's more, *I'll* come with you to your island—if there is such a place."

"Hear you, fat pigs of the sea. Who comes with me to the Sea Cow's tunnel? Answer, or I shall teach you again," roared Kotick.

There was a murmur like the ripple of the tide all up and down the beaches. "We will come," said thousands of tired voices. "We will follow Kotick, the White Seal."

Then Kotick dropped his head between his shoulders and shut his eyes proudly. He was not a white seal any more, but red from head to tail. All the same he would have scorned to look at or touch one of his wounds.

A week later he and his army (nearly ten thousand holluschickie and old seals) went away north to the Sea Cow's tunnel, Kotick leading them,

and the seals that stayed at Novastoshnah called them idiots. But next spring, when they all met off the fishing banks of the Pacific, Kotick's seals told such tales of the new beaches beyond Sea Cow's tunnel that more and more seals left Novastoshnah. Of course it was not all done at once, for the seals are not very clever, and they need a long time to turn things over in their minds, but year after year more seals went away from Novastoshnah, and Lukannon, and the other nurseries, to the quiet, sheltered beaches where Kotick sits all the summer through, getting bigger and fatter and stronger each year, while the holluschickie play around him, in that sea where no man comes.

8. LUKANNON

This is the great deep-sea song that all the St. Paul seals sing when they are heading back to their beaches in the summer. It is a sort of very sad seal National Anthem.

I met my mates in the morning (and, oh, but I am old!)
Where roaring on the ledges the summer ground-swell
 rolled;
I heard them lift the chorus that drowned the breakers'
 song—
The Beaches of Lukannon—two million voices strong.

The song of pleasant stations beside the salt lagoons,
The song of blowing squadrons that shuffled down the
 dunes,
The song of midnight dances that churned the sea to
 flame—
The Beaches of Lukannon—before the sealers came!

I met my mates in the morning (I'll never meet them more!);
They came and went in legions that darkened all the shore.
And o'er the foam-flecked offing as far as voice could reach
We hailed the landing-parties and we sang them up the
 beach.

The Beaches of Lukannon—the winter wheat so tall—
The dripping, crinkled lichens, and the sea-fog drenching all!
The platforms of our playground, all shining smooth and
 worn!
The Beaches of Lukannon—the home where we were born!

I met my mates in the morning, a broken, scattered band.
Men shoot us in the water and club us on the land;

Men drive us to the Salt House like silly sheep and tame,
And still we sing Lukannon—before the sealers came.

Wheel down, wheel down to southward; oh, Gooverooska,
 go!
And tell the Deep-Sea Viceroys the story of our woe;
Ere, empty as the shark's egg the tempest flings ashore,
The Beaches of Lukannon shall know their sons no more!

9. "RIKKI-TIKKI-TAVI"

At the hole where he went in
Red-Eye called to Wrinkle-Skin.
Hear what little Red-Eye saith:
"Nag, come up and dance with death!"

Eye to eye and head to head,
 (Keep the measure, Nag.)
This shall end when one is dead;
 (At thy pleasure, Nag.)
Turn for turn and twist for twist—
 (Run and hide thee, Nag.)
Hah! The hooded Death has missed!
 (Woe betide thee, Nag!)

This is the story of the great war that Rikki-tikki-tavi fought single-handed, through the bath-rooms of the big bungalow in Segowlee cantonment. Darzee, the Tailorbird, helped him, and Chuchundra, the musk-rat, who never comes out into the middle of the floor, but always creeps round by the wall, gave him advice, but Rikki-tikki did the real fighting.

He was a mongoose, rather like a little cat in his fur and his tail, but quite like a weasel in his head and his habits. His eyes and the end of his restless nose were pink. He could scratch himself anywhere he pleased with any leg, front or back, that he chose to use. He could fluff up his tail till it looked like a bottle brush, and his war cry as he scuttled through the long grass was: "*Rikk-tikk-tikki-tikki-tchk!*"

One day, a high summer flood washed him out of the burrow where he lived with his father and mother, and carried him, kicking and clucking, down a roadside ditch. He found a little wisp of grass floating there, and clung to it till he lost his senses. When he revived, he was lying in the hot sun on the middle of a garden path, very draggled indeed, and a small boy was saying, "Here's a dead mongoose. Let's have a funeral."

"No," said his mother, "let's take him in and dry him. Perhaps he isn't really dead."

They took him into the house, and a big man picked him up between his finger and thumb and said he was not dead but half choked. So they wrapped him in cotton wool, and warmed him over a little fire, and he opened his eyes and sneezed.

"Now," said the big man (he was an Englishman who had just moved into the bungalow), "don't frighten him, and we'll see what he'll do."

It is the hardest thing in the world to frighten a mongoose, because he is eaten up from nose to tail with curiosity. The motto of all the mongoose family is "Run and find out," and Rikki-tikki was a true mongoose. He looked at the cotton wool, decided that it was not good to eat, ran all round the table, sat up and put his fur in order, scratched himself, and jumped on the small boy's shoulder.

"Don't be frightened, Teddy," said his father. "That's his way of making friends."

"Ouch! He's tickling under my chin," said Teddy.

Rikki-tikki looked down between the boy's collar and neck, snuffed at his ear, and climbed down to the floor, where he sat rubbing his nose.

"Good gracious," said Teddy's mother, "and that's a wild creature! I suppose he's so tame because we've been kind to him."

"All mongooses are like that," said her husband. "If Teddy doesn't pick him up by the tail, or try to put him in a cage, he'll run in and out of the house all day long. Let's give him something to eat."

They gave him a little piece of raw meat. Rikki-tikki liked it immensely, and when it was finished he went out into the veranda and sat in the sunshine and fluffed up his fur to make it dry to the roots. Then he felt better.

"There are more things to find out about in this house," he said to himself, "than all my family could find out in all their lives. I shall certainly stay and find out."

He spent all that day roaming over the house. He nearly drowned himself in the bath-tubs, put his nose into the ink on a writing table, and burned it on the end of the big man's cigar, for he climbed up in the big man's lap to see how writing was done. At nightfall he ran into Teddy's

nursery to watch how kerosene lamps were lighted, and when Teddy went to bed Rikki-tikki climbed up too. But he was a restless companion, because he had to get up and attend to every noise all through the night, and find out what made it. Teddy's mother and father came in, the last thing, to look at their boy, and Rikki-tikki was awake on the pillow. "I don't like that," said Teddy's mother. "He may bite the child." "He'll do no such thing," said the father. "Teddy's safer with that little beast than if he had a bloodhound to watch him. If a snake came into the nursery now—"

But Teddy's mother wouldn't think of anything so awful.

Early in the morning Rikki-tikki came to early breakfast in the veranda riding on Teddy's shoulder, and they gave him banana and some boiled egg. He sat on all their laps one after the other, because every well-brought-up mongoose always hopes to be a house mongoose some day and have rooms to run about in; and Rikki-tikki's mother (she used to live in the general's house at Segowlee) had carefully told Rikki what to do if ever he came across white men.

Then Rikki-tikki went out into the garden to see what was to be seen. It was a large garden, only half cultivated, with bushes, as big as summer-houses, of Marshal Niel roses, lime and orange trees, clumps of bamboos, and thickets of high grass. Rikki-tikki licked his lips. "This is a splendid hunting-ground," he said, and his tail grew bottle-brushy at the thought of it, and he scuttled up and down the garden, snuffing here and there till he heard very sorrowful voices in a thorn-bush.

It was Darzee, the Tailorbird, and his wife. They had made a beautiful nest by pulling two big leaves together and stitching them up the edges with fibers, and had filled the hollow with cotton and downy fluff. The nest swayed to and fro, as they sat on the rim and cried.

"What is the matter?" asked Rikki-tikki.

"We are very miserable," said Darzee. "One of our babies fell out of the nest yesterday and Nag ate him."

"H'm!" said Rikki-tikki, "that is very sad—but I am a stranger here. Who is Nag?"

Darzee and his wife only cowered down in the nest without answering, for from the thick grass at the foot of the bush there came

a low hiss—a horrid cold sound that made Rikki-tikki jump back two clear feet. Then inch by inch out of the grass rose up the head and spread hood of Nag, the big black cobra, and he was five feet long from tongue to tail. When he had lifted one-third of himself clear of the ground, he stayed balancing to and fro exactly as a dandelion tuft balances in the wind, and he looked at Rikki-tikki with the wicked snake's eyes that never change their expression, whatever the snake may be thinking of.

"Who is Nag?" said he. "*I* am Nag. The great God Brahm put his mark upon all our people, when the first cobra spread his hood to keep the sun off Brahm as he slept. Look, and be afraid!"

He spread out his hood more than ever, and Rikki-tikki saw the spectacle-mark on the back of it that looks exactly like the eye part of a hook-and-eye fastening. He was afraid for the minute, but it is impossible for a mongoose to stay frightened for any length of time, and though Rikki-tikki had never met a live cobra before, his mother had fed him on dead ones, and he knew that all a grown mongoose's business in life was to fight and eat snakes. Nag knew that too and, at the bottom of his cold heart, he was afraid.

"Well," said Rikki-tikki, and his tail began to fluff up again, "marks or no marks, do you think it is right for you to eat fledglings out of a nest?"

Nag was thinking to himself, and watching the least little movement in the grass behind Rikki-tikki. He knew that mongooses in the garden meant death sooner or later for him and his family, but he wanted to get Rikki-tikki off his guard. So he dropped his head a little, and put it on one side.

"Let us talk," he said. "You eat eggs. Why should not I eat birds?"

"Behind you! Look behind you!" sang Darzee.

Rikki-tikki knew better than to waste time in staring. He jumped up in the air as high as he could go, and just under him whizzed by the head of Nagaina, Nag's wicked wife. She had crept up behind him as he was talking, to make an end of him. He heard her savage hiss as the stroke missed. He came down almost across her back, and if he had been an old mongoose he would have known that then was the time to break her back with one bite; but he was afraid of the terrible lashing return

THE JUNGLE BOOK

stroke of the cobra. He bit, indeed, but did not bite long enough, and he jumped clear of the whisking tail, leaving Nagaina torn and angry.

"Wicked, wicked Darzee!" said Nag, lashing up as high as he could reach toward the nest in the thorn-bush. But Darzee had built it out of reach of snakes, and it only swayed to and fro.

Rikki-tikki felt his eyes growing red and hot (when a mongoose's eyes grow red, he is angry), and he sat back on his tail and hind legs like a little kangaroo, and looked all round him, and chattered with rage. But Nag and Nagaina had disappeared into the grass. When a snake misses its stroke, it never says anything or gives any sign of what it means to do next. Rikki-tikki did not care to follow them, for he did not feel sure that he could manage two snakes at once. So he trotted off to the gravel path near the house, and sat down to think. It was a serious matter for him.

If you read the old books of natural history, you will find they say that when the mongoose fights the snake and happens to get bitten, he runs off and eats some herb that cures him. That is not true. The victory is only a matter of quickness of eye and quickness of foot—snake's blow against mongoose's jump—and as no eye can follow the motion of a snake's head when it strikes, this makes things much more wonderful than any magic herb. Rikki-tikki knew he was a young mongoose, and it made him all the more pleased to think that he had managed to escape a blow from behind. It gave him confidence in himself, and when Teddy came running down the path, Rikki-tikki was ready to be petted.

But just as Teddy was stooping, something wriggled a little in the dust, and a tiny voice said: "Be careful. I am Death!" It was Karait, the dusty brown snakeling that lies for choice on the dusty earth; and his bite is as dangerous as the cobra's. But he is so small that nobody thinks of him, and so he does the more harm to people.

Rikki-tikki's eyes grew red again, and he danced up to Karait with the peculiar rocking, swaying motion that he had inherited from his family. It looks very funny, but it is so perfectly balanced a gait that you can fly off from it at any angle you please, and in dealing with snakes this is an advantage. If Rikki-tikki had only known, he was doing a much more dangerous thing than fighting Nag, for Karait is so small,

and can turn so quickly, that unless Rikki bit him close to the back of the head, he would get the return stroke in his eye or his lip. But Rikki did not know. His eyes were all red, and he rocked back and forth, looking for a good place to hold. Karait struck out. Rikki jumped sideways and tried to run in, but the wicked little dusty gray head lashed within a fraction of his shoulder, and he had to jump over the body, and the head followed his heels close.

Teddy shouted to the house: "Oh, look here! Our mongoose is killing a snake." And Rikki-tikki heard a scream from Teddy's mother. His father ran out with a stick, but by the time he came up, Karait had lunged out once too far, and Rikki-tikki had sprung, jumped on the snake's back, dropped his head far between his forelegs, bitten as high up the back as he could get hold, and rolled away. That bite paralyzed Karait, and Rikki-tikki was just going to eat him up from the tail, after the custom of his family at dinner, when he remembered that a full meal makes a slow mongoose, and if he wanted all his strength and quickness ready, he must keep himself thin.

He went away for a dust bath under the castor-oil bushes, while Teddy's father beat the dead Karait. "What is the use of that?" thought Rikki-tikki. "I have settled it all;" and then Teddy's mother picked him up from the dust and hugged him, crying that he had saved Teddy from death, and Teddy's father said that he was a providence, and Teddy looked on with big scared eyes. Rikki-tikki was rather amused at all the fuss, which, of course, he did not understand. Teddy's mother might just as well have petted Teddy for playing in the dust. Rikki was thoroughly enjoying himself.

That night at dinner, walking to and fro among the wine-glasses on the table, he might have stuffed himself three times over with nice things. But he remembered Nag and Nagaina, and though it was very pleasant to be patted and petted by Teddy's mother, and to sit on Teddy's shoulder, his eyes would get red from time to time, and he would go off into his long war cry of "*Rikk-tikk-tikki-tikki-tchk!*"

Teddy carried him off to bed, and insisted on Rikki-tikki sleeping under his chin. Rikki-tikki was too well bred to bite or scratch, but as soon as Teddy was asleep he went off for his nightly walk round the

house, and in the dark he ran up against Chuchundra, the musk-rat, creeping around by the wall. Chuchundra is a broken-hearted little beast. He whimpers and cheeps all the night, trying to make up his mind to run into the middle of the room. But he never gets there.

"Don't kill me," said Chuchundra, almost weeping. "Rikki-tikki, don't kill me!"

"Do you think a snake-killer kills muskrats?" said Rikki-tikki scornfully.

"Those who kill snakes get killed by snakes," said Chuchundra, more sorrowfully than ever. "And how am I to be sure that Nag won't mistake me for you some dark night?"

"There's not the least danger," said Rikki-tikki. "But Nag is in the garden, and I know you don't go there."

"My cousin Chua, the rat, told me—" said Chuchundra, and then he stopped.

"Told you what?"

"H'sh! Nag is everywhere, Rikki-tikki. You should have talked to Chua in the garden."

"I didn't—so you must tell me. Quick, Chuchundra, or I'll bite you!"

Chuchundra sat down and cried till the tears rolled off his whiskers. "I am a very poor man," he sobbed. "I never had spirit enough to run out into the middle of the room. H'sh! I mustn't tell you anything. Can't you *hear*, Rikki-tikki?"

Rikki-tikki listened. The house was as still as still, but he thought he could just catch the faintest *scratch-scratch* in the world—a noise as faint as that of a wasp walking on a window-pane—the dry scratch of a snake's scales on brick-work.

"That's Nag or Nagaina," he said to himself, "and he is crawling into the bath-room sluice. You're right, Chuchundra; I should have talked to Chua."

He stole off to Teddy's bath-room, but there was nothing there, and then to Teddy's mother's bathroom. At the bottom of the smooth plaster wall there was a brick pulled out to make a sluice for the bath water, and as Rikki-tikki stole in by the masonry curb where the bath

is put, he heard Nag and Nagaina whispering together outside in the moonlight.

"When the house is emptied of people," said Nagaina to her husband, "*he* will have to go away, and then the garden will be our own again. Go in quietly, and remember that the big man who killed Karait is the first one to bite. Then come out and tell me, and we will hunt for Rikki-tikki together."

"But are you sure that there is anything to be gained by killing the people?" said Nag.

"Everything. When there were no people in the bungalow, did we have any mongoose in the garden? So long as the bungalow is empty, we are king and queen of the garden; and remember that as soon as our eggs in the melon bed hatch (as they may to-morrow), our children will need room and quiet."

"I had not thought of that," said Nag. "I will go, but there is no need that we should hunt for Rikki-tikki afterward. I will kill the big man and his wife, and the child if I can, and come away quietly. Then the bungalow will be empty, and Rikki-tikki will go."

Rikki-tikki tingled all over with rage and hatred at this, and then Nag's head came through the sluice, and his five feet of cold body followed it. Angry as he was, Rikki-tikki was very frightened as he saw the size of the big cobra. Nag coiled himself up, raised his head, and looked into the bathroom in the dark, and Rikki could see his eyes glitter.

"Now, if I kill him here, Nagaina will know; and if I fight him on the open floor, the odds are in his favour. What am I to do?" said Rikki-tikki-tavi.

Nag waved to and fro, and then Rikki-tikki heard him drinking from the biggest water-jar that was used to fill the bath. "That is good," said the snake. "Now, when Karait was killed, the big man had a stick. He may have that stick still, but when he comes in to bathe in the morning he will not have a stick. I shall wait here till he comes. Nagaina—do you hear me?—I shall wait here in the cool till daytime."

There was no answer from outside, so Rikki-tikki knew Nagaina had gone away. Nag coiled himself down, coil by coil, round the bulge

at the bottom of the water jar, and Rikki-tikki stayed still as death. After an hour he began to move, muscle by muscle, toward the jar. Nag was asleep, and Rikki-tikki looked at his big back, wondering which would be the best place for a good hold. "If I don't break his back at the first jump," said Rikki, "he can still fight. And if he fights—O Rikki!" He looked at the thickness of the neck below the hood, but that was too much for him; and a bite near the tail would only make Nag savage.

"It must be the head"' he said at last; "the head above the hood. And, when I am once there, I must not let go."

Then he jumped. The head was lying a little clear of the water jar, under the curve of it; and, as his teeth met, Rikki braced his back against the bulge of the red earthenware to hold down the head. This gave him just one second's purchase, and he made the most of it. Then he was battered to and fro as a rat is shaken by a dog—to and fro on the floor, up and down, and around in great circles, but his eyes were red and he held on as the body cart-whipped over the floor, upsetting the tin dipper and the soap dish and the flesh brush, and banged against the tin side of the bath. As he held he closed his jaws tighter and tighter, for he made sure he would be banged to death, and, for the honour of his family, he preferred to be found with his teeth locked. He was dizzy, aching, and felt shaken to pieces when something went off like a thunderclap just behind him. A hot wind knocked him senseless and red fire singed his fur. The big man had been wakened by the noise, and had fired both barrels of a shotgun into Nag just behind the hood.

Rikki-tikki held on with his eyes shut, for now he was quite sure he was dead. But the head did not move, and the big man picked him up and said, "It's the mongoose again, Alice. The little chap has saved *our* lives now."

Then Teddy's mother came in with a very white face, and saw what was left of Nag, and Rikki-tikki dragged himself to Teddy's bedroom and spent half the rest of the night shaking himself tenderly to find out whether he really was broken into forty pieces, as he fancied.

When morning came he was very stiff, but well pleased with his doings. "Now I have Nagaina to settle with, and she will be worse than

five Nags, and there's no knowing when the eggs she spoke of will hatch. Goodness! I must go and see Darzee," he said.

Without waiting for breakfast, Rikki-tikki ran to the thornbush where Darzee was singing a song of triumph at the top of his voice. The news of Nag's death was all over the garden, for the sweeper had thrown the body on the rubbish-heap.

"Oh, you stupid tuft of feathers!" said Rikki-tikki angrily. "Is this the time to sing?"

"Nag is dead—is dead—is dead!" sang Darzee. "The valiant Rikki-tikki caught him by the head and held fast. The big man brought the bang-stick, and Nag fell in two pieces! He will never eat my babies again."

"All that's true enough. But where's Nagaina?" said Rikki-tikki, looking carefully round him.

"Nagaina came to the bathroom sluice and called for Nag," Darzee went on, "and Nag came out on the end of a stick—the sweeper picked him up on the end of a stick and threw him upon the rubbish heap. Let us sing about the great, the red-eyed Rikki-tikki!" And Darzee filled his throat and sang.

"If I could get up to your nest, I'd roll your babies out!" said Rikki-tikki. "You don't know when to do the right thing at the right time. You're safe enough in your nest there, but it's war for me down here. Stop singing a minute, Darzee."

"For the great, the beautiful Rikki-tikki's sake I will stop," said Darzee. "What is it, O Killer of the terrible Nag?"

"Where is Nagaina, for the third time?"

"On the rubbish heap by the stables, mourning for Nag. Great is Rikki-tikki with the white teeth."

"Bother my white teeth! Have you ever heard where she keeps her eggs?"

"In the melon bed, on the end nearest the wall, where the sun strikes nearly all day. She hid them there weeks ago."

"And you never thought it worth while to tell me? The end nearest the wall, you said?"

"Rikki-tikki, you are not going to eat her eggs?"

"Not eat exactly; no. Darzee, if you have a grain of sense you will fly off to the stables and pretend that your wing is broken, and let Nagaina chase you away to this bush. I must get to the melon-bed, and if I went there now she'd see me."

Darzee was a feather-brained little fellow who could never hold more than one idea at a time in his head. And just because he knew that Nagaina's children were born in eggs like his own, he didn't think at first that it was fair to kill them. But his wife was a sensible bird, and she knew that cobra's eggs meant young cobras later on. So she flew off from the nest, and left Darzee to keep the babies warm, and continue his song about the death of Nag. Darzee was very like a man in some ways.

She fluttered in front of Nagaina by the rubbish heap and cried out, "Oh, my wing is broken! The boy in the house threw a stone at me and broke it." Then she fluttered more desperately than ever.

Nagaina lifted up her head and hissed, "You warned Rikki-tikki when I would have killed him. Indeed and truly, you've chosen a bad place to be lame in." And she moved toward Darzee's wife, slipping along over the dust.

"The boy broke it with a stone!" shrieked Darzee's wife.

"Well! It may be some consolation to you when you're dead to know that I shall settle accounts with the boy. My husband lies on the rubbish heap this morning, but before night the boy in the house will lie very still. What is the use of running away? I am sure to catch you. Little fool, look at me!"

Darzee's wife knew better than to do *that*, for a bird who looks at a snake's eyes gets so frightened that she cannot move. Darzee's wife fluttered on, piping sorrowfully, and never leaving the ground, and Nagaina quickened her pace.

Rikki-tikki heard them going up the path from the stables, and he raced for the end of the melon patch near the wall. There, in the warm litter above the melons, very cunningly hidden, he found twenty-five eggs, about the size of a bantam's eggs, but with whitish skin instead of shell.

"I was not a day too soon," he said, for he could see the baby cobras curled up inside the skin, and he knew that the minute they were

hatched they could each kill a man or a mongoose. He bit off the tops of the eggs as fast as he could, taking care to crush the young cobras, and turned over the litter from time to time to see whether he had missed any. At last there were only three eggs left, and Rikki-tikki began to chuckle to himself, when he heard Darzee's wife screaming:

"Rikki-tikki, I led Nagaina toward the house, and she has gone into the veranda, and—oh, come quickly—she means killing!"

Rikki-tikki smashed two eggs, and tumbled backward down the melon-bed with the third egg in his mouth, and scuttled to the veranda as hard as he could put foot to the ground. Teddy and his mother and father were there at early breakfast, but Rikki-tikki saw that they were not eating anything. They sat stone-still, and their faces were white. Nagaina was coiled up on the matting by Teddy's chair, within easy striking distance of Teddy's bare leg, and she was swaying to and fro, singing a song of triumph.

"Son of the big man that killed Nag," she hissed, "stay still. I am not ready yet. Wait a little. Keep very still, all you three! If you move I strike, and if you do not move I strike. Oh, foolish people, who killed my Nag!"

Teddy's eyes were fixed on his father, and all his father could do was to whisper, "Sit still, Teddy. You mustn't move. Teddy, keep still."

Then Rikki-tikki came up and cried, "Turn round, Nagaina. Turn and fight!"

"All in good time," said she, without moving her eyes. "I will settle my account with *you* presently. Look at your friends, Rikki-tikki. They are still and white. They are afraid. They dare not move, and if you come a step nearer I strike."

"Look at your eggs," said Rikki-tikki, "in the melon bed near the wall. Go and look, Nagaina!"

The big snake turned half around, and saw the egg on the veranda. "Ah-h! Give it to me," she said.

Rikki-tikki put his paws one on each side of the egg, and his eyes were blood-red. "What price for a snake's egg? For a young cobra? For a young king cobra? For the last—the very last of the brood? The ants are eating all the others down by the melon bed."

Nagaina spun clear round, forgetting everything for the sake of the one egg. Rikki-tikki saw Teddy's father shoot out a big hand, catch Teddy by the shoulder, and drag him across the little table with the tea-cups, safe and out of reach of Nagaina.

"Tricked! Tricked! Tricked! *Rikk-tck-tck!*" chuckled Rikki-tikki. "The boy is safe, and it was I—I—I that caught Nag by the hood last night in the bathroom." Then he began to jump up and down, all four feet together, his head close to the floor. "He threw me to and fro, but he could not shake me off. He was dead before the big man blew him in two. I did it! *Rikki-tikki-tck-tck!* Come then, Nagaina. Come and fight with me. You shall not be a widow long."

Nagaina saw that she had lost her chance of killing Teddy, and the egg lay between Rikki-tikki's paws. "Give me the egg, Rikki-tikki. Give me the last of my eggs, and I will go away and never come back," she said, lowering her hood.

"Yes, you will go away, and you will never come back. For you will go to the rubbish heap with Nag. Fight, widow! The big man has gone for his gun! Fight!"

Rikki-tikki was bounding all round Nagaina, keeping just out of reach of her stroke, his little eyes like hot coals. Nagaina gathered herself together and flung out at him. Rikki-tikki jumped up and backward. Again and again and again she struck, and each time her head came with a whack on the matting of the veranda and she gathered herself together like a watch spring. Then Rikki-tikki danced in a circle to get behind her, and Nagaina spun round to keep her head to his head, so that the rustle of her tail on the matting sounded like dry leaves blown along by the wind.

He had forgotten the egg. It still lay on the veranda, and Nagaina came nearer and nearer to it, till at last, while Rikki-tikki was drawing breath, she caught it in her mouth, turned to the veranda steps, and flew like an arrow down the path, with Rikki-tikki behind her. When the cobra runs for her life, she goes like a whip-lash flicked across a horse's neck.

Rikki-tikki knew that he must catch her, or all the trouble would begin again. She headed straight for the long grass by the thorn-bush,

and as he was running Rikki-tikki heard Darzee still singing his foolish little song of triumph. But Darzee's wife was wiser. She flew off her nest as Nagaina came along, and flapped her wings about Nagaina's head. If Darzee had helped they might have turned her, but Nagaina only lowered her hood and went on. Still, the instant's delay brought Rikki-tikki up to her, and as she plunged into the rat-hole where she and Nag used to live, his little white teeth were clenched on her tail, and he went down with her—and very few mongooses, however wise and old they may be, care to follow a cobra into its hole. It was dark in the hole; and Rikki-tikki never knew when it might open out and give Nagaina room to turn and strike at him. He held on savagely, and stuck out his feet to act as brakes on the dark slope of the hot, moist earth.

Then the grass by the mouth of the hole stopped waving, and Darzee said, "It is all over with Rikki-tikki! We must sing his death song. Valiant Rikki-tikki is dead! For Nagaina will surely kill him underground."

So he sang a very mournful song that he made up on the spur of the minute, and just as he got to the most touching part, the grass quivered again, and Rikki-tikki, covered with dirt, dragged himself out of the hole leg by leg, licking his whiskers. Darzee stopped with a little shout. Rikki-tikki shook some of the dust out of his fur and sneezed. "It is all over," he said. "The widow will never come out again." And the red ants that live between the grass stems heard him, and began to troop down one after another to see if he had spoken the truth.

Rikki-tikki curled himself up in the grass and slept where he was—slept and slept till it was late in the afternoon, for he had done a hard day's work.

"Now," he said, when he awoke, "I will go back to the house. Tell the Coppersmith, Darzee, and he will tell the garden that Nagaina is dead."

The Coppersmith is a bird who makes a noise exactly like the beating of a little hammer on a copper pot; and the reason he is always making it is because he is the town crier to every Indian garden, and tells all the news to everybody who cares to listen. As Rikki-tikki went up the path, he heard his "attention" notes like a tiny dinner gong, and then the

steady "*Ding-dong-tock!* Nag is dead—*dong*! Nagaina is dead! *Ding-dong-tock!*" That set all the birds in the garden singing, and the frogs croaking, for Nag and Nagaina used to eat frogs as well as little birds.

When Rikki got to the house, Teddy and Teddy's mother (she looked very white still, for she had been fainting) and Teddy's father came out and almost cried over him; and that night he ate all that was given him till he could eat no more, and went to bed on Teddy's shoulder, where Teddy's mother saw him when she came to look late at night.

"He saved our lives and Teddy's life," she said to her husband. "Just think, he saved all our lives."

Rikki-tikki woke up with a jump, for the mongooses are light sleepers.

"Oh, it's you," said he. "What are you bothering for? All the cobras are dead. And if they weren't, I'm here."

Rikki-tikki had a right to be proud of himself. But he did not grow too proud, and he kept that garden as a mongoose should keep it, with tooth and jump and spring and bite, till never a cobra dared show its head inside the walls.

10. DARZEE'S CHAUNT

(Sung in honour of Rikki-tikki-tavi)

Singer and tailor am I—
Doubled the joys that I know—
Proud of my lilt to the sky,
Proud of the house that I sew—
Over and under, so weave I my music—so weave I the house
 that I sew.

Sing to your fledglings again,
Mother, oh lift up your head!
Evil that plagued us is slain,
Death in the garden lies dead.
Terror that hid in the roses is impotent—flung on the dung-
 hill and dead!

Who has delivered us, who?
Tell me his nest and his name.
Rikki, the valiant, the true,
Tikki, with eyeballs of flame,
Rikk-tikki-tikki, the ivory-fanged, the hunter with eyeballs
 of flame!

Give him the Thanks of the Birds,
Bowing with tail feathers spread!
Praise him with nightingale words—
Nay, I will praise him instead.
Hear! I will sing you the praise of the bottle-tailed Rikki,
 with eyeballs of red!

(Here Rikki-tikki interrupted, and the rest of the song is lost.)

11. TOOMAI OF THE ELEPHANTS

I will remember what I was, I am sick of rope and chain—
I will remember my old strength and all my forest affairs.
I will not sell my back to man for a bundle of sugar-cane:
I will go out to my own kind, and the wood-folk in their lairs.

I will go out until the day, until the morning break—
Out to the wind's untainted kiss, the water's clean caress;
I will forget my ankle-ring and snap my picket stake.
I will revisit my lost loves, and playmates masterless!

Kala Nag, which means Black Snake, had served the Indian Government in every way that an elephant could serve it for forty-seven years, and as he was fully twenty years old when he was caught, that makes him nearly seventy—a ripe age for an elephant. He remembered pushing, with a big leather pad on his forehead, at a gun stuck in deep mud, and that was before the Afghan War of 1842, and he had not then come to his full strength.

His mother Radha Pyari,—Radha the darling,—who had been caught in the same drive with Kala Nag, told him, before his little milk tusks had dropped out, that elephants who were afraid always got hurt. Kala Nag knew that advice was good, for the first time that he saw a shell burst he backed, screaming, into a stand of piled rifles, and the bayonets pricked him in all his softest places. So, before he was twenty-five, he gave up being afraid, and so he was the best-loved and the best-looked-after elephant in the service of the Government of India. He had carried tents, twelve hundred pounds' weight of tents, on the march in Upper India. He had been hoisted into a ship at the end of a steam crane and taken for days across the water, and made to carry a mortar on his back in a strange and rocky country very far from India, and had seen the Emperor Theodore lying dead in Magdala, and had come back again in the steamer entitled, so the soldiers said, to the Abyssinian War

medal. He had seen his fellow elephants die of cold and epilepsy and starvation and sunstroke up at a place called Ali Musjid, ten years later; and afterward he had been sent down thousands of miles south to haul and pile big balks of teak in the timberyards at Moulmein. There he had half killed an insubordinate young elephant who was shirking his fair share of work.

After that he was taken off timber-hauling, and employed, with a few score other elephants who were trained to the business, in helping to catch wild elephants among the Garo hills. Elephants are very strictly preserved by the Indian Government. There is one whole department which does nothing else but hunt them, and catch them, and break them in, and send them up and down the country as they are needed for work.

Kala Nag stood ten fair feet at the shoulders, and his tusks had been cut off short at five feet, and bound round the ends, to prevent them splitting, with bands of copper; but he could do more with those stumps than any untrained elephant could do with the real sharpened ones. When, after weeks and weeks of cautious driving of scattered elephants across the hills, the forty or fifty wild monsters were driven into the last stockade, and the big drop gate, made of tree trunks lashed together, jarred down behind them, Kala Nag, at the word of command, would go into that flaring, trumpeting pandemonium (generally at night, when the flicker of the torches made it difficult to judge distances), and, picking out the biggest and wildest tusker of the mob, would hammer him and hustle him into quiet while the men on the backs of the other elephants roped and tied the smaller ones.

There was nothing in the way of fighting that Kala Nag, the old wise Black Snake, did not know, for he had stood up more than once in his time to the charge of the wounded tiger, and, curling up his soft trunk to be out of harm's way, had knocked the springing brute sideways in mid-air with a quick sickle cut of his head, that he had invented all by himself; had knocked him over, and kneeled upon him with his huge knees till the life went out with a gasp and a howl, and there was only a fluffy striped thing on the ground for Kala Nag to pull by the tail.

"Yes," said Big Toomai, his driver, the son of Black Toomai who had taken him to Abyssinia, and grandson of Toomai of the Elephants

who had seen him caught, "there is nothing that the Black Snake fears except me. He has seen three generations of us feed him and groom him, and he will live to see four."

"He is afraid of *me* also," said Little Toomai, standing up to his full height of four feet, with only one rag upon him. He was ten years old, the eldest son of Big Toomai, and, according to custom, he would take his father's place on Kala Nag's neck when he grew up, and would handle the heavy iron *ankus*, the elephant goad, that had been worn smooth by his father, and his grandfather, and his great-grandfather.

He knew what he was talking of; for he had been born under Kala Nag's shadow, had played with the end of his trunk before he could walk, had taken him down to water as soon as he could walk, and Kala Nag would no more have dreamed of disobeying his shrill little orders than he would have dreamed of killing him on that day when Big Toomai carried the little brown baby under Kala Nag's tusks, and told him to salute his master that was to be.

"Yes," said Little Toomai, "he is afraid of *me*," and he took long strides up to Kala Nag, called him a fat old pig, and made him lift up his feet one after the other.

"Wah!" said Little Toomai, "thou art a big elephant," and he wagged his fluffy head, quoting his father. "The Government may pay for elephants, but they belong to us mahouts. When thou art old, Kala Nag, there will come some rich rajah, and he will buy thee from the Government, on account of thy size and thy manners, and then thou wilt have nothing to do but to carry gold earrings in thy ears, and a gold howdah on thy back, and a red cloth covered with gold on thy sides, and walk at the head of the processions of the King. Then I shall sit on thy neck, O Kala Nag, with a silver *ankus*, and men will run before us with golden sticks, crying, 'Room for the King's elephant!' That will be good, Kala Nag, but not so good as this hunting in the jungles."

"Umph!" said Big Toomai. "Thou art a boy, and as wild as a buffalo-calf. This running up and down among the hills is not the best Government service. I am getting old, and I do not love wild elephants. Give me brick elephant lines, one stall to each elephant, and big stumps to tie them to safely, and flat, broad roads to exercise upon, instead of

this come-and-go camping. Aha, the Cawnpore barracks were good. There was a bazaar close by, and only three hours' work a day."

Little Toomai remembered the Cawnpore elephant-lines and said nothing. He very much preferred the camp life, and hated those broad, flat roads, with the daily grubbing for grass in the forage reserve, and the long hours when there was nothing to do except to watch Kala Nag fidgeting in his pickets.

What Little Toomai liked was to scramble up bridle paths that only an elephant could take; the dip into the valley below; the glimpses of the wild elephants browsing miles away; the rush of the frightened pig and peacock under Kala Nag's feet; the blinding warm rains, when all the hills and valleys smoked; the beautiful misty mornings when nobody knew where they would camp that night; the steady, cautious drive of the wild elephants, and the mad rush and blaze and hullabaloo of the last night's drive, when the elephants poured into the stockade like boulders in a landslide, found that they could not get out, and flung themselves at the heavy posts only to be driven back by yells and flaring torches and volleys of blank cartridge.

Even a little boy could be of use there, and Toomai was as useful as three boys. He would get his torch and wave it, and yell with the best. But the really good time came when the driving out began, and the Keddah—that is, the stockade—looked like a picture of the end of the world, and men had to make signs to one another, because they could not hear themselves speak. Then Little Toomai would climb up to the top of one of the quivering stockade posts, his sun-bleached brown hair flying loose all over his shoulders, and he looking like a goblin in the torch-light. And as soon as there was a lull you could hear his high-pitched yells of encouragement to Kala Nag, above the trumpeting and crashing, and snapping of ropes, and groans of the tethered elephants. "*Mael, mael, Kala Nag!* (Go on, go on, Black Snake!) *Dant do!* (Give him the tusk!) *Somalo! Somalo!* (Careful, careful!) *Maro! Maro!* (Hit him, hit him!) Mind the post! *Arré ! Arré! Hai! Yai! Kya-a-ah!*" he would shout, and the big fight between Kala Nag and the wild elephant would sway to and fro across the Keddah, and the old elephant catchers would wipe the sweat out of their eyes,

and find time to nod to Little Toomai wriggling with joy on the top of the posts.

He did more than wriggle. One night he slid down from the post and slipped in between the elephants and threw up the loose end of a rope, which had dropped, to a driver who was trying to get a purchase on the leg of a kicking young calf (calves always give more trouble than full-grown animals). Kala Nag saw him, caught him in his trunk, and handed him up to Big Toomai, who slapped him then and there, and put him back on the post.

Next morning he gave him a scolding and said, "Are not good brick elephant lines and a little tent carrying enough, that thou must needs go elephant catching on thy own account, little worthless? Now those foolish hunters, whose pay is less than my pay, have spoken to Petersen Sahib of the matter." Little Toomai was frightened. He did not know much of white men, but Petersen Sahib was the greatest white man in the world to him. He was the head of all the Keddah operations—the man who caught all the elephants for the Government of India, and who knew more about the ways of elephants than any living man.

"What—what will happen?" said Little Toomai.

"Happen! The worst that can happen. Petersen Sahib is a madman. Else why should he go hunting these wild devils? He may even require thee to be an elephant catcher, to sleep anywhere in these fever-filled jungles, and at last to be trampled to death in the Keddah. It is well that this nonsense ends safely. Next week the catching is over, and we of the plains are sent back to our stations. Then we will march on smooth roads, and forget all this hunting. But, son, I am angry that thou shouldst meddle in the business that belongs to these dirty Assamese jungle folk. Kala Nag will obey none but me, so I must go with him into the Keddah, but he is only a fighting elephant, and he does not help to rope them. So I sit at my ease, as befits a mahout,—not a mere hunter,—a mahout, I say, and a man who gets a pension at the end of his service. Is the family of Toomai of the Elephants to be trodden underfoot in the dirt of a Keddah? Bad one! Wicked one! Worthless son! Go and wash Kala Nag and attend to his ears, and see that there are no thorns in his feet. Or else Petersen Sahib will surely catch thee and

make thee a wild hunter—a follower of elephant's foot tracks, a jungle bear. Bah! Shame! Go!"

Little Toomai went off without saying a word, but he told Kala Nag all his grievances while he was examining his feet. "No matter," said Little Toomai, turning up the fringe of Kala Nag's huge right ear. "They have said my name to Petersen Sahib, and perhaps—and perhaps—and perhaps—who knows? Hai! That is a big thorn that I have pulled out!"

The next few days were spent in getting the elephants together, in walking the newly caught wild elephants up and down between a couple of tame ones to prevent them giving too much trouble on the downward march to the plains, and in taking stock of the blankets and ropes and things that had been worn out or lost in the forest.

Petersen Sahib came in on his clever she-elephant Pudmini; he had been paying off other camps among the hills, for the season was coming to an end, and there was a native clerk sitting at a table under a tree, to pay the drivers their wages. As each man was paid he went back to his elephant, and joined the line that stood ready to start. The catchers, and hunters, and beaters, the men of the regular Keddah, who stayed in the jungle year in and year out, sat on the backs of the elephants that belonged to Petersen Sahib's permanent force, or leaned against the trees with their guns across their arms, and made fun of the drivers who were going away, and laughed when the newly caught elephants broke the line and ran about.

Big Toomai went up to the clerk with Little Toomai behind him, and Machua Appa, the head tracker, said in an undertone to a friend of his, "There goes one piece of good elephant stuff at least. 'Tis a pity to send that young jungle-cock to molt in the plains."

Now Petersen Sahib had ears all over him, as a man must have who listens to the most silent of all living things—the wild elephant. He turned where he was lying all along on Pudmini's back and said, "What is that? I did not know of a man among the plains-drivers who had wit enough to rope even a dead elephant."

"This is not a man, but a boy. He went into the Keddah at the last drive, and threw Barmao there the rope, when we were trying to get that young calf with the blotch on his shoulder away from his mother."

Machua Appa pointed at Little Toomai, and Petersen Sahib looked, and Little Toomai bowed to the earth.

"He throw a rope? He is smaller than a picket-pin. Little one, what is thy name?" said Petersen Sahib.

Little Toomai was too frightened to speak, but Kala Nag was behind him, and Toomai made a sign with his hand, and the elephant caught him up in his trunk and held him level with Pudmini's forehead, in front of the great Petersen Sahib. Then Little Toomai covered his face with his hands, for he was only a child, and except where elephants were concerned, he was just as bashful as a child could be.

"Oho!" said Petersen Sahib, smiling underneath his mustache, "and why didst thou teach thy elephant *that* trick? Was it to help thee steal green corn from the roofs of the houses when the ears are put out to dry?"

"Not green corn, Protector of the Poor,—melons," said Little Toomai, and all the men sitting about broke into a roar of laughter. Most of them had taught their elephants that trick when they were boys. Little Toomai was hanging eight feet up in the air, and he wished very much that he were eight feet underground.

"He is Toomai, my son, Sahib," said Big Toomai, scowling. "He is a very bad boy, and he will end in a jail, Sahib."

"Of that I have my doubts," said Petersen Sahib. "A boy who can face a full Keddah at his age does not end in jails. See, little one, here are four annas to spend in sweetmeats because thou hast a little head under that great thatch of hair. In time thou mayest become a hunter too." Big Toomai scowled more than ever. "Remember, though, that Keddahs are not good for children to play in," Petersen Sahib went on.

"Must I never go there, Sahib?" asked Little Toomai with a big gasp.

"Yes." Petersen Sahib smiled again. "When thou hast seen the elephants dance. That is the proper time. Come to me when thou hast seen the elephants dance, and then I will let thee go into all the Keddahs."

There was another roar of laughter, for that is an old joke among elephant-catchers, and it means just never. There are great cleared flat places hidden away in the forests that are called elephants' ball-rooms,

but even these are only found by accident, and no man has ever seen the elephants dance. When a driver boasts of his skill and bravery the other drivers say, "And when didst *thou* see the elephants dance?"

Kala Nag put Little Toomai down, and he bowed to the earth again and went away with his father, and gave the silver four-anna piece to his mother, who was nursing his baby brother, and they all were put up on Kala Nag's back, and the line of grunting, squealing elephants rolled down the hill path to the plains. It was a very lively march on account of the new elephants, who gave trouble at every ford, and needed coaxing or beating every other minute.

Big Toomai prodded Kala Nag spitefully, for he was very angry, but Little Toomai was too happy to speak. Petersen Sahib had noticed him, and given him money, so he felt as a private soldier would feel if he had been called out of the ranks and praised by his commander-in-chief.

"What did Petersen Sahib mean by the elephant dance?" he said, at last, softly to his mother.

Big Toomai heard him and grunted. "That thou shouldst never be one of these hill buffaloes of trackers. *That* was what he meant. Oh, you in front, what is blocking the way?"

An Assamese driver, two or three elephants ahead, turned round angrily, crying: "Bring up Kala Nag, and knock this youngster of mine into good behaviour. Why should Petersen Sahib have chosen *me* to go down with you donkeys of the rice fields? Lay your beast alongside, Toomai, and let him prod with his tusks. By all the Gods of the Hills, these new elephants are possessed, or else they can smell their companions in the jungle." Kala Nag hit the new elephant in the ribs and knocked the wind out of him, as Big Toomai said, "We have swept the hills of wild elephants at the last catch. It is only your carelessness in driving. Must I keep order along the whole line?"

"Hear him!" said the other driver. "*We* have swept the hills! Ho! Ho! You are very wise, you plains people. Anyone but a mud-head who never saw the jungle would know that *they* know that the drives are ended for the season. Therefore all the wild elephants to-night will— but why should I waste wisdom on a river-turtle?"

"What will they do?" Little Toomai called out.

"*Ohé*, little one. Art thou there? Well, I will tell thee, for thou hast a cool head. They will dance, and it behooves thy father, who has swept *all* the hills of *all* the elephants, to double-chain his pickets to-night."

"What talk is this?" said Big Toomai. "For forty years, father and son, we have tended elephants, and we have never heard such moonshine about dances."

"Yes; but a plainsman who lives in a hut knows only the four walls of his hut. Well, leave thy elephants unshackled tonight and see what comes. As for their dancing, I have seen the place where—*Bapree-bap!* How many windings has the Dihang River? Here is another ford, and we must swim the calves. Stop still, you behind there."

And in this way, talking and wrangling and splashing through the rivers, they made their first march to a sort of receiving camp for the new elephants. But they lost their tempers long before they got there.

Then the elephants were chained by their hind legs to their big stumps of pickets, and extra ropes were fitted to the new elephants, and the fodder was piled before them, and the hill drivers went back to Petersen Sahib through the afternoon light, telling the plains drivers to be extra careful that night, and laughing when the plains drivers asked the reason.

Little Toomai attended to Kala Nag's supper, and as evening fell, wandered through the camp, unspeakably happy, in search of a tom-tom. When an Indian child's heart is full, he does not run about and make a noise in an irregular fashion. He sits down to a sort of revel all by himself. And Little Toomai had been spoken to by Petersen Sahib! If he had not found what he wanted, I believe he would have been ill. But the sweetmeat seller in the camp lent him a little tom-tom—a drum beaten with the flat of the hand—and he sat down, cross-legged, before Kala Nag as the stars began to come out, the tom-tom in his lap, and he thumped and he thumped and he thumped, and the more he thought of the great honour that had been done to him, the more he thumped, all alone among the elephant fodder. There was no tune and no words, but the thumping made him happy.

The new elephants strained at their ropes, and squealed and trumpeted from time to time, and he could hear his mother in the camp

hut putting his small brother to sleep with an old, old song about the great God Shiv, who once told all the animals what they should eat. It is a very soothing lullaby, and the first verse says:

> Shiv, who poured the harvest and made the winds to blow,
> Sitting at the doorways of a day of long ago,
> Gave to each his portion, food and toil and fate,
> From the King upon the *guddee* to the Beggar at the gate.
> All things made he—Shiva the Preserver.
> Mahadeo! Mahadeo! He made all—
> Thorn for the camel, fodder for the kine,
> And mother's heart for sleepy head, O little son of mine!

Little Toomai came in with a joyous *tunk-a-tunk* at the end of each verse, till he felt sleepy and stretched himself on the fodder at Kala Nag's side. At last the elephants began to lie down one after another as is their custom, till only Kala Nag at the right of the line was left standing up; and he rocked slowly from side to side, his ears put forward to listen to the night wind as it blew very slowly across the hills. The air was full of all the night noises that, taken together, make one big silence—the click of one bamboo stem against the other, the rustle of something alive in the undergrowth, the scratch and squawk of a half-waked bird (birds are awake in the night much more often than we imagine), and the fall of water ever so far away. Little Toomai slept for some time, and when he waked it was brilliant moonlight, and Kala Nag was still standing up with his ears cocked. Little Toomai turned, rustling in the fodder, and watched the curve of his big back against half the stars in heaven, and while he watched he heard, so far away that it sounded no more than a pinhole of noise pricked through the stillness, the "hoot-toot" of a wild elephant.

All the elephants in the lines jumped up as if they had been shot, and their grunts at last waked the sleeping mahouts, and they came out and drove in the picket pegs with big mallets, and tightened this rope and knotted that till all was quiet. One new elephant had nearly grubbed up his picket, and Big Toomai took off Kala Nag's leg chain and shackled that elephant fore-foot to hind-foot, but slipped a loop of grass string

round Kala Nag's leg, and told him to remember that he was tied fast. He knew that he and his father and his grandfather had done the very same thing hundreds of times before. Kala Nag did not answer to the order by gurgling, as he usually did. He stood still, looking out across the moonlight, his head a little raised and his ears spread like fans, up to the great folds of the Garo hills.

"Tend to him if he grows restless in the night," said Big Toomai to Little Toomai, and he went into the hut and slept. Little Toomai was just going to sleep, too, when he heard the coir string snap with a little "tang," and Kala Nag rolled out of his pickets as slowly and as silently as a cloud rolls out of the mouth of a valley. Little Toomai pattered after him, barefooted, down the road in the moonlight, calling under his breath, "Kala Nag! Kala Nag! Take me with you, O Kala Nag!" The elephant turned, without a sound, took three strides back to the boy in the moonlight, put down his trunk, swung him up to his neck, and almost before Little Toomai had settled his knees, slipped into the forest.

There was one blast of furious trumpeting from the lines, and then the silence shut down on everything, and Kala Nag began to move. Sometimes a tuft of high grass washed along his sides as a wave washes along the sides of a ship, and sometimes a cluster of wild-pepper vines would scrape along his back, or a bamboo would creak where his shoulder touched it. But between those times he moved absolutely without any sound, drifting through the thick Garo forest as though it had been smoke. He was going uphill, but though Little Toomai watched the stars in the rifts of the trees, he could not tell in what direction.

Then Kala Nag reached the crest of the ascent and stopped for a minute, and Little Toomai could see the tops of the trees lying all speckled and furry under the moonlight for miles and miles, and the blue-white mist over the river in the hollow. Toomai leaned forward and looked, and he felt that the forest was awake below him—awake and alive and crowded. A big brown fruit-eating bat brushed past his ear; a porcupine's quills rattled in the thicket; and in the darkness between the tree stems he heard a hog-bear digging hard in the moist warm earth, and snuffing as it digged.

Then the branches closed over his head again, and Kala Nag began to go down into the valley—not quietly this time, but as a runaway gun goes down a steep bank—in one rush. The huge limbs moved as steadily as pistons, eight feet to each stride, and the wrinkled skin of the elbow points rustled. The undergrowth on either side of him ripped with a noise like torn canvas, and the saplings that he heaved away right and left with his shoulders sprang back again and banged him on the flank, and great trails of creepers, all matted together, hung from his tusks as he threw his head from side to side and plowed out his pathway. Then Little Toomai laid himself down close to the great neck lest a swinging bough should sweep him to the ground, and he wished that he were back in the lines again.

The grass began to get squashy, and Kala Nag's feet sucked and squelched as he put them down, and the night mist at the bottom of the valley chilled Little Toomai. There was a splash and a trample, and the rush of running water, and Kala Nag strode through the bed of a river, feeling his way at each step. Above the noise of the water, as it swirled round the elephant's legs, Little Toomai could hear more splashing and some trumpeting both up-stream and down—great grunts and angry snortings, and all the mist about him seemed to be full of rolling, wavy shadows.

"*Ai!*" he said, half aloud, his teeth chattering. "The elephant-folk are out tonight. It *is* the dance, then!"

Kala Nag swashed out of the water, blew his trunk clear, and began another climb. But this time he was not alone, and he had not to make his path. That was made already, six feet wide, in front of him, where the bent jungle-grass was trying to recover itself and stand up. Many elephants must have gone that way only a few minutes before. Little Toomai looked back, and behind him a great wild tusker with his little pig's eyes glowing like hot coals was just lifting himself out of the misty river. Then the trees closed up again, and they went on and up, with trumpetings and crashings, and the sound of breaking branches on every side of them.

At last Kala Nag stood still between two tree-trunks at the very top of the hill. They were part of a circle of trees that grew round

an irregular space of some three or four acres, and in all that space, as Little Toomai could see, the ground had been trampled down as hard as a brick floor. Some trees grew in the centre of the clearing, but their bark was rubbed away, and the white wood beneath showed all shiny and polished in the patches of moonlight. There were creepers hanging from the upper branches, and the bells of the flowers of the creepers, great waxy white things like convolvuluses, hung down fast asleep. But within the limits of the clearing there was not a single blade of green— nothing but the trampled earth.

The moonlight showed it all iron gray, except where some elephants stood upon it, and their shadows were inky black. Little Toomai looked, holding his breath, with his eyes starting out of his head, and as he looked, more and more and more elephants swung out into the open from between the tree trunks. Little Toomai could only count up to ten, and he counted again and again on his fingers till he lost count of the tens, and his head began to swim. Outside the clearing he could hear them crashing in the undergrowth as they worked their way up the hillside, but as soon as they were within the circle of the tree trunks they moved like ghosts.

There were white-tusked wild males, with fallen leaves and nuts and twigs lying in the wrinkles of their necks and the folds of their ears; fat, slow-footed she-elephants, with restless, little pinky black calves only three or four feet high running under their stomachs; young elephants with their tusks just beginning to show, and very proud of them; lanky, scraggy old-maid elephants, with their hollow anxious faces, and trunks like rough bark; savage old bull elephants, scarred from shoulder to flank with great weals and cuts of bygone fights, and the caked dirt of their solitary mud baths dropping from their shoulders; and there was one with a broken tusk and the marks of the full-stroke, the terrible drawing scrape, of a tiger's claws on his side.

They were standing head to head, or walking to and fro across the ground in couples, or rocking and swaying all by themselves—scores and scores of elephants.

Toomai knew that so long as he lay still on Kala Nag's neck nothing would happen to him, for even in the rush and scramble of a Keddah

drive a wild elephant does not reach up with his trunk and drag a man off the neck of a tame elephant. And these elephants were not thinking of men that night. Once they started and put their ears forward when they heard the chinking of a leg iron in the forest, but it was Pudmini, Petersen Sahib's pet elephant, her chain snapped short off, grunting, snuffling up the hillside. She must have broken her pickets and come straight from Petersen Sahib's camp; and Little Toomai saw another elephant, one that he did not know, with deep rope galls on his back and breast. He, too, must have run away from some camp in the hills about.

At last there was no sound of any more elephants moving in the forest, and Kala Nag rolled out from his station between the trees and went into the middle of the crowd, clucking and gurgling, and all the elephants began to talk in their own tongue, and to move about.

Still lying down, Little Toomai looked down upon scores and scores of broad backs, and wagging ears, and tossing trunks, and little rolling eyes. He heard the click of tusks as they crossed other tusks by accident, and the dry rustle of trunks twined together, and the chafing of enormous sides and shoulders in the crowd, and the incessant flick and *hissh* of the great tails. Then a cloud came over the moon, and he sat in black darkness. But the quiet, steady hustling and pushing and gurgling went on just the same. He knew that there were elephants all round Kala Nag, and that there was no chance of backing him out of the assembly; so he set his teeth and shivered. In a Keddah at least there was torchlight and shouting, but here he was all alone in the dark, and once a trunk came up and touched him on the knee.

Then an elephant trumpeted, and they all took it up for five or ten terrible seconds. The dew from the trees above spattered down like rain on the unseen backs, and a dull booming noise began, not very loud at first, and Little Toomai could not tell what it was. But it grew and grew, and Kala Nag lifted up one forefoot and then the other, and brought them down on the ground—one-two, one-two, as steadily as trip-hammers. The elephants were stamping all together now, and it sounded like a war drum beaten at the mouth of a cave. The dew fell from the trees till there was no more left to fall, and the booming went on, and the ground rocked and shivered, and Little Toomai put his

hands up to his ears to shut out the sound. But it was all one gigantic jar that ran through him—this stamp of hundreds of heavy feet on the raw earth. Once or twice he could feel Kala Nag and all the others surge forward a few strides, and the thumping would change to the crushing sound of juicy green things being bruised, but in a minute or two the boom of feet on hard earth began again. A tree was creaking and groaning somewhere near him. He put out his arm and felt the bark, but Kala Nag moved forward, still tramping, and he could not tell where he was in the clearing. There was no sound from the elephants, except once, when two or three little calves squeaked together. Then he heard a thump and a shuffle, and the booming went on. It must have lasted fully two hours, and Little Toomai ached in every nerve, but he knew by the smell of the night air that the dawn was coming.

The morning broke in one sheet of pale yellow behind the green hills, and the booming stopped with the first ray, as though the light had been an order. Before Little Toomai had got the ringing out of his head, before even he had shifted his position, there was not an elephant in sight except Kala Nag, Pudmini, and the elephant with the rope-galls, and there was neither sign nor rustle nor whisper down the hillsides to show where the others had gone.

Little Toomai stared again and again. The clearing, as he remembered it, had grown in the night. More trees stood in the middle of it, but the undergrowth and the jungle grass at the sides had been rolled back. Little Toomai stared once more. Now he understood the trampling. The elephants had stamped out more room—had stamped the thick grass and juicy cane to trash, the trash into slivers, the slivers into tiny fibers, and the fibers into hard earth.

"Wah!" said Little Toomai, and his eyes were very heavy. "Kala Nag, my lord, let us keep by Pudmini and go to Petersen Sahib's camp, or I shall drop from thy neck."

The third elephant watched the two go away, snorted, wheeled round, and took his own path. He may have belonged to some little native king's establishment, fifty or sixty or a hundred miles away.

Two hours later, as Petersen Sahib was eating early breakfast, his elephants, who had been double chained that night, began to trumpet,

and Pudmini, mired to the shoulders, with Kala Nag, very footsore, shambled into the camp. Little Toomai's face was gray and pinched, and his hair was full of leaves and drenched with dew, but he tried to salute Petersen Sahib, and cried faintly: "The dance—the elephant dance! I have seen it, and—I die!" As Kala Nag sat down, he slid off his neck in a dead faint.

But, since native children have no nerves worth speaking of, in two hours he was lying very contentedly in Petersen Sahib's hammock with Petersen Sahib's shooting-coat under his head, and a glass of warm milk, a little brandy, with a dash of quinine, inside of him, and while the old hairy, scarred hunters of the jungles sat three deep before him, looking at him as though he were a spirit, he told his tale in short words, as a child will, and wound up with:

"Now, if I lie in one word, send men to see, and they will find that the elephant folk have trampled down more room in their dance-room, and they will find ten and ten, and many times ten, tracks leading to that dance-room. They made more room with their feet. I have seen it. Kala Nag took me, and I saw. Also Kala Nag is very leg-weary!"

Little Toomai lay back and slept all through the long afternoon and into the twilight, and while he slept Petersen Sahib and Machua Appa followed the track of the two elephants for fifteen miles across the hills. Petersen Sahib had spent eighteen years in catching elephants, and he had only once before found such a dance-place. Machua Appa had no need to look twice at the clearing to see what had been done there, or to scratch with his toe in the packed, rammed earth.

"The child speaks truth," said he. "All this was done last night, and I have counted seventy tracks crossing the river. See, Sahib, where Pudmini's leg-iron cut the bark of that tree! Yes; she was there too."

They looked at one another and up and down, and they wondered. For the ways of elephants are beyond the wit of any man, black or white, to fathom.

"Forty years and five," said Machua Appa, "have I followed my lord, the elephant, but never have I heard that any child of man had seen what this child has seen. By all the Gods of the Hills, it is—what can we say?" and he shook his head.

When they got back to camp it was time for the evening meal. Petersen Sahib ate alone in his tent, but he gave orders that the camp should have two sheep and some fowls, as well as a double ration of flour and rice and salt, for he knew that there would be a feast.

Big Toomai had come up hotfoot from the camp in the plains to search for his son and his elephant, and now that he had found them he looked at them as though he were afraid of them both. And there was a feast by the blazing campfires in front of the lines of picketed elephants, and Little Toomai was the hero of it all. And the big brown elephant catchers, the trackers and drivers and ropers, and the men who know all the secrets of breaking the wildest elephants, passed him from one to the other, and they marked his forehead with blood from the breast of a newly killed jungle-cock, to show that he was a forester, initiated and free of all the jungles.

And at last, when the flames died down, and the red light of the logs made the elephants look as though they had been dipped in blood too, Machua Appa, the head of all the drivers of all the Keddahs—Machua Appa, Petersen Sahib's other self, who had never seen a made road in forty years: Machua Appa, who was so great that he had no other name than Machua Appa,—leaped to his feet, with Little Toomai held high in the air above his head, and shouted: "Listen, my brothers. Listen, too, you my lords in the lines there, for I, Machua Appa, am speaking! This little one shall no more be called Little Toomai, but Toomai of the Elephants, as his great-grandfather was called before him. What never man has seen he has seen through the long night, and the favour of the elephant-folk and of the Gods of the Jungles is with him. He shall become a great tracker. He shall become greater than I, even I, Machua Appa! He shall follow the new trail, and the stale trail, and the mixed trail, with a clear eye! He shall take no harm in the Keddah when he runs under their bellies to rope the wild tuskers; and if he slips before the feet of the charging bull elephant, the bull elephant shall know who he is and shall not crush him. *Aihai!* my lords in the chains,"—he whirled up the line of pickets—"here is the little one that has seen your dances in your hidden places,—the sight that never man saw! Give him honour, my lords! *Salaam karo*, my children. Make your salute to Toomai of

the Elephants! Gunga Pershad, ahaa! Hira Guj, Birchi Guj, Kuttar Guj, ahaa! Pudmini,—thou hast seen him at the dance, and thou too, Kala Nag, my pearl among elephants!—ahaa! Together! To Toomai of the Elephants. *Barrao!*"

And at that last wild yell the whole line flung up their trunks till the tips touched their foreheads, and broke out into the full salute— the crashing trumpet-peal that only the Viceroy of India hears, the Salaamut of the Keddah.

But it was all for the sake of Little Toomai, who had seen what never man had seen before—the dance of the elephants at night and alone in the heart of the Garo hills!

12. SHIV AND THE GRASSHOPPER

(The song that Toomai's mother sang to the baby)

Shiv, who poured the harvest and made the winds to blow,
Sitting at the doorways of a day of long ago,
Gave to each his portion, food and toil and fate,
From the King upon the *guddee* to the Beggar at the gate.
> *All things made he—Shiva the Preserver.*
> *Mahadeo! Mahadeo! He made all,—*
> *Thorn for the camel, fodder for the kine,*
> *And mother's heart for sleepy head, O little son of mine!*

Wheat he gave to rich folk, millet to the poor,
Broken scraps for holy men that beg from door to door;
Cattle to the tiger, carrion to the kite,
And rags and bones to wicked wolves without the wall at
 night.
Naught he found too lofty, none he saw too low—
Parbati beside him watched them come and go;
Thought to cheat her husband, turning Shiv to jest—
Stole the little grasshopper and hid it in her breast.
> *So she tricked him, Shiva the Preserver.*
> *Mahadeo! Mahadeo! Turn and see.*
> *Tall are the camels, heavy are the kine,*
> *But this was Least of Little Things, O little son of mine!*

When the dole was ended, laughingly she said,
"Master, of a million mouths, is not one unfed?"
Laughing, Shiv made answer, "All have had their part,
Even he, the little one, hidden 'neath thy heart."
From her breast she plucked it, Parbati the thief,
Saw the Least of Little Things gnawed a new-grown leaf!
Saw and feared and wondered, making prayer to Shiv,
Who hath surely given meat to all that live.

All things made he—Shiva the Preserver.
Mahadeo! Mahadeo! He made all,—
Thorn for the camel, fodder for the kine,
And mother's heart for sleepy head, O little son of mine!

13. HER MAJESTY'S SERVANTS

You can work it out by Fractions or by simple Rule of
 Three,
But the way of Tweedle-dum is not the way of Tweedle-dee.
You can twist it, you can turn it, you can plait it till you drop,
But the way of Pilly Winky's *not* the way of Winkie Pop!

It had been raining heavily for one whole month—raining on a camp
of thirty thousand men and thousands of camels, elephants, horses,
bullocks, and mules all gathered together at a place called Rawal Pindi,
to be reviewed by the Viceroy of India. He was receiving a visit from
the Amir of Afghanistan—a wild king of a very wild country. The
Amir had brought with him for a bodyguard eight hundred men and
horses who had never seen a camp or a locomotive before in their
lives—savage men and savage horses from somewhere at the back of
Central Asia. Every night a mob of these horses would be sure to break
their heel ropes and stampede up and down the camp through the mud
in the dark, or the camels would break loose and run about and fall over
the ropes of the tents, and you can imagine how pleasant that was for
men trying to go to sleep. My tent lay far away from the camel lines,
and I thought it was safe. But one night a man popped his head in and
shouted, "Get out, quick! They're coming! My tent's gone!"

I knew who "they" were, so I put on my boots and waterproof
and scuttled out into the slush. Little Vixen, my fox terrier, went out
through the other side; and then there was a roaring and a grunting and
bubbling, and I saw the tent cave in, as the pole snapped, and begin to
dance about like a mad ghost. A camel had blundered into it, and wet
and angry as I was, I could not help laughing. Then I ran on, because I
did not know how many camels might have got loose, and before long I
was out of sight of the camp, plowing my way through the mud.

At last I fell over the tail-end of a gun, and by that knew I was

somewhere near the artillery lines where the cannon were stacked at night. As I did not want to plowter about any more in the drizzle and the dark, I put my waterproof over the muzzle of one gun, and made a sort of wigwam with two or three rammers that I found, and lay along the tail of another gun, wondering where Vixen had got to, and where I might be.

Just as I was getting ready to go to sleep I heard a jingle of harness and a grunt, and a mule passed me shaking his wet ears. He belonged to a screw-gun battery, for I could hear the rattle of the straps and rings and chains and things on his saddle pad. The screw-guns are tiny little cannon made in two pieces, that are screwed together when the time comes to use them. They are taken up mountains, anywhere that a mule can find a road, and they are very useful for fighting in rocky country.

Behind the mule there was a camel, with his big soft feet squelching and slipping in the mud, and his neck bobbing to and fro like a strayed hen's. Luckily, I knew enough of beast language—not wild-beast language, but camp-beast language, of course—from the natives to know what he was saying.

He must have been the one that flopped into my tent, for he called to the mule, "What shall I do? Where shall I go? I have fought with a white thing that waved, and it took a stick and hit me on the neck." (That was my broken tent pole, and I was very glad to know it.) "Shall we run on?"

"Oh, it was you," said the mule, "you and your friends, that have been disturbing the camp? All right. You'll be beaten for this in the morning. But I may as well give you something on account now."

I heard the harness jingle as the mule backed and caught the camel two kicks in the ribs that rang like a drum. "Another time," he said, "you'll know better than to run through a mule battery at night, shouting 'Thieves and fire!' Sit down, and keep your silly neck quiet."

The camel doubled up camel-fashion, like a two-foot rule, and sat down whimpering. There was a regular beat of hoofs in the darkness, and a big troop-horse cantered up as steadily as though he were on parade, jumped a gun tail, and landed close to the mule.

"It's disgraceful," he said, blowing out his nostrils. "Those camels

have racketed through our lines again——the third time this week. How's a horse to keep his condition if he isn't allowed to sleep. Who's here?"

"I'm the breech-piece mule of number two gun of the First Screw Battery," said the mule, "and the other's one of your friends. He's waked me up too. Who are you?"

"Number Fifteen, E troop, Ninth Lancers——Dick Cunliffe's horse. Stand over a little, there."

"Oh, beg your pardon," said the mule. "It's too dark to see much. Aren't these camels too sickening for anything? I walked out of my lines to get a little peace and quiet here."

"My lords," said the camel humbly, "we dreamed bad dreams in the night, and we were very much afraid. I am only a baggage-camel of the 39th Native Infantry, and I am not as brave as you are, my lords."

"Then why didn't you stay and carry baggage for the 39th Native Infantry, instead of running all round the camp?" said the mule.

"They were such very bad dreams," said the camel. "I am sorry. Listen! What is that? Shall we run on again?"

"Sit down," said the mule, "or you'll snap your long stick-legs between the guns." He cocked one ear and listened. "Bullocks!" he said. "Gun-bullocks. On my word, you and your friends have waked the camp very thoroughly. It takes a good deal of prodding to put up a gun-bullock."

I heard a chain dragging along the ground, and a yoke of the great sulky white bullocks that drag the heavy siege guns when the elephants won't go any nearer to the firing, came shouldering along together. And almost stepping on the chain was another battery mule, calling wildly for "Billy."

"That's one of our recruits," said the old mule to the troop-horse. "He's calling for me. Here, youngster, stop squealing. The dark never hurt anybody yet."

The gun-bullocks lay down together and began chewing the cud, but the young mule huddled close to Billy.

"Things!" he said. "Fearful and horrible, Billy! They came into our lines while we were asleep. D'you think they'll kill us?"

"I've a very great mind to give you a number-one kicking," said

Billy. "The idea of a fourteen-hand mule with your training disgracing the battery before this gentleman!"

"Gently, gently!" said the troop-horse. "Remember they are always like this to begin with. The first time I ever saw a man (it was in Australia when I was a three-year-old) I ran for half a day, and if I'd seen a camel, I should have been running still."

Nearly all our horses for the English cavalry are brought to India from Australia, and are broken in by the troopers themselves.

"True enough," said Billy. "Stop shaking, youngster. The first time they put the full harness with all its chains on my back I stood on my forelegs and kicked every bit of it off. I hadn't learned the real science of kicking then, but the battery said they had never seen anything like it."

"But this wasn't harness or anything that jingled," said the young mule. "You know I don't mind that now, Billy. It was Things like trees, and they fell up and down the lines and bubbled; and my head-rope broke, and I couldn't find my driver, and I couldn't find you, Billy, so I ran off with—with these gentlemen."

"H'm!" said Billy. "As soon as I heard the camels were loose I came away on my own account. When a battery—a screw-gun mule calls gun-bullocks gentlemen, he must be very badly shaken up. Who are you fellows on the ground there?"

The gun-bullocks rolled their cuds, and answered both together: "The seventh yoke of the first gun of the Big Gun Battery. We were asleep when the camels came, but when we were trampled on we got up and walked away. It is better to lie quiet in the mud than to be disturbed on good bedding. We told your friend here that there was nothing to be afraid of, but he knew so much that he thought otherwise. Wah!"

They went on chewing.

"That comes of being afraid," said Billy. "You get laughed at by gun-bullocks. I hope you like it, young un."

The young mule's teeth snapped, and I heard him say something about not being afraid of any beefy old bullock in the world. But the bullocks only clicked their horns together and went on chewing.

"Now, don't be angry *after* you've been afraid. That's the worst

kind of cowardice," said the troop-horse. "Anybody can be forgiven for being scared in the night, *I* think, if they see things they don't understand. We've broken out of our pickets, again and again, four hundred and fifty of us, just because a new recruit got to telling tales of whip snakes at home in Australia till we were scared to death of the loose ends of our head-ropes."

"That's all very well in camp," said Billy. "I'm not above stampeding myself, for the fun of the thing, when I haven't been out for a day or two. But what do you do on active service?"

"Oh, that's quite another set of new shoes," said the troop-horse. "Dick Cunliffe's on my back then, and drives his knees into me, and all I have to do is to watch where I am putting my feet, and to keep my hind legs well under me, and be bridle-wise."

"What's bridle-wise?" said the young mule.

"By the Blue Gums of the Back Blocks," snorted the troop-horse, "do you mean to say that you aren't taught to be bridle-wise in your business? How can you do anything, unless you can spin round at once when the rein is pressed on your neck? It means life or death to your man, and of course that's life and death to you. Get round with your hind legs under you the instant you feel the rein on your neck. If you haven't room to swing round, rear up a little and come round on your hind legs. That's being bridle-wise."

"We aren't taught that way," said Billy the mule stiffly. "We're taught to obey the man at our head: step off when he says so, and step in when he says so. I suppose it comes to the same thing. Now, with all this fine fancy business and rearing, which must be very bad for your hocks, what do you *do*?"

"That depends," said the troop-horse. "Generally I have to go in among a lot of yelling, hairy men with knives—long shiny knives, worse than the farrier's knives—and I have to take care that Dick's boot is just touching the next man's boot without crushing it. I can see Dick's lance to the right of my right eye, and I know I'm safe. I shouldn't care to be the man or horse that stood up to Dick and me when we're in a hurry."

"Don't the knives hurt?" said the young mule.

"Well, I got one cut across the chest once, but that wasn't Dick's fault—"

"A lot I should have cared whose fault it was, if it hurt!" said the young mule.

"You must," said the troop-horse. "If you don't trust your man, you may as well run away at once. That's what some of our horses do, and I don't blame them. As I was saying, it wasn't Dick's fault. The man was lying on the ground, and I stretched myself not to tread on him, and he slashed up at me. Next time I have to go over a man lying down I shall step on him—hard."

"H'm!" said Billy. "It sounds very foolish. Knives are dirty things at any time. The proper thing to do is to climb up a mountain with a well-balanced saddle, hang on by all four feet and your ears too, and creep and crawl and wriggle along, till you come out hundreds of feet above anyone else on a ledge where there's just room enough for your hoofs. Then you stand still and keep quiet—never ask a man to hold your head, young un—keep quiet while the guns are being put together, and then you watch the little poppy shells drop down into the tree-tops ever so far below."

"Don't you ever trip?" said the troop-horse.

"They say that when a mule trips you can split a hen's ear," said Billy. "Now and again *per-haps* a badly packed saddle will upset a mule, but it's very seldom. I wish I could show you our business. It's beautiful. Why, it took me three years to find out what the men were driving at. The science of the thing is never to show up against the sky line, because, if you do, you may get fired at. Remember that, young un. Always keep hidden as much as possible, even if you have to go a mile out of your way. I lead the battery when it comes to that sort of climbing."

"Fired at without the chance of running into the people who are firing!" said the troop-horse, thinking hard. "I couldn't stand that. I should want to charge—with Dick."

"Oh, no, you wouldn't. You know that as soon as the guns are in position *they'll* do all the charging. That's scientific and neat. But knives—pah!"

The baggage-camel had been bobbing his head to and fro for some time past, anxious to get a word in edgewise. Then I heard him say, as he cleared his throat, nervously:

"I—I—I have fought a little, but not in that climbing way or that running way."

"No. Now you mention it," said Billy, "you don't look as though you were made for climbing or running—much. Well, how was it, old Hay-bales?"

"The proper way," said the camel. "We all sat down—"

"Oh, my crupper and breastplate!" said the troop-horse under his breath. "Sat down!"

"We sat down—a hundred of us," the camel went on, "in a big square, and the men piled our packs and saddles, outside the square, and they fired over our backs, the men did, on all sides of the square."

"What sort of men? Any men that came along?" said the troop-horse. "They teach us in riding school to lie down and let our masters fire across us, but Dick Cunliffe is the only man I'd trust to do that. It tickles my girths, and, besides, I can't see with my head on the ground."

"What does it matter who fires across you?" said the camel. "There are plenty of men and plenty of other camels close by, and a great many clouds of smoke. I am not frightened then. I sit still and wait."

"And yet," said Billy, "you dream bad dreams and upset the camp at night. Well, well! Before I'd lie down, not to speak of sitting down, and let a man fire across me, my heels and his head would have something to say to each other. Did you ever hear anything so awful as that?"

There was a long silence, and then one of the gun-bullocks lifted up his big head and said, "This is very foolish indeed. There is only one way of fighting."

"Oh, go on," said Billy. "*Please* don't mind me. I suppose you fellows fight standing on your tails?"

"Only one way," said the two together. (They must have been twins.) "This is that way. To put all twenty yoke of us to the big gun as soon as Two Tails trumpets." ("Two Tails" is camp slang for the elephant.)

"What does Two Tails trumpet for?" said the young mule.

"To show that he is not going any nearer to the smoke on the other side. Two Tails is a great coward. Then we tug the big gun all together—*Heya—Hullah! Heeyah! Hullah! We* do not climb like cats nor run like calves. We go across the level plain, twenty yoke of us, till we are unyoked again, and we graze while the big guns talk across the plain to some town with mud walls, and pieces of the wall fall out, and the dust goes up as though many cattle were coming home."

"Oh! And you choose that time for grazing?" said the young mule.

"That time or any other. Eating is always good. We eat till we are yoked up again and tug the gun back to where Two Tails is waiting for it. Sometimes there are big guns in the city that speak back, and some of us are killed, and then there is all the more grazing for those that are left. This is Fate. None the less, Two Tails is a great coward. That is the proper way to fight. We are brothers from Hapur. Our father was a sacred bull of Shiva. We have spoken."

"Well, I've certainly learned something tonight," said the troop-horse. "Do you gentlemen of the screw-gun battery feel inclined to eat when you are being fired at with big guns, and Two Tails is behind you?"

"About as much as we feel inclined to sit down and let men sprawl all over us, or run into people with knives. I never heard such stuff. A mountain ledge, a well-balanced load, a driver you can trust to let you pick your own way, and I'm your mule. But—the other things—no!" said Billy, with a stamp of his foot.

"Of course," said the troop-horse, "everyone is not made in the same way, and I can quite see that your family, on your father's side, would fail to understand a great many things."

"Never you mind my family on my father's side," said Billy angrily, for every mule hates to be reminded that his father was a donkey. "My father was a Southern gentleman, and he could pull down and bite and kick into rags every horse he came across. Remember that, you big brown Brumby!"

Brumby means wild horse without any breeding. Imagine the feelings of Sunol if a car-horse called her a "skate," and you can imagine how the Australian horse felt. I saw the white of his eye glitter in the dark.

"See here, you son of an imported Malaga jackass," he said between his teeth, "I'd have you know that I'm related on my mother's side to Carbine, winner of the Melbourne Cup, and where *I* come from we aren't accustomed to being ridden over roughshod by any parrot-mouthed, pig-headed mule in a pop-gun pea-shooter battery. Are you ready?"

"On your hind legs!" squealed Billy. They both reared up facing each other, and I was expecting a furious fight, when a gurgly, rumbly voice, called out of the darkness to the right—"Children, what are you fighting about there? Be quiet."

Both beasts dropped down with a snort of disgust, for neither horse nor mule can bear to listen to an elephant's voice.

"It's Two Tails!" said the troop-horse. "I can't stand him. A tail at each end isn't fair!"

"My feelings exactly," said Billy, crowding into the troop-horse for company. "We're very alike in some things."

"I suppose we've inherited them from our mothers," said the troop-horse. "It's not worth quarreling about. Hi! Two Tails, are you tied up?"

"Yes," said Two Tails, with a laugh all up his trunk. "I'm picketed for the night. I've heard what you fellows have been saying. But don't be afraid. I'm not coming over."

The bullocks and the camel said, half aloud, "Afraid of Two Tails—what nonsense!" And the bullocks went on, "We are sorry that you heard, but it is true. Two Tails, why are you afraid of the guns when they fire?"

"Well," said Two Tails, rubbing one hind leg against the other, exactly like a little boy saying a poem, "I don't quite know whether you'd understand."

"We don't, but we have to pull the guns," said the bullocks.

"I know it, and I know you are a good deal braver than you think you are. But it's different with me. My battery captain called me a Pachydermatous Anachronism the other day."

"That's another way of fighting, I suppose?" said Billy, who was recovering his spirits.

"*You* don't know what that means, of course, but I do. It means betwixt and between, and that is just where I am. I can see inside my head what will happen when a shell bursts, and you bullocks can't."

"I can," said the troop-horse. "At least a little bit. I try not to think about it."

"I can see more than you, and I *do* think about it. I know there's a great deal of me to take care of, and I know that nobody knows how to cure me when I'm sick. All they can do is to stop my driver's pay till I get well, and I can't trust my driver."

"Ah!" said the troop-horse. "That explains it. I can trust Dick."

"You could put a whole regiment of Dicks on my back without making me feel any better. I know just enough to be uncomfortable, and not enough to go on in spite of it."

"We do not understand," said the bullocks.

"I know you don't. I'm not talking to you. You don't know what blood is."

"We do," said the bullocks. "It is red stuff that soaks into the ground and smells."

The troop-horse gave a kick and a bound and a snort.

"Don't talk of it," he said. "I can smell it now, just thinking of it. It makes me want to run—when I haven't Dick on my back."

"But it is not here," said the camel and the bullocks. "Why are you so stupid?"

"It's vile stuff," said Billy. "I don't want to run, but I don't want to talk about it."

"There you are!" said Two Tails, waving his tail to explain.

"Surely. Yes, we have been here all night," said the bullocks.

Two Tails stamped his foot till the iron ring on it jingled. "Oh, I'm not talking to *you*. You can't see inside your heads."

"No. We see out of our four eyes," said the bullocks. "We see straight in front of us."

"If I could do that and nothing else, you wouldn't be needed to pull the big guns at all. If I was like my captain—he can see things inside his head before the firing begins, and he shakes all over, but he knows too much to run away—if I was like him I could pull the guns. But if I

were as wise as all that I should never be here. I should be a king in the forest, as I used to be, sleeping half the day and bathing when I liked. I haven't had a good bath for a month."

"That's all very fine," said Billy. "But giving a thing a long name doesn't make it any better."

"H'sh!" said the troop-horse. "I think I understand what Two Tails means."

"You'll understand better in a minute," said Two Tails angrily. "Now you just explain to me why you don't like *this*!"

He began trumpeting furiously at the top of his trumpet.

"Stop that!" said Billy and the troop-horse together, and I could hear them stamp and shiver. An elephant's trumpeting is always nasty, especially on a dark night.

"I shan't stop," said Two Tails. "Won't you explain that, please? *Hhrrmph! Rrrt! Rrrmph! Rrrhha!*" Then he stopped suddenly, and I heard a little whimper in the dark, and knew that Vixen had found me at last. She knew as well as I did that if there is one thing in the world the elephant is more afraid of than another it is a little barking dog. So she stopped to bully Two Tails in his pickets, and yapped round his big feet. Two Tails shuffled and squeaked. "Go away, little dog!" he said. "Don't snuff at my ankles, or I'll kick at you. Good little dog—nice little doggie, then! Go home, you yelping little beast! Oh, why doesn't someone take her away? She'll bite me in a minute."

"Seems to me," said Billy to the troop-horse, "that our friend Two Tails is afraid of most things. Now, if I had a full meal for every dog I've kicked across the parade-ground I should be as fat as Two Tails nearly."

I whistled, and Vixen ran up to me, muddy all over, and licked my nose, and told me a long tale about hunting for me all through the camp. I never let her know that I understood beast talk, or she would have taken all sorts of liberties. So I buttoned her into the breast of my overcoat, and Two Tails shuffled and stamped and growled to himself.

"Extraordinary! Most extraordinary!" he said. "It runs in our family. Now, where has that nasty little beast gone to?"

I heard him feeling about with his trunk.

"We all seem to be affected in various ways," he went on, blowing his nose. "Now, you gentlemen were alarmed, I believe, when I trumpeted."

"Not alarmed, exactly," said the troop-horse, "but it made me feel as though I had hornets where my saddle ought to be. Don't begin again."

"I'm frightened of a little dog, and the camel here is frightened by bad dreams in the night."

"It is very lucky for us that we haven't all got to fight in the same way," said the troop-horse.

"What I want to know," said the young mule, who had been quiet for a long time—"what *I* want to know is, why we have to fight at all."

"Because we're told to," said the troop-horse, with a snort of contempt.

"Orders," said Billy the mule, and his teeth snapped.

"*Hukm hai!*" (It is an order!), said the camel with a gurgle, and Two Tails and the bullocks repeated, "*Hukm hai!*"

"Yes, but who gives the orders?" said the recruit-mule.

"The man who walks at your head—Or sits on your back—Or holds the nose rope—Or twists your tail," said Billy and the troop-horse and the camel and the bullocks one after the other.

"But who gives them the orders?"

"Now you want to know too much, young un," said Billy, "and that is one way of getting kicked. All you have to do is to obey the man at your head and ask no questions."

"He's quite right," said Two Tails. "I can't always obey, because I'm betwixt and between. But Billy's right. Obey the man next to you who gives the order, or you'll stop all the battery, besides getting a thrashing."

The gun-bullocks got up to go. "Morning is coming," they said. "We will go back to our lines. It is true that we only see out of our eyes, and we are not very clever. But still, we are the only people to-night who have not been afraid. Good-night, you brave people."

Nobody answered, and the troop-horse said, to change the conversation, "Where's that little dog? A dog means a man somewhere about."

"Here I am," yapped Vixen, "under the gun tail with my man. You big, blundering beast of a camel you, you upset our tent. My man's very angry."

"Phew!" said the bullocks. "He must be white!"

"Of course he is," said Vixen. "Do you suppose I'm looked after by a black bullock-driver?"

"*Huah! Ouach! Ugh!*" said the bullocks. "Let us get away quickly."

They plunged forward in the mud, and managed somehow to run their yoke on the pole of an ammunition wagon, where it jammed.

"Now you *have* done it," said Billy calmly. "Don't struggle. You're hung up till daylight. What on earth's the matter?"

The bullocks went off into the long hissing snorts that Indian cattle give, and pushed and crowded and slued and stamped and slipped and nearly fell down in the mud, grunting savagely.

"You'll break your necks in a minute," said the troop-horse. "What's the matter with white men? I live with 'em."

"They—eat—us! Pull!" said the near bullock. The yoke snapped with a twang, and they lumbered off together.

I never knew before what made Indian cattle so scared of Englishmen. We eat beef—a thing that no cattle-driver touches—and of course the cattle do not like it.

"May I be flogged with my own pad-chains! Who'd have thought of two big lumps like those losing their heads?" said Billy.

"Never mind. I'm going to look at this man. Most of the white men, I know, have things in their pockets," said the troop-horse.

"I'll leave you, then. I can't say I'm over-fond of 'em myself. Besides, white men who haven't a place to sleep in are more than likely to be thieves, and I've a good deal of Government property on my back. Come along, young un, and we'll go back to our lines. Good-night, Australia! See you on parade to-morrow, I suppose. Good-night, old Hay-bale!—try to control your feelings, won't you? Good-night, Two Tails! If you pass us on the ground to-morrow, don't trumpet. It spoils our formation."

Billy the Mule stumped off with the swaggering limp of an old campaigner, as the troop-horse's head came nuzzling into my breast,

and I gave him biscuits, while Vixen, who is a most conceited little dog, told him fibs about the scores of horses that she and I kept.

"I'm coming to the parade to-morrow in my dog-cart," she said. "Where will you be?"

"On the left hand of the second squadron. I set the time for all my troop, little lady," he said politely. "Now I must go back to Dick. My tail's all muddy, and he'll have two hours' hard work dressing me for parade."

The big parade of all the thirty thousand men was held that afternoon, and Vixen and I had a good place close to the Viceroy and the Amir of Afghanistan, with high, big black hat of astrakhan wool and the great diamond star in the centre. The first part of the review was all sunshine, and the regiments went by in wave upon wave of legs all moving together, and guns all in a line, till our eyes grew dizzy. Then the cavalry came up, to the beautiful cavalry canter of "Bonnie Dundee," and Vixen cocked her ear where she sat on the dog-cart. The second squadron of the Lancers shot by, and there was the troop-horse, with his tail like spun silk, his head pulled into his breast, one ear forward and one back, setting the time for all his squadron, his legs going as smoothly as waltz music. Then the big guns came by, and I saw Two Tails and two other elephants harnessed in line to a forty-pounder siege gun, while twenty yoke of oxen walked behind. The seventh pair had a new yoke, and they looked rather stiff and tired. Last came the screw-guns, and Billy the mule carried himself as though he commanded all the troops, and his harness was oiled and polished till it winked. I gave a cheer all by myself for Billy the mule, but he never looked right or left.

The rain began to fall again, and for a while it was too misty to see what the troops were doing. They had made a big half circle across the plain, and were spreading out into a line. That line grew and grew and grew till it was three-quarters of a mile long from wing to wing—one solid wall of men, horses, and guns. Then it came on straight toward the Viceroy and the Amir, and as it got nearer the ground began to shake, like the deck of a steamer when the engines are going fast.

Unless you have been there you cannot imagine what a frightening

effect this steady come-down of troops has on the spectators, even when they know it is only a review. I looked at the Amir. Up till then he had not shown the shadow of a sign of astonishment or anything else. But now his eyes began to get bigger and bigger, and he picked up the reins on his horse's neck and looked behind him. For a minute it seemed as though he were going to draw his sword and slash his way out through the English men and women in the carriages at the back. Then the advance stopped dead, the ground stood still, the whole line saluted, and thirty bands began to play all together. That was the end of the review, and the regiments went off to their camps in the rain, and an infantry band struck up with—

> The animals went in two by two,
> > Hurrah!
> The animals went in two by two,
> The elephant and the battery mu-l',
> and they all got into the Ark
> > For to get out of the rain!

Then I heard an old grizzled, long-haired Central Asian chief, who had come down with the Amir, asking questions of a native officer.

"Now," said he, "in what manner was this wonderful thing done?"

And the officer answered, "An order was given, and they obeyed."

"But are the beasts as wise as the men?" said the chief.

"They obey, as the men do. Mule, horse, elephant, or bullock, he obeys his driver, and the driver his sergeant, and the sergeant his lieutenant, and the lieutenant his captain, and the captain his major, and the major his colonel, and the colonel his brigadier commanding three regiments, and the brigadier the general, who obeys the Viceroy, who is the servant of the Empress. Thus it is done."

"Would it were so in Afghanistan!" said the chief, "for there we obey only our own wills."

"And for that reason," said the native officer, twirling his mustache, "your Amir whom you do not obey must come here and take orders from our Viceroy."

14. PARADE SONG OF THE CAMP ANIMALS

ELEPHANTS OF THE GUN TEAMS

We lent to Alexander the strength of Hercules,
The wisdom of our foreheads, the cunning of our knees;
We bowed our necks to service: they ne'er were loosed
 again,—
Make way there—way for the ten-foot teams
Of the Forty-Pounder train!

GUN-BULLOCKS

Those heroes in their harnesses avoid a cannon-ball,
And what they know of powder upsets them one and all;
Then *we* come into action and tug the guns again—
Make way there—way for the twenty yoke
Of the Forty-Pounder train!

CAVALRY HORSES

By the brand on my shoulder, the finest of tunes
Is played by the Lancers, Hussars, and Dragoons,
And it's sweeter than "Stables" or "Water" to me—
The Cavalry Canter of "Bonnie Dundee"!
Then feed us and break us and handle and groom,
And give us good riders and plenty of room,
And launch us in column of squadron and see
The way of the war-horse to "Bonnie Dundee"!

SCREW-GUN MULES

As me and my companions were scrambling up a hill,

The path was lost in rolling stones, but we went forward
 still;
For we can wriggle and climb, my lads, and turn up
 everywhere,
Oh, it's our delight on a mountain height, with a leg or two
 to spare!
Good luck to every sergeant, then, that lets us pick our road;
Bad luck to all the driver-men that cannot pack a load:
For we can wriggle and climb, my lads, and turn up
 everywhere,
Oh, it's our delight on a mountain height, with a leg or two
 to spare!

COMMISSARIAT CAMELS

We haven't a camelty tune of our own
To help us trollop along,
But every neck is a hair trombone
(*Rtt-ta-ta-ta!* is a hair trombone!)
And this our marching-song:
Can't! Don't! Shan't! Won't!
Pass it along the line!
Somebody's pack has slid from his back,
Wish it were only mine!
Somebody's load has tipped off in the road—
Cheer for a halt and a row!
Urrr! Yarrh! Grr! Arrh!
Somebody's catching it now!

ALL THE BEASTS TOGETHER

Children of the Camp are we,
Serving each in his degree;
Children of the yoke and goad,
Pack and harness, pad and load.
See our line across the plain,
Like a heel-rope bent again,
Reaching, writhing, rolling far,

Sweeping all away to war!
While the men that walk beside,
Dusty, silent, heavy-eyed,
Cannot tell why we or they
March and suffer day by day.

> *Children of the Camp are we,*
> *Serving each in his degree;*
> *Children of the yoke and goad,*
> *Pack and harness, pad and load!*

The Second Jungle Book

1. HOW FEAR CAME

The stream is shrunk—the pool is dry,
And we be comrades, thou and I;
With fevered jowl and dusty flank
Each jostling each along the bank;
And by one drouthy fear made still,
Forgoing thought of quest or kill.
Now 'neath his dam the fawn may see,
The lean Pack-wolf as cowed as he,
And the tall buck, unflinching, note
The fangs that tore his father's throat.
The pools are shrunk—the streams are dry,
And we be playmates, thou and I,
Till yonder cloud—Good Hunting!—loose
The rain that breaks our Water Truce.

The Law of the Jungle—which is by far the oldest law in the world—has arranged for almost every kind of accident that may befall the Jungle People, till now its code is as perfect as time and custom can make it. You will remember that Mowgli spent a great part of his life in the Seeonee Wolf-Pack, learning the Law from Baloo, the Brown Bear; and it was Baloo who told him, when the boy grew impatient at the constant orders, that the Law was like the Giant Creeper, because it dropped across every one's back and no one could escape. "When thou hast lived as long as I have, Little Brother, thou wilt see how all the Jungle obeys at least one Law. And that will be no pleasant sight," said Baloo.

This talk went in at one ear and out at the other, for a boy who spends his life eating and sleeping does not worry about anything till it actually stares him in the face. But, one year, Baloo's words came true, and Mowgli saw all the Jungle working under the Law.

It began when the winter Rains failed almost entirely, and Ikki, the Porcupine, meeting Mowgli in a bamboo-thicket, told him that the wild yams were drying up. Now everybody knows that Ikki is ridiculously fastidious in his choice of food, and will eat nothing but the very best and ripest. So Mowgli laughed and said, What is that to me?"

"Not much *now*," said Ikki, rattling his quills in a stiff, uncomfortable way, "but later we shall see. Is there any more diving into the deep rock-pool below the Bee-Rocks, Little Brother?"

"No. The foolish water is going all away, and I do not wish to break my head," said Mowgli, who, in those days, was quite sure that he knew as much as any five of the Jungle People put together.

"That is thy loss. A small crack might let in some wisdom." Ikki ducked quickly to prevent Mowgli from pulling his nose-bristles, and Mowgli told Baloo what Ikki had said. Baloo looked very grave, and mumbled half to himself: "If I were alone I would change my hunting-grounds now, before the others began to think. And yet—hunting among strangers ends in fighting; and they might hurt the Man-cub. We must wait and see how the *mohwa* blooms."

That spring the *mohwa* tree, that Baloo was so fond of, never flowered. The greeny, cream-coloured, waxy blossoms were heat-killed before they were born, and only a few bad-smelling petals came down when he stood on his hind legs and shook the tree. Then, inch by inch, the untempered heat crept into the heart of the Jungle, turning it yellow, brown, and at last black. The green growths in the sides of the ravines burned up to broken wires and curled films of dead stuff; the hidden pools sank down and caked over, keeping the last least footmark on their edges as if it had been cast in iron; the juicy-stemmed creepers fell away from the trees they clung to and died at their feet; the bamboos withered, clanking when the hot winds blew, and the moss peeled off the rocks deep in the Jungle, till they were as bare and as hot as the quivering blue boulders in the bed of the stream.

The birds and the monkey-people went north early in the year, for they knew what was coming; and the deer and the wild pig broke far away to the perished fields of the villages, dying sometimes before the eyes of men too weak to kill them. Chil, the Kite, stayed and grew

fat, for there was a great deal of carrion, and evening after evening he brought the news to the beasts, too weak to force their way to fresh hunting-grounds, that the sun was killing the Jungle for three days' flight in every direction.

Mowgli, who had never known what real hunger meant, fell back on stale honey, three years old, scraped out of deserted rock-hives—honey black as a sloe, and dusty with dried sugar. He hunted, too, for deep-boring grubs under the bark of the trees, and robbed the wasps of their new broods. All the game in the jungle was no more than skin and bone, and Bagheera could kill thrice in a night, and hardly get a full meal. But the want of water was the worst, for though the Jungle People drink seldom they must drink deep.

And the heat went on and on, and sucked up all the moisture, till at last the main channel of the Waingunga was the only stream that carried a trickle of water between its dead banks; and when Hathi, the wild elephant, who lives for a hundred years and more, saw a long, lean blue ridge of rock show dry in the very centre of the stream, he knew that he was looking at the Peace Rock, and then and there he lifted up his trunk and proclaimed the Water Truce, as his father before him had proclaimed it fifty years ago. The deer, wild pig, and buffalo took up the cry hoarsely; and Chil, the Kite, flew in great circles far and wide, whistling and shrieking the warning.

By the Law of the Jungle it is death to kill at the drinking-places when once the Water Truce has been declared. The reason of this is that drinking comes before eating. Every one in the Jungle can scramble along somehow when only game is scarce; but water is water, and when there is but one source of supply, all hunting stops while the Jungle People go there for their needs. In good seasons, when water was plentiful, those who came down to drink at the Waingunga—or anywhere else, for that matter—did so at the risk of their lives, and that risk made no small part of the fascination of the night's doings. To move down so cunningly that never a leaf stirred; to wade knee-deep in the roaring shallows that drown all noise from behind; to drink, looking backward over one shoulder, every muscle ready for the first desperate bound of keen terror; to roll on the sandy margin, and

return, wet-muzzled and well plumped out, to the admiring herd, was a thing that all tall-antlered young bucks took a delight in, precisely because they knew that at any moment Bagheera or Shere Khan might leap upon them and bear them down. But now all that life-and-death fun was ended, and the Jungle People came up, starved and weary, to the shrunken river,—tiger, bear, deer, buffalo, and pig, all together,— drank the fouled waters, and hung above them, too exhausted to move off.

The deer and the pig had tramped all day in search of something better than dried bark and withered leaves. The buffaloes had found no wallows to be cool in, and no green crops to steal. The snakes had left the Jungle and come down to the river in the hope of finding a stray frog. They curled round wet stones, and never offered to strike when the nose of a rooting pig dislodged them. The river-turtles had long ago been killed by Bagheera, cleverest of hunters, and the fish had buried themselves deep in the dry mud. Only the Peace Rock lay across the shallows like a long snake, and the little tired ripples hissed as they dried on its hot side.

It was here that Mowgli came nightly for the cool and the companionship. The most hungry of his enemies would hardly have cared for the boy then, His naked hide made him seem more lean and wretched than any of his fellows. His hair was bleached to tow colour by the sun; his ribs stood out like the ribs of a basket, and the lumps on his knees and elbows, where he was used to track on all fours, gave his shrunken limbs the look of knotted grass-stems. But his eye, under his matted forelock, was cool and quiet, for Bagheera was his adviser in this time of trouble, and told him to go quietly, hunt slowly, and never, on any account, to lose his temper.

"It is an evil time," said the Black Panther, one furnace-hot evening, "but it will go if we can live till the end. Is thy stomach full, Man-cub?"

"There is stuff in my stomach, but I get no good of it. Think you, Bagheera, the Rains have forgotten us and will never come again?"

"Not I! We shall see the *mohwa* in blossom yet, and the little fawns all fat with new grass. Come down to the Peace Rock and hear the news. On my back, Little Brother."

"This is no time to carry weight. I can still stand alone, but—indeed we be no fatted bullocks, we two."

Bagheera looked along his ragged, dusty flank and whispered. "Last night I killed a bullock under the yoke. So low was I brought that I think I should not have dared to spring if he had been loose. *Wou!*"

Mowgli laughed. "Yes, we be great hunters now," said he. "I am very bold—to eat grubs," and the two came down together through the crackling undergrowth to the river-bank and the lace-work of shoals that ran out from it in every direction.

"The water cannot live long," said Baloo, joining them. "Look across. Yonder are trails like the roads of Man."

On the level plain of the farther bank the stiff jungle-grass had died standing, and, dying, had mummied. The beaten tracks of the deer and the pig, all heading toward the river, had striped that colourless plain with dusty gullies driven through the ten-foot grass, and, early as it was, each long avenue was full of first-comers hastening to the water. You could hear the does and fawns coughing in the snuff-like dust.

Up-stream, at the bend of the sluggish pool round the Peace Rock, and Warden of the Water Truce, stood Hathi, the wild elephant, with his sons, gaunt and gray in the moonlight, rocking to and fro—always rocking. Below him a little were the vanguard of the deer; below these, again, the pig and the wild buffalo; and on the opposite bank, where the tall trees came down to the water's edge, was the place set apart for the Eaters of Flesh—the tiger, the wolves, the panther, the bear, and the others.

"We are under one Law, indeed," said Bagheera, wading into the water and looking across at the lines of clicking horns and starting eyes where the deer and the pig pushed each other to and fro. "Good hunting, all you of my blood," he added, lying own at full length, one flank thrust out of the shallows; and then, between his teeth, "But for that which is the Law it would be *very* good hunting."

The quick-spread ears of the deer caught the last sentence, and a frightened whisper ran along the ranks. "The Truce! Remember the Truce!"

"Peace there, peace!" gurgled Hathi, the wild elephant. "The Truce holds, Bagheera. This is no time to talk of hunting."

"Who should know better than I?" Bagheera answered, rolling his yellow eyes up-stream. "I am an eater of turtles—a fisher of frogs. *Ngaa-yah!* Would I could get good from chewing branches!"

"*We* wish so, very greatly," bleated a young fawn, who had only been born that spring, and did not at all like it. Wretched as the Jungle People were, even Hathi could not help chuckling; while Mowgli, lying on his elbows in the warm water, laughed aloud, and beat up the scum with his feet.

"Well spoken, little bud-horn," Bagheera purred. "When the Truce ends that shall be remembered in thy favour," and he looked keenly through the darkness to make sure of recognising the fawn again.

Gradually the talking spread up and down the drinking-places. One could hear the scuffling, snorting pig asking for more room; the buffaloes grunting among themselves as they lurched out across the sand-bars, and the deer telling pitiful stories of their long foot-sore wanderings in quest of food. Now and again they asked some question of the Eaters of Flesh across the river, but all the news was bad, and the roaring hot wind of the Jungle came and went between the rocks and the rattling branches, and scattered twigs, and dust on the water.

"The men-folk, too, they die beside their ploughs," said a young *sambhur*. "I passed three between sunset and night. They lay still, and their Bullocks with them. We also shall lie still in a little."

"The river has fallen since last night," said Baloo. "O Hathi, hast thou ever seen the like of this drought?"

"It will pass, it will pass," said Hathi, squirting water along his back and sides.

"We have one here that cannot endure long," said Baloo; and he looked toward the boy he loved.

"I?" said Mowgli indignantly, sitting up in the water. "I have no long fur to cover my bones, but—but if *thy* hide were taken off, Baloo—"

Hathi shook all over at the idea, and Baloo said severely:

"Man-cub, that is not seemly to tell a Teacher of the Law. *Never* have I been seen without my hide."

"Nay, I meant no harm, Baloo; but only that thou art, as it were, like the cocoanut in the husk, and I am the same cocoanut all naked. Now that brown husk of thine—" Mowgli was sitting cross-legged, and explaining things with his forefinger in his usual way, when Bagheera put out a paddy paw and pulled him over backward into the water.

"Worse and worse," said the Black Panther, as the boy rose spluttering. "First Baloo is to be skinned, and now he is a cocoanut. Be careful that he does not do what the ripe cocoanuts do."

"And what is that?" said Mowgli, off his guard for the minute, though that is one of the oldest catches in the Jungle.

"Break thy head," said Bagheera quietly, pulling him under again.

"It is not good to make a jest of thy teacher," said the bear, when Mowgli had been ducked for the third time.

"Not good! What would ye have? That naked thing running to and fro makes a monkey-jest of those who have once been good hunters, and pulls the best of us by the whiskers for sport." This was Shere Khan, the Lame Tiger, limping down to the water. He waited a little to enjoy the sensation he made among the deer on the opposite to lap, growling: "The jungle has become a whelping-ground for naked cubs now. Look at me, Man-cub!"

Mowgli looked—stared, rather—as insolently as he knew how, and in a minute Shere Khan turned away uneasily. "Man-cub this, and Man-cub that," he rumbled, going on with his drink, "the cub is neither man nor cub, or he would have been afraid. Next season I shall have to beg his leave for a drink. *Augrh!*"

"That may come, too," said Bagheera, looking him steadily between the eyes. "That may come, too—Faugh, Shere Khan!—what new shame hast thou brought here?"

The Lame Tiger had dipped his chin and jowl in the water, and dark, oily streaks were floating from it down-stream.

"Man!" said Shere Khan coolly, "I killed an hour since." He went on purring and growling to himself.

The line of beasts shook and wavered to and fro, and a whisper went up that grew to a cry. "Man! Man! He has killed Man!" Then all looked towards Hathi, the wild elephant, but he seemed not to hear. Hathi

never does anything till the time comes, and that is one of the reasons why he lives so long.

"At such a season as this to kill Man! Was no other game afoot?" said Bagheera scornfully, drawing himself out of the tainted water, and shaking each paw, cat-fashion, as he did so.

"I killed for choice—not for food." The horrified whisper began again, and Hathi's watchful little white eye cocked itself in Shere Khan's direction. "For choice," Shere Khan drawled. "Now come I to drink and make me clean again. Is there any to forbid?"

Bagheera's back began to curve like a bamboo in a high wind, but Hathi lifted up his trunk and spoke quietly.

"Thy kill was from choice?" he asked; and when Hathi asks a question it is best to answer.

"Even so. It was my right and my Night. Thou knowest, O Hathi." Shere Khan spoke almost courteously.

"Yes, I know," Hathi answered; and, after a little silence, "Hast thou drunk thy fill?"

"For to-night, yes."

"Go, then. The river is to drink, and not to defile. None but the Lame Tiger would so have boasted of his right at this season when—when we suffer together—Man and Jungle People alike. Clean or unclean, get to thy lair, Shere Khan!"

The last words rang out like silver trumpets, and Hathi's three sons rolled forward half a pace, though there was no need. Shere Khan slunk away, not daring to growl, for he knew—what every one else knows—that when the last comes to the last, Hathi is the Master of the Jungle.

"What is this right Shere Khan speaks of?" Mowgli whispered in Bagheera's ear. "To kill Man is *always* shameful. The Law says so. And yet Hathi says—"

"Ask him. I do not know, Little Brother. Right or no right, if Hathi had not spoken I would have taught that lame butcher his lesson. To come to the Peace Rock fresh from a kill of Man—and to boast of it—is a jackal's trick. Besides, he tainted the good water."

Mowgli waited for a minute to pick up his courage, because no one cared to address Hathi directly, and then he cried: "What is Shere Khan's

right, O Hathi?" Both banks echoed his words, for all the People of the Jungle are intensely curious, and they had just seen something that none except Baloo, who looked very thoughtful, seemed to understand.

"It is an old tale," said Hathi; "a tale older than the Jungle. Keep silence along the banks and I will tell that tale."

There was a minute or two of pushing a shouldering among the pigs and the buffalo, and then the leaders of the herds grunted, one after another, "We wait," and Hathi strode forward, till he was nearly knee-deep in the pool by the Peace Rock. Lean and wrinkled and yellow-tusked though he was, he looked what the Jungle knew him to be—their master.

"Ye know, children," he began, "that of all things ye most fear Man;" and there was a mutter of agreement.

"This tale touches thee, Little Brother," said Bagheera to Mowgli.

"I? I am of the Pack—a hunter of the Free People," Mowgli answered. "What have I to do with Man?"

"And ye do not know why ye fear Man?" Hathi went on. "This is the reason. In the beginning of the Jungle, and none know when that was, we of the Jungle walked together, having no fear of one another. In those days there was no drought, and leaves and flowers and fruit grew on the same tree, and we ate nothing at all except leaves and flowers and grass and fruit and bark."

"I am glad I was not born in those days," said Bagheera. "Bark is only good to sharpen claws."

"And the Lord of the Jungle was Tha, the First of the Elephants. He drew the Jungle out of deep waters with his trunk; and where he made furrows in the ground with his tusks, there the rivers ran; and where he struck with his foot, there rose ponds of good water; and when he blew through his trunk,—thus,—the trees fell. That was the manner in which the Jungle was made by Tha; and so the tale was told to me."

"It has not lost fat in the telling," Bagheera whispered, and Mowgli laughed behind his hand.

"In those days there was no corn or melons or pepper or sugar-cane, nor were there any little huts such as ye have all seen; and the Jungle People knew nothing of Man, but lived in the Jungle together, making

one people. But presently they began to dispute over their food, though there was grazing enough for all. They were lazy. Each wished to eat where he lay, as sometimes we can do now when the spring rains are good. Tha, the First of the Elephants, was busy making new jungles and leading the rivers in their beds. He could not walk in all places; therefore he made the First of the Tigers the master and the judge of the Jungle, to whom the Jungle People should bring their disputes. In those days the First of the Tigers ate fruit and grass with the others. He was as large as I am, and he was very beautiful, in colour all over like the blossom of the yellow creeper. There was never stripe nor bar upon his hide in those good days when this the Jungle was new. All the Jungle People came before him without fear, and his word was the Law of all the Jungle. We were then, remember ye, one people.

"Yet upon a night there was a dispute between two bucks—a grazing-quarrel such as ye now settle with the horns and the fore-feet—and it is said that as the two spoke together before the First of the First of the Tigers lying among the flowers, a buck pushed him with his horns, and the First of the Tigers forgot that he was the master and judge of the Jungle, and, leaping upon that buck, broke his neck.

"Till that night never one of us had died, and the First of the Tigers, seeing what he had done, and being made foolish by the scent of the blood, ran away into the marshes of the North, and we of the Jungle, left without a judge, fell to fighting among ourselves; and Tha heard the noise of it and came back. Then some of us said this and some of us said that, but he saw the dead buck among the flowers, and asked who had killed, and we of the Jungle would not tell because the smell of the blood made us foolish. We ran to and fro in circles, capering and crying out and shaking our heads. Then Tha gave an order to the trees that hang low, and to the trailing creepers of the Jungle, that they should mark the killer of the buck so that he should know him again, and he said, 'Who will now be master of the Jungle People?' Then up leaped the Gray Ape who lives in the branches, and said, 'I will now be master of the Jungle.'"

At this Tha laughed, and said, "So be it," and went away very angry.

"Children, ye know the Gray Ape. He was then as he is now. At the

first he made a wise face for himself, but in a little while he began to scratch and to leap up and down, and when Tha came back he found the Gray Ape hanging, head down, from a bough, mocking those who stood below; and they mocked him again. And so there was no Law in the Jungle—only foolish talk and senseless words.

"Then Tha called us all together and said: 'The first of your masters has brought Death into the Jungle, and the second Shame. Now it is time there was a Law, and a Law that ye must not break. Now ye shall know Fear, and when ye have found him ye shall know that he is your master, and the rest shall follow.' Then we of the jungle said, 'What is Fear?' And Tha said, 'Seek till ye find.' So we went up and down the Jungle seeking for Fear, and presently the buffaloes—"

"Ugh!" said Mysa, the leader of the buffaloes, from their sand-bank.

"Yes, Mysa, it was the buffaloes. They came back with the news that in a cave in the Jungle sat Fear, and that he had no hair, and went upon his hind legs. Then we of the Jungle followed the herd till we came to that cave, and Fear stood at the mouth of it, and he was, as the buffaloes had said, hairless, and he walked upon his hinder legs. When he saw us he cried out, and his voice filled us with the fear that we have now of that voice when we hear it, and we ran away, tramping upon and tearing each other because we were afraid. That night, so it was told to me, we of the Jungle did not lie down together as used to be our custom, but each tribe drew off by itself—the pig with the pig, the deer with the deer; horn to horn, hoof to hoof,—like keeping to like, and so lay shaking in the Jungle.

"Only the First of the Tigers was not with us, for he was still hidden in the marshes of the North, and when word was brought to him of the Thing we had seen in the cave, he said. 'I will go to this Thing and break his neck.' So he ran all the night till he came to the cave; but the trees and the creepers on his path, remembering the order that Tha had given, let down their branches and marked him as he ran, drawing their fingers across his back, his flank, his forehead, and his jowl. Wherever they touched him there was a mark and a stripe upon his yellow hide. *And those stripes do his children wear to this day!* When he came to the cave, Fear, the Hairless One, put out his hand and called him 'The

Striped One that comes by night,' and the First of the Tigers was afraid
of the Hairless One, and ran back to the swamps howling."

Mowgli chuckled quietly here, his chin in the water.

"So loud did he howl that Tha heard him and said, 'What is the
sorrow?' And the First of the Tigers, lifting up his muzzle to the new-
made sky, which is now so old, said: 'Give me back my power, O Tha.
I am made ashamed before all the Jungle, and I have run away from a
Hairless One, and he has called me a shameful name.' 'And why?' said
Tha. 'Because I am smeared with the mud of the marshes,' said the
First of the Tigers. 'Swim, then, and roll on the wet grass, and if it be
mud it will wash away,' said Tha; and the First of the Tigers swam, and
rolled and rolled upon the grass, till the Jungle ran round and round
before his eyes, but not one little bar upon all his hide was changed, and
Tha, watching him, laughed. Then the First of the Tigers said: 'What
have I done that this comes to me?' Tha said, 'Thou hast killed the
buck, and thou hast let Death loose in the Jungle, and with Death has
come Fear, so that the people of the Jungle are afraid one of the other,
as thou art afraid of the Hairless One.' The First of the Tigers said,
'They will never fear me, for I knew them since the beginning.' Tha
said, 'Go and see.' And the First of the Tigers ran to and fro, calling
aloud to the deer and the pig and the *sambhur* and the porcupine and all
the Jungle Peoples, and they all ran away from him who had been their
judge, because they were afraid.

"Then the First of the Tigers came back, and his pride was broken
in him, and, beating his head upon the ground, he tore up the earth
with all his feet and said: 'Remember that I was once the Master of the
Jungle. Do not forget me, O Tha! Let my children remember that I
was once without shame or fear!' And Tha said: 'This much I will do,
because thou and I together saw the Jungle made. For one night in each
year it shall be as it was before the buck was killed—for thee and for
thy children. In that one night, if ye meet the Hairless One—and his
name is Man—ye shall not be afraid of him, but he shall be afraid of
you, as though ye were judges of the Jungle and masters of all things.
Show him mercy in that night of his fear, for thou hast known what
Fear is.'

"Then the First of the Tigers answered, 'I am content'; but when next he drank he saw the black stripes upon his flank and his side, and he remembered the name that the Hairless One had given him, and he was angry. For a year he lived in the marshes waiting till Tha should keep his promise. And upon a night when the jackal of the Moon [the Evening Star] stood clear of the Jungle, he felt that his Night was upon him, and he went to that cave to meet the Hairless One. Then it happened as Tha promised, for the Hairless One fell down before him and lay along the ground, and the First of the Tigers struck him and broke his back, for he thought that there was but one such Thing in the Jungle, and that he had killed Fear. Then, nosing above the kill, he heard Tha coming down from the woods of the North, and presently the voice of the First of the Elephants, which is the voice that we hear now—"

The thunder was rolling up and down the dry, scarred hills, but it brought no rain—only heat—lightning that flickered along the ridges—and Hathi went on: "*That* was the voice he heard, and it said: 'Is this thy mercy?' The First of the Tigers licked his lips and said: 'What matter? I have killed Fear.' And Tha said: 'O blind and foolish! Thou hast untied the feet of Death, and he will follow thy trail till thou diest. Thou hast taught Man to kill!'

"The First of the Tigers, standing stiffly to his kill, said. 'He is as the buck was. There is no Fear. Now I will judge the Jungle Peoples once more.'

"And Tha said: 'Never again shall the Jungle Peoples come to thee. They shall never cross thy trail, nor sleep near thee, nor follow after thee, nor browse by thy lair. Only Fear shall follow thee, and with a blow that thou canst not see he shall bid thee wait his pleasure. He shall make the ground to open under thy feet, and the creeper to twist about thy neck, and the tree-trunks to grow together about thee higher than thou canst leap, and at the last he shall take thy hide to wrap his cubs when they are cold. Thou hast shown him no mercy, and none will he show thee.'

"The First of the Tigers was very bold, for his Night was still on him, and he said: 'The Promise of Tha is the Promise of Tha. He will not take away my Night?' And Tha said: 'The one Night is thine, as I

have said, but there is a price to pay. Thou hast taught Man to kill, and he is no slow learner.'

"The First of the Tigers said: 'He is here under my foot, and his back is broken. Let the Jungle know I have killed Fear.'

"Then Tha laughed, and said: 'Thou hast killed one of many, but thou thyself shalt tell the Jungle—for thy Night is ended.'

"So the day came; and from the mouth of the cave went out another Hairless One, and he saw the kill in the path, and the First of the Tigers above it, and he took a pointed stick—"

"They throw a thing that cuts now," said Ikki, rustling down the bank; for Ikki was considered uncommonly good eating by the Gonds—they called him Ho-Igoo—and he knew something of the wicked little Gondee axe that whirls across a clearing like a dragon-fly.

"It was a pointed stick, such as they put in the foot of a pit-trap," said Hathi, "and throwing it, he struck the First of the Tigers deep in the flank. Thus it happened as Tha said, for the First of the Tigers ran howling up and down the Jungle till he tore out the stick, and all the Jungle knew that the Hairless One could strike from far off, and they feared more than before. So it came about that the First of the Tigers taught the Hairless One to kill—and ye know what harm that has since done to all our peoples—through the noose, and the pitfall, and the hidden trap, and the flying stick and the stinging fly that comes out of white smoke [Hathi meant the rifle], and the Red Flower that drives us into the open. Yet for one night in the year the Hairless One fears the Tiger, as Tha promised, and never has the Tiger given him cause to be less afraid. Where he finds him, there he kills him, remembering how the First of the Tigers was made ashamed. For the rest, Fear walks up and down the Jungle by day and by night."

"*Ahi! Aoo!*" said the deer, thinking of what it all meant to them.

"And only when there is one great Fear over all, as there is now, can we of the Jungle lay aside our little fears, and meet together in one place as we do now."

"For one night only does Man fear the Tiger?" said Mowgli.

"For one night only," said Hathi.

"But I—but we—but all the Jungle knows that Shere Khan kills Man twice and thrice in a moon."

"Even so. *Then* he springs from behind and turns his head aside as he strikes, for he is full of fear. If Man looked at him he would run. But on his one Night he goes openly down to the village. He walks between the houses and thrusts his head into the doorway, and the men fall on their faces, and there he does his kill. One kill in that Night."

"Oh!" said Mowgli to himself, rolling over in the water. "*Now* I see why it was Shere Khan bade me look at him! He got no good of it, for he could not hold his eyes steady, and—and I certainly did not fall down at his feet. But then I am not a man, being of the Free People."

"Umm!" said Bagheera deep in his furry throat. "Does the Tiger know his Night?"

"Never till the Jackal of the Moon stands clear of the evening mist. Sometimes it falls in the dry summer and sometimes in the wet rains— this one Night of the Tiger. But for the First of the Tigers, this would never have been, nor would any of us have known fear."

The deer grunted sorrowfully and Bagheera's lips curled in a wicked smile. "Do men know this—tale?" said he.

"None know it except the tigers, and we, the elephants—the children of Tha. Now ye by the pools have heard it, and I have spoken."

Hathi dipped his trunk into the water as a sign that he did not wish to talk.

"But—but—but," said Mowgli, turning to Baloo, "why did not the First of the Tigers continue to eat grass and leaves and trees? He did but break the buck's neck. He did not *eat*. What led him to the hot meat?"

"The trees and the creepers marked him, Little Brother, and made him the striped thing that we see. Never again would he eat their fruit; but from that day he revenged himself upon the deer, and the others, the Eaters of Grass," said Baloo.

"Then *thou* knowest the tale. Heh? Why have I never heard?"

"Because the Jungle is full of such tales. If I made a beginning there would never be an end to them. Let go my ear, Little Brother."

2. THE LAW OF THE JUNGLE

Just to give you an idea of the immense variety of the Jungle Law, I have translated into verse (Baloo always recited them in a sort of sing-song) a few of the laws that apply to the wolves. There are, of course, hundreds and hundreds more, but these will do for specimens of the simpler rulings.

Now this is the Law of the Jungle—as old and as true as the
 sky;
And the Wolf that shall keep it may prosper, but the Wolf
 that shall break it must die.
As the creeper that girdles the tree-trunk the Law runneth
 forward and back—
For the strength of the Pack is the Wolf, and the strength of
 the Wolf is the Pack.

Wash daily from nose-tip to tail-tip; drink deeply, but never too
 deep;
And remember the night is for hunting, and forget not the day is
 for sleep.

The jackal may follow the Tiger, but, Cub, when thy whiskers
 are grown,
Remember the Wolf is a hunter—go forth and get food of thine
 own.

Keep peace with the Lords of the Jungle—the Tiger, the
 Panther, the Bear;
And trouble not Hathi the Silent, and mock not the Boar in his
 lair.

When Pack meets with Pack in the Jungle, and neither will go
 from the trail,

Lie down till the leaders have spoken—it may be fair words shall prevail.

When ye fight with a Wolf of the Pack, ye must fight him alone and afar,
Lest others take part in the quarrel, and the Pack be diminished by war.

The Lair of the Wolf is his refuge, and where he has made him his home,
Not even the Head Wolf may enter, not even the Council may come.

The Lair of the Wolf is his refuge, but where he has digged it too plain,
The Council shall send him a message, and so he shall change it again.

If ye kill before midnight, be silent, and wake not the woods with your bay,
Lest ye frighten the deer from the crops, and the brothers go empty away.

Ye may kill for yourselves, and your mates, and your cubs as they need, and ye can;
But kill not for pleasure of killing, and seven times never kill man.

If ye plunder his Kill from a weaker, devour not all in thy pride;
Pack-Right is the right of the meanest; so leave him the head and the hide.

The Kill of the Pack is the meat of the Pack. Ye must eat where it lies;
And no one may carry away of that meat to his lair, or he dies.

The Kill of the Wolf is the meat of the Wolf. He may do what he will,

But, till he has given permission, the Pack may not eat of that Kill.

Cub-Right is the right of the Yearling. From all of his Pack he may claim
Full-gorge when the killer has eaten; and none may refuse him the same.

Lair-Right is the right of the Mother. From all of her year she may claim
One haunch of each kill for her litter, and none may deny her the same.

Cave-Right is the right of the Father—to hunt by himself for his own.
He is freed of all calls to the Pack; he is judged by the Council alone.

Because of his age and his cunning, because of his gripe and his paw,
In all that the Law leaveth open, the word of the Head Wolf is Law.

Now these are the Laws of the Jungle, and many and mighty are they;
But the head and the hoof of the Law and the haunch and the hump is—Obey!

3. THE MIRACLE OF PURUN BHAGAT

The night we felt the earth would move
We stole and plucked him by the hand,
Because we loved him with the love
That knows but cannot understand.

And when the roaring hillside broke,
And all our world fell down in rain,
We saved him, we the Little Folk;
But lo! he does not come again!

Mourn now, we saved him for the sake
Of such poor love as wild ones may.
Mourn ye! Our brother will not wake,
And his own kind drive us away!

—*Dirge of the Langurs*

There was once a man in India who was Prime Minister of one of the semi-independent native States in the north-western part of the country. He was a Brahmin, so high-caste that caste ceased to have any particular meaning for him; and his father had been an important official in the gay-coloured tag-rag and bobtail of an old-fashioned Hindu Court. But as Purun Dass grew up he felt that the old order of things was changing, and that if any one wished to get on in the world he must stand well with the English, and imitate all that the English believed to be good. At the same time a native official must keep his own master's favour. This was a difficult game, but the quiet, close-mouthed young Brahmin, helped by a good English education at a Bombay University, played it coolly, and rose, step by step, to be Prime Minister of the kingdom. That is to say, he held more real power than his master the Maharajah.

When the old king—who was suspicious of the English, their

railways and telegraphs—died, Purun Dass stood high with his young successor, who had been tutored by an Englishman; and between them, though he always took care that his master should have the credit, they established schools for little girls, made roads, and started State dispensaries and shows of agricultural implements, and published a yearly blue-book on the "Moral and Material Progress of the State," and the Foreign Office and the Government of India were delighted. Very few native States take up English progress altogether, for they will not believe, as Purun Dass showed he did, that what was good for the Englishman must be twice as good for the Asiatic. The Prime Minister became the honoured friend of Viceroys, and Governors, and Lieutenant-Governors, and medical missionaries, and common missionaries, and hard-riding English officers who came to shoot in the State preserves, as well as of whole hosts of tourists who travelled up and down India in the cold weather, showing how things ought to be managed. In his spare time he would endow scholarships for the study of medicine and manufactures on strictly English lines, and write letters to the *Pioneer*, the greatest Indian daily paper, explaining his master's aims and objects.

At last he went to England on a visit, and had to pay enormous sums to the priests when he came back; for even so high-caste a Brahmin as Purun Dass lost caste by crossing the black sea. In London he met and talked with every one worth knowing—men whose names go all over the world—and saw a great deal more than he said. He was given honorary degrees by learned universities, and he made speeches and talked of Hindu social reform to English ladies in evening dress, till all London cried, "This is the most fascinating man we have ever met at dinner since cloths were first laid."

When he returned to India there was a blaze of glory, for the Viceroy himself made a special visit to confer upon the Maharajah the Grand Cross of the Star of India—all diamonds and ribbons and enamel; and at the same ceremony, while the cannon boomed, Purun Dass was made a Knight Commander of the Order of the Indian Empire; so that his name stood Sir Purun Dass, K.C.I.E.

That evening, at dinner in the big Viceregal tent, he stood up with

the badge and the collar of the Order on his breast, and replying to the toast of his master's health, made a speech few Englishmen could have bettered.

Next month, when the city had returned to its sun-baked quiet, he did a thing no Englishman would have dreamed of doing; for, so far as the world's affairs went, he died. The jewelled order of his knighthood went back to the Indian Government, and a new Prime Minister was appointed to the charge of affairs, and a great game of General Post began in all the subordinate appointments. The priests knew what had happened, and the people guessed; but India is the one place in the world where a man can do as he pleases and nobody asks why; and the fact that Dewan Sir Purun Dass, K.C.I.E., had resigned position, palace, and power, and taken up the begging-bowl and ochre-coloured dress of a Sunnyasi, or holy man, was considered nothing extraordinary. He had been, as the Old Law recommends, twenty years a youth, twenty years a fighter,—though he had never carried a weapon in his life,— and twenty years head of a household. He had used his wealth and his power for what he knew both to be worth; he had taken honour when it came his way; he had seen men and cities far and near, and men and cities had stood up and honoured him. Now he would let those things go, as a man drops the cloak he no longer needs.

Behind him, as he walked through the city gates, an antelope skin and brass-handled crutch under his arm, and a begging-bowl of polished brown *coco-de-mer* in his hand, barefoot, alone, with eyes cast on the ground—behind him they were firing salutes from the bastions in honour of his happy successor. Purun Dass nodded. All that life was ended; and he bore it no more ill-will or good-will than a man bears to a colourless dream of the night. He was a Sunnyasi—a houseless, wandering mendicant, depending on his neighbours for his daily bread; and so long as there is a morsel to divide in India, neither priest nor beggar starves. He had never in his life tasted meat, and very seldom eaten even fish. A five-pound note would have covered his personal expenses for food through any one of the many years in which he had been absolute master of millions of money. Even when he was being lionised in London he had held before him his dream of peace

and quiet—the long, white, dusty Indian road, printed all over with bare feet, the incessant, slow-moving traffic, and the sharp-smelling wood smoke curling up under the fig-trees in the twilight, where the wayfarers sit at their evening meal.

When the time came to make that dream true the Prime Minister took the proper steps, and in three days you might more easily have found a bubble in the trough of the long Atlantic seas, than Purun Dass among the roving, gathering, separating millions of India.

At night his antelope skin was spread where the darkness overtook him—sometimes in a Sunnyasi monastery by the roadside; sometimes by a mud-pillar shrine of Kala Pir, where the Jogis, who are another misty division of holy men, would receive him as they do those who know what castes and divisions are worth; sometimes on the outskirts of a little Hindu village, where the children would steal up with the food their parents had prepared; and sometimes on the pitch of the bare grazing-grounds, where the flame of his stick fire waked the drowsy camels. It was all one to Purun Dass—or Purun Bhagat, as he called himself now. Earth, people, and food were all one. But unconsciously his feet drew him away northward and eastward; from the south to Rohtak; from Rohtak to Kurnool; from Kurnool to ruined Samanah, and then up-stream along the dried bed of the Gugger river that fills only when the rain falls in the hills, till one day he saw the far line of the great Himalayas.

Then Purun Bhagat smiled, for he remembered that his mother was of Rajput Brahmin birth, from Kulu way—a Hill-woman, always home-sick for the snows—and that the least touch of Hill blood draws a man in the end back to where he belongs.

"Yonder," said Purun Bhagat, breasting the lower slopes of the Sewaliks, where the cacti stand up like seven-branched candlesticks— "yonder I shall sit down and get knowledge"; and the cool wind of the Himalayas whistled about his ears as he trod the road that led to Simla.

The last time he had come that way it had been in state, with a clattering cavalry escort, to visit the gentlest and most affable of Viceroys; and the two had talked for an hour together about mutual friends in London, and what the Indian common folk really thought

of things. This time Purun Bhagat paid no calls, but leaned on the rail of the Mall, watching that glorious view of the Plains spread out forty miles below, till a native Mohammedan policeman told him he was obstructing traffic; and Purun Bhagat salaamed reverently to the Law, because he knew the value of it, and was seeking for a Law of his own. Then he moved on, and slept that night in an empty hut at Chota Simla, which looks like the very last end of the earth, but it was only the beginning of his journey.

He followed the Himalaya-Thibet road, the little ten-foot track that is blasted out of solid rock, or strutted out on timbers over gulfs a thousand feet deep; that dips into warm, wet, shut-in valleys, and climbs out across bare, grassy hill-shoulders where the sun strikes like a burning-glass; or turns through dripping, dark forests where the tree-ferns dress the trunks from head to heel, and the pheasant calls to his mate. And he met Thibetan herdsmen with their dogs and flocks of sheep, each sheep with a little bag of borax on his back, and wandering wood-cutters, and cloaked and blanketed Lamas from Thibet, coming into India on pilgrimage, and envoys of little solitary Hill-states, posting furiously on ring-streaked and piebald ponies, or the cavalcade of a Rajah paying a visit; or else for a long, clear day he would see nothing more than a black bear grunting and rooting below in the valley. When he first started, the roar of the world he had left still rang in his ears, as the roar of a tunnel rings long after the train has passed through; but when he had put the Mutteeanee Pass behind him that was all done, and Purun Bhagat was alone with himself, walking, wondering, and thinking, his eyes on the ground, and his thoughts with the clouds.

One evening he crossed the highest pass he had met till then—it had been a two-day's climb—and came out on a line of snow-peaks that banded all the horizon—mountains from fifteen to twenty thousand feet high, looking almost near enough to hit with a stone, though they were fifty or sixty miles away. The pass was crowned with dense, dark forest—deodar, walnut, wild cherry, wild olive, and wild pear, but mostly deodar, which is the Himalayan cedar; and under the shadow of the deodars stood a deserted shrine to Kali—who is Durga, who is Sitala, who is sometimes worshipped against the smallpox.

Purun Dass swept the stone floor clean, smiled at the grinning statue, made himself a little mud fireplace at the back of the shrine, spread his antelope skin on a bed of fresh pine-needles, tucked his *bairagi*—his brass-handled crutch—under his armpit, and sat down to rest.

Immediately below him the hillside fell away, clean and cleared for fifteen hundred feet, where a little village of stone-walled houses, with roofs of beaten earth, clung to the steep tilt. All round it the tiny terraced fields lay out like aprons of patchwork on the knees of the mountain, and cows no bigger than beetles grazed between the smooth stone circles of the threshing-floors. Looking across the valley, the eye was deceived by the size of things, and could not at first realise that what seemed to be low scrub, on the opposite mountain-flank, was in truth a forest of hundred-foot pines. Purun Bhagat saw an eagle swoop across the gigantic hollow, but the great bird dwindled to a dot ere it was half-way over. A few bands of scattered clouds strung up and down the valley, catching on a shoulder of the hills, or rising up and dying out when they were level with the head of the pass. And "Here shall I find peace," said Purun Bhagat.

Now, a Hill-man makes nothing of a few hundred feet up or down, and as soon as the villagers saw the smoke in the deserted shrine, the village priest climbed up the terraced hillside to welcome the stranger.

When he met Purun Bhagat's eyes—the eyes of a man used to control thousands—he bowed to the earth, took the begging-bowl without a word, and returned to the village, saying, "We have at last a holy man. Never have I seen such a man. He is of the Plains—but pale-coloured—a Brahmin of the Brahmins." Then all the housewives of the village said, "Think you he will stay with us?" and each did her best to cook the most savoury meal for the Bhagat. Hill-food is very simple, but with buckwheat and Indian corn, and rice and red pepper, and little fish out of the stream in the valley, and honey from the flue-like hives built in the stone walls, and dried apricots, and turmeric, and wild ginger, and bannocks of flour, a devout woman can make good things, and it was a full bowl that the priest carried to the Bhagat. Was he going to stay? asked the priest. Would he need a *chela*—a disciple—to beg for him? Had he a blanket against the cold weather? Was the food good?

Purun Bhagat ate, and thanked the giver. It was in his mind to stay. That was sufficient, said the priest. Let the begging-bowl be placed outside the shrine, in the hollow made by those two twisted roots, and daily should the Bhagat be fed; for the village felt honoured that such a man—he looked timidly into the Bhagat's face—should tarry among them.

That day saw the end of Purun Bhagat's wanderings. He had come to the place appointed for him—the silence and the space. After this, time stopped, and he, sitting at the mouth of the shrine, could not tell whether he were alive or dead; a man with control of his limbs, or a part of the hills, and the clouds, and the shifting rain and sunlight. He would repeat a Name softly to himself a hundred hundred times, till, at each repetition, he seemed to move more and more out of his body, sweeping up to the doors of some tremendous discovery; but, just as the door was opening, his body would drag him back, and, with grief, he felt he was locked up again in the flesh and bones of Purun Bhagat.

Every morning the filled begging-bowl was laid silently in the crutch of the roots outside the shrine. Sometimes the priest brought it; sometimes a Ladakhi trader, lodging in the village, and anxious to get merit, trudged up the path; but, more often, it was the woman who had cooked the meal overnight; and she would murmur, hardly above her breath. "Speak for me before the gods, Bhagat. Speak for such a one, the wife of so-and-so!" Now and then some bold child would be allowed the honour, and Purun Bhagat would hear him drop the bowl and run as fast as his little legs could carry him, but the Bhagat never came down to the village. It was laid out like a map at his feet. He could see the evening gatherings, held on the circle of the threshing-floors, because that was the only level ground; could see the wonderful unnamed green of the young rice, the indigo blues of the Indian corn, the dock-like patches of buckwheat, and, in its season, the red bloom of the amaranth, whose tiny seeds, being neither grain nor pulse, make a food that can be lawfully eaten by Hindus in time of fasts.

When the year turned, the roofs of the huts were all little squares of purest gold, for it was on the roofs that they laid out their cobs of the corn to dry. Hiving and harvest, rice-sowing and husking, passed before his eyes, all embroidered down there on the many-sided plots of

fields, and he thought of them all, and wondered what they all led to at the long last.

Even in populated India a man cannot a day sit still before the wild things run over him as though he were a rock; and in that wilderness very soon the wild things, who knew Kali's Shrine well, came back to look at the intruder. The *langurs*, the big gray-whiskered monkeys of the Himalayas, were, naturally, the first, for they are alive with curiosity; and when they had upset the begging-bowl, and rolled it round the floor, and tried their teeth on the brass-handled crutch, and made faces at the antelope skin, they decided that the human being who sat so still was harmless. At evening, they would leap down from the pines, and beg with their hands for things to eat, and then swing off in graceful curves. They liked the warmth of the fire, too, and huddled round it till Purun Bhagat had to push them aside to throw on more fuel; and in the morning, as often as not, he would find a furry ape sharing his blanket. All day long, one or other of the tribe would sit by his side, staring out at the snows, crooning and looking unspeakably wise and sorrowful.

After the monkeys came the *barasingh*, that big deer which is like our red deer, but stronger. He wished to rub off the velvet of his horns against the cold stones of Kali's statue, and stamped his feet when he saw the man at the shrine. But Purun Bhagat never moved, and, little by little, the royal stag edged up and nuzzled his shoulder. Purun Bhagat slid one cool hand along the hot antlers, and the touch soothed the fretted beast, who bowed his head, and Purun Bhagat very softly rubbed and ravelled off the velvet. Afterward, the *barasingh* brought his doe and fawn—gentle things that mumbled on the holy man's blanket—or would come alone at night, his eyes green in the fire-flicker, to take his share of fresh walnuts. At last, the musk-deer, the shyest and almost the smallest of the deerlets, came, too, her big rabbity ears erect; even brindled, silent *mushick-nabha* must needs find out what the light in the shrine meant, and drop out her moose-like nose into Purun Bhagat's lap, coming and going with the shadows of the fire. Purun Bhagat called them all "my brothers," and his low call of "*Bhai! Bhai!*" would draw them from the forest at noon if they were within ear shot. The Himalayan black bear, moody and suspicious—Sona, who

has the V-shaped white mark under his chin—passed that way more than once; and since the Bhagat showed no fear, Sona showed no anger, but watched him, and came closer, and begged a share of the caresses, and a dole of bread or wild berries. Often, in the still dawns, when the Bhagat would climb to the very crest of the pass to watch the red day walking along the peaks of the snows, he would find Sona shuffling and grunting at his heels, thrusting, a curious fore-paw under fallen trunks, and bringing it away with a *whoof* of impatience; or his early steps would wake Sona where he lay curled up, and the great brute, rising erect, would think to fight, till he heard the Bhagat's voice and knew his best friend.

Nearly all hermits and holy men who live apart from the big cities have the reputation of being able to work miracles with the wild things, but all the miracle lies in keeping still, in never making a hasty movement, and, for a long time, at least, in never looking directly at a visitor. The villagers saw the outline of the *barasingh* stalking like a shadow through the dark forest behind the shrine; saw the *minaul*, the Himalayan pheasant, blazing in her best colours before Kali's statue; and the *langurs* on their haunches, inside, playing with the walnut shells. Some of the children, too, had heard Sona singing to himself, bear-fashion, behind the fallen rocks, and the Bhagat's reputation as miracle-worker stood firm.

Yet nothing was farther from his mind than miracles. He believed that all things were one big Miracle, and when a man knows that much he knows something to go upon. He knew for a certainty that there was nothing great and nothing little in this world: and day and night he strove to think out his way into the heart of things, back to the place whence his soul had come.

So thinking, his untrimmed hair fell down about his shoulders, the stone slab at the side of the antelope skin was dented into a little hole by the foot of his brass-handled crutch, and the place between the tree-trunks, where the begging-bowl rested day after day, sunk and wore into a hollow almost as smooth as the brown shell itself; and each beast knew his exact place at the fire. The fields changed their colours with the seasons; the threshing-floors filled and emptied, and filled again

and again; and again and again, when winter came, the *langurs* frisked among the branches feathered with light snow, till the mother-monkeys brought their sad-eyed little babies up from the warmer valleys with the spring. There were few changes in the village. The priest was older, and many of the little children who used to come with the begging-dish sent their own children now; and when you asked of the villagers how long their holy man had lived in Kali's Shrine at the head of the pass, they answered, "Always."

Then came such summer rains as had not been known in the Hills for many seasons. Through three good months the valley was wrapped in cloud and soaking mist—steady, unrelenting downfall, breaking off into thunder-shower after thunder-shower. Kali's Shrine stood above the clouds, for the most part, and there was a whole month in which the Bhagat never caught a glimpse of his village. It was packed away under a white floor of cloud that swayed and shifted and rolled on itself and bulged upward, but never broke from its piers—the streaming flanks of the valley.

All that time he heard nothing but the sound of a million little waters, overhead from the trees, and underfoot along the ground, soaking through the pine-needles, dripping from the tongues of draggled fern, and spouting in newly-torn muddy channels down the slopes. Then the sun came out, and drew forth the good incense of the deodars and the rhododendrons, and that far-off, clean smell which the Hill people call "the smell of the snows." The hot sunshine lasted for a week, and then the rains gathered together for their last downpour, and the water fell in sheets that flayed off the skin of the ground and leaped back in mud. Purun Bhagat heaped his fire high that night, for he was sure his brothers would need warmth; but never a beast came to the shrine, though he called and called till he dropped asleep, wondering what had happened in the woods.

It was in the black heart of the night, the rain drumming like a thousand drums, that he was roused by a plucking at his blanket, and, stretching out, felt the little hand of a *langur*. "It is better here than in the trees," he said sleepily, loosening a fold of blanket; "take it and be warm." The monkey caught his hand and pulled hard. "Is it food,

then?" said Purun Bhagat. "Wait awhile, and I will prepare some." As he kneeled to throw fuel on the fire the *langur* ran to the door of the shrine, crooned and ran back again, plucking at the man's knee.

"What is it? What is thy trouble, Brother?" said Purun Bhagat, for the *langur's* eyes were full of things that he could not tell. "Unless one of thy caste be in a trap—and none set traps here—I will not go into that weather. Look, Brother, even the *barasingh* comes for shelter!"

The deer's antlers clashed as he strode into the shrine, clashed against the grinning statue of Kali. He lowered them in Purun Bhagat's direction and stamped uneasily, hissing through his half-shut nostrils.

"Hai! Hai! Hai!" said the Bhagat, snapping his fingers, "Is *this* payment for a night's lodging?" But the deer pushed him toward the door, and as he did so Purun Bhagat heard the sound of something opening with a sigh, and saw two slabs of the floor draw away from each other, while the sticky earth below smacked its lips.

"Now I see," said Purun Bhagat. "No blame to my brothers that they did not sit by the fire to-night. The mountain is falling. And yet— why should I go?" His eye fell on the empty begging-bowl, and his face changed. "They have given me good food daily since—since I came, and, if I am not swift, to-morrow there will not be one mouth in the valley. Indeed, I must go and warn them below. Back there, Brother! Let me get to the fire."

The *barasingh* backed unwillingly as Purun Bhagat drove a pine torch deep into the flame, twirling it till it was well lit. "Ah! ye came to warn me," he said, rising. "Better than that we shall do; better than that. Out, now, and lend me thy neck, Brother, for I have but two feet."

He clutched the bristling withers of the *barasingh* with his right hand, held the torch away with his left, and stepped out of the shrine into the desperate night. There was no breath of wind, but the rain nearly drowned the flare as the great deer hurried down the slope, sliding on his haunches. As soon as they were clear of the forest more of the Bhagat's brothers joined them. He heard, though he could not see, the *langurs* pressing about him, and behind them the *uhh! uhh!* of Sona. The rain matted his long white hair into ropes; the water splashed beneath his bare feet, and his yellow robe clung to his frail old body,

but he stepped down steadily, leaning against the *barasingh*. He was no longer a holy man, but Sir Purun Dass, K.C.I.E., Prime Minister of no small State, a man accustomed to command, going out to save life. Down the steep, plashy path they poured all together, the Bhagat and his brothers, down and down till the deer's feet clicked and stumbled on the wall of a threshing-floor, and he snorted because he smelt Man. Now they were at the head of the one crooked village street, and the Bhagat beat with his crutch on the barred windows of the blacksmith's house, as his torch blazed up in the shelter of the eaves. "Up and out!" cried Purun Bhagat; and he did not know his own voice, for it was years since he had spoken aloud to a man. "The hill falls! The hill is falling! Up and out, oh, you within!"

"It is our Bhagat," said the blacksmith's wife. "He stands among his beasts. Gather the little ones and give the call."

It ran from house to house, while the beasts, cramped in the narrow way, surged and huddled round the Bhagat, and Sona puffed impatiently.

The people hurried into the street—they were no more than seventy souls all told—and in the glare of the torches they saw their Bhagat holding back the terrified *barasingh*, while the monkeys plucked piteously at his skirts, and Sona sat on his haunches and roared.

"Across the valley and up the next hill!" shouted Purun Bhagat. "Leave none behind! We follow!"

Then the people ran as only Hill folk can run, for they knew that in a landslip you must climb for the highest ground across the valley. They fled, splashing through the little river at the bottom, and panted up the terraced fields on the far side, while the Bhagat and his brethren followed. Up and up the opposite mountain they climbed, calling to each other by name—the roll-call of the village—and at their heels toiled the big *barasingh*, weighted by the failing strength of Purun Bhagat. At last the deer stopped in the shadow of a deep pinewood, five hundred feet up the hillside. His instinct, that had warned him of the coming slide, told him he would he safe here.

Purun Bhagat dropped fainting by his side, for the chill of the rain and that fierce climb were killing him; but first he called to the scattered

torches ahead, "Stay and count your numbers"; then, whispering to the deer as he saw the lights gather in a cluster: "Stay with me, Brother. Stay—till—I—go!"

There was a sigh in the air that grew to a mutter, and a mutter that grew to a roar, and a roar that passed all sense of hearing, and the hillside on which the villagers stood was hit in the darkness, and rocked to the blow. Then a note as steady, deep, and true as the deep C of the organ drowned everything for perhaps five minutes, while the very roots of the pines quivered to it. It died away, and the sound of the rain falling on miles of hard ground and grass changed to the muffled drum of water on soft earth. That told its own tale.

Never a villager—not even the priest—was bold enough to speak to the Bhagat who had saved their lives. They crouched under the pines and waited till the day. When it came they looked across the valley and saw that what had been forest, and terraced field, and track-threaded grazing-ground was one raw, red, fan-shaped smear, with a few trees flung head-down on the scarp. That red ran high up the hill of their refuge, damming back the little river, which had begun to spread into a brick-coloured lake. Of the village, of the road to the shrine, of the shrine itself, and the forest behind, there was no trace. For one mile in width and two thousand feet in sheer depth the mountain-side had come away bodily, planed clean from head to heel.

And the villagers, one by one, crept through the wood to pray before their Bhagat. They saw the *barasingh* standing over him, who fled when they came near, and they heard the *langurs* wailing in the branches, and Sona moaning up the hill; but their Bhagat was dead, sitting cross-legged, his back against a tree, his crutch under his armpit, and his face turned to the north-east.

The priest said: "Behold a miracle after a miracle, for in this very attitude must all Sunnyasis be buried! Therefore where he now is we will build the temple to our holy man."

They built the temple before a year was ended—a little stone-and-earth shrine—and they called the hill the Bhagat's hill, and they worship there with lights and flowers and offerings to this day. But they do not know that the saint of their worship is the late Sir Purun Dass,

K.C.I.E., D.C.L., Ph.D., etc., once Prime Minister of the progressive and enlightened State of Mohiniwala, and honorary or corresponding member of more learned and scientific societies than will ever do any good in this world or the next.

4. A SONG OF KABIR

Oh, light was the world that he weighed in his hands!
Oh, heavy the tale of his fiefs and his lands!
He has gone from the *guddee* and put on the shroud,
And departed in guise of *bairagi* avowed!

Now the white road to Delhi is mat for his feet,
The *sal* and the *kikar* must guard him from heat;
His home is the camp, and the waste, and the crowd—
He is seeking the Way as *bairagi* avowed!

He has looked upon Man, and his eyeballs are clear
(There was One; there is One, and but One, saith Kabir);
The Red Mist of Doing has thinned to a cloud—
He has taken the Path for *bairagi* avowed!

To learn and discern of his brother the clod,
Of his brother the brute, and his brother the God.
He has gone from the council and put on the shroud
("Can ye hear?" saith Kabir), a *bairagi* avowed!

5. LETTING IN THE JUNGLE

Veil them, cover them, wall them round—
Blossom, and creeper, and weed—
Let us forget the sight and the sound,
The smell and the touch of the breed!

Fat black ash by the altar-stone,
Here is the white-foot rain,
And the does bring forth in the fields unsown,
And none shall affright them again;
And the blind walls crumble, unknown, o'erthrown
And none shall inhabit again!

You will remember that after Mowgli had pinned Shere Khan's hide to the Council Rock, he told as many as were left of the Seeonee Pack that henceforward he would hunt in the Jungle alone; and the four children of Mother and Father Wolf said that they would hunt with him. But it is not easy to change one's life all in a minute—particularly in the Jungle. The first thing Mowgli did, when the disorderly Pack had slunk off, was to go to the home-cave, and sleep for a day and a night. Then he told Mother Wolf and Father Wolf as much as they could understand of his adventures among men; and when he made the morning sun flicker up and down the blade of his skinning-knife,— the same he had skinned Shere Khan with,—they said he had learned something. Then Akela and Gray Brother had to explain their share of the great buffalo-drive in the ravine, and Baloo toiled up the hill to hear all about it, and Bagheera scratched himself all over with pure delight at the way in which Mowgli had managed his war.

It was long after sunrise, but no one dreamed of going to sleep, and from time to time, during the talk, Mother Wolf would throw up her head, and sniff a deep snuff of satisfaction as the wind brought her the smell of the tiger-skin on the Council Rock.

"But for Akela and Gray Brother here," Mowgli said, at the end,

"I could have done nothing. Oh, mother, mother! if thou hadst seen the black herd-bulls pour down the ravine, or hurry through the gates when the Man-Pack flung stones at me!"

"I am glad I did not see that last," said Mother Wolf stiffly. "It is not *my* custom to suffer my cubs to be driven to and fro like jackals. *I* would have taken a price from the Man-Pack; but I would have spared the woman who gave thee the milk. Yes, I would have spared her alone."

"Peace, peace, Raksha!" said Father Wolf, lazily. "Our Frog has come back again—so wise that his own father must lick his feet; and what is a cut, more or less, on the head? Leave Men alone." Baloo and Bagheera both echoed: "Leave Men alone."

Mowgli, his head on Mother Wolf's side, smiled contentedly, and said that, for his own part, he never wished to see, or hear, or smell Man again.

"But what," said Akela, cocking one ear—"but what if men do not leave thee alone, Little Brother?"

"We be *five*," said Gray Brother, looking round at the company, and snapping his jaws on the last word.

"We also might attend to that hunting," said Bagheera, with a little *switch-switch* of his tail, looking at Baloo. "But why think of men now, Akela?"

"For this reason," the Lone Wolf answered: "when that yellow chief's hide was hung up on the rock, I went back along our trail to the village, stepping in my tracks, turning aside, and lying down, to make a mixed trail in case one should follow us. But when I had fouled the trail so that I myself hardly knew it again, Mang, the Bat, came hawking between the trees, and hung up above me." Said Mang, "The village of the Man-Pack, where they cast out the Man-cub, hums like a hornet's nest."

"It was a big stone that I threw," chuckled Mowgli, who had often amused himself by throwing ripe paw-paws into a hornet's nest, and racing off to the nearest pool before the hornets caught him.

"I asked of Mang what he had seen. He said that the Red Flower blossomed at the gate of the village, and men sat about it carrying guns. Now *I* know, for I have good cause,"—Akela looked down at

the old dry scars on his flank and side,—"that men do not carry guns for pleasure. Presently, Little Brother, a man with a gun follows our trail—if, indeed, he be not already on it."

"But why should he? Men have cast me out. What more do they need?" said Mowgli angrily.

"Thou art a man, Little Brother," Akela returned. "It is not for *us*, the Free Hunters, to tell thee what thy brethren do, or *why*."

He had just time to snatch up his paw as the skinning-knife cut deep into the ground below. Mowgli struck quicker than an average human eye could follow but Akela was a wolf; and even a dog, who is very far removed from the wild wolf, his ancestor, can be waked out of deep sleep by a cart-wheel touching his flank, and can spring away unharmed before that wheel comes on.

"Another time," Mowgli said quietly, returning the knife to its sheath, "speak of the Man-Pack and of Mowgli in *two* breaths—not one."

"Phff! That is a sharp tooth," said Akela, snuffing at the blade's cut in the earth, "but living with the Man-Pack has spoiled thine eye, Little Brother. I could have killed a buck while thou wast striking."

Bagheera sprang to his feet, thrust up his head as far as he could, sniffed, and stiffened through every curve in his body. Gray Brother followed his example quickly, keeping a little to his left to get the wind that was blowing from the right, while Akela bounded fifty yards up wind, and, half-crouching, stiffened too. Mowgli looked on enviously. He could smell things as very few human beings could, but he had never reached the hair-trigger-like sensitiveness of a Jungle nose; and his three months in the smoky village had set him back sadly. However, he dampened his finger, rubbed it on his nose, and stood erect to catch the upper scent, which, though it is the faintest, is the truest.

"Man!" Akela growled, dropping on his haunches.

"Buldeo!" said Mowgli, sitting down. "He follows our trail, and yonder is the sunlight on his gun. Look!"

It was no more than a splash of sunlight, for a fraction of a second, on the brass clamps of the old Tower musket, but nothing in the Jungle

winks with just that flash, except when the clouds race over the sky. Then a piece of mica, or a little pool, or even a highly-polished leaf will flash like a heliograph. But that day was cloudless and still.

"I knew men would follow," said Akela triumphantly. "Not for nothing have I led the Pack."

The four cubs said nothing, but ran down hill on their bellies, melting into the thorn and under-brush as a mole melts into a lawn.

"Where go ye, and without word?" Mowgli called.

"H'sh! We roll his skull here before mid-day!" Gray Brother answered.

"Back! Back and wait! Man does not eat Man!" Mowgli shrieked.

"Who was a wolf but now? Who drove the knife at me for thinking he might be Man?" said Akela, as the four wolves turned back sullenly and dropped to heel.

"Am I to give reason for all I choose to do?" said Mowgli furiously.

"That is Man! There speaks Man!" Bagheera muttered under his whiskers. "Even so did men talk round the King's cages at Oodeypore. We of the Jungle know that Man is wisest of all. If we trusted our ears we should know that of all things he is most foolish." Raising his voice, he added, "The Man-cub is right in this. Men hunt in packs. To kill one, unless we know what the others will do, is bad hunting. Come, let us see what this Man means toward us."

"We will not come," Gray Brother growled. "Hunt alone, Little Brother. *We* know our own minds. The skull would have been ready to bring by now."

Mowgli had been looking from one to the other of his friends, his chest heaving and his eyes full of tears. He strode forward to the wolves, and, dropping on one knee, said: "Do I not know my mind? Look at me!"

They looked uneasily, and when their eyes wandered, he called them back again and again, till their hair stood up all over their bodies, and they trembled in every limb, while Mowgli stared and stared.

"Now," said he, "of us five, which is leader?"

"Thou art leader, Little Brother," said Gray Brother, and he licked Mowgli's foot.

"Follow, then," said Mowgli, and the four followed at his heels with their tails between their legs.

"This comes of living with the Man-Pack," said Bagheera, slipping down after them. "There is more in the Jungle now than Jungle Law, Baloo."

The old bear said nothing, but he thought many things.

Mowgli cut across noiselessly through the Jungle, at right angles to Buldeo's path, till, parting the undergrowth, he saw the old man, his musket on his shoulder, running up the trail of overnight at a dog-trot.

You will remember that Mowgli had left the village with the heavy weight of Shere Khan's raw hide on his shoulders, while Akela and Gray Brother trotted behind, so that the triple trail was very clearly marked. Presently Buldeo came to where Akela, as you know, had gone back and mixed it all up. Then he sat down, and coughed and grunted, and made little casts round and about into the Jungle to pick it up again, and, all the time he could have thrown a stone over those who were watching him. No one can be so silent as a wolf when he does not care to be heard; and Mowgli, though the wolves thought he moved very clumsily, could come and go like a shadow. They ringed the old man as a school of porpoises ring a steamer at full speed, and as they ringed him they talked unconcernedly, for their speech began below the lowest end of the scale that untrained human beings can hear. [The other end is bounded by the high squeak of Mang, the Bat, which very many people cannot catch at all. From that note all the bird and bat and insect talk takes on.]

"This is better than any kill," said Gray Brother, as Buldeo stooped and peered and puffed. "He looks like a lost pig in the Jungles by the river. What does he say?" Buldeo was muttering savagely.

Mowgli translated. "He says that packs of wolves must have danced round me. He says that he never saw such a trail in his life. He says he is tired."

"He will be rested before he picks it up again," said Bagheera coolly, as he slipped round a tree-trunk, in the game of blindman's-buff that they were playing. "*Now*, what does the lean thing do?"

"Eat or blow smoke out of his mouth. Men always play with their mouths," said Mowgli; and the silent trailers saw the old man fill and

light and puff at a water-pipe, and they took good note of the smell of the tobacco, so as to be sure of Buldeo in the darkest night, if necessary.

Then a little knot of charcoal-burners came down the path, and naturally halted to speak to Buldeo, whose fame as a hunter reached for at least twenty miles round. They all sat down and smoked, and Bagheera and the others came up and watched while Buldeo began to tell the story of Mowgli, the Devil-child, from one end to another, with additions and inventions. How he himself had really killed Shere Khan; and how Mowgli had turned himself into a wolf, and fought with him all the afternoon, and changed into a boy again and bewitched Buldeo's rifle, so that the bullet turned the corner, when he pointed it at Mowgli, and killed one of Buldeo's own buffaloes; and how the village, knowing him to be the bravest hunter in Seeonee, had sent him out to kill this Devil-child. But meantime the village had got hold of Messua and her husband, who were undoubtedly the father and mother of this Devil-child, and had barricaded them in their own hut, and presently would torture them to make them confess they were witch and wizard, and then they would be burned to death.

"When?" said the charcoal-burners, because they would very much like to be present at the ceremony.

Buldeo said that nothing would be done till he returned, because the village wished him to kill the Jungle Boy first. After that they would dispose of Messua and her husband, and divide their lands and buffaloes among the village. Messua's husband had some remarkably fine buffaloes, too. It was an excellent thing to destroy wizards, Buldeo thought; and people who entertained Wolf-children out of the Jungle were clearly the worst kind of witches.

But, said the charcoal-burners, what would happen if the English heard of it? The English, they had heard, were a perfectly mad people, who would not let honest farmers kill witches in peace.

Why, said Buldeo, the head-man of the village would report that Messua and her husband had died of snake-bite. *That* was all arranged, and the only thing now was to kill the Wolf-child. They did not happen to have seen anything of such a creature?

The charcoal-burners looked round cautiously, and thanked their

stars they had not; but they had no doubt that so brave a man as Buldeo would find him if any one could. The sun was getting rather low, and they had an idea that they would push on to Buldeo's village and see that wicked witch. Buldeo said that, though it was his duty to kill the Devil-child, he could not think of letting a party of unarmed men go through the Jungle, which might produce the Wolf-demon at any minute, without his escort. He, therefore, would accompany them, and if the sorcerer's child appeared—well, he would show them how the best hunter in Seeonee dealt with such things. The Brahmin, he said, had given him a charm against the creature that made everything perfectly safe.

"What says he? What says he? What says he?" the wolves repeated every few minutes; and Mowgli translated until he came to the witch part of the story, which was a little beyond him, and then he said that the man and woman who had been so kind to him were trapped.

"Does Man trap Man?" said Bagheera.

"So he says. I cannot understand the talk. They are all mad together. What have Messua and her man to do with me that they should be put in a trap; and what is all this talk about the Red Flower? I must look to this. Whatever they would do to Messua they will not do till Buldeo returns. And so——" Mowgli thought hard, with his fingers playing round the haft of the skinning-knife, while Buldeo and the charcoal-burners went off very valiantly in single file.

"I go hot-foot back to the Man-Pack," Mowgli said at last.

"And those?" said Gray Brother, looking hungrily after the brown backs of the charcoal-burners.

"Sing them home," said Mowgli, with a grin; "I do not wish them to be at the village gates till it is dark. Can ye hold them?"

Gray Brother bared his white teeth in contempt. "We can head them round and round in circles like tethered goats—if I know Man."

"That I do not need. Sing to them a little, lest they be lonely on the road, and, Gray Brother, the song need not be of the sweetest. Go with them, Bagheera, and help make that song. When night is shut down, meet me by the village—Gray Brother knows the place."

"It is no light hunting to work for a Man-cub. When shall I sleep?"

said Bagheera, yawning, though his eyes showed that he was delighted with the amusement. "Me to sing to naked men! But let us try."

He lowered his head so that the sound would travel, and cried a long, long, "Good hunting"—a midnight call in the afternoon, which was quite awful enough to begin with. Mowgli heard it rumble, and rise, and fall, and die off in a creepy sort of whine behind him, and laughed to himself as he ran through the Jungle. He could see the charcoal-burners huddled in a knot; old Buldeo's gun-barrel waving, like a banana-leaf, to every point of the compass at once. Then Gray Brother gave the *Ya-la-hi! Yalaha!* call for the buck-driving, when the Pack drives the nilghai, the big blue cow, before them, and it seemed to come from the very ends of the earth, nearer, and nearer, and nearer, till it ended in a shriek snapped off short. The other three answered, till even Mowgli could have vowed that the full Pack was in full cry, and then they all broke into the magnificent Morning-song in the Jungle, with every turn, and flourish, and grace-note that a deep-mouthed wolf of the Pack knows. This is a rough rendering of the song, but you must imagine what it sounds like when it breaks the afternoon hush of the Jungle:—

One moment past our bodies cast
No shadow on the plain;
Now clear and black they stride our track,
And we run home again.
In morning hush, each rock and bush
Stands hard, and high, and raw:
Then give the Call: *"Good rest to all
That keep The Jungle Law!"*

Now horn and pelt our peoples melt
In covert to abide;
Now, crouched and still, to cave and hill
Our Jungle Barons glide.
Now, stark and plain, Man's oxen strain,
That draw the new-yoked plough;
Now, stripped and dread, the dawn is red
Above the lit *talao*.

Ho! Get to lair! The sun's aflare
Behind the breathing grass:
And cracking through the young bamboo
The warning whispers pass.
By day made strange, the woods we range
With blinking eyes we scan;
While down the skies the wild duck cries:
"The Day—the Day to Man!"

The dew is dried that drenched our hide
Or washed about our way;
And where we drank, the puddled bank
Is crisping into clay.
The traitor Dark gives up each mark
Of stretched or hooded claw;
Then hear the Call: *"Good rest to all
That keep the Jungle Law!"*

But no translation can give the effect of it, or the yelping scorn the Four threw into every word of it, as they heard the trees crash when the men hastily climbed up into the branches, and Buldeo began repeating incantations and charms. Then they lay down and slept, for, like all who live by their own exertions, they were of a methodical cast of mind; and no one can work well without sleep.

Meantime, Mowgli was putting the miles behind him, nine to the hour, swinging on, delighted to find himself so fit after all his cramped months among men. The one idea in his head was to get Messua and her husband out of the trap, whatever it was; for he had a natural mistrust of traps. Later on, he promised himself, he would pay his debts to the village at large.

It was at twilight when he saw the well-remembered grazing-grounds, and the *dhak*-tree where Gray Brother had waited for him on the morning that he killed Shere Khan. Angry as he was at the whole breed and community of Man, something jumped up in his throat and made him catch his breath when he looked at the village roofs. He noticed that every one had come in from the fields unusually early, and

that, instead of getting to their evening cooking, they gathered in a crowd under the village tree, and chattered, and shouted.

"Men must always be making traps for men, or they are not content," said Mowgli. "Last night it was Mowgli—but that night seems many Rains ago. To-night it is Messua and her man. To-morrow, and for very many nights after, it will be Mowgli's turn again."

He crept along outside the wall till he came to Messua's hut, and looked through the window into the room. There lay Messua, gagged, and bound hand and foot, breathing hard, and groaning: her husband was tied to the gaily-painted bedstead. The door of the hut that opened into the street was shut fast, and three or four people were sitting with their backs to it.

Mowgli knew the manners and customs of the villagers very fairly. He argued that so long as they could eat, and talk, and smoke, they would not do anything else; but as soon as they had fed they would begin to be dangerous. Buldeo would be coming in before long, and if his escort had done its duty, Buldeo would have a very interesting tale to tell. So he went in through the window, and, stooping over the man and the woman, cut their thongs, pulling out the gags, and looked round the hut for some milk.

Messua was half wild with pain and fear (she had been beaten and stoned all the morning), and Mowgli put his hand over her mouth just in time to stop a scream. Her husband was only bewildered and angry, and sat picking dust and things out of his torn beard.

"I knew—I knew he would come," Messua sobbed at last. "Now do I *know* that he is my son!" and she hugged Mowgli to her heart. Up to that time Mowgli had been perfectly steady, but now he began to tremble all over, and that surprised him immensely.

"Why are these thongs? Why have they tied thee?" he asked, after a pause.

"To be put to the death for making a son of thee—what else?" said the man sullenly. "Look! I bleed."

Messua said nothing, but it was at *her* wounds that Mowgli looked, and they heard him grit his teeth when he saw the blood.

"Whose work is this?" said he. "There is a price to pay."

"The work of all the village. I was too rich. I had too many cattle. *Therefore* she and I are witches, because we gave thee shelter."

"I do not understand. Let Messua tell the tale."

"I gave thee milk, Nathoo; dost thou remember?" Messua said timidly. "Because thou wast my son, whom the tiger took, and because I loved thee very dearly. They said that I was thy mother, the mother of a devil, and therefore worthy of death."

"And what is a devil?" said Mowgli. "Death I have seen."

The man looked up gloomily, but Messua laughed. "See!" she said to her husband, "I knew—I said that he was no sorcerer. He is my son—my son!"

"Son or sorcerer, what good will that do us?" the man answered. "We be as dead already."

"Yonder is the road to the Jungle"—Mowgli pointed through the window. "Your hands and feet are free. Go now."

"We do not know the Jungle, my son, as—as thou knowest," Messua began. "I do not think that I could walk far."

"And the men and women would be upon our backs and drag us here again," said the husband.

"H'm!" said Mowgli, and he tickled the palm of his hand with the tip of his skinning-knife; "I have no wish to do harm to any one of this village—*yet*. But I do not think they will stay thee. In a little while they will have much else to think upon. Ah!" he lifted his head and listened to shouting and trampling outside. "So they have let Buldeo come home at last?"

"He was sent out this morning to kill thee," Messua cried. "Didst thou meet him?"

"Yes—we—I met him. He has a tale to tell and while he is telling it there is time to do much. But first I will learn what they mean. Think where ye would go, and tell me when I come back."

He bounded through the window and ran along again outside the wall of the village till he came within ear-shot of the crowd round the peepul-tree. Buldeo was lying on the ground, coughing and groaning, and every one was asking him questions. His hair had fallen about his shoulders; his hands and legs were skinned from climbing up trees,

and he could hardly speak, but he felt the importance of his position keenly. From time to time he said something about devils and singing devils, and magic enchantment, just to give the crowd a taste of what was coming. Then he called for water.

"Bah!" said Mowgli. "Chatter—chatter! Talk, talk! Men are blood-brothers of the *Bandar-log*. Now he must wash his mouth with water; now he must blow smoke; and when all that is done he has still his story to tell. They are very wise people—men. They will leave no one to guard Messua till their ears are stuffed with Buldeo's tales. And—I grow as lazy as they!"

He shook himself and glided back to the hut. Just as he was at the window he felt a touch on his foot.

"Mother," said he, for he knew that tongue well, "what dost *thou* here?"

"I heard my children singing through the woods, and I followed the one I loved best. Little Frog, I have a desire to see that woman who gave thee milk," said Mother Wolf, all wet with the dew.

"They have bound and mean to kill her. I have cut those ties, and she goes with her man through the Jungle."

"I also will follow. I am old, but not yet toothless." Mother Wolf reared herself up on end, and looked through the window into the dark of the hut.

In a minute she dropped noiselessly, and all she said was: "I gave thee thy first milk; but Bagheera speaks truth: Man goes to Man at the last."

"Maybe," said Mowgli, with a very unpleasant look on his face; "but to-night I am very far from that trail. Wait here, but do not let her see."

"*Thou* wast never afraid of *me*, Little Frog," said Mother Wolf, backing into the high grass, and blotting herself out, as she knew how.

"And now," said Mowgli cheerfully, as he swung into the hut again, "they are all sitting round Buldeo, who is saying that which did not happen. When his talk is finished, they say they will assuredly come here with the Red—with fire and burn you both. And then?"

"I have spoken to my man," said Messua. "Khanhiwara is thirty miles from here, but at Khanhiwara we may find the English—"

"And what Pack are they?" said Mowgli.

"I do not know. They be white, and it is said that they govern all the land, and do not suffer people to burn or beat each other without witnesses. If we can get thither to-night, we live. Otherwise we die."

"Live, then. No man passes the gates to-night. But what does *he* do?" Messua's husband was on his hands and knees digging up the earth in one corner of the hut.

"It is his little money," said Messua. "We can take nothing else."

"Ah, yes. The stuff that passes from hand to hand and never grows warmer. Do they need it outside this place also?" said Mowgli.

The man stared angrily. "He is a fool, and no devil," he muttered. "With the money I can buy a horse. We are too bruised to walk far, and the village will follow us in an hour."

"I say they will *not* follow till I choose; but a horse is well thought of, for Messua is tired." Her husband stood up and knotted the last of the rupees into his waist-cloth. Mowgli helped Messua through the window, and the cool night air revived her, but the Jungle in the starlight looked very dark and terrible.

"Ye know the trail to Khanhiwara?" Mowgli whispered.

They nodded.

"Good. Remember, now, not to be afraid. And there is no need to go quickly. Only—only there may be some small singing in the Jungle behind you and before."

"Think you we would have risked a night in the Jungle through anything less than the fear of burning? It is better to be killed by beasts than by men," said Messua's husband; but Messua looked at Mowgli and smiled.

"I say," Mowgli went on, just as though he were Baloo repeating an old Jungle Law for the hundredth time to a foolish cub—"I say that not a tooth in the Jungle is bared against you; not a foot in the Jungle is lifted against you. Neither man nor beast shall stay you till you come within eye-shot of Khanhiwara. There will be a watch about you." He turned quickly to Messua, saying, "*He* does not believe, but thou wilt believe?"

"Ay, surely, my son. Man, ghost, or wolf of the Jungle, I believe."

"*He* will be afraid when he hears my people singing. Thou wilt know and understand. Go now, and slowly, for there is no need of any haste. The gates are shut."

Messua flung herself sobbing at Mowgli's feet, but he lifted her very quickly with a shiver. Then she hung about his neck and called him every name of blessing she could think of, but her husband looked enviously across his fields, and said: "*If* we reach Khanhiwara, and I get the ear of the English, I will bring such a lawsuit against the Brahmin and old Buldeo and the others as shall eat the village to the bone. They shall pay me twice over for my crops untilled and my buffaloes unfed. I will have a great justice."

Mowgli laughed. "I do not know what justice is, but—come next Rains and see what is left."

They went off toward the Jungle, and Mother Wolf leaped from her place of hiding.

"Follow!" said Mowgli; "and look to it that all the Jungle knows these two are safe. Give tongue a little. I would call Bagheera."

The long, low howl rose and fell, and Mowgli saw Messua's husband flinch and turn, half minded to run back to the hut.

"Go on," Mowgli called cheerfully. "I said there might be singing. That call will follow up to Khanhiwara. It is Favour of the Jungle."

Messua urged her husband forward, and the darkness shut down on them and Mother Wolf as Bagheera rose up almost under Mowgli's feet, trembling with delight of the night that drives the Jungle People wild.

"I am ashamed of thy brethren," he said, purring. "What? Did they not sing sweetly to Buldeo?" said Mowgli.

"Too well! Too well! They made even *me* forget my pride, and, by the Broken Lock that freed me, I went singing through the Jungle as though I were out wooing in the spring! Didst thou not hear us?"

"I had other game afoot. Ask Buldeo if he liked the song. But where are the Four? I do not wish one of the Man-Pack to leave the gates to-night."

"What need of the Four, then?" said Bagheera, shifting from foot to foot, his eyes ablaze, and purring louder than ever. "I can hold them, Little Brother. Is it killing at last? The singing and the sight of

the men climbing up the trees have made me very ready. Who is Man that we should care for him—the naked brown digger, the hairless and toothless, the eater of earth? I have followed him all day—at noon—in the white sunlight. I herded him as the wolves herd buck. I am Bagheera! Bagheera! Bagheera! As I dance with my shadow, so danced I with those men. Look!" The great panther leaped as a kitten leaps at a dead leaf whirling overhead, struck left and right into the empty air, that sang under the strokes, landed noiselessly, and leaped again and again, while the half purr, half growl gathered head as steam rumbles in a boiler. "I am Bagheera—in the jungle—in the night, and my strength is in me. Who shall stay my stroke? Man-cub, with one blow of my paw I could beat thy head flat as a dead frog in the summer!"

"Strike, then!" said Mowgli, in the dialect of the village, *not* the talk of the Jungle, and the human words brought Bagheera to a full stop, flung back on haunches that quivered under him, his head just at the level of Mowgli's. Once more Mowgli stared, as he had stared at the rebellious cubs, full into the beryl-green eyes till the red glare behind their green went out like the light of a lighthouse shut off twenty miles across the sea; till the eyes dropped, and the big head with them—dropped lower and lower, and the red rasp of a tongue grated on Mowgli's instep.

"Brother—Brother—Brother!" the boy whispered, stroking steadily and lightly from the neck along the heaving back. "Be still, be still! It is the fault of the night, and no fault of thine."

"It was the smells of the night," said Bagheera penitently. "This air cries aloud to me. But how dost *thou* know?"

Of course the air round an Indian village is full of all kinds of smells, and to any creature who does nearly all his thinking through his nose, smells are as maddening as music and drugs are to human beings. Mowgli gentled the panther for a few minutes longer, and he lay down like a cat before a fire, his paws tucked under his breast, and his eyes half shut.

"Thou art of the Jungle and *not* of the Jungle," he said at last. "And I am only a black panther. But I love thee, Little Brother."

"They are very long at their talk under the tree," Mowgli said,

without noticing the last sentence. "Buldeo must have told many tales. They should come soon to drag the woman and her man out of the trap and put them into the Red Flower. They will find that trap sprung. Ho! ho!"

"Nay, listen," said Bagheera. "The fever is out of my blood now. Let them find *me* there! Few would leave their houses after meeting me. It is not the first time I have been in a cage; and I do not think they will tie *me* with cords."

"Be wise, then," said Mowgli, laughing; for he was beginning to feel as reckless as the panther, who had glided into the hut.

"Pah!" Bagheera grunted. "This place is rank with Man, but here is just such a bed as they gave me to lie upon in the King's cages at Oodeypore. Now I lie down." Mowgli heard the strings of the cot crack under the great brute's weight. "By the Broken Lock that freed me, they will think they have caught big game! Come and sit beside me, Little Brother; we will give them 'good hunting' together!"

"No; I have another thought in my stomach. The Man-Pack shall not know what share I have in the sport. Make thine own hunt. I do not wish to see them."

"Be it so," said Bagheera. "Ah, now they come!"

The conference under the peepul-tree had been growing noisier and noisier, at the far end of the village. It broke in wild yells, and a rush up the street of men and women, waving clubs and bamboos and sickles and knives. Buldeo and the Brahmin were at the head of it, but the mob was close at their heels, and they cried, "The witch and the wizard! Let us see if hot coins will make them confess! Burn the hut over their heads! We will teach them to shelter wolf-devils! Nay, beat them first! Torches! More torches! Buldeo, heat the gun-barrels!"

Here was some little difficulty with the catch of the door. It had been very firmly fastened, but the crowd tore it away bodily, and the light of the torches streamed into the room where, stretched at full length on the bed, his paws crossed and lightly hung down over one end, black as the Pit, and terrible as a demon, was Bagheera. There was one half-minute of desperate silence, as the front ranks of the crowd clawed and tore their way back from the threshold, and in that minute Bagheera raised

his head and yawned—elaborately, carefully, and ostentatiously—as he would yawn when he wished to insult an equal. The fringed lips drew back and up; the red tongue curled; the lower jaw dropped and dropped till you could see half-way down the hot gullet; and the gigantic dog-teeth stood clear to the pit of the gums till they rang together, upper and under, with the snick of steel-faced wards shooting home round the edges of a safe. Next instant the street was empty; Bagheera had leaped back through the window, and stood at Mowgli's side, while a yelling, screaming torrent scrambled and tumbled one over another in their panic haste to get to their own huts.

"They will not stir till day comes," said Bagheera quietly. "And now?"

The silence of the afternoon sleep seemed to have overtaken the village; but, as they listened, they could hear the sound of heavy grain-boxes being dragged over earthen floors and set down against doors. Bagheera was quite right; the village would not stir till daylight. Mowgli sat still, and thought, and his face grew darker and darker.

"What have I done?" said Bagheera, at last coming to his feet, fawning.

"Nothing but great good. Watch them now till the day. I sleep." Mowgli ran off into the Jungle, and dropped like a dead man across a rock, and slept and slept the day round, and the night back again.

When he waked, Bagheera was at his side, and there was a newly-killed buck at his feet. Bagheera watched curiously while Mowgli went to work with his skinning-knife, ate and drank, and turned over with his chin in his hands.

"The man and the woman are come safe within eye-shot of Khanhiwara," Bagheera said. "Thy lair mother sent the word back by Chil, the Kite. They found a horse before midnight of the night they were freed, and went very quickly. Is not that well?"

"That is well," said Mowgli.

"And thy Man-Pack in the village did not stir till the sun was high this morning. Then they ate their food and ran back quickly to their houses."

"Did they, by chance, see thee?"

"It may have been. I was rolling in the dust before the gate at dawn, and I may have made also some small song to myself. Now, Little Brother, there is nothing more to do. Come hunting with me and Baloo. He has new hives that he wishes to show, and we all desire thee back again as of old. Take off that look which makes even *me* afraid! The man and woman will not be put into the Red Flower, and all goes well in the Jungle. Is it not true? Let us forget the Man-Pack."

"They shall be forgotten in a little while. Where does Hathi feed to-night?"

"Where he chooses. Who can answer for the Silent One? But why? What is there Hathi can do which we cannot?"

"Bid him and his three sons come here to me."

"But, indeed, and truly, Little Brother, it is not—it is not seemly to say 'Come,' and 'Go,' to Hathi. Remember, he is the Master of the Jungle, and before the Man-Pack changed the look on thy face, he taught thee the Master-words of the Jungle."

"That is all one. I have a Master-word for him now. Bid him come to Mowgli, the Frog: and if he does not hear at first, bid him come because of the Sack of the Fields of Bhurtpore."

"The Sack of the Fields of Bhurtpore," Bagheera repeated two or three times to make sure. "I go. Hathi can but be angry at the worst, and I would give a moon's hunting to hear a Master-word that compels the Silent One."

He went away, leaving Mowgli stabbing furiously with his skinning-knife into the earth. Mowgli had never seen human blood in his life before till he had seen, and—what meant much more to him—smelled Messua's blood on the thongs that bound her. And Messua had been kind to him, and, so far as he knew anything about love, he loved Messua as completely as he hated the rest of mankind. But deeply as he loathed them, their talk, their cruelty, and their cowardice, not for anything the Jungle had to offer could he bring himself to take a human life, and have that terrible scent of blood back again in his nostrils. His plan was simpler, but much more thorough; and he laughed to himself when he thought that it was one of old Buldeo's tales told under the peepul-tree in the evening that had put the idea into his head.

"It *was* a Master-word," Bagheera whispered in his ear. "They were feeding by the river, and they obeyed as though they were bullocks. Look where they come now!"

Hathi and his three sons had arrived, in their usual way, without a sound. The mud of the river was still fresh on their flanks, and Hathi was thoughtfully chewing the green stem of a young plantain-tree that he had gouged up with his tusks. But every line in his vast body showed to Bagheera, who could see things when he came across them, that it was not the Master of the Jungle speaking to a Man-cub, but one who was afraid coming before one who was not. His three sons rolled side by side, behind their father.

Mowgli hardly lifted his head as Hathi gave him "Good hunting." He kept him swinging and rocking, and shifting from one foot to another, for a long time before he spoke; and when he opened his mouth it was to Bagheera, not to the elephants.

"I will tell a tale that was told to me by the hunter ye hunted to-day," said Mowgli. "It concerns an elephant, old and wise, who fell into a trap, and the sharpened stake in the pit scarred him from a little above his heel to the crest of his shoulder, leaving a white mark." Mowgli threw out his hand, and as Hathi wheeled the moonlight showed a long white scar on his slaty side, as though he had been struck with a red-hot whip. "Men came to take him from the trap," Mowgli continued, "but he broke his ropes, for he was strong, and went away till his wound was healed. Then came he, angry, by night to the fields of those hunters. And I remember now that he had three sons. These things happened many, many Rains ago, and very far away—among the fields of Bhurtpore. What came to those fields at the next reaping, Hathi?"

"They were reaped by me and by my three sons," said Hathi.

"And to the ploughing that follows the reaping?" said Mowgli.

"There was no ploughing," said Hathi.

"And to the men that live by the green crops on the ground?" said Mowgli.

"They went away."

"And to the huts in which the men slept?" said Mowgli.

"We tore the roofs to pieces, and the Jungle swallowed up the walls," said Hathi.

"And what more?" said Mowgli.

"As much good ground as I can walk over in two nights from the east to the west, and from the north to the south as much as I can walk over in three nights, the Jungle took. We let in the Jungle upon five villages; and in those villages, and in their lands, the grazing-ground and the soft crop-grounds, there is not one man to-day who takes his food from the ground. That was the Sack of the Fields of Bhurtpore, which I and my three sons did; and now I ask, Man-cub, how the news of it came to thee?" said Hathi.

"A man told me, and now I see even Buldeo can speak truth. It was well done, Hathi with the white mark; but the second time it shall be done better, for the reason that there is a man to direct. Thou knowest the village of the Man-Pack that cast me out? They are idle, senseless, and cruel; they play with their mouths, and they do not kill the weaker for food, but for sport. When they are full-fed they would throw their own breed into the Red Flower. This I have seen. It is not well that they should live here any more. I hate them!"

"Kill, then," said the youngest of Hathi's three sons, picking up a tuft of grass, dusting it against his fore-legs, and throwing it away, while his little red eyes glanced furtively from side to side.

"What good are white bones to me?" Mowgli answered angrily. "Am I the cub of a wolf to play in the sun with a raw head? I have killed Shere Khan, and his hide rots on the Council Rock; but—but I do not know whither Shere Khan is gone, and my stomach is still empty. Now I will take that which I can see and touch. Let in the Jungle upon that village, Hathi!"

Bagheera shivered, and cowered down. He could understand, if the worst came to the worst, a quick rush down the village street, and a right and left blow into a crowd, or a crafty killing of men as they ploughed in the twilight; but this scheme for deliberately blotting out an entire village from the eyes of man and beast frightened him. Now he saw why Mowgli had sent for Hathi. No one but the long-lived elephant could plan and carry through such a war.

"Let them run as the men ran from the fields of Bhurtpore, till we have the rain-water for the only plough, and the noise of the rain on the thick leaves for the pattering of their spindles—till Bagheera and I lair in the house of the Brahmin, and the buck drink at the tank behind the temple! Let in the Jungle, Hathi!"

"But I—but we have no quarrel with them, and it needs the red rage of great pain ere we tear down the places where men sleep," said Hathi doubtfully.

"Are ye the only eaters of grass in the Jungle? Drive in your peoples. Let the deer and the pig and the nilghai look to it. Ye need never show a hand's-breadth of hide till the fields are naked. Let in the Jungle, Hathi!"

"There will be no killing? My tusks were red at the Sack of the Fields of Bhurtpore, and I would not wake that smell again."

"Nor I. I do not wish even their bones to lie on the clean earth. Let them go and find a fresh lair. They cannot stay here. I have seen and smelled the blood of the woman that gave me food—the woman whom they would have killed but for me. Only the smell of the new grass on their door-steps can take away that smell. It burns in my mouth. Let in the Jungle, Hathi!"

"Ah!" said Hathi. "So did the scar of the stake burn on my hide till we watched the villages die under in the spring growth. Now I see. Thy war shall be our war. We will let in the jungle!"

Mowgli had hardly time to catch his breath—he was shaking all over with rage and hate before the place where the elephants had stood was empty, and Bagheera was looking at him with terror.

"By the Broken Lock that freed me!" said the Black Panther at last. "Art *thou* the naked thing I spoke for in the Pack when all was young? Master of the Jungle, when my strength goes, speak for me—speak for Baloo—speak for us all! We are cubs before thee! Snapped twigs under foot! Fawns that have lost their doe!"

The idea of Bagheera being a stray fawn upset Mowgli altogether, and he laughed and caught his breath, and sobbed and laughed again, till he had to jump into a pool to make himself stop. Then he swam round and round, ducking in and out of the bars of the moonlight like the frog, his namesake.

By this time Hathi and his three sons had turned, each to one point of the compass, and were striding silently down the valleys a mile away. They went on and on for two days' march—that is to say, a long sixty miles—through the Jungle; and every step they took, and every wave of their trunks, was known and noted and talked over by Mang and Chil and the Monkey-People and all the birds. Then they began to feed, and fed quietly for a week or so. Hathi and his sons are like Kaa, the Rock-python. They never hurry till they have to.

At the end of that time—and none knew who had started it—a rumour went through the Jungle that there was better food and water to be found in such and such a valley. The pig—who, of course, will go to the ends of the earth for a full meal—moved first by companies, scuffling over the rocks, and the deer followed, with the small wild foxes that live on the dead and dying of the herds; and the heavy-shouldered nilghai moved parallel with the deer, and the wild buffaloes of the swamps came after the nilghai. The least little thing would have turned the scattered, straggling droves that grazed and sauntered and drank and grazed again; but whenever there was an alarm some one would rise up and soothe them. At one time it would be Ikki the Porcupine, full of news of good feed just a little farther on; at another Mang would cry cheerily and flap down a glade to show it was all empty; or Baloo, his mouth full of roots, would shamble alongside a wavering line and half frighten, half romp it clumsily back to the proper road. Very many creatures broke back or ran away or lost interest, but very many were left to go forward. At the end of another ten days or so the situation was this. The deer and the pig and the nilghai were milling round and round in a circle of eight or ten miles radius, while the Eaters of Flesh skirmished round its edge. And the centre of that circle was the village, and round the village the crops were ripening, and in the crops sat men on what they call *machans*—platforms like pigeon-perches, made of sticks at the top of four poles—to scare away birds and other stealers. Then the deer were coaxed no more. The Eaters of Flesh were close behind them, and forced them forward and inward.

It was a dark night when Hathi and his three sons slipped down from the Jungle, and broke off the poles of the *machans* with their trunks;

they fell as a snapped stalk of hemlock in bloom falls, and the men that tumbled from them heard the deep gurgling of the elephants in their ears. Then the vanguard of the bewildered armies of the deer broke down and flooded into the village grazing-grounds and the ploughed fields; and the sharp-hoofed, rooting wild pig came with them, and what the deer left the pig spoiled, and from time to time an alarm of wolves would shake the herds, and they would rush to and fro desperately, treading down the young barley, and cutting flat the banks of the irrigating channels. Before the dawn broke the pressure on the outside of the circle gave way at one point. The Eaters of Flesh had fallen back and left an open path to the south, and drove upon drove of buck fled along it. Others, who were bolder, lay up in the thickets to finish their meal next night.

But the work was practically done. When the villagers looked in the morning they saw their crops were lost. And that meant death if they did not get away, for they lived year in and year out as near to starvation as the Jungle was near to them. When the buffaloes were sent to graze the hungry brutes found that the deer had cleared the grazing-grounds, and so wandered into the Jungle and drifted off with their wild mates; and when twilight fell the three or four ponies that belonged to the village lay in their stables with their heads beaten in. Only Bagheera could have given those strokes, and only Bagheera would have thought of insolently dragging the last carcass to the open street.

The villagers had no heart to make fires in the fields that night, so Hathi and his three sons went gleaning among what was left; and where Hathi gleans there is no need to follow. The men decided to live on their stored seed-corn until the rains had fallen, and then to take work as servants till they could catch up with the lost year; but as the grain-dealer was thinking of his well-filled crates of corn, and the prices he would levy at the sale of it, Hathi's sharp tusks were picking out the corner of his mud-house, and smashing open the big wicker chest, leeped with cow-dung, where the precious stuff lay.

When that last loss was discovered, it was the Brahmin's turn to speak. He had prayed to his own Gods without answer. It might be, he said, that, unconsciously, the village had offended some one of the

Gods of the Jungle, for, beyond doubt, the Jungle was against them. So they sent for the head-man of the nearest tribe of wandering Gonds— little, wise, and very black hunters, living in the deep Jungle, whose fathers came of the oldest race in India—the aboriginal owners of the land. They made the Gond welcome with what they had, and he stood on one leg, his bow in his hand, and two or three poisoned arrows stuck through his top-knot, looking half afraid and half contemptuously at the anxious villagers and their ruined fields. They wished to know whether his Gods—the Old Gods—were angry with them and what sacrifices should be offered. The Gond said nothing, but picked up a trail of the *Karela*, the vine that bears the bitter wild gourd, and laced it to and fro across the temple door in the face of the staring red Hindu image. Then he pushed with his hand in the open air along the road to Khanhiwara, and went back to his Jungle, and watched the Jungle People drifting through it. He knew that when the Jungle moves only white men can hope to turn it aside.

There was no need to ask his meaning. The wild gourd would grow where they had worshipped their God, and the sooner they saved themselves the better.

But it is hard to tear a village from its moorings. They stayed on as long as any summer food was left to them, and they tried to gather nuts in the Jungle, but shadows with glaring eyes watched them, and rolled before them even at mid-day; and when they ran back afraid to their walls, on the tree-trunks they had passed not five minutes before the bark would be stripped and chiselled with the stroke of some great taloned paw. The more they kept to their village, the bolder grew the wild things that gambolled and bellowed on the grazing-grounds by the Waingunga. They had no time to patch and plaster the rear walls of the empty byres that backed on to the Jungle; the wild pig trampled them down, and the knotty-rooted vines hurried after and threw their elbows over the new-won ground, and the coarse grass bristled behind the vines like the lances of a goblin army following a retreat. The unmarried men ran away first, and carried the news far and near that the village was doomed. Who could fight, they said, against the Jungle, or the Gods of the Jungle, when the very village cobra had left his hole

in the platform under the peepul-tree? So their little commerce with the outside world shrank as the trodden paths across the open grew fewer and fainter. At last the nightly trumpetings of Hathi and his three sons ceased to trouble them; for they had no more to be robbed of. The crop on the ground and the seed in the ground had been taken. The outlying fields were already losing their shape, and it was time to throw themselves on the charity of the English at Khanhiwara.

Native fashion, they delayed their departure from one day to another till the first Rains caught them and the unmended roofs let in a flood, and the grazing-ground stood ankle deep, and all life came on with a rush after the heat of the summer. Then they waded out—men, women, and children—through the blinding hot rain of the morning, but turned naturally for one farewell look at their homes.

They heard, as the last burdened family filed through the gate, a crash of falling beams and thatch behind the walls. They saw a shiny, snaky black trunk lifted for an instant, scattering sodden thatch. It disappeared, and there was another crash, followed by a squeal. Hathi had been plucking off the roofs of the huts as you pluck water-lilies, and a rebounding beam had pricked him. He needed only this to unchain his full strength, for of all things in the Jungle the wild elephant enraged is the most wantonly destructive. He kicked backward at a mud wall that crumbled at the stroke, and, crumbling, melted to yellow mud under the torrent of rain. Then he wheeled and squealed, and tore through the narrow streets, leaning against the huts right and left, shivering the crazy doors, and crumpling up the eaves; while his three sons raged behind as they had raged at the Sack of the Fields of Bhurtpore.

"The Jungle will swallow these shells," said a quiet voice in the wreckage. "It is the outer wall that must lie down," and Mowgli, with the rain sluicing over his bare shoulders and arms, leaped back from a wall that was settling like a tired buffalo.

"All in good time," panted Hathi. "Oh, but my tusks were red at Bhurtpore! To the outer wall, children! With the head! Together! Now!"

The four pushed side by side; the outer wall bulged, split, and fell, and the villagers, dumb with horror, saw the savage, clay-streaked heads of the wreckers in the ragged gap. Then they fled, houseless and

foodless, down the valley, as their village, shredded and tossed and trampled, melted behind them.

A month later the place was a dimpled mound, covered with soft, green young stuff; and by the end of the Rains there was the roaring jungle in full blast on the spot that had been under plough not six months before.

6. MOWGLI'S SONG
AGAINST PEOPLE

I will let loose against you the fleet-footed vines—
I will call in the Jungle to stamp out your lines!
The roofs shall fade before it,
The house-beams shall fall,
And the *Karela*, the bitter *Karela*,
Shall cover it all!

In the gates of these your councils my people shall sing,
In the doors of these your garners the Bat-folk shall
 cling;
And the snake shall be your watchman,
By a hearthstone unswept;
For the *Karela*, the bitter *Karela*,
Shall fruit where ye slept!

Ye shall not see my strikers; ye shall hear them and guess;
By night, before the moon-rise, I will send for my cess,
And the wolf shall be your herdsman
By a landmark removed,
For the *Karela*, the bitter *Karela*,
Shall seed where ye loved!

I will reap your fields before you at the hands of a host;
Ye shall glean behind my reapers, for the bread that is
 lost,
And the deer shall be your oxen
By a headland untilled,
For the *Karela*, the bitter *Karela*,
Shall leaf where ye build!

I have untied against you the club-footed vines,
I have sent in the Jungle to swamp out your lines.

The trees—the trees are on you!
The house-beams shall fall,
And the *Karela*, the bitter *Karela*,
Shall cover you all!

7. THE UNDERTAKERS

When ye say to Tabaqui, "My Brother!" when ye call
 the Hyena to meat,
Ye may cry the Full Truce with Jacala—the Belly that
 runs on four feet.

—*Jungle Law*

Respect the aged!"

It was a thick voice—a muddy voice that would have made
you shudder—a voice like something soft breaking in two. There was a
quaver in it, a croak and a whine.

"Respect the aged! O Companions of the River—respect the aged!"

Nothing could be seen on the broad reach of the river except a little
fleet of square-sailed, wooden-pinned barges, loaded with building-
stone, that had just come under the railway bridge, and were driving
down-stream. They put their clumsy helms over to avoid the sand-bar
made by the scour of the bridge-piers, and as they passed, three abreast,
the horrible voice began again:

"O Brahmins of the River—respect the aged and infirm!"

A boatman turned where he sat on the gunwale, lifted up his hand,
said something that was not a blessing, and the boats creaked on through
the twilight. The broad Indian river, that looked more like a chain of
little lakes than a stream, was as smooth as glass, reflecting the sandy-
red sky in mid-channel, but splashed with patches of yellow and dusky
purple near and under the low banks. Little creeks ran into the river in
the wet season, but now their dry mouths hung clear above water-line.
On the left shore, and almost under the railway bridge, stood a mud-
and-brick and thatch-and-stick village, whose main street, full of cattle
going back to their byres, ran straight to the river, and ended in a sort
of rude brick pier-head, where people who wanted to wash could wade
in step by step. That was the Ghaut of the village of Mugger-Ghaut.

Night was falling fast over the fields of lentils and rice and cotton in the low-lying ground yearly flooded by the river; over the reeds that fringed the elbow of the bend, and the tangled jungle of the grazing-grounds behind the still reeds. The parrots and crows, who had been chattering and shouting over their evening drink, had flown inland to roost, crossing the out-going battalions of the flying-foxes; and cloud upon cloud of water-birds came whistling and "honking" to the cover of the reed-beds. There were geese, barrel-headed and black-backed, teal, widgeon, mallard, and sheldrake, with curlews, and here and there a flamingo.

A lumbering Adjutant-crane brought up the rear, flying as though each slow stroke would be his last.

"Respect the aged! Brahmins of the River—respect the aged!"

The Adjutant half turned his head, sheered a little in the direction of the voice, and landed stiffly on the sand-bar below the bridge. Then you saw what a ruffianly brute he really was. His back view was immensely respectable, for he stood nearly six feet high, and looked rather like a very proper bald-headed parson. In front it was different, for his Ally Sloper-like head and neck had not a feather to them, and there was a horrible raw-skin pouch on his neck under his chin—a hold-all for the things his pick-axe beak might steal. His legs were long and thin and skinny, but he moved them delicately, and looked at them with pride as he preened down his ashy-gray tail-feathers, glanced over the smooth of his shoulder, and stiffened into "Stand at attention."

A mangy little Jackal, who had been yapping hungrily on a low bluff, cocked up his ears and tail, and scuttered across the shallows to join the Adjutant.

He was the lowest of his caste—not that the best of jackals are good for much, but this one was peculiarly low, being half a beggar, half a criminal—a cleaner-up of village rubbish-heaps, desperately timid or wildly bold, everlastingly hungry, and full of cunning that never did him any good.

"Ugh!" he said, shaking himself dolefully as he landed. "May the red mange destroy the dogs of this village! I have three bites for each flea upon me, and all because I looked—only looked, mark you—at an

old shoe in a cow-byre. Can I eat mud?" He scratched himself under his left ear.

"I heard," said the Adjutant, in a voice like a blunt saw going through a thick board—"I *heard* there was a new-born puppy in that same shoe."

"To hear is one thing; to know is another," said the Jackal, who had a very fair knowledge of proverbs, picked up by listening to men round the village fires of an evening.

"Quite true. So, to make sure, I took care of that puppy while the dogs were busy elsewhere."

"They were *very* busy," said the Jackal. "Well, I must not go to the village hunting for scraps yet awhile. And so there truly was a blind puppy in that shoe?"

"It is here," said the Adjutant, squinting over his beak at his full pouch. "A small thing, but acceptable now that charity is dead in the world."

"Ahai! The world is iron in these days," wailed the Jackal. Then his restless eye caught the least possible ripple on the water, and he went on quickly: "Life is hard for us all, and I doubt not that even our excellent master, the Pride of the Ghaut and the Envy of the River—"

"A liar, a flatterer, and a Jackal were all hatched out of the same egg," said the Adjutant to nobody in particular; for he was rather a fine sort of a liar on his own account when he took the trouble.

"Yes, the Envy of the River," the Jackal repeated, raising his voice. "Even he, I doubt not, finds that since the bridge has been built good food is more scarce. But on the other hand, though I would by no means say this to his noble face, he is so wise and so virtuous—as I, alas I am not—"

"When the Jackal owns he is gray, how black must the Jackal be!" muttered the Adjutant. He could not see what was coming.

"That *his* food never fails, and in consequence—"

There was a soft grating sound, as though a boat had just touched in shoal water. The Jackal spun round quickly and faced (it is always best to face) the creature he had been talking about. It was a twenty-four-foot crocodile, cased in what looked like treble-riveted boiler-plate,

studded and keeled and crested; the yellow points of his upper teeth just overhanging his beautifully fluted lower jaw. It was the blunt-nosed Mugger of Mugger-Ghaut, older than any man in the village, who had given his name to the village; the demon of the ford before the railway bridge, came—murderer, man-eater, and local fetish in one. He lay with his chin in the shallows, keeping his place by an almost invisible rippling of his tail, and well the Jackal knew that one stroke of that same tail in the water would carry the Mugger up the bank with the rush of a steam-engine.

"Auspiciously met, Protector of the Poor!" he fawned, backing at every word. "A delectable voice was heard, and we came in the hopes of sweet conversation. My tailless presumption, while waiting here, led me, indeed, to speak of thee. It is my hope that nothing was overheard."

Now the Jackal had spoken just to be listened to, for he knew flattery was the best way of getting things to eat, and the Mugger knew that the Jackal had spoken for this end, and the Jackal knew that the Mugger knew, and the Mugger knew that the Jackal knew that the Mugger knew, and so they were all very contented together.

The old brute pushed and panted and grunted up the bank, mumbling, "Respect the aged and infirm!" and all the time his little eyes burned like coals under the heavy, horny eyelids on the top of his triangular head, as he shoved his bloated barrel-body along between his crutched legs. Then he settled down, and, accustomed as the Jackal was to his ways, he could not help starting, for the hundredth time, when he saw how exactly the Mugger imitated a log adrift on the bar. He had even taken pains to lie at the exact angle a naturally stranded log would make with the water, having regard to the current of the season at the time and place. All this was only a matter of habit, of course, because the Mugger had come ashore for pleasure; but a crocodile is never quite full, and if the Jackal had been deceived by the likeness he would not have lived to philosophise over it.

"My child, I heard nothing," said the Mugger, shutting one eye. "The water was in my ears, and also I was faint with hunger. Since the railway bridge was built my people at my village have ceased to love me; and that is breaking my heart."

"Ah, shame!" said the Jackal. "So noble a heart, too! But men are all alike, to my mind."

"Nay, there are very great differences indeed," the Mugger answered gently. "Some are as lean as boat-poles. Others again are fat as young ja—dogs. Never would I causelessly revile men. They are of all fashions, but the long years have shown me that, one with another, they are very good. Men, women, and children—I have no fault to find with them. And remember, child, he who rebukes the World is rebuked by the World."

"Flattery is worse than an empty tin can in the belly. But that which we have just heard is wisdom," said the Adjutant, bringing down one foot.

"Consider, though, their ingratitude to this excellent one," began the Jackal tenderly.

"Nay, nay, not ingratitude!" the Mugger said. "They do not think for others; that is all. But I have noticed, lying at my station below the ford, that the stairs of the new bridge are cruelly hard to climb, both for old people and young children. The old, indeed, are not so worthy of consideration, but I am grieved—I am truly grieved—on account of the fat children. Still, I think, in a little while, when the newness of the bridge has worn away, we shall see my people's bare brown legs bravely splashing through the ford as before. Then the old Mugger will be honoured again."

"But surely I saw Marigold wreaths floating off the edge of the Ghaut only this noon," said the Adjutant.

Marigold wreaths are a sign of reverence all India over.

"An error—an error. It was the wife of the sweetmeat-seller. She loses her eyesight year by year, and cannot tell a log from me—the Mugger of the Ghaut. I saw the mistake when she threw the garland, for I was lying at the very foot of the Ghaut, and had she taken another step I might have shown her some little difference. Yet she meant well, and we must consider the spirit of the offering."

"What good are marigold wreaths when one is on the rubbish-heap?" said the Jackal, hunting for fleas, but keeping one wary eye on his Protector of the Poor.

"True, but they have not yet begun to make the rubbish-heap that shall carry *me*. Five times have I seen the river draw back from the village and make new land at the foot of the street. Five times have I seen the village rebuilt on the banks, and I shall see it built yet five times more. I am no faithless, fish-hunting Gavial, I, at Kasi to-day and Prayag to-morrow, as the saying is, but the true and constant watcher of the ford. It is not for nothing, child, that the village bears my name, and 'he who watches long,' as the saying is, 'shall at last have his reward.'"

"*I* have watched long—very long—nearly all my life, and my reward has been bites and blows," said the Jackal.

"Ho! ho! ho!" roared the Adjutant.

> "In August was the Jackal born;
> The Rains fell in September;
> 'Now such a fearful flood as this,'
> Says he, 'I can't remember!'"

There is one very unpleasant peculiarity about the Adjutant. At uncertain times he suffers from acute attacks of the fidgets or cramp in his legs, and though he is more virtuous to behold than any of the cranes, who are all immensely respectable, he flies off into wild, cripple-stilt war-dances, half opening his wings and bobbing his bald head up and down; while for reasons best known to himself he is very careful to time his worst attacks with his nastiest remarks. At the last word of his song he came to attention again, ten times adjutaunter than before.

The Jackal winced, though he was full three seasons old, but you cannot resent an insult from a person with a beak a yard long, and the power of driving it like a javelin. The Adjutant was a most notorious coward, but the Jackal was worse.

"We must live before we can learn," said the Mugger, "and there is this to say: Little jackals are very common, child, but such a mugger as I am is not common. For all that, I am not proud, since pride is destruction; but take notice, it is Fate, and against his Fate no one who swims or walks or runs should say anything at all. I am well contented with Fate. With good luck, a keen eye, and the custom of considering

whether a creek or a backwater has an outlet to it ere you ascend, much may be done."

"Once I heard that even the Protector of the Poor made a mistake," said the Jackal viciously.

"True; but there my Fate helped me. It was before I had come to my full growth—before the last famine but three (by the Right and Left of Gunga, how full used the streams to be in those days!). Yes, I was young and unthinking, and when the flood came, who so pleased as I? A little made me very happy then. The village was deep in flood, and I swam above the Ghaut and went far inland, up to the rice-fields, and they were deep in good mud. I remember also a pair of bracelets (glass they were, and troubled me not a little) that I found that evening. Yes, glass bracelets; and, if my memory serves me well, a shoe. I should have shaken off both shoes, but I was hungry. I learned better later. Yes. And so I fed and rested me; but when I was ready to go to the river again the flood had fallen, and I walked through the mud of the main street. Who but I? Came out all my people, priests and women and children, and I looked upon them with benevolence. The mud is not a good place to fight in. Said a boatman, 'Get axes and kill him, for he is the Mugger of the ford.' 'Not so,' said the Brahmin. 'Look, he is driving the flood before him! He is the godling of the village.' Then they threw many flowers at me, and by happy thought one led a goat across the road."

"How good—how very good is goat!" said the Jackal.

"Hairy—too hairy, and when found in the water more than likely to hide a cross-shaped hook. But that goat I accepted, and went down to the Ghaut in great honour. Later, my Fate sent me the boatman who had desired to cut off my tail with an axe. His boat grounded upon an old shoal which you would not remember."

"We are not *all* jackals here," said the Adjutant. "Was it the shoal made where the stone-boats sank in the year of the great drouth—a long shoal that lasted three floods?"

"There were two," said the Mugger; "an upper and a lower shoal."

"Ay, I forgot. A channel divided them, and later dried up again," said the Adjutant, who prided himself on his memory.

"On the lower shoal my well-wisher's craft grounded. He was sleeping in the bows, and, half awake, leaped over to his waist—no, it was no more than to his knees—to push off. His empty boat went on and touched again below the next reach, as the river ran then. I followed, because I knew men would come out to drag it ashore."

"And did they do so?" said the Jackal, a little awe-stricken. This was hunting on a scale that impressed him.

"There and lower down they did. I went no farther, but that gave me three in one day—well-fed *manjis* (boatmen) all, and, except in the case of the last (then I was careless), never a cry to warn those on the bank."

"Ah, noble sport! But what cleverness and great judgment it requires!" said the Jackal.

"Not cleverness, child, but only thought. A little thought in life is like salt upon rice, as the boatmen say, and I have thought deeply always. The Gavial, my cousin, the fish-eater, has told me how hard it is for him to follow his fish, and how one fish differs from the other, and how he must know them all, both together and apart. I say that is wisdom; but, on the other hand, my cousin, the Gavial, lives among his people. *My* people do not swim in companies, with their mouths out of the water, as Rewa does; nor do they constantly rise to the surface of the water, and turn over on their sides, like Mohoo and little Chapta; nor do they gather in shoals after flood, like Batchua and Chilwa."

"All are very good eating," said the Adjutant, clattering his beak.

"So my cousin says, and makes a great to-do over hunting them, but they do not climb the banks to escape his sharp nose. *My* people are otherwise. Their life is on the land, in the houses, among the cattle. I must know what they do, and what they are about to do; and adding the tail to the trunk, as the saying is, I make up the whole elephant. Is there a green branch and an iron ring hanging over a doorway? The old Mugger knows that a boy has been born in that house, and must some day come down to the Ghaut to play. Is a maiden to be married? The old Mugger knows, for he sees the men carry gifts back and forth; and she, too, comes down to the Ghaut to bathe before her wedding, and—he is there. Has the river changed its channel, and made new land where there was only sand before? The Mugger knows."

"Now, of what use is that knowledge?" said the Jackal. "The river has shifted even in my little life." Indian rivers are nearly always moving about in their beds, and will shift, sometimes, as much as two or three miles in a season, drowning the fields on one bank, and spreading good silt on the other.

"There is no knowledge so useful," said the Mugger, "for new land means new quarrels. The Mugger knows. Oho! the Mugger knows. As soon as the water has drained off, he creeps up the little creeks that men think would not hide a dog, and there he waits. Presently comes a farmer saying he will plant cucumbers here, and melons there, in the new land that the river has given him. He feels the good mud with his bare toes. Anon comes another, saying he will put onions, and carrots, and sugar-cane in such and such places. They meet as boats adrift meet, and each rolls his eye at the other under the big blue turban. The old Mugger sees and hears. Each calls the other 'Brother,' and they go to mark out the boundaries of the new land. The Mugger hurries with them from point to point, shuffling very low through the mud. Now they begin to quarrel! Now they say hot words! Now they pull turbans! Now they lift up their *lathis* (clubs), and, at last, one falls backward into the mud, and the other runs away. When he comes back the dispute is settled, as the iron-bound bamboo of the loser witnesses. Yet they are not grateful to the Mugger. No, they cry 'Murder!' and their families fight with sticks, twenty a-side. My people are good people—upland Jats—Malwais of the Bêt. They do not give blows for sport, and, when the fight is done, the old Mugger waits far down the river, out of sight of the village, behind the *kikar*-scrub yonder. Then come they down, my broad-shouldered Jats—eight or nine together under the stars, bearing the dead man upon a bed. They are old men with gray beards, and voices as deep as mine. They light a little fire—ah! how well I know that fire!—and they drink tobacco, and they nod their heads together forward in a ring, or sideways toward the dead man upon the bank. They say the English Law will come with a rope for this matter, and that such a man's family will be ashamed, because such a man must be hanged in the great square of the Jail. Then say the friends of the dead, 'Let him hang!' and the

talk is all to do over again—once, twice, twenty times in the long night. Then says one, at last, 'The fight was a fair fight. Let us take blood-money, a little more than is offered by the slayer, and we will say no more about it.' Then do they haggle over the blood-money, for the dead was a strong man, leaving many sons. Yet before *amratvela* (sunrise) they put the fire to him a little, as the custom is, and the dead man comes to me, and *he* says no more about it. Aha! my children, the Mugger knows—the Mugger knows—and my Malwah Jats are a good people!"

"They are too close—too narrow in the hand for my crop," croaked the Adjutant. "They waste not the polish on the cow's horn, as the saying is; and, again, who can glean after a Malwai?"

"Ah, I—glean—*them*," said the Mugger.

"Now, in Calcutta of the South, in the old days," the Adjutant went on, "everything was thrown into the streets, and we picked and chose. Those were dainty seasons. But to-day they keep their streets as clean as the outside of an egg, and my people fly away. To be clean is one thing; to dust, sweep, and sprinkle seven times a day wearies the very Gods themselves."

"There was a down-country jackal had it from a brother, who told me, that in Calcutta of the South all the jackals were as fat as otters in the Rains," said the Jackal, his mouth watering at the bare thought of it.

"Ah, but the white-faces are there—the English, and they bring dogs from somewhere down the river in boats—big fat dogs—to keep those same jackals lean," said the Adjutant.

"They are, then, as hard-hearted as these people? I might have known. Neither earth, sky, nor water shows charity to a jackal. I saw the tents of a white-face last season, after the Rains, and I also took a new yellow bridle to eat. The white-faces do not dress their leather in the proper way. It made me very sick."

"That was better than my case," said the Adjutant. "When I was in my third season, a young and a bold bird, I went down to the river where the big boats come in. The boats of the English are thrice as big as this village."

"He has been as far as Delhi, and says all the people there walk on

their heads," muttered the Jackal. The Mugger opened his left eye, and looked keenly at the Adjutant.

"It is true," the big bird insisted. "A liar only lies when he hopes to be believed. No one who had not seen those boats *could* believe this truth."

"*That* is more reasonable," said the Mugger. "And then?"

"From the insides of this boat they were taking out great pieces of white stuff, which, in a little while, turned to water. Much split off, and fell about on the shore, and the rest they swiftly put into a house with thick walls. But a boatman, who laughed, took a piece no larger than a small dog, and threw it to me. I—all my people—swallow without reflection, and that piece I swallowed as is our custom. Immediately I was afflicted with an excessive cold which, beginning in my crop, ran down to the extreme end of my toes, and deprived me even of speech, while the boatmen laughed at me. Never have I felt such cold. I danced in my grief and amazement till I could recover my breath and then I danced and cried out against the falseness of this world; and the boatmen derided me till they fell down. The chief wonder of the matter, setting aside that marvellous coldness, was that there was nothing at all in my crop when I had finished my lamentings!"

The Adjutant had done his very best to describe his feelings after swallowing a seven-pound lump of Wenham Lake ice, off an American ice-ship, in the days before Calcutta made her ice by machinery; but as he did not know what ice was, and as the Mugger and the Jackal knew rather less, the tale missed fire.

"Anything," said the Mugger, shutting his left eye again—"*anything* is possible that comes out of a boat thrice the size of Mugger-Ghaut. My village is not a small one."

There was a whistle overhead on the bridge, and the Delhi Mail slid across, all the carriages gleaming with light, and the shadows faithfully following along the river. It clanked away into the dark again; but the Mugger and the Jackal were so well used to it that they never turned their heads.

"Is that anything less wonderful than a boat thrice the size of Mugger-Ghaut?" said the bird, looking up.

"I saw that built, child. Stone by stone I saw the bridge-piers rise, and when the men fell off (they were wondrous sure-footed for the most part—but *when* they fell) I was ready. After the first pier was made they never thought to look down the stream for the body to burn. There, again, I saved much trouble. There was nothing strange in the building of the bridge," said the Mugger.

"But that which goes across, pulling the roofed carts! *That* is strange," the Adjutant repeated. "It is, past any doubt, a new breed of bullock. Some day it will not be able to keep its foothold up yonder, and will fall as the men did. The old Mugger will then be ready."

The Jackal looked at the Adjutant and the Adjutant looked at the Jackal. If there was one thing they were more certain of than another, it was that the engine was everything in the wide world except a bullock. The Jackal had watched it time and again from the aloe hedges by the side of the line, and the Adjutant had seen engines since the first locomotive ran in India. But the Mugger had only looked up at the thing from below, where the brass dome seemed rather like a bullock's hump.

"M—yes, a new kind of bullock," the Mugger repeated ponderously, to make himself quite sure in his own mind; and "Certainly it is a bullock," said the Jackal.

"And again it might be—" began the Mugger pettishly.

"Certainly—most certainly," said the Jackal, without waiting for the other to finish.

"What?" said the Mugger angrily, for he could feel that the others knew more than he did. "What might it be? *I* never finished my words. You said it was a bullock."

"It is anything the Protector of the Poor pleases. I am *his* servant—not the servant of the thing that crosses the river."

"Whatever it is, it is white-face work," said the Adjutant; "and for my own part, I would not lie out upon a place so near to it as this bar."

"You do not know the English as I do," said the Mugger. "There was a white-face here when the bridge was built, and he would take a boat in the evenings and shuffle with his feet on the bottom-boards, and whisper: 'Is he here? Is he there? Bring me my gun.' I could hear him before I could see him—each sound that he made—creaking

and puffing and rattling his gun, up and down the river. As surely as I had picked up one of his workmen, and thus saved great expense in wood for the burning, so surely would he come down to the Ghaut, and shout in a loud voice that he would hunt me, and rid the river of me—the Mugger of Mugger-Ghaut! *Me!* Children, I have swum under the bottom of his boat for hour after hour, and heard him fire his gun at logs; and when I was well sure he was wearied, I have risen by his side and snapped my jaws in his face. When the bridge was finished he went away. All the English hunt in that fashion, except when they are hunted."

"Who hunts the white-faces?" yapped the Jackal excitedly.

"No one now, but I have hunted them in my time."

"I remember a little of that Hunting. I was young then," said the Adjutant, clattering his beak significantly.

"I was well established here. My village was being builded for the third time, as I remember, when my cousin, the Gavial, brought me word of rich waters above Benares. At first I would not go, for my cousin, who is a fish-eater, does not always know the good from the bad; but I heard my people talking in the evenings, and what they said made me certain."

"And what did they say?" the Jackal asked.

"They said enough to make me, the Mugger of Mugger-Ghaut, leave water and take to my feet. I went by night, using the littlest streams as they served me; but it was the beginning of the hot weather, and all streams were low. I crossed dusty roads; I went through tall grass; I climbed hills in the moonlight. Even rocks did I climb, children— consider this well. I crossed the tail of Sirhind, the waterless, before I could find the set of the little rivers that flow Gungaward. I was a month's journey from my own people and the river that I knew. That was very marvellous!"

"What food on the way?" said the Jackal, who kept his soul in his little stomach, and was not a bit impressed by the Mugger's land travels.

"That which I could find—*cousin*," said the Mugger slowly, dragging each word.

Now you do not call a man a cousin in India unless you think you

can establish some kind of blood-relationship, and as it is only in old fairy-tales that the Mugger ever marries a jackal, the Jackal knew for what reason he had been suddenly lifted into the Mugger's family circle. If they had been alone he would not have cared, but the Adjutant's eyes twinkled with mirth at the ugly jest.

"Assuredly, Father, I might have known," said the Jackal. A mugger does not care to be called a father of jackals, and the Mugger of Mugger-Ghaut said as much—and a great deal more which there is no use in repeating here.

"The Protector of the Poor has claimed kinship. How can I remember the precise degree? Moreover, we eat the same food. He has said it," was the Jackal's reply.

That made matters rather worse, for what the Jackal hinted at was that the Mugger must have eaten his food on that land-march fresh and fresh every day, instead of keeping it by him till it was in a fit and proper condition, as every self-respecting mugger and most wild beasts do when they can. Indeed, one of the worst terms of contempt along the River-bed is "eater of fresh meat." It is nearly as bad as calling a man a cannibal.

"That food was eaten thirty seasons ago," said the Adjutant quietly. "If we talk for thirty seasons more it will never come back. Tell us, now, what happened when the good waters were reached after thy most wonderful land journey. If we listened to the howling of every jackal the business of the town would stop, as the saying is."

The Mugger must have been grateful for the interruption, because he went on, with a rush:

"By the Right and Left of Gunga! when I came there never did I see such waters!"

"Were they better, then, than the big flood of last season?" said the Jackal.

"Better! That flood was no more than comes every five years—a handful of drowned strangers, some chickens, and a dead bullock in muddy water with cross-currents. But the season I think of, the river was low, smooth, and even, and, as the Gavial had warned me, the dead English came down, touching each other. I got my girth in that

season—my girth and my depth. From Agra, by Etawah and the broad waters by Allahabad—"

"Oh, the eddy that set under the walls of the fort at Allahabad!" said the Adjutant. "They came in there like widgeon to the reeds, and round and round they swung—thus!"

He went off into his horrible dance again, while the Jackal looked on enviously. He naturally could not remember the terrible year of the Mutiny they were talking about. The Mugger continued:

"Yes, by Allahabad one lay still in the slack-water and let twenty go by to pick one; and, above all, the English were not cumbered with jewellery and nose-rings and anklets as my women are nowadays. To delight in ornaments is to end with a rope for a necklace, as the saying is. All the muggers of all the rivers grew fat then, but it was my Fate to be fatter than them all. The news was that the English were being hunted into the rivers, and by the Right and Left of Gunga! we believed it was true. So far as I went south I believed it to be true; and I went down-stream beyond Monghyr and the tombs that look over the river."

"I know that place," said the Adjutant. "Since those days Monghyr is a lost city. Very few live there now."

"Thereafter I worked up-stream very slowly and lazily, and a little above Monghyr there came down a boatful of white-faces—alive! They were, as I remember, women, lying under a cloth spread over sticks, and crying aloud. There was never a gun fired at us, the watchers of the fords in those days. All the guns were busy elsewhere. We could hear them day and night inland, coming and going as the wind shifted. I rose up full before the boat, because I had never seen white-faces alive, though I knew them well—otherwise. A naked white child kneeled by the side of the boat, and, stooping over, must needs try to trail his hands in the river. It is a pretty thing to see how a child loves running water. I had fed that day, but there was yet a little unfilled space within me. Still, it was for sport and not for food that I rose at the child's hands. They were so clear a mark that I did not even look when I closed; but they were so small that though my jaws rang true—I am sure of that—the child drew them up swiftly, unhurt. They must have passed between tooth and tooth—those small white hands. I should have caught him

cross-wise at the elbows; but, as I said, it was only for sport and desire to see new things that I rose at all. They cried out one after another in the boat, and presently I rose again to watch them. The boat was too heavy to push over. They were only women, but he who trusts a woman will walk on duckweed in a pool, as the saying is: and by the Right and Left of Gunga, that is truth!"

"Once a woman gave me some dried skin from a fish," said the Jackal. "I had hoped to get her baby, but horse-food is better than the kick of a horse, as the saying is. What did thy woman do?"

"She fired at me with a short gun of a kind I have never seen before or since. Five times, one after another" (the Mugger must have met with an old-fashioned revolver); "and I stayed open-mouthed and gaping, my head in the smoke. Never did I see such a thing. Five times, as swiftly as I wave my tail—thus!"

The Jackal, who had been growing more and more interested in the story, had just time to leap back as the huge tail swung by like a scythe.

"Not before the fifth shot," said the Mugger, as though he had never dreamed of stunning one of his listeners—"not before the fifth shot did I sink, and I rose in time to hear a boatman telling all those white women that I was most certainly dead. One bullet had gone under a neck-plate of mine. I know not if it is there still, for the reason I cannot turn my head. Look and see, child. It will show that my tale is true."

"I?" said the Jackal. "Shall an eater of old shoes, a bone-cracker, presume, to doubt the word of the Envy of the River? May my tail be bitten off by blind puppies if the shadow of such a thought has crossed my humble mind! The Protector of the Poor has condescended to inform me, his slave, that once in his life he has been wounded by a woman. That is sufficient, and I will tell the tale to all my children, asking for no proof."

"Over-much civility is sometimes no better than over-much discourtesy, for, as the saying is, one can choke a guest with curds. I do *not* desire that any children of thine should know that the Mugger of Mugger-Ghaut took his only wound from a woman. They will have much else to think of if they get their meat as miserably as does their father."

"It is forgotten long ago! It was never said! There never was a white woman! There was no boat! Nothing whatever happened at all."

The Jackal waved his brush to show how completely everything was wiped out of his memory, and sat down with an air.

"Indeed, very many things happened," said the Mugger, beaten in his second attempt that night to get the better of his friend. (Neither bore malice, however. Eat and be eaten was fair law along the river, and the Jackal came in for his share of plunder when the Mugger had finished a meal.) "I left that boat and went up-stream, and, when I had reached Arrah and the back-waters behind it, there were no more dead English. The river was empty for a while. Then came one or two dead, in red coats, not English, but of one kind all—Hindus and Purbeeahs—then five and six abreast, and at last, from Arrah to the North beyond Agra, it was as though whole villages had walked into the water. They came out of little creeks one after another, as the logs come down in the Rains. When the river rose they rose also in companies from the shoals they had rested upon; and the falling flood dragged them with it across the fields and through the Jungle by the long hair. All night, too, going North, I heard the guns, and by day the shod feet of men crossing fords, and that noise which a heavy cart-wheel makes on sand under water; and every ripple brought more dead. At last even I was afraid, for I said: 'If this thing happen to men, how shall the Mugger of Mugger-Ghaut escape?' There were boats, too, that came up behind me without sails, burning continually, as the cotton-boats sometimes burn, but never sinking."

"Ah!" said the Adjutant. "Boats like those come to Calcutta of the South. They are tall and black, they beat up the water behind them with a tail, and they—"

"Are thrice as big as my village. *My* boats were low and white; they beat up the water on either side of them and were no larger than the boats of one who speaks truth should be. They made me very afraid, and I left water and went back to this my river, hiding by day and walking by night, when I could not find little streams to help me. I came to my village again, but I did not hope to see any of my people there. Yet they were ploughing and sowing and reaping, and going to and fro in their fields, as quietly as their own cattle."

"Was there still good food in the river?" said the Jackal.

"More than I had any desire for. Even I—and I do not eat mud—even *I* was tired, and, as I remember, a little frightened of this constant coming down of the silent ones. I heard my people say in my village that all the English were dead; but those that came, face down, with the current were *not* English, as my people saw. Then my people said that it was best to say nothing at all, but to pay the tax and plough the land. After a long time the river cleared, and those that came down it had been clearly drowned by the floods, as I could well see; and though it was not so easy then to get food, I was heartily glad of it. A little killing here and there is no bad thing—but even the Mugger is sometimes satisfied, as the saying is."

"Marvellous! Most truly marvellous!" said the Jackal. "I am become fat through merely hearing about so much good eating. And afterward what, if it be permitted to ask, did the Protector of the Poor do?"

"I said to myself—and by the Right and Left of Gunga! I locked my jaws on that vow—I said I would never go roving any more. So I lived by the Ghaut, very close to my own people, and I watched over them year after year; and they loved me so much that they threw marigold wreaths at my head whenever they saw it lift. Yes, and my Fate has been very kind to me, and the river is good enough to respect my poor and infirm presence; only—"

"No one is all happy from his beak to his tail," said the Adjutant sympathetically. "What does the Mugger of Mugger-Ghaut need more?"

"That little white child which I did not get," said the Mugger, with a deep sigh. "He was very small, but I have not forgotten. I am old now, but before I die it is my desire to try one new thing. It is true they are a heavy-footed, noisy, and foolish people, and the sport would be small, but I remember the old days above Benares, and, if the child lives, he will remember still. It may be he goes up and down the bank of some river, telling how he once passed his hands between the teeth of the Mugger of Mugger-Ghaut, and lived to make a tale of it. My Fate has been very kind, but that plagues me sometimes in my dreams—the thought of the little white child in the bows of that boat." He yawned,

and closed his jaws. "And now I will rest and think. Keep silent, my children, and respect the aged."

He turned stiffly, and shuffled to the top of the sand-bar, while the Jackal drew back with the Adjutant to the shelter of a tree stranded on the end nearest the railway bridge.

"That was a pleasant and profitable life," he grinned, looking up inquiringly at the bird who towered above him. "And not once, mark you, did he think fit to tell me where a morsel might have been left along the banks. Yet I have told *him* a hundred times of good things wallowing down-stream. How true is the saying, 'All the world forgets the Jackal and the Barber when the news has been told!' Now he is going to sleep! *Arrh!*"

"How can a jackal hunt with a Mugger?" said the Adjutant coolly. "Big thief and little thief; it is easy to say who gets the pickings."

The Jackal turned, whining impatiently, and was going to curl himself up under the tree-trunk, when suddenly he cowered, and looked up through the draggled branches at the bridge almost above his head.

"What now?" said the Adjutant, opening his wings uneasily.

"Wait till we see. The wind blows from us to them, but they are not looking for us—those two men."

"Men, is it? My office protects me. All India knows I am holy." The Adjutant, being a first-class scavenger, is allowed to go where he pleases, and so this one never flinched.

"I am not worth a blow from anything better than an old shoe," said the Jackal, and listened again. "Hark to that footfall!" he went on. "That was no country leather, but the shod foot of a white-face. Listen again! Iron hits iron up there! It is a gun! Friend, those heavy-footed, foolish English are coming to speak with the Mugger."

"Warn him, then. He was called Protector of the Poor by some one not unlike a starving Jackal but a little time ago."

"Let my cousin protect his own hide. He has told me again and again there is nothing to fear from the white-faces. They must be white-faces. Not a villager of Mugger-Ghaut would dare to come after him. See, I said it was a gun! Now, with good luck, we shall feed before

daylight. He cannot hear well out of water, and—this time it is not a woman!"

A shiny barrel glittered for a minute in the moonlight on the girders. The Mugger was lying on the sand-bar as still as his own shadow, his fore-feet spread out a little, his head dropped between them, snoring like a—mugger.

A voice on the bridge whispered: "It's an odd shot—straight down almost—but as safe as houses. Better try behind the neck. Golly! what a brute! The villagers will be wild if he's shot, though. He's the *deota* [godling] of these parts."

"Don't care a rap," another voice answered; "he took about fifteen of my best coolies while the bridge was building, and it's time he was put a stop to. I've been after him in a boat for weeks. Stand by with the Martini as soon as I've given him both barrels of this."

"Mind the kick, then. A double four-bore's no joke."

"That's for him to decide. Here goes!"

There was a roar like the sound of a small cannon (the biggest sort of elephant-rifle is not very different from some artillery), and a double streak of flame, followed by the stinging crack of a Martini, whose long bullet makes nothing of a crocodile's plates. But the explosive bullets did the work. One of them struck just behind the Mugger's neck, a hand's-breadth to the left of the backbone, while the other burst a little lower down, at the beginning of the tail. In ninety-nine cases out of a hundred a mortally-wounded crocodile can scramble to deep water and get away; but the Mugger of Mugger-Ghaut was literally broken into three pieces. He hardly moved his head before the life went out of him, and he lay as flat as the Jackal.

"Thunder and lightning! Lightning and thunder!" said that miserable little beast. "Has the thing that pulls the covered carts over the bridge tumbled at last?"

"It is no more than a gun," said the Adjutant, though his very tail-feathers quivered. "Nothing more than a gun. He is certainly dead. Here come the white-faces."

The two Englishmen had hurried down from the bridge and across to the sand-bar, where they stood admiring the length of the Mugger.

Then a native with an axe cut off the big head, and four men dragged it across the spit.

"The last time that I had my hand in a Mugger's mouth," said one of the Englishmen, stooping down (he was the man who had built the bridge), "it was when I was about five years old—coming down the river by boat to Monghyr. I was a Mutiny baby, as they call it. Poor mother was in the boat, too, and she often told me how she fired dad's old pistol at the beast's head."

"Well, you've certainly had your revenge on the chief of the clan— even if the gun has made your nose bleed. Hi, you boatmen! Haul that head up the bank, and we'll boil it for the skull. The skin's too knocked about to keep. Come along to bed now. This was worth sitting up all night for, wasn't it?"

<p style="text-align:center">*　　　　*　　　　*　　　　*　　　　*</p>

Curiously enough, the Jackal and the Adjutant made the very same remark not three minutes after the men had left.

8. A RIPPLE SONG

Once a ripple came to land
In the golden sunset burning—
Lapped against a maiden's hand,
By the ford returning.

Dainty foot and gentle breast—
Here, across, be glad and rest.
"Maiden, wait," the ripple saith.
"Wait awhile, for I am Death!"

"Where my lover calls I go—
Shame it were to treat him coldly—
'Twas a fish that circled so,
Turning over boldly."

Dainty foot and tender heart,
Wait the loaded ferry-cart.
"Wait, ah, wait!" the ripple saith;
"Maiden, wait, for I am Death!"

"When my lover calls I haste—
Dame Disdain was never wedded!"
Ripple-ripple round her waist,
Clear the current eddied.

Foolish heart and faithful hand,
Little feet that touched no land.
Far away the ripple sped,
Ripple—ripple—running red!

9. THE KING'S ANKUS

These are the Four that are never content, that have never
 been filled since the Dews began—
Jacala's mouth, and the glut of the Kite, and the hands of the
 Ape, and the Eyes of Man.

—Jungle Saying

Kaa, the big Rock-python, had changed his skin for perhaps the two-hundredth time since his birth; and Mowgli, who never forgot that he owed his life to Kaa for a night's work at Cold Lairs, which you may perhaps remember, went to congratulate him. Skin-changing always makes a snake moody and depressed till the new skin begins to shine and look beautiful. Kaa never made fun of Mowgli any more, but accepted him, as the other Jungle People did, for the Master of the Jungle, and brought him all the news that a python of his size would naturally hear. What Kaa did not know about the Middle Jungle, as they call it,—the life that runs close to the earth or under it, the boulder, burrow, and the tree-bole life,—might have been written upon the smallest of his scales.

That afternoon Mowgli was sitting in the circle of Kaa's great coils, fingering the flaked and broken old skin that lay all looped and twisted among the rocks just as Kaa had left it. Kaa had very courteously packed himself under Mowgli's broad, bare shoulders, so that the boy was really resting in a living arm-chair.

"Even to the scales of the eyes it is perfect," said Mowgli, under his breath, playing with the old skin. "Strange to see the covering of one's own head at one's own feet!"

"Ay, but I lack feet," said Kaa; "and since this is the custom of all my people, I do not find it strange. Does thy skin never feel old and harsh?"

"Then go I and wash, Flathead; but, it is true, in the great heats I have wished I could slough my skin without pain, and run skinless."

"I wash, and *also* I take off my skin. How looks the new coat?"

Mowgli ran his hand down the diagonal checkerings of the immense back. "The Turtle is harder-backed, but not so gay," he said judgmatically. "The Frog, my name-bearer, is more gay, but not so hard. It is very beautiful to see—like the mottling in the mouth of a lily."

"It needs water. A new skin never comes to full colour before the first bath. Let us go bathe."

"I will carry thee," said Mowgli; and he stooped down, laughing, to lift the middle section of Kaa's great body, just where the barrel was thickest. A man might just, as well have tried to heave up a two-foot water-main; and Kaa lay still, puffing with quiet amusement. Then the regular evening game began—the Boy in the flush of his great strength, and the Python in his sumptuous new skin, standing up one against the other for a wrestling match—a trial of eye and strength. Of course, Kaa could have crushed a dozen Mowglis if he had let himself go; but he played carefully, and never loosed one-tenth of his power. Ever since Mowgli was strong enough to endure a little rough handling, Kaa had taught him this game, and it suppled his limbs as nothing else could. Sometimes Mowgli would stand lapped almost to his throat in Kaa's shifting coils, striving to get one arm free and catch him by the throat. Then Kaa would give way limply, and Mowgli, with both quick-moving feet, would try to cramp the purchase of that huge tail as it flung backward feeling for a rock or a stump. They would rock to and fro, head to head, each waiting for his chance, till the beautiful, statue-like group melted in a whirl of black-and-yellow coils and struggling legs and arms, to rise up again and again. "Now! now! now!" said Kaa, making feints with his head that even Mowgli's quick hand could not turn aside. "Look! I touch thee here, Little Brother! Here, and here! Are thy hands numb? Here again!"

The game always ended in one way—with a straight, driving blow of the head that knocked the boy over and over. Mowgli could never learn the guard for that lightning lunge, and, as Kaa said, there was not the least use in trying.

"Good hunting!" Kaa grunted at last; and Mowgli, as usual, was shot

away half a dozen yards, gasping and laughing. He rose with his fingers full of grass, and followed Kaa to the wise snake's pet bathing-place—a deep, pitchy-black pool surrounded with rocks, and made interesting by sunken tree-stumps. The boy slipped in, Jungle-fashion, without a sound, and dived across; rose, too, without a sound, and turned on his back, his arms behind his head, watching the moon rising above the rocks, and breaking up her reflection in the water with his toes. Kaa's diamond-shaped head cut the pool like a razor, and came out to rest on Mowgli's shoulder. They lay still, soaking luxuriously in the cool water.

"It is *very* good," said Mowgli at last, sleepily. "Now, in the Man-Pack, at this hour, as I remember, they laid them down upon hard pieces of wood in the inside of a mud-trap, and, having carefully shut out all the clean winds, drew foul cloth over their heavy heads and made evil songs through their noses. It is better in the Jungle."

A hurrying cobra slipped down over a rock and drank, gave them "Good hunting!" and went away.

"Sssh!" said Kaa, as though he had suddenly remembered something. "So the Jungle gives thee all that thou hast ever desired, Little Brother?"

"Not all," said Mowgli, laughing; "else there would be a new and strong Shere Khan to kill once a moon. *Now*, I could kill with my own hands, asking no help of buffaloes. And also I have wished the sun to shine in the middle of the Rains, and the Rains to cover the sun in the deep of summer; and also I have never gone empty but I wished that I had killed a goat; and also I have never killed a goat but I wished it had been buck; nor buck but I wished it had been nilghai. But thus do we feel, all of us."

"Thou hast no other desire?" the big snake demanded.

"What more can I wish? I have the Jungle, and the favour of the Jungle! Is there more anywhere between sunrise and sunset?"

"Now, the Cobra said—" Kaa began. "What cobra? He that went away just now said nothing. He was hunting."

"It was another."

"Hast thou many dealings with the Poison People? I give them their own path. They carry death in the fore-tooth, and that is not good—for they are so small. But what hood is this thou hast spoken with?"

Kaa rolled slowly in the water like a steamer in a beam sea. "Three or four moons since," said he, "I hunted in Cold Lairs, which place thou hast not forgotten. And the thing I hunted fled shrieking past the tanks and to that house whose side I once broke for thy sake, and ran into the ground."

"But the people of Cold Lairs do not live in burrows." Mowgli knew that Kaa was telling of the Monkey-People.

"This thing was not living, but seeking to live," Kaa replied, with a quiver of his tongue. "He ran into a burrow that led very far. I followed, and having killed, I slept. When I waked I went forward."

"Under the earth?"

"Even so, coming at last upon a White Hood [a white cobra], who spoke of things beyond my knowledge, and showed me many things I had never before seen."

"New game? Was it good hunting?" Mowgli turned quickly on his side.

"It was no game, and would have broken all my teeth; but the White Hood said that a man—he spoke as one that knew the breed—that a man would give the breath under his ribs for only the sight of those things."

"We will look," said Mowgli. "I now remember that I was once a man."

"Slowly—slowly. It was haste killed the Yellow Snake that ate the sun. We two spoke together under the earth, and I spoke of thee, naming thee as a man. Said the White Hood (and he is indeed as old as the Jungle): 'It is long since I have seen a man. Let him come, and he shall see all these things, for the least of which very many men would die.'"

"That *must* be new game. And yet the Poison People do not tell us when game is afoot. They are an unfriendly folk."

"It is *not* game. It is—it is—I cannot say what it is."

"We will go there. I have never seen a White Hood, and I wish to see the other things. Did he kill them?"

"They are all dead things. He says he is the keeper of them all."

"Ah! As a wolf stands above meat he has taken to his own lair. Let us go."

Mowgli swam to bank, rolled on the grass to dry himself, and the

two set off for Cold Lairs, the deserted city of which you may have heard. Mowgli was not the least afraid of the Monkey-People in those days, but the Monkey-People had the liveliest horror of Mowgli. Their tribes, however, were raiding in the Jungle, and so Cold Lairs stood empty and silent in the moonlight. Kaa led up to the ruins of the queens' pavilion that stood on the terrace, slipped over the rubbish, and dived down the half-choked staircase that went underground from the centre of the pavilion. Mowgli gave the snake-call,—"We be of one blood, ye and I,"—and followed on his hands and knees. They crawled a long distance down a sloping passage that turned and twisted several times, and at last came to where the root of some great tree, growing thirty feet overhead, had forced out a solid stone in the wall. They crept through the gap, and found themselves in a large vault, whose domed roof had been also broken away by tree-roots so that a few streaks of light dropped down into the darkness.

"A safe lair," said Mowgli, rising to his firm feet, "but over-far to visit daily. And now what do we see?"

"Am I nothing?" said a voice in the middle of the vault; and Mowgli saw something white move till, little by little, there stood up the hugest cobra he had ever set eyes on—a creature nearly eight feet long, and bleached by being in darkness to an old ivory-white. Even the spectacle-marks of his spread hood had faded to faint yellow. His eyes were as red as rubies, and altogether he was most wonderful.

"Good hunting!" said Mowgli, who carried his manners with his knife, and that never left him.

"What of the city?" said the White Cobra, without answering the greeting. "What of the great, the walled city—the city of a hundred elephants and twenty thousand horses, and cattle past counting—the city of the King of Twenty Kings? I grow deaf here, and it is long since I heard their war-gongs."

"The Jungle is above our heads," said Mowgli. "I know only Hathi and his sons among elephants. Bagheera has slain all the horses in one village, and—what is a King?"

"I told thee," said Kaa softly to the Cobra,—"I told thee, four moons ago, that thy city was not."

"The city—the great city of the forest whose gates are guarded by the King's towers—can never pass. They built it before my father's father came from the egg, and it shall endure when my son's sons are as white as I! Salomdhi, son of Chandrabija, son of Viyeja, son of Yegasuri, made it in the days of Bappa Rawal. Whose cattle are *ye?*"

"It is a lost trail," said Mowgli, turning to Kaa. "I know not his talk."

"Nor I. He is very old. Father of Cobras, there is only the Jungle here, as it has been since the beginning."

"Then who is *he*," said the White Cobra, "sitting down before me, unafraid, knowing not the name of the King, talking our talk through a man's lips? Who is he with the knife and the snake's tongue?"

"Mowgli they call me," was the answer. "I am of the Jungle. The wolves are my people, and Kaa here is my brother. Father of Cobras, who art thou?"

"I am the Warden of the King's Treasure. Kurrun Raja built the stone above me, in the days when my skin was dark, that I might teach death to those who came to steal. Then they let down the treasure through the stone, and I heard the song of the Brahmins my masters."

"Umm!" said Mowgli to himself. "I have dealt with one Brahmin already, in the Man-Pack, and—I know what I know. Evil comes here in a little."

"Five times since I came here has the stone been lifted, but always to let down more, and never to take away. There are no riches like these riches—the treasures of a hundred kings. But it is long and long since the stone was last moved, and I think that my city has forgotten."

"There is no city. Look up. Yonder are roots of the great trees tearing the stones apart. Trees and men do not grow together," Kaa insisted.

"Twice and thrice have men found their way here," the White Cobra answered savagely; "but they never spoke till I came upon them groping in the dark, and then they cried only a little time. But *ye* come with lies, Man and Snake both, and would have me believe the city is not, and that my wardship ends. Little do men change in the years. But *I* change never! Till the stone is lifted, and the Brahmins come down singing the songs that I know, and feed me with warm milk, and take

me to the light again, I—I—*I*, and no other, am the Warden of the King's Treasure! The city is dead, ye say, and here are the roots of the trees? Stoop down, then, and take what ye will. Earth has no treasure like to these. Man with the snake's tongue, if thou canst go alive by the way that thou hast entered it, the lesser Kings will be thy servants!"

"Again the trail is lost," said Mowgli coolly. "Can any jackal have burrowed so deep and bitten this great White Hood? He is surely mad. Father of Cobras, I see nothing here to take away."

"By the Gods of the Sun and Moon, it is the madness of death upon the boy!" hissed the Cobra. "Before thine eyes close I will allow thee this favour. Look thou, and see what man has never seen before!"

"They do not well in the Jungle who speak to Mowgli of favours," said the boy, between his teeth; "but the dark changes all, as I know. I will look, if that please thee."

He stared with puckered-up eyes round the vault, and then lifted up from the floor a handful of something that glittered.

"Oho!" said he, "this is like the stuff they play with in the Man-Pack: only this is yellow and the other was brown."

He let the gold pieces fall, and move forward. The floor of the vault was buried some five or six feet deep in coined gold and silver that had burst from the sacks it had been originally stored in, and, in the long years, the metal had packed and settled as sand packs at low tide. On it and in it and rising through it, as wrecks lift through the sand, were jewelled elephant-howdahs of embossed silver, studded with plates of hammered gold, and adorned with carbuncles and turquoises. There were palanquins and litters for carrying queens, framed and braced with silver and enamel, with jade-handled poles and amber curtain-rings; there were golden candlesticks hung with pierced emeralds that quivered on the branches; there were studded images, five feet high, of forgotten gods, silver with jewelled eyes; there were coats of mail, gold inlaid on steel, and fringed with rotted and blackened seed-pearls; there were helmets, crested and beaded with pigeon's-blood rubies; there were shields of lacquer, of tortoise-shell and rhinoceros-hide, strapped and bossed with red gold and set with emeralds at the edge; there were sheaves of diamond-hilted swords, daggers, and hunting-knives; there

were golden sacrificial bowls and ladles, and portable altars of a shape that never sees the light of day; there were jade cups and bracelets; there were incense-burners, combs, and pots for perfume, henna, and eye-powder, all in embossed gold; there were nose-rings, armlets, head-bands, finger-rings, and girdles past any counting; there were belts, seven fingers broad, of square-cut diamonds and rubies, and wooden boxes, trebly clamped with iron, from which the wood had fallen away in powder, showing the pile of uncut star-sapphires, opals, cat's-eyes, sapphires, rubies, diamonds, emeralds, and garnets within.

The White Cobra was right. No mere money would begin to pay the value of this treasure, the sifted pickings of centuries of war, plunder, trade, and taxation. The coins alone were priceless, leaving out of count all the precious stones; and the dead weight of the gold and silver alone might be two or three hundred tons. Every native ruler in India to-day, however poor, has a hoard to which he is always adding; and though, once in a long while, some enlightened prince may send off forty or fifty bullock-cart loads of silver to be exchanged for Government securities, the bulk of them keep their treasure and the knowledge of it very closely to themselves.

But Mowgli naturally did not understand what these things meant. The knives interested him a little, but they did not balance so well as his own, and so he dropped them. At last he found something really fascinating laid on the front of a howdah half buried in the coins. It was a three-foot ankus, or elephant-goad—something like a small boat-hook. The top was one round, shining ruby, and eight inches of the handle below it were studded with rough turquoises close together, giving a most satisfactory grip. Below them was a rim of jade with a flower-pattern running round it—only the leaves were emeralds, and the blossoms were rubies sunk in the cool, green stone. The rest of the handle was a shaft of pure ivory, while the point—the spike and hook—was gold-inlaid steel with pictures of elephant-catching; and the pictures attracted Mowgli, who saw that they had something to do with his friend Hathi the Silent.

The White Cobra had been following him closely.

"Is this not worth dying to behold?" he said. "Have I not done thee a great favour?"

"I do not understand," said Mowgli. "The things are hard and cold, and by no means good to eat. But this"—he lifted the ankus—"I desire to take away, that I may see it in the sun. Thou sayest they are all thine? Wilt thou give it to me, and I will bring thee frogs to eat?"

The White Cobra fairly shook with evil delight. "Assuredly I will give it," he said. "All that is here I will give thee—till thou goest away."

"But I go now. This place is dark and cold, and I wish to take the thorn-pointed thing to the Jungle."

"Look by thy foot! What is that there?" Mowgli picked up something white and smooth. "It is the bone of a man's head," he said quietly. "And here are two more."

"They came to take the treasure away many years ago. I spoke to them in the dark, and they lay still."

"But what do I need of this that is called treasure? If thou wilt give me the ankus to take away, it is good hunting. If not, it is good hunting none the less. I do not fight with the Poison People, and I was also taught the Master-word of thy tribe."

"There is but one Master-word here. It is mine!"

Kaa flung himself forward with blazing eyes. "Who bade me bring the Man?" he hissed.

"I surely," the old Cobra lisped. "It is long since I have seen Man, and this Man speaks our tongue."

"But there was no talk of killing. How can I go to the Jungle and say that I have led him to his death?" said Kaa.

"I talk not of killing till the time. And as to thy going or not going, there is the hole in the wall. Peace, now, thou fat monkey-killer! I have but to touch thy neck, and the Jungle will know thee no longer. Never Man came here that went away with the breath under his ribs. I am the Warden of the Treasure of the King's City!"

"But, thou white worm of the dark, I tell thee there is neither king nor city! The Jungle is all about us!" cried Kaa.

"There is still the Treasure. But this can be done. Wait awhile, Kaa of the Rocks, and see the boy run. There is room for great sport here. Life is good. Run to and fro awhile, and make sport, boy!"

Mowgli put his hand on Kaa's head quietly.

"The white thing has dealt with men of the Man-Pack until now. He does not know me," he whispered. "He has asked for this hunting. Let him have it." Mowgli had been standing with the ankus held point down. He flung it from him quickly and it dropped crossways just behind the great snake's hood, pinning him to the floor. In a flash, Kaa's weight was upon the writhing body, paralysing it from hood to tail. The red eyes burned, and the six spare inches of the head struck furiously right and left.

"Kill!" said Kaa, as Mowgli's hand went to his knife.

"No," he said, as he drew the blade; "I will never kill again save for food. But look you, Kaa!" He caught the snake behind the hood, forced the mouth open with the blade of the knife, and showed the terrible poison-fangs of the upper jaw lying black and withered in the gum. The White Cobra had outlived his poison, as a snake will.

"*Thuu*" ("It is dried up"),"* said Mowgli; and motioning Kaa away, he picked up the ankus, setting the White Cobra free.

"The King's Treasure needs a new Warden," he said gravely. "Thuu, thou hast not done well. Run to and fro and make sport, Thuu!"

"I am ashamed. Kill me!" hissed the White Cobra.

"There has been too much talk of killing. We will go now. I take the thorn-pointed thing, Thuu, because I have fought and worsted thee."

"See, then, that the thing does not kill thee at last. It is Death! Remember, it is Death! There is enough in that thing to kill the men of all my city. Not long wilt thou hold it, Jungle Man, nor he who takes it from thee. They will kill, and kill, and kill for its sake! My strength is dried up, but the ankus will do my work. It is Death! It is Death! It is Death!"

Mowgli crawled out through the hole into the passage again, and the last that he saw was the White Cobra striking furiously with his harmless fangs at the stolid golden faces of the gods that lay on the floor, and hissing, "It is Death!"

They were glad to get to the light of day once more; and when they were back in their own Jungle and Mowgli made the ankus glitter in the morning light, he was almost as pleased as though he had found a bunch of new flowers to stick in his hair.

* Literally, a rotted out tree-stump.

"This is brighter than Bagheera's eyes," he said delightedly, as he twirled the ruby. "I will show it to him; but what did the Thuu mean when he talked of death?"

"I cannot say. I am sorrowful to my tail's tail that he felt not thy knife. There is always evil at Cold Lairs—above ground or below. But now I am hungry. Dost thou hunt with me this dawn?" said Kaa.

"No; Bagheera must see this thing. Good hunting!" Mowgli danced off, flourishing the great ankus, and stopping from time to time to admire it, till he came to that part of the Jungle Bagheera chiefly used, and found him drinking after a heavy kill. Mowgli told him all his adventures from beginning to end, and Bagheera sniffed at the ankus between whiles. When Mowgli came to the White Cobra's last words, the Panther purred approvingly.

"Then the White Hood spoke the thing which is?" Mowgli asked quickly.

"I was born in the King's cages at Oodeypore, and it is in my stomach that I know some little of Man. Very many men would kill thrice in a night for the sake of that one big red stone alone."

"But the stone makes it heavy to the hand. My little bright knife is better; and—see! the red stone is not good to eat. Then *why* would they kill?"

"Mowgli, go thou and sleep. Thou hast lived among men, and—"

"I remember. Men kill because they are not hunting;—for idleness and pleasure. Wake again, Bagheera. For what use was this thorn-pointed thing made?"

Bagheera half opened his eyes—he was very sleepy—with a malicious twinkle.

"It was made by men to thrust into the head of the sons of Hathi, so that the blood should pour out. I have seen the like in the street of Oodeypore, before our cages. That thing has tasted the blood of many such as Hathi."

"But why do they thrust into the heads of elephants?"

"To teach them Man's Law. Having neither claws nor teeth, men make these things—and worse."

"Always more blood when I come near, even to the things the Man-

Pack have made," said Mowgli disgustedly. He was getting a little tired of the weight of the ankus. "If I had known this, I would not have taken it. First it was Messua's blood on the thongs, and now it is Hathi's. I will use it no more. Look!"

The ankus flew sparkling, and buried itself point down thirty yards away, between the trees. "So my hands are clean of Death," said Mowgli, rubbing his palms on the fresh, moist earth. "The Thuu said Death would follow me. He is old and white and mad."

"White or black, or death or life, *I* am going to sleep, Little Brother. I cannot hunt all night and howl all day, as do some folk."

Bagheera went off to a hunting-lair that he knew, about two miles off. Mowgli made an easy way for himself up a convenient tree, knotted three or four creepers together, and in less time than it takes to tell was swinging in a hammock fifty feet above ground. Though he had no positive objection to strong daylight, Mowgli followed the custom of his friends, and used it as little as he could. When he waked among the very loud-voiced peoples that live in the trees, it was twilight once more, and he had been dreaming of the beautiful pebbles he had thrown away.

"At least I will look at the thing again," he said, and slid down a creeper to the earth; but Bagheera was before him. Mowgli could hear him snuffing in the half light.

"Where is the thorn-pointed thing?" cried Mowgli.

"A man has taken it. Here is the trail."

"Now we shall see whether the Thuu spoke truth. If the pointed thing is Death, that man will die. Let us follow."

"Kill first," said Bagheera. "An empty stomach makes a careless eye. Men go very slowly, and the Jungle is wet enough to hold the lightest mark."

They killed as soon as they could, but it was nearly three hours before they finished their meat and drink and buckled down to the trail. The Jungle People know that nothing makes up for being hurried over your meals.

"Think you the pointed thing will turn in the man's hand and kill him?" Mowgli asked. "The Thuu said it was Death."

"We shall see when we find," said Bagheera, trotting with his head low. "It is single-foot" (he meant that there was only one man), "and the weight of the thing has pressed his heel far into the ground."

"Hai! This is as clear as summer lightning," Mowgli answered; and they fell into the quick, choppy trail-trot in and out through the checkers of the moonlight, following the marks of those two bare feet.

"Now he runs swiftly," said Mowgli. "The toes are spread apart." They went on over some wet ground. "Now why does he turn aside here?"

"Wait!" said Bagheera, and flung himself forward with one superb bound as far as ever he could. The first thing to do when a trail ceases to explain itself is to cast forward without leaving, your own confusing foot-marks on the ground. Bagheera turned as he landed, and faced Mowgli, crying, "Here comes another trail to meet him. It is a smaller foot, this second trail, and the toes turn inward."

Then Mowgli ran up and looked. "It is the foot of a Gond hunter," he said. "Look! Here he dragged his bow on the grass. That is why the first trail turned aside so quickly. Big Foot hid from Little Foot."

"That is true," said Bagheera. "Now, lest by crossing each other's tracks we foul the signs, let each take one trail. I am Big Foot, Little Brother, and thou art Little Foot, the Gond."

Bagheera leaped back to the original trail, leaving Mowgli stooping above the curious narrow track of the wild little man of the woods.

"Now," said Bagheera, moving step by step along the chain of footprints, "I, Big Foot, turn aside here. Now I hide me behind a rock and stand still, not daring to shift my feet. Cry thy trail, Little Brother."

"Now, I, Little Foot, come to the rock," said Mowgli, running up his trail. "Now, I sit down under the rock, leaning upon my right hand, and resting my bow between my toes. I wait long, for the mark of my feet is deep here."

"I also," said Bagheera, hidden behind the rock. "I wait, resting the end of the thorn-pointed thing upon a stone. It slips, for here is a scratch upon the stone. Cry thy trail, Little Brother."

"One, two twigs and a big branch are broken here," said Mowgli, in an undertone. "Now, how shall I cry *that*? Ah! It is plain now. I, Little Foot, go away making noises and tramplings so that Big Foot

may hear me." He moved away from the rock pace by pace among the trees, his voice rising in the distance as he approached a little cascade. "I—go, far—away—to—where—the—noise—of—falling-water—covers—my—noise; and—here—I—wait. Cry thy trail, Bagheera, Big Foot!"

The panther had been casting in every direction to see how Big Foot's trail led away from behind the rock. Then he gave tongue:

"I come from behind the rock upon my knees, dragging the thorn-pointed thing. Seeing no one, I run. I, Big Foot, run swiftly. The trail is clear. Let each follow his own. I run!"

Bagheera swept on along the clearly-marked trail, and Mowgli followed the steps of the Gond. For some time there was silence in the Jungle.

"Where art thou, Little Foot?" cried Bagheera. Mowgli's voice answered him not fifty yards to the right.

"Um!" said the Panther, with a deep cough. "The two run side by side, drawing nearer!"

They raced on another half-mile, always keeping about the same distance, till Mowgli, whose head was not so close to the ground as Bagheera's, cried: "They have met. Good hunting—look! Here stood Little Foot, with his knee on a rock—and yonder is Big Foot indeed!"

Not ten yards in front of them, stretched across a pile of broken rocks, lay the body of a villager of the district, a long, small-feathered Gond arrow through his back and breast.

"Was the Thuu so old and so mad, Little Brother?" said Bagheera gently. "Here is one death, at least."

"Follow on. But where is the drinker of elephant's blood—the red-eyed thorn?"

"Little Foot has it—perhaps. It is single-foot again now."

The single trail of a light man who had been running quickly and bearing a burden on his left shoulder held on round a long, low spur of dried grass, where each footfall seemed, to the sharp eyes of the trackers, marked in hot iron.

Neither spoke till the trail ran up to the ashes of a camp-fire hidden in a ravine.

"Again!" said Bagheera, checking as though he had been turned into stone.

The body of a little wizened Gond lay with its feet in the ashes, and Bagheera looked inquiringly at Mowgli.

"That was done with a bamboo," said the boy, after one glance. "I have used such a thing among the buffaloes when I served in the Man-Pack. The Father of Cobras—I am sorrowful that I made a jest of him—knew the breed well, as I might have known. Said I not that men kill for idleness?"

"Indeed, they killed for the sake of the red and blue stones," Bagheera answered. "Remember, *I* was in the King's cages at Oodeypore."

"One, two, three, four tracks," said Mowgli, stooping over the ashes. "Four tracks of men with shod feet. They do not go so quickly as Gonds. Now, what evil had the little woodman done to them? See, they talked together, all five, standing up, before they killed him. Bagheera, let us go back. My stomach is heavy in me, and yet it heaves up and down like an oriole's nest at the end of a branch."

"It is not good hunting to leave game afoot. Follow!" said the panther. "Those eight shod feet have not gone far."

No more was said for fully an hour, as they worked up the broad trail of the four men with shod feet.

It was clear, hot daylight now, and Bagheera said, "I smell smoke."

"Men are always more ready to eat than to run," Mowgli answered, trotting in and out between the low scrub bushes of the new Jungle they were exploring. Bagheera, a little to his left, made an indescribable noise in his throat.

"Here is one that has done with feeding," said he. A tumbled bundle of gay-coloured clothes lay under a bush, and round it was some spilt flour.

"That was done by the bamboo again," said Mowgli. "See! that white dust is what men eat. They have taken the kill from this one,—he carried their food,—and given him for a kill to Chil, the Kite."

"It is the third," said Bagheera.

"I will go with new, big frogs to the Father of Cobras, and feed him

fat," said Mowgli to himself. "The drinker of elephant's blood is Death himself—but still I do not understand!"

"Follow!" said Bagheera.

They had not gone half a mile farther when they heard Ko, the Crow, singing the death-song in the top of a tamarisk under whose shade three men were lying. A half-dead fire smoked in the centre of the circle, under an iron plate which held a blackened and burned cake of unleavened bread. Close to the fire, and blazing in the sunshine, lay the ruby-and-turquoise ankus.

"The thing works quickly; all ends here," said Bagheera. "How did *these* die, Mowgli? There is no mark on any."

A Jungle-dweller gets to learn by experience as much as many doctors know of poisonous plants and berries. Mowgli sniffed the smoke that came up from the fire, broke off a morsel of the blackened bread, tasted it, and spat it out again.

"Apple of Death," he coughed. "The first must have made it ready in the food for *these*, who killed him, having first killed the Gond."

"Good hunting, indeed! The kills follow close," said Bagheera.

"Apple of Death" is what the Jungle call thorn-apple or dhatura, the readiest poison in all India.

"What now?" said the panther. "Must thou and I kill each other for yonder red-eyed slayer?"

"Can it speak?" said Mowgli in a whisper. "Did I do it a wrong when I threw it away? Between us two it can do no wrong, for we do not desire what men desire. If it be left here, it will assuredly continue to kill men one after another as fast as nuts fall in a high wind. I have no love to men, but even I would not have them die six in a night."

"What matter? They are only men. They killed one another, and were well pleased," said Bagheera. "That first little woodman hunted well."

"They are cubs none the less; and a cub will drown himself to bite the moon's light on the water. The fault was mine," said Mowgli, who spoke as though he knew all about everything. "I will never again bring into the Jungle strange things—not though they be as beautiful as flowers. This"—he handled the ankus gingerly—"goes back to the

Father of Cobras. But first we must sleep, and we cannot sleep near these sleepers. Also we must bury *him*, lest he run away and kill another six. Dig me a hole under that tree."

"But, Little Brother," said Bagheera, moving off to the spot, "I tell thee it is no fault of the blood-drinker. The trouble is with the men."

"All one," said Mowgli. "Dig the hole deep. When we wake I will take him up and carry him back."

* * * * *

Two nights later, as the White Cobra sat mourning in the darkness of the vault, ashamed, and robbed, and alone, the turquoise ankus whirled through the hole in the wall, and clashed on the floor of golden coins.

"Father of Cobras," said Mowgli (he was careful to keep the other side of the wall), "get thee a young and ripe one of thine own people to help thee guard the King's Treasure, so that no man may come away alive any more."

"Ah-ha! It returns, then. I said the thing was Death. How comes it that thou art still alive?" the old Cobra mumbled, twining lovingly round the ankus-haft.

"By the Bull that bought me, I do not know! That thing has killed six times in a night. Let him go out no more."

10. THE SONG OF THE LITTLE HUNTER

Ere Mor the Peacock flutters, ere the Monkey-People cry,
Ere Chil the Kite swoops down a furlong sheer,
Through the Jungle very softly flits a shadow and a sigh—
He is Fear, O Little Hunter, he is Fear!
Very softly down the glade runs a waiting, watching shade,
And the whisper spreads and widens far and near;
And the sweat is on thy brow, for he passes even now—
He is Fear, O Little Hunter, he is Fear!

Ere the moon has climbed the mountain, ere the rocks are
 ribbed with light,
When the downward-dipping trails are dank and drear,
Comes a breathing hard behind thee—*snuffle-snuffle*
 through the night—
It is Fear, O Little Hunter, it is Fear!
On thy knees and draw the bow; bid the shrilling arrow go;
In the empty, mocking thicket plunge the spear;
But thy hands are loosed and weak, and the blood has left thy
 cheek—
It is Fear, O Little Hunter, it is Fear!

When the heat-cloud sucks the tempest, when the slivered
 pine-trees fall,
When the blinding, blaring rain-squalls lash and veer;
Through the war-gongs of the thunder rings a voice more
 loud than all—
It is Fear, O Little Hunter, it is Fear!
Now the spates are banked and deep; now the footless
 boulders leap—
Now the lightning shows each littlest leaf-rib clear—
But thy throat is shut and dried, and thy heart against thy
 side
Hammers: Fear, O Little Hunter—this is Fear!

11. QUIQUERN

The People of the Eastern Ice, they are melting like
 the snow—
They beg for coffee and sugar; they go where the white
 men go.
The People of the Western Ice, they learn to steal
 and fight;
They sell their furs to the trading-post: they sell their
 souls to the white.

The People of the Southern Ice, they trade with the
 whaler's crew;
Their women have many ribbons, but their tents are
 torn and few.
But the People of the Elder Ice, beyond the white
 man's ken—
Their spears are made of the narwhal-horn, and they
 are the last of the Men!

 —*Translation*

He has opened his eyes. Look!"

"Put him in the skin again. He will be a strong dog. On the fourth month we will name him."

"For whom?" said Amoraq.

Kadlu's eye rolled round the skin-lined snow-house till it fell on fourteen-year-old Kotuko sitting on the sleeping-bench, making a button out of walrus ivory. "Name him for me," said Kotuko, with a grin. "I shall need him one day."

Kadlu grinned back till his eyes were almost buried in the fat of his flat cheeks, and nodded to Amoraq, while the puppy's fierce mother whined to see her baby wriggling far out of reach in the little sealskin pouch hung above the warmth of the blubber-lamp. Kotuko went on with his carving, and Kadlu threw a rolled bundle of leather dog-harnesses into a tiny little room that opened from one side of the house,

slipped off his heavy deerskin hunting-suit, put it into a whalebone-net that hung above another lamp, and dropped down on the sleeping-bench to whittle at a piece of frozen seal-meat till Amoraq, his wife, should bring the regular dinner of boiled meat and blood-soup. He had been out since early dawn at the seal-holes, eight miles away, and had come home with three big seal. Half-way down the long, low snow passage or tunnel that led to the inner door of the house you could hear snappings and yelpings, as the dogs of his sleigh-team, released from the day's work, scuffled for warm places.

When the yelpings grew too loud Kotuko lazily rolled off the sleeping-bench, and picked up a whip with an eighteen-inch handle of springy whalebone, and twenty-five feet of heavy, plaited thong. He dived into the passage, where it sounded as though all the dogs were eating him alive; but that was no more than their regular grace before meals. When he crawled out at the far end, half a dozen furry heads followed him with their eyes as he went to a sort of gallows of whale-jawbones, from which the dog's meat was hung; split off the frozen stuff in big lumps with a broad-headed spear; and stood, his whip in one hand and the meat in the other. Each beast was called by name, the weakest first, and woe betide any dog that moved out of his turn; for the tapering lash would shoot out like thonged lightning, and flick away an inch or so of hair and hide. Each beast growled, snapped, choked once over his portion, and hurried back to the protection of the passage, while the boy stood upon the snow under the blazing Northern Lights and dealt out justice. The last to be served was the big black leader of the team, who kept order when the dogs were harnessed; and to him Kotuko gave a double allowance of meat as well as an extra crack of the whip.

"Ah!" said Kotuko, coiling up the lash, "I have a little one over the lamp that will make a great many howlings. *Sarpok!* Get in!"

He crawled back over the huddled dogs, dusted the dry snow from his furs with the whalebone beater that Amoraq kept by the door, tapped the skin-lined roof of the house to shake off any icicles that might have fallen from the dome of snow above, and curled up on the bench. The dogs in the passage snored and whined in their sleep, the boy-baby in Amoraq's deep fur hood kicked and choked and gurgled,

and the mother of the newly-named puppy lay at Kotuko's side, her eyes fixed on the bundle of sealskin, warm and safe above the broad yellow flame of the lamp.

And all this happened far away to the north, beyond Labrador, beyond Hudson's Strait, where the great tides heave the ice about, north of Melville Peninsula—north even of the narrow Fury and Hecla Straits—on the north shore of Baffin Land, where Bylot's Island stands above the ice of Lancaster Sound like a pudding-bowl wrong side up. North of Lancaster Sound there is little we know anything about, except North Devon and Ellesmere Land; but even there live a few scattered people, next door, as it were, to the very Pole.

Kadlu was an Inuit,—what you call an Esquimau,—and his tribe, some thirty persons all told, belonged to the Tununirmiut—"the country lying at the back of something." In the maps that desolate coast is written Navy Board Inlet, but the Inuit name is best, because the country lies at the very back of everything in the world. For nine months of the year there is only ice and snow, and gale after gale, with a cold that no one can realise who has never seen the thermometer even at zero. For six months of those nine it is dark; and that is what makes it so horrible. In the three months of the summer it only freezes every other day and every night, and then the snow begins to weep off on the southerly slopes, and a few ground-willows put out their woolly buds, a tiny stonecrop or so makes believe to blossom, beaches of fine gravel and rounded stones run down to the open sea, and polished boulders and streaked rocks lift up above the granulated snow. But all that is gone in a few weeks, and the wild winter locks down again on the land; while at sea the ice tears up and down the offing, jamming and ramming, and splitting and hitting, and pounding and grounding, till it all freezes together, ten feet thick, from the land outward to deep water.

In the winter Kadlu would follow the seal to the edge of this land-ice, and spear them as they came up to breathe at their blow-holes. The seal must have open water to live and catch fish in, and in the deep of winter the ice would sometimes run eighty miles without a break from the nearest shore. In the spring he and his people retreated from the floes to the rocky mainland, where they put up tents of skins, and snared

the sea-birds, or speared the young seal basking on the beaches. Later, they would go south into Baffin Land after the reindeer, and to get their year's store of salmon from the hundreds of streams and lakes of the interior; coming back north in September or October for the musk-ox hunting and the regular winter sealery. This travelling was done with dog-sleighs, twenty and thirty miles a day, or sometimes down the coast in big skin "woman-boats," when the dogs and the babies lay among the feet of the rowers, and the women sang songs as they glided from cape to cape over the glassy, cold waters. All the luxuries that the Tununirmiut knew came from the south—driftwood for sleigh-runners, rod-iron for harpoon-tips, steel knives, tin kettles that cooked food much better than the old soap-stone affairs, flint and steel, and even matches, as well as coloured ribbons for the women's hair, little cheap mirrors, and red cloth for the edging of deerskin dress-jackets. Kadlu traded the rich, creamy, twisted narwhal horn and musk-ox teeth (these are just as valuable as pearls) to the Southern Inuit, and they, in turn, traded with the whalers and the missionary-posts of Exeter and Cumberland Sounds; and so the chain went on, till a kettle picked up by a ship's cook in the Bhendy Bazaar might end its days over a blubber-lamp somewhere on the cool side of the Arctic Circle.

Kadlu, being a good hunter, was rich in iron harpoons, snow-knives, bird-darts, and all the other things that make life easy up there in the great cold; and he was the head of his tribe, or, as they say, "the man who knows all about it by practice." This did not give him any authority, except now and then he could advise his friends to change their hunting-grounds; but Kotuko used it to domineer a little, in the lazy, fat Inuit fashion, over the other boys, when they came out at night to play ball in the moonlight, or to sing the Child's Song to the Aurora Borealis.

But at fourteen an Inuit feels himself a man, and Kotuko was tired of making snares for wild-fowl and kit-foxes, and most tired of all of helping the women to chew seal-and deer-skins (that supples them as nothing else can) the long day through, while the men were out hunting. He wanted to go into the *quaggi*, the Singing-House, when the hunters gathered there for their mysteries, and the *angekok*, the

sorcerer, frightened them into the most delightful fits after the lamps were put out, and you could hear the Spirit of the Reindeer stamping on the roof; and when a spear was thrust out into the open black night it came back covered with hot blood. He wanted to throw his big boots into the net with the tired air of the head of a family, and to gamble with the hunters when they dropped in of an evening and played a sort of home-made roulette with a tin pot and a nail. There were hundreds of things that he wanted to do, but the grown men laughed at him and said, "Wait till you have been in the buckle, Kotuko. Hunting is not *all* catching."

Now that his father had named a puppy for him, things looked brighter. An Inuit does not waste a good dog on his son till the boy knows something of dog-driving; and Kotuko was more than sure that he knew more than everything.

If the puppy had not had an iron constitution he would have died from over-stuffing and over-handling. Kotuko made him a tiny harness with a trace to it, and hauled him all over the house-floor, shouting: "Aua! Ja aua!" (Go to the right!) "Choiachoi! Ja choiachoi!" (Go to the left!) "Ohaha!" (Stop!) The puppy did not like it at all, but being fished for in this way was pure happiness beside being put to the sleigh for the first time. He just sat down on the snow, and played with the seal-hide trace that ran from his harness to the *pitu*, the big thong in the bows of the sleigh. Then the team started, and the puppy found the heavy ten-foot sleigh running up his back, and dragging him along the snow, while Kotuko laughed till the tears ran down his face. There followed days and days of the cruel whip that hisses like the wind over ice, and his companions all bit him because he did not know his work, and the harness chafed him, and he was not allowed to sleep with Kotuko any more, but had to take the coldest place in the passage. It was a sad time for the puppy.

The boy learned, too, as fast as the dog; though a dog-sleigh is a heart-breaking thing to manage. Each beast is harnessed, the weakest nearest to the driver, by his own separate trace, which runs under his left fore-leg to the main thong, where it is fastened by a sort of button and loop which can be slipped by a turn of the wrist, thus freeing one

dog at a time. This is very necessary, because young dogs often get the trace between their hind legs, where it cuts to the bone. And they one and all *will* go visiting their friends as they run, jumping in and out among the traces. Then they fight, and the result is more mixed than a wet fishing-line next morning. A great deal of trouble can be avoided by scientific use of the whip. Every Inuit boy prides himself as being a master of the long lash; but it is easy to flick at a mark on the ground, and difficult to lean forward and catch a shirking dog just behind the shoulders when the sleigh is going at full speed. If you call one dog's name for "visiting," and accidentally lash another, the two will fight it out at once, and stop all the others. Again, if you travel with a companion and begin to talk, or by yourself and sing, the dogs will halt, turn round, and sit down to hear what you have to say. Kotuko was run away from once or twice through forgetting to block the sleigh when he stopped; and he broke many lashings, and ruined a few thongs before he could be trusted with a full team of eight and the light sleigh. Then he felt himself a person of consequence, and on smooth, black ice, with a bold heart and a quick elbow, he smoked along over the levels as fast as a pack in full cry. He would go ten miles to the seal-holes, and when he was on the hunting-grounds he would twitch a trace loose from the *pitu*, and free the big black leader, who was the cleverest dog in the team. As soon as the dog had scented a breathing-hole, Kotuko would reverse the sleigh, driving a couple of sawed-off antlers, that stuck up like perambulator-handles from the back-rest, deep into the snow, so that the team could not get away. Then he would crawl forward inch by inch, and wait till the seal came up to breathe. Then he would stab down swiftly with his spear and running-line, and presently would haul his seal up to the lip of the ice, while the black leader came up and helped to pull the carcass across the ice to the sleigh. That was the time when the harnessed dogs yelled and foamed with excitement, and Kotuko laid the long lash like a red-hot bar across all their faces, till the carcass froze stiff. Going home was the heavy work. The loaded sleigh had to be humoured among the rough ice, and the dogs sat down and looked hungrily at the seal instead of pulling. At last they would strike the well-worn sleigh-road to the

village, and toodle-kiyi along the ringing ice, heads down and tails up, while Kotuko struck up the "An-gutivaun tai-na tau-na-ne taina" (The Song of the Returning Hunter), and voices hailed him from house to house under all that dim, star-littern sky.

When Kotuko the dog came to his full growth he enjoyed himself too. He fought his way up the team steadily, fight after fight, till one fine evening, over their food, he tackled the big, black leader (Kotuko the boy saw fair play), and made second dog of him, as they say. So he was promoted to the long thong of the leading dog, running five feet in advance of all the others: it was his bounden duty to stop all fighting, in harness or out of it, and he wore a collar of copper wire, very thick and heavy. On special occasions he was fed with cooked food inside the house, and sometimes was allowed to sleep on the bench with Kotuko. He was a good seal-dog, and would keep a musk-ox at bay by running round him and snapping at his heels. He would even—and this for a sleigh-dog is the last proof of bravery—he would even stand up to the gaunt Arctic wolf, whom all dogs of the North, as a rule, fear beyond anything that walks the snow. He and his master—they did not count the team of ordinary dogs as company—hunted together, day after day and night after night, fur-wrapped boy and savage, long-haired, narrow-eyed, white-fanged, yellow brute. All an Inuit has to do is to get food and skins for himself and his family. The women-folk make the skins into clothing, and occasionally help in trapping small game; but the bulk of the food—and they eat enormously—must be found by the men. If the supply fails there is no one up there to buy or beg or borrow from. The people must die.

An Inuit does not think of these chances till he is forced to. Kadlu, Kotuko, Amoraq, and the boy-baby who kicked about in Amoraq's fur hood and chewed pieces of blubber all day, were as happy together as any family in the world. They came of a very gentle race—an Inuit seldom loses his temper, and almost never strikes a child—who did not know exactly what telling a real lie meant, still less how to steal. They were content to spear their living out of the heart of the bitter, hopeless cold; to smile oily smiles, and tell queer ghost and fairy tales of evenings, and eat till they could eat no more, and sing the endless

woman's song: "Amna aya, aya amna, ah! ah!" through the long lamp-lighted days as they mended their clothes and their hunting-gear.

But one terrible winter everything betrayed them. The Tununirmiut returned from the yearly salmon-fishing, and made their houses on the early ice to the north of Bylot's Island, ready to go after the seal as soon as the sea froze. But it was an early and savage autumn. All through September there were continuous gales that broke up the smooth seal-ice when it was only four or five feet thick, and forced it inland, and piled a great barrier, some twenty miles broad, of lumped and ragged and needly ice, over which it was impossible to draw the dog-sleighs. The edge of the floe off which the seal were used to fish in winter lay perhaps twenty miles beyond this barrier, and out of reach of the Tununirmiut. Even so, they might have managed to scrape through the winter on their stock of frozen salmon and stored blubber, and what the traps gave them, but in December one of their hunters came across a *tupik* (a skin-tent) of three women and a girl nearly dead, whose men had come down from the far North and been crushed in their little skin hunting-boats while they were out after the long-horned narwhal. Kadlu, of course, could only distribute the women among the huts of the winter village, for no Inuit dare refuse a meal to a stranger. He never knows when his own turn may come to beg. Amoraq took the girl, who was about fourteen, into her own house as a sort of servant. From the cut of her sharp-pointed hood, and the long diamond pattern of her white deer-skin leggings, they supposed she came from Ellesmere Land. She had never seen tin cooking-pots or wooden-shod sleighs before; but Kotuko the boy and Kotuko the dog were rather fond of her.

Then all the foxes went south, and even the wolverine, that growling, blunt-headed little thief of the snow, did not take the trouble to follow the line of empty traps that Kotuko set. The tribe lost a couple of their best hunters, who were badly crippled in a fight with a musk-ox, and this threw more work on the others. Kotuko went out, day after day, with a light hunting-sleigh and six or seven of the strongest dogs, looking till his eyes ached for some patch of clear ice where a seal might perhaps have scratched a breathing-hole. Kotuko the dog ranged far and wide, and in the dead stillness of the ice-fields Kotuko the boy could hear his

half-choked whine of excitement, above a seal-hole three miles away, as plainly as though he were at his elbow. When the dog found a hole the boy would build himself a little, low snow wall to keep off the worst of the bitter wind, and there he would wait ten, twelve, twenty hours for the seal to come up to breathe, his eyes glued to the tiny mark he had made above the hole to guide the downward thrust of his harpoon, a little seal-skin mat under his feet, and his legs tied together in the *tutareang* (the buckle that the old hunters had talked about). This helps to keep a man's legs from twitching as he waits and waits and waits for the quick-eared seal to rise. Though there is no excitement in it, you can easily believe that the sitting still in the buckle with the thermometer perhaps forty degrees below zero is the hardest work an Inuit knows. When a seal was caught, Kotuko the dog would bound forward, his trace trailing behind him, and help to pull the body to the sleigh, where the tired and hungry dogs lay sullenly under the lee of the broken ice.

A seal did not go very far, for each mouth in the little village had a right to be filled, and neither bone, hide, nor sinew was wasted. The dogs' meat was taken for human use, and Amoraq fed the team with pieces of old summer skin-tents raked out from under the sleeping-bench, and they howled and howled again, and waked to howl hungrily. One could tell by the soap-stone lamps in the huts that famine was near. In good seasons, when blubber was plentiful, the light in the boat-shaped lamps would be two feet high—cheerful, oily, and yellow. Now it was a bare six inches: Amoraq carefully pricked down the moss wick, when an unwatched flame brightened for a moment, and the eyes of all the family followed her hand. The horror of famine up there in the great cold is not so much dying, as dying in the dark. All the Inuit dread the dark that presses on them without a break for six months in each year; and when the lamps are low in the houses the minds of people begin to be shaken and confused.

But worse was to come.

The underfed dogs snapped and growled in the passages, glaring at the cold stars, and snuffing into the bitter wind, night after night. When they stopped howling the silence fell down again as solid and heavy as a snowdrift against a door, and men could hear the beating of their blood

in the thin passages of the ear, and the thumping of their own hearts, that sounded as loud as the noise of sorcerers' drums beaten across the snow. One night Kotuko the dog, who had been unusually sullen in harness, leaped up and pushed his head against Kotuko's knee. Kotuko patted him, but the dog still pushed blindly forward, fawning. Then Kadlu waked, and gripped the heavy wolf-like head, and stared into the glassy eyes. The dog whimpered and shivered between Kadlu's knees. The hair rose about his neck, and he growled as though a stranger were at the door; then he barked joyously, and rolled on the ground, and bit at Kotuko's boot like a puppy.

"What is it?" said Kotuko; for he was beginning to be afraid.

"The sickness," Kadlu answered. "It is the dog sickness." Kotuko the dog lifted his nose and howled and howled again.

"I have not seen this before. What will he do?" said Kotuko.

Kadlu shrugged one shoulder a little, and crossed the hut for his short stabbing-harpoon. The big dog looked at him, howled again, and slunk away down the passage, while the other dogs drew aside right and left to give him ample room. When he was out on the snow he barked furiously, as though on the trail of a musk-ox, and, barking and leaping and frisking, passed out of sight. His trouble was not hydrophobia, but simple, plain madness. The cold and the hunger, and, above all, the dark, had turned his head; and when the terrible dog-sickness once shows itself in a team, it spreads like wild-fire. Next hunting-day another dog sickened, and was killed then and there by Kotuko as he bit and struggled among the traces. Then the black second dog, who had been the leader in the old days, suddenly gave tongue on an imaginary reindeer-track, and when they slipped him from the *pitu* he flew at the throat of an ice-cliff, and ran away as his leader had done, his harness on his back. After that no one would take the dogs out again. They needed them for something else, and the dogs knew it; and though they were tied down and fed by hand, their eyes were full of despair and fear. To make things worse, the old women began to tell ghost-tales, and to say that they had met the spirits of the dead hunters lost that autumn, who prophesied all sorts of horrible things.

Kotuko grieved more for the loss of his dog than anything else; for

though an Inuit eats enormously he also knows how to starve. But the hunger, the darkness, the cold, and the exposure told on his strength, and he began to hear voices inside his head, and to see people who were not there, out of the tail of his eye. One night—he had unbuckled himself after ten hours' waiting above a "blind" seal-hole, and was staggering back to the village faint and dizzy—he halted to lean his back against a boulder which happened to be supported like a rocking-stone on a single jutting point of ice. His weight disturbed the balance of the thing, it rolled over ponderously, and as Kotuko sprang aside to avoid it, slid after him, squeaking and hissing on the ice-slope.

That was enough for Kotuko. He had been brought up to believe that every rock and boulder had its owner (its *inua*), who was generally a one-eyed kind of a Woman-Thing called a *tornaq*, and that when a *tornaq* meant to help a man she rolled after him inside her stone house, and asked him whether he would take her for a guardian spirit. (In summer thaws the ice-propped rocks and boulders roll and slip all over the face of the land, so you can easily see how the idea of live stones arose.) Kotuko heard the blood beating in his ears as he had heard it all day, and he thought that was the *tornaq* of the stone speaking to him. Before he reached home he was quite certain that he had held a long conversation with her, and as all his people believed that this was quite possible, no one contradicted him.

"She said to me, 'I jump down, I jump down from my place on the snow,'" cried Kotuko, with hollow eyes, leaning forward in the half-lighted hut. "She said, 'I will be a guide.' She said, 'I will guide you to the good seal-holes.' To-morrow I go out, and the *tornaq* will guide me."

Then the *angekok*, the village sorcerer, came in, and Kotuko told him the tale a second time. It lost nothing in the telling.

"Follow the *tornait* [the spirits of the stones], and they will bring us food again," said the *angekok*.

Now the girl from the North had been lying near the lamp, eating very little and saying less for days past; but when Amoraq and Kadlu next morning packed and lashed a little hand-sleigh for Kotuko, and loaded it with his hunting-gear and as much blubber and frozen seal-

meat as they could spare, she took the pulling-rope, and stepped out boldly at the boy's side.

"Your house is my house," she said, as the little bone-shod sleigh squeaked and bumped behind them in the awful Arctic night.

"My house is your house," said Kotuko; "but *I* think that we shall both go to Sedna together."

Now Sedna is the Mistress of the Underworld, and the Inuit believe that every one who dies must spend a year in her horrible country before going to Quadliparmiut, the Happy Place, where it never freezes and the fat reindeer trot up when you call.

Through the village people were shouting: "The *tornait* have spoken to Kotuko. They will show him open ice. He will bring us the seal again!" Their voices were soon swallowed up by the cold, empty dark, and Kotuko and the girl shouldered close together as they strained on the pulling-rope or humoured the sleigh through the ice in the direction of the Polar Sea. Kotuko insisted that the *tornaq* of the stone had told him to go north, and north they went under Tuktuqdjung the Reindeer—those stars that we call the Great Bear.

No European could have made five miles a day over the ice-rubbish and the sharp-edged drifts; but those two knew exactly the turn of the wrist that coaxes a sleigh round a hummock, the jerk that nearly lifts it out of an ice-crack, and the exact strength that goes to the few quiet strokes of the spear-head that make a path possible when everything looks hopeless.

The girl said nothing, but bowed her head, and the long wolverine-fur fringe of her ermine hood blew across her broad, dark face. The sky above them was an intense velvety black, changing to bands of Indian red on the horizon, where the great stars burned like street-lamps. From time to time a greenish wave of the Northern Lights would roll across the hollow of the high heavens, flick like a flag, and disappear; or a meteor would crackle from darkness to darkness, trailing a shower of sparks behind. Then they could see the ridged and furrowed surface of the floe tipped and laced with strange colours—red, copper, and bluish; but in the ordinary starlight everything turned to one frost-bitten gray. The floe, as you will remember, had been battered and tormented by

the autumn gales till it was one frozen earthquake. There were gullies and ravines, and holes like gravel-pits, cut in ice; lumps and scattered pieces frozen down to the original floor of the floe; blotches of old black ice that had been thrust under the floe in some gale and heaved up again; roundish boulders of ice; saw-like edges of ice carved by the snow that flies before the wind; and sunken pits where thirty or forty acres lay below the level of the rest of the field. From a little distance you might have taken the lumps for seal or walrus, overturned sleighs or men on a hunting expedition, or even the great Ten-legged White Spirit-Bear himself; but in spite of these fantastic shapes, all on the very edge of starting into life, there was neither sound nor the least faint echo of sound. And through this silence and through this waste, where the sudden lights flapped and went out again, the sleigh and the two that pulled it crawled like things in a nightmare—a nightmare of the end of the world at the end of the world.

When they were tired Kotuko would make what the hunters call a "half-house," a very small snow hut, into which they would huddle with the travelling-lamp, and try to thaw out the frozen seal-meat. When they had slept, the march began again—thirty miles a day to get ten miles northward. The girl was always very silent, but Kotuko muttered to himself and broke out into songs he had learned in the Singing-House—summer songs, and reindeer and salmon songs—all horribly out of place at that season. He would declare that he heard the *tornaq* growling to him, and would run wildly up a hummock, tossing his arms and speaking in loud, threatening tones. To tell the truth, Kotuko was very nearly crazy for the time being; but the girl was sure that he was being guided by his guardian spirit, and that everything would come right. She was not surprised, therefore, when at the end of the fourth march Kotuko, whose eyes were burning like fire-balls in his head, told her that his *tornaq* was following them across the snow in the shape of a two-headed dog. The girl looked where Kotuko pointed, and something seemed to slip into a ravine. It was certainly not human, but everybody knew that the *tornait* preferred to appear in the shape of bear and seal, and such like.

It might have been the Ten-legged White Spirit-Bear himself, or it

might have been anything, for Kotuko and the girl were so starved that their eyes were untrustworthy. They had trapped nothing, and seen no trace of game since they had left the village; their food would not hold out for another week, and there was a gale coming. A Polar storm can blow for ten days without a break, and all that while it is certain death to be abroad. Kotuko laid up a snow-house large enough to take in the hand-sleigh (never be separated from your meat), and while he was shaping the last irregular block of ice that makes the key-stone of the roof, he saw a Thing looking at him from a little cliff of ice half a mile away. The air was hazy, and the Thing seemed to be forty feet long and ten feet high, with twenty feet of tail and a shape that quivered all along the outlines. The girl saw it too, but instead of crying aloud with terror, said quietly, "That is Quiquern. What comes after?"

"He will speak to me," said Kotuko; but the snow-knife trembled in his hand as he spoke, because however much a man may believe that he is a friend of strange and ugly spirits, he seldom likes to be taken quite at his word. Quiquern, too, is the phantom of a gigantic toothless dog without any hair, who is supposed to live in the far North, and to wander about the country just before things are going to happen. They may be pleasant or unpleasant things, but not even the sorcerers care to speak about Quiquern. He makes the dogs go mad. Like the Spirit-Bear, he has several extra pairs of legs,—six or eight,—and this Thing jumping up and down in the haze had more legs than any real dog needed. Kotuko and the girl huddled into their hut quickly. Of course if Quiquern had wanted them, he could have torn it to pieces above their heads, but the sense of a foot-thick snow-wall between themselves and the wicked dark was great comfort. The gale broke with a shriek of wind like the shriek of a train, and for three days and three nights it held, never varying one point, and never lulling even for a minute. They fed the stone lamp between their knees, and nibbled at the half-warm seal-meat, and watched the black soot gather on the roof for seventy-two long hours. The girl counted up the food in the sleigh; there was not more than two days' supply, and Kotuko looked over the iron heads and the deer-sinew fastenings of his harpoon and his seal-lance and his bird-dart. There was nothing else to do.

"We shall go to Sedna soon—very soon," the girl whispered. "In three days we shall lie down and go. Will your *tornaq* do nothing? Sing her an *angekok's* song to make her come here."

He began to sing in the high-pitched howl of the magic songs, and the gale went down slowly. In the middle of his song the girl started, laid her mittened hand and then her head to the ice floor of the hut. Kotuko followed her example, and the two kneeled, staring into each other's eyes, and listening with every nerve. He ripped a thin sliver of whalebone from the rim of a bird-snare that lay on the sleigh, and, after straightening, set it upright in a little hole in the ice, firming it down with his mitten. It was almost as delicately adjusted as a compass-needle, and now instead of listening they watched. The thin rod quivered a little—the least little jar in the world; then it vibrated steadily for a few seconds, came to rest, and vibrated again, this time nodding to another point of the compass.

"Too soon!" said Kotuko. "Some big floe has broken far away outside."

The girl pointed at the rod, and shook her head. "It is the big breaking," she said. "Listen to the ground-ice. It knocks."

When they kneeled this time they heard the most curious muffled grunts and knockings, apparently under their feet. Sometimes it sounded as though a blind puppy were squeaking above the lamp; then as if a stone were being ground on hard ice; and again, like muffled blows on a drum; but all dragged out and made small, as though they travelled through a little horn a weary distance away.

"We shall not go to Sedna lying down," said Kotuko. "It is the breaking. The *tornaq* has cheated us. We shall die."

All this may sound absurd enough, but the two were face to face with a very real danger. The three days' gale had driven the deep water of Baffin's Bay southerly, and piled it on to the edge of the far-reaching land-ice that stretches from Bylot's Island to the west. Also, the strong current which sets east out of Lancaster Sound carried with it mile upon mile of what they call pack-ice—rough ice that has not frozen into fields; and this pack was bombarding the floe at the same time that the swell and heave of the storm-worked sea was weakening and

undermining it. What Kotuko and the girl had been listening to were the faint echoes of that fight thirty or forty miles away, and the little tell-tale rod quivered to the shock of it.

Now, as the Inuit say, when the ice once wakes after its long winter sleep, there is no knowing what may happen, for solid floe-ice changes shape almost as quickly as a cloud. The gale was evidently a spring gale sent out of time, and anything was possible.

Yet the two were happier in their minds than before. If the floe broke up there would be no more waiting and suffering. Spirits, goblins, and witch-people were moving about on the racking ice, and they might find themselves stepping into Sedna's country side by side with all sorts of wild Things, the flush of excitement still on them. When they left the hut after the gale, the noise on the horizon was steadily growing, and the tough ice moaned and buzzed all round them.

"It is still waiting," said Kotuko.

On the top of a hummock sat or crouched the eight-legged Thing that they had seen three days before—and it howled horribly.

"Let us follow," said the girl. "It may know some way that does not lead to Sedna"; but she reeled from weakness as she took the pulling-rope. The Thing moved off slowly and clumsily across the ridges, heading always toward the westward and the land, and they followed, while the growling thunder at the edge of the floe rolled nearer and nearer. The floe's lip was split and cracked in every direction for three or four miles inland, and great pans of ten-foot-thick ice, from a few yards to twenty acres square, were jolting and ducking and surging into one another, and into the yet unbroken floe, as the heavy swell took and shook and spouted between them. This battering-ram ice was, so to speak, the first army that the sea was flinging against the floe. The incessant crash and jar of these cakes almost drowned the ripping sound of sheets of pack-ice driven bodily under the floe as cards are hastily pushed under a tablecloth. Where the water was shallow these sheets would be piled one atop of the other till the bottommost touched mud fifty feet down, and the discoloured sea banked behind the muddy ice till the increasing pressure drove all forward again. In addition to the floe and the pack-ice, the gale and the currents were bringing down

true bergs, sailing mountains of ice, snapped off from the Greenland side of the water or the north shore of Melville Bay. They pounded in solemnly, the waves breaking white round them, and advanced on the floe like an old-time fleet under full sail. A berg that seemed ready to carry the world before it would ground helplessly in deep water, reel over, and wallow in a lather of foam and mud and flying frozen spray, while a much smaller and lower one would rip and ride into the flat floe, flinging tons of ice on either side, and cutting a track half a mile long before it was stopped. Some fell like swords, shearing a raw-edged canal; and others splintered into a shower of blocks, weighing scores of tons apiece, that whirled and skirted among the hummocks. Others, again, rose up bodily out of the water when they shoaled, twisted as though in pain, and fell solidly on their sides, while the sea threshed over their shoulders. This trampling and crowding and bending and buckling and arching of the ice into every possible shape was going on as far as the eye could reach all along the north line of the floe. From where Kotuko and the girl were, the confusion looked no more than an uneasy, rippling, crawling movement under the horizon; but it came toward them each moment, and they could hear, far away to landward a heavy booming, as it might have been the boom of artillery through a fog. That showed that the floe was being jammed home against the iron cliffs of Bylot's Island, the land to the southward behind them.

"This has never been before," said Kotuko, staring stupidly. "This is not the time. How can the floe break *now?*"

"Follow *that!*" the girl cried, pointing to the Thing half limping, half running distractedly before them. They followed, tugging at the hand-sleigh, while nearer and nearer came the roaring march of the ice. At last the fields round them cracked and starred in every direction, and the cracks opened and snapped like the teeth of wolves. But where the Thing rested, on a mound of old and scattered ice-blocks some fifty feet high, there was no motion. Kotuko leaped forward wildly, dragging the girl after him, and crawled to the bottom of the mound. The talking of the ice grew louder and louder round them, but the mound stayed fast, and, as the girl looked at him, he threw his right elbow upward and outward, making the Inuit sign for land in the shape of an island. And

land it was that the eight-legged, limping Thing had led them to—some granite-tipped, sand-beached islet off the coast, shod and sheathed and masked with ice so that no man could have told it from the floe, but at the bottom solid earth, and not shifting ice! The smashing and rebound of the floes as they grounded and splintered marked the borders of it, and a friendly shoal ran out to the northward, and turned aside the rush of the heaviest ice, exactly as a ploughshare turns over loam. There was danger, of course, that some heavily squeezed ice-field might shoot up the beach, and plane off the top of the islet bodily; but that did not trouble Kotuko and the girl when they made their snow-house and began to eat, and heard the ice hammer and skid along the beach. The Thing had disappeared, and Kotuko was talking excitedly about his power over spirits as he crouched round the lamp. In the middle of his wild sayings the girl began to laugh, and rock herself backward and forward.

Behind her shoulder, crawling into the hut crawl by crawl, there were two heads, one yellow and one black, that belonged to two of the most sorrowful and ashamed dogs that ever you saw. Kotuko the dog was one, and the black leader was the other. Both were now fat, well-looking, and quite restored to their proper minds, but coupled to each other in an extraordinary fashion. When the black leader ran off, you remember, his harness was still on him. He must have met Kotuko the dog, and played or fought with him, for his shoulder-loop had caught in the plaited copper wire of Kotuko's collar, and had drawn tight, so that neither could get at the trace to gnaw it apart, but each was fastened sidelong to his neighbour's neck. That, with the freedom of hunting on their own account, must have helped to cure their madness. They were very sober.

The girl pushed the two shamefaced creatures towards Kotuko, and, sobbing with laughter, cried, "That is Quiquern, who led us to safe ground. Look at his eight legs and double head!"

Kotuko cut them free, and they fell into his arms, yellow and black together, trying to explain how they had got their senses back again. Kotuko ran a hand down their ribs, which were round and well clothed. "They have found food," he said, with a grin. "I do not think we shall go to Sedna so soon. My *tornaq* sent these. The sickness has left them."

As soon as they had greeted Kotuko, these two, who had been forced to sleep and eat and hunt together for the past few weeks, flew at each other's throat, and there was a beautiful battle in the snow-house. "Empty dogs do not fight," Kotuko said. "They have found the seal. Let us sleep. We shall find food."

When they waked there was open water on the north beach of the island, and all the loosened ice had been driven landward. The first sound of the surf is one of the most delightful that the Inuit can hear, for it means that spring is on the road. Kotuko and the girl took hold of hands and smiled, for the clear, full roar of the surge among the ice reminded them of salmon and reindeer time and the smell of blossoming ground-willows. Even as they looked, the sea began to skim over between the floating cakes of ice, so intense was the cold; but on the horizon there was a vast red glare, and that was the light of the sunken sun. It was more like hearing him yawn in his sleep than seeing him rise, and the glare lasted for only a few minutes, but it marked the turn of the year. Nothing, they felt, could alter that.

Kotuko found the dogs fighting over a fresh-killed seal who was following the fish that a gale always disturbs. He was the first of some twenty or thirty seal that landed on the island in the course of the day, and till the sea froze hard there were hundreds of keen black heads rejoicing in the shallow free water and floating about with the floating ice.

It was good to eat seal-liver again; to fill the lamps recklessly with blubber, and watch the flame blaze three feet in the air; but as soon as the new sea-ice bore, Kotuko and the girl loaded the hand-sleigh, and made the two dogs pull as they had never pulled in their lives, for they feared what might have happened in their village. The weather was as pitiless as usual; but it is easier to draw a sleigh loaded with good food than to hunt starving. They left five-and-twenty seal carcasses buried in the ice of the beach, all ready for use, and hurried back to their people. The dogs showed them the way as soon as Kotuko told them what was expected, and though there was no sign of a landmark, in two days they were giving tongue outside Kadlu's house. Only three dogs answered them; the others had been eaten, and the houses were all dark. But when

Kotuko shouted, "Ojo!" (boiled meat), weak voices replied, and when he called the muster of the village name by name, very distinctly, there were no gaps in it.

An hour later the lamps blazed in Kadlu's house; snow-water was heating; the pots were beginning to simmer, and the snow was dripping from the roof, as Amoraq made ready a meal for all the village, and the boy-baby in the hood chewed at a strip of rich nutty blubber, and the hunters slowly and methodically filled themselves to the very brim with seal-meat. Kotuko and the girl told their tale. The two dogs sat between them, and whenever their names came in, they cocked an ear apiece and looked most thoroughly ashamed of themselves. A dog who has once gone mad and recovered, the Inuit say, is safe against all further attacks.

"So the *tornaq* did not forget us," said Kotuko. "The storm blew, the ice broke, and the seal swam in behind the fish that were frightened by the storm. Now the new seal-holes are not two days distant. Let the good hunters go to-morrow and bring back the seal I have speared— twenty-five seal buried in the ice. When we have eaten those we will all follow the seal on the floe."

"What do *you* do?" said the sorcerer in the same sort of voice as he used to Kadlu, richest of the Tununirmiut.

Kadlu looked at the girl from the North, and said quietly, "*We* build a house." He pointed to the north-west side of Kadlu's house, for that is the side on which the married son or daughter always lives.

The girl turned her hands palm upward, with a little despairing shake of her head. She was a foreigner, picked up starving, and could bring nothing to the housekeeping.

Amoraq jumped from the bench where she sat, and began to sweep things into the girl's lap—stone lamps, iron skin-scrapers, tin kettles, deer-skins embroidered with musk-ox teeth, and real canvas-needles such as sailors use—the finest dowry that has ever been given on the far edge of the Arctic Circle, and the girl from the North bowed her head down to the very floor.

"Also these!" said Kotuko, laughing and signing to the dogs, who thrust their cold muzzles into the girl's face.

"Ah," said the *angekok*, with an important cough, as though he had

been thinking it all over. "As soon as Kotuko left the village I went to the Singing-House and sang magic. I sang all the long nights, and called upon the Spirit of the Reindeer. *My* singing made the gale blow that broke the ice and drew the two dogs toward Kotuko when the ice would have crushed his bones. *My* song drew the seal in behind the broken ice. My body lay still in the *quaggi*, but my spirit ran about on the ice, and guided Kotuko and the dogs in all the things they did. *I* did it."

Everybody was full and sleepy, so no one contradicted; and the *angekok*, by virtue of his office, helped himself to yet another lump of boiled meat, and lay down to sleep with the others in the warm, well-lighted, oil-smelling home.

* * * * *

Now Kotuko, who drew very well in the Inuit fashion, scratched pictures of all these adventures on a long, flat piece of ivory with a hole at one end. When he and the girl went north to Ellesmere Land in the year of the Wonderful Open Winter, he left the picture-story with Kadlu, who lost it in the shingle when his dog-sleigh broke down one summer on the beach of Lake Netilling at Nikosiring, and there a Lake Inuit found it next spring and sold it to a man at Imigen who was interpreter on a Cumberland Sound whaler, and he sold it to Hans Olsen, who was afterward a quartermaster on board a big steamer that took tourists to the North Cape in Norway. When the tourist season was over, the steamer ran between London and Australia, stopping at Ceylon, and there Olsen sold the ivory to a Cingalese jeweller for two imitation sapphires. I found it under some rubbish in a house at Colombo, and have translated it from one end to the other.

12. "ANGUTIVAUN TAINA"

(This is a very free translation of the Song of the Returning Hunter, as the men used to sing it after seal-spearing. The Inuit always repeat things over and over again.)

> Our gloves are stiff with the frozen blood,
> Our furs with the drifted snow,
> As we come in with the seal—the seal!
> In from the edge of the floe.
>
> *Au jana! Aua! Oha! Haq!*
> And the yelping dog-teams go,
> And the long whips crack, and the men come back,
> Back from the edge of the floe!
>
> We tracked our seal to his secret place,
> We heard him scratch below,
> We made our mark, and we watched beside,
> Out on the edge of the floe.
>
> We raised our lance when he rose to breathe,
> We drove it downward—so!
> And we played him thus, and we killed him thus,
> Out on the edge of the floe.
> Our gloves are glued with the frozen blood,
> Our eyes with the drifting snow;
> But we come back to our wives again,
> Back from the edge of the floe!
>
> Au jana! Aua! Oha! Haq!
> *And the* loaded *dog-teams go,*
> *And the wives can hear their men come back.*
> *Back from the edge of the floe!*

263

13. RED DOG

For our white and our excellent nights—for the nights
 of swift running.
Fair ranging, far seeing, good hunting, sure cunning!
For the smells of the dawning, untainted, ere dew
 has departed!
For the rush through the mist, and the quarry blind-
 started!
For the cry of our mates when the *sambhur* has wheeled
 and is standing at bay,
For the risk and the riot of night!
For the sleep at the lair-mouth by day,
It is met, and we go to the fight.
Bay! O Bay!

It was after the letting in of the Jungle that the pleasantest part of
Mowgli's life began. He had the good conscience that comes from
paying debts; all the Jungle was his friend, and just a little afraid of
him. The things that he did and saw and heard when he was wandering
from one people to another, with or without his four companions,
would make many many stories, each as long as this one. So you will
never be told how he met the Mad Elephant of Mandla, who killed
two-and-twenty bullocks drawing eleven carts of coined silver to the
Government Treasury, and scattered the shiny rupees in the dust; how
he fought Jacala, the Crocodile, all one long night in the Marshes of the
North, and broke his skinning-knife on the brute's back-plates; how
he found a new and longer knife round the neck of a man who had
been killed by a wild boar, and how he tracked that boar and killed him
as a fair price for the knife; how he was caught up once in the Great
Famine, by the moving of the deer, and nearly crushed to death in the
swaying hot herds; how he saved Hathi the Silent from being once more
trapped in a pit with a stake at the bottom, and how, next day, he himself
fell into a very cunning leopard-trap, and how Hathi broke the thick

wooden bars to pieces above him; how he milked the wild buffaloes in the swamp, and how—

But we must tell one tale at a time. Father and Mother Wolf died, and Mowgli rolled a big boulder against the mouth of their cave, and cried the Death Song over them; Baloo grew very old and stiff, and even Bagheera, whose nerves were steel and whose muscles were iron, was a shade slower on the kill than he had been. Akela turned from gray to milky white with pure age; his ribs stuck out, and he walked as though he had been made of wood, and Mowgli killed for him. But the young wolves, the children of the disbanded Seeonee Pack, throve and increased, and when there were about forty of them, masterless, full-voiced, clean-footed five-year-olds, Akela told them that they ought to gather themselves together and follow the Law, and run under one head, as befitted the Free People.

This was not a question in which Mowgli concerned himself, for, as he said, he had eaten sour fruit, and he knew the tree it hung from; but when Phao, son of Phaona (his father was the Gray Tracker in the days of Akela's headship), fought his way to the leadership of the Pack, according to the Jungle Law, and the old calls and songs began to ring under the stars once more, Mowgli came to the Council Rock for memory's sake. When he chose to speak the Pack waited till he had finished, and he sat at Akela's side on the rock above Phao. Those were days of good hunting and good sleeping. No stranger cared to break into the jungles that belonged to Mowgli's people, as they called the Pack, and the young wolves grew fat and strong, and there were many cubs to bring to the Looking-over. Mowgli always attended a Looking-over, remembering the night when a black panther bought a naked brown baby into the pack, and the long call, "Look, look well, O Wolves," made his heart flutter. Otherwise, he would be far away in the Jungle with his four brothers, tasting, touching, seeing, and feeling new things.

One twilight when he was trotting leisurely across the ranges to give Akela the half of a buck that he had killed, while the Four jogged behind him, sparring a little, and tumbling one another over for joy of being alive, he heard a cry that had never been heard since the bad days

of Shere Khan. It was what they call in the Jungle the *pheeal*, a hideous kind of shriek that the jackal gives when he is hunting behind a tiger, or when there is a big killing afoot. If you can imagine a mixture of hate, triumph, fear, and despair, with a kind of leer running through it, you will get some notion of the *pheeal* that rose and sank and wavered and quavered far away across the Waingunga. The Four stopped at once, bristling and growling. Mowgli's hand went to his knife, and he checked, the blood in his face, his eyebrows knotted.

"There is no Striped One dare kill here," he said.

"That is not the cry of the Forerunner," answered Gray Brother. "It is some great killing. Listen!"

It broke out again, half sobbing and half chuckling, just as though the jackal had soft human lips. Then Mowgli drew deep breath, and ran to the Council Rock, overtaking on his way hurrying wolves of the Pack. Phao and Akela were on the Rock together, and below them, every nerve strained, sat the others. The mothers and the cubs were cantering off to their lairs; for when the *pheeal* cries it is no time for weak things to be abroad.

They could hear nothing except the Waingunga rushing and gurgling in the dark, and the light evening winds among the tree-tops, till suddenly across the river a wolf called. It was no wolf of the Pack, for they were all at the Rock. The note changed to a long, despairing bay; and "Dhole!" it said, "Dhole! dhole! dhole!" They heard tired feet on the rocks, and a gaunt wolf, streaked with red on his flanks, his right fore-paw useless, and his jaws white with foam, flung himself into the circle and lay gasping at Mowgli's feet.

"Good hunting! Under whose Headship?" said Phao gravely.

"Good hunting! Won-tolla am I," was the answer. He meant that he was a solitary wolf, fending for himself, his mate, and his cubs in some lonely lair, as do many wolves in the south. Won-tolla means an Outlier—one who lies out from any Pack. Then he panted, and they could see his heart-beats shake him backward and forward.

"What moves?" said Phao, for that is the question all the Jungle asks after the *pheeal* cries.

"The dhole, the dhole of the Dekkan—Red Dog, the Killer! They

came north from the south saying the Dekkan was empty and killing out by the way. When this moon was new there were four to me—my mate and three cubs. She would teach them to kill on the grass plains, hiding to drive the buck, as we do who are of the open. At midnight I heard them together, full tongue on the trail. At the dawn-wind I found them stiff in the grass—four, Free People, four when this moon was new. Then sought I my Blood-Right and found the dhole."

"How many?" said Mowgli quickly; the Pack growled deep in their throats.

"I do not know. Three of them will kill no more, but at the last they drove me like the buck; on my three legs they drove me. Look, Free People!"

He thrust out his mangled fore-foot, all dark with dried blood. There were cruel bites low down on his side, and his throat was torn and worried.

"Eat," said Akela, rising up from the meat Mowgli had brought him, and the Outlier flung himself on it.

"This shall be no loss," he said humbly, when he had taken off the first edge of his hunger. "Give me a little strength, Free People, and I also will kill. My lair is empty that was full when this moon was new, and the Blood Debt is not all paid."

Phao heard his teeth crack on a haunch-bone and grunted approvingly.

"We shall need those jaws," said he. "Were there cubs with the dhole?"

"Nay, nay. Red Hunters all: grown dogs of their Pack, heavy and strong for all that they eat lizards in the Dekkan."

What Won-tolla had said meant that the dhole, the red hunting-dog of the Dekkan, was moving to kill, and the Pack knew well that even the tiger will surrender a new kill to the dhole. They drive straight through the Jungle, and what they meet they pull down and tear to pieces. Though they are not as big nor half as cunning as the wolf, they are very strong and very numerous. The dhole, for instance, do not begin to call themselves a pack till they are a hundred strong; whereas forty wolves make a very fair pack indeed. Mowgli's wanderings had taken

him to the edge of the high grassy downs of the Dekkan, and he had seen the fearless dholes sleeping and playing and scratching themselves in the little hollows and tussocks that they use for lairs. He despised and hated them because they did not smell like the Free People, because they did not live in caves, and, above all, because they had hair between their toes while he and his friends were clean-footed. But he knew, for Hathi had told him, what a terrible thing a dhole hunting-pack was. Even Hathi moves aside from their line, and until they are killed, or till game is scarce, they will go forward.

Akela knew something of the dholes, too, for he said to Mowgli quietly, "It is better to die in a Full Pack than leaderless and alone. This is good hunting, and—my last. But, as men live, thou hast very many more nights and days, Little Brother. Go north and lie down, and if any live after the dhole has gone by he shall bring thee word of the fight."

"Ah," said Mowgli, quite gravely, "must I go to the marshes and catch little fish and sleep in a tree, or must I ask help of the *Bandar-log* and crack nuts, while the Pack fight below?"

"It is to the death," said Akela. "Thou hast never met the dhole—the Red Killer. Even the Striped One—"

"*Aowa! Aowa!*" said Mowgli pettingly. "I have killed one striped ape, and sure am I in my stomach that Shere Khan would have left his own mate for meat to the dhole if he had winded a pack across three ranges. Listen now: There was a wolf, my father, and there was a wolf, my mother, and there was an old gray wolf (not too wise: he is white now) was my father and my mother. Therefore I—" he raised his voice, "I say that when the dhole come, and if the dhole come, Mowgli and the Free People are of one skin for that hunting; and I say, by the Bull that bought me—by the Bull Bagheera paid for me in the old days which ye of the Pack do not remember—I say, that the Trees and the River may hear and hold fast if I forget; *I* say that this my knife shall be as a tooth to the Pack—and I do not think it is so blunt. This is my Word which has gone from me."

"Thou dost not know the dhole, man with a wolf's tongue," said Won-tolla. "I look only to clear the Blood Debt against them ere they have me in many pieces. They move slowly, killing out as they go, but

in two days a little strength will come back to me and I turn again for the Blood Debt. But for *ye*, Free People, my word is that ye go north and eat but little for a while till the dhole are gone. There is no meat in this hunting."

"Hear the Outlier!" said Mowgli with a laugh. "Free People, we must go north and dig lizards and rats from the bank, lest by any chance we meet the dhole. He must kill out our hunting-grounds, while we lie hid in the north till it please him to give us our own again. He is a dog—and the pup of a dog—red, yellow-bellied, lairless, and haired between every toe! He counts his cubs six and eight at the litter, as though he were Chikai, the little leaping rat. Surely we must run away, Free People, and beg leave of the peoples of the north for the offal of dead cattle! Ye know the saying: 'North are the vermin; south are the lice. *We* are the Jungle.' Choose ye, O choose. It is good hunting! For the Pack—for the Full Pack—for the lair and the litter; for the in-kill and the out-kill; for the mate that drives the doe and the little, little cub within the cave; it is met!—it is met!—it is met!"

The Pack answered with one deep, crashing bark that sounded in the night like a big tree falling. "It is met!" they cried. "Stay with these," said Mowgli to the Four. "We shall need every tooth. Phao and Akela must make ready the battle. I go to count the dogs."

"It is death!" Won-tolla cried, half rising. "What can such a hairless one do against the Red Dog? Even the Striped One, remember—"

"Thou art indeed an Outlier," Mowgli called back; "but we will speak when the dholes are dead. Good hunting all!"

He hurried off into the darkness, wild with excitement, hardly looking where he set foot, and the natural consequence was that he tripped full length over Kaa's great coils where the python lay watching a deer-path near the river.

"*Kssha!*" said Kaa angrily. "Is this jungle-work, to stamp and tramp and undo a night's hunting—when the game are moving so well, too?"

"The fault was mine," said Mowgli, picking himself up. "Indeed I was seeking thee, Flathead, but each time we meet thou art longer and broader by the length of my arm. There is none like thee in the Jungle, wise, old, strong, and most beautiful Kaa."

"Now whither does *this* trail lead?" Kaa's voice was gentler. "Not a moon since there was a Manling with a knife threw stones at my head and called me bad little tree-cat names, because I lay asleep in the open."

"Ay, and turned every driven deer to all the winds, and Mowgli was hunting, and this same Flathead was too deaf to hear his whistle, and leave the deer-roads free," Mowgli answered composedly, sitting down among the painted coils.

"Now this same Manling comes with soft, tickling words to this same Flathead, telling him that he is wise and strong and beautiful, and this same old Flathead believes and makes a place, thus, for this same stone-throwing Manling, and—Art thou at ease now? Could Bagheera give thee so good a resting-place?"

Kaa had, as usual, made a sort of soft half-hammock of himself under Mowgli's weight. The boy reached out in the darkness, and gathered in the supple cable-like neck till Kaa's head rested on his shoulder, and then he told him all that had happened in the Jungle that night.

"Wise I may be," said Kaa at the end; "but deaf I surely am. Else I should have heard the *pheeal*. Small wonder the Eaters of Grass are uneasy. How many be the dhole?"

"I have not yet seen. I came hot-foot to thee. Thou art older than Hathi. But oh, Kaa,"—here Mowgli wriggled with sheer joy,—"it will be good hunting. Few of us will see another moon."

"Dost *thou* strike in this? Remember thou art a Man; and remember what Pack cast thee out. Let the Wolf look to the Dog. Thou art a Man."

"Last year's nuts are this year's black earth," said Mowgli. "It is true that I am a Man, but it is in my stomach that this night I have said that I am a Wolf. I called the River and the Trees to remember. I am of the Free People, Kaa, till the dhole has gone by."

"Free People," Kaa grunted. "Free thieves! And thou hast tied thyself into the death-knot for the sake of the memory of the dead wolves? This is no good hunting."

"It is my Word which I have spoken. The Trees know, the River knows. Till the dhole have gone by my Word comes not back to me."

"*Ngssh!* This changes all trails. I had thought to take thee away with

me to the northern marshes, but the Word—even the Word of a little, naked, hairless Manling—is the Word. Now I, Kaa, say—"

"Think well, Flathead, lest thou tie thyself into the death-knot also. I need no Word from thee, for well I know—"

"Be it so, then," said Kaa. "I will give no Word; but what is in thy stomach to do when the dhole come?"

"They must swim the Waingunga. I thought to meet them with my knife in the shallows, the Pack behind me; and so stabbing and thrusting, we a little might turn them down-stream, or cool their throats."

"The dhole do not turn and their throats are hot," said Kaa. "There will be neither Manling nor Wolf-cub when that hunting is done, but only dry bones."

"*Alala!* If we die, we die. It will be most good hunting. But my stomach is young, and I have not seen many Rains. I am not wise nor strong. Hast thou a better plan, Kaa?"

"I have seen a hundred and a hundred Rains. Ere Hathi cast his milk-tushes my trail was big in the dust. By the First Egg, I am older than many trees, and I have seen all that the Jungle has done."

"But *this* is new hunting," said Mowgli. "Never before have the dhole crossed our trail."

"What is has been. What will be is no more than a forgotten year striking backward. Be still while I count those my years."

For a long hour Mowgli lay back among the coils, while Kaa, his head motionless on the ground, thought of all that he had seen and known since the day he came from the egg. The light seemed to go out of his eyes and leave them like stale opals, and now and again he made little stiff passes with his head, right and left, as though he were hunting in his sleep. Mowgli dozed quietly, for he knew that there is nothing like sleep before hunting, and he was trained to take it at any hour of the day or night.

Then he felt Kaa's back grow bigger and broader below him as the huge python puffed himself out, hissing with the noise of a sword drawn from a steel scabbard.

"I have seen all the dead seasons," Kaa said at last, "and the great

trees and the old elephants, and the rocks that were bare and sharp-pointed ere the moss grew. Art *thou* still alive, Manling?"

"It is only a little after moonset," said Mowgli. "I do not understand——"

"*Hssh!* I am again Kaa. I knew it was but a little time. Now we will go to the river, and I will show thee what is to be done against the dhole."

He turned, straight as an arrow, for the main stream of the Waingunga, plunging in a little above the pool that hid the Peace Rock, Mowgli at his side.

"Nay, do not swim. I go swiftly. My back, Little Brother."

Mowgli tucked his left arm round Kaa's neck, dropped his right close to his body, and straightened his feet. Then Kaa breasted the current as he alone could, and the ripple of the checked water stood up in a frill round Mowgli's neck, and his feet were waved to and fro in the eddy under the python's lashing sides. A mile or two above the Peace Rock the Waingunga narrows between a gorge of marble rocks from eighty to a hundred feet high, and the current runs like a mill-race between and over all manner of ugly stones. But Mowgli did not trouble his head about the water; little water in the world could have given him a moment's fear. He was looking at the gorge on either side and sniffing uneasily, for there was a sweetish-sourish smell in the air, very like the smell of a big ant-hill on a hot day. Instinctively he lowered himself in the water, only raising his head to breathe from time to time, and Kaa came to anchor with a double twist of his tail round a sunken rock, holding Mowgli in the hollow of a coil, while the water raced on.

"This is the Place of Death," said the boy. "Why do we come here?"

"They sleep," said Kaa. "Hathi will not turn aside for the Striped One. Yet Hathi and the Striped One together turn aside for the dhole, and the dhole they say turn aside for nothing. And yet for whom do the Little People of the Rocks turn aside? Tell me, Master of the Jungle, who is the Master of the Jungle?"

"These," Mowgli whispered. "It is the Place of Death. Let us go."

"Nay, look well, for they are asleep. It is as it was when I was not the length of thy arm."

The split and weatherworn rocks of the gorge of the Waingunga

had been used since the beginning of the Jungle by the Little People of the Rocks—the busy, furious, black wild bees of India; and, as Mowgli knew well, all trails turned off half a mile before they reached the gorge. For centuries the Little People had hived and swarmed from cleft to cleft, and swarmed again, staining the white marble with stale honey, and made their combs tall and deep in the dark of the inner caves, where neither man nor beast nor fire nor water had ever touched them. The length of the gorge on both sides was hung as it were with black shimmery velvet curtains, and Mowgli sank as he looked, for those were the clotted millions of the sleeping bees. There were other lumps and festoons and things like decayed tree-trunks studded on the face of the rock, the old combs of past years, or new cities built in the shadow of the windless gorge, and huge masses of spongy, rotten trash had rolled down and stuck among the trees and creepers that clung to the rock-face. As he listened he heard more than once the rustle and slide of a honey-loaded comb turning over or failing away somewhere in the dark galleries; then a booming of angry wings, and the sullen drip, drip, drip, of the wasted honey, guttering along till it lipped over some ledge in the open air and sluggishly trickled down on the twigs. There was a tiny little beach, not five feet broad, on one side of the river, and that was piled high with the rubbish of uncounted years. There were dead bees, drones, sweepings, and stale combs, and wings of marauding moths that had strayed in after honey, all tumbled in smooth piles of the finest black dust. The mere sharp smell of it was enough to frighten anything that had no wings, and knew what the Little People were.

Kaa moved up-stream again till he came to a sandy bar at the head of the gorge.

"Here is this season's kill," said he. "Look!" On the bank lay the skeletons of a couple of young deer and a buffalo. Mowgli could see that neither wolf nor jackal had touched the bones, which were laid out naturally.

"They came beyond the line; they did not know the Law," murmured Mowgli, "and the Little People killed them. Let us go ere they wake."

"They do not wake till the dawn," said Kaa. "Now I will tell thee. A hunted buck from the south, many, many Rains ago, came hither from

the south, not knowing the Jungle, a Pack on his trail. Being made blind by fear, he leaped from above, the Pack running by sight, for they were hot and blind on the trail. The sun was high, and the Little People were many and very angry. Many, too, were those of the Pack who leaped into the Waingunga, but they were dead ere they took water. Those who did not leap died also in the rocks above. But the buck lived."

"How?"

"Because he came first, running for his life, leaping ere the Little People were aware, and was in the river when they gathered to kill. The Pack, following, was altogether lost under the weight of the Little People."

"The buck lived?" Mowgli repeated slowly.

"At least he did not die *then*, though none waited his coming down with a strong body to hold him safe against the water, as a certain old fat, deaf, yellow Flathead would wait for a Manling—yea, though there were all the dholes of the Dekkan on his trail. What is in thy stomach?" Kaa's head was close to Mowgli's ear; and it was a little time before the boy answered.

"It is to pull the very whiskers of Death, but—Kaa, thou art, indeed, the wisest of all the Jungle."

"So many have said. Look now, if the dhole follow thee—"

"As surely they will follow. Ho! ho! I have many little thorns under my tongue to prick into their hides."

"If they follow thee hot and blind, looking only at thy shoulders, those who do not die up above will take water either here or lower down, for the Little People will rise up and cover them. Now the Waingunga is hungry water, and they will have no Kaa to hold them, but will go down, such as live, to the shallows by the Seeonee Lairs, and there thy Pack may meet them by the throat."

"*Ahai! Eowawa!* Better could not be till the Rains fall in the dry season. There is now only the little matter of the run and the leap. I will make me known to the dholes, so that they shall follow me very closely."

"Hast thou seen the rocks above thee? From the landward side?"

"Indeed, no. That I had forgotten."

"Go look. It is all rotten ground, cut and full of holes. One of thy clumsy feet set down without seeing would end the hunt. See, I leave thee here, and for thy sake only I will carry word to the Pack that they may know where to look for the dhole. For myself, I am not of one skin with *any* wolf."

When Kaa disliked an acquaintance he could be more unpleasant than any of the Jungle People, except perhaps Bagheera. He swam down-stream, and opposite the Rock he came on Phao and Akela listening to the night noises.

"*Hssh!* Dogs," he said cheerfully. "The dholes will come down-stream. If ye be not afraid ye can kill them in the shallows."

"When come they?" said Phao. "And where is my Man-cub?" said Akela.

"They come when they come," said Kaa. "Wait and see. As for *thy* Man-cub, from whom thou hast taken a Word and so laid him open to Death, *thy* Man-cub is with *me*, and if he be not already dead the fault is none of thine, bleached dog! Wait here for the dhole, and be glad that the Man-cub and I strike on thy side."

Kaa flashed up-stream again, and moored himself in the middle of the gorge, looking upward at the line of the cliff. Presently he saw Mowgli's head move against the stars, and then there was a whizz in the air, the keen, clean *schloop* of a body falling feet first, and next minute the boy was at rest again in the loop of Kaa's body.

"It is no leap by night," said Mowgli quietly. "I have jumped twice as far for sport; but that is an evil place above—low bushes and gullies that go down very deep, all full of the Little People. I have put big stones one above the other by the side of three gullies. These I shall throw down with my feet in running, and the Little People will rise up behind me, very angry."

"That is Man's talk and Man's cunning," said Kaa. "Thou art wise, but the Little People are always angry."

"Nay, at twilight all wings near and far rest for a while. I will play with the dhole at twilight, for the dhole hunts best by day. He follows now Won-tolla's blood-trail."

"Chil does not leave a dead ox, nor the dhole the blood-trail," said Kaa.

"Then I will make him a new blood-trail, of his own blood, if I can, and give him dirt to eat. Thou wilt stay here, Kaa, till I come again with my dholes?"

"Ay, but what if they kill thee in the Jungle, or the Little People kill thee before thou canst leap down to the river?"

"When to-morrow comes we will kill for to-morrow," said Mowgli, quoting a Jungle saying; and again, "When I am dead it is time to sing the Death Song. Good hunting, Kaa!"

He loosed his arm from the python's neck and went down the gorge like a log in a freshet, paddling toward the far bank, where he found slack-water, and laughing aloud from sheer happiness. There was nothing Mowgli liked better than, as he himself said, "to pull the whiskers of Death," and make the Jungle know that he was their overlord. He had often, with Baloo's help, robbed bees' nests in single trees, and he knew that the Little People hated the smell of wild garlic. So he gathered a small bundle of it, tied it up with a bark string, and then followed Won-tolla's blood-trail, as it ran southerly from the Lairs, for some five miles, looking at the trees with his head on one side, and chuckling as he looked.

"Mowgli the Frog have I been," said he to himself; "Mowgli the Wolf have I said that I am. Now Mowgli the Ape must I be before I am Mowgli the Buck. At the end I shall be Mowgli the Man. Ho!" and he slid his thumb along the eighteen-inch blade of his knife.

Won-tolla's trail, all rank with dark blood-spots, ran under a forest of thick trees that grew close together and stretched away north-eastward, gradually growing thinner and thinner to within two miles of the Bee Rocks. From the last tree to the low scrub of the Bee Rocks was open country, where there was hardly cover enough to hide a wolf. Mowgli trotted along under the trees, judging distances between branch and branch, occasionally climbing up a trunk and taking a trial leap from one tree to another till he came to the open ground, which he studied very carefully for an hour. Then he turned, picked up Won-tolla's trail where he had left it, settled himself in a tree with an outrunning branch

some eight feet from the ground, and sat still, sharpening his knife on the sole of his foot and singing to himself.

A little before mid-day, when the sun was very warm, he heard the patter of feet and smelt the abominable smell of the dhole-pack as they trotted pitilessly along Won-tolla's trail. Seen from above, the red dhole does not look half the size of a wolf, but Mowgli knew how strong his feet and jaws were. He watched the sharp bay head of the leader snuffing along the trail, and gave him "Good hunting!"

The brute looked up, and his companions halted behind him, scores and scores of red dogs with low-hung tails, heavy shoulders, weak quarters, and bloody mouths. The dholes are a very silent people as a rule, and they have no manners even in their own Jungle. Fully two hundred must have gathered below him, but he could see that the leaders sniffed hungrily on Won-tolla's trail, and tried to drag the Pack forward. That would never do, or they would be at the Lairs in broad daylight, and Mowgli meant to hold them under his tree till dusk.

"By whose leave do ye come here?" said Mowgli.

"All Jungles are our Jungle," was the reply, and the dhole that gave it bared his white teeth. Mowgli looked down with a smile, and imitated perfectly the sharp chitter-chatter of Chikai, the leaping rat of the Dekkan, meaning the dholes to understand that he considered them no better than Chikai. The Pack closed up round the tree-trunk and the leader bayed savagely, calling Mowgli a tree-ape. For an answer Mowgli stretched down one naked leg and wriggled his bare toes just above the leader's head. That was enough, and more than enough, to wake the Pack to stupid rage. Those who have hair between their toes do not care to be reminded of it. Mowgli caught his foot away as the leader leaped up, and said sweetly: "Dog, red dog! Go back to the Dekkan and eat lizards. Go to Chikai thy brother—dog, dog—red, red dog! There is hair between every toe!" He twiddled his toes a second time.

"Come down ere we starve thee out, hairless ape!" yelled the Pack, and this was exactly what Mowgli wanted. He laid himself down along the branch, his cheek to the bark, his right arm free, and there he told the Pack what he thought and knew about them, their manners, their customs, their mates, and their puppies. There is no speech in the world

so rancorous and so stinging as the language the Jungle People use to show scorn and contempt. When you come to think of it you will see how this must be so. As Mowgli told Kaa, he had many little thorns under his tongue, and slowly and deliberately he drove the dholes from silence to growls, from growls to yells, and from yells to hoarse slavery ravings. They tried to answer his taunts, but a cub might as well have tried to answer Kaa in a rage; and all the while Mowgli's right hand lay crooked at his side, ready for action, his feet locked round the branch. The big bay leader had leaped many times in the air, but Mowgli dared not risk a false blow. At last, made furious beyond his natural strength, he bounded up seven or eight feet clear of the ground. Then Mowgli's hand shot out like the head of a tree-snake, and gripped him by the scruff of his neck, and the branch shook with the jar as his weight fell back, almost wrenching Mowgli to the ground. But he never loosed his grip, and inch by inch he hauled the beast, hanging like a drowned jackal, up on the branch. With his left hand he reached for his knife and cut off the red, bushy tail, flinging the dhole back to earth again. That was all he needed. The Pack would not go forward on Won-tolla's trail now till they had killed Mowgli or Mowgli had killed them. He saw them settle down in circles with a quiver of the haunches that meant they were going to stay, and so he climbed to a higher crotch, settled his back comfortably, and went to sleep.

After three or four hours he waked and counted the Pack. They were all there, silent, husky, and dry, with eyes of steel. The sun was beginning to sink. In half an hour the Little People of the Rocks would be ending their labours, and, as you know, the dhole does not fight best in the twilight.

"I did not need such faithful watchers," he said politely, standing up on a branch, "but I will remember this. Ye be true dholes, but to my thinking over much of one kind. For that reason I do not give the big lizard-eater his tail again. Art thou not pleased, Red Dog?"

"I myself will tear out thy stomach!" yelled the leader, scratching at the foot of the tree.

"Nay, but consider, wise rat of the Dekkan. There will now be many litters of little tailless red dogs, yea, with raw red stumps that sting when

the sand is hot. Go home, Red Dog, and cry that an ape has done this. Ye will not go? Come, then, with me, and I will make you very wise!"

He moved, *Bandar-log* fashion, into the next tree, and so on into the next and the next, the Pack following with lifted hungry heads. Now and then he would pretend to fall, and the Pack would tumble one over the other in their haste to be at the death. It was a curious sight—the boy with the knife that shone in the low sunlight as it sifted through the upper branches, and the silent Pack with their red coats all aflame, huddling and following below. When he came to the last tree he took the garlic and rubbed himself all over carefully, and the dholes yelled with scorn. "Ape with a wolf's tongue, dost thou think to cover thy scent?" they said. "We follow to the death."

"Take thy tail," said Mowgli, flinging it back along the course he had taken. The Pack instinctively rushed after it. "And follow now—to the death."

He had slipped down the tree-trunk, and headed like the wind in bare feet for the Bee Rocks, before the dholes saw what he would do.

They gave one deep howl, and settled down to the long, lobbing canter that can at the last run down anything that runs. Mowgli knew their pack-pace to be much slower than that of the wolves, or he would never have risked a two-mile run in full sight. They were sure that the boy was theirs at last, and he was sure that he held them to play with as he pleased. All his trouble was to keep them sufficiently hot behind him to prevent their turning off too soon. He ran cleanly, evenly, and springily; the tailless leader not five yards behind him; and the Pack tailing out over perhaps a quarter of a mile of ground, crazy and blind with the rage of slaughter. So he kept his distance by ear, reserving his last effort for the rush across the Bee Rocks.

The Little People had gone to sleep in the early twilight, for it was not the season of late blossoming flowers; but as Mowgli's first footfalls rang hollow on the hollow ground he heard a sound as though all the earth were humming. Then he ran as he had never run in his life before, spurned aside one—two—three of the piles of stones into the dark, sweet-smelling gullies; heard a roar like the roar of the sea in a cave; saw with the tail of his eye the air grow dark behind him; saw the

current of the Waingunga far below, and a flat, diamond-shaped head in the water; leaped outward with all his strength, the tailless dhole snapping at his shoulder in mid-air, and dropped feet first to the safety of the river, breathless and triumphant. There was not a sting upon him, for the smell of the garlic had checked the Little People for just the few seconds that he was among them. When he rose Kaa's coils were steadying him and things were bounding over the edge of the cliff—great lumps, it seemed, of clustered bees falling like plummets; but before any lump touched water the bees flew upward and the body of a dhole whirled down-stream. Overhead they could hear furious short yells that were drowned in a roar like breakers—the roar of the wings of the Little People of the Rocks. Some of the dholes, too, had fallen into the gullies that communicated with the underground caves, and there choked and fought and snapped among the tumbled honeycombs, and at last, borne up, even when they were dead, on the heaving waves of bees beneath them, shot out of some hole in the river-face, to roll over on the black rubbish-heaps. There were dholes who had leaped short into the trees on the cliffs, and the bees blotted out their shapes; but the greater number of them, maddened by the stings, had flung themselves into the river; and, as Kaa said, the Waingunga was hungry water.

Kaa held Mowgli fast till the boy had recovered his breath.

"We may not stay here," he said. "The Little People are roused indeed. Come!"

Swimming low and diving as often as he could, Mowgli went down the river, knife in hand.

"Slowly, slowly," said Kaa. "One tooth does not kill a hundred unless it be a cobra's, and many of the dholes took water swiftly when they saw the Little People rise."

"The more work for my knife, then. *Phai!* How the Little People follow!" Mowgli sank again. The face of the water was blanketed with wild bees, buzzing sullenly and stinging all they found.

"Nothing was ever yet lost by silence," said Kaa—no sting could penetrate his scales—"and thou hast all the long night for the hunting. Hear them howl!"

Nearly half the pack had seen the trap their fellows rushed into, and turning sharp aside had flung themselves into the water where the gorge broke down in steep banks. Their cries of rage and their threats against the "tree-ape" who had brought them to their shame mixed with the yells and growls of those who had been punished by the Little People. To remain ashore was death, and every dhole knew it. Their pack was swept along the current, down to the deep eddies of the Peace Pool, but even there the angry Little People followed and forced them to the water again. Mowgli could hear the voice of the tailless leader bidding his people hold on and kill out every wolf in Seeonee. But he did not waste his time in listening.

"One kills in the dark behind us!" snapped a dhole. "Here is tainted water!"

Mowgli had dived forward like an otter, twitched a struggling dhole under water before he could open his mouth, and dark rings rose as the body plopped up, turning on its side. The dholes tried to turn, but the current prevented them, and the Little People darted at the heads and ears, and they could hear the challenge of the Seeonee Pack growing louder and deeper in the gathering darkness. Again Mowgli dived, and again a dhole went under, and rose dead, and again the clamour broke out at the rear of the pack; some howling that it was best to go ashore, others calling on their leader to lead them back to the Dekkan, and others bidding Mowgli show himself and be killed.

"They come to the fight with two stomachs and several voices," said Kaa. "The rest is with thy brethren below yonder, The Little People go back to sleep. They have chased us far. Now I, too, turn back, for I am not of one skin with *any* wolf. Good hunting, Little Brother, and remember the dhole bites low."

A wolf came running along the bank on three legs, leaping up and down, laying his head sideways close to the ground, hunching his back, and breaking high into the air, as though he were playing with his cubs. It was Won-tolla, the Outlier, and he said never a word, but continued his horrible sport beside the dholes. They had been long in the water now, and were swimming wearily, their coats drenched and heavy, their bushy tails dragging like sponges, so tired and shaken that

they, too, were silent, watching the pair of blazing eyes that moved abreast.

"This is no good hunting," said one, panting.

"Good hunting!" said Mowgli, as he rose boldly at the brute's side, and sent the long knife home behind the shoulder, pushing hard to avoid the dying snap.

"Art thou there, Man-cub?" said Won-tolla across the water.

"Ask of the dead, Outlier," Mowgli replied. "Have none come down-stream? I have filled these dogs' mouths with dirt; I have tricked them in the broad daylight, and their leader lacks his tail, but here be some few for thee still. Whither shall I drive them?"

"I will wait," said Won-tolla. "The night is before me."

Nearer and nearer came the bay of the Seeonee wolves. "For the Pack, for the Full Pack it is met!" and a bend in the river drove the dholes forward among the sands and shoals opposite the Lairs.

Then they saw their mistake. They should have landed half a mile higher up, and rushed the wolves on dry ground. Now it was too late. The bank was lined with burning eyes, and except for the horrible *pheeal* that had never stopped since sundown, there was no sound in the Jungle. It seemed as though Won-tolla were fawning on them to come ashore; and "Turn and take hold!" said the leader of the dholes. The entire Pack flung themselves at the shore, threshing and squattering through the shoal water, till the face of the Waingunga was all white and torn, and the great ripples went from side to side, like bow-waves from a boat. Mowgli followed the rush, stabbing and slicing as the dholes, huddled together, rushed up the river-beach in one wave.

Then the long fight began, heaving and straining and splitting and scattering and narrowing and broadening along the red, wet sands, and over and between the tangled tree-roots, and through and among the bushes, and in and out of the grass clumps; for even now the dholes were two to one. But they met wolves fighting for all that made the Pack, and not only the short, high, deep-chested, white-tusked hunters of the Pack, but the anxious-eyed lahinis—the she-wolves of the lair, as the saying is—fighting for their litters, with here and there a yearling wolf, his first coat still half woolly, tugging and grappling

by their sides. A wolf, you must know, flies at the throat or snaps at the flank, while a dhole, by preference, bites at the belly; so when the dholes were struggling out of the water and had to raise their heads, the odds were with the wolves. On dry land the wolves suffered; but in the water or ashore, Mowgli's knife came and went without ceasing. The Four had worried their way to his side. Gray Brother, crouched between the boy's knees, was protecting his stomach, while the others guarded his back and either side, or stood over him when the shock of a leaping, yelling dhole who had thrown himself full on the steady blade bore him down. For the rest, it was one tangled confusion—a locked and swaying mob that moved from right to left and from left to right along the bank; and also ground round and round slowly on its own centre. Here would be a heaving mound, like a water-blister in a whirlpool, which would break like a water-blister, and throw up four or five mangled dogs, each striving to get back to the centre; here would be a single wolf borne down by two or three dholes, laboriously dragging them forward, and sinking the while; here a yearling cub would be held up by the pressure round him, though he had been killed early, while his mother, crazed with dumb rage, rolled over and over, snapping, and passing on; and in the middle of the thickest press, perhaps, one wolf and one dhole, forgetting everything else, would be manoeuvring for first hold till they were whirled away by a rush of furious fighters. Once Mowgli passed Akela, a dhole on either flank, and his all but toothless jaws closed over the loins of a third; and once he saw Phao, his teeth set in the throat of a dhole, tugging the unwilling beast forward till the yearlings could finish him. But the bulk of the fight was blind flurry and smother in the dark; hit, trip, and tumble, yelp, groan, and worry-worry-worry, round him and behind him and above him. As the night wore on, the quick, giddy-go-round motion increased. The dholes were cowed and afraid to attack the stronger wolves, but did not yet dare to run away. Mowgli felt that the end was coming soon, and contented himself with striking merely to cripple. The yearlings were growing bolder; there was time now and again to breathe, and pass a word to a friend, and the mere flicker of the knife would sometimes turn a dog aside.

"The meat is very near the bone," Gray Brother yelled. He was bleeding from a score of flesh-wounds.

"But the bone is yet to be cracked," said Mowgli. "*Eowawa! Thus* do we do in the Jungle!" The red blade ran like a flame along the side of a dhole whose hind-quarters were hidden by the weight of a clinging wolf.

"My kill!" snorted the wolf through his wrinkled nostrils. "Leave him to me."

"Is thy stomach still empty, Outlier?" said Mowgli. Won-tolla was fearfully punished, but his grip had paralysed the dhole, who could not turn round and reach him.

"By the Bull that bought me," said Mowgli, with a bitter laugh, "it is the tailless one!" And indeed it was the big bay-coloured leader.

"It is not wise to kill cubs and lahinis," Mowgli went on philosophically, wiping the blood out of his eyes, "unless one has also killed the Outlier; and it is in my stomach that this Won-tolla kills thee."

A dhole leaped to his leader's aid; but before his teeth had found Won-tolla's flank, Mowgli's knife was in his throat, and Gray Brother took what was left.

"And thus do we do in the Jungle," said Mowgli.

Won-tolla said not a word, only his jaws were closing and closing on the backbone as his life ebbed. The dhole shuddered, his head dropped, and he lay still, and Won-tolla dropped above him.

"*Huh!* The Blood Debt is paid," said Mowgli. "Sing the song, Won-tolla."

"He hunts no more," said Gray Brother; "and Akela, too, is silent this long time."

"The bone is cracked!" thundered Phao, son of Phaona. "They go! Kill, kill out, O hunters of the Free People!"

Dhole after dhole was slinking away from those dark and bloody sands to the river, to the thick Jungle, up-stream or down-stream as he saw the road clear.

"The debt! The debt!" shouted Mowgli. "Pay the debt! They have slain the Lone Wolf! Let not a dog go!"

He was flying to the river, knife in hand, to check any dhole who

dared to take water, when, from under a mound of nine dead, rose Akela's head and fore-quarters, and Mowgli dropped on his knees beside the Lone Wolf.

"Said I not it would be my last fight?" Akela gasped. "It is good hunting. And thou, Little Brother?"

"I live, having killed many."

"Even so. I die, and I would—I would die by thee, Little Brother."

Mowgli took the terrible scarred head on his knees, and put his arms round the torn neck.

"It is long since the old days of Shere Khan, and a Man-cub that rolled naked in the dust."

"Nay, nay, I am a wolf. I am of one skin with the Free People," Mowgli cried. "It is no will of mine that I am a man."

"Thou art a man, Little Brother, wolfling of my watching. Thou art a man, or else the Pack had fled before the dhole. My life I owe to thee, and to-day thou hast saved the Pack even as once I saved thee. Hast thou forgotten? All debts are paid now. Go to thine own people. I tell thee again, eye of my eye, this hunting is ended. Go to thine own people."

"I will never go. I will hunt alone in the Jungle. I have said it."

"After the summer come the Rains, and after the Rains comes the spring. Go back before thou art driven."

"Who will drive me?"

"Mowgli will drive Mowgli. Go back to thy people. Go to Man."

"When Mowgli drives Mowgli I will go," Mowgli answered.

"There is no more to say," said Akela. "Little Brother, canst thou raise me to my feet? I also was a leader of the Free People."

Very carefully and gently Mowgli lifted the bodies aside, and raised Akela to his feet, both arms round him, and the Lone Wolf drew a long breath, and began the Death Song that a leader of the Pack should sing when he dies. It gathered strength as he went on, lifting and lifting, and ringing far across the river, till it came to the last "Good hunting!" and Akela shook himself clear of Mowgli for an instant, and, leaping into the air, fell backward dead upon his last and most terrible kill.

Mowgli sat with his head on his knees, careless of anything else,

while the remnant of the flying dholes were being overtaken and run down by the merciless lahinis. Little by little the cries died away, and the wolves returned limping, as their wounds stiffened, to take stock of the losses. Fifteen of the Pack, as well as half a dozen lahinis, lay dead by the river, and of the others not one was unmarked. And Mowgli sat through it all till the cold daybreak, when Phao's wet, red muzzle was dropped in his hand, and Mowgli drew back to show the gaunt body of Akela.

"Good hunting!" said Phao, as though Akela were still alive, and then over his bitten shoulder to the others: "Howl, dogs! A Wolf has died to-night!"

But of all the Pack of two hundred fighting dholes, whose boast was that all jungles were their Jungle, and that no living thing could stand before them, not one returned to the Dekkan to carry that word.

14. CHIL'S SONG

(This is the song that Chil sang as the kites dropped down one after another to the river-bed, when the great fight was finished. Chil is good friends with everybody, but he is a cold-blooded kind of creature at heart, because he knows that almost everybody in the Jungle comes to him in the long-run.)

> These were my companions going forth by night—
> *(For Chil! Look you, for Chil!)*
> Now come I to whistle them the ending of the fight.
> *(Chil! Vanguards of Chil!)*
> Word they gave me overhead of quarry newly slain,
> Word I gave them underfoot of buck upon the plain.
> Here's an end of every trail—they shall not speak again!
> They that called the hunting-cry—they that followed fast—
> *(For Chil! Look you, for Chil!)*
> They that bade the *sambhur* wheel, or pinned him as he
> passed—
> *(Chil! Vanguards of Chil!)*
> They that lagged behind the scent—they that ran before,
> They that shunned the level horn—they that overbore.
> Here's an end of every trail—they shall not follow more.
> These were my companions. Pity 'twas they died!
> *(For Chil! Look you, for Chil!)*
> Now come I to comfort them that knew them in their pride.
> *(Chil! Vanguards of Chil!)*
> Tattered flank and sunken eye, open mouth and red,
> Locked and lank and lone they lie, the dead upon their dead.
> Here's an end of every trail—and here my hosts are fed.

15. THE SPRING RUNNING

Man goes to Man! Cry the challenge through the Jungle!
He that was our Brother goes away.
Hear, now, and judge, O ye People of the Jungle,—
Answer, who shall turn him—who shall stay?

Man goes to Man! He is weeping in the Jungle:
He that was our Brother sorrows sore!
Man goes to Man! (Oh, we loved him in the Jungle!)
To the Man-Trail where we may not follow more.

The second year after the great fight with Red Dog and the death of Akela, Mowgli must have been nearly seventeen years old. He looked older, for hard exercise, the best of good eating, and baths whenever he felt in the least hot or dusty, had given him strength and growth far beyond his age. He could swing by one hand from a top branch for half an hour at a time, when he had occasion to look along the tree-roads. He could stop a young buck in mid-gallop and throw him sideways by the head. He could even jerk over the big, blue wild boars that lived in the Marshes of the North. The Jungle People who used to fear him for his wits feared him now for his strength, and when he moved quietly on his own affairs the mere whisper of his coming cleared the wood-paths. And yet the look in his eyes was always gentle. Even when he fought, his eyes never blazed as Bagheera's did. They only grew more and more interested and excited; and that was one of the things that Bagheera himself did not understand.

He asked Mowgli about it, and the boy laughed and said. "When I miss the kill I am angry. When I must go empty for two days I am very angry. Do not my eyes talk then?"

"The mouth is hungry," said Bagheera, "but the eyes say nothing. Hunting, eating, or swimming, it is all one—like a stone in wet or dry weather." Mowgli looked at him lazily from under his long eyelashes, and, as usual, the panther's head dropped. Bagheera knew his master.

They were lying out far up the side of a hill overlooking the Waingunga, and the morning mists hung below them in bands of white and green. As the sun rose it changed into bubbling seas of red gold, churned off, and let the low rays stripe the dried grass on which Mowgli and Bagheera were resting. It was the end of the cold weather, the leaves and the trees looked worn and faded, and there was a dry, ticking rustle everywhere when the wind blew. A little leaf tap-tap-tapped furiously against a twig, as a single leaf caught in a current will. It roused Bagheera, for he snuffed the morning air with a deep, hollow cough, threw himself on his back, and struck with his fore-paws at the nodding leaf above.

"The year turns," he said. "The Jungle goes forward. The Time of New Talk is near. That leaf knows. It is very good."

"The grass is dry," Mowgli answered, pulling up a tuft. "Even Eye-of-the-Spring [that is a little trumpet-shaped, waxy red flower that runs in and out among the grasses]—even Eye-of-the Spring is shut, and... Bagheera, *is* it well for the Black Panther so to lie on his back and beat with his paws in the air, as though he were the tree-cat?"

"Aowh?" said Bagheera. He seemed to be thinking of other things.

"I say, *is* it well for the Black Panther so to mouth and cough, and howl and roll? Remember, we be the Masters of the Jungle, thou and I."

"Indeed, yes; I hear, Man-cub." Bagheera rolled over hurriedly and sat up, the dust on his ragged black flanks. (He was just casting his winter coat.) "We be surely the Masters of the Jungle! Who is so strong as Mowgli? Who so wise?" There was a curious drawl in the voice that made Mowgli turn to see whether by any chance the Black Panther were making fun of him, for the Jungle is full of words that sound like one thing, but mean another. "I said we be beyond question the Masters of the Jungle," Bagheera repeated. "Have I done wrong? I did not know that the Man-cub no longer lay upon the ground. Does he fly, then?"

Mowgli sat with his elbows on his knees, looking out across the valley at the daylight. Somewhere down in the woods below a bird was trying over in a husky, reedy voice the first few notes of his spring song.

It was no more than a shadow of the liquid, tumbling call he would be pouring later, but Bagheera heard it.

"I said the Time of New Talk is near," growled the panther, switching his tail.

"I hear," Mowgli answered. "Bagheera, why dost thou shake all over? The sun is warm."

"That is Ferao, the scarlet woodpecker," said Bagheera. "*He* has not forgotten. Now I, too, must remember my song," and he began purring and crooning to himself, harking back dissatisfied again and again.

"There is no game afoot," said Mowgli.

"Little Brother, are *both* thine ears stopped? That is no killing-word, but my song that I make ready against the need."

"I had forgotten. I shall know when the Time of New Talk is here, because then thou and the others all run away and leave me alone." Mowgli spoke rather savagely.

"But, indeed, Little Brother," Bagheera began, "we do not always—"

"I say ye do," said Mowgli, shooting out his forefinger angrily. "Ye *do* run away, and I, who am the Master of the Jungle, must needs walk alone. How was it last season, when I would gather sugar-cane from the fields of a Man-Pack? I sent a runner—I sent thee!—to Hathi, bidding him to come upon such a night and pluck the sweet grass for me with his trunk."

"He came only two nights later," said Bagheera, cowering a little; "and of that long, sweet grass that pleased thee so he gathered more than any Man-cub could eat in all the nights of the Rains. That was no fault of mine."

"He did not come upon the night when I sent him the word. No, he was trumpeting and running and roaring through the valleys in the moonlight. His trail was like the trail of three elephants, for he would not hide among the trees. He danced in the moonlight before the houses of the Man-Pack. I saw him, and yet he would not come to me; and *I* am the Master of the Jungle!"

"It was the Time of New Talk," said the panther, always very humble. "Perhaps, Little Brother, thou didst not that time call him by a Master-word? Listen to Ferao, and be glad!"

Mowgli's bad temper seemed to have boiled itself away. He lay back with his head on his arms, his eyes shut. "I do not know—nor do I care," he said sleepily. "Let us sleep, Bagheera. My stomach is heavy in me. Make me a rest for my head."

The panther lay down again with a sigh, because he could hear Ferao practising and repractising his song against the Springtime of New Talk, as they say.

In an Indian Jungle the seasons slide one into the other almost without division. There seem to be only two—the wet and the dry; but if you look closely below the torrents of rain and the clouds of char and dust you will find all four going round in their regular ring. Spring is the most wonderful, because she has not to cover a clean, bare field with new leaves and flowers, but to drive before her and to put away the hanging-on, over-surviving raffle of half-green things which the gentle winter has suffered to live, and to make the partly-dressed stale earth feel new and young once more. And this she does so well that there is no spring in the world like the Jungle spring.

There is one day when all things are tired, and the very smells, as they drift on the heavy air, are old and used. One cannot explain this, but it feels so. Then there is another day—to the eye nothing whatever has changed—when all the smells are new and delightful, and the whiskers of the Jungle People quiver to their roots, and the winter hair comes away from their sides in long, draggled locks. Then, perhaps, a little rain falls, and all the trees and the bushes and the bamboos and the mosses and the juicy-leaved plants wake with a noise of growing that you can almost hear, and under this noise runs, day and night, a deep hum. *That* is the noise of the spring—a vibrating boom which is neither bees, nor falling water, nor the wind in tree-tops, but the purring of the warm, happy world.

Up to this year Mowgli had always delighted in the turn of the seasons. It was he who generally saw the first Eye-of-the-Spring deep down among the grasses, and the first bank of spring clouds, which are like nothing else in the Jungle. His voice could be heard in all sorts of wet, star-lighted, blossoming places, helping the big frogs through their choruses, or mocking the little upside-down owls that hoot through the

white nights. Like all his people, spring was the season he chose for his flittings—moving, for the mere joy of rushing through the warm air, thirty, forty, or fifty miles between twilight and the morning star, and coming back panting and laughing and wreathed with strange flowers. The Four did not follow him on these wild ringings of the Jungle, but went off to sing songs with other wolves. The Jungle People are very busy in the spring, and Mowgli could hear them grunting and screaming and whistling according to their kind. Their voices then are different from their voices at other times of the year, and that is one of the reasons why spring in the Jungle is called the Time of New Talk.

But that spring, as he told Bagheera, his stomach was changed in him. Ever since the bamboo shoots turned spotty-brown he had been looking forward to the morning when the smells should change. But when the morning came, and Mor the Peacock, blazing in bronze and blue and gold, cried it aloud all along the misty woods, and Mowgli opened his mouth to send on the cry, the words choked between his teeth, and a feeling came over him that began at his toes and ended in his hair—a feeling of pure unhappiness, so that he looked himself over to be sure that he had not trod on a thorn. Mor cried the new smells, the other birds took it over, and from the rocks by the Waingunga he heard Bagheera's hoarse scream—something between the scream of an eagle and the neighing of a horse. There was a yelling and scattering of *Bandar-log* in the new-budding branches above, and there stood Mowgli, his chest, filled to answer Mor, sinking in little gasps as the breath was driven out of it by this unhappiness.

He stared all round him, but he could see no more than the mocking *Bandar-log* scudding through the trees, and Mor, his tail spread in full splendour, dancing on the slopes below.

"The smells have changed," screamed Mor. "Good hunting, Little Brother! Where is thy answer?"

"Little Brother, good hunting!" whistled Chil the Kite and his mate, swooping down together. The two baffed under Mowgli's nose so close that a pinch of downy white feathers brushed away.

A light spring rain—elephant-rain they call it—drove across the Jungle in a belt half a mile wide, left the new leaves wet and nodding

behind, and died out in a double rainbow and a light roll of thunder. The spring hum broke out for a minute, and was silent, but all the Jungle Folk seemed to be giving tongue at once. All except Mowgli.

"I have eaten good food," he said to himself. "I have drunk good water. Nor does my throat burn and grow small, as it did when I bit the blue-spotted root that Oo the Turtle said was clean food. But my stomach is heavy, and I have given very bad talk to Bagheera and others, people of the Jungle and my people. Now, too, I am hot and now I am cold, and now I am neither hot nor cold, but angry with that which I cannot see. Huhu! It is time to make a running! To-night I will cross the ranges; yes, I will make a spring running to the Marshes of the North, and back again. I have hunted too easily too long. The Four shall come with me, for they grow as fat as white grubs."

He called, but never one of the Four answered. They were far beyond earshot, singing over the spring songs—the Moon and *Sambhur* Songs—with the wolves of the pack; for in the spring-time the Jungle People make very little difference between the day and the night. He gave the sharp, barking note, but his only answer was the mocking *maiou* of the little spotted tree-cat winding in and out among the branches for early birds' nests. At this he shook all over with rage, and half drew his knife. Then he became very haughty, though there was no one to see him, and stalked severely down the hillside, chin up and eyebrows down. But never a single one of his people asked him a question, for they were all too busy with their own affairs.

"Yes," said Mowgli to himself, though in his heart he knew that he had no reason. "Let the Red Dhole come from the Dekkan, or the Red Flower dance among the bamboos, and all the Jungle runs whining to Mowgli, calling him great elephant-names. But now, because Eye-of-the-Spring is red, and Mor, forsooth, must show his naked legs in some spring dance, the Jungle goes mad as Tabaqui.…By the Bull that bought me! am I the Master of the Jungle, or am I not? Be silent! What do ye here?"

A couple of young wolves of the Pack were cantering down a path, looking for open ground in which to fight. (You will remember that the Law of the Jungle forbids fighting where the Pack can see.) Their

neck-bristles were as stiff as wire, and they bayed furiously, crouching for the first grapple. Mowgli leaped forward, caught one outstretched throat in either hand, expecting to fling the creatures backward as he had often done in games or Pack hunts. But he had never before interfered with a spring fight. The two leaped forward and dashed him aside, and without word to waste rolled over and over close locked.

Mowgli was on his feet almost before he fell, his knife and his white teeth were bared, and at that minute he would have killed both for no reason but that they were fighting when he wished them to be quiet, although every wolf has full right under the Law to fight. He danced round them with lowered shoulders and quivering hand, ready to send in a double blow when the first flurry of the scuffle should be over; but while he waited the strength seemed to ebb from his body, the knife-point lowered, and he sheathed the knife and watched.

"I have surely eaten poison," he sighed at last. "Since I broke up the Council with the Red Flower—since I killed Shere Khan—none of the Pack could fling me aside. And these be only tail-wolves in the Pack, little hunters! My strength is gone from me, and presently I shall die. Oh, Mowgli, why dost thou not kill them both?"

The fight went on till one wolf ran away, and Mowgli was left alone on the torn and bloody ground, looking now at his knife, and now at his legs and arms, while the feeling of unhappiness he had never known before covered him as water covers a log.

He killed early that evening and ate but little, so as to be in good fettle for his spring running, and he ate alone because all the Jungle People were away singing or fighting. It was a perfect white night, as they call it. All green things seemed to have made a month's growth since the morning. The branch that was yellow-leaved the day before dripped sap when Mowgli broke it. The mosses curled deep and warm over his feet, the young grass had no cutting edges, and all the voices of the Jungle boomed like one deep harp-string touched by the moon—the Moon of New Talk, who splashed her light full on rock and pool, slipped it between trunk and creeper, and sifted it through a million leaves. Forgetting his unhappiness, Mowgli sang aloud with pure delight as he settled into his stride. It was more like flying than

anything else, for he had chosen the long downward slope that leads to the Northern Marshes through the heart of the main Jungle, where the springy ground deadened the fall of his feet. A man-taught man would have picked his way with many stumbles through the cheating moonlight, but Mowgli's muscles, trained by years of experience, bore him up as though he were a feather. When a rotten log or a hidden stone turned under his foot he saved himself, never checking his pace, without effort and without thought. When he tired of ground-going he threw up his hands monkey-fashion to the nearest creeper, and seemed to float rather than to climb up into the thin branches, whence he would follow a tree-road till his mood changed, and he shot downward in a long, leafy curve to the levels again. There were still, hot hollows surrounded by wet rocks where he could hardly breathe for the heavy scents of the night flowers and the bloom along the creeper buds; dark avenues where the moonlight lay in belts as regular as checkered marbles in a church aisle; thickets where the wet young growth stood breast-high about him and threw its arms round his waist; and hilltops crowned with broken rock, where he leaped from stone to stone above the lairs of the frightened little foxes. He would hear, very faint and far off, the *chug-drug* of a boar sharpening his tusks on a bole; and would come across the great gray brute all alone, scribing and rending the bark of a tall tree, his mouth dripping with foam, and his eyes blazing like fire. Or he would turn aside to the sound of clashing horns and hissing grunts, and dash past a couple of furious *sambhur*, staggering to and fro with lowered heads, striped with blood that showed black in the moonlight. Or at some rushing ford he would hear Jacala the Crocodile bellowing like a bull, or disturb a twined knot of the Poison People, but before they could strike he would be away and across the glistening shingle, and deep in the Jungle again.

So he ran, sometimes shouting, sometimes singing to himself, the happiest thing in all the Jungle that night, till the smell of the flowers warned him that he was near the marshes, and those lay far beyond his farthest hunting-grounds.

Here, again, a man-trained man would have sunk overhead in three strides, but Mowgli's feet had eyes in them, and they passed him from

tussock to tussock and clump to quaking clump without asking help from the eyes in his head. He ran out to the middle of the swamp, disturbing the duck as he ran, and sat down on a moss-coated tree-trunk lapped in the black water. The marsh was awake all round him, for in the spring the Bird People sleep very lightly, and companies of them were coming or going the night through. But no one took any notice of Mowgli sitting among the tall reeds humming songs without words, and looking at the soles of his hard brown feet in case of neglected thorns. All his unhappiness seemed to have been left behind in his own Jungle, and he was just beginning a full-throat song when it came back again—ten times worse than before.

This time Mowgli was frightened. "It is here also!" he said half aloud. "It has followed me," and he looked over his shoulder to see whether the It were not standing behind him. "There is no one here." The night noises of the marsh went on, but never a bird or beast spoke to him, and the new feeling of misery grew.

"I have surely eaten poison," he said in an awe-stricken voice. "It must be that carelessly I have eaten poison, and my strength is going from me. I was afraid—and yet it was not *I* that was afraid—Mowgli was afraid when the two wolves fought. Akela, or even Phao, would have silenced them; yet Mowgli was afraid. That is true sign I have eaten poison....But what do they care in the Jungle? They sing and howl and fight, and run in companies under the moon, and I—*Hai-mai!*—I am dying in the marshes, of that poison which I have eaten." He was so sorry for himself that he nearly wept. "And after," he went on, "they will find me lying in the black water. Nay, I will go back to my own Jungle, and I will die upon the Council Rock, and Bagheera, whom I love, if he is not screaming in the valley—Bagheera, perhaps, may watch by what is left for a little, lest Chil use me as he used Akela."

A large, warm tear splashed down on his knee, and, miserable as he was, Mowgli felt happy that he was so miserable, if you can understand that upside-down sort of happiness. "As Chil the Kite used Akela," he repeated, "on the night I saved the Pack from Red Dog." He was quiet for a little, thinking of the last words of the Lone Wolf, which you, of course, remember. "Now Akela said to me many foolish things before

he died, for when we die our stomachs change. He said...None the less, I *am* of the Jungle!"

In his excitement, as he remembered the fight on Waingunga bank, he shouted the last words aloud, and a wild buffalo-cow among the reeds sprang to her knees, snorting, "Man!"

"Uhh!" said Mysa the Wild Buffalo (Mowgli could hear him turn in his wallow), "*That* is no man. It is only the hairless wolf of the Seeonee Pack. On such nights runs he to and fro."

"Uhh!" said the cow, dropping her head again to graze, "I thought it was Man."

"I say no. Oh, Mowgli, is it danger?" lowed Mysa.

"Oh, Mowgli, is it danger?" the boy called back mockingly. "That is all Mysa thinks for: Is it danger? But for Mowgli, who goes to and fro in the Jungle by night, watching, what do ye care?"

"How loud he cries!" said the cow. "Thus do they cry," Mysa answered contemptuously, "who, having torn up the grass, know not how to eat it."

"For less than this," Mowgli groaned to himself, "for less than this even last Rains I had pricked Mysa out of his wallow, and ridden him through the swamp on a rush halter." He stretched a hand to break one of the feathery reeds, but drew it back with a sigh. Mysa went on steadily chewing the cud, and the long grass ripped where the cow grazed. "I will not die *here*," he said angrily. "Mysa, who is of one blood with Jacala and the pig, would see me. Let us go beyond the swamp and see what comes. Never have I run such a spring running—hot and cold together. Up, Mowgli!"

He could not resist the temptation of stealing across the reeds to Mysa and pricking him with the point of his knife. The great dripping bull broke out of his wallow like a shell exploding, while Mowgli laughed till he sat down.

"Say now that the hairless wolf of the Seeonee Pack once herded thee, Mysa," he called.

"Wolf! *Thou?*" the bull snorted, stamping in the mud. "All the jungle knows thou wast a herder of tame cattle—such a man's brat as shouts in the dust by the crops yonder. *Thou* of the Jungle! What hunter would

have crawled like a snake among the leeches, and for a muddy jest—a jackal's jest—have shamed me before my cow? Come to firm ground, and I will—I will…" Mysa frothed at the mouth, for Mysa has nearly the worst temper of any one in the Jungle.

Mowgli watched him puff and blow with eyes that never changed. When he could make himself heard through the pattering mud, he said: "What Man-Pack lair here by the marshes, Mysa? This is new Jungle to me."

"Go north, then," roared the angry bull, for Mowgli had pricked him rather sharply. "It was a naked cow-herd's jest. Go and tell them at the village at the foot of the marsh."

"The Man-Pack do not love jungle-tales, nor do I think, Mysa, that a scratch more or less on thy hide is any matter for a council. But I will go and look at this village. Yes, I will go. Softly now. It is not every night that the Master of the Jungle comes to herd thee."

He stepped out to the shivering ground on the edge of the marsh, well knowing that Mysa would never charge over it and laughed, as he ran, to think of the bull's anger.

"My strength is not altogether gone," he said. "It may be that the poison is not to the bone. There is a star sitting low yonder." He looked at it between his half-shut hands. "By the Bull that bought me, it is the Red Flower—the Red Flower that I lay beside before—before I came even to the first Seeonee Pack! Now that I have seen, I will finish the running."

The marsh ended in a broad plain where a light twinkled. It was a long time since Mowgli had concerned himself with the doings of men, but this night the glimmer of the Red Flower drew him forward.

"I will look," said he, "as I did in the old days, and I will see how far the Man-Pack has changed."

Forgetting that he was no longer in his own Jungle, where he could do what he pleased, he trod carelessly through the dew-loaded grasses till he came to the hut where the light stood. Three or four yelping dogs gave tongue, for he was on the outskirts of a village.

"Ho!" said Mowgli, sitting down noiselessly, after sending back a deep wolf-growl that silenced the curs. "What comes will come.

Mowgli, what hast thou to do any more with the lairs of the Man-Pack?" He rubbed his mouth, remembering where a stone had struck it years ago when the other Man-Pack had cast him out.

The door of the hut opened, and a woman stood peering out into the darkness. A child cried, and the woman said over her shoulder, "Sleep. It was but a jackal that waked the dogs. In a little time morning comes."

Mowgli in the grass began to shake as though he had fever. He knew that voice well, but to make sure he cried softly, surprised to find how man's talk came back, "Messua! O Messua!"

"Who calls?" said the woman, a quiver in her voice.

"Hast thou forgotten?" said Mowgli. His throat was dry as he spoke.

"If it be *thou*, what name did I give thee? Say!" She had half shut the door, and her hand was clutching at her breast.

"Nathoo! Ohé, Nathoo!" said Mowgli, for, as you remember, that was the name Messua gave him when he first came to the Man-Pack.

"Come, my son," she called, and Mowgli stepped into the light, and looked full at Messua, the woman who had been good to him, and whose life he had saved from the Man-Pack so long before. She was older, and her hair was gray, but her eyes and her voice had not changed. Woman-like, she expected to find Mowgli where she had left him, and her eyes travelled upward in a puzzled way from his chest to his head, that touched the top of the door.

"My son," she stammered; and then, sinking to his feet: "But it is no longer my son. It is a Godling of the Woods! Ahai!"

As he stood in the red light of the oil-lamp, strong, tall, and beautiful, his long black hair sweeping over his shoulders, the knife swinging at his neck, and his head crowned with a wreath of white jasmine, he might easily have been mistaken for some wild god of a jungle legend. The child half asleep on a cot sprang up and shrieked aloud with terror. Messua turned to soothe him, while Mowgli stood still, looking in at the water-jars and the cooking-pots, the grain-bin, and all the other human belongings that he found himself remembering so well.

"What wilt thou eat or drink?" Messua murmured. "This is all thine. We owe our lives to thee. But art thou him I called Nathoo, or a Godling, indeed?"

"I am Nathoo," said Mowgli, "I am very far from my own place. I saw this light, and came hither. I did not know thou wast here."

"After we came to Khanhiwara," Messua said timidly, "the English would have helped us against those villagers that sought to burn us. Rememberest thou?"

"Indeed, I have not forgotten."

"But when the English Law was made ready, we went to the village of those evil people, and it was no more to be found."

"That also I remember," said Mowgli, with a quiver of his nostril.

"My man, therefore, took service in the fields, and at last—for, indeed, he was a strong man—we held a little land here. It is not so rich as the old village, but we do not need much—we two."

"Where is he the man that dug in the dirt when he was afraid on that night?"

"He is dead—a year."

"And he?" Mowgli pointed to the child.

"My son that was born two Rains ago. If thou art a Godling, give him the Favour of the Jungle, that he may be safe among thy—thy people, as we were safe on that night."

She lifted up the child, who, forgetting his fright, reached out to play with the knife that hung on Mowgli's chest, and Mowgli put the little fingers aside very carefully.

"And if thou art Nathoo whom the tiger carried away," Messua went on, choking, "he is then thy younger brother. Give him an elder brother's blessing."

"*Hai-mai!* What do I know of the thing called a blessing? I am neither a Godling nor his brother, and—O mother, mother, my heart is heavy in me." He shivered as he set down the child.

"Like enough," said Messua, bustling among the cooking-pots. "This comes of running about the marshes by night. Beyond question, the fever had soaked thee to the marrow." Mowgli smiled a little at the idea of anything in the Jungle hurting him. "I will make a fire, and thou shalt drink warm milk. Put away the jasmine wreath: the smell is heavy in so small a place."

Mowgli sat down, muttering, with his face in his hands. All manner

of strange feelings that he had never felt before were running over him, exactly as though he had been poisoned, and he felt dizzy and a little sick. He drank the warm milk in long gulps, Messua patting him on the shoulder from time to time, not quite sure whether he were her son Nathoo of the long ago days, or some wonderful Jungle being, but glad to feel that he was at least flesh and blood.

"Son," she said at last,—her eyes were full of pride,—"have any told thee that thou art beautiful beyond all men?"

"Hah?" said Mowgli, for naturally he had never heard anything of the kind. Messua laughed softly and happily. The look in his face was enough for her.

"I am the first, then? It is right, though it comes seldom, that a mother should tell her son these good things. Thou art very beautiful. Never have I looked upon such a man."

Mowgli twisted his head and tried to see over his own hard shoulder, and Messua laughed again so long that Mowgli, not knowing why, was forced to laugh with her, and the child ran from one to the other, laughing too.

"Nay, thou must not mock thy brother," said Messua, catching him to her breast. "When thou art one-half as fair we will marry thee to the youngest daughter of a king, and thou shalt ride great elephants."

Mowgli could not understand one word in three of the talk here; the warm milk was taking effect on him after his long run, so he curled up and in a minute was deep asleep, and Messua put the hair back from his eyes, threw a cloth over him, and was happy. Jungle-fashion, he slept out the rest of that night and all the next day; for his instincts, which never wholly slept, warned him there was nothing to fear. He waked at last with a bound that shook the hut, for the cloth over his face made him dream of traps; and there he stood, his hand on his knife, the sleep all heavy in his rolling eyes, ready for any fight.

Messua laughed, and set the evening meal before him. There were only a few coarse cakes baked over the smoky fire, some rice, and a lump of sour preserved tamarinds—just enough to go on with till he could get to his evening kill. The smell of the dew in the marshes made him hungry and restless. He wanted to finish his spring running, but the child

insisted on sitting in his arms, and Messua would have it that his long, blue-black hair must be combed out. So she sang, as she combed, foolish little baby-songs, now calling Mowgli her son, and now begging him to give some of his jungle power to the child. The hut door was closed, but Mowgli heard a sound he knew well, and saw Messua's jaw drop with horror as a great gray paw came under the bottom of the door, and Gray Brother outside whined a muffled and penitent whine of anxiety and fear.

"Out and wait! Ye would not come when I called," said Mowgli in Jungle-talk, without turning his head, and the great gray paw disappeared.

"Do not—do not bring thy—thy servants with thee," said Messua. "I—we have always lived at peace with the Jungle."

"It is peace," said Mowgli, rising. "Think of that night on the road to Khanhiwara. There were scores of such folk before thee and behind thee. But I see that even in springtime the Jungle People do not always forget. Mother, I go."

Messua drew aside humbly—he was indeed a wood-god, she thought; but as his hand was on the door the mother in her made her throw her arms round Mowgli's neck again and again.

"Come back!" she whispered. "Son or no son, come back, for I love thee—Look, he too grieves."

The child was crying because the man with the shiny knife was going away.

"Come back again," Messua repeated. "By night or by day this door is never shut to thee."

Mowgli's throat worked as though the cords in it were being pulled, and his voice seemed to be dragged from it as he answered, "I will surely come back."

"And now," he said, as he put by the head of the fawning wolf on the threshold, "I have a little cry against thee, Gray Brother. Why came ye not all four when I called so long ago?"

"So long ago? It was but last night. I—we—were singing in the Jungle the new songs, for this is the Time of New Talk. Rememberest thou?"

"Truly, truly."

"And as soon as the songs were sung," Gray Brother went on earnestly, "I followed thy trail. I ran from all the others and followed hot-foot. But, O Little Brother, what hast *thou* done, eating and sleeping with the Man-Pack?"

"If ye had come when I called, this had never been," said Mowgli, running much faster.

"And now what is to be?" said Gray Brother. Mowgli was going to answer when a girl in a white cloth came down some path that led from the outskirts of the village. Gray Brother dropped out of sight at once, and Mowgli backed noiselessly into a field of high-springing crops. He could almost have touched her with his hand when the warm, green stalks closed before his face and he disappeared like a ghost. The girl screamed, for she thought she had seen a spirit, and then she gave a deep sigh. Mowgli parted the stalks with his hands and watched her till she was out of sight.

"And now I do not know," he said, sighing in his turn. "*Why* did ye not come when I called?"

"We follow thee—we follow thee," Gray Brother mumbled, licking at Mowgli's heel. "We follow thee always, except in the Time of the New Talk."

"And would ye follow me to the Man-Pack?" Mowgli whispered.

"Did I not follow thee on the night our old Pack cast thee out? Who waked thee lying among the crops?"

"Ay, but again?"

"Have I not followed thee to-night?"

"Ay, but again and again, and it may be again, Gray Brother?"

Gray Brother was silent. When he spoke he growled to himself, "The Black One spoke truth."

"And he said?"

"Man goes to Man at the last. Raksha, our mother, said—"

"So also said Akela on the night of Red Dog," Mowgli muttered.

"So also says Kaa, who is wiser than us all."

"What dost thou say, Gray Brother?"

"They cast thee out once, with bad talk. They cut thy mouth with stones. They sent Buldeo to slay thee. They would have thrown thee

into the Red Flower. Thou, and not I, hast said that they are evil and senseless. Thou, and not I—I follow my own people—didst let in the Jungle upon them. Thou, and not I, didst make song against them more bitter even than our song against Red Dog."

"I ask thee what *thou* sayest?"

They were talking as they ran. Gray Brother cantered on a while without replying, and then he said,—between bound and bound as it were,—"Man-cub—Master of the Jungle—Son of Raksha, Lair-brother to me—though I forget for a little while in the spring, thy trail is my trail, thy lair is my lair, thy kill is my kill, and thy death-fight is my death-fight. I speak for the Three. But what wilt thou say to the Jungle?"

"That is well thought. Between the sight and the kill it is not good to wait. Go before and cry them all to the Council Rock, and I will tell them what is in my stomach. But they may not come—in the Time of New Talk they may forget me."

"Hast thou, then, forgotten nothing?" snapped Gray Brother over his shoulder, as he laid himself down to gallop, and Mowgli followed, thinking.

At any other season the news would have called all the Jungle together with bristling necks, but now they were busy hunting and fighting and killing and singing. From one to another Gray Brother ran, crying, "The Master of the Jungle goes back to Man! Come to the Council Rock." And the happy, eager People only answered, "He will return in the summer heats. The Rains will drive him to lair. Run and sing with us, Gray Brother."

"But the Master of the Jungle goes back to Man," Gray Brother would repeat.

"*Eee—Yoawa?* Is the Time of New Talk any less sweet for that?" they would reply. So when Mowgli, heavy-hearted, came up through the well-remembered rocks to the place where he had been brought into the Council, he found only the Four, Baloo, who was nearly blind with age, and the heavy, cold-blooded Kaa coiled around Akela's empty seat.

"Thy trail ends here, then, Manling?" said Kaa, as Mowgli threw

himself down, his face in his hands. "Cry thy cry. We be of one blood, thou and I—man and snake together."

"Why did I not die under Red Dog?" the boy moaned. "My strength is gone from me, and it is not any poison. By night and by day I hear a double step upon my trail. When I turn my head it is as though one had hidden himself from me that instant. I go to look behind the trees and he is not there. I call and none cry again; but it is as though one listened and kept back the answer. I lie down, but I do not rest. I run the spring running, but I am not made still. I bathe, but I am not made cool. The kill sickens me, but I have no heart to fight except I kill. The Red Flower is in my body, my bones are water—and—I know not what I know."

"What need of talk?" said Baloo slowly, turning his head to where Mowgli lay. "Akela by the river said it, that Mowgli should drive Mowgli back to the Man-Pack. I said it. But who listens now to Baloo? Bagheera—where is Bagheera this night?—he knows also. It is the Law."

"When we met at Cold Lairs, Manling, I knew it," said Kaa, turning a little in his mighty coils. "Man goes to Man at the last, though the Jungle does not cast him out."

The Four looked at one another and at Mowgli, puzzled but obedient.

"The Jungle does not cast me out, then?" Mowgli stammered.

Gray Brother and the Three growled furiously, beginning, "So long as we live none shall dare—" But Baloo checked them.

"I taught thee the Law. It is for me to speak," he said; "and, though I cannot now see the rocks before me, I see far. Little Frog, take thine own trail; make thy lair with thine own blood and pack and people; but when there is need of foot or tooth or eye, or a word carried swiftly by night, remember, Master of the Jungle, the Jungle is thine at call."

"The Middle Jungle is thine also," said Kaa. "I speak for no small people."

"*Hai-mai,* my brothers," cried Mowgli, throwing up his arms with a sob. "I know not what I know! I would not go; but I am drawn by both feet. How shall I leave these nights?"

"Nay, look up, Little Brother," Baloo repeated. "There is no shame in this hunting. When the honey is eaten we leave the empty hive."

"Having cast the skin," said Kaa, "we may not creep into it afresh. It is the Law."

"Listen, dearest of all to me," said Baloo. "There is neither word nor will here to hold thee back. Look up! Who may question the Master of the Jungle? I saw thee playing among the white pebbles yonder when thou wast a little frog; and Bagheera, that bought thee for the price of a young bull newly killed, saw thee also. Of that Looking Over we two only remain; for Raksha, thy lair-mother, is dead with thy lair-father; the old Wolf-Pack is long since dead; thou knowest whither Shere Khan went, and Akela died among the dholes, where, but for thy wisdom and strength, the second Seeonee Pack would also have died. There remains nothing but old bones. It is no longer the Man-cub that asks leave of his Pack, but the Master of the Jungle that changes his trail. Who shall question Man in his ways?"

"But Bagheera and the Bull that bought me," said Mowgli. "I would not—"

His words were cut short by a roar and a crash in the thicket below, and Bagheera, light, strong, and terrible as always, stood before him.

"*Therefore,*" he said, stretching out a dripping right paw, "I did not come. It was a long hunt, but he lies dead in the bushes now—a bull in his second year—the Bull that frees thee, Little Brother. All debts are paid now. For the rest, my word is Baloo's word." He licked Mowgli's foot. "Remember, Bagheera loved thee," he cried, and bounded away. At the foot of the hill he cried again long and loud, "Good hunting on a new trail, Master of the Jungle! Remember, Bagheera loved thee."

"Thou hast heard," said Baloo. "There is no more. Go now; but first come to me. O wise Little Frog, come to me!"

"It is hard to cast the skin," said Kaa as Mowgli sobbed and sobbed, with his head on the blind bear's side and his arms round his neck, while Baloo tried feebly to lick his feet.

"The stars are thin," said Gray Brother, snuffing at the dawn wind. "Where shall we lair to-day? for from now, we follow new trails."

*　　　*　　　*　　　*　　　*

And this is the last of the Mowgli stories.

16. THE OUTSONG

(This is the song that Mowgli heard behind him in the Jungle till he came to Messua's door again.)

BALOO—

For the sake of him who showed
One wise Frog the Jungle-Road,
Keep the Law the Man-Pack make—
For thy blind old Baloo's sake!
Clean or tainted, hot or stale,
Hold it as it were the Trail,
Through the day and through the night,
Questing neither left nor right.
For the sake of him who loves
Thee beyond all else that moves,
When thy Pack would make thee pain,
Say: "Tabaqui sings again."
When thy Pack would work thee ill,
Say: "Shere Khan is yet to kill."
When the knife is drawn to slay,
Keep the Law and go thy way.
(Root and honey, palm and spathe,
Guard a cub from harm and scathe!)
Wood and Water, Wind and Tree,
Jungle-Favour go with thee!

KAA—

Anger is the egg of Fear—
Only lidless eyes are clear.
Cobra-poison none may leech.
Even so with Cobra-speech.
Open talk shall call to thee

Strength, whose mate is Courtesy.
Send no lunge beyond thy length;
Lend no rotten bough thy strength.
Gauge thy gape with buck or goat,
Lest thine eye should choke thy throat,
After gorging, wouldst thou sleep?
Look thy den is hid and deep,
Lest a wrong, by thee forgot,
Draw thy killer to the spot.
East and West and North and South,
Wash thy hide and close thy mouth.
(Pit and rift and blue pool-brim,
Middle-Jungle follow him!)
Wood and Water, Wind and Tree,
Jungle-Favour go with thee!

BAGHEERA—

In the cage my life began;
Well I know the worth of Man.
By the Broken Lock that freed—
Man-cub, 'ware the Man-cub's breed!
Scenting-dew or starlight pale,
Choose no tangled tree-cat trail.
Pack or council, hunt or den,
Cry no truce with Jackal-Men.
Feed them silence when they say:
"Come with us an easy way."
Feed them silence when they seek
Help of thine to hurt the weak.
Make no banaar's boast of skill;
Hold thy peace above the kill.
Let nor call nor song nor sign
Turn thee from thy hunting-line.
(Morning mist or twilight clear,
Serve him, Wardens of the Deer!)
Wood and Water, Wind and Tree,
Jungle-Favour go with thee!

THE THREE—

On the trail that thou must tread
To the thresholds of our dread,
Where the Flower blossoms red;
Through the nights when thou shalt lie
Prisoned from our Mother-sky,
Hearing us, thy loves, go by;
In the dawns when thou shalt wake
To the toil thou canst not break,
Heartsick for the Jungle's sake:
Wood and Water, Wind and Tree,
Wisdom, Strength, and Courtesy,
Jungle-Favour go with thee!

Word Cloud Classics

Word Cloud Classics

Madame Bovary

Mansfield Park

*The Merry Adventures of
Robin Hood*

Moby-Dick

My Ántonia

*Narrative of the Life of Frederick
Douglass and Other Works*

Northanger Abbey

Odyssey

Persuasion

Peter Pan

The Phantom of the Opera

The Picture of Dorian Gray

The Poetry of Emily Dickinson

Pride and Prejudice

The Prince and Other Writings

*The Red Badge of Courage
and Other Stories*

The Romantic Poets

The Scarlet Letter

The Secret Garden

*Selected Works of
Alexander Hamilton*

Sense and Sensibility

*Shakespeare's Sonnets and
Other Poems*

*Strange Case of Dr. Jekyll and
Mr. Hyde & Other Stories*

*Tarzan of the Apes &
The Return of Tarzan*

The Three Musketeers

Treasure Island

*Twenty Thousand Leagues
Under the Sea*

*Uncle Tom's Cabin, or Life
Among the Lowly*

*The U.S. Constitution and Other
Key American Writings*

Walden and Civil Disobedience

The Wizard of Oz

Wuthering Heights